❧ Literature in America ❧

Literature in America

ᢒ An Illustrated History ᢒ

Peter Conn

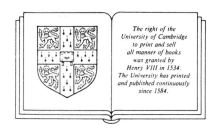

The right of the
University of Cambridge
to print and sell
all manner of books
was granted by
Henry VIII in 1534.
The University has printed
and published continuously
since 1584.

CAMBRIDGE UNIVERSITY PRESS

Cambridge • New York • Port Chester • Melbourne • Sydney

Published by the Press Syndicate of the University of Cambridge
The Pitt Building, Trumpington Street, Cambridge CB2 1RP
40 West 20th Street, New York, NY 10011, USA
10 Stamford Road, Oakleigh, Melbourne 3166 Australia

First published 1989

Printed in the United States of America

Library of Congress Cataloging-in-Publication Data
Conn, Peter
Literature in America.
Includes index.
1. American literature – History and criticism.
I. Title.
PS88.C65   1989   810'.9   88–30505

ISBN 0 521 30373 7

British Library Cataloguing in Publication applied for.

For Terry, again,

and for Jennifer, Alison, David, and Steven, too

❧ Contents ❧

Preface   page   ix

Acknowledgments   xi

List of illustrations   xv

ONE: THE COLONIAL EXPERIENCE   I
    Puritan prose, including sermons, diaries, histories ❧
    Puritan poetry, including Anne Bradstreet and Edward
    Taylor ❧ *The middle and southern colonies*

TWO: FORGING A NATIONAL LITERATURE   77
    Benjamin Franklin and the literature of independence
    ❧ *Early American novels* ❧ *American Romanticism*

THREE: DEMOCRATIC VISTAS   141
    Writers of New England ❧ *Transcendentalism: Ralph*
    Waldo Emerson, Henry David Thoreau, Margaret
    Fuller ❧ *Historians and utopians* ❧ *Nathaniel*
    Hawthorne and Herman Melville ❧ *Walt Whitman and*
    the Civil War ❧ *Emily Dickinson*

FOUR: AN AGE OF LITERARY ENTERPRISE   231
    Realism: Henry James, Samuel Clemens, William
    Dean Howells, Rebecca Harding Davis ❧ *Writers of*
    the local scene ❧ *Naturalism: Stephen Crane,*
    Charlotte Perkins Gilman, Frank Norris

FIVE: MODERNISTS AND MUCKRAKERS   295
    Cosmopolitans: Henry Adams, Henry James, Edith
    Wharton ❧ *Theodore Dreiser* ❧ *The muckrakers* ❧
    Black writers: Booker T. Washington, W. E. B. Du Bois,

Charles Chesnutt, Paul Laurence Dunbar ❧ Modernism: Gertrude Stein, Ezra Pound, T. S. Eliot

Six: BETWEEN THE WARS 348

Postwar reaction and literary experiments: Sinclair Lewis, Ernest Hemingway, Marianne Moore, Wallace Stevens, Eugene O'Neill ❧ The Harlem Renaissance ❧ F. Scott Fitzgerald ❧ The Depression and proletarian writing ❧ Southern literature: William Faulkner, Zora Neale Hurston, Richard Wright ❧ Nathanael West

Seven: MIDCENTURY AND BEYOND 443

Poetry ❧ Drama ❧ Fiction and nonfiction

Literary chronology 537

Chronology of American events 543

Books for further reading 557

Index 569

❧ *Preface* ❧

Literature in America is addressed to all readers who are interested in the history and variety of literary achievement in the United States.

In a time of energetic cultural debate, when the assumptions that govern literary preferences and interpretations are being subjected to unprecedented scrutiny, a one-volume history of American literature requires a word or two of explanation. My purposes in this book can be stated briefly: to describe literary movements within a roughly chronological framework; to suggest something of the connections between literary texts and their historical contexts; to define and exemplify in some detail the work of a large cross section of writers.

Many of the authors discussed in these pages have long been familiar to readers of American literature; others have been rather more recently recovered. While the contents of any one-volume history will necessarily be selective, my aim has been to offer a relatively spacious account of American literature, a survey that acknowledges both the diversity and the excellence that have typified America's literary experience. I have been guided by the assumption that American literature is best conceived as a dialogue involving many and plural voices.

As to method, I have chosen to avoid appealing either to unanchored generalizations or to indigestible lists of proper names. Rather, I have kept the focus on particulars, summarizing the distinctive literary accomplishment of each writer and locating literary work within its relevant settings. My intentions in the book have been primarily descriptive, but I have not been reluctant to include estimates and evaluations of much of the work I discuss.

Within these assumptions and objectives, the book's illustrations serve several purposes. In their variety – landscape paintings and portraits, photographs, drawings, woodcuts, engravings, posters, broadsides, cartoons, title pages, manuscript pages, dust jackets, dramatic scenes, statues, and buildings – the illustrations offer a broad sampling of America's accomplishments in the visual arts. Many of the major artists and photographers who have lived and worked in the United States over the past several centuries are represented in these pages.

Aside from recalling what some of America's writers looked like and reproducing examples of their work in its original forms, the illustrations add a visual dimension to my descriptions of literary themes and movements. The almost two hundred figures and plates comprise an anthology of images that provide glimpses of the changing American scene and analogs for literary statements. In short, text and pictures are intended to illuminate each other throughout the book.

❧ Acknowledgments ❧

A project of this scope comprises a large act of collaboration. My primary indebtedness is acknowledged in the list of suggested readings included in the back pages of this book. In addition, I have received the courteous and useful assistance of literally hundreds of people, and I want to thank some of them by name:

Kathleen E. Abbott, Dartmouth College Library; Sharon Bangert, Washington University; Georgia Barnhill, American Antiquarian Society; Edmund Berkeley, Curator of Manuscripts, University of Virginia Library; Ann E. Billesbach, Curator, Cather Historical Center; Linda Buck, New American Library; Eileen Cahill, Assistant Curator, Rosenbach Museum and Library; Caron Caswell, New York Graphic Society; William Clark, National Park Service; Deb Cohen, *Life* Picture Services; David Coleman; Joel Conarroe; Terry, Steven, David, Alison, and Jennifer Conn; William Cox, Smithsonian Institution Archives; William Cuffe, Yale University Art Gallery; Ruth Degenhardt, Berkshire Atheneum; David DeLaura; Anne Denlinger, Bryn Mawr Library; Grace Dinkins, National Portrait Gallery (Washington, D.C.); Robert Dumont, New York Public Library; Anita Duquette, Whitney Museum of American Art; Tom Ehrlich; David Espey; Bruce English, President, Poe Foundation; Linda Fiske, Assistant Director, Pace-MacGill Gallery; Sally Fitzgerald; Walter Frankel, Rare Books Division, Free Library of Philadelphia; Ray W. Frantz, University Librarian, University of Virginia; Mary Kay Freedman, National Museum of American Art; Barbara Puorro Galasso, George Eastman House; Allen Ginsberg; Joan Givner; Jerry Gold, Director, Man Ray Foundation; Marie-Helene Gold, Schlesinger Library, Radcliffe College; Jeff Goldman, Maryland Historical Society; Elizabeth Gombosi, Fogg Art Museum, Harvard University; Thomas B. Greenslade, Kenyon College; Vartan Gregorian; Sandra Petri Hachey, Worcester Art Museum; Virginius Halls, Virginia Historical Society; Thomas S. Hays, President, Edith Wharton Restoration; Wyman Hilscine; H. T. Holmes, Head, Special Collections, Mississippi Department of History; Ann Hopkins, Special Collections, Amherst College Library; Alexander James; Neil Jordahl, Enoch Pratt Free Library; William L. Joyce, Associate Director, Princeton University Library; Cybele Katz; Susan Kismaric, Museum of Modern Art; Mardi Leland, DeYoung Memorial Museum; Daniel Lombardo, Curator, Special Collections, Jones Library; Robert F. Lucid; Strawberry Luck, Vanderbilt University; Nora Magid; Mme. Juliette Man Ray; Michael McIntyre; Sandra M. Mongeon, Museum of Fine Arts, Boston; Prentiss Moore, Ransom Humanities Research Center, University of Texas, Austin; Leslie Morris, Curator of Printed Books and Manuscripts, Rosenbach Museum and Library; Bettsy Mosimann, University of Pennsylvania Library; Katherine Naylor, New-York Historical Society; Carolyn Park, Pennsylvania Historical Society; Raymond Petke, Wadsworth Atheneum; Ruth Pollak, Educational Film Center; Judith Prendergast, National Portrait Gallery (London); Jennie Rathbun, Houghton Reading Room, Harvard University; Ellie Reichlin, Curator, Society for the Preservation of New England Antiquities; Beth Rhoads, Philadelphia Museum of Art; Gregory Rodowski, Farrar, Straus & Giroux; Patricia Rose; Christine Ruggere, University of Pennsylvania Library; Mark Scala, Virginia State Library; Linda Seidman, University of Massachusetts, Amherst; Jack Siggins, Deputy University Librarian, Yale University; Marjorie Sly, Sophia Smith Collection, Smith College; Kristy Stewart, Art Institute of Chicago; Kathleen Stocking, New York State Historical Association; Roger Stoddard, Houghton Library, Harvard University; Chom and Robert Storey; Dorothy L. Swerdlove, Curator, Billy Rose Theater Collection; Bob Taylor, Curator, Museum of the City of New York Theater Collection; Anastasio Teodoro, Department of Rare Books and Manuscripts, New York Public Library; Richard L. Tooke, Museum of Modern Art; Daniel Traister, Curator of Special Collections, University of Pennsylvania Library; Louis L. Tucker, Director, Massachusetts Historical Society; Ross Urquhart, Massachusetts Historical Society; Laura Vassell, Mark Twain Memorial; Carolee Walker, Philadelphia Museum of Art; Ellen Wallenstein, Museum of the City of New York; Gerald Weales;

Eudora Welty; Patricia Willis, Curator of American Literature, Beinecke Library, Yale University; Georgianna Ziegler, Curator, Furness Collection, University of Pennsylvania Library.

The following individuals and institutions have provided illustrations and have given permission for reproduction:
American Antiquarian Society: figures 5, 11, 13, 15, 16, 24; Amherst College: figures 81, 82; The Art Institute of Chicago: figure 126; Artists Rights Society: Figure 120; Beinecke Library, Yale University: figures 110, 111, 132, 158; Berkshire Atheneum: Figure 75; Bettmann Archives: Figure 88; Boston Globe Photo: Figure 155; Dr. Edward Burns: Figure 120; Butler Library, Columbia University: Figure 136; Cedar Rapids Museum of Art: Figure 142; Helen Krich Chinoy: Figure 145; Dartmouth College Library: Figure 166; Edgar Allan Poe Museum of the Poe Foundation, Inc.: Figure 56; Enoch Pratt Free Library: Figure 131; Farrar, Straus & Giroux: figures 167, 182; Free Library of Philadelphia: Figure 57; Harvard University Art Museums: Plate 1; Harvard University, Fine Arts Library: Figure 106; Wyman Hilscine: Figure 105; Historical Society of Pennsylvania: figures 29, 31; Houghton Library, Harvard University: figures 94, 122; Houghton Mifflin Company: Figure 149; International Museum of Photography, George Eastman House: Figure 108; Thomas Jefferson University: Plate 3; Jones Library: Figure 123; Kenyon College Archives: Figure 165; Alfred A. Knopf and Company: Figure 139; Library of Congress: figures 2, 18, 34, 39, 40, 59, 62, 69, 79, 83, 85, 101, 148; Life Picture Service: figures 174, 175; Allan I. Ludwig (Ludwig Portfolios): Figure 17; Mark Twain Memorial Foundation: figures 91, 93; Maryland Historical Society: Figure 28; Massachusetts Historical Society: figures 9, 12, 72; Fred McDarrah: Figure 177; Metropolitan Museum of Art: figures 22, 61, 84, plates 5, 6; Minneapolis Institute of the Arts: Figure 55; Mississippi Department of Archives and History: Figure 172; Josephine Morris: Figure 162; Museum of the City of New York: figures 41, 99, (Theater Collection) 144, 146; Museum of Fine Arts, Boston: Figure 8, Plate 2; Museum of Modern Art: Figure 125;

National Archives: Figure 151; National Gallery of Art (Washington, D.C.): figures 32, 48, 113, Plate 8; National Museum of American Art: Figure 54; National Park Service: Figure 70; National Portrait Gallery (London): Figure 107; National Portrait Gallery (Washington, D.C.): figures 36, 47; Nebraska State Historical Society: Figure 117; New Hampshire Historical Society: Figure 73; New-York Historical Society: figures 38, 45, 67; New York Public Library: figures 1, 3, 33, 37, 52, 58, 60, 63, 74, 77, 89, 90, 130, (Theater Collection) 169; New York State Historical Association: figures 50, 51; Pace-MacGill Galleries: Figure 164; Pennsylvania Academy of the Fine Arts: figures 53, 65, 78, Plate 4; Philadelphia Museum of Art: figures 27, 97; Plymouth Plantation: Figure 6; Princeton University Library: Figure 141; Harry Ransom Humanities Center, University of Texas: Figure 170; Rosenbach Museum and Library: figures 76, 138; Fine Arts Museum, San Francisco: Figure 21; Schlesinger Library, Radcliffe College: Figure 104; Smith College: Figure 66; Smithsonian Institution: figures 100, 152; Society for the Preservation of New England Antiquities: Figure 4; University of Massachusetts, Amherst: Figure 119; University of Pennsylvania Library: figures 43, 80, 86, 98, 102, 114, 127, 128, 129, 147; Vanderbilt University Photographic Archives: figures 154, 173; University of Virginia Library: figures 96, 153; Virginia Historical Society: Figure 25; Virginia State Library: Figure 35; Wadsworth Atheneum: Figure 44; Washington University Gallery of Art: Figure 46; Whitney Museum of American Art: Figure 150; Jonathan Williams: Figure 163; Dr. William Eric Williams: Figure 137; Worcester Art Museum: Figure 14, Plate 7; Yale University Art Gallery: figures 23, 30, 42; Yale University Library: Figure 20.

❧ Illustrations ❧

CHAPTER ONE

1	Robert Johnson, *Nova Britannia*	2
2	John Smith, *General Historie of Virginia*	4
3	John Smith, *A Description of New England*	7
4	Harvard College	8
5	John Winthrop	9
6	Plymouth Plantation	11
7	Cotton Mather, sermon on the death of Mrs. Hannah Sewall	13
8	Samuel Sewall	21
9	Manuscript page from Samuel Sewall's *Diary*	22
10	Edward Johnson, *The Wonder-working Providence of Sion's Saviour in New England*	28
11	Richard Mather	32
12	Increase Mather	32
13	Cotton Mather	32
14	Thomas Smith, self-portrait	37
15	Slave auction broadside	38
16	Title page, *Bay Psalm Book*	43
17	The Joseph Tapping stone (1678), King's Chapel, Boston	46
18	Anne Bradstreet	54
19	Anne Bradstreet, *The Tenth Muse*	55
20	Edward Taylor, "Meditation," I, 38	61
21	*The Mason Children*	65
22	Matthew Pratt, *The American School*	66
23	Jonathan Edwards	67
24	*New England Primer*	69
25	William Byrd II	71
26	William Bartram drawing	75

CHAPTER TWO

27	Benjamin West, *Benjamin Franklin with Kite and Key*	78

28   Benjamin Banneker's *Almanac*   80
29   *Poor Richard's Almanack*   81
30   *Bowles's Moral Pictures*   82
31   Franklin's snake device   82
32   Thomas Paine   86
33   Thomas Paine, *Common Sense*   86
34   Thomas Jefferson, Declaration of
        Independence   87
35   Virginia State Capitol   88
36   George Washington   89
37   Phillis Wheatley, *Poems*   91
38   Gustavus Vassa (Olaudah Equiano)   93
39   Diagram, eighteenth-century British slave ship   94
40   Joel Barlow   98
41   Frontispiece from Royall Tyler, *The Contrast*   100
42   John Trumbull, *The Death of General Warren
        at the Battle of Bunker's Hill, June 17, 1775*   102
43   Susanna Rowson, *Charlotte Temple*   104
44   Eighteenth-century crewelwork   106
45   Eastman Johnson, *Old Kentucky Home*   109
46   George Caleb Bingham, *Daniel Boone*   110
47   Christian Schussele, *Washington Irving and His
        Friends*   114
48   John Quidor, *The Return of Rip Van Winkle*   117
49   F. O. C. Darley, *Ichabod Crane*   118
50   James Fenimore Cooper   119
51   Scene from *The Spy*   120
52   Asher Durand, *Kindred Spirits*   127
53   William Sidney Mount, *The Painter's Triumph*   128
54   George Catlin, *The Buffalo's Back Fat*   130
55   Shoshoni elk-hide painting   132
56   Edgar Allan Poe   134
57   Edgar Allan Poe, "Annabel Lee"   137

CHAPTER THREE

58   Title page and table of contents, *The Pioneer*   150
59   James Russell Lowell   152
60   Headpiece, *The Liberator*   154
61   Original architect's sketch of "Glen Ellen"   156
62   Ralph Waldo Emerson   164
63   Henry David Thoreau   174
64   Title page, *Walden*   176
65   Horace Pippin, *John Brown Going to His
        Hanging*   181
66   Cover, *Anti-Slavery Almanac*   183

67   Advertisement, *Uncle Tom's Cabin*   184
68   Title page, *Incidents in the Life of a Slave Girl*   187
69   Theodore R. Davis, *A Slave Auction at the
     South*   188
70   Frederick Douglass   189
71   Illustration from Mason Weems, *The Life of
     George Washington*   191
72   *Brook Farm in 1844*   196
73   Nathaniel Hawthorne   200
74   Sophia Hawthorne, illustration for "The
     Gentle Boy"   202
75   Herman Melville   204
76   Title page, Hawthorne's copy of Melville's
     Moby-Dick   208
77   Frontispiece portrait, first edition of *Leaves of
     Grass*   211
78   Walt Whitman   215
79   Abraham Lincoln   218
80   Alexander Gardner, *Home of a Rebel
     Sharpshooter*   220
81   Emily Dickinson   224
82   Emily Dickinson, "A little madness in the
     spring"   228

CHAPTER FOUR

83   New York City dry goods district, 1880s   232
84   Corliss Engine, Hall of Machinery,
     Philadelphia Centennial Exposition   235
85   John Dost, *American Progress*   236
86   Illustration from Horatio Alger, *Herbert
     Carter's Legacy; or, The Inventor's Son*   239
87   Thomas Nast, *The Tammany Tiger Loose*   240
88   Henry and William James   243
89   Bret Harte, *The Heathen Chinee*   252
90   Illustration from George Washington Harris,
     Sut Lovingood's Yarns   253
91   The American Humorists: Petroleum V.
     Nasby, Mark Twain, Josh Billings   255
92   E. W. Kemble, illustration from *Huckleberry
     Finn*   258
93   351 Farmington Avenue, Hartford,
     Connecticut   259
94   William Dean Howells   262
95   Illustration from Charles W. Caryl, *New Era*   267
96   Mary E. Wilkins Freeman   270

97 Thomas Hovenden, *Breaking Home Ties* 274
98 Lafcadio Hearn, cartoon for *Creole Sketches* 276
99 Jacob Riis, *Bandit's Roost* 280
100 Court of Honor, World's Columbian
 Exposition 281
101 Advertisement, Buffalo Bill's Wild West Show 284
102 Frederic Remington, *Mounting a Wild One* 285
103 Frontispiece, F. Marion Crawford, *Via Crucis* 286
104 Charlotte Perkins Gilman 291

CHAPTER FIVE

105 Augustus Saint-Gaudens, *Adams Memorial* 300
106 The Nave at Chartres, from Henry Adams,
 Mont-Saint-Michel and Chartres 301
107 Henry James 302
108 Alvin Langdon Coburn, *Portland Place* 305
109 Hester Street 306
110 Edith Wharton 307
111 The Mount 307
112 Illustration from *The House of Mirth* 310
113 George Bellows, *The Lone Tenement* 313
114 Theodore Dreiser 314
115 John Sloan, cover of *The Masses* 319
116 Jack London 321
117 Willa Cather 322
118 Frontispiece, Booker T. Washington, *The
 Story of My Life and Work* 324
119 W. E. B. Du Bois and founders of the Niagara
 Movement 326
120 Gertrude Stein and Alice B. Toklas 331
121 Ezra Pound 333
122 T. S. Eliot 335
123 Robert Frost 337
124 Frank Lloyd Wright, drawing from *The
 Wasmuth Portfolio* 340
125 Edward Steichen, photomontage of Carl
 Sandburg 342
126 Sherwood Anderson 344
127 Map from *Winesburg, Ohio* 346

CHAPTER SIX

128 Jacket, E. E. Cummings, *The Enormous Room* 351
129 Frontispiece and title page, Ernest
 Hemingway, *In Our Time* 353
130 George Jean Nathan and H. L. Mencken 359

131 Sinclair Lewis 362
132 Sauk Centre, Minnesota 363
133 Eugene O'Neill 367
134 Scene from *Long Day's Journey into Night* 370
135 Hart Crane 371
136 William Carlos Williams 374
137 Marianne Moore 378
138 Marianne Moore, sketch of a diamondback
    turtle 379
139 Wallace Stevens 380
140 Writers of the Harlem Renaissance 385
141 The Fitzgeralds: F. Scott, Zelda, and Scottie 387
142 Grant Wood, *Overmantel Decoration* 393
143 Linocut from Giacomo Patri, *White Collar* 396
144 Scene from Lillian Hellman, *The Children's
    Hour* 397
145 Directors of the Group Theatre 399
146 Scene from Clifford Odets, *Waiting for Lefty* 400
147 Cover, Anzia Yezierska, *Bread Givers* 401
148 Walker Evans, photograph from *Let Us Now
    Praise Famous Men* 407
149 Reginald Marsh, drawing for *U.S.A.* 410
150 Raphael Soyer, *The Mission* 412
151 John Steinbeck 414
152 Dorothy Lange, *Ditched, Stalled, and Stranded,
    San Joaquin Valley, California* 416
153 Ellen Glasgow 419
154 The Fugitives 421
155 Katherine Anne Porter 425
156 William Faulkner, *Pierrot Standing*, from *The
    Marionettes* 427
157 William Faulkner, map of Yoknapatawpha
    County 430
158 Zora Neale Hurston 435
159 Richard Wright, as Bigger Thomas 438
160 Nathanael West 439
161 Trylon and Perisphere, New York World's Fair 441

CHAPTER SEVEN

162 Levittown, Long Island, in the 1950s 446
163 Wright Morris, photograph from *The Home
    Place* 448
164 Martin Luther King, Jr., Washington, D.C.,
    August 1963 449
165 Charles Olson at Black Mountain 453

166 Allen Ginsberg 455
167 Kenyon College English faculty 457
168 Augustus Saint-Gaudens, *The Shaw Memorial* 459
169 Ben Shahn, drawing for John Berryman,
    Homage to Mistress Bradstreet 460
170 Adrienne Rich 468
171 Set for Arthur Miller, *Death of a Salesman* 471
172 Scene from Tennessee Williams, *A Streetcar
    Named Desire* 476
173 John Updike 485
174 Robert Penn Warren 489
175 Photograph from Eudora Welty, *One Time,
    One Place* 492
176 Flannery O'Connor 494
177 Saul Bellow 500
178 Philip Roth 505
179 James Baldwin 511
180 Alice Walker 514
181 Toni Morrison 515
182 Illustration from Donald Barthelme, "At the
    Tolstoy Museum" 523
183 The March on the Pentagon 531
184 Norman Mailer 532
185 Joyce Carol Oates 533

❧ Color Plates ❧   *following page* 140

1 John Singleton Copley, *Mrs. Thomas Boylston*
2 Fitz Hugh Lane, *Owl's Head, Penobscot Bay,
    Maine*
3 Thomas Eakins, *The Gross Clinic*
4 Winslow Homer, *The Fox Hunt*
5 Georgia O'Keeffe, *Black Iris*
6 Charles Demuth, *I Saw the Figure 5 in Gold*
7 Jacob Armstead Lawrence, *They Live in Fire
    Traps*
8 Jackson Pollock, *Number 1, 1950 (Lavender
    Mist)*

CHAPTER ONE

❧ *The colonial experience* ❧

I
N THE BEGINNING," wrote the English philosopher John Locke, echoing the familiar words of Genesis, "all the world was America." Like the Garden of Eden before the Fall, America seemed to Locke, and to many others in the Old World, to stand at the dawn of a new history, radiant with the hope of new opportunities. This was a myth that endured for centuries, providing the standard against which the facts of America's experience have been measured. Indeed, the contest between the idealized image of the New World and the realities of New World history has defined one of the principal themes of America's literary culture from its beginnings. For generations, the hopeful dreams of new settlers have made up the largest cargo carried to the shores of America.

Following centuries of intermittent exploration, the English, French, and Spanish began to colonize the New World in the 1500s. For the first time, Europeans in large numbers came to America with the intention of settling permanently. Nothing quite like this more or less voluntary migration had happened before. Indeed, the idea of colonization – the word itself – was a new one in the sixteenth century. A whole continent was taken from its native occupants and repeopled. Among those who came, some sought adventure, while others were seeking to escape from bankruptcy or criminal charges. Some cast a calculating eye at the potential profits of the New World's rivers and forests and offshore fisheries, and still others sought a haven from religious persecution. Many of the settlers, of course, responded to several motives at once. Adventurers might find homes, and pious Christians might become shrewd merchants.

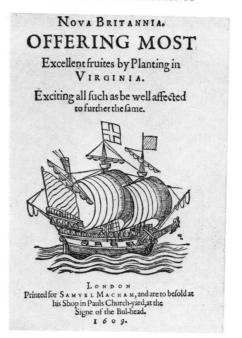

FIGURE I 🙠 The title page of Robert Johnson's *Nova Britannia* (1609), one of the many early tracts which promoted English emigration and settlement in the New World.

The economic and political pressures that beset contemporary Europe probably made the migration to America inevitable. Nonetheless, the settlers were urged on by a literature of exploration, a series of popular books and pamphlets that pictured America as a fruitful garden, a land teeming with fish and game and opportunity (Figure 1). America's native peoples appeared in these texts but almost always in terms of one-dimensional caricatures. To the white settlers, the hundreds of Indian languages all sounded unintelligibly alike, and the diverse forms of cultural expression all seemed equivalently barbaric. Complex traditional chants, songs, and dances were dismissed as symptoms of savage frenzy. The native tribes represented exotic otherness, and they also stood in the way of white expansion and development. Prejudice, self-interest, and genuine Christian zeal reinforced each other in the military campaigns that settlers waged against Indian populations, which were pursued by threats of conversion or extermination.

The most famous episode in the early encounters between Europeans and Native Americans was reported by Captain John Smith, who was also one of the earliest and busiest promoters of the New World. Condemned to death by the Chesapeake king

Powhatan, Smith was purportedly rescued by the intervention of Powhatan's daughter, Pocahontas. Whether the story is true or not (Smith does not mention it in his initial accounts), the tale became a romantic parable bespeaking the inevitability of white triumph over Indian opposition. Smith's 1608 account of Virginia was the first book written in English in America, and his *Description of New England* followed several years later. According to Smith, the rewards of settlement in America far outnumber the difficulties, including the resistance of the Indians. In the New World, Smith promises, a person need only work three days out of the seven to earn an ample living. Crops and vines multiply more plentifully than in England. It is "a very bad fisher," writes Smith, who cannot take two hundred or even three hundred codfish a day from New England waters. The labors of subsistence become nearly enjoyable in the presence of such natural bounty. "What pleasure can be more than . . . to recreate themselves before their own doors in their own boats upon the sea where man, woman, and child, with a small hook and line, by angling, may take diverse sorts of excellent fish at their pleasures." In short, Smith assures his readers that a modest diligence will be repaid with independence and even comfort (Figure 2).

Francis Higginson came with the initial group of Puritans to Salem in 1629, and he was one of the first settlers to publish an eyewitness account of the virtues of the New World. Higginson's pamphlet, *New Englands Plantation* (1630), includes a catalog of contrasts demonstrating the superiority of America to England: the climate is healthier, the soil is richer, the fish and fowls more plentiful and bigger. America's turkeys are "exceeding fat, sweet, and fleshy," and American partridges are so heavy that they can hardly fly. In short, writes Higginson, "A sup of New England's air is better than a whole draft of old England's ale."

Poets, too, made their contributions to the task of propagandizing for the New World. Richard Ruth, for example, testified to America's bounty in his versified "Newes from Virginie":

> There is no feare of hunger here,
>   for Corne much store here growes,
> Much fish the gallant Rivers yield,
>   tis truth, without suppose.

FIGURE 2 ❧ Several engravings from John Smith's *General Historie of Virginia* (1624). The unknown engraver, who derived many of his images from an earlier publication, Theodor de Bry's *America*, made the most of Smith's captures and escapes. The story of the captain's rescue by Pocahontas is the subject of the dramatic scene at the lower right.

Such versified reports, many from eyewitnesses, claimed to anchor the myth of American abundance in fact. These jovial celebrations of the New World's green and pleasant land are thin poetry, but they are the earliest body of literature that took America as its subject. Trumpeting the virtues of a country that barely existed yet in any political sense, the literature of promotion anticipated a major theme of American letters throughout the next several centuries: a fascination with America's identity and its proper place in the world of nations.

In jog-trotting couplets, John Holme offered what he called "A True Relation of the Flourishing State of Pennsylvania." Though Pennsylvania, except for Philadelphia, was still largely a wilderness outpost when Holme wrote, he nonetheless had no trouble identifying the New World's superiority to the Old. For one thing, the land is more productive:

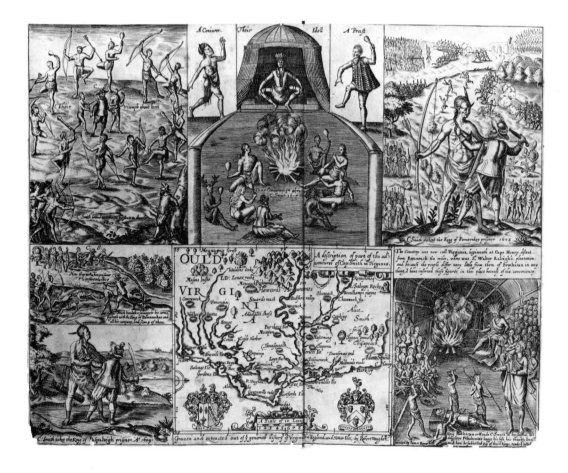

The soil is good, as plainly doth appear,
What grows in England doth or may grow here;
Yea here are many things grow for our use
Which we know English ground will not produce.

In addition, opportunity lies at the hand of the industrious poor, who would not find such chances in Europe:

This land is large and cheap, as is well known,
So that each poor man may make some his own,
Enjoy it while he lives, and at the end
Bestow it on his children or his friend.

Finally, America is a haven from the brutality of European wars. Holme puts this pacific boast at the center of his conclusion:

But here they'll bide and safely hide
    Whilst Europe broils in war;
The fruit of the curse which may prove worse
    Than hath been yet by far.

Abundance, opportunity, peace. The elements of American exceptionalism – the belief in the special and sanctified character of the New World – are already visible in the lumbering doggerel of such versifiers as Ruth and Holme.

The job of settlement proved, however, to be a rather more difficult matter than the promotional poems and tracts foretold. There were indeed space and opportunity, but the first colonists also found disease, crop failure, and hunger. They shivered in the cold of New England winters, sweltered in the heat of southern summers, and met the armed resistance of the native Indian populations. Many of the early settlers faced starvation and saw their numbers decimated. In the 1580s, three consecutive attempts were made to settle Roanoake Island, off the coast of North Carolina. All failed. The first contingent of settlers returned to England, the second group was killed by the Indians, and the fate of the third – 117 men, women, and children who landed in 1587 – has never been learned. The initial settlers of Virginia starved to death. In Massachusetts the people known to history as the Pilgrims lost nearly half of their original company during their first winter in Plymouth in 1620–1.

The Pilgrims landed fully forty years after the first English efforts to colonize the New World. Most of the earlier attempts, going back to the 1570s and 1580s, had ended in failure. The sustained business of settlement began after a group of London merchants received a license to colonize "Virginia," the name for the whole eastern seaboard claimed by England. The Royal Council for Virginia was granted authority over two joint-stock companies, the London Company, which was to colonize the southern regions, and the Plymouth Company, which was given the north. These were essentially commercial enterprises. The first charter referred to the virtues of Christianity and addressed the obligations of the companies to lift "the Infidels and Savages, living in those Parts, to human civility," but the more important emphasis was on each company's right "to dig, mine, and search for all Manner of Mines of Gold, Silver, and Copper." Jamestown, the first permanent English colony in America, was founded under this grant in May 1607. Other colonies soon followed. Some of them, such as Plymouth and Massachusetts in New England, were corporate undertakings, while others were organized by individuals or small groups. Beginning in 1634, Maryland was settled under a charter granted to Lord Baltimore by Charles I. New Amsterdam was taken from the Dutch and renamed New York in 1664, and New Jersey was created in the same year. William Penn received title to the land he would name Pennsylvania in 1681. From the tobacco crops of the South to the fisheries of New England, each of these colonies found a distinctive economic base. So also they followed separate political histories. What they demonstrated collectively was that by the mid-seventeenth century, English domination of the whole coast between present-day Newfoundland and Florida was assured (Figure 3).

Throughout the first century of English settlement, most of the literary achievement of the colonies was the work of New England's Puritans. The Puritans were, quite simply, the most literate of the English colonists, the best-educated, and the most firmly committed to intellectual pursuits. If their learning was narrow in focus, it was nonetheless substantial. With Cambridge University in mind as a model, the leaders of Massachusetts Bay Colony founded Harvard College in 1636, just a few years after the colony itself was established (Figure 4). The first printing press was set up at Harvard in 1639. The Puritans produced an immense quantity of writing, most of it in defense or explanation of their religious beliefs.

The Puritans who settled Massachusetts Bay had much in common with the Plymouth Pilgrims. Both groups were dissatisfied with the government of the English church under the Stuart monarchs, and both had felt the sting of ecclesiastical persecution. Unlike the Pilgrims, however, the Puritans for many years insisted that their theology was nonseparatist: their announced program was to reform the Church of England, not break from it as the Pilgrims had done. They intended the Bible Commonwealth they were going to build in the New World to remain spiritually linked to the English homeland. They maintained this sense of participation until 1660, when

FIGURE 3 ❧ A portrait of John Smith and his map of the Massachusetts coast were reproduced in the volume *A Description of New England* (1616). As the map indicates, many of the region's place names were established years before the arrival of permanent settlers.

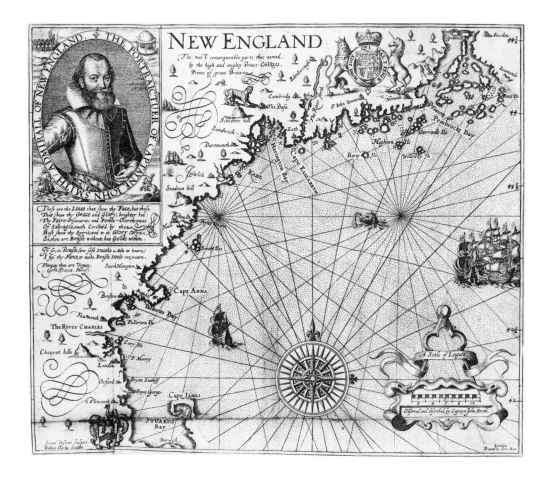

FIGURE 4 🙰 A conjectural restoration of the building that housed Harvard College in the seventeenth century. The drawing is by H. R. Shurtleff.

the restoration of Charles II to the English throne brought the final collapse of Puritan political hopes in England.

The principal leader of Massachusetts Bay in its first two decades was John Winthrop. Winthrop was a man of considerable importance in England, an attorney and a justice of the peace. He led the first group of Puritans to Massachusetts in 1630, and his leadership of the Massachusetts Bay Company had much to do with its success. For most of the last twenty years of his life, he served as governor or deputy governor of the colony. On the journey to New England aboard the *Arbella*, Winthrop preached a lay-sermon in which he urged his followers to create a colony that would be "A Model of Christian Charity." He invoked the covenant that had been drawn up between the colonists and God. This notion of a sort of spiritual contract binding the parties together would become the cornerstone of Puritan theology and politics for the first several generations of New England settlement. Elaborating on the colonists' responsibilities under the covenant, Winthrop declared that the world would be watching this experiment in New England. "We must consider," said Winthrop in a famous image, "that we shall be as a city upon a hill, the eyes of all people are upon us; so that if we shall deal falsely with our God in this work we have undertaken

FIGURE 5 ❧ Portrait of Governor John Winthrop. The artist is unknown.

and so cause him to withdraw his present help from us, we shall be made a story and a by-word through the world" (Figure 5).

By likening the new community to a city on a hill, Winthrop presumed to transform a colonial outpost into the center of European attention. God had sent his new chosen people on a decisive errand into the New World wilderness. This vaunting definition of the Puritan experience would reverberate through centuries of America's political history. At the same time, Winthrop's image reveals the extent to which the Puritans of New England initially thought of themselves in relation to the Old World. The eyes that would watch them were European, and the significance of the errand would be measured in its European consequences. Like all immigrants, the men and women who came to Massachusetts brought their culture with them. Except in the matter of church government, innovation was not their conscious policy; indeed, they were in most respects quite conservative. The evolution that turned these transplanted Europeans into Americans was gradual and generally unintended. The cultural history of the next several generations is essentially a story of adaptation, as imported ideas and material forms were altered under the pressure of America's different conditions.

Colonial law, for example, though not a mere transcription of the statutes of England, depended heavily on the body of English common law, as well as on medieval theories of natural law. Among other things, the early legal codes of New England acknowledged and incorporated the hierarchy of class divisions. John Winthrop defined the terms upon which the godly commonwealth would be governed when he affirmed that "God Almighty in his most holy and wise providence hath so disposed of the Condition of mankind, as in all times some must be rich, some poor, some high and eminent in power and dignity; others mean and in subjection." According to Winthrop, the freedom of citizens resided in their freedom to obey their magistrates. John Cotton, the most influential preacher of the first Puritan generation, expressed New England's commitment to traditional ideas of authority in a letter to Lord Say and Seal in 1636. "Democracy," wrote Cotton, "I do not conceive that ever God did ordain as a fit government either for church or commonwealth. If the people be governors, who shall be governed? As for monarchy, and aristocracy, they are both of them clearly approved, and directed in scripture." It was Cotton who drafted the first proposed legal code, an adaptation of Mosaic law called "a model of Moses his Judicials," but this was rejected by the Massachusetts General Court in favor of a "Body of Liberties" that more closely resembled the common law of England.

The institutions of public and private life, the systems of laws and customs, the houses in which families lived, the clothes they wore, and, perhaps most important, the language they spoke: all these the colonists carried with them from the Old World (Figure 6). The most valuable possession these men and women brought to New England, in their own view at least, was their theology. In religion, they were the heirs of both the Reformation and of medieval Christianity. Their version of Protestantism, with its emphases on the exclusive authority of the Bible in matters of faith and on the contractual nature of God's election of saints, had been formulated and taught at Cambridge University in the late sixteenth and early seventeenth centuries. English divines such as William Ames and William Perkins devised the theological structure which the early Puritan settlers transmitted to America. For generations, these beliefs would touch every work of Puritan culture, including its literature.

Above all, the Puritans committed themselves to the Bible. They were preeminently a people of the Book. They believed that the Bible was the revealed word of God, a repository of literal truth about every subject, from church government and morality to rules of dress and banking. Since Scripture lay at the heart of their religion, scriptural preaching became nearly the sole focus of their worship services. In the Puritan meetinghouse, it was often said, pulpit had replaced altar. The reciprocal acts of preaching and hearing were the indispensable elements in the life of the Puritan con-

FIGURE 6 &a A reconstruction of Leyden Street, in the Plymouth Plantation, in the 1620s.

gregation. Puritan theologians went so far as to insist that the efficacy of the sacraments depended upon preaching. "Affectionate, faithful preaching and setting forth of Christ," declared John Cotton, "stirreth up in others a saving knowledge of Christ, and hearty affection to him." Preaching was a means of grace, and Puritan preachers were vehicles of the Word. They were also the chief intellectual figures in their communities. Though they were prohibited from holding public office, their advice was invariably sought by the secular leaders of government.

The preacher gave authoritative voice to the collective aspirations and needs of the godly commonwealth. In addition to his regular sermons on Sundays and in weekday lectures, the minister would be called on to speak on the community's behalf at moments of tragedy or crisis. In times of peril, such as drought or storm or Indian attack, the preacher drew out the lesson of the Lord's chastisement and exhorted his congregation to repentance and renewed religious zeal. When death struck down one of the faithful, the preacher spoke at the funeral, subduing mourning in the consolation of redemption and transforming the biography of the departed man or woman into a saint's life. The preacher also stood next to criminals at their executions. With the scaffold for a pulpit and the condemned person as his object lesson, the preacher pressed home the hard truths of guilt and punishment (Figure 7).

The sermons that Puritan preachers delivered can be regarded as the first substantial literary genre produced in the English-speaking New World. Puritans had strong opinions about the rhetoric that was appropriate for the pulpit. They insisted on a "plain style," one that subordinated decoration to substance, and they valued logic and clarity above all. Thomas Hooker, in the preface to his *Survey of the Sum of Church Discipline*, avows that "plainness and perspicuity, both for nature and manner of expression, are the things that I have conscientiously endeavored in the whole debate." Hooker's reasoning would have found wide assent: "I have ever thought writings that come abroad, they are not to dazzle, but direct the apprehension of the meanest; and I have accounted it the chiefest part of judicious learning, to make a hard point easy and familiar in explication." Along with other Puritan preachers and writers of the first generations, Hooker was striving for a sort of religious utilitarianism. He chose to communicate in a plain style so that the

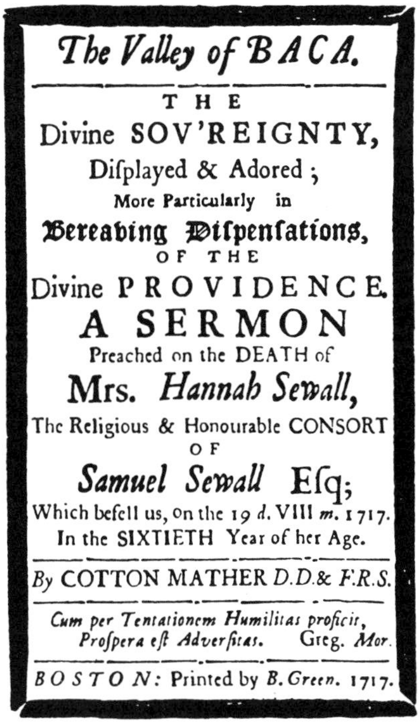

The Valley of BACA.

THE
Divine SOV'REIGNTY,
Difplayed & Adored ;
More Particularly in
𝔅ereaving 𝔇ifpenfations,
OF THE
Divine PROVIDENCE.
A SERMON
Preached on the DEATH of
Mrs. *Hannah Sewall,*
The Religious & Honourable CONSORT
O F
Samuel Sewall Efq;
Which befell us, On the 19 *d.* VIII *m.* 1717.
In the SIXTIETH Year of her Age.

By COTTON MATHER *D.D.*& *F.R.S.*

Cum per Tentationem Humilitas proficit,
Profpera eft Adverfitas. Greg. *Mor*.

BOSTON: Printed by *B. Green.* 1717.

FIGURE 7 &. The title page of Cotton Mather's funeral sermon on the death of Mrs. Hannah Sewall. Hannah Hull and Samuel Sewall had been married for forty-one years at the time of Hannah's death.

hard places of the Scriptures and theology would be made easy, and so that people of all levels of education and intelligence – including the lowest – could comprehend and live by the truth. The flowers of rhetoric might lead listeners away from holiness; like stained-glass windows, ornaments in sermons were dangerously sensuous. The great English divine, Richard Baxter, wrote that "painted obscure Sermons (like the painted glass in the windows that keeps out the Light) are too oft the marks of painted Hypocrites. The paint upon the glass may feed the fancy, but the room is not well lighted by it." John Cotton's famous catechism, *Milk for Babes,* since it was written especially for the instruction of children, is predictably couched in the simplest possible terms. But many of the sermons of early New England, and much of the rest of Puritan literature, exhibit a style that is quite deliberately plain.

At the same time, in spite of their stern simplicity, Puritan sermons are often artful and even dramatic. William Ames, the English divine whose theology had great influence on the New England settlers, exhorted preachers above all to effectiveness; they must stir up their hearers and prepare them to receive Christ:

Men are to be pricked to the quick, that they may feel in every one of them what the Apostle saith, namely that the Word of the Lord is a two edged sword, that pierceth into the inward thoughts and affections, and goeth through unto the joining together of the bones and the marrow. Preaching therefore ought not to be dead, but lively and effectual, so that an unbeliever coming into the Congregation of the faithful he ought to be affected, and as it were digged through with the very hearing of the Word.

The format for these sermons was standardized and was invariably based on the "opening," or exposition, of biblical verses. Beginning with a reading of the verse which formed the basis of his talk, the preacher would first define the doctrine contained in the text, then explain the meaning of each word and phrase, link the passage to others in the Bible, and conclude by enumerating the "uses" – the practical applications of the verse to everyday life. The commitment to plainness did not preclude an abundant use of allusions and similes in support of each argument. "Similitudes," as they were called, were permissible in preaching, provided their intent was to "win the hearer by plain and evident demonstrations," as one English Puritan put it. Members of the congregations actually took notes during the sermons; many of their notebooks have survived, and they suggest how attentively the sermons in the Puritan meetinghouses were received. Like their preachers, the Puritan faithful valued the Scriptures above all human discourse, but they also relished the concrete particularity that gave the sermons much of their energy. The vivid imagery of Puritan preaching came from two sources: the ordinary events of daily life, and the Bible. Thus, John Cotton spoke at length about the idea of vocation, or "calling." God is the instrument of the call, Cotton explained, and faith must cooperate: "Faith saith not, Give me such a calling and turn me loose to it; but faith looks up to heaven for skill and ability, though strong and able, yet it looks to all its abilities as a dead work, as like braided wares in a shop, as such as will be lost and rust, unless God refresh and renew his breath in them."

Thomas Hooker, along with Shepard and Cotton one of the most powerful of early Puritan preachers, described meditation in terms that capture both the difficulty and the value of the exercise: "The Goldsmith observes that it is not the laying of the fire, but the blowing of it that melts the metal: So with meditation, it breathes upon any truth that is applied, and that makes it really sink and soak into the soul." Such preaching as this gave a sense of immediacy and reality to the abstract tenets of the Christian doctrine. Ransacking history and classical literature as well as Scripture for examples and illustrations, the Puritan sermon was designed as a pious monument to the Christian faith. The sermons were monumental in scale, too. Sermons of over an hour's duration were common, and Edward Johnson records his undivided attention as Thomas Shepard spoke through two turnings of the hourglass. The biblical texts were almost literally inexhaustible. John Cotton, to give just one example, preached a sequence of sermons on the brief First Epistle of John. In a modern reprint, Cotton's text reaches nearly six hundred pages; and he did not quite get to the end of the epistle.

Through their combination of biblical imagery and homely facts the Puritan sermons would exert a permanent influence upon America's later writers, who would adapt the Bible's stories and cadences to the telling of secular tales. The Puritans' ample use of analogies would also affect the literature of later centuries. The Puritans themselves believed that their analogies were far more than ornamental devices. Rather, analogical connections were based on the vast system of correspondences that inhered in the whole created universe. The world is Word, sacrament, a system of signs revealing God's power and his design. To the Puritan imagination, God's hand was visible not only in the ultimate direction of events but also in each detail and episode of daily life. All earthly and human affairs take on a double reference. Beyond their literal existence in time, they also serve as emblems or shadows of divine and timeless things. Thus, a page from a Puritan sermon – or a diary or a volume of history – does not merely report events. Each occurrence, whether death or Indian attack or thunderstorm, is accompanied by a commentary revealing the spiritual significance of what has happened. This view of the world gave rise to the allegorical turn of the Puritan mind. Long after the dogmas of Puritanism had been eroded, this fascination with the emblematic nature of the visible world would continue to influence the American literary imagination.

The truths that Puritan preaching elaborated had been forged in the heat of several generations of European debate. At the center of Puritan doctrine lay a set of Augustinian and Calvinist convictions concerning the absolute depravity of human nature and the absolute necessity of free grace for salvation. The God of this theology is a being utterly remote and incomprehensible, as distant and unknowable as the sun. Puritan writers agreed in particularly emphasizing God's sovereignty. Theirs was a God of power, who had specifically decreed every event that has occurred or will occur in human history.

Among the choices God has made was the arbitrary election of some men and women to receive the irresistible gift of regeneration, which the Puritans called "justification." The New England divine Thomas Hooker described the consequences of justification:

> There is a moral change in justification, a man [was] bound to the Law, and liable to the penalty of it, and guilty of the breach of it. Now God the Father in Jesus Christ, acquits a man of this guilt, and delivers him from this revenging power of the Law, and that's not all, but withal he puts holiness into the heart, and wisdom into the mind.

The moment of conversion was the most profound and sacred in a saint's life, and it became the focus of constant analysis and introspection. Much time and anxiety were invested in the effort to answer what Puritans regarded as the most important question they faced in life: "how a man may know whether he be saved or not," as one of their preachers summarized it. Their unceasing concern with salvation earned for the Puritans a reputation for moral rigor. It also led them into a habit of daily spiritual examination, and they filled their diaries with the results of their investigations. With striking immediacy, the diaries offer glimpses into daily Puritan experience.

The Puritans were neither the first nor the only men and women to write down the stories of their interior and exterior lives. But the sheer scale of their effort, and the involvement of so many of them in it, makes the Puritans the great autobiographers of the early modern world. They spent a portion of each day engaged in searching inquiries into the state of their souls. These men and women bequeathed to American culture a preoccupation with self, along with the habit of recording their observations and judgments of themselves.

Though Puritan dogma insisted upon the irrelevance of human effort in the transactions of grace, the Puritan community demanded righteous behavior. The paradox is only superficial. Good deeds might not be the instrument of achieving justification, but they were a sign of it. Men and women who were effectually saved would conduct their lives accordingly. They studied their spiritual accomplishments and failures to find evidence of God's favor or blame. The strenuous inward searchings recorded in the diaries have a single motive: Puritan men and women wanted to transcribe the details of each pilgrim's progress toward the heavenly city. Keeping a journal or diary was probably a means of creating the assurance they so diligently sought. The regularity of the exercise lent a sense of purpose and stability to the daily life of the anxious believer, and the very fact of the accumulating pages may have symbolized the reality of personal sanctity. Especially in the first and second generations, the diaries can be seen as the Puritans' effort not just to live saintly lives but to be the authors of their own saintly biographies.

Because they have so much in common, the Puritan diaries tend toward a likeness that can be repetitive and even stylized. Similarly, their fixation on the subjective life means that in many of them the outside world – the physical world of getting and spending and daily doing – is frustratingly absent. Nevertheless, the most memorable of them display a good deal of personality and distinction. Three examples will serve to illustrate the characteristics of this important Puritan genre.

Thomas Shepard was the only one of the first group of Puritan leaders and pioneers to have left both a journal and an autobiography. A comparison reveals instructive differences. The autobiography is a more polished and better-organized piece of work. It is also retrospective and thus perhaps loses in immediacy what it gains in coherence. Shepard wrote his autobiography to be read by others – it is addressed to his son, for his instruction – and a fair amount of effort has clearly gone into the verbal style, the selection and arrangement of the parts, and the balance between incident and moral or religious exhortation.

Shepard led a relatively eventful life, especially during the years of his dispute with Archbishop Laud and the rest of the anti-Puritan religious establishment in England. On a number of occasions, he made hair-raising escapes from Laud's agents. After narrating each of these episodes in his autobiography, he pauses to explain the spiritual significance. Just as he was ready to embark for New England in 1635, for instance, he suffered a delay of six weeks because his ship was not ready. They were frightened weeks, just a step ahead of the law, but in retrospect the delay points a moral: "I learnt from that time never to go about a sad business in the dark, unless God's call within as well as that without be very strong and clear and comfortable." And, describing one of his near shipwrecks, Shepard tells of his amazement that the ship was saved by its anchor. As he says, with a deliberate literary flourish: "The cable was let out so far that a little rope held the cable, and the cable the little anchor, and the little anchor the great ship in this great storm."

Shepard's journal, which he did not prepare for other readers, does not display this kind of effort toward verbal felicity. It is much more spontaneous, since its entries were probably inscribed at the time of the events recorded and not afterward. Consequently, the journal, though awkward and repetitive, is a more informal and revealing document than the autobiography. Nonetheless, both of Shepard's accounts of himself disclose some of the same commanding preoccupations: above all, an anxiety over his election and a conviction that every event, both in one's own life and in the world at large, was at once a part of God's plan and a part too of God's communication of that plan. To pick an instance almost at random, Shepard interprets the sicknesses of his firstborn son as a sign: "The Lord showed me my weak faith, want of fear, pride, carnal content, immoderate love of creatures and of my child especially." Similarly, the long and quite poignant description Shepard gives of the death of his second wife concludes with the observation that "God hath visited and scourged me for my sins and sought to wean me from this world."

There is surely a sinister egotism in this reduction of other human beings and their tragedies into a system of signals directed toward oneself. At the same time, such a translation – and there is a good deal of it in the diaries of these self-absorbed Puritan men and women – was theologically consistent. In addition, incorporating suffering into patterns also provided a means of controlling grief. If the death of a loved one is perceived as a purposeful rebuke from God, then that death, though no less painful, becomes rational and meaningful.

A journal entry from April 15, 1640, provides an indication of how demanding Shepard was in judging his own behavior. "When I looked over the day," he writes, "I saw how I fell short of God and Christ, and how I had spent one hour unprofitably. And why? Because though the thing I did was good, yet because I intended not my God in it as my end . . . therefore I was unprofitable and so desired to be humbled for it."

This sort of zeal and sobriety and self-reproach fills Shepard's journal. Nonetheless, his self-analysis seems practically lighthearted in comparison with the diary of Michael Wigglesworth. Wigglesworth, remembered today as the author of *The Day of Doom*, is perhaps the man who conforms most closely to the popular view of the Puritan as a grim and relentless spiritual scourge. Wigglesworth, whose diary covers the mid–1650s, wrote it while he was in his twenties and a student and tutor at Harvard. The volume is a bleak and almost unrelieved succession of complaints in which Wigglesworth records for whole days practically nothing but the unregenerate state of his soul. Even the occasional concrete detail or episode is included only to illustrate his degeneracy.

On June 24, 1653, Wigglesworth records that he scolded one of the younger Harvard students for misbehavior, and he says along the way: "I told him also of the dangers of pleasure and how they had like to have been my ruin." That sentence rather nicely summarizes Wigglesworth's attitude throughout his diary. On September 14 of the same year, he writes: "I fall short and have nothing compared to my sins." And then he adds, in a sentence that quite specifically appears to link gloom and salvation: "And that's the reason I attain not redemption, because not weary and heavy laden with my sin." In spite of this disclaimer, weariness and self-reproach sit heavily upon these pages.

September 11, 1653: "I found much deadness and little brokenness of heart for my sins this day, and some risings of Atheistic thoughts." September 28: "I am unworthy to lift up mine eyes to heaven, because proud and vain and forgetful of God." January 9, 1654: "Monday. I found pride monstrously prevailing, for which I am ashamed and know not what to do." Again and again, day after day, Wigglesworth torments himself with self-condemnation, sometimes in a distastefully lurid language. This, for instance, from November 9, 1653: "Look down and see my plague sores which I spread before thee, my savior; wounds and old putrified sores which provoke the Lord, stink in his nostrils, and poison the peace and comfort of my own soul. Behold I am vile; when thou showest me my face, I abhor myself. Who can bring a clean thing out of filthiness?"

It is difficult to discern much in the way of either spiritual or literary refreshment in this kind of performance, especially when it is multiplied literally hundreds of times. On one occasion, Wigglesworth actually composed an itemized list of his sins: first, a blind mind, often questioning the most palpable truths; second, carnal security and hardness of heart. And so on, down through: fifth, pride; sixth, sloth; seventh, vain distractions in holy duties. The dreary catalog finally ends at ten.

If Wigglesworth's diary is impressive for any reason, it might be for his sheer spiritual tenacity. He expended an exceptional quantity of energy indicting himself for the same offenses week after week, yet the sense of crisis is ultimately diminished rather than intensified by reiteration. Wigglesworth was probably altogether sincere as he went about his inward religious excavations, but his ideas and images are so repetitive that they begin to seem routine. Even fear and trembling lose their urgency when they become too predictable.

Whereas Wigglesworth seems the most formidable, one-dimensional, and distant of all the major New England Puritans, Samuel Sewall is probably the only Puritan whom many modern readers find nearly congenial. Part of the reason for this, as his diary makes clear, is quite simply that Sewall does not at all exemplify rigorous and orthodox Puritan values. His diary covers about as many years in the eighteenth century as in the seventeenth, but in ways other than mere chronology Sewall represents a more modern temperament than either Thomas Shepard or Michael Wigglesworth. His diary reveals a man trying, sometimes comically, sometimes with dignity, to sustain the plainer ideals of his fathers while, willy-nilly, becoming an eighteenth-century gentleman.

Sewall was the son of a prosperous landowner, and he multiplied his inheritance through shrewd commerce. Merchant, elected official, chief judge of the Massachusetts Superior Court, husband and father several times each, Sewall was a man of considerable colonial importance for several decades. At the same time, he was a Harvard classmate of the poet Edward Taylor, he showed a lifelong interest in books and learning, and he followed theological debates with knowledgeable attention (Figure 8).

In most respects, both politically and religiously, Sewall was a conventional and conservative man of his time. Two choices, however, set him apart from his contemporaries. The first was his public confession of guilt for having handed down death sentences in the Salem witch trials of 1692. On Fast Day, January 1697, Sewall stood up in church and listened along with the congregation as the minister read aloud the declaration of remorse that Sewall had composed. His second remarkable act was to write and publish *The Selling of Joseph: A Memorial*, in 1700. This was the first antislavery tract to be printed in New England. Part of Sewall's argument in his pamphlet is based on appeals to common sense and natural law. Men and women should not be arbitrarily deprived of their freedom, Sewall writes, because "liberty is in real value next unto Life." Furthermore, the "continual aspiring after their forbidden Liberty" turns slaves into "Unwilling Servants." Pragmatism and logic thus

FIGURE 8 ❧ John Smibert, portrait of Samuel Sewall (ca. 1730). This portrait of Sewall appeared in the exhibition with which Smibert opened his Boston studio in 1730, the first organized art show in the New World.

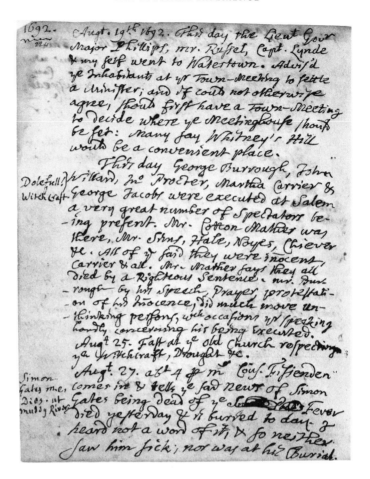

FIGURE 9 ❧ Manuscript page from Samuel Sewall's *Diary* showing the entry for August 19, 1692. On this page Sewall records the execution of George Burroughs, John Williams, John Proctor, Martha Carrier, and George Jacobs as witches. His marginal comment, "Doleful Witchcraft!", was added later.

oppose slavery. But Sewall also invokes Scripture in his argument; indeed much of his tract is given over to a refutation of the so-called biblical defense of slavery.

These acts of Sewall's – his recantation of his role in the witch trials and his attack on slavery – brought him notoriety; they made a prominent man even more prominent. His diary, on the other hand, which he kept for over half a century and by which he is best remembered today, was unknown to his contemporaries. It was published more than a century after his death (Figure 9).

Sewall's belief in God is a prominent theme in his diary, as are his spiritual doubts and longings. Many of the entries in the diary are still inscribed within familiar Puritan perspectives. For example, Sewall's world still consists of a system of readable signs which body forth the presence and the plans of God. Thus, his observations are often followed by some question or comment concerning the spiritual significance of what he sees. On October 1, 1697, Sewall notes that a glass of spirits standing on a stool fell and broke. He adds: "I said 'twas a lively emblem of our fragility and mortality." Again, on October 25, 1713, he writes: "I was startled because I had spilled a whole can of water just before we went to bed and made the reflection that our lives would shortly be spilt." Such remarks seem more like perfunctory moral tags than thoughtful meditations, but they document at least a vestigial trace of sacramental conviction.

However, competing with these conventional religious attitudes on every page, and finally shouldering them aside altogether, is a different discourse, revealing quite a different side of Sewall's personality, the attitudes of an inquisitive, secular, attentive man of the world. Though most of his contemporaries did not know it, Sewall was a tireless collector of facts and impressions, which he wrote down in his diary. Without intending to do so, he produced a literary work of a high order, evoking at once a whole society and a good many of its individual members.

Sewall tells stories about murderers and militiamen; he grouses about prices and periwigs; he provides notations upon just about every nook and cranny of the colony's politics, economy, and social life. This note is dated August 6, 1695: "Mr. Obinson's wife comes to me and complains of her husband's ill usage of her; kicked her out of bed last night, lets her have nothing but water to drink, won't let her have Clothes or victuals." On October 24, 1706, Sewall laments that "Mr. Wadsworth appears at lectures in his perriwig. Mr. Chiever is grieved at it." So too is Sewall grieved at Mr. Wadsworth's indecorous behavior.

In the midst of all his years and pages, the most engrossing parts of Sewall's diary relate his several middle-aged courtships, especially the addresses he made, when in his sixties and twice widowed, to Mrs. Winthrop. When he bestows gifts on her, he itemizes them, along with their cost. "I gave her Dr. Preston['s book], The Church's Marriage and the Church's Carriage, which cost me 6ˢ at the Sale." That from October 12, 1720; and this from November 2: "Gave her about ½ pound of Sugar Almonds, cost 3ˢ per pound." Sometimes he complains to his diary about her personal appearance: "In the evening I visited Madam Winthrop, who treated me courteously, but not in clean linen as sometimes" (October 17, 1720). And, as the next entry indicates, Sewall did not always find friendly treatment at Mrs. Winthrop's hands: "I asked when our proceedings should be made public. She said they were like to be no more public than they were already. Offered me no wine that I remember. I rose up at eleven a-clock to come away, saying I would put on my coat; She offered not to help me. I prayed her that Juno [Mrs. Winthrop's servant] might light me home; she opened the shutter, and said 'twas pretty light abroad; Juno was weary and gone to bed. So I came home by starlight as well as I could." Sewall and the lady argue about proposed cash settlements and about expenses. He says that she spoke "earnestly about keeping a Coach. I said 'twould cost £100 per annum; she said 'twould cost but £40." On one or two occasions, Sewall even sounds like a New England version of a Restoration gallant. I asked her "to acquit me of Rudeness if I drew off her glove. When she enquired the reason, I told her 'twas great odds between handling a dead goat and a living lady." But, at last, all of Sewall's gifts and wit and arguments were in vain. Mrs. Winthrop refused him, and several years later the diary ends.

Private and sometimes interestingly idiosyncratic, the Puritans' diaries tell their individual stories. Their collective and public story can be found in the books of history they wrote. These comprise what might be called the communal autobiography of the Puritan colonists. The Puritans brought to their historical craft both a lively interest in the classical historians and a particular religious perspective. They shared with their Renaissance contemporaries an enthusiasm for the moralizing chronicles of Livy, Tacitus, and Plutarch, and they inherited from medieval Christianity a providential conception of human history, the belief that earthly events move inexorably toward the fulfillment of a divine plan. All Christian historians assume a didactic responsibility: to explain how the facts of the past illuminate God's intentions. The Puritan historians went farther. They placed themselves and their New World experiment at the focus of providential history. They depicted themselves as a latter-day chosen people, enacting in the New World Zion the decisive chapters of human history.

Since the Puritans perceived themselves as having undertaken a uniquely providential mission, they concluded that their collective affairs were worth preserving and passing on. After all, they were acting not simply as secular men and women but as agents of God. In 1673, Urian Oakes spoke for the first several generations of Puritans when he explained the providential basis of their history. Oakes affirmed that "God has shewn us almost unexampled... mercy. And it were very well if there were a memorial of these things faithfully drawn up, and transmitted to Posterity." Because they had been the recipients of God's special benevolence, it was their "great duty to be the Lords *Remembrancers*." The story of the Puritan errand, in short, is not the mere record of human deeds but tells of God's purposeful presence in the New World. Such assumptions give a formulaic predictability to much Puritan history, but they also engender a sense of drama and high purpose. From the Puritans' providential vantage point, fact is transformed into myth.

The first of the New England historians was William Bradford, who began writing *Of Plymouth Plantation* in 1630 and continued working on it for two decades. Bradford was the leading figure in the Plymouth colony; he was elected governor after the death of John Carver in 1621 and served in that position for most of the rest of his life. *Of Plymouth Plantation* was not published until the nineteenth century, but it circulated in manuscript and exerted a considerable influence on writers of the second and third generations of New England settlement. Bradford opens his history by declaring that he will write in "a plain style, with singular regard unto the simple truth in all things, at least as near as my slender judgment can attain the same." These may have been Bradford's intentions, but the style of the history is not always plain, nor is the truth always simple. Rather, the book is a kind of sacred melodrama in which the piety and courage of the saints are repeatedly tested by danger and treachery. *Of Plymouth Plantation* bears witness to a people of destiny. Looking back, for example, to the moment in 1620 when the Pilgrims were first put ashore in the New World, Bradford summons an image enveloped in the aura of heroism and endurance:

> But here I cannot but stay and make a pause, and stand half amazed at this poor people's present condition; and so I think will the reader, too, when he well considers the same. Being thus passed the vast ocean, and a sea of troubles . . . they had now no friends to welcome them nor inns to entertain or refresh their weather-beaten bodies; no houses or much less towns to repair to, to seek for succour. It is recorded in Scripture as a mercy to the Apostle and his ship-wrecked company, that the barbarians showed them no small kindness in refreshing them, but these savage barbarians, when they met with them . . . were readier to fill their sides full of arrows than otherwise. What could they see but a hideous and desolate wilderness, full of wild beasts and wild men – and what multitudes there might be of them they knew not. Neither could they, as it were go up to the top of Pisgah to view from this wilderness a more goodly country to feed their hopes; for which way soever they turned their eyes (save upward to the heavens) they could have little solace or content in respect of any outward objects. For summer being done, all things stand upon them with a weather-beaten face, and the whole country, full of woods and thickets, represented a wild and savage hue. If they looked behind them, there was the mighty ocean which they had passed and was now as a main bar and gulf to separate them from all the civil parts the world.
>
> What could now sustain them but the Spirit of God and His Grace?

In this well-known passage, Bradford renders the Pilgrim's first encounter with the wilderness that was to be their new home. The settlers under his command are shown to be beleaguered but faithful Christians, facing unprecedented perils with unshakable resolve. The biblical references link the Pilgrims to heroes of the Old and New Testaments: Moses and Saint Paul. In short, *Of Plymouth Plantation* is not merely history; it is a religious epic. The story it tells is filled with a sense of God's providential design and the unique place of the Pilgrims in carrying out that plan. Thus, Bradford's purpose is only incidentally to create a record of events. He intends to celebrate the triumphant saints and to enshrine their righteous mission.

Despite Bradford's proud and pious hopes, Plymouth did not survive to the end of its first century. Increasingly overshadowed by its larger neighbor to the north, the Plymouth Plantation was officially absorbed into Massachusetts in 1691. But the story of the

Pilgrims endured as picturesque legend. Bradford's rhetoric endured as well, contributing its indelible share to the emerging myth of America's special mission and its exceptional place in the community of nations.

The New England colonies produced historians in abundance. The significance of the holy errand demanded documentation. Furthermore, the theological and political enemies of the Puritans published slanders against the saints that called forth volumes of historical self-defense. The New Englanders were accustomed to attack; the name "Puritan" itself had initially been a label applied to them with a sneer by their opponents in Europe. In the New World, the most pernicious of their enemies was Thomas Morton. In the 1620s, Morton presided over a tiny settlement near Plymouth that outraged his godly neighbors. Merry Mount, as Morton called his cluster of huts, seemed to Bradford and his followers a haven of loose living and deviant theology. It also seemed dangerous, because Morton sold guns and liquor to the Indians. In 1628, Morton provoked the Pilgrims by setting up a maypole. He was arrested by Captain Myles Standish and deported to England. As Bradford wrote, Morton's house was torn down, "that it might be no longer a roost for such unclean birds to nestle in." Morton refused to repent. He met puritanical piety with ribald contempt. Several years after the events at Merry Mount, Morton published his book *New England Canaan*, in which he held the spiritual rigor of the Pilgrims up to ridicule. In his account, the short and red-faced Myles Standish becomes Captain Shrimp, and the other Pilgrim leaders are derisively honored as the Nine Worthies. The whole saintly community is populated by "precise Separatists," as Morton calls them, men and women who "keep much ado about the tithe of meat and cumin, troubling their brains more than reason would require about things that are indifferent."

The Puritans frequently met with such antagonism as Morton's; it provided their chroniclers with an added polemical motive. By demonstrating the sanctity of the mission, the Puritan historian could dispose of the hostile criticism of outsiders. In addition, as time went by and the communal sense of purpose waned, the historians could provide a means of collective self-assurance, periodic recollections of past heroism coupled with reaffirmations of communal integrity.

Aside from William Bradford, most of the colonial chroniclers were residents of Massachusetts. Among the earliest settlers, for example, was Edward Johnson, who emigrated to Boston in 1630, spent the remaining forty years of his life in New England, and held several important positions in the colony, including a term as speaker of the Massachusetts House of Deputies. His history was published anonymously in London in 1653, and the title could serve as a summary of the Puritans' sense of historical identity. Johnson called his book *The Wonder-working Providence of Sion's Saviour in New England* (Figure 10).

Like all the Puritan historians, Johnson insists on the religious motives that impelled the colonial settlements. Thus, the migration of the saints to the New World became necessary when "England began to decline in Religion" and complied with "Popery," rather than purging it. In Johnson's reckoning, New England was to be the place where sacred and earthly history would converge, where "the Lord will create a new Heaven, and a new Earth, new Churches, and a new Common-wealth." This language suggests the apocalyptic temper that Johnson's book shares with so much of Puritan historical writing. The errand in the New England wilderness opens the decisive last encounter

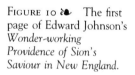

FIGURE 10 ❧ The first page of Edward Johnson's *Wonder-working Providence of Sion's Saviour in New England.*

CHAP. I.   I

VVonder-working PROVIDENCE
OF
SIONS *SAVIOUR*.

Being a Relation of the first planting in *New England,*
in the Yeare, 1628.

CHAP. I.

The sad Condition of England, when this People removed.

 HEN *England* began to decline in Religion, like luke-warme *Laodicea,* and instead of purging out Popery, a farther compliance was sought not onely in vaine Idolatrous Ceremonies, but also in prophaning the Sabbath, and by Proclamation throughout their Parish churches, exasperating lewd and prophane persons to celebrate a Sabbath like the Heathen to *Venus, Baccus* and *Ceres;* in so much that the multitude of irreligious lascivious and popish affected persons spred the whole land like *Grashoppers,* in this very time Christ the glorious King of his Churches, raises an Army out of our *English* Nation, for freeing his people from their long servitude under usurping Prelacy; and because every corner of *England* was filled with the fury of malignant adversaries, Christ creates a New *England* to muster up the first of his Forces in; Whose low condition, little number, and remotenesse of place made

B   these

between the armies of the Lord and those of evil. Johnson's prose practically marches to the conviction that New England history and sacred history are one.

> Who would not be a Soldier on Christ's side, where there is such a certainty of victory? Nay I can tell you a farther word of encouragement, every true-hearted Soldier that falls by the sword in this fight, shall not lie dead long, but stand upon his feet again, and be made partaker of the triumph of this Victory: and none can be overcome but by turning his back in flight. And for a word of terror to the enemy, let them know, Christ will never give over the raising of fresh Forces, till they are overthrown root and branch.

As he reconstructs the story of Puritan settlement, Johnson repeatedly invokes biblical precedents. The harassment of the saints by King Charles I is like the pursuit of David by Saul; the pain of separation caused by the departure from old England recalls the sorrow felt by David and Jonathan; the Puritan leaders resemble Moses and Aaron.

These analogies exemplify a recurrent pattern in Johnson's book, the application of biblical parallels to Puritan circumstances. Like William Bradford, and Puritan historians generally, Johnson was adapting a typological method of reading history and the Bible. Typology involves the relationship between the Old and the New Testaments. Briefly, it is a method of biblical interpretation devised early in the Christian era through which the meaning of the Old Testament is made partly dependent upon correspondences between the Old Testament and the New. Events and persons in the Old Testament, although they retain their own literal and historical truth, gain further significance because they are thought to anticipate episodes and figures in the New Testament. So, for instance, Adam becomes a *type* of Christ: Christ is the new Adam, whose death brings redemption and the expiation of the first Adam's sin. Or, the bread and wine used by the Old Testament prophet Melchizedek is thought to foreshadow the Last Supper. The three days Jonah spent in the whale's belly prophesy Christ's three-day harrowing of hell between the Crucifixion and Resurrection.

Through all sorts of linkages, the Puritans adopted typology for their own history. Their journey across the ocean became the Exodus; the New World was perceived by turns as wilderness and promised land; and their leaders, especially Bradford and Winthrop, were likened to Moses leading the new nation of Israel out of the Babylon (sometimes the Egypt) of Old World depravity. The Puritans dealt with their history as if it were a sort of third Testament, fulfilling the promises of both the Old and New Testaments and approaching the end of secular history.

Mary Rowlandson's narrative of her captivity by Indians illustrates how such perceptions guided the interpretation of personal as well as communal events. Rowlandson's book gives an account of her capture by the Narragansett Indians in February 1675 and her sufferings during three months of captivity. In the raid in which she was taken, Rowlandson saw her town put to the torch and several men, women, and children murdered. In the subsequent months, she took part in several forced marches through the New England woods, surviving through a combination of good fortune and her own shrewd competence. Her exciting story has enjoyed three centuries of popularity, primarily because of the vivid particularity with which she recreated her adventures. Her main purposes in the narrative, however, were pious and didactic. Entitled *The Sovereignty and Goodness of God, Together with the Faithfulness of His Promises Displayed*, her book transforms her adventures into a sustained allegory declaring the presence of God in human affairs. Thus, the Indians are the servants of the devil, a role often assigned to them by English settlers. Rowlandson herself is the imperiled Christian pilgrim, threatened by satanic snares and finally delivered by Providence. Throughout her narrative, Rowlandson uses biblical citations to comment on each episode. In the end, she likens herself to David, grateful for the scourge of her afflictions, and then to Moses, whose exodus anticipated her own.

The same providential assumptions underlie the most ambitious of Puritan histories, Cotton Mather's seven-volume *Magnalia Christi Americana* (1702). Mather was a leading figure in New England's third Puritan generation, and his family was among the most distinguished in Massachusetts. He was the grandson of both John Cotton and Richard Mather, two of the leading ministers of the colony's early years, and he was the son of Increase Mather, the teacher of Boston's Second Church and president of Harvard College

(Figure 11, Figure 12). Cotton Mather's lineage was matched by his own great gifts – he enrolled in Harvard before his twelfth birthday, and he mastered several ancient and modern languages. He made a prominent, controversial career, but he labored throughout his life under the heavy burden that his family and talents created. Along with his preaching and writing, Mather was active as a doer of good works, including the support of schools for the children of slaves. He also took an influential part in all the debates that shook Massachusetts in his lifetime, from the witchcraft trials of the 1690s to the arguments over smallpox vaccination thirty years later. By the time of his death in 1728, he had played a leading role in the colony's life for over forty years. But Mather's life of public achievement was shadowed by private tragedy and self-doubt. He suffered an assortment of physical and nervous afflictions, buried two wives and thirteen of his fifteen children, and saw his third wife drift into insanity (Figure 13).

Mather was the most productive scholar and author that the New World produced in its first century. He published over four hundred separate books, tracts, and pamphlets, most of them theological but some of them on subjects ranging from natural science to politics. From the vantage point of posterity, his most notorious publication is probably his book *Wonders of the Invisible World*, which he brought out in 1692, in the midst of the witchcraft trials in Salem. As a result of those trials, twenty women and men were executed: nineteen of them were hanged, and one, an old man named Giles Corey, was "pressed" to death under heavy weights. Mather was not solely responsible for the moral climate that produced the witchcraft hysteria, but in the months before the trials he campaigned tirelessly to convince New England that witchcraft presented a real and present danger to the well-being of the community. His first book on the subject, *Memorable Providences, Relating to Witchcraft and Possessions*, had appeared three years before the tragedy in Salem and had attracted notice in Massachusetts and England.

To be sure, belief in witches had been current throughout the Christian world for centuries. Nor was Mather's position uncommon, even in the late seventeenth century. The spiritual world was understood to be invisible but real, and its agents could intrude into earthly affairs at any moment. However, despite the vitality of

Mr. Richard Mather.

FIGURE 11 ᕙ John Foster's likeness of Richard Mather (ca. 1670) is the first known engraved portrait made in the English-speaking New World.

FIGURE 12 ᕙ Jan Vanderspriet, portrait of Increase Mather (1688).

FIGURE 13 ᕙ Peter Pelham, mezzotint portrait of Cotton Mather (1727).

demonic belief throughout the colonies, formal accusations of witchcraft were relatively rare, and trials were even fewer. The witchcraft
outbreak at Salem was by far the worst such episode in the history
of the New World. Thus, if traditional concepts of the spirit world
provide the background for the events in Salem, they do not explain
why the hysteria attacked where and when it did. Many suggestions
have been offered, ranging from the sexual pathology of a repressive
society to the anxieties caused by the revocation of the Massachusetts charter in 1691, which threatened the colony's legal status and
the validity of property titles. To Cotton Mather, at least initially,
the rise of witchcraft in Salem had an obvious explanation. It was
both a test of the colony's mettle and a rebuke for the community's
moral backsliding.

The quality of justice dispensed by the Massachusetts court is
suggested by the chilling transcripts that have survived. Sarah Good,
in this representative exchange, found herself trapped between the
accusations of the young girls who brought the witchcraft charges
and the suspicions of her judges:

Q. Sarah Good, what evil spirit have you familiarity with?
A. None.
Q. Have you made no contract with the devil?
Good answered no.
Q. Why do you hurt these children?
A. I do not hurt them. I scorn it.
Q. Who do you employ, then, to do it?
A. I employ nobody.
Q. What creature do you employ, then?
A. No creature. But I am falsely accused.
Q. Why did you go away muttering from Mr. Parris's house?
   [Samuel Parris was pastor of the church in Salem village.]
A. I did not mutter, but I thanked him for what he gave
   my child.
Q. Have you made no contract with the devil?
A. No.
H[Judge William Hathorne] desired the children, all of them, to
look upon her and see if this were the person that had hurt them,
and so they all did look upon her and said this was one of the persons
that did torment them. Presently they were all tormented.
Q. Sarah Good, do you not see now what you have done?
   Why do you not tell us the truth? Why do you thus
   torment these poor children?

A. I do not torment them.
Q. Who do you employ then?
A. I employ nobody. I scorn it.

Within a few months of the first accusations, hundreds of men and women were in Massachusetts jails under indictment for witchcraft. However, the mass executions provoked widespread repugnance; in the fall of 1692, almost as suddenly as they began, the convulsions ended.

Cotton Mather's role in this darkest episode in New England's colonial history was equivocal. Although he counseled caution in the evaluation of testimony and warned against relying on spectral evidence, he also demanded the vigorous prosecution of witches. The special sanctity of New England was actually proved, in Mather's estimation, by the epidemic of witchcraft. The Puritans had taken over the devil's territories and turned them to holy uses; in consequence, as Mather wrote in *The Wonders of the Invisible World*, "the devil was exceedingly disturbed... and is now making one more attempt upon us." The witches were enemies within the gates of the city, conscious agents of a powerful and hidden adversary: The frenzied scenes Cotton Mather described and his orthodox but unsavory defense of repression would echo across three centuries of American experience. "Witch-hunt" would become a metaphor, loose-fitting but quite proper, for government's recurrent efforts to punish difference and impose conformity.

Mather's health and reputation both suffered as a result of the trials in Salem. The attacks he suffered contributed to what he saw as a lifelong pattern of misunderstanding and rejection. Nonetheless, he remained at his ministerial post for three more decades, carrying out his preaching duties and publishing his views at a prodigious rate. Among all his many works, the most enduring has been *Magnalia Christi Americana*, his encyclopedic history of New England (or, as the title suggests, the history of Christ's great deeds in America). Filling eight hundred oversize pages and divided into seven volumes, the *Magnalia* combines a history of the colony and of Harvard College, lives of governors and ministers, polemical accounts of theological debates, and copious examples of God's special providences toward his saints. Despite the assurance of its title, the

Magnalia is as much elegy as history, a vast monument to vanished glory. Mather intended that his book might help in "keeping *Alive* ... the Interests of *Dying Religion* in our Churches," but a sense of belatedness, of an irrecoverable loss, pervades his pages. If Massachusetts remains a city upon a hill, its high eminence lingers mainly in memory and myth. What is still vital endures in the recovered past: "Whether *New England* may *Live* any where else or no, it must *Live* in our *History!*"

The dozens of biographies that Mather included in the *Magnalia* serve both to exemplify the shining legacy of the ancestors and to counterpoint the gloomy facts of present decline. The "old New England Way" has come to an end. By reading Mather's history, the lesser men and women of the eighteenth century could find "the *Graves* of their *Dead Fathers*" and recall their heroic ancestors.

Plymouth's William Bradford, for example, was in Mather's view the Moses that a people in a wilderness needed. The perils of early colonization might have proved beyond solution without the providential guidance of Bradford's strength and unerring common sense. Furthermore, along with his talent for governing, Bradford was notable for piety. He taught himself Hebrew so that he could "see with his own eyes the ancient oracles of God in their native beauty." Combining in himself the active and contemplative in abundant measure, Bradford emerges from Mather's pages as a man of mythic proportions. John Winthrop was the American Nehemiah, the reference recalling the governor of Judea who rebuilt the walls of Jerusalem after their destruction by Nebuzaradan. In Mather's pious portrait, Winthrop also resembles but surpasses the lawgivers and governors of Greece and Rome. Among the other heroes of the early years of the godly commonwealth, Mather commemorates his grandfathers, Richard Mather and John Cotton; the legendary schoolmaster Ezekiel Cheever, who taught the young boys of Boston, New Haven, Ipswich, and Charlestown for sixty years; and John Eliot, apostle to the Indians, who "shone as the *Moon* among the lesser *Stars*."

These portraits in the *Magnalia* exemplify the interweaving of the Puritan arts of history and biography. The career of the American covenant is embodied both in the godly community and in the righteous persons whose lives the community embraces. A similar if less ambitious use of individuals as representative figures can also be seen in the painting of early New England. Captain Thomas Smith's rough but quite powerful self-portrait, for example, is more an allegorical image of sober gravity, social hierarchy, and moral preachment than a likeness. Caressing a death's head, the traditional emblem of mortality, Captain Smith broods on the transience of life. At the same time, Smith's strong features fill the center of the picture; his face perched atop a cravat of fine, expensive fabric. The open window offers a glimpse of the sea, once the route of the exodus, now the pathway of commerce. The picture captures something at once of the personal and public character of seventeenth-century Massachusetts. Mercantile instincts and piety coexist, bridging the future and the past of the colony (Figure 14).

Cotton Mather's long life spanned a period of profound change in the British settlements in the New World. In the years following the Stuart Restoration of 1660, the Crown made considerable administrative exertions in the effort to draw its disparate American outposts into a more connected imperial unit. The political history of the eighteenth century resulted in large measure from the tensions between the centralizing ambition of England and the increasingly independent inclinations of the New World. Those tensions were exacerbated by the rise of an Anglo-American aristocracy, individuals and families who had prospered on America's soil and whose self-interest corresponded with an enlarged American self-government. The emerging elite put strains on colonial society as well. Though Europe's grinding poverty was absent from America, the gulf between rich and poor widened, and slavery ominously grew. Most property holders held title to small claims, but a man like Robert ("King") Carter of Virgina, who died in 1732, left an estate including three hundred thousand acres, ten thousand pounds in cash, and one hundred twenty-five slaves (Figure 15).

America's numbers grew rapidly. The population reached a quarter of a million by 1720, then quintupled by the time of the Revolution. The country remained agrarian, but cities were growing. A small but increasing proportion of the colonies' citizens lived in New York, Boston, and Philadelphia, the last of which became, by midcentury, the second-largest metropolis in the English-speaking world. These cities, along with Charleston and Newport, were the chief seaports and the commercial centers of the colonies. Enter-

FIGURE 14 ❧ Captain Thomas Smith, self-portrait (1690).

prising merchants accumulated fortunes and competed with large landowners for dominance. Religion would remain prominent in the rhetoric of America's public life, but the contest for colonial leadership and ultimately for national sovereignty shifted irreversibly to the secular arena of politics.

A prophetic glimpse of the nation's future course can be found in one of Cotton Mather's last important publications, *Bonifacius* (1710), usually called by the abbreviated title *"Essays to Do Good."*

The book is an extended meditation upon the civic obligations of Christians, along with detailed suggestions for useful service. Among other things, Mather proposes that charitable undertakings should be addressed through voluntary organizations; that the poor and the sick should be relieved; that education should be made widely available. Though religion provides the basis upon which Mather builds in *Bonifacius*, the spirit of a later and more secular philanthropy has often been discerned in the volume. Benjamin Franklin wrote that *Bonifacius* influenced him "through life; for I have always set a greater value on the character of a doer of good, than on any other kind of reputation; and if I have been a useful citizen, the Public owes the advantage of it to that book." Franklin was four years old when *Bonifacius* was published; his tribute to the book identifies the continuity as well as the changes that would mark the eighteenth-century course of New England's intellectual and social history. The Puritan virtues of industry, sobriety, and fidelity to one's calling would persist but would find worldly outlets.

FIGURE 15 🍂
Newspaper notices, posters, and broadsides were used to advertise slave sales. This broadside was circulated in South Carolina.

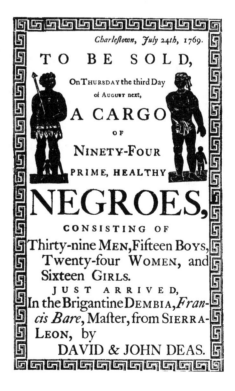

࿔

The enormous canon of Mather's writings includes examples of virtually every nonfictional genre; he even attempted a number of halting verses. Poetry was much written in colonial New England, though most of it was, like Mather's, derivative, pious, and wooden. Poetry was merely another part, and a small one, of the Old World legacy the Puritans brought with them to America. The education that many of them had received included sound training in the classics. For generations, though much verse was published by the colonists, only that of Anne Bradstreet rose above mediocrity. Edward Taylor's several hundred poems were not published, nor even discovered, until the twentieth century.

Not all Puritan poetry was religious. Like other men and women of the seventeenth century, the New England colonists found occasion to versify a good deal of their experience. The day-to-day concerns of an agrarian and commercial society are often visible in early Puritan poetry. To pick a representative instance, there appears in the Boston *Almanac* for 1671 a verse calendar by Daniel Russell in which the twelve months of the year are apostrophized at considerable length. The entire poem presents an immense exhibition of mythological reference, without a single mention of Christianity. This stanza describes the month of June:

> The smiling Fields, attired in their Suits
> Of Taste-delighting, and Eye-pleasing Fruits;
> Their Strawb'ry Mantles now begin to wear,
> And many Orchards Cherry-cheeked appear.
> Now *Sol* in's Crabbed Throne doth take his place.
> Where he performs his Longest daily Race:
> Soon after which, the days length 'gins to fade,
> And *Phoebus, Cancer*-like turns Retrograde.

This is neither identifiably Puritan nor even religious. It resembles any number of other rather hackneyed, pastoral exercises produced in English in the seventeenth century. And countless examples of this sort, revealing the Puritans as competent, uninspired humanists, can be discovered in any collection of Puritan literature. Such collections also reveal the frequency with which the Puritans turned their poetic attention to local politics, weather conditions, court-ship, and simple gossip.

Nonetheless, although the Puritans scribbled volumes of secular verse, it is also undeniable that religion, and especially the distinctive tenets of reformed Christianity, provided the greatest single imperative and subject for Puritan poetry. As always, the Bible claimed the center of attention, providing at once a major source of ideas and imagery, a model for style and method, and the justification for poetry itself. The Puritans characteristically dedicated their literary practice to their religious commitment, and their most typical poems are devotional and didactic. Jonathan Mitchell praised the religious power of poetry in a prefatory poem he wrote for Wigglesworth's *Day of Doom*:

> A Verse may find him who a sermon flies,
> Saith Herbert well. Great truths to dress in Meter
> Becomes a Preacher, who men's Souls doth prize.

In Mitchell's view, Wigglesworth's verses avoided the frivolity of worldly poetry and achieved a noble spiritual purpose:

> In costly Verse, and most laborious Rhymes,
> Are dish'd up here Truths worthy most regard:
> No Toys, nor Fables (Poets' wonted crimes)
> Here be, but things of worth, with wit prepar'd.

The New England colonists never produced a systematic exposition of their literary theory, but Mitchell's tongue-tied tribute to Wigglesworth fairly represents what might be called a Puritan poetics. Poetry served its most productive purposes when it was directed toward religious edification. The stylistic consequences of that religious motive included a suspicion of sensuous imagery and of "witty conceits," those knotty extended metaphors through which the English metaphysical poets turned their verses into dazzling arguments.

A brief but important statement of Puritan literary attitudes is contained in the preface to the *Bay Psalm Book*. Issued in 1640, this volume of translations was the first book published in the English-speaking New World. John Cotton composed a preface which justified the poetry as an aid to religious practice. Repeatedly Cotton insists that the criteria by which the translations should be judged are religious, not literary. *The Whole Book of Psalms Faithfully Translated into English Meter*, to give its full title, was intended to replace an earlier translation of the psalms by Sternhold and Hopkins. This had been published in 1562, was soon added to the Prayer Book, and remained widely popular among Anglicans throughout the seventeenth century. Puritan disapproval of these translations was not based on matters of style or art. Rather, the Puritans objected because Sternhold and Hopkins "presented a paraphrase" instead of the words of David and often added to and subtracted from the sacred texts. As for the new translation, Cotton writes that the precise meaning of David's words, and not the requirements of sound or rhythm, has guided every verbal choice. The validity of poetry rests on its accuracy as a record of scriptural language.

Cotton acknowledged the artistic price that such priorities entail; his tone is sometimes defensive, sometimes pugnacious.

> If therefore the verses are not always so smooth and elegant as some may desire or expect; let them consider that God's Altar needs not our polishings: Exodus 20, for we have respected rather a plain translation, than to smooth our verses with the sweetness of any paraphrase, and so have attended Conscience rather than Elegance, fidelity rather than poetry, in translating the Hebrew words into English language, and David's poetry into English meter; so that we may sing in Sion the Lord's song of praise according to his own will.

The translations in the *Bay Psalm Book* are indeed unpolished. Whatever their fidelity to the Hebrew originals, as poems they are consistently awkward and unharmonious. A comparison with the King James Bible (1611) is perhaps unfair but certainly decisive. In the King James Bible, for example, the opening verses of the Twenty-Third Psalm are rendered with the elegance that Cotton has belittled:

> The Lord is my shepherd; I shall not want.
> He maketh me to lie down in green pastures: he leadeth me
>   beside the still waters.
> He restoreth my soul: he leadeth me in the paths of
>   righteousness for his name's sake.

> Yea, though I walk through the valley of the shadow of
> death, I will fear no evil: for thou art with me; thy rod
> and thy staff they comfort me.

The restrained dignity of this translation is cast into bold relief by comparison with the singsong couplets in the *Bay Psalm Book*:

> The Lord to me a shepherd is, want therefore shall not I.
> He in the folds of tender grass, doth cause me down to lie:
>   To waters calm me gently leads
> Restore my soul doth he: he doth in paths of righteousness:
>   for his name's sake lead me.
> Yea though in valley of death's shade I walk, none ill I'll
>   fear: because thou art with me, thy rod, and staff my
>   comfort are.

When the *Bay Psalm Book* was revised in 1651, the new editors, President Henry Dunster of Harvard and Richard Lyon, claimed to consult taste as well as gravity in their work. The results do not prove a major aesthetic advance, but the approval of what Dunster and Lyon call "sweetness" does suggest the relatively early intrusion of less doctrinaire norms into Puritan poetic discussion (Figure 16).

The circumstances under which the colonists wrote were unfriendly to serious artistic effort. They lived on a rough frontier, absorbed in the demands of mere physical subsistence and spiritual survival, separated from any literary society. A survey of Puritan poetry would enumerate a great many minor names, among them John Saffin, John Fiske, and Benjamin Tompson. Roger Williams included poems in praise of the Indians in his midcentury book on the language of the Narragansett tribe. Richard Steere published anti-Catholic satire and a prayerful account of Christ's nativity. Philip Pain wrote a series of sixty-four brief and rather unorthodox meditations, describing them as "Quotidian Preparations for, and Considerations of Death and Eternity." Meditation 26 is typical of the striking and sometimes slightly shocking quality of Pain's imagery:

> Alas, what's Sorrow? 'tis our portion here;
> The Christian's portion, Trouble, Grief, and Fear:
> He is The Man of Sorrows here below

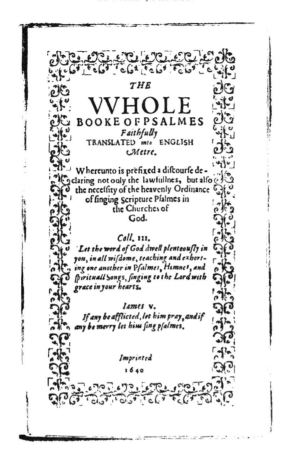

FIGURE 16 ❧ The title page of the *Bay Psalm Book* (1640). Produced on the press of Stephen Daye in Cambridge, Massachusetts, this was the first book printed in what is now the United States.

Of all the men on earth; yet let us know,
    Christ left his Grave-clothes, that we might when grief
    Draws tears, or blood, not want an Handkerchief.

The historian Edward Johnson included a number of poems in his *Wonder-Working Providence*. One of them follows this prefatory apology: "Let no man be offended at the Author's rude verse, penned of purpose to keep in memory the Names of such worthies as Christ made strong for himself, in this unwonted work of his." Johnson here admits the slender accomplishment of his own verse; more significantly, he acknowledges the traditional power of poetry to confer immortality. Johnson's commendatory portrait of the minister John Eliot is a versified saint's life. Eliot taught "heathen people" to find Christ and to overcome their savage blindness of heart. The same intentions that guided the colonists' prose also shaped their verse. Puritan poetry set out to define some aspect of New England's religious system, or to provide instruction in what the authors regard as right belief, or to record personal religious experience. Many poems, like Johnson's admiring memorial of Eliot, celebrated the lives of the ministers and leaders.

Johnson also wrote the earliest American epic, a poem called "Good News from New England." In several hundred primitive lines, he translated the providential convictions of the Puritans into verse. The familiar story of English persecution, perilous exodus, and heroic mastery of the wilderness is retold, now in scores of clumsy couplets.

> In unknown depths, and pathless Seas, there nights and days they
>   spend,
>   'Mongst stormy winds and mountain waves long time no land
>   they kend.
> At ships mast doth Christs Pastors preach, while waves like
>   Prelates proud,
>   Would fling them from their pulpits place as not by them
>   allowed.
> The swelling surges raging come to stop their mouths with foam,
>   For publishing of every truth that by God's word is known.
> But Christ as once, so now he says peace ye waves, and be still,
>   For all their height they fall down flat, obey they must his
>   will.
> And now the Seas like meadows green, whose ground and grass
>   even are,
>   Doth gently lead their ships as sheep from place to place afar.

The hand of Christ is everywhere visible, and nature is pressed into poetic service. The ocean signifies, first, the persecuting prelates of the English church from whom the colonists are escaping, and then, the promise of green harmony which lies before them. Johnson's poem contains an abundance of vivid scenes such as this one. Thus, despite its rudimentary artistic control and the manacles of its meter, "Good News from New England" reproduces something of the exaltation of the Puritan first settlement. It often manages as well to coordinate image and idea in a sustained millennial allegory.

The Puritans produced examples of poetry in virtually all the traditional genres, except for drama, which was forbidden by the same iconoclasm that led to the vandalism of shattered stained glass and mutilated statues in the churches of old England. Epic, satire, lyric, and even love poems received regular if characteristically rough-hewn treatment. During the first century of settlement, elegies had particularly wide currency. Most were circulated privately, but others were printed as broadsides and distributed as gifts, along with the customary rings and scarves, at burial services. Many of the elegies hardly rose above the jingling epitaphs carved on some colonial gravestones (Figure 17). This lament for Thomas Dudley, beginning with a clumsy anagram formed out of its subject's name, turns Dudley's fate into a threadbare warning of mortality:

> Thomas Dudley
> ah! old, must die
> A death's head on your hand you needs not wear
> a dying hand you on your shoulders bear
> you need not one to mind you, you must die
> you in your name may spell mortality
> young men may die, but old men these die must
> t'will not be long before you turn to dust.
> before you turn to dust! ah! must; old! die!

New England elegies were often far more elaborate than this anonymous memento mori. Elegies served the same purposes in colonial New England as they have in other cultures, channeling emotion into comforting patterns. The elegy enrolled the deceased man or woman in the company of departed saints, and it thereby drew consolation out of sorrow. Most Puritan elegies are stylized and even routine in their language and form, but such familiarity was itself a source of reassurance. The repetitive conventions of memorial tributes reminded readers and listeners that holiness shaped the lives of saints in quite similar and recognizable ways.

Elegies were the verse counterparts of funeral sermons, and they resembled as well the admiring biographies that filled Puritan histories. Like the biographies, elegies forged strong providential links between the individual and the community. In many elegies, the sanctity commemorated belongs not only to the individual whose death is the poem's explicit subject but equally to the covenanted commonwealth. This sort of moral calculus can lead the elegist, paradoxically but quite logically, from sorrow to satisfaction and even joy. Benjamin Woodbridge, for example, betrays hardly a hint of mourning in his poem on John Cotton. Cotton is presented first as a series of personified virtues; then he is the sun, whose retirement will permit the lesser stars to be seen. He is, furthermore, a "living breathing Bible," a metaphor that leads to an extended display of Woodbridge's wit:

> His very Name a *Title Page*; and next,
> His Life a *Commentary* on the Text.
> O what a Monument of glorious worth,
> When in a *New Edition* he comes forth

FIGURE 17 ᵂ The Joseph Tapping stone (1678), King's Chapel, Boston. Many of the emblems of mortality that Puritan carvers used on gravestones appear here: the winged skull and hourglass; the candle of life being snuffed out by a skeleton armed with a spear; the bearded and winged figure of Time carrying a scythe and hourglass.

> Without *Errata's*, may we think he'll be,
> In *Leaves* and *Covers* of Eternity!

Glancing forward to the wit of Franklin's famous epitaph, a stanza like this suggests the literary exuberance that often coexisted with piety in the Puritan imagination.

Among the handful of New England's finest elegies, the most enduring is probably Urian Oakes's tribute of 1677 to Thomas Shepard, son of the first generation's famous minister. The younger Shepard was also a minister, for many years serving the congregation of Charlestown, Massachusetts. When he died, according to Cotton Mather, "the whole Country was fill'd with Lamentations." Oakes's elegy, in fifty-two numbered stanzas, derives its strength from a combination of technical skill and controlled but palpable emotion.

> My Dearest, Inmost, Bosom-Friend is Gone!
> Gone is my sweet Companion, Soul's delight!
> Now in an Huddling Crowd I'm all alone,
> And almost could bid all the World Goodnight:
> Blest be my Rock! God lives: Oh let him be,
> As He is All, so All in All to me.

As a man, a companion, and preacher, Shepard was learned and wise: "Serious but not Sour." Oakes deftly knits together a sequence of metaphorical compliments to express the scale of the fallen saint's heroism. Shepard was a soldier defending the colony's spiritual barricades, a saint wrestling with angels, one of the pillars of New England. He was also God's ambassador, and his death may thus be a grim portent for the community. Oakes reminds his readers that kings call their ambassadors home when they intend war; Shepard's death may therefore signal God's intention to end his treaty with the Puritans. The death of Shepard, like the blaze of comets or other "Portentous Prodigies," obliges Oakes to anticipate "some approaching woe . . . some grievous inundation."

This prophetic thesis exemplifies another use of the elegy, especially in the latter part of the seventeenth century. The connection between individual and community is still vital but is here put to more censorious purposes. The death of the saint is interpreted as punishment for general misconduct or the decline of collective zeal. Such elegies become versions of jeremiad, rebuking their readers for religious and moral backsliding and demanding root-and-branch reformation as the only way to appease God's impatience and avoid his just retribution. Versions of these apocalyptic warnings were common in seventeenth-century Puritan preaching, and they infiltrated poetry as well. The Puritan consciousness, like that of other late-medieval Christians, was often absorbed in meditation upon the end of things. Feeling that they knew history's inevitable destination, Puritan believers searched for millennial signs and often found them. They anticipated the outcome with a mixture of excitement and dread, and they expressed their apocalyptic expectations in a language that superimposed the imagery of the Bible's prophetic books upon the phenomena of New England experience. In particular, they scoured the Book of Revelation for insight into the expected end. From that source they borrowed and repeatedly invoked an anthology of theatrical events that would accompany the earth's final hours: hideous thunder and lightning, sounding trumpets, a blood-stained moon, falling stars. Millennial preoccupations fixed themselves firmly in the American imagination. Stripped of their original religious substance, images of apocalypse would endure for centuries as the dark glass through which the American literary imagination perceived the history of the New World.

Sermons, poems, and diary entries beyond numbering were penetrated by the stereotyped vocabulary and structure of the end of the world, but the most sensational was Michael Wigglesworth's *Day of Doom.* Wigglesworth grew up in the wilds of New Haven, graduated first in his Harvard class, stayed on to take a master's degree in 1656, and then accepted the ministry of Malden, Massachusetts. His dispiriting diary offers a portrait of Puritanism's more lugubrious face. In stature he was, according to Cotton Mather, "a feeble, little shadow of a man," but he remained in Malden for nearly half a century, serving his congregation as both preacher and physician. He also became an influential writer. In 1662, he completed "God's Controversy with New-England. Written in the time of the great drought." The argument of this poem was that God had turned New England into "a waste and howling wilderness" to punish the spiritually bankrupt behavior of his chosen people. Several years later Wigglesworth published "Meat out of the Eater," whose purpose is declared in the remainder of its title: "Meditations concerning the necessity, end, and usefulness of afflictions unto God's children, all tending to prepare them for and comfort them under the Cross."

While these poems brought Wigglesworth a degree of notoriety, *The Day of Doom* conferred on him an odd, unsavory immortality. Here was the most popular poem in seventeenth-century New England, quite literally that century's best-selling American book. In 224 rocking stanzas of fourteener verse, this "Poetical Description of the Great and Last Judgment" tells of Christ's second coming and the just doom he brings to an evil and complacent world. After describing how the "vile wretches" of the world lay carelessly wallowing in sin, Wigglesworth presents the terror that Christ's appearance arouses:

> Mean men lament, great men do rent their Robes, and tear
> > their hair:
> > They do not spare their flesh to tear through horrible
> > > despair.
> All Kindreds wail: all hearts do fail: horror the world doth
> > fill
> > With weeping eyes, and loud out-cries, yet knows not
> > > how to kill.

The poem lingers over Christ's judgments of the guilty, titillating its readers with the reminder that all sins will be disclosed, no matter how deeply they have been concealed from neighbors and family:

> All filthy facts, and secret acts, however closly done,
> > And long conceal'd, are there reveal'd before the
> > > mid-day Sun.
> Deeds of the night shunning the light, which darkest
> > corners sought,
> > To fearful blame, and endless shame, are there most
> > > justly brought.

Although *The Day of Doom* derives a good deal of its considerable energy from narrative and descriptive passages such as these, in fact most of the poem is given over to quite detailed theological debate, as Christ explains to each class of sinners the particular grounds of its damnation. One of the more celebrated of these macabre conversations occurs when Christ is approached by those who died in infancy and had therefore never sinned. As Christ himself observes, "God doth such doom forbid, that men should dye eternally for what they never did." However, as Christ goes on to explain in a fiercely dogmatic gloss on original sin, these reprobate infants are guilty after all: "Had you been made in Adam's stead, you would like things have wrought, / and so into the self-same wo, your selves and yours have brought." Christ concludes by agreeing that the sins of these infants are less than the sins of those who lived longer; he therefore assigns them to "the easiest room in Hell." The poem concludes with glimpses of the suffering of the damned and the contrasted joys of the elect.

The Day of Doom is almost surely the most reviled poem ever written in America. The relentless sameness of its couplets never rises above the level of doctrinaire doggerel. In its scowling meagerness, Wigglesworth's writing demonstrates the aesthetic penalties that Puritanism could inflict on poetry. Nonetheless, the poem accomplished its didactic purposes. It appeared in numerous editions for over a century, and generations of New England schoolchildren actually committed it to memory. Thus, while it barely escapes self-parody, *The Day of Doom* retains historical importance as an extraordinary instance of versified Puritan orthodoxy allied with an eccentrically gothic use of plain style.

Despite its contemporary popularity, Wigglesworth's narrow achievement does not adequately illustrate the potential range or depth of Puritan verse. The first century of Puritan settlement also produced poetry of more abiding significance; in particular, the work of Anne Bradstreet and Edward Taylor first gave voice to the possibilities of an authentic American poetry.

As a child in England, Anne Bradstreet was a member of the Earl of Lincoln's Puritan household; her father, Thomas Dudley, was manager of the earl's extensive estates. From early on, the young Anne Dudley was surrounded by the religion, family, politics, and literary culture that would provide the themes of the poetry she wrote in New England. She married Simon Bradstreet in 1628, and the couple sailed for America on April 8, 1630, members of John Winthrop's first group of migrating saints. She later recalled that when she first "came into this country," she found a "new world and new manners," at which her "heart rose" in distaste. She was apparently referring to the rule that candidates for admission to colonial congregations earn their acceptance through personal narratives, because she adds: "After I was convinced it was the way of God, I submitted to it and joined the church at Boston." Bradstreet spent the remaining forty-two years of her life in Massachusetts, remaining longest in the town of Andover, a mere outpost when she moved there, still a backwater community at the end of her life.

The life and writing of Anne Bradstreet both need to be considered in the context of Puritan attitudes toward women. Among the cluster of values inherited by the New England colonists from medieval Christianity was a systematic subordination of women in theory and fact. In old England, especially in the 1650s, some of the smaller radical sects did inch toward a more humane conception of gender, but on the question of woman's place there was little to differentiate the various Protestant denominations from Rome. When a Boston preacher referred to the family as the "root whence church and commonwealth come," the family he had in mind conformed to venerable European ideas. Relationships within the family were patriarchal. The preeminent status of the husband was anchored both in custom and in biblical sources. Colonial statutes admonished wives to submit themselves to the direction of their husbands, and authority over children and servants rested ultimately with the father. Because of the initial absence of other established institutions, the family played perhaps an even more central role in the colonies than it had in England. Not surprisingly, under such circumstances, traditional definitions of the family's structure and its members' obligations were reaffirmed.

An entry in John Winthrop's journal vividly illustrates the iron weight of convention that pressed down upon any effort women might make to reach beyond their permissible roles.

> April 13, 1645. Mr. Hopkins, the governor of Hartford upon Connecticut, came to Boston, and brought his wife with him,

(a godly young woman, and of special parts), who was fallen
into a sad infirmity, the loss of her understanding and reason,
which had been growing upon her divers years, by occasion of
her giving herself wholly to reading and writing, and had written many books. Her husband, being very loving and tender
of her, was loath to grieve her; but he saw his error, when it
was too late. For if she had attended her household affairs, and
such things as belong to women, and not gone out of her way
and calling to meddle in such things as are proper for men,
whose minds are stronger, etc., she had kept her wits, and
might have improved them usefully and honorably in the place
God had set her. He brought her to Boston, and left her with
her brother, one Mr. Yale, a merchant, to try what means
might be had here for her. But no help could be had.

Undoubtedly, Winthrop had this recent scandal in mind when he
addressed the General Court on July 3, 1645, and reaffirmed the
traditional comparison between the church's subordination to Christ
and the wife's subordination to her husband. "A true wife," Winthrop reminded his hearers, "accounts her subjection her honor and
freedom, and would not think her condition safe and free, but in
her subjection to her husband's authority. Such is the liberty of the
church under the authority of Christ."

Resistance to the aspirations or even to the equal humanity of
women sometimes took more punishing forms. Two of the most
disruptive political events that punctuated the seventeenth century
– the antinomian crisis and the witchcraft trials in Salem – were
defined in large measure by issues of gender. The first of these
occurred in 1636, when Anne Hutchinson was accused by the General Court of propagating ideas that were considered both heretical
and seditious. Hutchinson had emigrated to New England in 1634
and had quickly attracted attention by her keen intellect, compelling
personality, and serious interest in theology. Men as well as women
attended her twice-weekly discussions in considerable numbers, and
they heard her energetically defend her version of the covenant of
grace. Her position was in many ways quite close to orthodox doctrine. In the eyes of the authorities, however, she represented a
species of antinomian rebellion against religious and civil order. At
her trial, the prosecution was led by John Winthrop, serving at that
time as deputy governor. Winthrop was abetted by John Cotton,

who had been Hutchinson's religious mentor in England. Hutchinson conducted her defense with impressive scholarship and voluble courage – Winthrop himself called her "a woman of ready wit and bold spirit" – but she was hectored for days, worn down, and finally convicted. John Cotton pronounced the sentence "with great solemnity, and with much zeal and detestation of her errors and pride of spirit." Banished from Massachusetts, she fled to Portsmouth, then to Long Island, where she was killed in an Indian uprising.

Hutchinson's ideas would have been suppressed regardless of her sex. Roger Williams, for example, insisted too loudly on the separation of the colony's churches from those of England. His views, which resembled Hutchinson's only insofar as they were considered equally objectionable, brought him contempt and exile. Nonetheless, the harsh treatment that Hutchinson received from the Bay Colony's leaders was undoubtedly sharpened because she was a woman. Learned and self-reliant, she shocked the Puritans by teaching, lecturing, disputing. All of this seemed unnatural to men like Winthrop and Cotton, and it multiplied the threat which Hutchinson presented to the harmony of the community.

Two generations after Anne Hutchinson's trial, women again found themselves mortally harassed by the machinery of New England's theocratic justice. A handful of Salem's accused and executed witches were men, but the substantial majority were women. Many of the victims and accusers were also women and girls. Whatever local circumstances may have determined the details of the hysteria in Salem, the disproportionate prominence of women conformed to centuries of Old World experience. Satan himself was male, but the culture of late seventeenth-century Massachusetts assumed that most of his earthly coconspirators were female.

If Anne Bradstreet made any comment on the prosecution of Anne Hutchinson, it has not survived, and she died two decades before the witch trials. Nonetheless, the values implied by those events, and by such comments as Winthrop's on Edward Hopkins's book-crazed wife, defined the atmosphere of denial and subordination within which Bradstreet wrote. Many of her poems are impersonal and derivative and inert. Others, however, usually briefer and occasional, create a splendidly personal, dramatic voice. In these Bradstreet records both the satisfactions and sorrows of her

FIGURE 18 🙲 No authenticated likeness of Anne Bradstreet is known. This stained-glass tributary portrait is part of a window in Saint Botolph's Church, Boston, Lincolnshire, England.

life, and some of them give evidence of the struggle between her religious commitment and the disappointments she faced as a Christian and a woman (Figure 18).

The volume in which Bradstreet's poetry first appeared was also the first book of poems published by a resident of the New World. Bradstreet's brother-in-law, John Woodbridge, carried a manuscript copy of the poetry to England and there, apparently without her knowledge, arranged for publication. *The Tenth Muse, Lately Sprung Up In America*, as the volume was called, appeared in London in 1650. The verses attracted wide and approving notice on both sides of the Atlantic, though much of the praise was also patronizing. Nathaniel Ward, for example, instead of merely pointing out Bradstreet's debt to Sylvester's translation of Du Bartas's *Divine Weeks*, chose to call her "a right Du Bartas girl." Ward also allowed that "it half revives my chill frost-bitten blood / To see a woman once do ought that's good." Cotton Mather offered a weightier tribute in the *Magnalia* when he wrote that Bradstreet's poems would serve as "a Monument for her Memory beyond the Stateliest Marbles." And the second edition of *The Tenth Muse* (1678) was the only volume of poems in Edward Taylor's library. She was treated with condescension, but she was also read (Figure 19).

In several places in her poems, Bradstreet makes explicit reference to the opposition her poetry would meet because of her sex. In a poetic "Prologue" to the first poem in *The Tenth Muse*, she sketches the several kinds of hostility she expects her writing to provoke:

> I am obnoxious to each carping tongue
> Who says my hand a needle better fits.
> A poet's pen all scorn I should thus wrong,
> For such despite they cast on female wits:
> If what I do prove well, it won't advance,
> They'll say it's stol'n, or else it was by chance.

Unequal to the high call of poetry, a woman should cling to her domestic tasks. If she persists, and if she writes a good poem, the

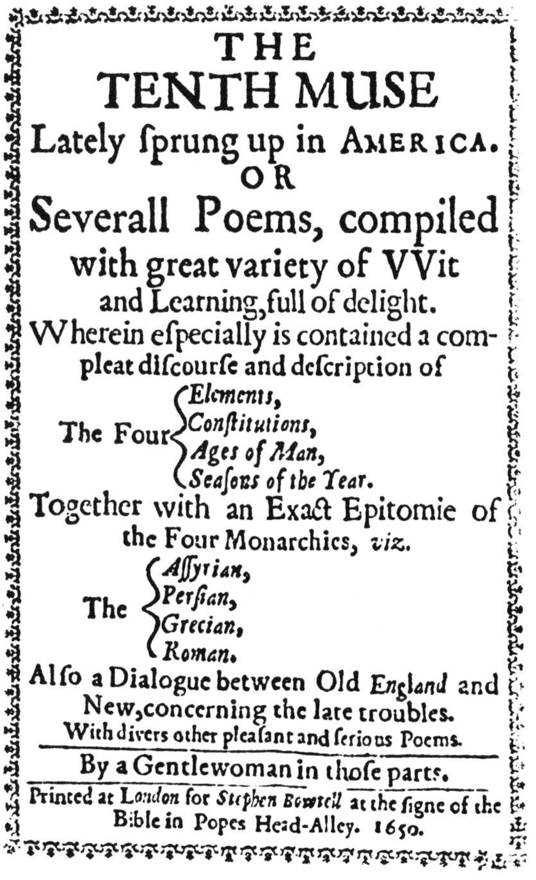

THE
TENTH MUSE
Lately ſprung up in AMERICA.
OR
Severall Poems, compiled
with great variety of VVit
and Learning, full of delight.
Wherein eſpecially is contained a compleat diſcourſe and deſcription of
The Four { *Elements, Conſtitutions, Ages of Man, Seaſons of the Year.* }
Together with an Exact Epitomie of
the Four Monarchies, *viz.*
The { *Aſſyrian, Perſian, Grecian, Roman.* }
Alſo a Dialogue between Old *England* and
New, concerning the late troubles.
With divers other pleaſant and ſerious Poems.
By a Gentlewoman in thoſe parts.
Printed at *London* for *Stephen Bowtell* at the ſigne of the
Bible in Popes Head-Alley. 1650.

FIGURE 19 ❧ The title page of Anne Bradstreet's *Tenth Muse* (1650).

outcome must be accident or plagiarism. Bradstreet's rejoinders to these mean-spirited but familiar jibes was sometimes defensive, sometimes defiant, usually restrained, and often witty. Her elegy on Queen Elizabeth, whose leadership exemplified the talents of women, includes a sly historical reminder by way of warning to male prejudice: "Let such as say our sex is void of reason, / Know 'tis a slander now but once was treason."

The most ambitious of the poems in *The Tenth Muse* is a series of "quarternions," sequences of pentameter couplets devoted respectively to the four elements, the four humors, the four ages, and the four seasons. The longest of all her poems, a survey of the four monarchies, is in large part a versified redaction of Sir Walter Raleigh's history of the world. All these compositions labor under imitative structures and commonplace themes, though they also contain isolated passages of spirited feeling and direct observation. The best of them is probably "The Four Seasons," in which the stylized apparatus of pastoral, including European nightingales and classical shepherds, alternate with sidelong but evocative glances at New England's landscape and weather.

Anne Bradstreet bore eight children and had the management of a large and relatively prosperous household. Some of her finest poems transcribe the joys and sorrows she felt in childbirth and in her home and family. She wrote a number of poems to her husband, playful and passionate by turns, which dance with a lively affection. In one of them, Simon is the sun whose heat has stirred and quickened her; in another, he is the treasure that she has sought and found. In yet another, wife longs for husband with the candid ardor of a natural creature:

> As loving hind that (hartless) wants her deer,
> Scuds through the woods and fern with hark'ning ear,
> Perplext, in every bush and nook doth pry,
> Her dearest deer, might answer ear or eye;
> So doth my anxious soul, which now doth miss
> A dearer deer (far dearer heart) than this.

Like other Puritans, Bradstreet made a record of her inner life, intended for the instruction of her children. In pages of this notebook, she reiterates her piety and numbers God's mercies toward her, but she also confesses some of her doubts. "I have often been perplexed," she writes, "that I have not found that constant Joy in my Pilgrimage and refreshing which I supposed most of the servants of God have." She questioned, among other things, those sectarian divisions which provoked so much bloodshed throughout the seventeenth century. Allowing that the Bible contains the true word of God, nonetheless Bradstreet asks, "Why may not the Popish Religion be the right? They have the same God, the same Christ, the same word: they only interpret it one way, we another." Encompassing both conviction and moments of uncertainty, Bradstreet's spiritual drama fairly typically represents the religious experience of contemporary Christians. Fundamentally, she was a woman of orthodox temperament, who desired to rest in the security of "this Rock Christ Jesus": "And if I perish, I perish."

Bradstreet's poetry occasionally documents her inner debate. The verses she wrote on the burning of her house, for example, conclude with religiously correct sentiments: property is mere vanity, God is preparing a heavenly house for her in heaven. The most moving passages in the poem, however, are surely those in which Bradstreet recalls all the homely pleasures that now lie in ashes. No guests will visit here again, no old tales will be told over dinner, no marriages will be celebrated. The human suffering is movingly rendered, and the pain of her loss is presented with affecting dignity. Similarly, the elegies she wrote on her grandchildren lead only with difficulty toward the consolation that religion offers. Her grandson Simon, who died at the age of one month and one day in 1669, was the third of her grandchildren to die in four years. The rhythms of the opening lines of the elegy Bradstreet wrote suggest a reluctant submission to God's inscrutable will:

> No sooner came, but gone, and fall'n asleep,
> Acquaintance short, yet parting caused us weep;
> Three flowers, two scarcely blown, the last i' th' bud,
> Cropt by th' Almighty's hand; yet is He good.

The simile of the cropped flower is a conventional figure for the death of a child, but in this poem Bradstreet's bewildered grief carries her far beyond predictable emblems and moral tags. Her compliance with God's justice seems close to irony; her head is bowed more in resignation or even bitterness than in reverence:

With dreadful awe before Him let's be mute,
Such was His will, but why, let's not dispute,
With humble hearts and mouths put in the dust,
Let's say He's merciful as well as just.

Lacerated by the deaths of so many children, Bradstreet's devotion collapses into exhausted acquiescence. She outlived her grandchildren by only a few years. In one of the last poems she wrote, she presents herself as a "weary pilgrim," perplexed and laden with cares, eager to lay her "corrupt carcass" down in its grave and wait for the splendor of the Resurrection.

When Bradstreet died, in 1672, Edward Taylor was a young man of thirty who had just graduated from Harvard and accepted the call to serve as minister in the frontier town of Westfield, across the Connecticut River in central Massachusetts. Taylor grew up in England, under the congenial rule of the Puritan Commonwealth. The details of his English education are uncertain, but he acquired enough training to take up a career as a schoolteacher. Shortly after the Stuart Restoration in 1660, teachers were compelled to subscribe to the Act of Uniformity, which demanded allegiance to Anglican liturgy and creed. Taylor was unwilling to submit, lost his job, and emigrated to Massachusetts. This early history accurately suggests his unbending commitment to Puritan principles. It was a posture he maintained throughout the rest of his life.

Taylor remained in Westfield for fifty-eight years, preaching, writing, counseling, and consoling. Like many colonial ministers, he also served his congregation as physician, since he alone in the community had any sort of medical training. Along with his abundant public duties, Taylor's domestic life was equally full. He was the father of fourteen children, eight with his first wife, Elizabeth Fitch, who died in 1689, and six more with his second wife, Ruth Wyllys. Among his grandchildren was Ezra Stiles, one of the early presidents of Yale College. Stiles recalled his grandfather as "an incessant student, but used no spectacles to his death. . . . He was small of stature, but firm; of quick passions, yet serious and grave; exemplary in piety and for a very sacred observance of the Lord's day."

Taylor's life seemed in most outward aspects busy, but typical of a colonial preacher. However, in parallel with his ministry Taylor pursued a productive, hidden career as a poet. He wrote enough poetry to fill a substantial volume, but he concealed his poetic practice from his contemporaries, probably out of some combination of diffidence and theological scruple. He also left instructions to his heirs not to publish his work. Consequently, the existence of his poems was not even suspected for over two centuries after his death. His handwritten manuscripts were discovered in 1937, and the publication of his poetry required a new estimation not just of his own achievement but of early American literature.

Taylor's longest single poem, filling nearly one hundred pages in a modern edition, is a versified tract painstakingly entitled *God's Determinations Touching His Elect: and The Elects Combat in Their Conversion, and Coming up to God in Christ Together with the Comfortable Effects Thereof.* The argument of *God's Determinations* is conducted through more than thirty separate speeches and debates, in the course of which the Christian is led from a sight of sin to the consolation of Christ. The poem employs a varied but accessible plain style throughout, and its simple, inexorable plot recalls *Pilgrim's Progress* as well as the morality plays that edified and entertained medieval audiences. Beginning with a homespun sketch of infinite power, *God's Determinations* takes up a series of issues important to the Puritan conscience, above all the permanently anxious search for personal salvation. Like *Paradise Lost*, Taylor's poem undertakes in its immeasurably smaller way to "justify the ways of God" to Christian men and women. The poem's tones are several, ranging from its charming translation of the Creator into a colonial carpenter, to the drama of temptation and spiritual struggle, to tendentious and often legalistic definitions of assorted Calvinist doctrines. Personified abstractions, such as Justice and Mercy, alternately threaten and comfort the soul. Satan rages colorfully, and Christ reiterates the dogma of election. In the midst of all this, Taylor traces the spiritual career of harried souls, representative Christians who exemplify but frequently transcend their emblematic function. Early in the poem, for example, one sinner is so frightened by his own corruption that he is "Stretcht upon the Wrack of Woe . . . Bereaved of Reason":

Betakes himselfe unto his Heels in haste,
Runs like a Madman till his Spirits waste,
Then like a Child that fears the Poker Clap
Him on his face doth on his Mothers lap
Doth hold his breath, lies still for fear least he
Should by his breathing loud discover'd be.
Thus on his face doth see no outward thing
But still his heart for Fear doth pant within.
Doth make its Drummer beat so loud it makes
The Very Bulwarks of the City quake:
Yet gets no aid: wherefore the Spirits they
Are ready all to leave, and run away.

Taylor's poetic strengths and weaknesses declare themselves immediately in passages like this. The drama of a soul's frantic search for security is reproduced in a lively, colloquial diction and charming images. At the same time, the maladroit rhythms and stumbling syntax betray the consequences of frontier isolation. All of Taylor's poetry is marked by the same self-tutored quality, a combination of striking literary talent hobbled by primitive formal training.

Taylor's other major sequence, his *Preparatory Meditations*, consists of poems apparently composed as private exercises preceding the communion service. The more than two hundred poems that make up the *Meditations* were composed during a period of more than forty years. The evidence of Taylor's extant sermons indicates that the meditations were written as verse responses to the same biblical texts on which he was preaching. Where the sermons "open" the Bible texts methodically, however, proceeding from doctrine to application, the poems usually focus on the single subject of Taylor's own sinfulness and his hope for saving grace. And in place of the formal architecture of the sermon, the meditations offer images, often in clusters, which reproduce the alternately anxious and ecstatic psychology of Puritan belief. Taken as a group, these poems are among the most remarkable verse sequences in American literature (Figure 20).

Built on an unvarying six-line stanza, the meditations are organized in relatively consistent patterns. Behind Taylor's poems lie several generations of Catholic and Protestant writers who had given

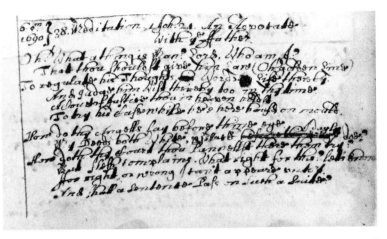

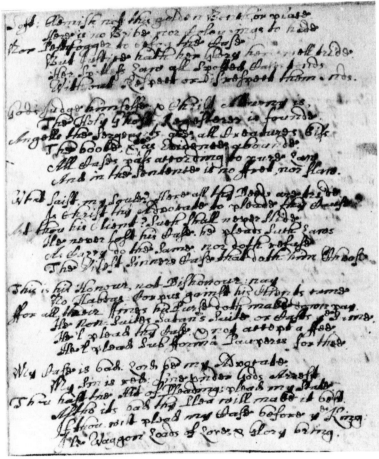

FIGURE 20   The manuscript of Edward Taylor's "Meditation," I, 38.

prominence to the exercise of meditation. Taylor was heir to a religious tradition that widely influenced poets on both sides of the Atlantic. His work also exhibits many of the characteristics of English metaphysical poetry. Like the earlier poems of Donne and especially Herbert, his meditations are introspective, knotty, and complex. They combine the imagery of the Bible, the abstruse diction of theology, and the colloquial terms of farm and workplace. They rely on metaphors, some of them daring and extravagant, to produce their effects. Compared to Herbert, Taylor often sounds raw and strident, but his lack of control can itself be a source of emotional power. In Taylor's meditations, the direct, personal and unmediated relation between the individual soul and Christ is transformed from a theological hypothesis into a sustained, dramatic encounter.

The intensely inward quality of these poems removes them almost completely from the external facts of New England history or even of Taylor's biography. Battles and journeys, feasts and marriages abound, but all of them are spiritual and allegorical. The subject is always and everywhere the soul's preparation to meet Christ in the sacrament of the Lord's Supper. Taylor remained constant to that purpose for four decades. At the rate of about one poem every two months, he wrote a series of forty-nine numbered poems (now called the First Series), then for unknown reasons began again at number one and produced over one hundred fifty more (the Second Series). The biblical texts upon which the meditations are based come principally from a small number of sources: the Gospels, the epistles of Paul and John, the Book of Revelation, and the Song of Solomon (which Taylor referred to as Canticles). Within their unchanging intentions, the length, tone, and emphasis of the meditations vary considerably. Some consist of just three stanzas, while others include a dozen or more. Many open with a confession of unworthiness, including hyperbolic self-reproach, and then progress with more or less assurance to declare the hope of salvation that Christ's mercy brings. Others record the surprised exultation Taylor feels in the good fortune of knowing Christ's love. Still others take Taylor's poetry as their subject, insisting on the inadequacy of his verse, or indeed any verse, to address Christ properly or to communicate his glory.

Though no single meditation is altogether typical of Taylor's craft, Meditation 38 of the First Series exemplifes many of his characteristic devices. The poem is based on a text from the First Epistle of John, in which Christ is invoked as "An Advocate with the Father," an ally who will speak for sinful men and women before the throne of God. In the seven stanzas of the meditation, Taylor expands this brief figure into a full courtroom drama, crowded with jury, witnesses, opposing attorneys, even a court stenographer. Taylor continues to elaborate on the biblical text for several stanzas, enriching the terse suggestion of John's initial image with a cascade of witty conceits. Along the way, Taylor even manages a bit of social satire, contrasting the unblemished justice of God's court with the corruption of the human judiciary: "Here is no bribe, nor colorings to hide / Nor pettifogger to befog the case." The soul's hope lies in Christ's skill as a barrister and his willingness to accept apparently desperate cases. In the final stanza, Taylor returns directly to the biblical text and calls on Christ for aid in three lines whose strong central pauses underscore the depth of feeling:

> My case is bad. Lord, be my advocate.
> My sin is red: I'm under God's arrest.
> Thou hast the hint of pleading; plead my state.

Audaciously, Taylor offers to pay Christ with "wagonloads of love and glory."

Along with the work of Anne Bradstreet, Taylor's verses prove that poetry could coexist with the discipline of Puritan obedience. Whatever its substantial merits, however, Taylor's poetry principally demonstrates the isolation and impoverishment that literary culture faced in early America. Taylor outlived Locke and Newton, but his cosmology was rooted in the Middle Ages. Even more than his American contemporary Cotton Mather, Taylor remained absorbed in the past. Mather, a resident of bustling Boston, pursued a serious interest in science while he was defending the New England way of his grandfathers. Taylor, out on the frontier, devoted himself wholly to his spiritual errand. His poetry has a similarly old-fashioned character. The years during which he slowly produced his meditations coincided with the achievements of Restoration wit and of Augustan elegance and satire. All of Dryden's work was published in Taylor's lifetime, and much of the major work of Swift and Pope.

Taylor almost surely never read any of these volumes, nor would they have interested him. His meditations are purposefully and systematically backward looking, and they find their models in writers of the earlier seventeenth century. Taylor is, in short, the last metaphysical poet in English, writing at least two generations after his nearest predecessors had laid down their pens.

※

The shopworn odor that attaches to all of Taylor's ideas and forms of expression is only partially explained by his single-minded religious commitment. Cultural belatedness was a general and inescapable consequence of America's colonial experience. Painting offers an analogous example. As with literature, a variety of absences retarded the emergence of a recognizable school and inhibited the development of talented individuals. Without teachers or academies or patronage, colonial painting was doomed to copy European models that were usually out of date by the time they became fashionable in the New World. The strongest influences on American painting were black-and-white mezzotints from England, along with the irrepressible popular demand for realistic likenesses. As a result, scores of colonial men and women have achieved a rather odd-looking immortality, awkwardly posed amid all the props of English portraiture. Nothing of America's native energy, idiosyncracy, or landscape intrudes to confess that the sitter and the scene might actually be found in Philadelphia or Boston or New York (Figure 21).

Painting would become more sophisticated as the eighteenth century wore on. A rapidly growing and more affluent population created a large enough market to attract several competent European artists to America, and the quality of painting gradually rose. Nonetheless, the two finest artists America produced before the Revolutionary War, Benjamin West and John Singleton Copley, both felt it necessary to emigrate to England in order to pursue their careers (Figure 22). America offered neither the fellowship nor the financial support that a serious artistic vocation required. (John

FIGURE 21 🕊 *The Mason Children* (1670), attributed to the Freake-Gibbs painter.

Singleton Copley's portrait of Mrs. Thomas Boylston is reproduced as Plate 1.)

The belatedness that stamped colonial literature and painting was also characteristic of America's intellectual development. The several political and theological structures that governed the first settlements were frank importations, adapted only under the pressures of time and circumstance. The continuing power of European precedent was demonstrated again, in the mid-eighteenth century, in the work of Jonathan Edwards. The most gifted and innovative of colonial philosophers, Edwards was also the most consciously tied to the past. He carefully studied the work of Newton and Locke but subordinated their purposes to his, gleaning from their physics and psychology insights that reaffirmed his reverent idealism. He put his originality at the service of reclaiming a restored and purified Calvinism. Edwards was the last Puritan but also, in an important sense, the first one. He was the almost exact contemporary of Benjamin Franklin. Between them, these two men may be said to summarize the struggle in eighteenth-century America between the theocentric past and the secular future. Edwards was as zealous in defending the sanctity of religion as Franklin would be in promoting public service and devising ways to wealth (Figure 23).

Like several of his Puritan predecessors, Edwards demonstrated his brilliance early. He graduated from Yale College at seventeen, soon became senior tutor there, and was chief minister of the important church in Northampton, Massachusetts, before he was thirty. Soon thereafter he earned his first celebrity, and notoriety, when his preaching provoked the explosive beginnings of the Great Awakening. Like all religious revivals, this one undoubtedly had its origins both in the emotional and social facts of its time and place, and in a reaction to the advancing materialism of colonial culture. It was neither the first nor the last tumultuous communal rediscovery of saving grace, but it gained wide visibility because of its violence and length and because of the number of its reputed converts. In

FIGURE 22 &. Matthew Pratt, *The American School: Benjamin West Instructing His Pupils* (1765). In his London studios, West gave instruction to three generations of American artists. He is shown here, palette in hand, advising one of his students, perhaps Matthew Pratt.

FIGURE 23 ❧ Joseph Badger, portrait of Jonathan Edwards.

May 1734 the episode came to a tragic, though only temporary, halt when Edwards's uncle Joseph Hawley committed suicide by cutting his throat.

Within a few years, this time under the prodding of the Methodist George Whitefield, the revival stirred again. It was then, on July 8, 1741, at Enfield, Connecticut, that Edwards delivered the best-known of all American sermons, "Sinners in the Hands of an Angry God." In the large canon of his work, this is the single item by which Edwards is best remembered. It is a call to repentance, in which a powerful, marching logic is allied with vivid and even sensational metaphors. "Their foot shall slide in due time" (Deut. 32.35): Earlier Puritan preachers had also used this text to warn against backsliding, but none had so fully explored its melodramatic implications. None had uttered the grim doctrines of human depravity and divine sovereignty with such remorseless conviction or embellished them with such care.

Slowly, methodically, Edwards "opens" the verse. Sinners will fall into hell inevitably, suddenly, justly: no power can turn away the wrath of God. His anger is like "great waters that are dammed for the present; they increase more and more"; it is like a bow bent, "the arrow made ready on the string, and justice bends the arrow at your heart." In the sermon's most famous passages, Edwards lingers over the peril that all sinners face:

> O sinner! Consider the fearful danger you are in: it is a great furnace of wrath, a wide and bottomless pit, full of the fire of wrath, that you are held over in the hand of God, whose wrath is provoked and incensed as much against you, as against many of the damned in hell. You hang by a slender thread, with the flames of divine wrath flashing about it, and ready every moment to singe it, and burn it asunder; and you have no interest in any Mediator, and nothing to lay hold of to save yourself, nothing to keep off the flames of wrath, nothing of your own, nothing that you ever have done, nothing that you can do, to induce God to spare you one moment.

Edwards wanted Christians to feel their religion as a stirring experience; merely assenting in some vaguely sanctimonious way to abstract truths was not enough. Firsthand accounts suggest that his preaching roused the men and women of his congregation to uncommon enthusiasm. This injured Edwards's reputation with more moderate clergymen and has distorted his image in the eyes of posterity. He was a thinker of genuine learning and subtlety, and the lurid drama of the Enfield sermon is not typical of his rhetoric. Yet a consistent intention provides the thread and motive that knit together much of Edwards's work, including his autobiographical "Personal Narrative," his sermons, and the more challenging philosophical essays he wrote near the end of his life. He wanted to unite head and heart, matter and spirit, in a grand restatement of the Calvinist doctrine, a synthesis at once sacred and scientific. History had a different outcome in store. In the event, his writing proved epitaph to the old New England way he had set out to revive.

Edwards, who died just a generation before the Revolution, had continued to grapple with the old questions of theology. Many of his contemporaries, however, had long since turned their attention to issues of politics and culture. After a century and a half of colonization, the settlements along the Atlantic coast had multiplied in number and diversity. Regional differences in language, costume, and manners were becoming as marked as the variations in climate and geography that set each section apart. Travelers from one colony to another sometimes felt that they were entering foreign lands. Though political requirements would soon mold these separate commonwealths into a reluctant confederation, a national consciousness emerged more gradually. To be sure, the belief in a distinctive American identity can be traced back to the promotional literature and Puritan histories of the seventeenth century. Furthermore, loyalty to the old homelands became attenuated with passing years. By the time of the Revolution, some Americans were fourth-generation residents of their country. Nonetheless, the definition of America, a land of plural societies and cultures, remained more problematic than assured (Figure 24).

FIGURE 24 &. First published in about 1690, the *New England Primer* circulated in three million copies over the next century and a half. Called "The Little Bible of New England," the *Primer*'s rhymes were used in both home and school to inculcate the received truths of religion, family, and politics.

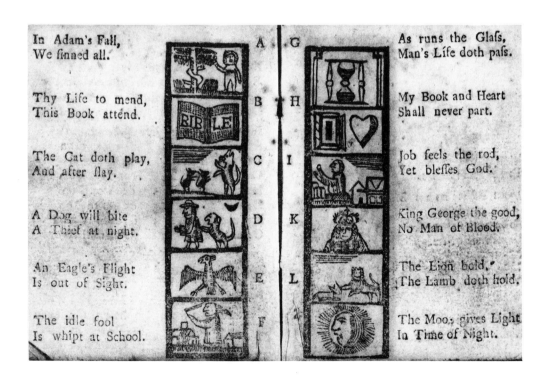

In Adam's Fall, We finned all.	A	G	As runs the Glafs, Man's Life doth pafs.
Thy Life to mend, This Book attend.	B	H	My Book and Heart Shall never part.
The Cat doth play, And after flay.	C	I	Job feels the rod, Yet bleffes God.
A Dog will bite A Thief at night.	D	K	King George the good, No Man of Blood.
An Eagle's Flight Is out of Sight.	E	L	The Lion bold, The Lamb doth hold.
The idle fool Is whipt at School.	F		The Moon gives Light In Time of Night.

Except as an extension of Europe, America had little history. One consequence, acknowledged by most inhabitants of the New World, was cultural backwardness. Indeed, fretfulness over England's cultural advantages was among the chief themes in the artistic consciousness of the colonies. The moral superiority of the fresh New World to the senescent old one could be smugly decreed, and passing time collaborated with transatlantic distance to nurture an increasingly independent political identity. However, in all the smaller and larger matters of taste that attend a civilized society, in the domains of literature and music and decoration, the New World keenly felt its modest stature. There were important exceptions – some writers who depicted civilization's westward course as an accomplished fact of the present rather than a prophecy. But a yearning for European cultivation is a more common motif, particularly in the relatively small body of colonial literature produced outside New England. Perhaps because it lacked the counterweight of religious mythmaking, the literature of the South and the middle colonies more frequently strikes the note of cultural deprivation.

Richard Lewis, for example, who had taught at Eton College, admired the New World's foliage and scenery, but he found little cultural sustenance in the colonial wilderness. In an early eighteenth-century poem praising Maryland's Lord Calvert, Lewis contrasts the artistic fertility of Europe with the barrenness of America. For centuries, the kind climate of the Mediterranean has inspired the Muse with "Thoughts sublime, and gay poetic Fire." Virgil, Ovid, and Horace exemplify the unapproachable excellence of the past and of Italy:

> *There*, PAINTURE breathes, *There*, STATUARY lives,
> And MUSIC most delighted Rapture gives:
> *There*, pompous Piles of *Building* pierce the Skies,
> And endless Scenes of *Pleasure* court the Eyes.
> While *Here*, rough Woods embrown the Hills and Plains,
> Mean are the *Buildings*, artless are the Swains:
> 'To raise the *Genius*,' we no Time can spare,
> A *bare Subsistence* claims our utmost Care.

In the debate over colonial identity, America was the New Jerusalem to some of its settlers, while others predicted that each of its cities

FIGURE 25 ❧ Portrait of William Byrd II.

would become a New World Athens. Lewis speaks for a third point of view. To him, America is a vacant place, whose deficiencies serve chiefly to remind him of the Old World's achievements. Echoes of this complaint would be heard across the succeeding decades, as writers from James Fenimore Cooper to Henry James complained of America's commercial atmosphere and its thin artistic soil.

The Virginia planter William Byrd II seldom grumbled about the impoverished cultural life of the New World. Byrd's diary, however, complements Lewis's verses perfectly. It is the self-portrait of a prosperous English gentleman making the best of his parochial American circumstances by recreating as much of England as he can. Byrd gathered the largest library in the colonies – larger than Cotton Mather's – and tried to spend some time each day reading in it. He studied to keep up his skill in three or four languages. At the same time, he was perpetually busy, a successful farmer and a figure of influence in Virginia politics (Figure 25). The pages of Byrd's diary reveal little of Puritan gravity or soul-searching. Rather, his laconic daily entries record the routine of a man of property and pleasure: what time he rose, what he read and ate, the journeys he took, and the visitors he received.

> April 7, 1709. The men began to work this day to dig for brick. I settled my accounts and read Italian. I reproached my wife with ordering the old beef to be kept and the fresh beef used first, contrary to good management, on which she was pleased to be very angry and this put me out of humor. I ate nothing but boiled beef for dinner. I went away presently after dinner to look after my people. When I returned I read more Italian and then my wife came and begged my pardon and we were friends again. I read in Dr. Lister again very late. I said my prayers. I had good health, good thoughts, and bad humor, unlike a philosopher.

> April 21, 1710. About 8 o'clock I went to see the President and then went to court. I settled some accounts first. Two of the negroes were tried and convicted for treason. I wrote a letter to England and then went to court again. About 3 o'clock I returned to my chambers again and found above a girl who I persuaded to go with me into my chambers but she would not. I ate some cake and cheese and then went to Mr. Bland's where I ate some boiled beef. Then I went to the President's where we were merry till 11 o'clock. Then I stole away. I said a short prayer but notwithstanding committed uncleanness in bed. I had good health, bad thoughts, and good humor, thanks be to God Almighty.

A comparison of this with Michael Wigglesworth's diary suggests in abbreviated form the differences between two colonial cultures. Wigglesworth's entries are dark and inward, tenacious in spiritual focus, indifferent to the concrete events that distinguish one day from another. Byrd, by contrast, looks only outward. Where Wigglesworth subjected himself to feverish introspection, Byrd observes and names virtually everything around him, genially indifferent to behavior that would have shriveled Wigglesworth's soul. Byrd's diary is a cornucopia of important and trivial details. Out of his pages roll all the items of Virginia's daily life: clothing, farming practices, diet, religious and sexual attitudes, relations between master and slave, backstairs political intrigue, and more.

Byrd had grown up in England, and he returned there whenever he could. England was synonymous with civilization and all of its attendant pleasures; the New World was a cultural desert. That invidious judgment was given one of its funniest and most embittered statements in Ebenezer Cooke's narrative poem "The Sot-weed Factor." Cooke was the self-styled "poet laureate" of Maryland, and he evidently detested every inch of his colonial home. His poem is a sustained rebuke to the raw and unsavory quality of America's wilderness life. The title character (a "sot-weed factor" is a tobacco merchant) is, in Cooke's opinion, grotesque beyond describing, the barbarous descendant of murderous Cain. And the factor is thus a representative Maryland citizen. Cooke's adventures lead him from one rogue to another, sodden men and sluttish women, hardly human, all living in tumbledown shanties and faithful only to dirt and drunkenness. This is the scene in a typical town:

> I thought it proper to provide,
> A Lodging for myself and Guide,
> So to our Inn we march'd away,
> Which at a little distance lay;
> Where all things were in such Confusion,
> I thought the World at its conclusion:
> A Herd of Planters on the ground,
> O'er-whelm'd with Punch, dead drunk we found:
> Others were fighting and contending,
> Some burnt their Cloaths to save the mending.

The miscreants of Cooke's poem live in a land as unappetizing as themselves, a dreary wasteland of damp forests, treacherous rivers, howling wolves, croaking frogs, elephantine mosquitoes, and poisonous snakes. Jingling couplets bury the myth of the New World Eden beneath layers of bumptious satire.

The landscape that provoked Cooke's dyspeptic irony more typically encouraged admiration and even reverence. From early on, the native beauty and variety of the New World's scenes promised felicity and the hope that all expectations might be met. Anne Bradstreet derived much of her religious contentment from contemplating the "wonderous works" of nature, "the vast frame of the heaven and the earth, the order of all things, night and day, summer and winter, spring and autumn." This is rather general, to be sure, but some of her poetry joins similar sentiments to closer observation.

Samuel Sewall, in an optimistically prophetic account of New England published in 1697, included a lyrical tribute to Plum Island. Sewall confidently connects New England's religious prospects with its natural abundance. Proudly, even lovingly, he names the birds and fish and animals of this "New Earth": The future is secure as long as "any salmon or sturgeon shall swim in the streams of Merrimac, or any perch or pickerel in Crane Pond . . . as long as any cattle shall be fed with the grass growing in the meadows, which do humbly bow down themselves before Turkey-Hill; as long as any sheep shall walk upon Old-Town Hills, and shall from thence pleasantly look down upon the River Parker."

In passages like this, colonists began to share their discovery of America as an imaginative opportunity. Landscape is no mere physical setting but a place of indwelling significance. In some measure, this attitude derived from the medieval cosmology of the Puritans, but long after the Puritan doctrine had retreated the land maintained its grip on the American imagination. Nature's appeal was at once sensuous and spiritual, and the landscape eventually assumed the place that orthodoxy once occupied. Each generation would search out the real and symbolic geography of America. The literature of exploration and travel became a substantial genre. Sarah Kemble Knight's early eighteenth-century journals include thickly detailed reports of her travels across New England to New York. William Byrd kept his diary secret, but in 1728 he published *Histories of the Dividing Line*, a witty and circumstantial account of the survey that drew the line between Virginia and North Carolina. Later in the century, the botanist William Bartram toured the South and published his findings, illustrated with his own drawings of animals and plants, under the title *Travels through North and South Carolina, Georgia, East and West Florida* (Figure 26). Bartram first saw the Mississippi in August 1777. His evocation of the river as it flows through Louisiana splendidly illustrates the characteristic mixture of science and mysticism that would so often mark the imaginative response of Americans to nature:

> The depth of the river here, even in this season, at its lowest
> ebb, is astonishing, not less than forty fathoms; and the width
> about a mile or somewhat less: but it is not expansion of surface
> alone that strikes us with ideas of magnificence; the altitude
> and theatrical accents of its . . . banks, the steady course of the

mighty flood, the trees, high forests, even every particular
object, as well as societies, bear the stamp of superiority and
excellence; all unite or combine in exhibiting a prospect of
the grand sublime.

By the mid-eighteenth century, the tasks that confronted Americans
were to forge a political identity and a cultural achievement commensurate with the "grand sublime" of the New World geography
that Bartram and others had mapped. Writing in 1743, Benjamin

FIGURE 26 🙊 William
Bartram, drawing of the
American lotus. John
Bartram had been, along
with Benjamin Franklin,
one of the original nine
members of the
American Philosophical
Society. His son
William, the first artist-
naturalist born in the
colonies, also became a
botanist of distinction;
William's *Travels through
North and South Carolina,
Georgia, East and West
Florida* (1791) was widely
admired on both sides of
the Atlantic. This
drawing of an American
lotus, along with a Venus
flytrap and an unscaled
blue heron, probably
dates from the late 1760s
or early 1770s.

Franklin declared that the "first Drudgery" of settling the new colonies was "now pretty well over" and that the time had therefore come "to cultivate the finer Arts, and improve the common Stock of Knowledge."

CHAPTER TWO

❧ Forging a national literature ❧

B ENJAMIN FRANKLIN himself was the first American who answered the New World's need to prove its cultural worthiness. He was the colonies' first world citizen, receiving
homage on both sides of the Atlantic as the man who personified
the peculiar genius of America. Self-reliant, unpretentious yet thoroughly accomplished, Franklin seemed to be the long-awaited "new
man." A French contemporary, paying double tribute, addressed
Franklin as the man who "snatched the lightning from the sky and
the scepter from the tyrant." He was born in Boston early in the
eighteenth century, in the twilight of Puritan predominance. His
career is a bridge connecting America's past and future. He became
Philadelphia's most famous adopted son, a writer, businessman, and
scientist of international stature. Late in his long career, he played
a leading role in the struggle for independence and then served as
a senior officer of the new nation he had helped to create. His life
story, an almost archetypal journey from ordinary beginnings to
luminous success, has been etched permanently into America's folklore. More than any other early American, Franklin invented the
vocabulary in which the New World's aspirations would henceforth
express themselves (Figure 27).

Franklin started working for his father, a Boston soap and candle
maker, at the age of ten. Two years later he was apprenticed to his
half brother James, the editor of a newspaper, the *New England
Courant*. It was in the *Courant* that Franklin, still in his teens,
published the "Dogood Papers," a series of essays in the fashion of
the *Spectator*. Written over the signature of Silence Dogood, the
widow of a parson, fourteen essays appeared between March and

FIGURE 27 🎗️ Benjamin West, *Benjamin Franklin with Kite and Key.* Painted in 1805, fifteen years after Franklin's death, West's idealized painting captures the strength, sobriety, and scientific ingenuity particularly associated with Franklin.

October 1722. The titles of the Dogood Papers suggest their range, from "Freedom of Thought," to "Drunkenness," to "Pride and Hoop Petticoats."

Franklin's shrewd common sense, his humor, and his free-thinking irreverence are already visible in these precocious essays. In the seventh paper, for example, he dismantled the Puritan elegy. A century of relentless elegizing had reduced that honorable Puritan genre to arid formulas and hackneyed similes. Franklin expressed his amused contempt by offering Mistress Dogood's "Receipt to Make a New-England Funeral Elegy." For the subject, she confides, any recently departed neighbor will serve, though "it will be best if he

went away suddenly, being Kill'd, Drown'd, or Frose to Death."
Rehearse all the excellences of the deceased, and "if he have not
enough, you may borrow some to make up a sufficient Quantity."
Finally, make ample use of "double Rhimes such as power, flower;
quiver, shiver; grieve us, leave us . . . expeditions, physicians; fatigue
him, intrigue him, &c. You must spread all upon Paper, and if you
can procure a Scrap of Latin to put at the End, it will garnish it
mightily."

Within a year of publishing the Dogood Papers, and following
a dispute with his brother, Franklin left Boston and embarked on
his legendary pilgrimage to Philadelphia. There he made his reputation and his fortune, establishing himself as the city's leading
printer and, eventually, its leading citizen. For a quarter of a century,
until 1758, he published annual installments of *Poor Richard's Almanack*. Almanacs, which were essentially calendars surrounded by
serious and frivolous information, were popular throughout the colonies. *Poor Richard* became the most successful of the almanacs, but
it is also typical, in its mixture of science and proverbs, curiosities
and humor (Figure 28, Figure 29). Franklin's literary technique in
the almanacs consists principally in the multiplication of aphorisms,
some of them original, others borrowed. Capitalizing on the popularity of the almanacs, Franklin later published a discourse known
as "The Way to Wealth," in which his adages were strung together
and put in the mouth of an old man called Father Abraham.

> If Time be of all things the most precious, wasting Time must
> be, as Poor Richard says, the greatest Prodigality; since, as he
> elsewhere tells us, Lost time is never found again; and what
> we call Time enough, always proves little enough: Let us then
> up and be doing, and doing to the Purpose; so by Diligence
> shall we do more with less Perplexity. Sloth makes all Things
> difficult, but Industry all easy, as Poor Richard says; and He
> that riseth late must trot all Day, and shall scarce overtake his
> Business at Night; while Laziness travels so slowly, that Poverty
> soon overtakes him, as we read in Poor Richard, who adds,
> Drive thy Business, let not that Drive thee; and Early to Bed
> and Early to Rise, makes a Man healthy, wealthy, and wise.

Franklin's homely encyclopedia of bourgeois virtues teeters toward
self-parody in its jaunty optimism and its commitment to the main
chance (Figure 30).

The Franklin of "The Way to Wealth" is indeed the benevolent materialist who presides rather smugly over America's imagination of success, yet this represents only one side of his complex character. Franklin was the most fully developed American example of the eighteenth-century Enlightenment. He was a member of the prestigious Royal Society of England – the only colonist since Cotton Mather to be so honored – and in the course of his long life he took the whole range of science and politics for his proper study. Like his Enlightenment contemporaries in Europe, Franklin believed in the ultimate good order of the universe and in the progress of humanity. He believed that the lives of ordinary men and women could be altered and improved by the intervention of science and

FIGURE 28 ❧ Title page of Benjamin Banneker's *Almanac* (1795). Like Franklin, Banneker (or Bannaker) was an inventor and scientist as well as an editor and journalist.

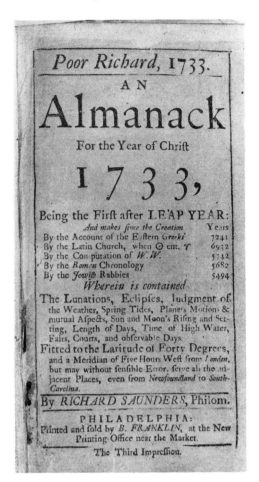

FIGURE 29 🙰 Title
page of one of the early
editions of Benjamin
Franklin's *Poor Richard's
Almanack* (1733).

good sense. His essays and letters contain the records of experiments
on heat, earthquakes, optics, music, lightning, and electricity. He
invented a more efficient stove, bifocal glasses, a popular harmonica;
he set up America's first public library, first city hospital, first learned
society; he published one of the colonies' first political cartoons
(Figure 31). He founded the school that eventually became the
University of Pennsylvania. In short, Franklin was equally devoted
to self-promotion and the common good.

Franklin's rise to international prominence signaled the end of
Puritan hegemony, yet the residual influence of Puritan ideology is
everywhere visible in his life and writings, as it would be in America's
subsequent intellectual history. Franklin's sense of American mission and his conception of the public responsibility of private persons

FIGURE 30 ❧ Franklin's aphorisms long enjoyed a wide popularity. These late eighteenth-century engravings, taken from a book called *Bowles's Moral Pictures, or Poor Richard Illustrated*, offer edifying "lessons for the young and old on Industry, Temperance, Frugality."

FIGURE 31 ❧ Franklin's snake device (1754). Published by Franklin on the eve of the Albany Congress, the broken but dangerous snake was adopted over the succeeding twenty years as a symbol of stiffening colonial resistance to England.

BENJAMIN FRANKLIN

both derive in some measure from his Puritan heritage. Franklin's *Autobiography*, his best-known work, shows the influence of his Puritan predecessors. Several of the virtues he praises, among them industry and thrift and temperance, are legacies from earlier New England culture. In addition, the introspective journals and the saintly biographies of men and women like John Winthrop, Thomas Shepard, and Anne Bradstreet, while they are distant in spirit from Franklin's book, are quite similar in design and structure. Like the earlier Puritans, Franklin offers his life as a representative instance, a model of trial, pilgrimage, and success intended for the edification and instruction of others. The determinative difference, of course, is that Franklin's *Autobiography* narrates a purely secular journey, in which reason has become his guide, the rewards have become earthly, and heaven has become a vaguely evocative metaphor for the unknowable and therefore peripheral beyond.

Within its worldly context, the self-portrait Franklin paints has a figurative and even allegorical significance. In this remarkable story, the strands of the American myth converge. Here is the poor boy who finds the way to wealth, the chartered servant who earns his freedom, the colonial subject who takes up the cause of national independence.

Franklin began writing the *Autobiography* in 1771 and worked on it intermittently until 1788. Since he traces his life only up to 1757, his tale is one of vigor and promise and first success. That is undoubtedly one reason for the book's two centuries of popularity: nothing of old age or decline intrudes, and young America finds a young hero. Furthermore, Franklin devised a style to match his subject. His chief legacy to American letters is the strong, lucid prose in which the *Autobiography* is written, a prose stripped of excess ornament, which captures the accents of real speech. Franklin's description of his arrival in Philadelphia exemplifies his style. On a Sunday morning in October 1723, he stepped out of the boat that had brought him from New Jersey and found himself on the Market Street wharf:

> I was in my working Dress, my best Clothes being to come round by Sea. I was dirty from my Journey; my Pockets were stuff'd out with Shirts and Stockings; I knew no Soul, nor where to look for Lodging. I was fatigu'd with Travelling, Rowing and Want of Rest. I was very hungry, and my whole

> Stock of Cash consisted of a Dutch Dollar and about a Shilling
> in Copper.

The scene recalls Bradford's doleful memory of pilgrims washed
ashore on the unfriendly New England coast, but answers Bradford's
fears with hope.

> I walk'd up the Street, gazing about, till near the Market House
> I met a Boy with Bread. I had made many a Meal on Bread,
> and inquiring where he got it, I went immediately to the Baker's
> he directed me to in Second Street; and ask'd for Biscuit,
> intending such as we had in Boston, but they it seems were
> not made in Philadelphia, then I ask'd for a three-penny Loaf,
> and was told they had none such: so not considering or knowing
> the Difference of Money and the greater Cheapness nor the
> Names of his Bread, I bad him give me three pennyworth of
> any sort. He gave me accordingly three great Puffy Rolls. I was
> surpris'd at the Quantity, but took it, and having no Room in
> my Pockets, walk'd off, with a Roll under each Arm, and eating
> the other. Thus I went up Market Street.

As he walked up Market Street into history and myth, Franklin
created one of the most durable scenes in America's literary record.

The scientific, rational, and deistic temperament that Franklin
exemplified was shared to one extent or another by many of the
politicians and writers who shaped America's fortunes in the decisive
last third of the eighteenth century. Whatever sources the American
Revolution had in personal ambition and economic issues, it was
also an event impelled and guided by ideas. On both sides of the
Atlantic, writers such as Voltaire, Diderot, Hume, Jefferson, and
Franklin proclaimed the tenets of the Age of Reason. The French
philosophes and their European and American contemporaries
called for relief from religious superstition, and they celebrated the
utopian possibilities that could follow from a rationally grounded
science and politics.

Much of the most impressive literature of the period was explicitly political in its subject matter. From the 1760s onward, literary and cultural aspirations were linked to revolutionary politics.
In this sense, the political and artistic ambitions of the colonists
ran parallel and even converged. The deepening crisis that divided

America and England found its energetic expression in a growing body of polemical and theoretical pamphlets and essays. The most influentially belligerent of those documents was produced by Thomas Paine, the English radical who came to Philadelphia at Franklin's invitation in 1774 (Figure 32).

Paine's *Common Sense*, published in January 1776, was an unqualified appeal for complete political independence. Paine's rhetorical power lay in his mastery of the plain style. "It is my design," he insisted, "to make those who can scarcely read understand" and to write in a language "as plain as the alphabet." He strove to adapt thinking and "the turn of language to the subject, so as to bring out a clear conclusion." That conclusion – the decadence of monarchy and the superiority of democracy – was clear enough. *Common Sense* was instantly successful; over one hundred thousand copies were sold by the end of March. Two centuries have not cooled the passion of Paine's rhetoric. "Of more worth is one honest man to society, and in the sight of God," he writes in a typical passage, "than all the crowned ruffians that ever lived." And again, "Everything that is right or reasonable pleads for separation. The blood of the slain, the weeping voice of Nature cries, 'TIS TIME TO PART.' " Righteous in tone but closely reasoned, Paine's argument powerfully molded opinion in the months before the Revolutionary War began (Figure 33).

Poetry, too, was pressed into the service of nationalism. Hugh Henry Brackenridge coauthored with classmate Philip Freneau an effusive graduation poem called "The Rising Glory of America," read at the Princeton commencement of 1771. "Paradise anew / Shall flourish, by no second Adam lost," declared the two young nationalists, the first of whom founded the *United States Magazine* in 1779, while the second went on to become the bitterly productive Poet of the American Revolution. Freneau was a prolific propagandist in democracy's cause, clever, contentious, and provocative. Jefferson said that he had saved the constitution when it was "galloping into monarchy." Freneau produced, among many other poems, a rather moving testament "To the Memory of the Brave Americans," a savage attack, drawn from his own experience, on conditions in a British prison ship. He was also the author of a versified tribute to Paine's *Rights of Man*. It was Paine, Freneau wrote, who enthroned Reason in politics and pulled down kings. Paine's democratic principles assured America's future happiness, a version of what might be called the apocalyptic sublime:

> Without a king, the laws maintain their sway,
> While honor bids each generous heart obey. . . .
> So shall our nation, formed on Virtue's plan,
> Remain the guardian of the Rights of Man,
> A vast Republic, famed through every clime,
> Without a king, to see the end of time.

FIGURE 32 ☙ John Wesley Jarvis, Portrait of Thomas Paine (1806).

FIGURE 33 ☙ Title page of Thomas Paine's *Common Sense* (1776). Though Paine was widely known to have written this pamphlet, his name did not appear on the title page of early editions. Some of the early impressions identified the author only as "An Englishman."

Though much verse was written in the last decades of the eighteenth century, the best literary work was, as the example of Thomas Paine suggests, in prose – the essays, pamphlets, letters, and public documents provoked by the Revolutionary cause. The correspondence of men and women like John and Abigail Adams, Thomas Jefferson, and James Madison eloquently memorializes a dangerous and pivotal period in history. The debates over independence and forms of government achieved a measure of clarity and skill un-

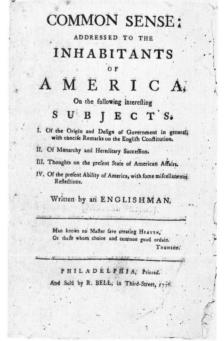

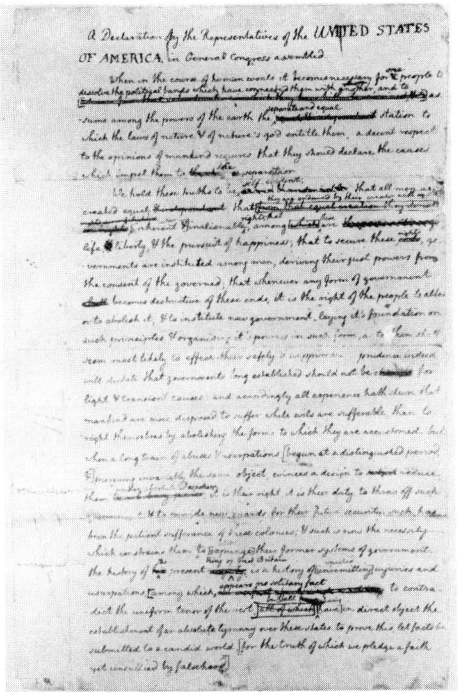

A Declaration by the Representatives of the UNITED STATES OF AMERICA, in General Congress assembled.

When in the course of human events it becomes necessary for one people to dissolve the political bands which have connected them with another, and to assume among the powers of the earth the separate and equal station to which the laws of nature & of nature's god entitle them, a decent respect to the opinions of mankind requires that they should declare the causes which impel them to the separation.

FIGURE 34 ❧ Thomas Jefferson, Declaration of Independence. This first page of Jefferson's draft includes alterations and corrections in the handwriting of Jefferson, John Adams, and Benjamin Franklin.

matched before or since in the political discourse of the nation. Out of this speaking and writing emerged the Declaration of Independence and the Constitution, documents of momentous political importance which have earned an equally high place in the history of American letters. The claims made by the Declaration on behalf of human rights have nurtured the aspirations of men and women around the world for two centuries:

> We hold these truths to be self-evident: that all men are created equal; that they are endowed by their Creator with inalienable rights; that among these are life, liberty, and the pursuit of happiness; that to secure these rights, governments are instituted among men, deriving their just powers from the consent of the governed; that whenever any form of government becomes destructive of these ends, it is the right of the people to alter or to abolish it, and to institute new government.

Officially, the Declaration was drafted by a committee; in fact, it was principally the work of Thomas Jefferson (Figure 34). Jefferson, though descended from aristocratic Virginia families and the owner of forty-five thousand acres and two hundred slaves, emerged before and after the Revolution as one of the new nation's most articulate democratic voices. Serving successively as secretary of state, vice-president, and president, Jefferson made bold and decisive contributions to American politics for a generation. He was, like Franklin, an enthusiastic scientific amateur, and he was also devoted to music and literature. His library of ten thousand volumes served as the foundation of the Library of Congress, and his writings and buildings strongly influenced America's taste in architecture. The Virginia State Capitol, which he began to design within two years of the Revolution's end, was based on the Maison Carrée, a Roman temple still standing in Nîmes, France. This and Jefferson's other neoclassical buildings were intended as symbolic statements in which the new nation declared its heroic descent from republican Rome. Jefferson had studied the works of the architect and theorist Palladio and was familiar with Palladio's contention that "ancient architecture gives us a certain idea of Roman virtue and greatness." Jefferson undoubtedly believed, as architects before and after him have done, that buildings can shape attitudes and behavior. He hoped that

FIGURE 35 &ul; *A South West View of the Capitol in Richmond, Virginia.* This engraving of 1802 is the earliest known view of the capitol building.

FIGURE 36 Gilbert Stuart, portrait of George Washington (1796). Stuart painted three likenesses of Washington from life. This one, called the "Atheneum Portrait," became the most famous image of Washington and the most widely familiar icon in the United States in the nineteenth century.

Roman buildings might nourish Roman virtue in the politicians of his new country (Figure 35).

The appeal to Roman precedent was universal in the early days of the Republic. It provided a dignified ancestry for a rashly innovative system, and it also provided a well-known set of allegorical references. George Washington was regularly called a "Roman hero" in his own lifetime. He was likened to Cincinnatus, the farmer who reluctantly left his plow to take up the sword, and to Fabius, who defeated Hannibal in the Second Punic War. Washington called Freneau a rascal, but Freneau called Washington the savior of "New Albion's Freedom," an immortal Roman hero. Portraits of Washington were the most widely circulated and familiar images in America; like Jefferson's architecture, they mingled classical reference and nationalism (Figure 36).

T he Constitution adopted by the new nation incorporated the limits as well as the strengths of the American Enlightenment. Beliefs about equality did not encompass women or blacks; women were excluded from the vote, and blacks were denied even the dignity of being considered human beings. They were property, to be counted as "fractions" of whites for census purposes. Many of the early national leaders publicly protested against slavery and acknowledged the appalling contradiction between slave ownership and the ideology of equality. A dozen years before the Declaration, in a pamphlet called *The Rights of the British Colonies Asserted and Proved*, James Otis, Jr., had insisted on the equality of all people, regardless of race. "Does it follow that 'tis right to enslave a man because he is black?" The dissent of such thinkers as Otis and the Philadelphia physician Benjamin Rush was unavailing. Hostility against blacks, combined with perceptions of economic self-interest, decreed the survival of the slave system. By a deliberate evasion, the word "slavery" never appears in the constitution, but the affirmation of slavery was the price that had to be paid to southern states for their ratification of the Constitution. Jefferson, who publicly denounced slavery while giving up neither his slaves nor his belief in black inferiority, was a typical but particularly prominent instance.

The first slave ship, the *Jesus*, had arrived in Virginia in 1619, a year before the arrival of Bradford's Pilgrims, and just a few days after the first meeting of the Virginia House of Burgesses. By the time of the Revolution, slavery had spread across much of the colonial North and all of the South. Under conditions of unimaginable difficulty, a richly varied body of Afro-American expression took shape and grew. Uprooted from their homelands and torn from their families, subject to brutal and capricious violence, slaves and free black men and women preserved and transmitted their heritage. This was primarily an oral culture, a world of songs, chants, tales, and folklore, embodying communal memories, resistance, and aspirations toward freedom. White America's European culture was adapted, often subverted, and then also found its way into early Afro-American songs and stories. Biblical talk of freedom, for example, was an article of religious faith for some blacks, but for others it was a political vehicle, a statement anticipating and demanding release from worldly bondage.

Phillis Wheatley, the only black writer who gained recognition in the colonial years, exemplifies a more cooperative relationship to the white society and theology that enslaved her. In 1760, when she was seven years old, she was purchased by a

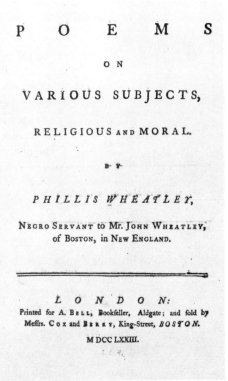

prosperous Boston tailor, John Wheatley, as a servant for his wife. An apt student of English and Latin literature, she began to publish poetry while she was still in her teens. She became something of a celebrity in Boston and also in London, which she visited in 1773. In that same year, her book of poetry was published, under the title *Poems on Various Occasions, Religious and Moral* (Figure 37). A condescending prefatory note, signed by Massachusetts governor Thomas Hutchinson and other New England dignitaries, assures the reader that the poems in the volume were indeed written by "Phillis, a young Negro girl." The poems themselves are modestly accomplished, conventional in form and diction, and bathed in irreproachable patriotic and Christian sentiments. A poem of 1775, for example, hails General Washington as the "great chief" and urges him forward in the name of all Americans. Wheatley's references to race are infrequent and self-effacing. "On Being Brought from Africa to

FIGURE 37 🍂 Frontispiece and title page of the first edition of Phillis Wheatley's *Poems* (1773).

America," for example, records her thanks for the good fortune of her transportation to New England, and her conversion:

> 'Twas mercy brought me from my pagan land,
> Taught my benighted soul to understand
> That there's a God, that there's a Savior too:
> Once I redemption neither sought nor knew.
> Some view our sable race with scornful eye,
> "Their color is a diabolic dye."
> Remember, Christians, Negroes, black as Cain,
> May be refined, and join the angelic train.

Such lines come perilously near echoing the racism of Wheatley's masters. Over half a century earlier, in *The Negro Christianized* (1706), Cotton Mather had called on "all that have any NEGROES in your Houses" to bring them "to the knowledge of God and the belief of Christ." The conversion of Africans offers a pious opportunity "to try whether you may not be the happy instruments of converting the blackest instances of blindness and baseness into admirable candidates for Eternal Blessedness." Jupiter Hammon was another slave whose poetry dwelt in an acceptance of his inferior status and in gratitude for the gift of Christianity. In "The Kind Master and the Dutiful Servant," the servant finds his "whole delight" in doing the master's pleasure, and he obeys the master's call to follow Christ and find salvation.

An altogether different response to servitude can be found in the life and writing of Olaudah Equiano, known as Gustavus Vassa. Taken from Africa and enslaved as a child, Equiano eventually earned his freedom and became a leading figure in the eighteenth-century abolition movement. He wrote and published the story of his life, *The Interesting Narrative of the Life of Olaudah Equiano, or Gustavus Vassa, the African* (1789) (Figure 38). An early example of the important genre of black autobiography, Equiano's *Narrative* offers a survivor's account of the middle passage and of life in bondage, grim memories that gave the lie to the pretence that slavery was compatible with any shred of humanity. Two generations before the first novels of the plantation school appeared, defending racism with sanitized fantasies of slavery's contentments, Equiano had described the cruelty of the slave trade. On the slave ships, he writes, white greed encouraged the barbarous overcrowding of blacks in the unventilated, pestilential holds below decks (Figure 39). Many slaves were killed by heat, sickness, and mistreatment: "This wretched situation was again aggravated by the galling of the chains, [and] now became insupportable... [Especially appalling was] the filth of the necessary tubs, into which the children often fell, and were almost suffocated.... The shrieks of the women, and the groans of the dying, rendered the whole a scene of horror almost inconceivable." Equiano's *Narrative* was published in the year of Washington's inauguration as America's first president. The almost incalculable human distance between those two events measured the new nation's democratic task. The promises of the Declaration and Constitution remained potent but unfulfilled.

GUSTAVUS VASSA,

OR

Olaudah Equiano.

FIGURE 38 An engraved portrait of Gustavus Vassa (Olaudah Equiano). The eighteenth-century caption under this engraving of Vassa identifies him as "a Native African from the Coast of Guinea who, after being freed from American slavery, made voyages to Europe, the West Indies, etc., and accompanied an Expedition to explore a North West passage. He was a worthy, pious, and enlightened Negro, and published his own Narrative dedicated to the British Parliament." In this portrait, Vassa has the New Testament open to the Book of Acts.

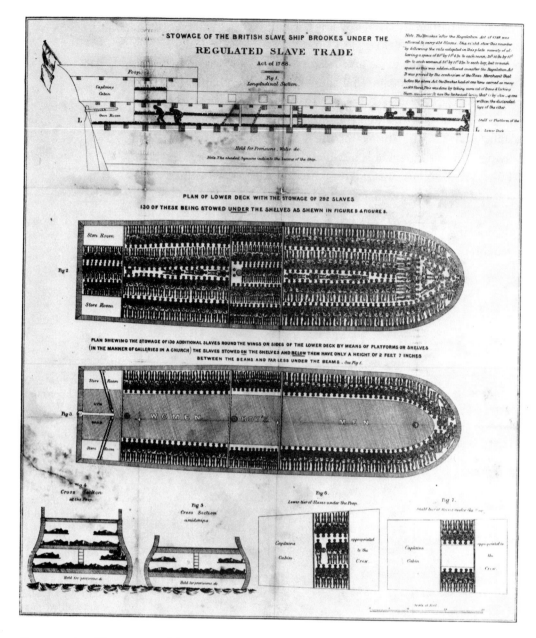

FIGURE 39 & The stowage of slaves was regulated by an act of 1788. This diagram illustrates how 454 human beings could be lawfully stowed aboard the slave ship *Brookes*.

Near the end of the American Revolution, Ezra Stiles, president of Yale College, preached a sermon entitled "The United States Elevated to Glory and Honor." In Stiles's grandiloquent opinion, the new nation that had emerged miraculously from its colonial status incorporated a significance that reached beyond worldly politics. The United States deserved reverence as "God's American Israel." Many patriots were eager to affirm the link between national identity and theology and to interpret the unfolding history of America as a chapter in sacred history as well. The rhetoric of biblical analogy, a legacy of the Puritan errand, would characterize American political discourse for generations.

At the same time, if Americans believed that they could find their sources and analogs in biblical history, they also felt themselves to be "new" men and women. St. Jean De Crèvecoeur famously asked, "What is an American?" and answered his own question by appealing to "a new race of men." De Crèvecoeur was French by birth, and a citizen by turns of England, Canada, and America. He spent the years before the Revolution working on his farm, Pine Hill, in upstate New York. Tory in sentiment, De Crèvecoeur returned to Europe shortly after the war began. During his New York years, he had written a series of essays which he published in London in 1782. These *Letters from an American Farmer* were instantly successful, and they made De Crèvecoeur a celebrity. His reports include an acknowledgment of the "horrors of slavery" and affecting descriptions of white planter brutality. For most of their length, however, De Crèvecoeur's essays render an idealized vision of the New World, offering images of peace and plenty not unlike the promotional literature of two centuries earlier. George Washington said the book was "too flattering" to be accurate, but he admired it nonetheless. In Letter III, where De Crèvecoeur set out to define this "new race" of men, he itemized many of the constituent elements of the American dream. In place of Europe's arbitrary power, its hostile castles, and haughty mansions, America is a "modern society," a nation of yeoman farmers bound together by the "silken bands of mild government." De Crèvecoeur's America is a haven, a refuge for the dispossessed of Europe. Freed of Old World trammels, Americans are revealing the strength of democracy as they build "the most perfect society now existing in the world."

Many of America's inhabitants – women, blacks, Indians, the poor and disenfranchised of all regions – might have detected a measure of unintended irony in De Crèvecoeur's hymn to the nation's excellence. Perhaps only one in ten of the people of America was actually embraced within the formulas of equality and power. Nevertheless, *Letters from an American Farmer* codified the celebratory elements of America's public discourse. Furthermore, if De Crèvecoeur's utopian pronouncements overstated the facts of the case, at the same time such rhetoric provided a vigorous spur to egalitarian aspirations throughout the next two centuries. The men and women of succeeding generations who struggled to give life to America's promises were urged on by their vision of the nation's unfolding democratic vistas.

One of the principal tasks confronting the newly independent country was to define a culture commensurate with its sovereign political status. In an essay of about 1800, Fisher Ames, a conservative Massachusetts farmer and sometime congressman, observed that "few speculative subjects have exercised the passions more . . . than the inquiry, what rank our country is to maintain in the world for genius and literary attainments." Ames went on to summarize the alternative possibilities: "Whether in point of intellect we are equal to Europeans, or only a race of degenerate creoles; whether our artists and authors have already performed much and promise every thing; whether the muses, like the nightingales, are too delicate to cross the salt water, or sicken and mope without song if they do, are themes upon which we Americans are privileged to be eloquent and loud."

As Ames's colorful rhetoric suggests, opinions on the subject of America's literary prospects were deeply divided, as they would continue to be through the nineteenth century. On the one side were the tribes of literary nationalists, steadfast in their conviction that the superiority of America's land and politics ensured the emergence of an equivalently superior literary art. The westward march of civilization, which brought with it America's "rising glory," would also bring poets who would discover the triumphant new voice that the New World required. Ranged against such optimism was a more conservative and skeptical opinion, a suspicion that America's commitment to democracy and its willful separation from the history and traditions of the Old World guaranteed an enduring artistic mediocrity. In this view, furthermore, the prevalent utilitarianism and the frankly antiintellectual cast of America's public discourse seemed antithetical to the understanding and patient encouragement that literary and visual art demand.

One of the busiest groups of literary nationalists in the late eighteenth century was a band of New England poets and essayists known as the Connecticut (or Hartford) Wits. These men, including such figures as Timothy Dwight, Lemuel Hopkins, and John Trumbull, shared a Yale connection, most of them having been students there in the 1760s and 1770s, and many of them later serving on the faculty. Among them they produced satires, epics and mock epics, elegies, and hymns to the New World landscape. Typically conservative and Federalist in temperament, they intended to announce America's arrival on the international literary stage, but in doing so they relied on imitations of various English models. Thus, they described American subjects in the manner of an assortment of English writers, including Pope, Addison, and Goldsmith.

Joel Barlow, one of the youngest of the Connecticut Wits, followed a rather different political path. After graduating from Yale, he served as a chaplain in the American army. He moved to Europe in 1788 and spent most of his remaining years there. In that time, he made a substantial fortune as a land-company agent, and his conservatism gave way to enthusiastic support for the French Revolution. He published a volume of essays, *Advice to the Privileged Orders* (1792), obviously influenced by his friend Thomas Paine, which argued for the rights of all citizens and classes and defended the revolution in France as "the work of argument and rational conviction". Anticipating a formulation of Lincoln two generations later, Barlow declared that the French Revolution was "designed for the benefit of the people, it originated in the people, and was conducted by the people." Like so many of his contemporaries in the early national years, Barlow took his subjects from politics, and he combined literary work with an active public life. He served in Washington's administration as consul to Algiers and later accepted an appointment from Madison as minister to France (Figure 40).

The best of Barlow's poems is probably *The Hasty Pudding*, which he wrote in the 1790s. Invoking muses and classical precedents in the approved mock-epic manner, Barlow celebrates the virtues of his title subject, the ubiquitous cornmeal mush eaten in rustic homes all across the new American nation.

> I sing the sweets I know, the charms I feel,
> My morning incense, and my evening meal –
> The sweets of Hasty Pudding. Come, dear bowl,
> Glide o'er my palate, and inspire my soul.

With straight-faced solemnity, Barlow traces the Indian lineage of the dish, enumerates its virtues, and offers instruction in its preparation and eating. Lighthearted in its tone, *The Hasty Pudding* nonetheless has a satiric point. It exemplifies one of the most prevalent themes of early national literature, the contrast between New World America and the nations of the Old World. Nutritious hasty pudding – hearty, democratic, unpretentious – is a comic but slyly effective emblem of America's vigorous superiority.

Comparisons between Europe and America can of course be traced back to the earliest promotional literature. Predictably, the motif of contrast became an especially prominent genre in the years immediately following the Revolution, when partisans of the new

FIGURE 40 🕿 Engraved portrait of Joel Barlow.

nation felt the need to justify the rebellion and warfare out of which it had been born. Poems, plays, newspaper commentary, even the private correspondence of men otherwise so unlike as Jefferson and John Trumbull, exulted in opposing New World vitality to Old World senescence. Even temporary contact with Europe was denounced as dangerous. Timothy Dwight marshaled heroic couplets to warn young Americans away from the lures of foreign travel. In Dwight's grumbling view, Europe is a "foul harlot," and its pleasures are those of "Circe's sensual bowl." The impressionable American who falls into these mythic snares will "with eye estrang'd, from fair Columbia turn, / Her youth, her innocence, and beauty scorn." Similarly, in a letter to a friend Jefferson wrote that "of all the errors which can possibly be committed in the education of youth, that of sending them to Europe is the most fatal."

The cluster of self-serving formulas that early American propagandists regularly summoned up in their quarrel with Europe would flourish for generations. America is portrayed as the land of rough-hewn individualism and unaffected honesty. Europe, on the other hand, is a haven for idlers and prancing fops. One of the more extended instances of this theme can be found in *The Contrast*, a play which Royall Tyler wrote and produced in 1787. Loosely modeled on Sheridan's *School for Scandal*, Tyler's comedy was the first significant play written in America and the first to be professionally staged. Within a predictable plot about matchmaking, the play's principal contrast is that between the bluff and honorable Colonel Manly, an upright veteran of the Revolution, and Mr. Dimple, a fluttering popinjay who defers to European manners and takes his sartorial and moral cues from the letters of Lord Chesterfield. "Believe me, Colonel," chirps Dimple, "when you have seen the brilliant exhibitions of Europe, you will learn to despise the amusements of this country as much as I do." To which Colonel Manly responds, will all the gravity of his stout republic virtue: "Therefore I do not wish to see them; for I can never esteem that knowledge valuable, which tends to give me a distaste for my native country" (Figure 41).

Dimple sneers that Manly is "unpolished," but Manly has the last word when he sententiously announces that probity and honesty do not require "the polish of Europe." A century and a half earlier, the preface to the *Bay Psalm Book* had declared that "God's altar

FIGURE 41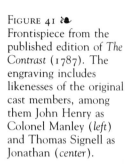
Frontispiece from the
published edition of *The
Contrast* (1787). The
engraving includes
likenesses of the original
cast members, among
them John Henry as
Colonel Manley (*left*)
and Thomas Signell as
Jonathan (*center*).

needs not our polishing." Though Tyler was not intentionally echoing the Puritan metaphor, his use of it recapitulates a major American theme. For the seventeenth-century Calvinists, it was God and
his truth who rose above mere aesthetic considerations. For the
early national patriot, it is the undecorated integrity of the Yankee
hero that defies ornament. The focus has shifted from the supernatural to the secular, but the two cases illustrate the New World's
continuing and characteristic impatience with elegance, along with
the subordination of stylistic questions to allegedly weightier
matters.

As they formulated their diverse definitions of themselves and
their country, Americans exhibited two different and even paradoxical attitudes toward the past. On the one hand, they delighted
in their collective youthfulness, and they regularly assailed European
decrepitude. Noah Webster typically and somewhat gleefully asserted that "Europe is grown old in folly, corruption, and tyranny"
and that "for America in her infancy to adopt the present maxims
of the old would be to stamp the wrinkles of decrepit age upon the

bloom of youth and to plant the seeds of decay in a vigorous constitution. . . . A durable and stately edifice can never be erected upon the moldering pillars of antiquity." At the same time, however, the novelty of America's national situation also induced a sustained anxiety. Though they had made a successful revolution, the men and women of the new nation shared the eighteenth century's suspicion of innovation. The atmosphere of independence was exhilarating but thin and even dangerous. Americans wanted to anchor their grand experiment in history and thus provide the United States with the legitimacy of a lineage. In their strenuous efforts to construct pasts that would enhance the stature of the new country, they appealed by turns to the Bible, to classical myth, and to the heroes of ancient Greece and Rome. In these accounts, America took on a messianic cast, entering on the human stage as mankind's long-awaited destination, the inevitable last chapter of civilization's political and cultural story.

Painters joined writers in embellishing America's history. John Trumbull, the leading painter-historian of the Revolution, regarded the war for American independence as "the noblest series of actions which have ever presented themselves in the history of man." Trumbull was the son of a Connecticut governor, and he served as a soldier for the first two years of the Revolution. Beginning in the mid–1780s and continuing through the remainder of his life, he painted dozens of canvases reproducing the battles and heroes of the war. These were the episodes, as Trumbull put it, "in which were laid the foundation of that free government, which secures our national and individual happiness." Trumbull shared with classical theorists the notion that art ought to instruct and elevate its audience. At the same time, however, his paintings subverted classical theory, which subordinated facts to generalizations and abstractions. Instead, he committed himself to seeking out and depicting the factual and specific and linked his images to confident prophecies about the forthcoming New World millennium. Trumbull intended his pictures to aid in forging America's national identity, and he appealed, like other Americans, to both past and future (Figure 42).

The alchemy of patriotic purpose transformed history into legend. The mythmaking needs of the new nation reached back to embrace the whole era of European exploration. Thus, Christopher

FIGURE 42 🪶 John Trumbull, *The Death of General Warren at the Battle of Bunker's Hill, June 17, 1775.* Trumbull projected twelve canvases in celebration of the American Revolution and completed eight. This scene, the first of the series, was painted in 1786 and depicts the only battle in the war at which Trumbull was present. At the center of the picture, the British victor, Major Small, protects his wounded American adversary, General Warren, from additional injury.

Columbus, an enterprising Italian who had served the colonial ambitions of monarchical Spain, became the unlikely forefather of an English-speaking democracy. In 1807, for example, Joel Barlow published *The Columbiad*, a long and tedious narrative in heroic couplets which he and his contemporaries regarded as his most significant literary work: it was praised as a "tremendous epic." The poem's preface summarizes Barlow's intentions: to promote the love of national liberty and to "show that on the basis of republican principle all good morals, as well as good government and hopes of permanent peace, must be founded." *The Columbiad* was an expanded version of a poem Barlow had written in the 1780s, called *The Vision of Columbus.* That earlier title describes the work's structure in both versions. Columbus, sitting in a Spanish prison, forecasts the future history of the New World and the triumph of the Revolution. Needless to say, the historical Columbus would have found the vision Barlow grants him bizarre. Nonetheless, his appearance as the genius of American democracy allows Barlow to trace the Amer-

ican story back to its earliest European chapters and thereby to secure the nation's pedigree. Barlow's Columbian mythmaking was reinforced and surpassed by Timothy Dwight, who gave the name "Columbia" to the new nation. At the moment America became Columbia, Columbus changed sex, transcended history, and entered the pantheon of gods and goddesses, taking America with him. In both guises, as the idealized historical character and the feminized deity, Columbus would remain a central and recurring figure in America's imagination.

Despite the optimism of the nationalists, literature of importance was slow to emerge in the New World. This was as true of fiction as of poetry. Residual Puritanism encouraged disapproval of story-telling, and the cultures of western frontier, southern plantation, and northern commerce provided stony soil for the nurture of fictional art. In addition, the primitive state of copyright law encouraged the pirating of popular English books. It was simply more profitable for American publishers to reprint the novels of Richardson and Fielding (and, later in the nineteenth century, Dickens) than to pay royalties to native writers. Finally, the writers of the new nation faced the basic and inescapable dilemma of working within linguistic codes and literary conventions bequeathed by a country from which they had deliberately separated themselves. The baggage of colonial dependence encumbered the American imagination for decades following the Revolution.

The American novels that did appear amid these inhospitable circumstances necessarily betrayed their derivation from European precedents, but they also initiated several important New World traditions. Susanna Haswell Rowson, for example, earned a considerable success with several novels, especially *Charlotte Temple, a Tale of Truth*, which was published in 1791. Rowson's tale is a melodramatic narrative of seduction and desertion; the heroine of the novel dies in poverty. Hannah Foster's *Coquette* (1797), an epistolary novel told in seventy-four letters, also tells a story of intrigue and abandonment and similarly ends with the death of its heroine. Both books are chronicles of romance and adventure, theatrical in language and mechanical in plot. Both, nonetheless, possessed a larger importance than their subsequent reputations suggest. Dismissed for supposed sentimentality, *Charlotte Temple* and *The*

FIGURE 43 ❧ Title page of Susanna Rowson's *Charlotte [Temple], A Tale of Truth*. Published first in England in 1791 and then in America three years later, *Charlotte Temple* became the first American fictional bestseller. Over fifty thousand copies were sold by 1810; the novel eventually appeared in perhaps two hundred editions. The author of many novels and plays, Rowson also founded a boarding school for girls in 1797. Hanna Evans, who owned the copy of the novel whose title page is reproduced here, was a nineteenth-century Pennsylvania portrait and miniature painter.

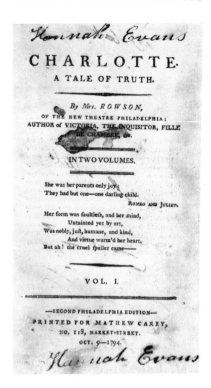

Coquette in fact stand at the head of a tradition of domestic fiction in which the lives and circumstances of women were studied with serious attention (Figure 43).

In the decades preceding the Civil War, novels and romances by women constituted America's most popular fiction. Catharine Sedgwick, E.D.E.N. Southworth, Susan Warner, Anna Warner, and scores of others offered the dramas of women who, like their female reading public, seek fulfillment in a society that bars their way to property, the professions, power – to virtually all the opportunities that came to men by right of male birth. These writers were reviled for the impertinence of success (Hawthorne muttered about "the damned mob of scribbling women" and the "ink-stained Amazons") and were subsequently dismissed from literary history on charges of sentimentality and melodrama. In fact, rendering the world from the vantage point of the hearth and kitchen rather than the wilderness, they made good on Emerson's democratic claims for American literature long before Emerson's more famous disciples. "What would we really know the meaning of?" Emerson asked.

"The meal in the firkin; the milk in the pan; the ballad in the street; the news of the boat; the glance of the eye; the form and gait of the body." In antebellum America, these homely things were more likely to be found in the fiction of women than anywhere else. Along with a body of once widely read fiction, women also left a legacy of imaginative work in nonliterary forms, in their quilting, crewelwork, recipes, and gardening manuals. Adapting tradition and myth to their talents and circumstances, they ornamented the utilitarian dimensions of their lives (Figure 44).

Charles Brockden Brown, who published prodigiously on subjects from the rights of women to geography to Roman history, contributed to a different tradition by wedding European gothic to American materials. Keats called Brown a "strange American scion of the German trunk. Powerful genius – accomplish'd horror." More significantly, in such novels as *Wieland* (1798), *Arthur Mervyn* (1800), and *Edgar Huntley* (1801), Brown set meandering stories of mystery and violence in relatively specific American circumstances. Yellow fever, for example, was a disease that only afflicted American cities – Jefferson called it "peculiar to our country." An early and virulent outbreak carried off one-tenth of Philadelphia's population in 1793. Frightful enough in its own medical terms, an epidemic of yellow fever takes on sinister and even supernatural overtones in *Arthur Mervyn*:

> Death seemed to hover over this scene, and I dreaded that the floating pestilence had already lighted on my frame. I approached a house before which stood a hearse. Presently a coffin borne by two men issued from the house. One of them, as he assisted in thrusting the coffin into the cavity provided it, said: "I'll be d——d if I think the poor dog was quite dead. . . . It was n't quite right to put him in his coffin before the breath was fairly gone. I thought the last look he gave me told me to stay a few minutes."

Brown's interest in somnambulism and psychic abnormality and his intimations of premature burial recall the earlier English work of Godwin and Walpole and also anticipate Poe's preoccupations with extremity.

Exploring yet another fictional territory, Hugh Henry Brackenridge took the novel to the American frontier. *Modern Chivalry*

FIGURE 44 ᴁ Mary Sarah Titcomb, Adam and Eve (crewelwork, 1760).

is a huge work that appeared in sections from 1792 to 1815. Subtitled *The Adventures of Captain Farrago and Teague O'Regan*, the novel follows its two title characters in their frankly plotless wandering across the American backwoods. Captain Farrago is a thoughtful, moderate Jeffersonian; his servant Teague O'Regan is an engagingly ignorant Irish scoundrel. Their misadventures, in which O'Regan is awarded one undeserved honor or office after another, reveal the narrow limits and the self-importance of a raw democratic society. In its satiric tone, its episodic shapelessness, and its roguish main character O'Regan, *Modern Chivalry* declares its descent from the sprawling picaresque tales of Sterne and Fielding, and especially from Cervantes's *Don Quixote*. Brackenridge's rough humor was intended to improve American democracy by lampooning its excesses, and in this *Modern Chivalry* initiated one of the central topics of the new nation's literature. Measuring the distance between the tub-thumping rhetoric of New World exceptionalism and the more vulgar realities of American life would remain a continuing preoccupation of American writers.

The South revered learning and aspired to a sort of literary culture. The nation's second-oldest college, William and Mary, had been founded in Virginia in 1693, and that state had provided much of the nation's intellectual leadership in the eighteenth and early nineteenth centuries. Increasingly dependent upon slavery, especially after the introduction of the cotton gin, the South's antebellum writers were driven either to propagandizing in defense of the indefensible institution or to indulging in escapist fantasy. Yielding to no other region in its admiration for Sir Walter Scott, the South produced a shelf of glutinous romance fictions, chivalric melodramas in which cardboard heroes and heroines address each other with maladroit formality. The best southern fiction included the work of William Gilmore Simms, whose romances of the frontier and of South Carolina's history include pages of quite vivid writing. *The Yemassee* (1835), one of Simms's "border romances," is enfeebled by its inert and stereotyped main characters, but the book makes an approach to lively realism in some of its descriptions and in the talk of some of its common folk.

An indigenous southern genre was the plantation novel, which turned the brutality of slavery into a sunny daydream of white benevolence and black loyalty. John Pendleton Kennedy published the first such novel, *Swallow Barn: or, A Sojourn in the Old Dominion*, in 1832. The book's forty-nine related sketches created most of the images and types that would recur in plantation novels written before and long after the Civil War, from the nostalgia of Thomas Nelson Page at the end of the century to *Gone with the Wind*. In all of these books, slavery is subsumed in the picturesque charm of magnolia and pleasant weather. In one of *Swallow Barn*'s typical scenes, the wise and amiable planter Frank Meriwether gallantly allows his aged black stablehand, Carey, to have the best of an argument over the care of horses: " 'Well, tie up your tongue, you old mastiff,' replied Frank, as he walked out of the stable, 'and cease growling, since you will have it your own way';—and then, as we left the old man's presence, he added, with an affectionate chuckle—'a faithful old cur, too, that snaps at me out of pure honesty; he has not many years left, and it does no harm to humor him!' "

In the decade before the Civil War, the antislavery uproar caused by the success of *Uncle Tom's Cabin* (1852) provoked a spasm of southern propaganda. John Esten Cooke's *Virginia Comedians: or, Old Days in the Old Dominion* (1854) is set in the late eighteenth century, just before the Revolution; the book includes Patrick Henry among its heroes. Cooke documents southern virtue and at the same time evades the looming turmoil by returning to the mystified chivalry and unsullied romance of an earlier struggle, when loyalty to the South was synonymous with fidelity to the nation. George Fitzhugh's tract, *Cannibals All! or, Slaves without Masters* (1857), argued that the wage slavery by which white workers were manacled in the North was a far worse bondage than the chattel slavery of the South. This was a commonplace of prewar polemic. A versified argument along similar lines was contained in William Grayson's popular poem, "The Hireling and the Slave" (1854). Grayson's image of happy slaves in rustic cabins turned bondage into a species of pastoral retirement:

> The cabin home, not comfortless, though rude,
> Light daily labor, and abundant food.
> The sturdy health that temperate habits yield,
> The cheerful song that rings in every field,
> The long, loud laugh, that freedmen seldom share.

The ersatz contentments of Grayson's scenes sometimes found visual

counterparts in antebellum genre painting. Eastman Johnson's most popular picture, *Old Kentucky Home* (1859), is a cloudless Land of Cockaigne, a pleasant scene of racial harmony from which the brutality of lash and forced labor have conveniently disappeared (Figure 45).

FIGURE 45 ❧ Eastman Johnson, *Old Kentucky Home* (1859).

Although America's antebellum culture seemed conspicuously meager, the country's economic and political centrality among the community of nations was quickly assured. What had begun as a chancy experiment on the margins of European

FIGURE 46 🕿 George Caleb Bingham, *Daniel Boone Escorting a Band of Pioneers into the Western Country* (1852).

hegemony rapidly transformed itself into a prosperous competitor on the world stage. In the three generations from independence to the Civil War, America expanded its geographical boundaries at a breathtaking rate. Jefferson's purchase of the Louisiana Territory from France in 1803 doubled the new nation's size, and a combination of war and bellicose diplomacy added the vast areas of Texas, California, and Oregon. By 1860, nearly twenty new states had entered the Union. Furthermore, while all of the thirteen original states had been washed by the Atlantic, America's new Pacific frontier was almost as far from the East Coast as London was. The country's population grew at a similar, extraordinary pace. In each decade, the country's population increased by a third. A high birth rate early in the century and increasing immigration in the 1840s and later combined to double the nation's population every twenty to twenty-five years.

Land meant opportunity, and many of America's new citizens moved westward, spreading over the Appalachian Mountains into the Mississippi Valley and across the Great Plains (Figure 46). De Tocqueville was not the only visitor who marveled at American restlessness and who discerned both strength and weakness in the national appetite for land and mobility. The needs of commerce encouraged the development of transport systems to link the regions of the huge country together. The first turnpike opened between Philadelphia and Lancaster in 1791; stage coaches could complete the seventy-mile journey in a slow and uncomfortable twelve hours. Turnpikes were built throughout the eastern half of the country; though the perils of weather and of poor road conditions were notorious, the whole nation seemed to climb onto wagons and move west. One British traveler wrote from the Cumberland Road that "old America seems to be breaking up and moving westward. We are seldom out of sight, as we travel towards the Ohio, of family groups behind us and before us."

Hazardous to persons and inefficient for goods, turnpikes soon found competition from water transport. Flatboats, keelboats, and packet boats plied the rivers of the East, South, and Midwest. By one estimate, over twelve thousand flatboats floated down the Mississippi to New Orleans in the years from 1805 to 1820. Steamboats, which allowed travel upstream as well as down, multiplied inland navigation, as did canals, beginning with the fabulously successful Erie Canal in the 1820s. Finally, it was the railroad that bound nineteenth-century America together, guided and shaped much of its economic development, and permitted the nation to meet the simultaneous challenges of expansion and consolidation. Sam Slick, the Yankee clock peddler, wryly observed that to Americans the railroad was "river, bridge, road, and canal, all in one." The humor was not far off the mark. Before midcentury, over nine thousand miles of track were in use, most of them joining the northern and western sections of the country. The railroad served both as cause and symbol of northern industrial dominance, sharpening its rivalry with the agrarian South and eventually doing much to determine the outcome of the Civil War. By the war's end, tracks had been laid for thirty-five thousand miles.

Unchecked speculation, incoherent federal regulatory attitudes, and recurrent bitter debates over the currency propelled the country through cycles of boom and bust. In 1819, 1837, and 1857, financial panic swept through the nation's banks and countinghouses, wiping out large and small investors indiscriminately. More important, in the view of many observers, the nation's attention seemed to have shifted from its earlier sense of mission toward calculations of profit and loss. Belief in American exceptionalism survived the onrushing tides of commercial expansion, but it was jostled by accelerating doubts. America appeared less a redeemer nation than a nest of confidence men and grasping opportunists. Economist Samuel Blodget might declare that commerce was a virtue, "the most sublime gift of heaven, wherewith to harmonize and enlarge society," but many Americans were uneasy with such bluster.

The contest between self-confidence and anxiety was symbolized by the deaths of John Adams and Thomas Jefferson, both of whom died on July 4, 1826, the fiftieth anniversary of the Declaration of Independence. This uncanny coincidence seemed weighted with significance, though interpretations sharply differed. Some saw the long lives of the patriarchs and their simultaneous, peaceful deaths as the blessing of Providence upon the American experiment; others read the deaths as a warning, an emblem of the nation's decline from the nobility of its founders. This much was clear: an era had come to an end, and the Revolutionary past had given way to the unpredictable future.

The multiplying states numbered the nation's growth, but the more significant political reality was the development of distinct regions. The towns of the North, plantations of the South, and prairies of the West symbolized the separate and often conflicting economic and cultural sections into which the country was inexorably divided. The great issues of antebellum America were polarized along the lines of regional loyalties. Debates over tariff and trade, commerce and currency, threatened to tear the growing country permanently apart. Above all, Americans faced each other with increasing bitterness as they pondered and legislated the shameful facts of slavery. Though the importation of slaves was forbidden after 1808, the slave populations grew tremendously in the years before the Civil War, from 1.5 million, in 1820, to upwards of 4 million in 1860. Much of the political history of those decades consists in the assorted compromises through which the nation despairingly refused to eliminate its most evil institution. With characteristic prescience, de Tocqueville observed in 1831: "If ever America undergoes great revolutions, they will be brought about by the presence of the black race on the soil of the United States; that is to say, they will owe their origin, not to the equality, but to the inequality of condition."

While the crime of slavery hung like a sword over America's destiny, the nation's citizens pursued their frantic commercial undertakings. The country's absorption in its moneymaking, along with its dizzying growth in size and numbers, was often invoked by American patriots to explain the paucity of culture. In 1843, a New Hampshire writer named J. N. Bellows defended the United States from the slurs of European critics by insisting that Americans were simply too busy for cultivated pastimes. "But a few years ago," Bellows wrote, "the country we inhabit was a wilderness. Hardly was the land cleared on the coast, and dotted with towns and villages; hardly had New York, and Boston, and Philadelphia assumed the name and character of cities, before the great west became an object of interest to our own people, and to the immigrant from foreign lands." Nation building was a full-time job. Visitors and natives alike remarked on the distinctive tone of American life, a tone that might be called moralizing utilitarianism. Philistinism conspired with dour piety in demanding an art and literature that would put themselves at the service of patriotism or moral uplift.

In the face of such constraints, America's early national literature seemed at best a matter of confident prophecy rather than of present accomplishment. In December 1818, the English critic Sydney Smith peered condescendingly down on American letters from the high vantage point of the influential *Edinburgh Review*:

> Literature the Americans have none – no native literature, we mean. It is all imported. They had a Franklin, indeed; and may afford to live for half a century on his fame. There is, or was, a Mr. Dwight, who wrote some poems; and his baptismal name was Timothy. There is also a small account of Virginia by Jefferson, and an epic by Joel Barlow – and some pieces of pleasantry by Mr. Irving. But why should the Americans write books, when a six weeks' passage brings them in our own tongue, our sense, science and genius, in bales and hogsheads?

Although it was not literally true, Smith's patronizing survey of

America's literary accomplishments elicited assent on both sides of the Atlantic. "In the four quarters of the globe," asked Smith, "who reads an American book?"

The question was being answered even as Smith asked it. In 1820, Washington Irving gathered together some of his "pieces of pleasantry" and published them as *The Sketch Book of Geoffrey Crayon, Gent.* The book earned an immediate success, both in America and in England, and Irving's personal triumph conferred esteem on America as well. Irving's appearance seemed an auspicious demonstration of America's cultural potential. Born in April 1783, within weeks of the British surrender at Yorktown, and named for the greatest of American heroes, Irving was the first literary representative of the post-Revolutionary generation. His fame brought the promise of a general American flowering, and for many years he did what he could to hearten and promote the work of other writers. When he died in 1859, on the eve of the Civil War, Irving

FIGURE 47 ✥ Christian Schussele, *Washington Irving and His Literary Friends at Sunnyside.* Writers represented include (*left to right*): Henry Tuckerman, Oliver Wendell Holmes, William Gilmore Simms, Fitz-Greene Halleck, Nathaniel Hawthorne, Henry Wadsworth Longfellow, Nathaniel Parker Willis, William H. Prescott, Washington Irving, James K. Paulding, Ralph Waldo Emerson, William Cullen Bryant, James Fenimore Cooper, George Bancroft.

had occupied the leading place of antebellum literary culture throughout the last four decades of his life (Figure 47).

Edgar Allan Poe resented Irving's eminence and argued that his talent had been overrated by a culture that had badly needed a pioneer. It was a view that would ultimately prevail. In any case, though Irving's priority was undeniable, the importance of his career was more complex. He did not so much surmount as embody the many questions and ambiguities which the new nation's nascent culture confronted. The son of a Scottish father and an English mother, Irving found his literary models in Addison's *Spectator* papers and in the works of Oliver Goldsmith and Laurence Sterne. In style, subject, and point of view he was a transitional figure, a man as much of the Old World as of the New. Significantly, beginning in 1815, Irving spent seventeen of his most productive years in Europe, enjoying the admiration of Coleridge and Byron and the friendship of Sir Walter Scott. He served as diplomatic attaché in Spain in the late 1820s, then became secretary to the American legation in London, and received the Gold Medal of the Society of Literature as well as an honorary doctorate from Oxford. When he returned to the United States in 1832, he was a public figure on both sides of the Atlantic, courted alike by campaigning politicians and aspiring writers. He went back to Europe in the 1840s, spent three years as minister to Spain, and then retired to live out his last, prosperous years at his New York home, Sunnyside, receiving homage and working on his final book, an immense biography of George Washington. As his friend Thackeray said in a commemorative tribute, Irving was the first "ambassador" from the "New World of Letters" to the "Old."

Irving had first come to literary notice while he was still in his teens with his precocious "Letters of Jonathan Oldstyle, Gent." (1802–3), genial satires on society in turn-of-the-century New York. A few years later, with his brother William and J. K. Paulding, he helped edit *Salmagundi: or, The Whim-Whams and Opinions of Launcelot Langstaff, Esq. and Others.* The essays and stories in these pamphlets combined generally pleasant attacks on contemporary manners with a Federalist distaste for Jeffersonian "mobocracy." A similar point of view defined Irving's next work, an elaborate fictional hoax entitled *The History of New York from the Beginning of the World to the End of the Dutch Dynasty* (1809). Advertised as the work of one Diedrich Knickerbocker, the *History* purports to contrast the decadence of the contemporary New York scene with the "golden age" of early Dutch settlement and rule. The Federalist satire of the *History*, closely attached to the now-vanished details of bygone politics, has grown rather stale.

The comic intentions that motivated Irving's mock-heroic history of New York disclose his misgivings about the quality of the American past. A nation without roots exhausts its few fictional resources in humor and genial gossip. *The Sketch Book*, the volume that secured Irving's reputation, is based on the same assumptions. *The Sketch Book* is a potpourri of thirty or so essays and tales, many of which take up English subjects from the point of view of an American visitor, Geoffrey Crayon. Given Irving's temperament, English subject matter was inevitable. In America, as Crayon complains, "local tales are trampled underfoot by the shifting throng . . . [and] ghosts have scarcely time to turn themselves in their graves, before their surviving friends have travelled away from the neighborhood." Thus, Crayon's accounts of Westminster Abbey, Stratford-on-Avon, and "The Christmas Dinner" are studiously picturesque, dappled in the carefully wrought charm that has lured generations of American travelers to England's small towns and old buildings. As Crayon says in the book's first essay, he finds his native country full only of youthful promise, while Europe possesses the treasures of age. Ruins display the history of times gone by, and moldering stones are chronicles. Here is the tribute paid by New World talent to Old World aesthetic resources, and especially to the imaginative opportunities represented by Europe's romantically encrusted past: "I longed to wander over the scenes of renowned achievement, – to tread, as it were, in the footsteps of antiquity, – to loiter about the ruined castle, – to meditate on the falling tower, – to escape, in short, from the commonplace realities of the present, and lose myself among the shadowy grandeurs of the past."

Only a handful of Geoffrey Crayon's sketches deal with American materials, but they include two of Irving's most durable stories, "Rip Van Winkle" and "The Legend of Sleepy Hollow." Like the amiable English anecdotes that surround them, these two tales also reveal Irving's antiquarian impulse and his fascination with the picturesque. In "Sleepy Hollow," he reiterates his complaint that America has no past, and he suggests ironically that the setting of the tale, "some thirty years ago," is "a remote period of American history." Furthermore, the sources of both the New York sketches were German folktales to which Irving had been directed by Sir Walter Scott. In spite of all this, however, Irving endowed his New World settings with something of the twilight and mystery he usually reserved for European scenes, and he distilled out of his Germanic raw materials memorable images of America's emergent and uncertain identity. Rip Van Winkle, who sleeps through the Revolution, and Ichabod Crane, who is frightened out of both his wits and his home by what he takes to be a headless horseman, personify in their different ways the intertwined social and cultural dilemmas the new nation faced. Derivative and oddly un-American as they are, these characters have long since entered the pantheon of American folklore and fiction (Figure 48, Figure 49).

In a pattern that other American writers would duplicate, Irving's early work was his best. His success coincided with diminishing powers and achievements. His later, feebler books of sketches, such as *Bracebridge Hall* and *Tales of a Traveller*; his copybook hymns to Spain, among them *The Alhambra* and *A Chronicle of the Conquest*

FIGURE 48 ❧ John Quidor, *The Return of Rip Van Winkle*. Probably completed in 1849, Quidor's painting illustrates Rip Van Winkle's confusion when he returns to his Catskills village after a twenty-year sleep. Much that he saw, including the fluttering flag with its assemblage of stars and stripes, was incomprehensible. "He recognized on the sign, however, the ruby face of King George, . . . but . . . the head was decorated with a cocked hat, and underneath was painted in large characters, GENERAL WASHINGTON."

FIGURE 49 ❧ F. O. C.
Darley, *Ichabod Crane.*
Irving's tales and
sketches attracted a large
number of illustrators, of
whom Felix Darley was
perhaps the most
successful. This rendering
of Ichabod Crane, which
became the definitive
image of Irving's ill-fated
schoolmaster, was
produced for the revised
edition of *The Legend of
Sleepy Hollow* (1848).

of Granada; and his enormous biographies of Columbus and Washington, all demonstrated more of Irving's commitments than his
skills. Yet his hold on the contemporary audience was durable. His
fascination with the picturesque and noble past seems irrelevant to
the pressing concerns of antebellum America, but it may have awakened a welcoming response from a people whose energies and efforts
were being poured so prodigally into the future. Irving's glimpses of
harmony matched a recurrent antebellum theme. His stories and
essays offered relief from the tumult of getting and spending in the
seductive byways of folktale, fable, and myth.

The year 1820, in which *The Sketch Book* appeared, also saw
the publication of James Fenimore Cooper's first novel, *Precaution.*
More belligerently American than Irving, and more single-minded
in his use of native materials, Cooper was also more unforgiving of
America's materialism and bad taste. Cooper was the son of a large
landholder, the son-in-law of a Tory squire, and a lifelong defender
of property. In his skeptical opinion, the democratic belief "that
'one man is as good as another' is true in neither nature, revealed

FIGURE 50 ❧ John Wesley Jarvis, portrait of James Fenimore Cooper.

morals, or political theory." The leveling politics that reached their apotheosis in Andrew Jackson provoked Cooper's virtually aristo-cratic impatience. Caught between his admiration for America's natural virtues and his uneasiness about its political pretension and social inadequacy, Cooper devised New World myth out of his own ambivalence. His characters are typically flat, his language stilted, and his landscapes sentimentalized, but he invented several of the genres and themes to which much of later American fiction would remain loyal (Figure 50).

Though Cooper was just six years younger than Irving, the lit-erary distance between them was considerably greater. Irving started publishing his work before he was twenty, whereas Cooper came belatedly to his vocation as a writer. *Precaution* was a mechanically derivative, briefly popular comedy of English manners, which Cooper wrote mainly to show that he could. His next novel, *The Spy*, was stronger and far more successful, and with it he began to map out his characteristic fictional territory. Influenced toward na-tional history by the example of Sir Walter Scott, Cooper turned to the American Revolution for a story of intrigue and military exploit, a tale at once patriotic and genuinely exciting. The idea for the novel apparently came from Cooper's friend, former chief justice John Jay, but the New York State setting and the title character, Harvey Birch, were Cooper's inventions. *The Spy* had an unprecedented sale for a work of American fiction, and it determined Cooper's career (Figure 51). By 1823, Cooper had also produced *The Pilot*, a romance of the sea based loosely on the career of John Paul Jones, and *The Pioneers*, set on the New York State frontier in the years after the Revolution, the first of the Leather-Stocking volumes. Within just four years, Cooper had established himself as a popular writer in several distinct types of fiction; he had produced novels of history, the frontier, and the sea. He had also moved to New York City and founded the Bread and Cheese Club, a gathering of Knickerbocker writers and artists, including William Cullen Bryant, Fitz-Greene Halleck, and Samuel F. B. Morse.

The remaining three decades of Cooper's life included seven years in Europe, primarily in France, where he held the largely honorific position of consul at Lyons. His output of novels, travel books, and essays was prodigious. Among his literally scores of books, the most important were the five volumes in the Leather-

FIGURE 51 &❧ William Dunlap, scene from James Fenimore Cooper, *The Spy*. In this scene from the dramatization of Cooper's novel, the loyalist Harry Wharton removes his disguise and surrenders to Captain Lawton. Dunlap, who completed this painting in 1823, was himself a well-known playwright.

Stocking series: *The Pioneers* (1823), *The Last of the Mohicans* (1826), *The Prairie* (1827), *The Pathfinder* (1840), and *The Deerslayer* (1841). In these novels, which coincided with the rapid westward march of American settlement and the taming of the frontier, Cooper presented the idealized likeness of the woodsman. Natty Bumppo is Cooper's memorial to unfettered individualism and natural aristocracy. The five novels picture Natty Bumppo at various stages of his life, from youth to old age, always presenting him as a man of instinctive honesty, matchless courage, and abounding generosity. Through Natty, Cooper explored his most evocative theme, the struggle between wilderness and the encroachments of civilization. The landscapes of the Leather-Stocking tales have their sources in the magic places of romance. If Cooper's hills and valleys are inadequately specified, they are suffused in an aura of myth.

Cooper understood the innovative significance of his fiction. In a book he published in 1828, *Notions of the Americans*, he somewhat apologetically explained the difficulties facing American writers. Like others before and after him, he called attention to the new nation's "poverty of materials." There are, he wrote in a famous list, "no annals for the historian; no follies (beyond the most vulgar and common place) for the satirist; no manners for the dramatist; no obscure fictions for the writer of romance; no gross and hardy offences against decorum for the moralist; nor any of the rich artificial auxiliaries of poetry." Cooper acknowledged the literary mediocrity that attended such multiplied absences, and he claimed to place his hope in the genius of the future. In fact, his own novels made imaginative use of some of the resources that lay waiting in the American scene, and they provided precedents of character and theme around which a significant body of later American writing would revolve. Natty Bumppo is a quintessentially American figure, engaging and masterful in unexpected ways that broke with European precedent and anticipated what lay ahead. Natty is heroic in spite of himself. In all of his guises, as Hawkeye, Deerslayer, and Pathfinder, Natty instructs America by opposing his primitive virtues to the nation's drift. His ragged clothing rebukes artifice, as his unlearned wisdom embodies a caution against bookishness. Natty Bumppo is a sample of the romantic primitivism that was disrupting literary culture on both sides of the Atlantic. He speaks in the untutored accents of the natural aristocrat. Here, for example, from

The Pioneers, is Natty's angry defense of himself when he is arrested on a trumped-up charge of assault: " 'You've driven God's creaters from the wilderness, where his providence had put them for his own pleasure: and you've brought in the troubles and divilities of the law, where no man was ever known to disturb another. You have driven me, that have lived forty long years of my appointed time in this very spot, from my home and the shelter of my head.' "

Cooper once wrote that "it takes a first class aristocrat to make a first class Democrat," and while he abhorred the feudal structures of Europe, his lifelong preference was for a limited franchise based on talent and property. D. H. Lawrence, in his *Studies in Classic American Literature*, used the broad brush of overstatement to capture something of Cooper's divided sympathies:

> In actuality, Fenimore loved the genteel continent of Europe, and waited gasping for the newspapers to praise his WORK.
> In another actuality he loved the tomahawking continent of America, and imagined himself Natty Bumppo.
> Now Natty and Fenimore, arm-in-arm, are an odd couple.
> You can see Fenimore: blue coat, silver buttons, silver-and-diamond buckle shoes, ruffles.
> You see Natty Bumppo: a grizzled, uncouth old renegade, with gaps in his old teeth and a drop on the end of his nose.
> But Natty was Fenimore's great wish: his wishfulfillment.

Cooper grew increasingly alienated from the tone and texture of Jacksonian democracy. In his fiction and nonfiction, as well as in his personal life, he identified himself with a pinched conservatism. The notoriety he achieved in literary controversy was reinforced by the numerous lawsuits he brought against his Cooperstown neighbors, usually in defense of his property rights. By the time of his death, a few years before Irving's, Cooper's name had become a synonym for cranky eccentricity and sharp practice. He had lost the place of high favor his early novels had won for him.

The critical reaction against Cooper reached its spectacular climax a half-century after his death when Samuel Clemens published "Fenimore Cooper's Literary Offenses." This is an excruciatingly funny essay, in which Clemens dismantled Cooper's plots, prose, characters, grammar, even his individual word choices. "Cooper's art has some defects," Clemens writes. "In one place in Deerslayer, and in the restricted space of two-thirds of a page, Cooper has scored 114 offences against literary art out of a possible 115. It breaks the record." Among the "eighteen rules" that govern the art of the literary romance, Clemens enumerates these:

> They require that the episodes of a tale shall be necessary parts of the tale, and shall help develop it. But as the *Deerslayer* tale is not a tale, and accomplishes nothing and arrives nowhere, the episodes have no rightful place in the work, since there was nothing for them to develop.
>
> They require that the personages in a tale shall be alive, except in the case of corpses, and that always the reader shall be able to tell the corpses from the others. But this detail has often been overlooked in the *Deerslayer* tale.

And so on, for a dozen pages. Cooper's reputation was entombed in the vault of Clemens's scorn. His fiction became a byword for coincidence, contrivance, and slipshod writing.

Nonetheless, while Cooper sounded no elemental depths, his renderings of woods and woodsman have force. The combat between simplicity and sophistication, a central preoccupation of Romanticism on both sides of the Atlantic, received a durable statement in Cooper's scenes. The excesses of his prose derived in part from his proprietary anger: the land he loved was under siege. Thus, his weak plots were nothing more than creaking mechanisms to transport his characters from one symbolic confrontation to another. In one such episode in *The Pioneers*, huge flocks of passenger pigeons, which had flown across the New York wilderness unmolested from time immemorial, are massacred by townsmen using the cannons of war. Natty Bumppo speaks Cooper's lament for the destruction of the natural by the engines of a so-called civilization. "This comes of settling a country," Natty complains: nature is violated and subdued, and nature's laws give way to the "divilities" of pettifogging legal systems. Inevitably, a sense of anxious belatedness turns Cooper's natural lyricism toward elegy. The wilderness whose brooding presence he reveres is inevitably vanishing, and with it the values that might have separated America from the crowded, corrupt societies of the Old World.

ぞ

Cooper's awkward but devoted embrace of nature exemplifies the emergence of American Romanticism. Romanticism eludes compact definition, but it encompassed a reaction against the Age of Reason, a large-scale shift in sensibility that began in the late eighteenth century and stormed across the first half of the nineteenth. This transatlantic cultural phenomenon usually involved the subordination of rationality to emotion and intuition and professed to locate the center of human interest and value in the individual. Subjective and inward-looking, Romanticism spurned the problem-solving, daylit world of the Enlightenment and chose rather the mysterious, darker realms of the psyche and of unspoiled nature or of moonlit ruins. Nature, indeed, was reconceived, becoming the source of spiritual refreshment and even – in some versions at least – the dwelling place of divinity. In Wordsworth's "Tintern Abbey," nature's harmony and joy make the human eye "quiet" and confer the power to "see into the life of things." Against dogmas in science and religion, Romantic artists declared the integrity of the individual and of instinct. Wisdom was associated with the innocence of children or with childlike elderly figures: the "simple Child" of Wordsworth's "We Are Seven," for example, or the old man of "Michael."

European for the most part in its genesis, Romanticism found a fertile seedbed in a New World imagination that had long since attached high privilege to the special and even sanctified qualities of the American landscape. So too did Romanticism's preference for the common man and woman awaken welcoming echoes stirred by democratic aspirations. Among the earliest of America's poets to exhibit an explicit response to English Romanticism was William Cullen Bryant. The earliest poetic influences that Bryant felt were those of Thomas Gray, Robert Blair, and other members of the eighteenth-century English graveyard school. Bryant remained in many ways allied with the preceding century throughout his poetic career. However, between the first draft of "Thanatopsis" (1811) and the final version, ten years later, Bryant underwent a Wordsworthian conversion. He read *Lyrical Ballads* and reported that it caused "a thousand springs . . . to gush up at once into my heart, and the face of Nature, of a sudden, to change into a strange freshness and life." In consequence of this metamorphosis, Bryant added an introductory group of sixteen or seventeen lines to "Thanatopsis," directing the reader to assume toward nature a posture of affectionate reciprocity not unlike Wordsworth's:

> To him who in the love of Nature holds
> Communion with her visible forms, she speaks
> A various language. . . .
>
> .   .   .   .
>
> Go forth, under the open sky, and list
> To Nature's teachings, while from all around –
> Earth and her waters, and the depths of air –
> Comes a still voice.

Born in 1794, when Washington was still president, Bryant was reared in an orthodox Puritanism that he eventually exchanged for deism and then for Unitarianism. His political odyssey was rather similar. He wrote an anti-Jeffersonian satire called "The Embargo" when he was just thirteen but soon left his conservative Federalist inclinations behind and, over a long lifetime, espoused a variety of liberal causes. As editor of the New York *Evening Post* for almost half a century, from 1829 until his death in 1878, Bryant proved himself one of the leading progressive newspapermen of the nineteenth century. He championed free trade and the right of workers to form unions, to engage in collective bargaining, and to strike. His editorials supported prison reform, the ending of imprisonment for debt, and, most important, the abolition of slavery. He was a leader of the antislavery Free Soil movement inside the Democratic party until this position became untenable, and then he took part in the formulation of the Republican party and supported Lincoln in 1860.

Although Bryant was acclaimed in his own day as America's first major poet, his significance seems, in retrospect, less conspicuous. Among his minor contemporaries, Bryant's poems deserved their relative eminence. Certainly nothing in the work of Freneau or Barlow or Halleck matches the best work Bryant did. His first thin volume, *Poems*, appeared in 1821, just a year after Irving published *The Sketch Book* and Cooper produced his first novel. Like those writers of fiction, Bryant offered the new nation a measure of literary reassurance. Unfortunately, his talent was too often put at the service of predictable, genteel sentiments. His admirable stoicism often subsides into heavy-footed gravity, and his meters become soporific. James Russell Lowell made fun of Bryant in approximately these terms in A *Fable for Critics*: "Bryant, as quiet, as cool, and as dignified / As a smooth, silent iceberg, that never is ignified." As Lowell suggests, Bryant too often wrote a chilly, bloodless verse. Despite his fervent appeals to Wordsworth, Bryant's poetry seldom achieves the poised urgency of Wordsworth's great meditations on nature and humanity. Indeed, Bryant's view of nature's benevolent tutelage has its sources as much in an attenuated Puritan sacramentalism as in English or Continental Romanticism. Nonetheless, his poems have strengths, among them a sober restraint, a generally unpretentious diction, a technical competence no American poet had previously exhibited, and a response to the New World's landscape that begins in bookish gestures but ends in wonder. These lines are from "A Forest Hymn" (1825):

> This mighty oak,
> By whose immovable stem I stand and seem
> Almost annihilated – not a prince,
> In all that proud old world beyond the deep,
> E'er wore his crown as loftily as he
> Wears the green coronal of leaves.

In 1849, Asher B. Durand painted his famous double portrait, *Kindred Spirits*, in which William Cullen Bryant stands with his friend Thomas Cole on a rocky outcropping amid the cliffs and trees of the Hudson River valley (Figure 52). Durand's painting was intended primarily as a memorial to Cole, who had died the previous year, but it testifies as well to an important cultural development in antebellum America. In 1800, painters had found little market for landscape. Starting in the 1820s – perhaps specifically in 1825, when Cole made a sketching trip up the Hudson – painting joined poetry in discovering and celebrating America's natural scenes. Durand's picture is no less a "forest hymn" than Bryant's poem. In the painting, Cole and Bryant are enclosed within the Catskill scenery, signifying the intimacy between nature and artist that defines the center of the Romantic vision. Beauty and truth are here identified; the foreground birches arch across the top of the scene like the leafy roof of a natural cathedral, and the two friends stand in attitudes

FIGURE 52 ❧ Asher Durand, *Kindred Spirits* (1849).

of respectful, even worshipful, attention. The title itself defines a theme of contemplative serenity by replacing names with a vocabulary of communal, enveloping spirituality: kindred spirits, Cole and Bryant are also kin to the genius of the natural scene.

The geographies of American painting expanded almost as rapidly as the nation itself. Painters reproduced the landscape in all of its variety, the rugged crags and wooded glens of the Hudson River valley, the great western rivers of Mississippi and Missouri, the sublimity of Niagara and the Rockies. In most cases, topographical accuracy was regarded as less important than a fidelity to the feeling and spirit of each place, and these values usually combined delight in the natural panorama with an implied or explicit affirmation of the national dream. A nation blessed with such beauty could confidently assume its worthiness. American scenery became the prototypical subject of antebellum painting, the vehicle through which the country sought its own visual identity and the means by which it would seek recognition from others.

The exploration of the land was accompanied by a new interest in local scenes and in the men and women who peopled them. A distinctively American species of genre painting seemed counterpart and testimony to the impulses of Jacksonian democracy. George Caleb

FIGURE 53 ❧ William Sidney Mount, *The Painter's Triumph* (1838).

Bingham and William Sidney Mount, among others, conferred an egalitarian immortality on the country's most ordinary citizens. Fur trappers, farmers, boatmen, and fiddlers provided the subjects, and their faces, clothing, pastimes, and work were consistently rendered without resort to caricature or condescension. In Mount's famous picture of 1838, *The Painter's Triumph*, the artist points with pride to what is surely some realistically rendered native scene (Figure 53). His neighbor, a simply dressed representative of America's plain people, shares the painter's delight, while the Apollo Belvedere in the drawing on the back wall turns his head away, morosely or indignantly. Mount spoke for a major tradition in American painting and literature: "There has been enough written on ideality and the grand style of Art, etc., to divert the artist from the true study of natural objects. Forever after let me read the volume of nature – a lecture always ready and bound by the Almighty."

American interest in the wilderness and its people received predictably Romantic expression in the decision of several antebellum artists to make a record of the American Indian. Indians had been the target of continuous mythmaking since the earliest white settlement: they were imagined usually as demonic, sometimes as noble, but rarely as merely human. George Catlin, who began his work in 1830 and eventually painted over five hundred portraits, was the best of the artists who turned to the Indians for his material (Figure 54). Like so many of his predecessors, he too observed them through the veil of piety that he brought with him. In Catlin's view, Indian society was superior in its robust integrity to the complex and artificial civilization of whites. The enduring American myth of simplicity once again demonstrates its powerful appeal in Catlin's work. Furthermore, a tone of elegy, similar to Cooper's, informs Catlin's pictures. He knew that the way of life he was commemorating in watercolor and pigment was doomed to extinction; his task was to leave a faithful but sympathetic account before the men and women he portrayed had vanished from the land.

A less humane impulse also promoted the imaginative use of America's Indians. The reaction against neoclassical conventions excited an interest in the exotic, and the Indians were exploited to satisfy the self-indulgent curiosity of white culture. The history of relations between whites and Indians, from the first English settlements through the nineteenth century, was a compound of white appetite for

FIGURE 54 ✤ George Catlin, *The Buffalo's Back Fat, Head Chief of the Blackfeet* (1832). Catlin's letters and journals record the westward march of white civilization's "juggernaut," which was bringing a "sweeping desolation" to the Native American people. "I have stood amidst these unsophisticated people," Catlin wrote, "and contemplated with feelings of deepest regret the certain approach of this overwhelming system, which will inevitably march on and prosper, until reluctant tears have watered every rod of this fair land."

Indian lands and white contempt for Indian civilization. Indians would either accept white values or be exterminated: "Soap and education," Samuel Clemens wrote, "are not as sudden as a massacre, but they are more deadly in the long run." Temporary alliances and promises of amity were invariably succeeded by violated treaties, warfare, and further white expansion. Looking back from the vantage point of 1877, President Rutherford B. Hayes declared with admirable candor that "many, if not most, of our Indian wars have had their origin in broken promises and acts of injustice on our part."

Aside from their relation to the land, their regional identifications, and their common vulnerability to white encroachments, the scores of Indian tribes and nations were separate and distinct. During their centuries of habitation in the continent of North America, they created a rich and diverse oral literature: songs, chants, fables, and stories that incorporated the traditional lore of creation, the trials and joys of life, the riddle of death. Indian literatures were ignored by the troopers who fought them and the hustlers and politicians who bargained their rights away. Academic students of Indian culture, including anthropologists, first brought the songs and tales of the original Americans to serious notice. Intractable linguistic problems stand discouragingly between English-speaking readers and Indian literature, but some of the brief songs collected and translated by the Smithsonian Institution may convey hints of the subtlety and evocative grace of the originals.

Love Song

A loon I thought it was
But it was
My love's
Splashing oar.
(Chippewa)

Song of Failure

A wolf
I considered myself,
But the owls are hooting
And the night
I fear.
(Teton Sioux)

The contours of the Indian imagination can perhaps be more im-

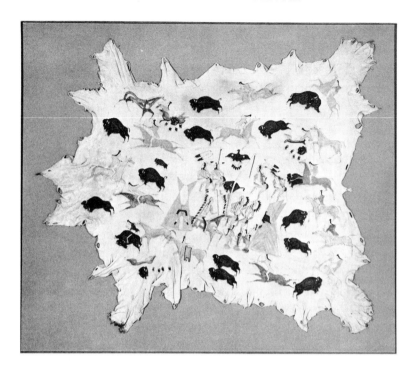

FIGURE 55 ❧ Shoshoni elk-hide painting. The Sun Dance, a midsummer ritual dedicated to the hunt for buffalo, was among the major ceremonies of the Plains Indians for over two hundred years. Young men danced without stopping for several days around the severed head of a buffalo, seeking to ensure the tribe's welfare by revitalizing the links between the natural and spiritual realms. This nineteenth-century painting depicts both the hunt (around the borders of the elk hide) and the dance (at the center).

mediately apprehended by non-Indians through the evidence of designs and drawings. Here the history and myths of the tribes, inscribed on the skins of the animals around which much of Indian life revolved, were given visual and symbolic statement (Figure 55). Despite its variety and strength, the cultural achievement of the Indians was beside the point to America's domestic imperialists. White pioneers, land agents, and railroad builders regarded the Indian as an impediment to progress, and the myth of savagery usefully buttressed economic opportunism. The Indians took their doomed and unwitting place in a white drama of continental domination and control.

The stereotypes that encumbered the Indians were inflamed by Romanticism. Decimated by the disease and warfare that attended Manifest Destiny, Indians were also trapped in the colorful categories through which the Romantic imagination seized and organized the world. Romanticism brought with it a cluster of complementary desires, yearnings downward and backward toward the picturesque, the antique, the inexplicable. The eighteenth century, with its tales of gothic horror and its taste for gothic ruins, had anticipated this development. In painting, Benjamin West's historical and religious canvases included such expeditions into the mysterious sublime as the influential *Saul and the Witch of Endor*. In literature, a number of writers excavated in the rich and sometimes dank soil of the gothic and grotesque. Irving himself was one of the earliest, but the most significant was Edgar Allan Poe.

Passionate controversy has always surrounded Poe's life and work. In Europe, the man called "Edgarpo" was a nineteenth-century cult figure, idolized for his unyielding aesthetic commitment and for the glamour of his poverty and early death. The French Symbolist poets Charles Baudelaire and Stéphane Mallarmé reverently translated Poe's works and maintained a hushed witness to his memory. English Pre-Raphaelites, too, found confirmation of their attitudes and beliefs in Poe's verses and tales and especially in his poetic theories. Americans, on the other hand, have approached Poe with edgy skepticism. Ralph Waldo Emerson allegedly called him "the jingle man," and Henry James suggested that enthusiasm for Poe was "the mark of a decidedly primitive stage of reflection. It seems to us," James continued, "that to take him with more than a certain degree of seriousness is to lack seriousness one's self." More recently, T. S. Eliot added his own famous rebuke, when he said that Poe's intellect was that of "a highly gifted young person before puberty."

Resistance to Poe began during his lifetime, in predictable response to the combative and often savage reviews in which he relentlessly scourged his contemporaries. He made an enemy with every stroke of his pen. However, the legend of Poe the evil and probably demented genius can be traced to the memoir published by the Reverend Rufus W. Griswold after Poe's death. Weaving half-truth, unsupported slander, and outright forgery together, Griswold reduced Poe to an unsavory monster, unscrupulous, pathological, even murderous – a villain, in short, from one of his own tales. Later scholarship would disprove much of what Griswold wrote, but an odor of scandal persists. In part this may disclose an American need for melodrama and a prurience that coexists with canons of prim respectability. At the same time, Poe's life was in fact remarkably disordered and repeatedly touched by tragedy.

The illegitimate son of traveling actors, he was born in Boston in 1809. Within two years both his parents were dead, and Edgar was taken in by a wealthy Richmond, Virginia, merchant, John Allan. The early years of Poe's life were punctuated by bitter disputes with Allan, who eventually disclaimed any responsibility for the young man. Poe's efforts to make a career were met with the same failure that shadowed his personal life. He showed academic talent but was forced to leave the University of Virginia for drinking and gambling debts. He joined the army under the name Edgar A. Perry but then resigned. He maneuvered an appointment to West Point, soon regretted it, and engineered his own dismissal by misbehaving. His first books of poetry, *Tamerlane* (1827) and *Al Aaraaf* (1829), commanded only scant recognition. The remaining twenty years of his brief life were given over to literature, to the daily grind of hackwork, and also to the stories, poems, and theoretical essays on which his subsequent reputation was built. *Tales of the Grotesque and Arabesque* (1840) received fairly wide comment, and Poe even enjoyed a moment of acclaim when he published "The Raven" in 1845. But neither the stories nor the poem brought him an income. Indeed, aside from an occasional prize for one or another of his tales, Poe earned little from his writing, and his heavy drinking

FIGURE 56 ❧ The "Ultima Thule" portrait of Edgar Allan Poe. This daguerreotype was taken in Providence in 1848. A friend who found it shocking said that the image revealed Poe "immediately after being snatched back from the ultimate world's end of horror."

made him unable to hold the several editorial jobs he found. His wife Virginia, a cousin whom he married when she was just thirteen, succumbed to tuberculosis in 1846. Three years later, Poe died in Baltimore, under mysterious circumstances (Figure 56).

Most of the literary notice Poe managed to acquire during his lifetime attached to his gothic tales and his criticism. Poe's critical judgments were often hobbled by opportunism, as he mustered the small influence of his reviews in the service of self-promotion. Furthermore, Poe could be petulant, hasty, and flatly dishonest in his appraisals. He was capable, nonetheless, of estimating contemporary literature with intelligence and insight. In a period when American criticism barely existed except as a minor bureau for the exchange of miscellaneous pleasantries and insults, Poe brought rigorous standards to the job of literary evaluation. He was often right. It was Poe, in a famous review in *Graham's Magazine* in 1842, who first paid tribute to Hawthorne's achievement in *Twice-Told Tales*. Poe's high sense of purpose stimulated his efforts to construct a theoretical basis upon which literature could be written and judged. Throughout his unhappy life, Poe held fast to a conception of literature as a profoundly serious vocation, a calling of virtually religious significance. This commitment was ultimately more important than the precision of his individual opinions. It was a point of view with little precedent in America, and it intensified his estrangement from the literary ethos of the day.

In a society hypnotized by commerce and common sense, Poe stood rapt in the contemplation of beauty. Where others called for a patriotically useful art, Poe (plagiarizing Coleridge) proclaimed that the object of poetry was pleasure. He inveighed against what he called "the heresy of the didactic," describing this heresy at some length in "The Poetic Principle," a lecture he gave in the last months of his life. The ultimate object of all poetry, he insisted, has erroneously been assumed to be truth. "Every poem, it is said, should inculcate a moral; and by this moral is the poetical merit of the work to be adjudged. We Americans especially have patronised this happy idea." In fact, he maintained, it is not truth but beauty, and beauty alone, that constitutes the bone and marrow of poetry. Dividing the world of the mind into parts, he assigned truth to the intellect and duty to the moral sense. It is the third part of the mind, what Poe called "taste," that "informs us of the Beautiful."

As a psychological model, this three-part scheme looks merely quaint. However, it conveyed a challenging and even polemical message, especially within the framework of America's workaday antebellum culture. By ascribing equal rank to the faculty of taste, Poe was also insisting on the coequal status of beauty with truth and moral obligation, the other purposes of the mind. This leads to one of Poe's florid passages of poetic overstatement:

> An immortal instinct, deep within the spirit of man, is thus, plainly, a sense of the Beautiful. . . . We have a thirst unquenchable [which] belongs to the immortality of Man. It is at once a consequence and an indication of his perennial existence. It is the desire of the moth for the star. It is no mere appreciation of the Beauty before us – but a wild effort to reach the Beauty above. Inspired by an ecstatic prescience of the glories beyond the grave, we struggle, by multiform combinations among the things and thoughts of Time, to attain a portion of that Loveliness whose very elements, perhaps, appertain to eternity alone.

This interweaving of beauty with vague intimations of immortality exemplifies the funereal aura that edges much of Poe's literary theorizing. "All experience has shown," he wrote, that in the highest expressions of beauty "the tone is one of sadness. Beauty of whatever kind, in its supreme development, invariably excites the sensitive soul to tears. Melancholy is thus the most legitimate of all the poetic tones." Lying like a dark incandescence at the core of Poe's beliefs about poetry was an impatience with the limits imposed by the flesh and a conviction that the way to beauty led through the grave. With a certain sort of logic, Poe deduced from these premises his sensationally vulgar conclusion about the "most poetical" of all subjects:

> I asked myself – "of all melancholy topics, what, according to the universal understanding of mankind, is the most melancholy?" Death – was the obvious reply. "And when," I said, "is this most melancholy of topics most poetical?" From what I have already explained at some length, the answer here also is obvious – "When it most closely allies itself to Beauty": the death, then, of a beautiful woman is, unquestionably, the most poetical topic in the world.

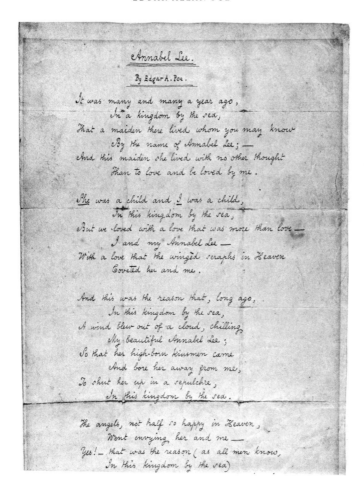

FIGURE 57 ❧ Edgar
Allan Poe, "Annabel
Lee." The first page of a
copy of the poem in
Poe's handwriting.

Taking his own advice, Poe dramatized the death of women in
many of his poems. The speaker of "Ulalume" mournfully discovers
his lover's tomb. "The Raven" commemorates the dead Lenore.
The woman in "The Sleeper" has fallen into a deep and lasting
sleep: "Soft may the worms about her creep." And, at the end of
"Annabel Lee," the poet broods over his dead lover's seaside tomb:

> And so, all the night tide, I lie down by the side
> Of my darling – my darling – my life and my bride,
>   In her sepulchre there by the sea –
>   In her tomb by the sounding sea.

In such poems as these, the dead female body is elevated to a macabre platonic apotheosis. This sinister coordination of women, death, and eroticism is not merely a Romantic figure of speech. It confesses a sexual anxiety, a fascinated fear of women except as ruthlessly sentimentalized objects (Figure 57).

Claiming Francis Bacon as his authority, Poe observed that beauty always has some element of strangeness in it. Whether his medium was poetry or prose, whether his subject was dead maidens or cities beneath the sea, that strangeness filled Poe's most representative work. He talked at length about the importance of what he called "unity of effect:" a single emotional response to which all the parts of a poem or tale contribute. The effect he usually sought was terror, and the results were notoriously mixed. No one in American literature wrote so much that was by turns ludicrous and unforgettable. His range was narrow, and he often confused the sublime with the gasps and groans that attended theatrical excess. There is some reason to believe that Poe was himself uncertain about the significance of his fiction. He wrote, with more candor than clarity, that most of his tales "were *intended* for half-banter, half-satire – although I might not acknowledge this to be their aim even to myself."

Nevertheless, and perhaps in spite of his own bantering intentions, the alien territories Poe invented have proved durable beyond the more prosaic imaginings of other writers. His maelstroms and pits and haunted castles and black cats are etched indelibly into America's literary memory. The narrator of "The Fall of the House of Usher" describes a scene of luxuriant gloominess that can stand for all of Poe's interiors:

> The room in which I found myself was very large and lofty. The windows were long, narrow, and pointed, and at so vast a distance from the black oaken floor as to be altogether inaccessible from within. Feeble gleams of encrimsoned light made their way through the trellissed panes, and served to render sufficiently distinct the more prominent objects around; the eye, however, struggled in vain to reach the remoter angles of the chamber, or the recesses of the vaulted and fretted ceiling. Dark draperies hung upon the walls.

Within the grim chamber the narrator finds his old friend, Roderick Usher, whom he has not seen in years. Usher has been terribly altered by unknown experiences; cadaverous, barely breathing, reeking of the tomb, he is a man who now evokes feelings of pity and awe. Commenting on scenes like this in his work, Poe somewhat imperiously claimed that "my terror is not from Germany but of the soul." Though he was not always so original as that remark implies, his stories are permeated with the atmosphere of nightmare or hallucination. The bad dreams that torment Poe's characters almost always lead to death, and they are furnished with the small, precise details that bring fantasy to morbid half-life. What remains convincing in Poe, after all the gruesome machinery of premature burials and crimson-tinted rooms is stripped away, are his images of fear and pain, of men and women threatened by forces that are mysterious, unavoidable, and evil.

Along with his gothic tales, Poe also produced stories of detection and science fiction that have strongly influenced popular literature on both sides of the Atlantic. Poe has with some justice been credited with inventing the detective story and with devising almost all the conventions of the form. His detective, the M. Dupin of "Murders in the Rue Morgue" and "The Purloined Letter," among other stories, is both mathematician and poet. That is to say, he is a man at once of stern logic and penetrating intuition. He is accompanied by a credulous and somewhat thick-witted friend who anticipates all the dense companions of detectives over the next century and a half. Dupin sees what others look past and solves baffling mysteries with an ease that appears to ordinary mortals either godlike or demonic.

Insofar as they affirm order rather than anarchy, Poe's detective stories differ sharply from his tales of terror. What all his fictions share, on the other hand, is an evident irritation with the commonplace and a preference for intellectual and emotional extremity. In this way, his stories, though they were divorced from America's public affairs in any literal sense, record his dissent from the democratic politics that were sweeping across America during his adult years. He nursed an aristocrat's contempt for the common man and woman; he defended the institution of slavery; he ridiculed reform movements. His heightened aesthetic self-consciousness made his failures more galling even as they confirmed his low estimate of American taste. Yet it was precisely Poe's posture of radical isolation that signaled his value for later artists, even those who had little sympathy for the rigmarole of his hysterical narrators and his theories of poetic irrationality. At a ceremony at Poe's grave in 1875, Walt Whitman described a dream in which he had watched

> one of those superb little schooner yachts I had often seen lying anchor'd, rocking so jauntily, in the waters around New York, or up Long Island sound – now flying uncontroll'd with torn sails and broken spars through the wild sleet and winds and waves of the night. On the deck was a slender, slight, beautiful figure, a dim man, apparently enjoying all the terror, the murk, and the dislocation of which he was the center and the victim. That figure . . . might stand for Edgar Poe, his spirit, his fortunes, and his poems.

Whitman had little interest in Poe's work: he had said earlier that Poe's verses "belong among the electric lights of imaginative literature, brilliant and dazzling, but with no heat." However, Whitman's dream is an illuminating testimony to the magnetism that Poe's strange life and writing radiated. Furthermore, Whitman's images yoke inward and outward turmoil together and suggest that Poe, far from being an odd enigma in nineteenth-century American literary culture, was in fact an emblematic figure. An America engrossed in its headlong expansion and flight from the past might itself have been described as "flying uncontroll'd with torn sails . . . apparently enjoying all the terror, the murk, and the dislocation" of its unprecedented national story. In short, it is a provocative paradox that Poe, this most willfully alienated of men, was also one of the most representative.

Plate 1. John Singleton Copley, *Mrs. Thomas Boylston* (1766).

Plate 2. Fitz Hugh Lane, *Owl's Head, Penobscot Bay, Maine* (1862).

Plate 3. Thomas Eakins, *The Gross Clinic* (1875).

Plate 4. Winslow Homer, *The Fox Hunt* (1893).

Plate 5. Georgia O'Keeffe, *Black Iris* (1926).

Plate 6. Charles Demuth, *I Saw the Figure 5 in Gold* (1928).

Plate 7. Jacob Armstead Lawrence, *They Live in Fire Traps* (1943).

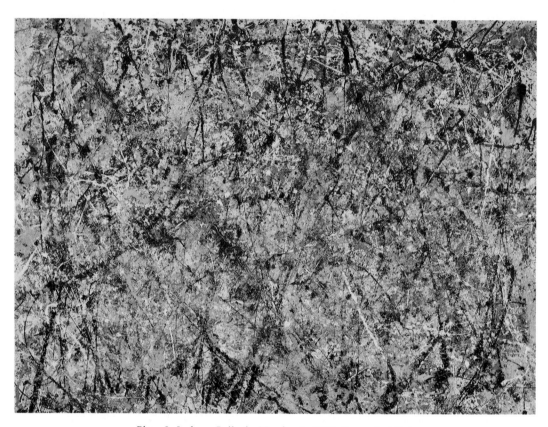

Plate 8. Jackson Pollock, *Number 1, 1950 (Lavender Mist)*.

CHAPTER THREE

❧ *Democratic vistas* ❧

THE SUCCESS that eluded Poe descended abundantly upon
several of his New England contemporaries, chief among
them Henry Wadsworth Longfellow. While Poe was
scratching out his hand-to-mouth existence in Baltimore, Richmond, Philadelphia, and New York, Longfellow presided over
American letters from Craigie House, his large and comfortable
Cambridge residence. His academic and poetic success had begun
while he was still a student at Bowdoin. Shortly after graduation,
he was appointed Bowdoin's first professor of modern languages. He
assumed the same post at Harvard before he was thirty and continued
in it for twenty years, until he resigned in 1854 to devote all his
time to writing. His textbooks and anthologies exerted a wide influence, and his poems brought consistent approval. His volumes
of verse enjoyed unusual sales and were translated into a dozen
languages (including Latin). When he traveled to England after the
Civil War, he was invited to a personal audience with Queen Victoria. Longfellow knew tragedy: his first wife died after miscarrying,
and his second wife died from injuries in a fire. But his career as
poet, professor, translator was an extraordinary series of triumphs.
He was for many years admired as America's principal poet, an
estimate that would endure until the early twentieth century.

The subsequent steep decline in Longfellow's reputation coincided with a wholesale revision of the culture he represented, the
genteel Brahmin society of antebellum Boston. In the years before
the Civil War, Boston rested securely in its position as the capital
of American culture. The city's authority derived from an intellectual heritage that went back to the learned preachers and school-

masters of the seventeenth century. The rest of the country might
be an unkempt wilderness; Boston was a town of tidy streets and
families whose residence was counted in generations rather than
years. Boston had a past: in 1836, when Chicago was a collection
of rough shacks huddled on the muddy shores of Lake Michigan,
Harvard solemnly observed its two-hundredth anniversary. Bostonians could share the enthusiasm of their countrymen for America's
special identity, but they remained more reserved, and closer in
their cultural affinities to Europe. For them, more than for other
Americans, England was "our old home." Their sensitivity to European excellence gave them an admirable sense of proportion, and
it gave them as well a respect for learning and art that too many
other Americans lacked. But Bostonian concern for standards also
had something to do with the timid reticence of the literary work
they produced. Refinement seemed to count for more than energy,
and decorum fetched a higher price than genius. Earnestness con-
gealed into conventions beneath which feeling struggled for breath.
There was something priggish in James Russell Lowell's boast that
it was "better to be a good fellow than a good poet." And Charles
Eliot Norton, in a letter to a friend later in the nineteenth century,
confessed more than he intended when he wrote "I wonder whether
you would agree with me that the set of men of letters . . . whom
we have known is a good deal the best that the world has seen; not
the greatest, perhaps, but the pleasantest to live with. . . . There are
no such liars as Pope, or cynics as Swift, or vulgarians as Gay, or
sycophants as Young, or mockers as Sterne."

Longfellow was one of the pleasant men Norton had in mind,
and his life and writing summarized both the strength and weakness
of Brahmin culture. He took literature seriously and had indeed
determined on a poetic career while he was still an undergraduate
at Bowdoin. In a letter to his father, a strong-willed lawyer who
intended his son for the same career, the young man wrote: "The
fact is . . . I most eagerly aspire after future eminence in literature,
my whole soul burns most ardently after it, and every earthly thought
centers in it. There may be something visionary in this, but I flatter
myself that I have prudence enough to keep my enthusiasm from
defeating its own object by too great haste." This outburst sounds
rather like the youthful effusions of schoolboy romanticism. Furthermore, Longfellow's subordination of enthusiasm to prudence

offers an uncanny insight into his own values and a forecast of his later work. Nonetheless, with all that granted, it was a bold act to declare allegiance to literature in such a place as rural Maine, at such a time as the 1820s. Within his limits, Longfellow maintained this allegiance through the years of a long and hardworking lifetime. His scholarship was legitimate and influenced his own work. His languages and foreign travel gave him a cosmopolitan attitude and a respect for the poetic achievement of such countries as Italy, Germany, and even Finland. He had a virtuoso command of the mechanics of poetry; few Americans have successfully manipulated as many different metrical and rhyme schemes.

Unfortunately, Longfellow's talent too frequently exhausted itself in pursuit of small objects and familiar effects. A schoolroom diligence touches much of his verse, along with a cautious respect for seemly limits. Emotions have little more than an adjectival reality, and metaphors often seem smugly calculated. "The Bridge," (1845), for example, is an exercise in poetic melancholy that exemplifies Longfellow's facility for creating impersonal, unfelt suffering:

> How often, oh how often,
> I had wished that the ebbing tide
> Would bear me away on its bosom
> O'er the ocean wild and wide!
>
> For my heart was hot and restless,
> And my life was full of care,
> And the burden laid upon me
> Seemed greater than I could bear.

Despite their exclamation marks and talk of wildness and heat, these lines remain incorrigibly inert. Similar passages occur throughout Longfellow's poems, making up a small anthology of premeditated but unconvincing effects. Any risk of turbulence or self-exposure is subdued by professorial propriety. Emerson said as much when he wrote to Longfellow that "I have always one foremost satisfaction in reading your books – that I am safe. I am in variously skillful hands, but first of all they are safe hands."

Emerson was speaking specifically of *Hiawatha* (1855), but his comment has a broad relevance. It was Longfellow, after all, who paid sentimental tribute to "The Village Blacksmith," who inflicted "Paul Revere's Ride" on generations of American children, and who declaimed in "A Psalm of Life" that "Life is real – life is earnest / And the grave is not its goal." In a few poems, however, Longfellow found subjects suitable to his inclinations and talent. On those occasions, sometimes for the length of an entire poem, more often for a stanza or two, his temperate mood achieves a convincing authority, and his restraint rises to quiet eloquence. Dignity balances pathos, for example, in "The Jewish Cemetery at Newport" (1852), and "Hawthorne" (1864) is at once a fitting memorial and a handsome response to the peculiar qualities of Hawthorne's fiction. In "The Fire of Drift-Wood" (1849), the speaker tells of a long and cold New England day spent with an old friend, the two of them simply talking before a driftwood fire. The poem's conclusion is marred by Longfellow's laborious explanation of the fire's symbolism, but earlier stanzas inscribe a poignant record of the meaning of friendship and memory and change.

> We spake of many a vanished scene,
>   Of what we once had thought and said,
> Of what had been and might have been,
>   And who was changed and who was dead;
>
> And all that fills the hearts of friends,
>   When first they feel, with secret pain,
> Their lives thenceforth have separate ends,
>   And never can be one again.

The risks and the achievement here are equally modest, and such verses hint more of good nature than of genius. At the same time, in choosing friendship for its subject, the poem offers a glimpse into the values of the literary culture that lay behind it. In the years before the Civil War, the boundaries of America's acknowledged literary society were narrowly drawn. Many of the young nation's writers knew each other well, and even more of them had shared at least a few dinners.

In Philadelphia and New York, but especially in New England, companionship channeled the currents of imagination; acquaintanceship and sometimes intimacy had much to do with defining literary taste. New York editor Evert Duyckinck, whose *Literary*

World was a leading weekly in the years from 1847 to 1853, opened his house as well as his magazine to such writers as Irving, Cooper, Bryant, and Herman Melville. Later in the 1850s, Pfaff's Cellar, a saloon on lower Broadway, served as a rendezvous for some of New York's self-styled bohemian artists and writers, including Bayard Taylor, Louis Gottschalk, and Ada Clare. It was in Pfaff's that Walt Whitman famously welcomed the young William Dean Howells, newly arrived from the Midwest. The gatherings in tavern and parlor sometimes took on more self-conscious form in the dozens of literary clubs whose murmur of conversation lingers as the half-heard background of early national culture. To their members, the clubs offered like-minded friends and access to influence. Literally and figuratively, the clubs represented the warmth of appreciation in a commercial climate of wintry indifference. Some of the groups, such as Cooper's early Bread and Cheese Club, were located in New York and elsewhere on the Atlantic coast. Predictably, however, most of the clubs were to be found in Boston and its vicinity. Of these, the most significant were perhaps the Saturday Club and the Transcendental Club.

The Saturday Club descended from the short-lived Town and Country Club, which Emerson had helped to found in 1849. The membership of the Town and Country Club was large, including Longfellow, James Russell Lowell, the publisher James T. Fields, and the liberal clergyman Theodore Parker. Several of the club's members had taken antislavery positions, but radicalism on public questions did not alter the parochial composition of the club itself. Frederick Douglass was unable to gain admission, apparently because of the opposition of Emerson. (Lowell, who had intended to pay Douglass's entrance fees, resigned with the sarcastic announcement that he himself was "an unfit companion for people too good to associate" with Douglass.) As the exclusion of Douglass indicates, the literary clubs of the nineteenth century denied as much as they gave. Blacks, Jews, Catholics, and immigrants were unwelcome, and only a few women gained entrance. The clubs were cozy, but their rooms were inaccessible, small, badly lit, and the air in them was slightly stale. Poe's sneering reference to Boston as "Frogpondium" could have been even more aptly directed to Boston's clubs.

After the Town and Country Club broke up, a few of its members continued to eat Saturday dinners at Boston's Parker House. The meetings were eventually regularized as the Saturday Club, which enrolled twenty-three men by the time of the Civil War, among them Emerson, Longfellow, Lowell, John Greenleaf Whittier, Oliver Wendell Holmes, Richard Henry Dana, Jr., and the historian John Lothrop Motley. Hawthorne sometimes joined the club as an invited guest. Frog pond or not, the Saturday Club harbored a wide range of opinion and temperament. From slavery to the status of women to the future of American art, there were few political or literary issues on which the club's members would have agreed. A capacity for vigorous debate and independence leavened the relations of antebellum New England intellectuals. In the century and more since their flowering, it has become commonplace to insist on Brahmin limits. Later critics like V. L. Parrington harried the New England writers for their refinement and their pallid withdrawal from the world. There is surely some justice in the accusations. Indeed, the Brahmins were themselves quite capable of ironic self-appraisal. It was Oliver Wendell Holmes, after all, himself a member of this social and literary elite, who first used the term "Brahmin." In his novel, *Elsie Venner* (1861), Holmes wrote of "the harmless, inoffensive, untitled aristocracy" of Boston, which "has grown to be a caste by the repetition of the same influences generation after generation." Henry Adams concurred, as he looked back in old age at the nervous introspection of the antebellum Bostonians: "Improvised Europeans we were, and – Lord God – how thin!"

Holmes was himself perhaps the quintessential representative of New England's elite culture. Throughout his life, he moved easily among Boston's several worlds, a figure of academic distinction and public influence. He was known for decades as a genial essayist and intelligent critic, and his speeches and poems were much in demand on important public occasions. Suitably, Holmes grew up in an old house facing the Boston Common, the parsonage of the First Congregational Church, of which his father was pastor. He graduated from Harvard College in 1829, studied law briefly, and then decided on medicine as a career. From 1847 until his retirement in 1882, he held the Parkman chair of anatomy at Harvard. He leaped into literary prominence at the age of twenty-one with the publication of "Old Ironsides," his versified plea for the preservation of the venerable frigate, USS *Constitution*. "Ay, tear her tattered ensign down," Holmes demanded with broad sarcasm, and thousands of schoolchildren took up the cry. The *Constitution* was saved, and Holmes was famous. Written in simple measures and appealing to comfortable emotions, "Old Ironsides" anticipated the rest of Holmes's poetry. In 1836, he wrote a "Song" for Harvard's bicentennial, a jovial and unreflective tribute to the college and its Puritan founders. "God bless the ancient Puritans," the progenitors of "our true-born Yankee stuff," Holmes happily proclaimed. Of such contented sentiments are poets laureate made, and Holmes performed the laureate's function for his small, insular Boston.

Holmes amiably embodied the salons and clubs in which he played such a leading role. His talent for good conversation achieved a minor immortality in *The Autocrat of the Breakfast Table*, a collection of miscellaneous essays published in 1858. Holmes felt his chief literary affinities drawing him toward the decorum and wit of the eighteenth century, and the *Autocrat* bears the mark of his admiration for Pope, Addison, and Goldsmith. The essays of the *Autocrat* first appeared in the new *Atlantic Monthly*, at the urging of the magazine's first editor, Holmes's friend James Russell Lowell. (Two original papers had been published in the *New England Magazine* a quarter-century earlier but were never reprinted.) Set in a boardinghouse dining room, the essays record the table talk of the entertaining, infallible, semiautobiographical Autocrat, a man of robustly genteel views on every imaginable nineteenth-century subject. Displays of the Autocrat's Holmesian wit provide all the structure and rationale that the essays possess. Plot is microscopic, and the Autocrat's interlocutors, the other boarders who join him at the table, are not characters but pasteboard conveniences. The Schoolmistress, the Landlady, the Divinity Student, and the others merely punctuate the Autocrat's brilliant torrent of talk with self-effacing questions or timorous opinions. The point and pleasure of the prose lie in the Autocrat's monologues. In the fourth essay, for example, he offers this droll gloss on a seventeenth-century volume of Erasmus:

> Look at the precious little black, ribbed-backed, clean-typed, vellum-papered 32mo. "Desiderii Erasmi Colloquia Amstelodami. Typis Ludovici Elzevirii. 1650." Various names written on the title-page. Most conspicuous this: Gul. Cookeson, E. Coll. Omn. Anim. 1725. Oxon.
> – O William Cookeson, of All-Souls College, Oxford, –

then writing as I now write, – now in the dust, where I shall lie, – is this line all that remains to thee of earthly remembrance? Thy name is at least once more spoken by living men; – is it a pleasure to thee? Thou shalt share with me my little draught of immortality, – its week, its month, its year, – whatever it may be, – and then we will go together into the solemn archives of Oblivion's Uncatalogued Library!

The arcane references, the tone of mock solemnity, and the carefully balanced rhythms all typify Holmes's mandarin playfulness. An atmosphere of picturesque obsolescence envelops most of his work, hinting that he found what he needed of contact with reality in medicine and that literature's proper place was on the more pleasant periphery. Something of his experience as a physician can be found in his three novels, *Elsie Venner*, *The Guardian Angel* (1867), and *A Mortal Antipathy* (1885), psychological studies of no particular literary distinction that furiously debunk Calvinist explanations of human behavior. However, Holmes's more characteristic work was the series of commemorative odes he produced in honor of his Harvard classmates at their reunions.

George Santayana would later complain of the bloodless reserve that shackled Brahmin effort. The members of the "genteel tradition" too often chose tradition over energy and revered respectability at the expense of human warmth. And yet, to reduce the New England aristocracy to the narrow marginality of caricature deprives the group of its interest. To begin with, while the Brahmins could certainly be complacent, the self-critical assessments of Holmes and Adams demonstrate a capacity for irony that was missing from much of the rest of American literary culture. Furthermore, the New Englanders carried on a more strenuous engagement with a larger number of serious cultural and political issues than almost any of their contemporaries. Although too much respect for European achievements could prove debilitating, too little could lead to the substitution of patriotism for aesthetic judgment. Unseemly praise of native work became a major thesis of nineteenth-century American letters, and the New England writers set themselves resolutely against the resulting confusion of standards. James Russell Lowell, for example, devoted his monthly magazine the *Pioneer* to the cause of American literature, but he insisted that literature could not be simply decreed out of chauvinist sentiment. Though the *Pioneer* floundered after three issues in 1843, Lowell had made his theoretical position clear in the first number of the magazine. "We are," Lowell wrote, "the farthest from wishing to see what many so ardently pray for – namely a *National* literature. . . . But we do long for a *natural* literature." Lowell repeatedly protested against simplifying nationalist assumptions, sometimes using his acid wit as a solvent against pretension. For example, in his review of the poet James Gates Percival, Lowell parodied the American inclination to confuse landscape and literature: "If that little dribble of an Avon had succeeded in engendering Shakespeare, what a giant might we not look for from the mighty womb of Mississippi! Physical geography for the first time took her rightful place as the tenth and most inspiring Muse" (Figure 58).

Lowell was one of the leading editors of the American midcentury, a chief spokesman for cultivated opinion. After the failure of the *Pioneer*, he served as editor of the *National Anti-slavery Standard* (1848–52), as first editor of the *Atlantic Monthly* (1857–61), and then as coeditor of the venerable *North American Review*, beginning in 1864. The weight of Lowell's views derived in part from his editorial authority but in larger part from the representative shape of a long career that moved from youthful radicalism to later conservatism. He was born in Cambridge, the descendant of an important colonial family, attended Harvard College, and graduated as class poet in 1838. He stayed at Harvard to take a law degree, but his real interests lay in poetry and politics. Lowell's career was divided by the Civil War. His major achievements, both in literature and public affairs, were concentrated in the antebellum years, when he wrote his most interesting poems and served as one of the most articulate radical voices in the debate over slavery. In his later years, Lowell's pace slowed from the quickstep of reform to the easier cadence of comfort and fame. He succeeded Longfellow as Harvard's Smith Professor of French and Spanish in 1855 and held the post for over thirty years (though he did little teaching after 1876). His prominence and his Republican loyalty earned him appointments as minister to Spain (1877–80) and England (1880–5). The affable conservatism of his old age was a matter of nostalgia rather than ideology. In England, he slipped contentedly into the leisurely upper-class life of club and country house, becoming better known for the number of dinner invitations he accepted than for his di-

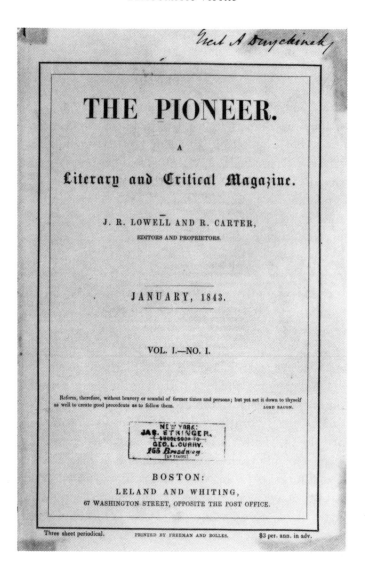

FIGURE 58 ❧ Title page and table of contents, *The Pioneer* (January, 1843).

plomacy. He outlived his achievement and his ambition by several decades (Figure 59).

Forty years before, in the 1830s and 1840s, a younger Lowell had confidently tested himself against America's artistic and political challenges. Just three years after his graduation from Harvard, he brought out his first collection of poetry, *A Year's Life* (1841). His poems exhibited undeniable talent, and they elicited a generous critical response. Poe, who would later change his mind, declared that Lowell's early work put him "at the very head of the poets of

THE PIONEER.

JANUARY, 1843.

EMBELLISHMENTS.

CIRCE GOING TO MEET ULYSSES; from Flaxman's Odyssey; engraved by J. Andrews.
TWO HUNDRED YEARS AGO; engraved by J. Andrews.
THE ROSE; a Ballad, Illustrated on Wood. By J. G. Chandler.

TABLE OF CONTENTS.

INTRODUCTION, ... 1	THE POET AND APOLLO, . . . 31
HUDSON RIVER. By T. W. PARSONS, 3	THE PLAYS OF THOMAS MIDDLETON. By
VOLTAIRE, ... 5	J. R. LOWELL, ... 32
AARON BURR. By JOHN NEAL, . 6	THE ROSE, ... 40
THE FOLLOWER, ... 11	
THE COLD SPRING IN NORTH SALEM. By	LITERARY NOTICES.
JONES VERY, ... 12	1. Hawthorne's Historical Tales for Youth, 42
SIXTEENTH EXHIBITION OF PAINTINGS AT	2. La Fontaine's Fables, . . . 42
THE BOSTON ATHENÆUM, 1842. By I.	3. Nature, a Parable, ... 43
B. WRIGHT, ... 12	4. The Salem Belle, ... 44
ACCEPTABLE WORSHIP. By W. H. BUR-	5. The Career of Puffer Hopkins, . 44
LEIGH, ... 16	6. American Notes, for General Circulation, 45
THE ARMENIAN'S DAUGHTER, . . 17	7. The Rights of Conscience and of Pro-
SONNET. By J. R. LOWELL, . . 25	perty, ... 45
ACADEMY OF MUSIC — BEETHOVEN'S SYM-	8. Sparks's Life of Washington, . 46
PHONIES. By J. S. DWIGHT, . . 26	9. American Criminal Trials, . . 46
LONGING. By W. W. STORY, . . 29	10. Confessions of St. Augustine, . 46
THE TELL-TALE HEART. By EDGAR A.	11. Life in Mexico, ... 46
POE, ... 29	FOREIGN LITERARY INTELLIGENCE, . 47

THE PIONEER is published monthly by LELAND & WHITING, 67 Washington Street, to whom all orders, subscriptions, and communications for the Editors, may be addressed, *post paid.*
TERMS.—Three dollars per annum, invariably in advance. Two copies for five dollars. The usual discount allowed to agents.
LELAND & WHITING also publish the *Religious* and *Literary Gem*, a Monthly Magazine, each number containing thirty-two pages royal octavo, with splendid steel engravings. Terms, $1,50 per annum. The Pioneer and Gem will be furnished to one subscription for four dollars per annum.

America." In fact, Lowell's first poems, typically bland in tone and meliorist in outlook, are accomplished but minor verses that are hobbled by his reverence for Wordsworth, Tennyson, and Shakespeare.

In the early 1840s, Lowell turned his attention and his considerable polemical skill toward the antislavery cause. Responding in part to the urgings of his wife, the abolitionist Maria White, Lowell came to regard slavery as the gravest issue confronting the young nation, the mortal illness that mocked its health and optimism. In 1820, Jefferson had written of slavery in tones of dire prophecy: "This momentous question, like a fire bell in the night, awakened and filled me with terror. I considered it at once the knell of the

FIGURE 59 🐟 Matthew Brady, photograph of James Russell Lowell. Lowell was thirty-eight years old at the time of this portrait.

Union." Among the countless shades of abolitionist opinion, Lowell aligned himself with the so-called "zealots," those who rejected compromise and gradualism in dealing with slavery. This was essentially the position of William Lloyd Garrison, activist and editor of the *Liberator*, the most influential of the abolitionist periodicals. Echoing Jefferson's metaphor, Garrison and Lowell argued that to "go slow" in ridding the nation of slavery would be the same as going slow in saving one's house from the fire that was burning it down. Impatient with delay, Lowell applied his lash to northern as well as southern defenders of "the peculiar institution." He understood that northern resistance to abolition was not merely tactical but had its sources in a myopic reverence for property rights and a widely shared belief in black inferiority (Figure 60).

Along with abolition, Lowell spoke out with memorable urgency on woman suffrage, child labor, temperance, and capital punishment. His passion for reform invaded his poetry, often with more emotion than his talent could accommodate. Duyckinck complained that Lowell was "one-sided, a preacher in verse and declamatory," and the justice of the charge is documented in such benevolent but inert lines as these, from *Poems* (1844), Lowell's second volume:

The hope of Truth grows stronger, day by day;
I hear the soul of Man around me waking,
Like a great sea, its frozen fetters breaking,
And flinging up to heaven its sunlit spray.

Lowell called this the "poetry of progress," but he also recognized the modest poetic quality of his work. Perhaps ironically, it was in the *Biglow Papers*, two series of verses in Yankee dialect, that he came closest to finding a distinctive poetic voice for his political statements. Both series consist of letters attributed to Lowell's fictional spokesman, the New England farmer Hosea Biglow. The first, a group of nine letters published in the *Boston Courier* and the *National Anti-slavery Standard* beginning in 1846, reflects Lowell's opposition to the Mexican War; the second was printed in the *Atlantic Monthly* during the Civil War and contains Lowell's support for the Union cause.

"Ez fer war," Hosea Biglow wrote in his first letter; "I call it murder, – / There you hev it plain an' flat." Like many of his New England contemporaries, Biglow condemned the war against Mexico as nothing more than imperialism in the service of slavery. Talk of "Manifest Destiny" – the phrase was invented by John L. O'Sullivan in 1845 – represented an arrogant attempt to inflate American privilege and open millions of acres to the profiteering of southern slaveholders:

> They may talk o' Freedom's airy
>   Tell they're pupple in the face, –
> It's a grand gret cemetary
>   Fer the birthrights of our race;
> They just want this Californy
>   So's to lug new slave-States in
> To abuse ye, an' to scorn ye,
>   An' to plunder ye like sin.

Three of the letters in the first series purport to come from the pen of Biglow's friend, Birdofredom Sawin, a patriotic young man who gullibly follows the flag but finds his illusions stripped away by experience: "Nimepunce a day fer killin' folks comes kind o' low fer murder."

Though Lowell's use of dialect in the *Biglow Papers* is halting and contrived, the great success of the poems enlarged the scope of America's literary vocabulary. One of the principal tasks of nineteenth-century writers was to liberate the artistic energy of colloquial expression. Lowell played his part both by example and by precept. In his introduction to the second series of *Biglow Papers*, he argued eloquently that the nation's strongest language was spoken by the uneducated plain people. Here could be found, said Lowell, speech "racy with life and vigor and originality." He professed to believe that the "first postulate of an original literature is that a people should use their language instinctively and unconsciously, as if it were a lively part of their growth and personality, not as the mere torpid boon of education and inheritance." Although this premise may have been self-consciously democratic, it could nonetheless serve as epigraph to subsequent literary developments. True to his critical tenets, Lowell late in life offered his considerable support to Edward Eggleston's sentimental but colloquial accounts of backwoods Indiana life in *The Hoosier Schoolmaster* (1871).

FIGURE 60 &
Headpiece, *The Liberator*. These contrasted scenes, in which the barbarism of the slave auction is replaced by the new day of freedom, appeared at the head of each issue of *The Liberator*.

In 1848, the same year Lowell gathered the first series of *Biglow Papers* and published them as a volume, he also published three other books: *Poems . . . Second Series*, *The Vision of Sir Launfal*, and *A Fable for Critics*. Not yet thirty years old, he had consolidated his literary reputation as a poet, critic, and journalist. The new poems exhibited the same facile craftsmanship as Lowell's earlier verses

and the same tendency to subordinate precision of feeling to grand axiomatic designs. (As Lowell himself later wrote: "I shall never be a poet till I get out of the pulpit.") *The Vision of Sir Launfal* at least demonstrated Lowell's pleasant versatility. Sir Launfal pursues the Holy Grail through a two-part iambic tetrameter fable and finds comfort in the end when Christ reveals himself to him. The legend is borrowed from Malory, though it is tailored somewhat awkwardly to fit nineteenth-century philanthropic requirements. Lowell's use of medieval materials in the *Vision* derived from his assumption that Malory's world had pertinence to modern concerns. The poem thus contributed its portion to the first American Gothic Revival, an amalgam of imported architectural and literary theory that exerted considerable influence on antebellum culture. This was a gothic that aspired toward antiquity rather than gloom, the gothic not of Poe but of Pugin, that tireless propagandist of medieval superiority, who instructed several generations of European and American artists.

As early as 1771, the intellectually restless Jefferson had sketched a crenelated tower for a site near Monticello, and he later considered building "a small Gothic temple of antique appearance" as a suitable ornament for his family graveyard. Just before the eighteenth century ended, Benjamin Henry Latrobe built Sedgeley, the first American

house with gothic elements, for a wealthy Philadelphia industrialist. However, the gothic made its visible mark on America in the two or three decades before the Civil War. A plan for a gothic house that appeared in Andrew Jackson Downing's *Cottage Residences* was perhaps the most frequently imitated domestic design ever published. Downing was a landscape architect whose ambition was to redesign the whole of America as a medieval country; he became in his books and articles the most vocal of antebellum American Goths. Born in 1815, Downing had been named for the hero of the Battle of New Orleans. He held utterly different political and cultural views from those of citizen-president Jackson but felt obligated, as so many other American artists have, to defend his style in the vocabulary of democracy and republic. In answer to the unsurprising charge that medieval buildings had no place in democratic America, Downing fiercely insisted that gothic forms provided appropriate correlatives for the rough grandeur of the American spirit. He announced the passing, in 1846, of what he called "the Greek temple disease," and he watched with satisfaction as gothic houses, churches, colleges, and even prisons multiplied in cities and countryside from Maine to Georgia.

FIGURE 61 ❧ Original architect's sketch of "Glen Ellen." In 1832, the important firm of Town and Davis produced this drawing of Glen Ellen, the future Maryland home of Robert Gilmor. For reasons of expense, the third floor was eliminated when the building was constructed.

Alexander Jackson Davis, the most prolific antebellum gothic architect, built Glen Ellen, his first medieval house, in 1832, shortly after returning from a visit to Sir Walter Scott's Abbotsford (Figure 61). Many American pilgrims paid homage to Scott, whose tastes in buildings and literature penetrated America's culture at several points. Samuel Clemens blamed Scott for the disastrously misplaced chivalry that clung to southern attitudes like an ill-fitting adhesive. In fact, Americans north and south felt the allure of the medieval past. Architects would discover the gothic repeatedly in the nineteenth and twentieth centuries. In literature, Lowell's *Vision of Sir Launfal* would be followed by countless other American excursions into the Middle Ages, from Longfellow's translation of *The Divine Comedy*, to Henry Adams's rhapsodies on Mont-Saint Michel and Chartres, to Edwin Arlington Robinson's brooding, blank-verse epic meditations on Lancelot and Tristram.

Sir Launfal proved to be among the most ephemeral of American knights errant. The *Vision* exemplified Lowell's belief that poetry ought to lift us "out of the dungeon of daily life," but it unintentionally underscored the truth that whatever literary abilities Lowell possessed were better suited to satire than to narrative or lyric. A *Fable for Critics*, published just a few months before the *Vision*, was Lowell's principal literary performance, and it remains his best known. In the course of the *Fable's* several hundred lines, Lowell offered capsule descriptions and estimates of a whole gallery of his literary contemporaries. The poem's rhymes are often outrageous – "cabinet . . . dab in it" – but the opinions they embellish typically display a vigorous common sense. Emerson, for example, is presented as a hybrid of Plotinus and Montaigne; he has a "Greek head on right Yankee shoulders," and he lurches from Olympus to the stock market. Thus does Lowell salute Emerson's characteristic mixture of pragmatism and spirit. He goes on to a comment on the sort of bemused discipleship that the Concord Sage inspired:

> All admire, and yet scarcely six converts he's got
> To I don't (nor they either) exactly know what;
> For though he builds glorious temples, 'tis odd
> He leaves never a doorway to get in a god.

Lowell's survey alternates between literary criticism and more personal observations. Thus, Hawthorne combines power and tenderness in rare balance – a genius "so shrinking and rare / That you hardly at first see the strength that is there." Cooper has drawn one original character, Natty Bumppo, and has done nothing but copy himself ever since. Even Cooper's Indians are just Natty, "daubed over with red." Irving is credited with a fine brain and "a true poet-heart," together with the talents of Addison and Steele. Lowell argues that elegance, at least in Longfellow's case, can also be force. And Poe is raised to a dubious apotheosis in Lowell's most memorable epigram: "There comes Poe, with his raven, like Barnaby Rudge, / Three fifths of him genius and two fifths sheer fudge." Lowell was equally astute in assessing his own gifts. The *Fable* ends with a canny self-portrait, Lowell's ironic confession that his lyrical and ideological commitments may have interfered with each other:

> There is Lowell, who's striving Parnassus to climb
> With a whole bale of *isms* together with rhyme,
> He might get on alone, spite of brambles and boulders,
> But he can't with that bundle he has on his shoulders,
> The top of the hill he will ne'er come nigh reaching
> Till he learns the distinction 'twixt singing and preaching.

At the conclusion of this exuberant self-parody, Lowell makes a witty but revealing reference to the utopian and even apocalyptic dreams that propelled him:

> His lyre has some chords that would ring pretty well,
> But he'd rather by half make a drum of the shell,
> And rattle away till he's old as Methusalem,
> At the head of a march to the last new Jerusalem.

Like many of his contemporaries, Lowell believed that the contest of antebellum politics was being waged for mortal stakes. Standing like a mountain between American aspirations and the New Jerusalem was the paradox and crime of slavery. "Liberty and slavery cannot dwell in harmony together": this was the self-evident truth that John Greenleaf Whittier declared in the pamphlet *Justice and Expediency*, which he published at his own expense in 1833.

Whittier was one of the most fervent of the many writers whose productive lives were dominated by the struggle against slavery. He was a Quaker, the son of relatively poor Massachusetts farmers. Since the hard work of the farm allowed only a little time for formal education, Whittier was instructed by his parents' piety and by the Bible, from which the family read every day. When he was fifteen, he heard a friend read from the work of Robert Burns, whose vernacular poetry commemorated the lives and the talk of Scottish peasants. This early introduction to Burns, Whittier later said, "had a lasting influence on me." Burns spoke to Whittier's rooted instincts and encouraged his poetic ambitions. Like his Scottish predecessor, Whittier endeavored to make poetry out of the ordinary experiences of ordinary men and women. His respect for America's common people was no democratic hypothesis but a birthright, and his poems take both their homely sincerity and their cloying sentimentality from his lifelong devotion to the values of rural New England.

Whittier's first poem, "The Exile's Departure," was published in the Newburyport *Free Press* in 1826 by a young editor named William Lloyd Garrison. Whittier quickly entered Garrison's orbit, taking up the journalism and abolitionist activism that would occupy him for the next thirty-five years. He was the spiritual and moral heir of John Woolman, the eighteenth-century Quaker whose commitment to the abolition of slavery formed the principal axis of his entire career. (Several years after the Civil War, Whittier published an edition of Woolman's autobiographical *Journal*.) Whittier's political and literary convictions were joined along the seam of his stubborn loyalty to justice and to the shared humanity of all persons. His politics made him a conspicuous public figure, revered and scorned by opposing partisans in the struggle over slavery. He was elected to the Massachusetts legislature in 1835, but he was also stoned and pelted with eggs in Pennsylvania and New Hampshire. A collection of his antislavery writings, *Voices of Freedom* (1846), enhanced his reputation among abolitionists and led to his appointment as corresponding editor of the important Washington, D.C., journal, the *National Era*.

For three decades, Whittier devoted his rhymes resolutely to the service of the antislavery cause. In "Song of Slaves in the Desert" (1847), a bewildered group of female captives plead with their God for deliverance. Though based on a historical incident, the poem's traffic in pathos and the singsong regularity of its meter diminish its power. "Massachusetts to Virginia" (1843) is better suited to

Whittier's oratorical inclinations. This is a shrill and angry warning, representative of Whittier's polemical verse and an index as well to the moralizing bitterness of sectional disputes:

> Hold, while ye may, your struggling slaves, and burden
>   God's free air
> With woman's shriek beneath the lash, and manhood's wild
>   despair;
> Cling closer to the "cleaving curse" that writes upon your
>   plains
> The blasting of Almighty wrath against a land of chains.

Along with other New Englanders, Whittier reacted to the Compromise of 1850 and its Fugitive Slave Law with disbelieving outrage; he was especially embarrassed by Massachusetts senator Daniel Webster's support of the legislation. In what he called one of his "saddest moments," he wrote the poem "Ichabod," in which Webster is pilloried as a morally abandoned man whose single act of perfidy has cost him the light and glory of a lifetime.

Whittier's pacifism, the legacy of his Quaker beliefs, eventually led to a break with Garrison over the question of antislavery tactics. Whittier diligently searched for political solutions, exhibiting a reluctance toward militant dissent that Garrison condemned as cowardly and worse. Whittier clung to his position until the eve of the war. Unlike many other abolitionists, he disapproved of John Brown's raid at Harper's Ferry in October of 1859: "The distinction should be made clear between the natural sympathy with the man and approval of his mad, and, as I think, most dangerous and unjustifiable act."

Throughout his decades of abolitionist activity, Whittier continued to write poems celebrating the scenes and people of rural New England. "Maud Muller" and "The Barefoot Boy," both collected in *The Panorama and Other Poems* (1856), offer warmhearted and rather slack sketches of country life, gestures of nostalgic mythmaking that are more reverent than animated. They nonetheless prepared for Whittier's finest poem, "Snowbound," which appeared shortly after the war's conclusion, in 1866. Almost alone among Whittier's poems, "Snowbound" balances its wistfully remembered scenes with an angular realism. At the center of the poem is the farmhouse Whittier grew up in, besieged

by a fierce winter storm. Family members and a few friends cluster around the fire and are recalled in turn, each portrait finding
its place in the mosaic of recollection. His father tells tales of
Canadian adventures, his mother reads from books of Quaker devotion. Uncle, aunt, and visitors add their stories. Whittier likens his genre scenes to "Flemish pictures of old days," and they
do possess the charm if not the solidity of Steen or de Hooch. In
"Snowbound," the past of countryside and childhood is alluring,
but the summoned images collaborate dramatically, offering scope
for mature meditation. Childish elation is circumscribed within
the reminders of later loss. Thus, the young Whittier who, late
in the poem, climbs into bed with his brother on the night of
the storm, is also the old man who has already described his own
and his brother's physical decline. The dual perspective knits
memory and the future complexly together:

> We heard the loosened clapboards tost,
> The board-nails snapping in the frost;
> And on us, through the unplastered wall,
> Felt the light sifted snowflakes fall.
> But sleep stole on, as sleep will do
> When hearts are light and life is new.

The poem looks back across personal suffering and across the collective catastrophe of the Civil War to an earlier, recognizably more
naive wholeness. Time and reverseless change become the lenses
through which the light of memory is focused.

Whittier and his New England contemporaries brought a
serious, sustained attention to the chief political and
moral issues of the antebellum years. Their exertions
document at once their descent and their distance from the earlier
world of Puritan theology. They had roots in Calvinism, but theirs
was a Calvinism transmuted into something else, a set of principles
rather than a body of dogma, an ethical point of view more than a
theological system. The high moral purposes of the older religion

remained intact, but the theological scaffolding had been dismantled. Unitarianism was one version of the newer attitudes. Liberal,
benevolent, and rationalistic, Unitarianism represented an alternative to the grim doctrines of human depravity, predestination,
and eternal punishment. Respectability and a sense of social obligation marked the boundaries of the Unitarian world-picture. Sectarian jealousy, so much a part of the colonial religious scene,
retreated before less demanding appeals to tolerance, decency, and
common sense. The men and women of earlier New England had
peered anxiously into events, hoping to catch a glimpse of God's
design. The Unitarians, molded by Enlightenment science and Romantic optimism, came by clarity more easily than their ancestors
and took for granted a broader scope for human will. Unitarians
were waggishly defined as people who believed "in one God – at
most," and their creed was derided as a feather bed for Christians
to fall into. Rejecting notions of inherited guilt, Unitarianism affirmed human competence. Insisting on personal responsibility,
Unitarianism offered partnership with God, who had once signified
inscrutable power, but who now became a cooperative and even
friendly companion.

The revision of Calvinism was the work of many preachers and
authors. Among them, none was more influential than William
Ellery Channing, who began a long career as pastor of a Congregational church in Boston in 1803. Trained to orthodoxy, Channing
emerged from ministerial obscurity in the 1820s and 1830s to become
the leading voice of Unitarian dissent. Commencing with his sermon
at the ordination of Jared Sparks in 1819, Channing announced his
break with Calvin and his intention to delineate a new dispensation.
In *The Moral Argument against Calvinism* (1820), he proposed that
the spirit of Christianity is "love, charity, benevolence. Christianity
. . . is designed to manifest God as perfect benevolence, and to bring
men to love and imitate him." Calvinism, on the other hand, with
its fixation on doom and hellfire, its hatred alike of reason and the
flesh, is a cruel "perversion" of true Christianity, an "outrage"
against conscience and intelligence, a system that aspires to "convert
us into monsters." The *Moral Argument* and Channing's other writings radiate with his confidence in the "progress of the human
mind." Channing never abandoned his belief in the mild God of
love he preached, but in demystifying God he prepared the way for

successors who would translate religion into completely secular terms. His eloquence did much to awaken transcendentalism and reform. Most significantly, he helped bring Emerson to a boil.

The 1830s and 1840s were the years of "the American newness," and it was Ralph Waldo Emerson who gave commanding meaning to that phrase. In his poems, lectures, and essays, Emerson produced the vocabulary and the images through which the confident expectancy of the rising nation declared itself. Given the inchoate state of American culture, it is perhaps more appropriate than odd that Emerson achieved his centrality without ever perfecting any of the usual literary forms. He wrote no plays or fiction; his poems, with a few exceptions, are modestly accomplished; and the essays on which his reputation rests are loosely constructed and sometimes frankly shapeless. Rather than formal excellence or even logical consistency, what Emerson provided was a vision and a voice. His essays are clad in the garments of prophecy, and they announce the nation's destiny in terms that repeatedly rise to the scale of myth. What Emerson learned as a student of theology, art, and commerce he embedded in a rhetoric of unprecedented energy that recapitulated America for itself. There was much that he neglected or did not see, but what he saw he expressed authoritatively, even decisively. On subjects ranging from poetry to individualism, from nature to national culture, Emerson helped to invent America, and much of his prose retains its original freshness and urgency (Figure 62).

Born in 1803, Ralph Waldo Emerson was one of the five surviving sons of a minister and an uneducated but strong-willed mother. Emerson's father died when the boy was nine years old, and his mother took on the job of ensuring the independence of her sons. Among other things, she managed a series of boardinghouses and was able to send four of the five brothers to Harvard (the fifth was mentally retarded). Emerson graduated from Harvard without distinction in 1821. After a few diligent but unsuccessful years as a schoolmaster, he entered the ministry and was ordained in 1829 as junior pastor of Boston's Second Church. Both Increase and Cotton Mather had preached in the Second Church generations earlier, and it was perhaps fitting that the setting which had signaled Puritan hegemony over America's spiritual culture should witness Emerson's transformation of the Puritan legacy into the secular terms that would characterize nineteenth-century discourse. Sometime in

FIGURE 62 🖎
Photograph of Ralph
Waldo Emerson.
Emerson was about forty-
five years old when this
photograph was made.

1830 or 1831, Emerson underwent a profound religious experience,
comparable to the conversions of so many reformed Christians but
leading the young preacher away from rather than into the church.
His spiritual crisis coincided with the death of his young first wife,
Ellen Tucker, who succumbed to tuberculosis at nineteen. Within
a year, Emerson created a sensation by resigning his pastorate because he had decided that he could no longer administer the Lord's
Supper. He traveled to Europe, where he met Wordsworth, Carlyle,
and Coleridge, through whom he became familiar with European
Romanticism in both its English and German forms. When he
returned, he exchanged pulpit for podium, embarking on the lecturing that would bring him his income and his fame. Out of those
lectures, he produced the remarkable sequence of essays that declared his point of view and conferred international recognition on
his opinions. Two ideas impressed themselves on everything Emerson wrote in those early, productive years: the tutelary benevolence
of nature, and the sanctity and autonomy of the individual. Repeatedly, he embraced and elaborated these two themes.

In 1835, Emerson remarried, this time to Lydia Jackson, and

settled in Concord. Here he presided over an extraordinary circle of acquaintance, a group of writers and intellectuals including Thoreau, Bronson Alcott (Louisa May Alcott's father), Margaret Fuller, Jones Very, and Orestes Brownson. These were the so-called transcendentalists, the men and women whom Emerson called "the party of the Future," loose in doctrine but aspiring to replace the shriveled rationalism of Unitarian decorum with passionate, intuitive appeals to a splendor beyond the grasp of dogmas and formulas. The clergyman F. H. Hedge, one of the principal participants in the transcendentalist meetings, said that these men and women met to consult "on the state of current opinion in theology and philosophy, which we agreed in thinking very unsatisfactory.... What was strongly felt was dissatisfaction with the reigning sensuous philosophy, dating from Locke, on which our Unitarian theology was based."

The group ("movement" is too strong a term) took its name from Kant, but its sources were as various as the reading of its members. Along with the German philosophers Fichte, Schleiermacher, and Schelling, the German writers Goethe, Novalis, and Richter, and the English Romantics, the transcendentalists were influenced by Plato, Plotinus, the Cambridge Platonists of the seventeenth century, the writings of Confucius, the Upanishads and the Bhagavad Gita, Buddhism of several sorts, Thomas à Kempis, and Pascal. As might be expected from such eclecticism, transcendentalism was more a potpourri than a system; nonetheless, a few leading ideas can be discerned. Divinity dwells in the world, not separately from it; the human soul also participates in that divinity; individuals are the best guarantors of their own conduct and probity; nature and the mind nurture and mirror each other; logic leads to a lower order of truth than insight.

In spite of its international and even exotic genealogy, transcendentalism was at bottom a local phenomenon with local roots. It represented an effort to smuggle emotion and a sense of wonder back into the religious life of antebellum New England, to rediscover at least something of the mystery that had attended the ineffable God of earlier Puritanism. At the same time, the transcendentalists rejected the terror that lay at the core of the old religion. They wanted a God who inspired awe rather than indifference, but they held onto the liberal idea of divine benevolence. They wanted zest without zeal, a high-spirited answer to complacency without too much risk. God would vacate the easy chair in the Unitarian front parlor but would remain routinely accessible. One of their contemporaries famously said that transcendentalism was like "going to heaven on a swing." Two generations later, Henry Adams looked back and found the whole undertaking fatuous. Nevertheless, the cluster of ideas, attitudes, and gestures summed up in the transcendentalist ferment provided an axis around which much of antebellum intellectual activity revolved.

Like so many of their literary contemporaries, the transcendentalists organized themselves loosely into a club. They called themselves the Symposium, the name an act of mild homage to Plato and a suggestion of their enthusiasm for talk. Their conversation eventually spilled over into the pages of the *Dial*, a quarterly magazine that grew out of their meetings. The *Dial* survived for less than four years, from July 1840 through April 1844, but it engendered consequences out of proportion to its brief life and tiny circulation. In part, the magazine's significance derived from its contents. Among the essays that appeared in its pages were Emerson's "Man the Reformer," Thoreau's "Friendship," Margaret Fuller's "Goethe," and Theodore Parker's "German Literature." However, the *Dial* earned its permanent place as much for the stance it assumed as for the talents of its contributors. The magazine promoted the idea of criticism as a legitimate activity in a democratic society, and thus it foreshadowed the numberless dissenting and utopian literary journals that were to become a continuing feature of America's cultural scene.

Just a few days before the transcendentalists' first meeting in 1836, Emerson published *Nature*, a small volume adopted by the group as a manifesto, and a work that has long survived the men and women whom it originally inspired. The book was first published anonymously and only slowly impressed itself on the reading public outside New England (fewer than five hundred copies were sold in ten years). From its unforgettable opening lines, however, *Nature* marked an epoch, blazing the path along which the search for American literary identity would lead:

> Our age is retrospective. It builds on the sepulchres of the fathers. It writes biographies, histories, and criticism. The fore-

going generations beheld God and nature face to face; we, through their eyes. Why should not we also enjoy an original relation to the universe? Why should not we have a poetry and philosophy of insight and not of tradition, and a religion by revelation to us, and not the history of theirs? . . .

The sun shines today also.

Carlyle called *Nature* "a true Apocalypse," and to many readers it was indeed a revelation. In eight brief chapters, the book exhorts Americans to throw off the burdens of past and precedent and immerse themselves in the liberation promised by inner authority and natural beauty. Often rhapsodic, the accents of the book are also democratic, as when Emerson hymns the ecstatic opportunities that ordinary experience offers: "Crossing a bare common, in snow puddles, at twilight, under a clouded sky, without having in my thoughts any occurrence of special good fortune, I have enjoyed a perfect exhilaration." To the alleged barrenness of American culture, Emerson answers with the festival of nature and the assured delights of harmony between the soul and the whole visible world. The appointed task of the citizens of a new nation is to tear off the blindfold of the past and turn their eyes toward what lies all around them. "The ruin or the blank that we see when we look at nature, is in our own eye," Emerson writes near the end of *Nature*. Mechanical philosophies have dwarfed humanity and occluded human sight. Similarly, the brokenness and seeming deadness of nature has its source in the internal divisions of men and women. Emerson beckons the people of the New World to repair themselves and thus grow into their full stature.

In one of the book's best-known passages, Emerson suggests some of the linguistic implications of the spiritual union between the soul and nature:

1. Words are signs of natural facts.
2. Particular natural facts are symbols of particular spiritual facts.
3. Nature is the symbol of spirit.

Here, in its most influential secular version, is the sacramental legacy bequeathed to antebellum New England by its Puritan ancestors. Everything natural and human finds its place in a seamless fabric of correspondences, a web of creation bodying forth the divinity that resides within all of the world's facts. To see those points of connection was to understand the unity that lay behind the miscellany of existence. Such was the goal of Reason, the faculty that Emerson defined, vaguely following the Germans, as higher than mere rational Understanding.

On August 31, 1837, a year after the publication of *Nature*, Emerson stood before the Phi Beta Kappa Society at Harvard and delivered the address that he later called "The American Scholar," the speech history has come to regard as America's declaration of literary independence. "We have listened too long to the courtly muses of Europe," Emerson said, and he stirred those who heard him. "Our day of dependence, our long apprenticeship to the learning of other lands, draws to a close." "The American Scholar" explores one of the principal themes of *Nature*, that modern society has replaced human wholeness with varieties of narrow specialization and division, and that each person has shrunk from human fullness to mere function. The scholar, who ought to be "Man Thinking," has declined into mere pedantry, becoming the "parrot of other men's thinking." Thus the tyranny of the past, and of books, which receive the reverence that ought to be reserved for the men and women who wrote them. "Each age," Emerson insists, "must write its own books. . . . The books of an older period will not fit this." Thus, while the "theory of books is noble," in practice books slow humanity's progress, adding their obsolete weight to the other impediments that stand between the eye and nature. Speaking in the midst of the panic of 1837, Emerson sneers at the "principles on which business is managed" and mourns the young men who turn into drudges in the service of commerce or die of disgust. As the antidote, he proposes the life of the scholar, which, rightly understood, has nothing to do with "man as bookworm" but demands a self-reliant, unfettered engagement with all of experience.

Less than a year after he lectured on the American scholar, Emerson returned to Harvard again, this time to address the seniors in the Divinity School. He put Christianity under the Emersonian lens and indicted the received creeds and ecclesiastical institutions as outworn, stultifying, and fraudulent. He demanded an original relation to divinity and welcomed the end of practices and beliefs whose only sanction is tradition, the dead hand of the past. He contrasted the church and the soul and declared that redemption should be sought in the soul. "Man is the wonder-worker. . . . The assumption that the age of inspiration is past, that the Bible is closed; the fear of degrading the character of Jesus by representing him as a man; indicate with sufficient clearness the falsehood of our theology." These opinions, while predictable, were such a scandal to the pious that the lecture proved to be Emerson's last at the college for over thirty years. Andrews Norton immortalized his outrage in an attack entitled "The Latest Form of Infidelity," and old John Quincy Adams grumbled that Emerson preached "wild and visionary phantasies," which threatened "the most important and solemn duties of the Christian faith."

Both Norton and Adams were more or less right, but their shock was not universally shared. Many of those who heard Emerson found him irresistible. Though the details of his program were typically uncertain, his appeal was almost literally electric. Years later, James Russell Lowell left a record of what it was like to listen to an Emerson lecture:

> Emerson's oration . . . began nowhere and ended everywhere and yet, as always with that divine man, it left you feeling that something beautiful had passed that way – something more beautiful than anything else, like the rising and setting of stars. . . . There was a tone in it that awakened all elevating associations. . . . It was as if a creature from some fairer world had lost his way in our fogs, and it was *our* fault, not his. It was chaotic, but it was all such stuff as stars are made of, and you couldn't help feeling that, if you waited awhile, all that was nebulous would be whirled into planets, and would assume the mathematical gravity of system.

Lowell's recollection conveys a glimpse of the excitement of Emersonian eloquence, but it also documents the disconnected quality of the rhetoric. It is not true that Emerson was simply inept or uninterested in the organizational demands his essays presented. He cautioned against what he called "immethodical harangues," and he acknowledged the importance of structure. At the same time, his essays continually disclose their origins in his lectures, and the lectures in turn were quarried from the journal he kept from his college days onward. In the end, it is not his essays but his sentences that have engraved themselves upon the cultural memory of his country. They are sentences by turns aphoristic, epigrammatic, pulsing with imagistic and metaphorical life, prodigious acts of compression that are themselves the best testimony of the vitality they affirm. Not surprisingly, he once named Montaigne, Francis Bacon, and the Book of Proverbs as his favorite literary models.

Whether he was working in prose or verse, Emerson considered himself a poet: "of a low class without doubt yet a poet. That is my nature & vocation." For Emerson, it was the highest calling, a status he illuminated in the dazzling essay, "The Poet," first published in 1844. The poet, Emerson writes, "is representative. He stands among partial men for the complete man, apprises us not of his wealth, but of the commonwealth. . . . The poet . . . is the man without impediment, who sees and handles that which others dream of, traverses the whole scale of experience." Poetry, then, is no matter of mere technique, of rhyme or meter. Rather, it is the act through which the deep truth of things declares itself. In that exalted sense, poets are "liberating gods." Furthermore, in line with his other essays, Emerson contends that the poetic calling is democratically available to all, since all men and women carry their portion of divinity. He acknowledged that no artist equal to America's splendid opportunity had yet appeared, but he insisted that the day was not far off. In the meantime, his own job was to prepare the ground, and to enumerate the materials that lay in wait:

> We have yet had no genius in America, with tyrannous eye, which knew the value of our incomparable materials, and saw, in the barbarism and materialism of the times, another carnival of the same gods whose picture he so much admires in Homer; then in the middle age; then in Calvinism. Banks and tariffs, the newspaper and caucus, methodism and unitarianism, are flat and dull to dull people, but rest on the same foundations of wonder as the town of Troy, and the temple of Delphos, and are as swiftly passing away. Our logrolling, our stumps and their politics, our fisheries, our Negroes, and Indians, our boasts and our repudiations, the wrath of rogues, and the pusillanimity of honest men, the northern trade, the southern planting, the western clearing, Oregon, and Texas, are yet unsung. Yet America is a poem in our eyes; its ample geography dazzles the imagination, and it will not wait long for metres.

It is a bravura paragraph that remains among Emerson's most memorable. Within a dozen years, the young Walt Whitman, stirred by Emerson, would take it on himself to produce the poetry foretold here.

The immense confidence that informs Emerson's eloquence often seems delusory, but it was probably more calculated than naive. He knew perfectly well the difference between the gleam of his vaulting lyricism and the stained, shabby facts of life. In the essay "Love," he wrote that "everything is beautiful seen from the point of the intellect. . . . But all is sour, if seen as experience. . . . In the actual world – the painful kingdom of time and place – dwell care, and canker, and fear." Emerson summoned infinity, and rhapsodized about nature, the oversoul, and self-reliance, as a cultural strategy, not as a statement of prosaic fact. He talked not of what America was, but of what it might become, when it was peopled by citizens worthy of their possibilities. In so doing he created a type, a theme that would permanently mark American artistic expression. If his work now seems insulated from the turmoil of a rising industrial democracy, his comrades and followers found his message utterly relevant to the times. He was slow to involvement in reform, notoriously slow to accept the national duty of abolition. At the same time, his words inspired others to action. The fiery John Jay Chapman said that Emerson had done more than any other antebellum thinker "to rescue the youth of the next generation and fit them for the fierce times to follow. It will not be denied that he sent ten thousand sons to the war."

The tributes and jibes of persons as diverse as John Quincy Adams and John Jay Chapman bear witness to the power of Emerson's influence upon the American imagination across much of the nineteenth century. He often kindled other minds into more muscular engagement than his own. Among those he touched was Margaret Fuller, the first editor of the *Dial* (from 1840 to 1842). Fuller was one of the most remarkable members of the transcendentalist group. Edgar Allan Poe, who knew her in New York, divided the world into men, women, and Margaret Fuller. If Poe intended his witticism as insulting, it nonetheless captured something of Fuller's singularity. She was, to begin with, a person of unusual learning for any nineteenth-century American, male or female. From an early age she was a voracious consumer of books: Emerson said that she read "at a rate like Gibbon's." Emerson's temperament was more pallid than Fuller's, but their friendship, while vexed on both sides, was fruitful. It was from Emerson, Fuller wrote, that she "first learned what is meant by an inward light."

During her years of membership in the Transcendental Club, Fuller also presided over gatherings of cultivated, well-read women who met in Elizabeth Peabody's rooms in West Street, Boston. They proposed in their discussions "to pass in review the departments of thought and knowledge, and endeavor to place them in due relation to one another in our mind." The English traveler, Harriet Martineau, criticized these women for the refined irrelevance of their salon to the hurly-burly of American life. While Margaret Fuller and "her adult pupils" sat talking about Plato and Goethe, Martineau complained, "the liberties of the republic were running out." The charge is less than half-true. Aside from the declaration made by the West Street meetings about the intellectual capacities of women, these sessions were also part of the backdrop to Fuller's landmark book, *Woman in the Nineteenth Century* (1845). This was a pathbreaking volume, the first full-scale American feminist inquiry, and one that had much influence on feminist theory and women's history. Among other things, Fuller's book helped to prepare opinion for the Seneca Falls Convention of 1848, to which can be dated the organized struggle for women's equal rights, including the right to vote. To be sure, feminist theorizing can be traced back to earlier writings, including those of Judith Sargent Murray, who argued vigorously for female education and self-reliance in the years just after the Revolution. The publication of such insights, however, was intermittent and isolated, more a prophecy of nineteenth-century developments than a source. Lacking a continuous tradition, pioneers followed each other in the quest for a workable feminist framework. *Woman in the Nineteenth Century* is itself more successful as an urgent call to consciousness and female solidarity than as a sustained investigation of its several political and economic subjects. In a culture in which women were reserved for the allegedly "higher" duties of domesticity and were therefore denied access to the worlds of commerce and politics, Fuller's concluding affirmations rang like a trumpet: "If you ask what offices [women] may fill, I reply – any. I do not care what case you put." Her most famous statement, for which she gained a lingering notoriety, was a deliberate provocation challenging the stereotypes that hemmed in women's scope: "Let [women] be sea-captains, if you will!"

Fuller's politics became increasingly radical in the last few years of her life, in particular when she traveled to Europe and found herself sympathetically swept up in the revolutionary events of 1848. By the time she died two years later, in a shipwreck off Fire Island, she had outdistanced most of her transcendentalist colleagues in her tough-minded appraisal of social structures. She had, in her own words, discovered the concrete facts of life and could stop wasting her strength on the evasions of abstractions. Emerson, above all, stood for such abstractions. Nonetheless, Fuller continued to acknowledge Emerson as her first and decisive mentor, and in this recognition she typified a generation of American intellectuals.

In differing degrees, all the transcendentalist writers embraced the notion that spirit dwelt within the physical. Indeed, in an age when spiritualism and religious revival were epidemic, even Americans not directly touched by Emerson would have assented to his definition of what he called "the relation between mind and matter." Seen aright, Emerson wrote in *Nature*, "the universe becomes transparent, and the light of higher laws than its own shines through it." Some contemporary painting presented visual expression of similar themes. In particular, the painters known as the "luminists" deployed an enveloping light that simultaneously delineated and transformed their landscapes and seascapes. In the work of Fitz Hugh Lane and Martin Johnson Heade, to name just two examples, scrupulous respect for surfaces coexists with a momentous and generalizing reverence. The burden of such paintings as Heade's *Salt Marshes: Newport, Rhode Island* and Lane's *Owl's Head, Penobscot Bay* (Plate 2) is to show that the ideal inheres in the real. In these canvases, appearance and essence seem to merge, and the transitory is subsumed in timelessness.

Both these paintings are typical of luminist practice in the absence or radical subordination of human figures. In this, they perhaps more closely resemble the thought of Emerson's younger colleague, his sometime acolyte Henry David Thoreau. It was Thoreau who wrote in 1852: "I would fain let man go by and behold a universe in which man is but a grain of sand. . . . I do not value any view of the universe into which man and the institutions of man enter very largely and absorb much of the attention. Man is but the place

where I stand." In the same year, Thoreau measured the distance between himself and his former mentor in a wonderfully revealing image: "I doubt," Thoreau confided to his journal, "if Emerson could trundle a wheelbarrow through the streets." It is indeed hard to imagine Emerson pushing a wheelbarrow, and the ironic figure might be taken as Thoreau's shorthand way of specifying the difference between the two men. Emerson's account of nature was stirring but theoretical and rather disembodied. Thoreau, on the other hand, had trundled wheelbarrows, worked as a day laborer and handyman, tilled the soil of gardens, surveyed property, painted houses, even built a cabin. He accepted the physical and abandoned himself to his senses with an exuberance Emerson hardly understood; in his prose he rendered the visible world in all its minute particularity. At Thoreau's funeral in 1862, Emerson delivered a eulogy in which he proposed, with a kind of awe, that Thoreau's powers of observation "seemed to indicate additional senses. He saw as with a microscope, heard as with an ear-trumpet, and his memory was a photographic register of all he saw and heard" (Figure 63).

Thoreau's death ended twenty-five tangled years of connection with Emerson, years in which discipleship had matured into friendship and then yielded to mutual frustration and estrangement. Thoreau was a senior at Harvard when *Nature* appeared, and the book had shaken him to his foundations. For the rest of his life, he would wrestle with the questions Emerson had raised. He shared Emerson's conviction that the natural world was the legible script of divinity, and shared as well his optimism about the depthless potential of the New World's men and women. With Emerson, he scorned the pushing, grasping materialism of nineteenth-century commercial culture. At the same time, Thoreau often stepped across borders of behavior from which Emerson typically shrank. Although Emerson preached self-reliance and contempt for conformity, his own conduct remained respectable and even rather prim. Thoreau offended his middle-class neighbors (including Emerson) with his apparent lack of ambition and with the uncompromising militance of his political dissent. It was Emerson who wrote that the poet was "isolated by truth and by his art," but it was Thoreau, far more than the relatively sociable Emerson, who found his best companionship in solitude and whose sojourn at Walden Pond became a metaphor for self-sufficiency.

Thoreau moved into the cabin he had built at Walden on July 4, 1845. On that day, while his fellow citizens gave themselves up to noisy and often drunken celebration, Thoreau quietly declared his independence. On that day as well, Margaret Fuller published in the New York *Daily Tribune* an essay called "Fourth of July," a sardonic dissent from the easy patriotism usually elicited by the occasion. In Fuller's opinion, the solemn promises made by America's founders had been betrayed, and she scolded America for its greed and especially for its tolerance of slavery. She called for a return to "the narrow, thorny path where Integrity leads."

Thoreau shared Fuller's disappointment with the morally besotted state of American affairs. He found in the narrow tracks of Walden's woods the path "where Integrity leads." He was twenty-eight years old when he moved into his cabin, and he had spent several years avoiding a career or even a steady job. He had lived for two years with the Emersons and been their man-of-all-work, and he had traveled to New York City for several unhappy months, during which he tried his hand at journalism and tutored Emerson's nephew. When he returned to Concord, he was determined to undertake the project of living in the woods, in order to see how economically and simply life could in fact be lived. Emerson owned the fourteen acres on which Thoreau's cabin stood, a piece of property more domestic than wild, located an easy walk from Concord. There Thoreau conducted his "experiment in living." He lived by the pond for two years, two months, and two days, and he returned with the testimony of his own experience. The book that resulted several years later was little noticed at first. Eventually, however, *Walden* gained a tenacious grip on the American imagination, valued as an unexampled statement of personal freedom, a rebuke to luxury, and a reminder of the priorities that make the good life possible.

It took Thoreau several drafts, written over nearly ten years, to complete the book. He shaped and reshaped the material continually, testing and discarding different strategies of organization. The most important choice he made had to do with time. In the book, the twenty-six months he spent at Walden are compressed into one year, from a summer to the following spring. By way of this obvious but profound alteration, Thoreau imposed upon his account the elemental, annual rhythm of the seasons. "My facts shall be falsehoods to the common sense," he wrote. "I would so state facts that they shall be significant, shall be mythic or mythologic." The ma-

FIGURE 64 🎐 Title page, Henry David Thoreau, *Walden*, first edition.

WALDEN;

OR,

LIFE IN THE WOODS.

BY HENRY D. THOREAU,

AUTHOR OF "A WEEK ON THE CONCORD AND MERRIMACK RIVERS."

I do not propose to write an ode to dejection, but to brag as lustily as chanticleer in the morning, standing on his roost, if only to wake my neighbors up. — Page 92.

BOSTON:
TICKNOR AND FIELDS.
M DCCC LIV.

nipulated facts of *Walden*'s chronology create a narrative structure that vivifies the myth of reciprocity between self and nature, between the particular and the universal. *Walden* in effect grows out of the seasons of the year and gains authenticy from the natural cycle of which it is the record (Figure 64).

"Economy" is the title of the book's first chapter, and Thoreau's definition of that term recapitulates the lesson he learned from his life in the woods. The natural world everywhere exhibits a simplicity and a fit proportion between ends and means that contrast at every point with the clutter and excess of civilization. Only by escaping from the baggage of possessions and worldly ambition can men and women regain their insight into the divinity that resides within nature and themselves. The woods teach the difference between price and value: "The cost of a thing is the amount of what I will call life which is required to be exchanged for it, immediately or in the long run." Thoreau dismissed the material comforts of life as "positive hindrances to the elevation of mankind." He argued that the necessities of existence, among them food, clothing, and shelter, could all be acquired without submitting oneself to the tyranny of wage slavery. In his own case, he attests that six weeks' work provided his maintenance for a year.

Thoreau's exaltation of the simple life was an attitude he assumed rather too easily. A lifelong bachelor, he avoided the adult responsibilities that confine most men and women, and he had ready access to friends and relatives who would rescue him from any real calamity. James Russell Lowell framed an angry indictment against Thoreau for playing a hypocritical game in *Walden*: "He squatted on another man's land; he borrows an ax; his boards, his nails, his bricks, his mortar, his books, his lamp, his fishhooks, his plough, his hoe, all turn state's evidence against him as an accomplice in the sin of that artificial civilization." When Thoreau visited the nearby family of John Fields, which lived in squalor by circumstance rather than by choice, their hunger and tattered clothes refuted his romantic call to voluntary poverty with wordless eloquence. Thoreau's detachment from pedestrian duties could shade into disdain and even a kind of spiritual miserliness: "I feel that my connections with and obligations to society are still very slight and transient." Versions of that statement recur in Thoreau's writing. A decade before Thoreau moved to Walden, de Tocqueville had written warningly: "Not only does democracy make each man forget his ancestors, but it hides his descendants and separates his contemporaries from him; it throws him back upon himself alone and threatens in the end to confine him entirely within the solitude of his own heart." Thoreau's failure of generosity can be discerned in de Tocqueville's reproof.

Thoreau's limits and the discrepancies in his book both deserve notice. Lingering over them, however, would confuse the biographical Thoreau with the persona he created. *Walden* is the tonic, incontrovertible reply to a culture hypnotized by money, always willing to subordinate integrity to success. Thoreau summons his readers with the fervor of an impatient preacher, asking them to break through the sterile surfaces of convention in order to rediscover the best in themselves. Thoreau's contemporary, the architect and landscape planner Andrew Jackson Downing, once wrote that "to find a really original man living in an original and characteristic house . . . is as satisfactory as to find an eagle's nest built on top of a mountain crag." Downing did not have Thoreau in mind, but his romantic simile could be applied to the task Thoreau took upon himself in Walden's woods.

Thoreau did not insist that others follow his example. However, like so many of his intellectual forebears, from the Mathers to Benjamin Franklin, he imagined his life as representative. *Walden* stands in America's autobiographical tradition, transformed to serve Thoreau's transcendental purposes. The book tells of a quest, neither for salvation in the next world nor for prosperity in this, but for personal liberation. Thus, while the vocabularies of religion and business permeate the text, they are put to new and ultimately subversive purposes. The language of religion demonstrates the universal scale of Thoreau's intentions and bespeaks the unfeigned holiness that invests the relation between soul and nature. The language of business – the book is filled with talk of economy, trade, commerce – represents Thoreau's ironic appropriation of the speech of the marketplace. Such language asserts the practical importance of Thoreau's errand into the wilderness, asserts indeed that Thoreau is as sensitive to matters of fact as the worldly Franklin. Thoreau's famous lists, of building materials, expenses, meteorological data, are even more scrupulous than Franklin's, but they coexist with a reality that escapes measurement and counting. In *Walden*, objects enter into the alliance Thoreau announces between physical and spiritual: "The feathers and wings of birds are still drier and thinner leaves. Thus, also, you pass from the lumpish grub in the earth to the airy and fluttering butterfly. The very globe continually transcends and translates itself, and becomes winged in its orbit." Scientific inquiry and visionary lyric collaborate to declare Emerson's proposition, more convincingly than Emerson ever did, that "nature is the symbol of spirit."

There are moments of ambivalence in *Walden*'s account of nature. Occasionally, Thoreau acknowledges the darkness and the competitive savagery of the natural world. Far more typically, however, he holds firm to pastoral values that insist on the higher laws that nature embodies. The woods, and especially the lakes that he calls the chief beauty of the landscape, declare a harmony that humbles the calculations of the commercial world. Timeless and serene, Walden Pond is at once perpetually fresh and also older than human history: "Perhaps on that spring morning when Adam and Eve were driven out of Eden Walden Pond was already in existence, and even then breaking up in a gentle spring rain accompanied with mist and a southerly wind, and covered with myriads of ducks and geese, which had not heard of the fall."

Alluding to Eden, to the world before the Fall, Thoreau evokes the elegy that hovers behind the reverence of *Walden*. The sun may be only "a morning star," as Thoreau avows in his buoyant conclusion, but the natural scene to which he appeals in the book was vanishing even as he wrote. Not only in Concord and its environs, but across the continent, the equipoise between humanity and nature upon which Thoreau grounded his vision was shifting. The process of industrial transformation was irresistibly under way; nature was in retreat. The railroad – what Thoreau calls "the devilish Iron Horse" – was a brute fact, but it also served as symbol for the new order that was emerging. "The whistle of the locomotive penetrates my woods summer and winter," Thoreau writes. The railroad battered his privacy and soiled the wilderness with debris. It was the clangorous agent of the cities and their crowded confusion.

Machinery and systems alike represented threats to human autonomy. Emerson spoke of Thoreau's contrariness, his need to feel himself in continuous opposition. The estimate acutely describes *Walden*. The book is governed by Thoreau's antagonism to government and to all the institutions of antebellum American society.

In a chapter called "The Village," he writes that "wherever a man goes, men will pursue and paw him with their dirty institutions, and, if they can, constrain him to belong to their desperate odd-fellow society." Courts and schools, churches and corporations, are engaged in a continuous conspiracy to shackle the nation's men and women. Above all, Thoreau denounced slavery, insisting that the legality of the "peculiar institution" proved the corruption of American law itself. To signal his resistance to slavery, he refused to pay a portion of his taxes and was arrested. He spent only one night in jail (his fine was paid by an unidentified friend), but the episode has survived as one of the most potent gestures of dissent in American history.

Thoreau put an uncompromising voice at the service of the antislavery cause. During his lifetime, his best-known writings were undoubtedly his vigorous abolitionist polemics, among them "Slavery in Massachusetts," delivered as a speech on the Fourth of July, 1854, and reprinted by Garrison in the *Liberator*. Under the hateful Fugitive Slave Law, passed as part of the Compromise of 1850, two escaped slaves had been returned by Massachusetts authorities to their southern masters. Thomas Sims had been sent back to Georgia in 1851, Anthony Burns to Virginia in 1854, just a few weeks before Thoreau spoke. His outrage barely under control, Thoreau pressed the shameful contrast between the requirements of simple humanity and the sordid facts of the slave system. The Fugitive Slave Law, Thoreau said, "has its life only in the dust and mire . . . and he who walks with freedom, and does not with Hindoo mercy avoid treading on every venomous reptile, will inevitably tread it under foot, — and Webster its maker, with it." Like Garrison, who burned a copy of the Constitution because it sanctioned slavery, Thoreau made his appeal to the superior law of conscience: "What is wanted is men, not of policy, but of probity – who recognize a higher law than the Constitution, or the decision of the majority."

Three years later, Thoreau met John Brown and concluded that he had found a man whose righteousness lifted him above the debased dead level of antebellum politics. On October 16, 1859, Brown and a handful of young followers attacked the federal arsenal at Harper's Ferry, Virginia; their goal was to provoke slave insurrection across the South. The raiders were put down within two days, but Brown's capture and imprisonment incited protests

FIGURE 65 ❧ Horace Pippin, *John Brown Going to His Hanging* (1942).

throughout the northern states, especially in Massachusetts. Thoreau's impassioned defense of Brown, in a speech delivered in Concord on October 30, solidly aligned him with the most radical sector of abolitionist opinion. The man evoked in "A Plea for Captain John Brown" is an American hero, a man who could not have been tried by a jury of his peers, because he had no peers. He was "like the best of those who stood at Concord Bridge once, on Lexington Common, and on Bunker Hill, only he was firmer and higher principled." In memorializing Brown (not yet dead, but obviously doomed), Thoreau enrolled him in the transcendentalist ranks: "A man of rare common sense and directness of speech, as of action; a transcendentalist above all, a man of ideas and principles." Emerson, who sometimes regarded Thoreau's incendiary politics with nervous caution, agreed. The hanging of John Brown, Emerson said, made "the gallows glorious like the Cross" (Figure 65).

In short, transcendentalism ought to lead to action. It had affinities with the myriad reform movements that agitated antebellum America, but the kinship was seldom announced as explicitly or as controversially as by Thoreau. He pursued transcendentalist logic to explosive outcomes that most of his New England comrades preferred to ignore. His influence on contemporary events was slight. However, in the years following his death, his arguments in support of principled dissent found a reception all over the world. "Civil Disobedience" (published anonymously as "Resistance to Civil Government" in 1849) became the most widely read of all American essays. Women and men as diverse as Emma Goldman, Gandhi, and Martin Luther King, Jr., revered Thoreau as a progenitor. Each of them learned something of tactics from Thoreau. More important, each took encouragement from his inspiriting conception of the sanctity of individuals and their liberty. "There will never be," Thoreau writes near the end of the essay, "a really free and enlightened State, until the State comes to recognize the individual as a higher and independent power, from which all its own power and authority are derived, and treats him accordingly." In the century and more since Thoreau wrote these words, the state has grown larger, and the individual smaller, than he could have imagined. Nonetheless, his work has heartened succeeding generations of men and women who share his vision of a social existence grounded on uncoerced cooperation.

Thoreau's commitment to antislavery politics was slow to coalesce, but his admiration for John Brown followed from the logically inescapable fact that slavery represented the most coercive of institutions. Thoreau's intellectual and moral progress was not unusual. In the decades that led up to secession and Civil War, the debate over slavery moved inexorably from the margins to the center of national consciousness. Territorial expansion repeatedly raised the question of slavery's extension beyond the borders of the original slaveholding South. Sectional tensions were heightened by a variety of differences between North and South, but the future of slavery increasingly became the dominant question faced by antebellum politics. Though abolitionism never commanded the support of a majority of northern Americans in the years before the Civil War, antislavery sentiment grew steadily, in part because of the newspapers, books, and pamphlets that appeared in such profusion.

Women played decisive roles in the abolitionist movement, providing most of the members of abolitionist societies, much of the day-to-day work, and a good deal of the leadership. Some of the abolitionist women, appealing to the "natural" female tendency toward care and nurturing, invoked the same stereotypes of difference that hobbled their own opportunities. Other women insisted on equality. The reluctance of their male counterparts to accept women as partners contributed to the development of antebellum feminism. The sisters Angelina and Sara Grimké, for example, who had traveled and spoken tirelessly in the abolitionist cause throughout the 1830s, were rebuked for lecturing to men and turned their considerable argumentative skills toward the rights of women (Figure 66).

Opposition to slavery was catalyzed by Harriet Beecher Stowe's *Uncle Tom's Cabin*, the most popular novel published in nineteenth-century America, and the most influential as well. Stowe, the daughter, sister, and wife of ministers, was born and raised in New England, but she lived for nearly two decades in Cincinnati. She began

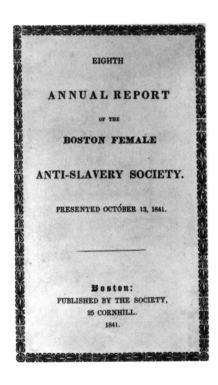

FIGURE 66 ᕫ Cover, *Anti-Slavery Almanac.* The Boston Female Anti-Slavery Society was organized in 1833. This is the cover of the society's eighth annual report.

FIGURE 67 🔊
Advertisement for
Harriet Beecher Stowe,
Uncle Tom's Cabin. This
poster, which appeared
within a few months
after the book was
published, shows the
large size of the novel's
immediate sale.

her career as a writer inconspicuously, publishing magazine stories
in the 1830s and 1840s and enjoying both the notoriety of authorship
and the small income she earned. Her return to New England in
1850, when her husband took up a professorship at Bowdoin, coincided with passage of the Fugitive Slave Law. Her revulsion from
that law – along with a vision she later reported seeing of a slave
being beaten to death and forgiving his murderers – provided the
inspiration for *Uncle Tom's Cabin, or Life among the Lowly.* The
novel was first published serially in the abolitionist *National Era*
from June 1851 through April 1852. When it appeared as a book,
first-year sales exceeded three hundred thousand copies. *Uncle Tom's
Cabin* has been continuously in print, in as many as forty languages,
from the day of its publication. Dozens of stage adaptations followed,
making Stowe's fiction America's most popular play for decades,

long after the Civil War had been fought and slavery abolished (Figure 67).

Uncle Tom's Cabin may not, as Lincoln reportedly said, have sparked the Civil War, but the novel's climactic scenes – the death of little Eva and the murder of Tom – have become universally recognized emblems for the fate of innocence in the hands of corruption. Stowe's victims have power, but it is the power of love and Christian forgiveness. The monstrous cruelty of the slave system, personified in the reprobate drunkard, Simon Legree, is opposed and ultimately mastered by forbearance and charity. In accepting his death and blessing his murderer, Tom becomes like Christ, "whose suffering changed an instrument of torture, degradation and shame, into a symbol of glory, honor, and immortal life." Stowe used the religious and moral premises of the American majority to indict the injustice of America's laws and the indecency of America's acquiescence in the crime of slavery.

The antislavery vanguard included a large number of black abolitionists, some working in groups and some individually. By 1830, there were at least fifty black antislavery societies molding opinion throughout the North. Some of the men and women in the movement had been born free, while others had seized their own freedom. The fugitive Harriet Tubman, for example, reportedly made a dozen dangerous trips into the South and helped more than two hundred slaves escape to the North and Canada. Sojourner Truth, in a long career as orator and organizer, led campaigns for abolition and for women's rights. Some black clergymen, such as Alexander Crummell and Bishop Richard Allen, head of the African Methodist Episcopal Church of Philadelphia, were influential abolitionist preachers who spread the gospel of freedom from their pulpits.

Blacks were the authors of several key documents in the antislavery struggle, among them David Walker's landmark pamphlet, *Appeal to the Colored Citizens of the World*, published in 1829. Walker was a self-educated and well-traveled man, born the son of a free black woman in North Carolina, and therefore free himself according to that state's laws. His *Appeal* marshalls history, classical rhetoric, and the Bible on behalf of a sustained and bitter denunciation of the inhumanity of slavery. Those Christians who put faith at the service of slavery are "ten times more cruel, avaricious, and unmerciful" than those who have no religion at all. Walker's observations of the slave system and its racism tempted him to the suspicion that whites were perhaps "not as good by nature" as blacks. Of more immediate political significance, Walker defended black rebellion. Invoking Jefferson with angry irony, Walker quoted the Declaration of Independence on behalf of black freedom. He prophesied that the "crushing arm of power" would avenge the wrongs blacks had suffered at white hands, and the wide circulation of the *Appeal* among slaves was seen by fearful whites as a call to insurrection. Revolution seemed imminent throughout the Western Hemisphere. In 1831, Nat Turner led a revolt of his fellow slaves in Southampton County, Virginia, that cost between fifty and sixty white lives. An uprising in Jamaica resulted in Parliament's abolition of slavery throughout the British Empire. Both black and white abolitionists began to call more frequently for a violent response to the violence of the slave system.

David Walker died, probably a murder victim, within a year of publishing the *Appeal*. Among those who were stirred by his example was Henry Highland Garnet, an escaped slave from Maryland who had become a minister and a celebrated abolitionist orator. Garnet republished the *Appeal*, along with a biographical sketch of Walker, in 1848. Garnet's own antislavery polemics included an influential speech called "An Address to the Slaves of the United States of America," which was first delivered to a Buffalo convention of free blacks in 1843. The speech is a ringing call for "resistance, resistance, resistance": "No oppressed people have ever secured their liberty without resistance." Garnet advises against armed insurrection, but only because it would be "inexpedient. Your numbers are too small." Nonetheless, Garnet's address includes a roll call of heroes who have earned their immortality by choosing liberty even at the cost of death: Denmark Vezey, who "died a martyr to freedom"; Nat Turner, "goaded to desperation by wrong and injustice"; and Joseph Cinque, who emancipated "a whole ship-load of his fellow men on the high seas."

The personal testimony of slaves and former slaves imparted the flesh and blood of human suffering to the literature of abolition (Figure 68). *The Narrative of the Adventures and Escape of Moses Roper, from American Slavery*, which was published in 1837, went through ten editions in the next two decades. The book is an episodic, artless, but moving revelation of life and death inside slavery's empire. Grounded securely on the authority of experience, Roper's narrative is couched in a plain style that casts his outrage and his anguish into vivid relief. The story's structure is chronological, following Roper's repeated attempts to escape and the tortures and punishments that followed each recapture. Along the way, Roper glances at the systemic cruelty and the legal codes within which slaves faced their masters. After recounting how a young slave was flogged to death for the "crime" of picking cotton on Sunday, for example, Roper comments: "The general custom in this respect is, that if a man kills his own slave, no notice is taken of it by the civil functionaries; but if a man kills a slave belonging to another master, he is compelled to pay the worth of the slave." Denied recourse to justice or to decency, Roper could only deploy his courage, tenacity, and agile intelligence to meet the relentless violence imposed on him (Figure 69).

The most widely read black autobiography was written by Frederick Douglass, who was also the leading figure in the black antislavery movement. *Narrative of the Life of Frederick Douglass, an American Slave* appeared in 1845 and sold thirteen thousand copies

INCIDENTS

IN THE

LIFE OF A SLAVE GIRL.

WRITTEN BY HERSELF.

Linda Brent

"Northerners know nothing at all about Slavery. They think it is perpetual bondage only. They have no conception of the depth of *degradation* involved in that word, SLAVERY; if they had, they would never cease their efforts until so horrible a system was overthrown."
            A WOMAN OF NORTH CAROLINA.

"Rise up, ye women that are at ease! Hear my voice, ye careless daughters! Give ear unto my speech."
            ISAIAH xxxii. 8.

EDITED BY L. MARIA CHILD.

BOSTON:
PUBLISHED FOR THE AUTHOR.
1861.

FIGURE 68 ❧ Title page, *Incidents in the Life of a Slave Girl: Written by Herself.* Harriet Jacobs was the author of *Incidents,* which was edited by the abolitionist writer Lydia Maria Child and was originally published under the pseudonym "Linda Brent."

within a year. This first version of his autobiography (he published a second in 1855 and a third in 1881) takes his story from birth to his escape from slavery in 1838. Douglass was born into slavery in Maryland in about 1817. The date is uncertain; it was part of slavery's strategy to deprive blacks of all the elements of identity, even a birthday. "By far the larger part of the slaves know as little of their ages as horses know of theirs," Douglass writes in the opening lines of the *Narrative*, "and it is the wish of most masters within my knowledge to keep their slaves thus ignorant." Slaves rarely came nearer to identifying their birth dates than "planting-time, harvest-time, cherry-time, spring-time, fall-time." Denying slaves their birth dates encapsulated the entire system of oppressing minds as well as bodies. Knowledge was denied to the slave because it would bring discontent. Douglass agreed with that hypothesis: his hunger for freedom sharpened when he learned to read. The stages of his liberation – from learning, to resistance, to escape, to anti-slavery leadership – define one of the remarkable careers of the nineteenth century. He lived his life as a struggle against the forces arrayed in concert against his dignity and humanity (Figure 70).

The *Narrative* is constructed out of the verbal materials Douglass had at hand. Like most of his radical contemporaries, black and

FIGURE 69 ❧ Theodore R. Davis, *A Slave Auction at the South*. This engraving, from Davis's drawing, appeared in *Harper's Weekly* in July 1861, three months after Confederate guns fired on Fort Sumter.

<figure>FIGURE 70 🙣
Photograph of Frederick
Douglass. Douglass was
in his sixties when this
photograph was made.</figure>

white, he adhered to relatively conventional religious and political
beliefs. Douglass interpreted his own career as a vindication, rather
than a denial, of America's premises. He was one of many Americans
who had concluded that democracy and Christianity, though they
had been deformed by slavery, remained doctrines worthy of allegiance. At the same time, his use of Christian images and vocabulary
can be complex in its design and effect. For example, the *Narrative*
has at its center a kind of conversion experience resembling the
rebirth of evangelical Christianity, but it occurs in a secular and
violent context. Douglass was sent to work as a field hand for a Mr.
Covey in 1833. After long abuse by this sadistic overseer, Douglass
decided on the dangerous course of resistance. The beating he gave
Covey was the turning point of his life:

> The gratification afforded by the triumph was a full compen-
> sation for whatever else might follow, even death itself. He
> only can understand the deep satisfaction which I experienced,
> who has himself repelled by force the bloody arm of slavery. I
> felt as I never felt before. It was a glorious resurrection, from
> the tomb of slavery, to the heaven of freedom. My long-crushed
> spirit rose, cowardice departed, bold defiance took its place;
> and I now resolved that, however long I might remain a slave

in form, the day had passed forever when I could be a slave
in fact. I did not hesitate to let it be known of me, that the
white man who expected to succeed in whipping, must also
succeed in killing me.

It is masterful rhetoric, breathing with a recollected anger which is
held in check and ordered by the symmetry of opposing clauses. An
exhilarating act of self-creation is announced through the appropriation of central Christian motifs: by means of his just violence,
Douglass lifts himself from the grave of bondage to the heaven of
liberty.

&

Whatever their Christian or transcendentalist inclinations, Douglass and Thoreau, Stowe and Emerson, all
imagined human choice to be the fulcrum and lever of
historical process. "There is properly no History," Emerson wrote
in 1841, "only Biography." The belief that persons and personalities
are the agents of historical change was widely shared on both sides
of the Atlantic: Thomas Carlyle, for instance, wrote that the "history of the world is but the biography of great men." However, the
distinctively American sources of this view lay in the venerable
Puritan identification of saint and community. The specially ordained role bestowed on such colonial leaders as John Winthrop
and William Bradford was bequeathed in the nineteenth century to
Washington and the rest of the nation's founders. Predictably, facts
usually counted for less than patriotic ideology and mythmaking,
and biographies of American heroes were often mere exercises in
secular piety and hero worship. The most famous example was the
largely fanciful *Life and Memorable Actions of George Washington*, by
the Reverend Mason Weems. This little book appeared in the first
of its many editions in 1800, just a year after Washington's death.
The fifth edition (1806) is the source of the enduring but apocryphal
cherry tree episode (Figure 71).

Better historians than Weems shared with him the assumption
that the meaning of the past could best be deciphered through the

SURRENDER OF LORD CORNWALLIS

FIGURE 71 🙋
Illustration from Mason
Locke Weems, *The Life
of George Washington:
with Curious Anecdotes,
Equally Honorable to
Himself, and Exemplary to
His Young Countrymen.*
Weems's audience is
suggested by the "Young
Countrymen" of his
subtitle.

lives and statements of the nation's leaders. Jared Sparks, who in
1839 was named by Harvard to the first chair of history in any
American university, had edited twelve volumes of Washington's
writings, written reverent biographies of Washington and Franklin,
and enthroned the American Revolution and its leaders at the apex
of human progress. Sparks set out to put national self-consciousness
on a more secure scholarly footing. Though his research was lamed
by his genteel temperament and his patriotic commitments, he
worked tirelessly in the archives of early America, preserving much
that would have been lost and setting an important example for
professional historians.

The most influential nineteenth-century historians, among them
William Hickling Prescott, John Lothrop Motley, and Francis Parkman, practiced history as a branch of literature. They invested
enormous amounts of time, energy, and money in travel and documentary research, but they combined scholarship with literary premeditation. While they were scrupulous about facts, and
indefatigable in searching them out, they were interested finally in

the themes and the dramatic designs through which they believed the past most usefully revealed itself. They each relied on familiar narrative techniques to reproduce the march and unfolding of historical events over time. They evoked settings with painstaking care, constructing places through copious details, because they believed that action and scene were intimately and causally intertwined. Furthermore, they were by their own description Romantics, who assumed that nature's indwelling significance served as a mirror of humanity. Parkman, for example, wrote that he had tried in his books "to include the whole course of the American conflict between France and England, or, in other words, the history of the American forest." Above all, these historians presented vivid sketches of their main characters, manipulating the thoughts, actions, and even the descriptions of heroes and villains as symbolic extensions of story and moral. They exploited contrast as an organizing device, playing off such figures as Cortés and Montezuma, Elizabeth and Isabella, Montcalm and Wolfe, to ratify their thematic purposes.

When young Henry Adams was planning his own future as a writer, he wrote a letter to Henry Cabot Lodge that reveals the profits and high repute that accompanied what he called "the historic-literary line":

> Now if you will think for a moment of the most respectable and respected products of our town of Boston, I think you will see at once that this profession does pay. No one has done better and won more in any business or pursuit, than has been acquired by men like Prescott, Motley, Frank Parkman, Bancroft, and so on in historical writing. . . . With it, comes social dignity, European reputation, and a foreign mission to close.

Prescott, Motley, and Parkman were graduates of Harvard, Brahmin in background and patrician in outlook. All three were freed from the demands of wage earning by family wealth; in addition, Prescott and Parkman were disabled from ordinary employment by bad eyes and poor health. Their lives were rather insulated from the commonplace and the contemporary. Thus, while they confidently read the annals of the past as the lesson of liberty's progress, all of them were uncomfortable with the raucous tone that nineteenth-century democracy was increasingly taking in America. None wrote extensively about the recent history of the United States; their major works included Prescott's *History of the Conquest of Mexico* (1843), Motley's *Rise of the Dutch Republic* (1856), and Parkman's multi-volume series on the struggle between France and England for control of North America.

Having read and admired the historical fiction of Sir Walter Scott, these men wanted to confer on historical materials the scope and the scale of Scott's romantic epics. Prescott's comments about the ambitions he brought to his history of Spain's conquest of Mexico could be applied to the designs of Parkman and Motley as well: "The true way of conceiving the subject is, not as a philosophical theme, but as an epic in prose, a romance of chivalry; as romantic and chivalrous as any which Boiardo or Ariosto ever fabled." Prescott demanded a historical conception equal to the sweep of great events, a prose style "which, while it combines all the picturesque features of the romantic school, is borne onward on a tide of destiny, like that which broods over the fiction of the Grecian poets."

Significantly, these literary historians tended to find subjects more suitable to epic in the past than the present. Vanished heroes people the pages of their histories as reminders and as rebukes to the meanness of contemporary political life. Parkman, in particular, looked with unfriendly skepticism at the expansion of popular democracy throughout the nineteenth century, and the corresponding decline of his own class. The cooperative rule of the able few was being replaced by the noisy incursions of the disenfranchised and of reformers. In one of his last books, *Montcalm and Wolfe* (1884), Parkman eloquently recalled the independent nation that had risen out of the British victory in North America, but he coupled his vision of America's emergent power with a warning about democratic limits. The British colonies, Parkman wrote, scarcely free from "the incubus of France" at the end of the French and Indian wars, immediately "showed symptoms of revolt." Resisting Parliament's taxations as insults to their rights as free citizens, the colonists audaciously "affronted the wrath of England in the hour of her triumph, forgot their jealousies and quarrels, joined hands in the common cause, fought, endured, and won. The disunited colonies became the United States. The string of discordant communities along the Atlantic coast has grown to a mighty people." The greatest danger America would face, in Parkman's conservative opinion, was "herself, destined to a majestic future," but only "if she will shun

the excess and perversion of the principles that made her great."
In short, the nation must "resist the mob" as it once resisted Parliament and king. Parkman's heroes were the antidotes to the social
changes he reviled, his answer to the demands of Irish immigrants
for a share of Boston's political power, of blacks for freedom, and
of women for the vote and property rights. During the Civil War,
Parkman scorned Lincoln as "the feeble and ungainly mouthpiece
of the North," a specimen of the vulgarity which an unchecked
democracy would spawn.

Evoking the shades of bygone heroes was in part an effort to
impose some sort of order on the multiplying discord of the years
before the Civil War. The Brahmin historians were unnerved by
the accelerating urbanization and the dramatic technological ad-
vances that were transforming antebellum society. Arguments over
the meaning of the family and the place and role of women were
being waged with increased intensity. The unresolved question of
slavery took on a growing political and moral urgency. This welter
of change and uncertainty elicited deeply ambivalent responses,
which might be described as a debate over the competing claims of
past and future. On the one hand were those, like Parkman, who
recoiled from the shock of the culture's several dislocations and
turned to the past for idealized images. Other men and women
believed that the logic of the American experiment led inevitably
toward the perfected future, the millennium in which the liberating
potential of democratic aspirations would be realized. Political reformers were joined in this view by spokesmen for the new industries.
As early as the latter part of the eighteenth century, propagandists
for the American manufacturing system confidently promised that
machinery would break the chains that bound working people to
their toil. By the nineteenth century, such predictions were commonplace. In 1831, for example, the lawyer and writer Timothy
Walker defended "Mechanism" as an aid to human fulfillment:

> In the absolute perfection of machinery, were that attainable,
> we might realize the absolute perfection of mind. In other
> words, if machines could be so improved and multiplied, that
> all our corporeal necessities could be entirely gratified, without
> the intervention of human labor, there would be nothing to
> hinder all mankind from becoming philosophers, poets, and
> votaries of art. The whole time and thought of the whole

human race could be given to inward culture, to spiritual advancement.

Dreams of perfection lay behind the dozens of utopian communities that were founded in the first half of the nineteenth century. Reforming energy often reached beyond pragmatic restraint and produced blueprints for the perfect society. "Not a reading man but has a draft of a new community in his waistcoat pocket," Emerson wrote to Carlyle, with only a little exaggeration. Some of the earliest utopias were set up by religious groups. The ascetic and socially radical Shakers, committed to celibacy and to equality between the sexes, settled New Lebanon, New York, in 1787. Shaker colonies spread to eight states over the next sixty years. The Mormons, harassed in New York for their practice of polygamy, made the long journey to Utah, where they founded their New Zion in the 1840s. In addition to such religious groups, other utopias were designed to secular specifications. What most of these hopeful schemes had in common was the ineradicable belief that human perversity was not the legacy of original sin but of environments that stunted the moral as well as the physical growth of the people who lived in them. Healthy living spaces and workplaces would shape healthy men and women. The immigrant industrialist Robert Owen, for example, established New Harmony, Indiana, in 1825 as a cooperative community based on handicraft and barter. John Humphrey Noyes founded "Perfectionist" settlements of Bible communists in Putney, Vermont, and Oneida, New York. Perfectionists became notorious for their doctrine of "complex marriage," which opponents derided as a euphemism for free love. In 1843, Bronson Alcott founded Fruitlands as a model socialist community. The venture immediately collapsed under the weight of its own extreme integrity. In *Transcendental Wild Oats*, Louisa May Alcott erected a parodic memorial to her father's scheme; Fruitlands becomes "Apple Slump," an eccentric haven for theorizing men and hardworking women.

The most notable of the scores of visionary collectives was organized at Brook Farm in West Roxbury, Massachusetts. The founder was a Unitarian minister named George Ripley, and the membership included farmers, artisans, and several of the transcendentalists. Loosely socialist in plan, Brook Farm was intended as a setting in which agriculture, handicrafts, and art would all have a place and in which manual labor would be amiably shared. The colony survived for only about six years, from 1841 to 1847, but its literary associations ensured that the undertaking had a large subsequent fame. Nathaniel Hawthorne was one of the original investors; he committed fifteen hundred dollars to the project and moved to the farm in April 1841, shortly after it opened. Initially he took part enthusiastically, accepting more than his share of the community's barnyard tasks. "He is our prince," Ripley's wife wrote of him, "despising no labor, and very athletic and able-bodied." Disillusionment quickly followed; within seven months, Hawthorne had left Brook Farm. For the rest of his life, he referred to the episode as a romantic daydream (Figure 72).

FIGURE 72 🥨 *Brook Farm in 1844*. Buildings are absorbed harmoniously into the landscape in this idealized contemporary painting of Brook Farm.

Hawthorne's departure from Brook Farm was less surprising than his joining it in the first place. He was not disposed to submit to a communal regime. More seriously, his deepest views of life were not in accord with the buoyant transcendentalism upon which the experiment was based. He often insisted on the distance between himself and transcendentalist opinions. His experiences at Brook

Farm itself provided some of the materials for his third novel, *The Blithedale Romance* (1852), an ironic assessment of the naive pretensions of the farm's inhabitants and, by implication, of all similar reformers. Earlier, in 1843, shortly after he left the farm, he published "The Celestial Railroad," which unmasks the defects of assorted liberal ideologies. In this story, transcendentalism is satirically personified as a fantastic giant, German by birth, indescribable even by his followers, an ill-proportioned heap of fog and duskiness. He fattens his disciples on meals of smoke, mist, moonshine, raw potatoes, and sawdust.

In fact, Hawthorne's response to the transcendentalists was more complex than this broad comedy would suggest. He was neighbor to most of the group, friend to some, and he acknowledged their cultural importance. In a paragraph affixed to the beginning of "Rappaccini's Daughter" (1844), he conceded that the transcendentalists "have their share in all the current literature of the world." Whatever his reservations, he was attracted by the moral earnestness of the transcendentalists and by their dissatisfaction with materialism and conventions. Like them, he was inquisitive about the intermixture of world and spirit, and he pondered the visible as a sign of the invisible.

At the same time, Hawthorne's romantic cast of mind was accompanied by an incorrigible irony that hung like a curtain between himself and his transcendentalist contemporaries. Unlike them, he was cautious about schemes for human perfection, and he was skeptical of any project that depended for success upon throwing off the burden of the past. The past had a far stronger hold on him than the future. His ancestral roots went back to the founding of Massachusetts, a heritage of two centuries that bore witness only to the ubiquity of human frailty. William Hathorne (it was Nathaniel who added the *w* to the family's name) was among John Winthrop's company aboard the *Arbella* in 1630. William is the "bearded, sable-cloaked, and steeple-crowned progenitor" to whom Hawthorne looks back, with feelings at once of awe and alienation, in "The Custom House" essay prefaced to *The Scarlet Letter*. William's battles for the Lord included the persecution of Quakers, among them a woman named Anne Coleman, whom he ordered beaten and banished. William bequeathed his puritanic rigor to his son John, who earned an unhappy immortality as one of the judges in the witchcraft

hysteria. Several generations later, the novelist's father, a merchant
sea captain, gathered a moiety of prosperity before drowning off the
coast of South America when Nathaniel was four years old.

The cramped circumstances of Hawthorne's childhood undoubtedly helped to mold his skepticism and his habitual air of detached
and wary observation. As a student at Bowdoin, from which he
graduated in 1825, he had already assumed an attitude of willful
isolation. A classmate, Jonathan Cilley, wrote: "I love Hawthorne;
I admire him; but I do not know him. He lives in a mysterious world
of thought and imagination which he never permits me to enter."
What might ordinarily be dismissed as undergraduate posturing
seems less theatrical in Hawthorne's case. He continued to live in
a mysterious imaginative world long after he left Bowdoin. In a
fabled act of disciplined retirement, he spent the dozen years after
his graduation sequestered in the attic of his mother's house in
Salem. In this "dismal chamber," as he called it, he spent his nights
and most of his days; here he read and thought and wrote, relentlessly
pursuing his artistic calling. English fiction and New England's history provided much of his reading, including the works of Spenser,
Bunyan, Cotton Mather, Fielding, Richardson, and Scott.

In 1837, Hawthorne published *Twice-Told Tales*, and with that
first volume he made his entry onto the American cultural scene.
Over the next quarter-century, he patiently produced just a half-
dozen more volumes, among them four novels and two or three
collections of stories. Authorship provided esteem but little income.
To support himself and his wife Sophia Peabody, whom he married
in 1842, he worked at a succession of jobs to which he was appointed
by political friends. He served as measurer in the Boston custom-
house for a few months in 1839–40, as surveyor in the Salem cus-
tomhouse from 1846 to 1849, and as U.S. consul at Liverpool from
1853 to 1857, during the administration of his friend and Bowdoin
classmate Franklin Pierce. The consulship was a reward for services
rendered to the Democratic party, including an adulatory biography
of Pierce that Hawthorne published during the campaign of 1852.
His last completed book, *Our Old Home* (1863), gathered the
sketches of England that he had written during his diplomatic tour
of duty.

For Hawthorne, the past that his family and region shared was
a moral tapestry interwoven of glory and shame, hope and decline.

Against transcendentalist uplift, he harbored a fixed conviction that men and women would always be pulled backward and downward by the taint that lay like a canker within human nature. The lesson taught by history was inescapable, and he summarized it in the opening pages of *The Scarlet Letter*, as he recreated New England's earliest days: "The founders of a new colony, whatever Utopia of human virtue and happiness they might originally project, have invariably recognized it among their earliest practical necessities to allot a portion of the virgin soil as a cemetery, and another portion as the site of a prison." The cadence of the prose matches Hawthorne's sober theme. Hope is a delusion fit only for the innocent, and innocence, as Henry James would also see, is disabling and even dangerous.

Human limits lie like a smudge across the promise of felicity. With almost compulsive frequency, Hawthorne explored the dilemmas of men and women cut off from the "magnetic chain of humanity," isolated by circumstance or by choice. His most typical stories are darkly lyrical meditations on the devastating consequences that follow when love is withdrawn, whether because of egotism or prejudice or a failure of sexual nerve. In "The Minister's Black Veil," the Reverend Mr. Hooper inexplicably covers his face with an opaque cloth, becoming for the rest of his brief life an emblem of secret guilt and loveless despair. In "The Birthmark" and "Rappacini's Daughter," men of science exchange human sympathy for a pernicious curiosity, ultimately murdering those they should love. In "Ethan Brand," the title character spends his life perversely seeking the unpardonable sin and finds it in the domination of humane feeling by manipulative intellect. Ethan Brand stands for all of Hawthorne's most malignant immoralists, a figure whose marble heart is merely an exotic symbol for the death of his human affections.

Almost all of Hawthorne's finest stories are remote in time or place. The glare of contemporary reality immobilized his imagination. He required shadows and half-light, and he sought a nervous equilibrium in ambiguity. Even his work that is set in the nineteenth century is usually marked by his characteristic preference for backward glances, for recovery and reconstruction. *The House of the Seven Gables* (1851) takes place in the Salem of Hawthorne's day, but the story's plot and the principal dramatic interest of the setting

FIGURE 73 ❧ G. P. A. Healy, portrait of Nathaniel Hawthorne (1852). Healy painted this portrait in his studio at the corner of West and Washington streets in Boston.

both depend upon the action of a seventeenth-century curse. Similarly, in *The Marble Faun* (1860), the present is overwhelmed by the long, lurid past of Rome. A history of ancient sin envelopes the book like the malarial fogs that settled on the city each summer. It was this history that Hawthorne evoked in the preface to the novel, when he contrasted the rich fictional opportunities of Italy's centuries with the relative emptiness of America's raw democracy:

> Italy, as the site of his Romance, was chiefly valuable to him as affording a sort of poetic or fairy precinct, where actualities would not be so terribly insisted upon as they are, and must needs be, in America. No author, without a trial, can conceive of the difficulty of writing a romance about a country where there is no shadow, no antiquity, no mystery, no picturesque and gloomy wrong, nor anything but a common place prosperity, in broad and simple daylight, as is happily the case with my dear native land. It will be very long, I trust, before romance-writers may find congenial and easily handled themes, either in the annals of our stalwart republic, or in any characteristic and probable events of our individual lives. Romance

and poetry, like ivy, lichens, and wall-flowers, need ruin to make them grow.

The irony here is of course multiple. Hawthorne's complaints about his "dear native land" were familiar enough, and they would be echoed and repeated throughout the following decades. Painters and sculptors in some numbers, among them Robert W. Weir, Horatio Greenough, and Hiram Powers, set up studios in Italy for longer or shorter periods in order to root themselves in the tradition they could not discover at home. Hawthorne, however, despite his disclaimers, had long since discovered in the early history of his own New England the ruins and gloomy wrongs he found congenial. The elusive geography of romance, that landscape in which imagination and reality could collaborate in acts of transformation, had perhaps disappeared from the bustling commercial world of Jackson, Van Buren, and Pierce, but it remained accessible to the historical imagination (Figure 73).

The Puritan ancestors who provided Hawthorne with his amplest materials also gave him his angle of vision and instructed him in his technique. He once planned to call a group of his stories "Allegories of the Heart," and in that unused title he summed up much of his method and his subject. His chosen terrain lay between the realms of theology and psychology, and allegory provided the means of his explorations. Christianity as such had no appeal for him. Nonetheless, within a culture of religious crisis, from which traditional verities and their consolations had been dismissed, Hawthorne continued to feel the enduring relevance of spiritual evil as a subject for fictional inquiry. He felt as well the tug of explanations beyond the mundane and rational. He was a secularized Puritan symbolist, who recovered the dramas enacted in cases of conscience by tracing the lines that bound men and women to their motives (Figure 74). Concerned with individuals as specimens or types, he endowed his characters with solemnly stylized features and then studied their anxiety, or doubt, or guilt. He placed them amid settings and objects that gave symbolic expression to their inward states.

Where traditional allegory was secured in certitude, however, Hawthorne's allegorical proceedings yield only restlessness and doubt. The stable system of correspondences that tied allegory's

THE GENTLE BOY

The boy had hushed his wailing at once and turned his face upward to the stranger.

FIGURE 74 🙵 Sophia
Hawthorne, illustration
for "The Gentle Boy."
"The Gentle Boy" was
reprinted in a separate
edition in 1839.
Hawthorne's wife Sophia
produced this drawing for
the frontispiece.

images and ideas together was lodged squarely upon the religious orthodoxy that Hawthorne rejected. In his belated version of the sacramental world, the links binding visible to spirit have become vexed and problematic. Henry James wrote that he found in Hawthorne's work evidence of "the constant struggle which must have gone on between his shyness and his desire to know something of life; between what may be called his evasive and inquisitive tendencies." James's antitheses quite adroitly capture Hawthorne's peculiar version of allegory. The flickering, uncertain revelations offered by the physical world in Hawthorne's fiction allow simultaneously for confession and concealment, for discovery and disguise. This doubleness generates tensions that can be felt throughout

Hawthorne's work, most memorably in his masterpiece, *The Scarlet Letter* (1850). The three great scaffold scenes that rise like spires in the architecture of the novel render fundamental human confrontations in which conflicting moral judgments find corollaries in contradictory views of reality itself. In the second of these scenes, Reverend Dimmesdale climbs the scaffold to confess his crime to an empty midnight square. The sky overhead is suddenly filled with the blaze of a meteor, whose intense, momentary glow lights the scene "with a singularity of aspect that seemed to give another moral interpretation to the things of this world than they had ever borne before." The alien grandeur of the scene confers a tragic nobility on the choices that Dimmesdale and Hester Prynne and Roger Chillingworth make. In the vanished New England of the seventeenth century, Hawthorne found the contrast and rebuke to the melancholy decay of his own generation.

He often chided himself for being an idler and mere scribbler. Though he never deserted his artistic allegiance, the looming specter of his grim, nation-building Puritan predecessors caused him to flinch apologetically from time to time. Furthermore, he was out of step with the prevailing entrepreneurial sentiments of his era, uneasy with what Henry James called the "genius of America." It was a genius, as James said dryly, that "has not, as a whole, been literary." These comments are taken from James's critical biography of Hawthorne, published in 1879, which was the first book-length study of an American writer. James's tone throughout the book is condescending: Hawthorne's achievement is pronounced modest, and in its modesty is summoned to prove how little could be produced in the inhospitable environment of the New World. Nonetheless, James accords Hawthorne a certain grudging eminence, and in doing so he followed the example of earlier critics, among them Poe and Melville.

Melville, reviewing Hawthorne's second volume of stories, *Mosses from an Old Manse*, in 1846, exulted in the "power of blackness" he found there. Melville (Figure 75) somewhat enthusiastically associated himself with what he took to be Hawthorne's belief in "that Calvinistic sense of Innate Depravity and Original Sin, from whose visitations, in some shape or other, no deeply thinking man is always and wholly free. For," Melville continued, "in certain moods, no man can weigh this world without throwing in some-

thing, somehow like Original Sin, to strike the uneven balance."
In acknowledging Hawthorne's mastery, Melville was offering sincere homage to a man fifteen years his senior, but he was also
disclosing his own longing for fraternity and affiliation. It might be
said that he needed to find his own deepest instincts verified in
Hawthorne's work. Even more thoroughly than Hawthorne, Melville had looked into the recesses of the human heart and found
uncertainty, violent struggle, and spiritual vacancy. "All men who
say *yes*, lie," he wrote in a letter to Hawthorne in 1851; "and all
men who say *no*, – why, they are in the happy condition of judicious,
unencumbered travellers in Europe; they cross the frontiers into
Eternity with nothing but a carpet-bag." Again, the comment is
ostensibly an estimate of Hawthorne, but its imagery and tone both
declare Melville's own imaginative allegiances.

His letters to Hawthorne disclose an ardent attraction; Hawthorne's responses, which have not survived, were apparently rather
cooler. Melville lunged toward affection with a forthright eagerness
that would have unsettled Hawthorne's considerable reserve. They
had a brief period of companionship, from the summer of 1850,
when Melville and his family moved from New York City to Pitts-

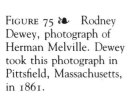

FIGURE 75 ☙ Rodney
Dewey, photograph of
Herman Melville. Dewey
took this photograph in
Pittsfield, Massachusetts,
in 1861.

field, Massachusetts, through the fall of 1851, when the Hawthornes left nearby Lenox. From first to last, the initiative was principally on Melville's side. It was a friendship without vitality, and it finally proved unsatisfactory to both men. Hawthorne was daunted by the tenacity of Melville's metaphysical speculations and simply puzzled by much of his writing. Some years later, after a visit from Melville in Liverpool, Hawthorne left this account of their conversation in his journal: "It is strange how he persists – and has persisted ever since I knew him, and probably long before – in wandering to and fro over these deserts, as dismal and monotonous as the sandhills amid which we were sitting. He can neither believe, nor be comfortable in his unbelief; and he is too honest and courageous not to try to do one or the other."

The sources of Melville's "unbelief" are of course unsearchable, but he had known something of the underside of the American experience and had seen firsthand the noose of circumstance that tightened around the lives of the poor and the unlucky. His own family's history illustrated de Tocqueville's reminder that America's celebrated mobility produced more losers than winners. Although Melville was descended on both sides from respectable and prosperous New York forebears, his father's bankruptcy and death when Melville was a child left the family in shabby dependency. He was unable to finish high school, and college was impossible; instead, as he later wrote, the sea was to be his Harvard and Yale, and his education began early. After desultory employment as a clerk and schoolteacher, he shipped for Liverpool as a common seaman when he was nineteen years old. The voyage produced a series of shocks and revelations: the unbending autocracy of the ship's chain of command; the casual cruelty of officers; the democratic camaraderie of the enlisted men before the mast; and, after landing in Liverpool, the poverty of English slums, human blight on a scale not yet known in America.

After returning to New York, Melville sought work unsuccessfully in the continuing depression that had followed the panic of 1837. In January 1841, he signed on as a hand aboard the *Acushnet*, a whaling ship bound for the South Seas. The next four years, which included hard usage under a tyrannical captain, desertion in the Marquesas Islands, captivity, and escape, provided the experiences and the material for reflection that sustained Melville through his first half-dozen novels. His first book, *Typee* (1846), was a fiction-alized account of his adventures in the Marquesas Islands, eked out with episodes alternately invented and plundered from the travel books of others. Melville more or less discovered the South Seas as a fictional subject, and in doing so he made his contribution to a widely popular genre. It was a time of exploration all over the globe, and the American audience showed a keen appetite for tales of the unknown and exotic. Poe's only novel, *The Narrative of Arthur Gordon Pym* (1838), carried its few readers on a fantastically unlikely expedition to the South Pole. In *Pym*, a rickety plot involving death ships, cannibalism, and an ersatz mysticism is superimposed on more sober material plagiarized from several factual reports of antarctic exploration. Two years later, Richard Henry Dana, Jr., published *Two Years before the Mast* (1840), a memoir of his own experiences as a sailor, a volume pioneering in its realism and detail. Dana was an affluent Bostonian who chose the rough life of an ordinary seaman and then wrote about what he had seen and heard with an amplitude and accuracy new to American letters. His intention, he wrote, was to "present the life of a common sailor as it really is." Dana's reports of shipboard life, his transcriptions of the sights and customs of Spanish California, and especially his portraits of his comrades, gave voice to a class of Americans previously unheard from.

Melville admired Dana's book, but his purposes in *Typee* were quite different. Subtitled "A Peep at Polynesian Life," *Typee* derives what thematic design it has from its pointed contrasts between the idyllic pleasures of native life and the barbarism brought by agents of white "civilization." Invoking Rousseau by name, Melville's nar-rator – an autobiographical surrogate named Tom – admiringly cat-alogs the abundance of the island and the health and beauty of its inhabitants. Melville brought back from the other side of the world a lesson not unlike the one Thoreau learned at Walden Pond, an insight into the superiority of simplicity and a need to fit life's means and ends to each other in humane proportion. Repeatedly Melville punctuates his descriptions of Typee happiness with bitter asides on the calamitous effects of European and American intrusions. Im-perialism has inflicted on the South Sea islanders the ravages of disease, the pettifoggery of legal systems, and above all the arrogance of Christian missionaries. "Among the islands of Polynesia, no sooner are the images overturned, the temples demolished, and the idolaters converted into *nominal* Christians, than disease, vice, and premature death make their appearance." Such is the fate of each peaceful island which suffers the invasion of those "rapacious hordes of enlightened individuals who settle themselves within its borders, and clamorously announce the progress of the Truth."

In the end, Melville was at home neither with the islanders nor with the values of white society. A sense of profound displacement offers the key to the book and to the shape of Melville's subsequent writing. At the same time, the volume's relative popularity became a burden to Melville as his literary reputation subsequently faded. "I shall be known only as a man who had lived among the cannibals," he wrote to Hawthorne with an affected heartiness. In retrospect, *Typee* seems prologue and footnote to *Moby-Dick*. It retains interest for the prophetic glimpses it offers of a man urgently in quest of answers to fundamental ethical and spiritual questions and probing beneath the deception of surfaces to find the bedrock of reality. In its combination of perilous voyage, metaphysical speculation, and social satire, and in its striking juxtaposition of realism and symbolic statement, *Typee* foreshadows many of Melville's chief concerns.

In the early years of his career, Melville published at a prodigious rate; seven novels appeared in the six years that separated *Typee* from *Pierre* (1852). In his own view, his sales depended on his conformity to the stereotypes and formulas of adventure fiction. His third book, *Mardi* (1849), elicited puzzled and even angry reviews, mainly because the straightforward journey that readers expected vanishes into several hundred pages of heavy-footed political allegory, the result of Melville's brooding on the fragility of American democracy and the failed European revolutions of 1848. *Mardi* was a commercial and critical disaster. The somewhat chastened Melville quickly produced two sea novels of a more conventional sort. In 1851, however, he published *Moby-Dick*, and with his greatest novel, he lost what remained of his public.

Moby-Dick is as massive as the beast Ahab seeks, but its plot, in Ishmael's laconic summary, is as simple as any adventure tale: "Here, then, was this grey-headed, ungodly old man, chasing with curses a Job's whale round the world, at the head of a crew, too, chiefly made up of mongrel renegades, and castaways, and cannibals." This rudimentary premise expands abundantly for one

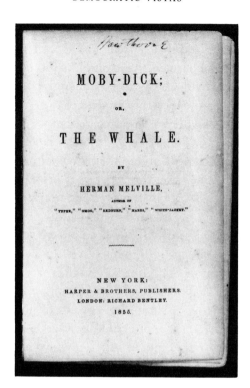

FIGURE 76 🎔 Title page, Hawthorne's copy of Melville's *Moby-Dick*.

hundred thirty-five chapters. The hunt for the white whale ultimately encompasses much of the political and economic history of America, and much of its interior disquietude as well. The book is a compound of lore, folktale, fact, and myth. Anchored in the business of whales and whaling, *Moby-Dick* is a primer on the growth of American industry, one of the few sustained and convincing representations in American literature of people actually working. At the same time, in the duel between Ahab and the whale, the book dramatizes a compelling encounter between the power of nature and the reach of the human will. Ahab stands before his men "with a crucifixion in his face; in all the nameless regal overbearing dignity of some mighty woe." The creature that leads him and his crew to their deaths is inscrutable in everything but magnitude and force. The whale's whiteness has the double signification of both good and evil; it "is at once the most meaning symbol in spiritual things . . . and yet it is the intensifying agent in things the most appalling to mankind" (Figure 76).

Near the end of the book, shortly before the final, fatal chase begins, Starbuck argues prudently and irrelevantly, that Ahab's pursuit of a mere animal, a "dumb thing," verges on blasphemy. Ahab's anguished answer confers an aura of evil legitimacy on his mad quest: "He tasks me; he heaps me; I see in him outrageous strength, with an inscrutable malice sinewing it. That inscrutable thing is chiefly what I hate; and be the white whale agent, or be the white whale principal, I will wreak that hate upon him. Talk not to me of blasphemy, man; I'd strike the sun if it insulted me." Starbuck's powerless common sense is no match for the authority of Ahab's rhetoric and his undeniable personal courage. Ahab bends the wills of his crew not only by his superior status but also because of his strength and mystery. His defeat merely testifies to the greater strength and mystery of a nature from which all the residue of benevolence has disappeared. In an epigraph to a later story, "The Bell-Tower," Melville wrote, "Seeking to conquer a larger liberty, man but extends the empire of necessity." Such is Ahab's fate. Gigantic in his scale and ambition, in the end he serves unknowable purposes beyond his own designing. Only Ishmael, who is needed to tell the tale, escapes the calamity that Ahab's rage precipitates.

The failure of *Moby-Dick* and of *Pierre* in close succession cast Melville's reputation into an eclipse from which it did not emerge until the twentieth century. In spite of his repeated disappointments, he produced much of the work for which he would later be admired in the 1850s. "Bartleby the Scrivener" presents a forlorn Wall Street clerk whose successive refusals – to work, to move, to eat – lead inexorably to his death in the New York City prison, the Tombs. It is a tale knit of barriers, blankness, and incomprehension, a disturbing study in radical alienation and death in the symbolic heart of commercial America. "Benito Cereno" dramatizes a slave mutiny and maps the transactions among innocence, self-deception, mystery, and evil that would reach a climactic extreme in the labyrinthine tangle of *The Confidence Man* (1857). None of these great works stirred the interest of critics or public. The last three decades of Melville's life were silent. He lived inconspicuously in New York City and spent twenty years working as a district inspector of customs there. "Billy Budd," a sort of final testament to the tragedy of innocence, lay unrevised among his unpublished papers. Several days after his death in 1891, the *Times* carried the obituary of a "Henry Melville," who was recalled as the author of *Typee*. His mordant prophecy to Hawthorne had been fulfilled; he was remembered – just barely – as the man who had lived among cannibals.

Despite all the differences of tone and attitude that separated Melville from the transcendentalists, he shared with them what might be termed their grandly paradoxical effort to yoke democracy and the sublime. Such an ambition also propelled Walt Whitman, whose steady belief in his own genius was matched by his devotion to the aesthetic value of America. On or around July 4, 1855, Whitman published the first edition of *Leaves of Grass* and permanently redirected the course of literary culture in America. It was a small book, ninety-five pages, published anonymously and at the author's own expense. Whitman shrewdly dispatched a complimentary copy to Emerson, whose five-page reply remains the most consequential act of sponsorship in the history of American letters. "I am not blind to the worth of the wonderful gift of 'Leaves of Grass,'" Emerson wrote:

> I find it the most extraordinary piece of wit & wisdom that America has yet contributed. I am very happy in reading it, as great power makes us happy. . . .
> I give you joy of your free & brave thought. I have great joy in it. I find incomparable things said incomparably well, as they must be. I find the courage of *treatment*, which so delights us, & which large perception only can inspire.
> I greet you at the beginning of a great career, which yet must have had a long foreground somewhere, for such a start.

Emerson was himself part of the long foreground, along with Whitman's experiences of childhood poverty, the countless odd jobs he had held, his work as a carpenter, printer, schoolmaster, and journalist, his love of the sea and of opera, his fascination with phrenology, astronomy, Egyptology, and animal magnetism, his absorption in the sights and sounds of the city, his homosexuality, his democratic politics, his delight in words. The man who looks out from the title page of *Leaves of Grass* is clothed in a jaunty confi-

FIGURE 77 ❧
Frontispiece portrait, first
edition of Walt
Whitman's *Leaves of
Grass* (1855).

dence. Slouch hat worn at a daring angle, shirt unbuttoned, one
hand on his hip and the other in his pocket: he is studiously indifferent to gentility and to the requirements of routine literary
convention. Many years later, Whitman said of this "carpenter"
photograph, whether in renunciation or pleasure: "I look so damned
flamboyant, as if I was hurling bolts at somebody – full of mad oaths
– saying defiantly, to hell with you!" (Figure 77).

Whitman wanted, he wrote, "to put a *Person*, a human being
(myself, in the latter half of the Nineteenth Century, in America),
freely, fully and truly on record." This would continue to be his
fundamental purpose through the remaining thirty-six years of his
life, during which he continually revised and expanded *Leaves of
Grass*. Nine editions of the book appeared, each longer than the
one before, each signaling Whitman's resistance to closure and completion. The volume grew with the man who wrote it and the nation
to which it gave voice. "The United States themselves are essentially
the greatest poem," Whitman wrote in the preface affixed to the
first edition. The tone of these double-columned, closely printed
introductory remarks is bumptiously patriotic. The essay is no preface

in the ordinary sense but a series of shouts on behalf of democracy, the American land, the common people. Energy is Whitman's unit of value, and by that measure he pronounces other nations tame compared to America's largeness and stir. This is the country that both nature and history have been waiting for, a nation at last correspondent with the doings of day and night themselves. America, with its "veins full of poetical stuff," needs poets to speak on its own mythy scale: "The American poets are to enclose old and new, for America is the race of races. Of them a bard is to be commensurate with a people. To him the other continents arrive as contributions. . . . He gives them reception for their sake and his own sake. His spirit responds to his country's spirit . . . he incarnates its geography and natural life and rivers and lakes."

The poem that would later be called "Song of Myself" was the longest of the dozen untitled selections printed in the first edition of *Leaves of Grass*. Triumphantly seeking and finding its own form, "Song of Myself" epitomizes Whitman's achievement. The poem simultaneously announces and exemplifies the potency of the liberated self; its opening lines mark the border between the past and future of America's literary achievement:

> I celebrate myself, and sing myself,
> And what I assume you shall assume,
> For every atom belonging to me as good belongs to you.

What Whitman assumes in the poem is nearly everything. All the nation's regions, classes, and races pass in review, and many of its trades and pastimes. Whitman's daring inclusiveness redefined the possibilities of poetry. Images and scenes are deployed in sequences that prove the theorem of American democracy:

> The pedler sweats with his pack on his back, (the purchaser
>   higgling about the odd cent;)
> The bride unrumples her white dress, the minute-hand of the
>   clock moves slowly,
> The opium-eater reclines with rigid head and just-open'd lips,
> The prostitute draggles her shawl, her bonnet bobs on her
>   tipsy and pimpled neck,
> The crowd laugh at her blackguard oaths, the men jeer and
>   wink to each other,

(Miserable! I do not laugh at your oaths nor jeer you;)
The President holding a cabinet council is surrounded by the
    great Secretaries.

Bride and prostitute, pedler and president are released from conventional hierarchy and make their equal contributions to the poetry
of the democratic nation. Where Emerson theorized about the power
of common speech, Whitman put that speech to revolutionary poetic use. The language of workplace and street enabled him to create
poetry unprecedented in its exuberance and empathic generosity.
Whitman called his first poem "a language experiment." He set out
to test the received limits of literary diction and to make use of a
vigorous, realistic vocabulary strong enough to chart his encounters
with self and love and death. In the "barbaric yawp" of "Song of
Myself" and his other poems, Whitman sang the visionary epic that
American culture had sought.

Whitman drew strength from a sympathy that extended to almost
every creature and person he saw. He once said that "what we call
poems" are "merely pictures." The "real poems," he insisted, are
men and women in all the variety of their human experience; it
was that reality Whitman yearned to express in *Leaves of Grass*. He
proudly insisted that he was the poet of the body as well as the soul.
Committed to reporting on life with unblinking candor, and stirred
by the joys and pathos of his own identity as a gay man, Whitman
virtually invented sexuality as a subject for American poetry.

Whitman repeatedly said that poetry must be organic, that it
must grow as naturally as flowers and plants. "Song of Myself"
exemplifies that romantic conception of aesthetic form. In place of
traditional structures, the poem moves according to a rhythm of
inner and outer discovery, creating a kaleidoscope of prophecy, lyric,
meditation, reportage, description, storytelling, and social comment. Expansion alternates with contraction, the turnings governed
by the poet's moods. Curiosity and sympathy may succeed each
other; despair or laughter can yield abruptly to the tug of desire. "I
am afoot with my vision," Whitman announces midway through
the poem, and in that phrase he gives perhaps the best summary
description of his design. The poem spans the continent, pausing
with literally hundreds of the men and women who people the cities,

farms, and plains, and offering glimpses of America's urban and natural landscape.

> Walking the path worn in the grass and beat through the
>   leaves of the brush,
> Where the quail is whistling betwixt the woods and the
>   wheat-lot,
> Where the bat flies in the Seventh-month eve, where the
>   great gold-bug drops through the dark,
> Where the brook puts out of the roots of the old tree and
>   flows to the meadow,
> Where cattle stand and shake away flies with the tremulous
>   shuddering of their hides,
> Where the cheese-cloth hangs in the kitchen, where
>   andirons straddle the hearth-slab, where cobwebs fall
>   in festoons from the rafters.

Whitman's catalogs can sometimes decline into mere lists. An exasperated Oliver Wendell Holmes complained that Whitman "carried the principle of republicanism through the whole world of created objects." This is witty, and it estimates some of Whitman's work accurately. On occasion, his itemized praise of what he called the "Democratic En-Masse" could be mechanical and inert. More often, however, his techniques unforgettably summon the manyness of America, taking poetry where it had not gone before, recording more of private experience and of the country's reality than anyone had yet done.

The third edition of *Leaves of Grass* appeared in 1860, and with its publication most of Whitman's greatest work was behind him. Along with "Song of Myself," he had in five years written the first versions of such masterpieces as "The Sleepers," "There Was a Child Went Forth," "As I Ebb'd with the Ocean of Life," and "Crossing Brooklyn Ferry." Each of these poems makes a distinctive contribution to that unfolding self whose revelation lies at the core of all Whitman's poetry. He assumes many guises in these poems, sometimes immersing himself in experience, sometimes standing aside in detached observation. Often the "real me" is distinguished from another, the "not me."

Whitman found an apt analogy for this drama of identity in the motion and changefulness of the sea. In *Specimen Days*, the "wayward, spontaneous, fragmentary" autobiographical reflections he published in 1882, he wrote that his imagination had been in thrall to the sea all his life. He was continually drawn to contemplation of the seashore, "that suggesting, dividing line, contact, juncture, the solid marrying the liquid." The seashore gave Whitman his image for the simultaneous allure of merger and separation, of communal mingling and solitude. The shifting, ceaseless contest between sea and shore came to seem "an invisible *influence*, a pervading gauge and tally," a sign of his own restless forays into the world. He was always, he wrote, going out and coming in (Figure 78).

The primal force of the sea offered rhythmic counterpoint to the most elemental human experiences, from birth to death. The sea was the womb of life, and its wet churning mirrored the embrace of lovers. Above all, the sea was the supreme hieroglyphic of death, the final mystery of existence. For Whitman, death was the meeting place of ecstasy and annihilation, and it became in a hundred variations the major theme of his poetry. He had his own example in mind when he called for great poets who would "make great poems of death." He regarded death with reverent fascination and derived from his meditations a mixture of terror and consolation. His imag-

FIGURE 78 ⁊ Thomas Eakins, portrait of Walt Whitman (1877).

ination of death aroused his deepest responses. The speaker in "Out of the Cradle Endlessly Rocking" recalls himself as a boy, searching along the shore for the word "superior to all," the "clew" that will unlock the riddle of life's purpose:

> Whereto answering, the sea,
> Delaying not, hurrying not,
> Whisper'd me through the night, and very plainly before
>   daybreak,
> Lisp'd to me the low and delicious word death,
> And again death, death, death, death,
> Hissing melodious.

In "Scented Herbage of My Breast," the poet says that nothing is finally beautiful except death and love, and of the two, death is identified as "the real reality."

Just a few months after Whitman wrote these lines, the Civil War brought the reality of death on a colossal scale. In the years before the war, he had aligned himself with Free Soil sentiments, but in general he took only a little interest in political questions. While his sympathy for slaves and fugitives was real enough, it coexisted with a commonplace racism and a voluble impatience with abolitionist agitators. The war's significance for Whitman was not ideological but personal; it brought him into daily and intimate contact with death. For three years, he served as a "wound-dresser," a kind of volunteer nurse, tending to the sick and dying, bringing companionship and comfort to literally hundreds of young men.

The bloodiness of the Civil War was unparalleled in American history. The "butcher's bill," as it was bitterly called, was over one million casualties – this at a time when the country's population had just passed thirty million. An appalling 60 percent of all the victims died. Sanitary conditions in the camps and hospitals were so primitive that more soldiers succumbed to disease and accident than to war wounds. A Confederate soldier wrote that "any one who goes over a battlefield after a battle, never cares to go over another. . . . I for one don't care if I am never near another fight again. . . . It is a sad sight to see the dead, and if possible more sad to see the wounded – shot in every possible way you can imagine." It was America's first "modern war," in which massed armies fought at close quarters and both sides made use of hugely destructive military technology. Thousands of men died in such battles as Shiloh, Gettysburg, and Spotsylvania. Twelve thousand Union soldiers fell at Cold Harbor in a single day; many had pinned their names and addresses to their uniforms so that those who found their dead bodies would be able more easily to notify their families. No American war before or since produced casualties on this scale.

Whitman wrote that "the real war will never get in the books." He felt that the war would remain unrecorded, because the scale of its carnage outweighed the bearing strength of words. In spite of that prophecy, Whitman himself produced in *Drum Taps* (1867) some of the war's preeminent memorials. "When Lilacs Last in the Dooryard Bloom'd," his tribute to the assassinated Lincoln, remains perhaps the most moving elegy ever written in America. Melville, too, wrote superb poetry in response to the war. He found in the national struggle the sort of epic subject his imagination demanded. *Battle-Pieces and Aspects of the War* (1866) is a sequence of meditations on the progress of events from John Brown's execution to Reconstruction.

The finest writer and speaker of the war was Abraham Lincoln. Poorly educated but well-read, Lincoln exploited his log-cabin origins and folksy appearance with shrewd calculation, and he brought a popular style to the conduct of the presidency. He was a master of image and rhythm, a superb storyteller who often deflected challenge and criticism with funny, sometimes ribald, anecdotes. In the most dangerous hours of the Civil War, he also crafted the prose in which commitment mastered despair. On the battlefield at Gettysburg, Lincoln delivered a speech that he described, with characteristic self-deprecation, only as "short, short, short." The whole text is just ten sentences long, and it probably took no more than five minutes to read, but Lincoln's tribute to the dead has remained a classic of American prose, a luminously simple and moving declaration of faith and solidarity. The ground on which the crowd had gathered, said Lincoln, had already been consecrated by the dead: "It is for us the living, rather, to be dedicated here to the

FIGURE 79 ❧
Photograph of Abraham
Lincoln (1865). This is
one of the last
photographs of Lincoln,
taken just four days
before his assassination.

unfinished work which they who fought here have thus far so nobly
advanced. It is rather for us to be here dedicated to the great task
remaining before us – that from these honored dead we take increased devotion to that cause for which they gave the last full
measure of devotion; that we here highly resolve that these dead
shall not have died in vain . . . " Lincoln made the scene at Gettysburg one of the rare state occasions when the burdens of a solemn
public moment received an adequate response (Figure 79).

As Lincoln's example correctly suggests, some of the most affecting literary records of the war are to be found in nonfictional
prose, including the eyewitness reports and the later recollections
of northern and southern participants. John William de Forest, for
example, who served as an officer in the Union army through the
war and into the early years of Reconstruction, sent a long and
remarkable series of letters to his wife. De Forest took part in some
of the war's most savage fighting, which he describes with the cool
detachment of a natural scientist:

> The nuisance of trench duty does not consist in the over-
> whelming amount of danger at any particular moment, but in

the fact that danger is perpetually present. The spring is always bent; the nerves never have a chance to recuperate; the elasticity of courage is slowly worn out. Every morning I was awakened by the popping of rifles and the whistling of balls; hardly a day passed that I did not hear the loud exclamations of the wounded, or see corpses borne to the rear. . . . It is a remark as old as sieges that trench duty has a tendency to unfit men for field fighting. The habit of taking cover becomes stronger than the habit of moving in unison; and, moreover, the health is enfeebled by confinement, and the nervous system shaken by incessant peril.

De Forest's stoic reflections on the waste around him alternate with an uncanny good humor and an irrepressible delight in the beauties of a summer day or the occasional full meal he managed to eat. Two years after the war, de Forest published *Miss Ravenel's Conversion from Secession to Loyalty*, a novel which William Dean Howells shrewdly praised as "the first to treat the war really and artistically." The realism of the battle scenes was strong enough to prevent the book's serial publication in *Harper's* magazine.

Private citizens, such as Mary Boykin Chesnut, and military commanders, among them Ulysses S. Grant and William T. Sherman, chronicled the war's progress at every scale of magnification. Chesnut's diary is the record of a highly placed Southerner, the wife of a Confederate general, a woman loyal to the cause and the values it represented but skeptical about all convictions that exact such a cost of death. Chesnut never published her diary, and her extensive revisions of it have raised questions about its value as a source. Nonetheless, the book offers arresting glimpses into the domestic lives of Southerners as they confronted the grim reality of inevitable and total defeat:

September 1st, 1864. The battle is raging at Atlanta, our fate hanging in the balance.

September 2nd. Atlanta is gone. Well, that agony is over. Like David, when the child was dead, I will get up from my knees, will wash my face and comb my hair. There is no hope, but we will try to have no fear. . . .

May 2nd, 1865. I am writing from the roadside below Blackstock's, en route to Camden. Since we left Chester, solitude;

FIGURE 80 ❧ Alexander Gardner, *Home of a Rebel Sharpshooter*. When Gardner published his photographs after the war, he wrote the accompanying titles and captions, usually including detailed information about the event represented. His comments on the picture he called *Home of a Rebel Sharpshooter, Gettysburg*, record two visits to the scene:

"On the Fourth of July, 1863, Lee's shattered army withdrew from Gettysburg, and started on its retreat from Pennsylvania to the Potomac. From Culp's Hill, on our right, to the forests that stretched away from Round Top, on the left, the fields were thickly strewn with Confederate dead and wounded, dismounted guns, wrecked caissons, and the debris of a broken army. The artist, in passing over the scene of the previous days' engagements, found in a lonely place the covert of a rebel sharpshooter, and photographed the scene presented here. The Confederate soldier had built up between two huge rocks, a stone wall, from the crevices of which he had directed his shots, and, in comparative security, picked off our officers. The side of the rock on the left shows, by the little white spots, how our sharpshooters and infantry had endeavored to dislodge him. The trees in the vicinity were splintered, and their branches cut off, while the front of the wall looked as if just recovering from an attack of geological small-pox.

The sharpshooter had evidently been wounded in the head by a fragment of shell which had exploded over him, and had laid down upon his blanket to await death. There was no means of judging how long he had lived after receiving his wound, but the disordered clothing shows that his sufferings must have been intense. Was he delirious with agony, or did death come slowly to his relief, while memories of home grew dearer as the field of carnage faded before him? What visions, of loved ones far away, may have hovered above his stony pillow! What familiar voices may he not have heard, like whispers beneath the roar of battle, as his eyes grew heavy in their long, last sleep!

"On the nineteenth of November, the artist attended the consecration of the Gettysburg Cemetery, and again visited the "Sharpshooter's Home." The musket, rusted by many storms, still leaned against the rock, and the skeleton of the soldier lay undisturbed within the mouldering uniform, as did the cold form of the dead four months before. None of those who went up and down the fields to bury the fallen, had found him. "Missing," was all that could have been known of him at home, and some mother may yet be patiently watching for the return of her boy, whose bones lie bleaching, unrecognized and alone, between the rocks at Gettysburg."

---

nothing but tall, blackened chimneys to show that any man has ever trod this road before us. This is Sherman's track. . . .

May 16. We are scattered, stunned.

Chesnut nursed Confederate casualties in South Carolina military hospitals and was appalled by the "loathesome wounds, distortion, stumps of limbs exhibited to all and not half cured." Like Whitman, she marveled at the persistence of courage and good humor in the midst of so much suffering.

The Personal Memoirs of U. S. Grant (1885) was written at the urging of Samuel Clemens and became one of the best-selling books of the nineteenth century. Grant's account clarifies the unfolding strategy of northern arms and conveys as well continuous glimpses of the war's human destruction. The restraint and dignity of Grant's prose lends authority to his staggering revelations. At one point,

he writes that bodies were lying so close together on the field at Shiloh that "it would have been possible to walk across the clearing, in any direction, stepping on dead bodies, without a foot touching the ground." In describing the Battle of Pittsburgh Landing, Grant recalls that he was caught outdoors one night during a pouring rain and so made his headquarters under a tree. He eventually sought shelter inside the only building in the area, a log house being used as a hospital: "All night wounded men were being brought in, their wounds dressed, a leg or an arm amputated as the case might require. . . . The sight was more unendurable than encountering the enemy's fire, and I returned to my tree in the rain." Grant's book stands at the juncture of journalism, history, and autobiography, and its enormous success owes much to the unexpected quality of the prose. Lacking in conscious artistic design, Grant's plain style gathers authority as it proceeds from one episode to the next, achieving the cumulative emphasis of unadorned statement. Samuel Clemens sincerely compared Grant's *Memoirs* to Caesar's *Commentaries*, insisting that it had a place with "the best purely narrative literature in the language." Over the years, good writers from William Dean Howells to Gertrude Stein concurred in that high estimate.

Memorials of the northern crusade to save the Union and the southern lost cause remained a major subject of American writing for decades after Appomattox, but almost all the books slipped immediately from the press into oblivion. The poetry of Melville and Whitman and a scattering of nonfiction prose comprise the war's scant literary testament. Ultimately, what Whitman called the "real war" found its most convincing voice not in words but in the battlefield photographs of Matthew Brady, Timothy O'Sullivan, and Alexander Gardner. It was perhaps fitting that the first American war to multiply slaughter through modern military technology should also be the first that was technologically documented. Brady and the others thought of themselves as entrepreneurs and craftsmen. They invented the techniques they used and intended to find a public for what they produced. Their equipment could only accommodate what was motionless or posed, which meant that their photographs included hundred of formal portraits. Partly for that reason, too, their supreme topic was death: the common soldiers of both sides pictured where they fell – in trenches, in open fields, sometimes in crowds, sometimes alone. These photographs stripped the war of its noise as well as its glamour, leaving only the pathos of the silent dead as the subject of contemplation (Figure 80).

Emily Dickinson called war "an oblique place," and the Civil War is rarely mentioned in her poems. The war encompassed the years of her most prodigious creativity; in 1862 and 1863, she was apparently writing at the rate of a poem each day. Yet the images of dissolution, slavery, and battle that recur in her poetry may have had their source as much in the religious traditions of New England as in the bloody struggles of Antietam and Gettysburg. The language of separation, servitude, and violent strife was the property of the preaching and singing that Dickinson grew up with.

She could never believe in the punishing God of her parents' faith: they worshipped "an Eclipse," she wrote, whom "they call their 'Father.'" Her own refusal to join in that worship came early. "When a Child and Fleeing from Sacrament I could hear the Clergyman saying 'All who loved the Lord Jesus Christ – were asked to remain' – My flight kept time to the Words." Nonetheless, though she ran from the church, Dickinson adapted the vocabulary of Christianity and the Bible, as she also made use of the common meter of the hymnbook. Ironically, her small poems come nearer to reproducing the ecstasy and terror of supernatural encounter than volumes of orthodox statement.

For generations, Dickinson was pent up in a set of trivializing myths, valued as a specimen of quaint eccentricity and harmless Yankee wit. In fact, her life was full, if not eventful. She was born in Amherst, Massachusetts, in 1830, died in the house in which she was born, seldom left Amherst, and traveled outside the state only once. She never married. She was often alone, but she was neither reclusive nor disengaged. To be sure, she contributed to the legends that surrounded her, sometimes slyly evading interrogation with a gentle irony that was taken literally. "You ask of my Companions," she wrote, "Hills – Sir – and the Sundown – and a Dog – large as myself, that my Father bought me – They are better than Beings – because they know – but do not tell – and the noise in the Pool, at Noon – excels my Piano." She had other companions than the hills, just as she had a better education than she confessed to. She was in touch with a wide circle of correspondents, and she bore a considerable responsibility for the supervision of a large home. Her existence was in most outward respects ordinary; in place of dramatic incident she lived inwardly with a rare intensity. She spent solitary hours, in her bedroom, pursuing the poetic vocation she so clearly felt. No one better than Dickinson exemplifies Marianne Moore's splendid description of the poet as a person for whom "there is society in solitude" (Figure 81).

Her lifelong habit of unflinching inquiry led her to discover the awe that resides within the compass of pantry and garden and the daily round of domestic life. In her poems, the routine of housekeeping can provide the emblems of the soul. Here, for example, is the experience of grief:

The Bustle in a House
The Morning after Death
Is solemnest of industries
Enacted upon Earth –

The Sweeping up the Heart
And putting Love away
We shall not want to use again
Until Eternity.

Dickinson's father was a severe and apparently joyless man, a lawyer "too busy with his Briefs," his daughter wrote, "to notice what we do – He buys me many Books – but begs me not to read

Daguerreotype of Emily Dickinson (1848). This is the only known photographic likeness of Emily Dickinson.

them – because he fears they joggle the Mind." She said that she "never had a mother," but she later acknowledged that caring for her mother during a long illness brought the two of them nearer: "We were never intimate Mother and Children while she was our Mother – but Mines in the same Ground meet by tunneling and when she became our Child, the Affection came." Dickinson reserved a less troubled love for her older brother Austin and her younger sister Lavinia, though even with them she guarded much. Lavinia Dickinson reported herself astonished to learn, after Emily's death, how much poetry her sister had written.

In addition to those she may have destroyed, Dickinson left over seventeen hundred poems. Only seven were published in her lifetime, denatured by well-meaning editors who smoothed them toward more regular rhyme and meter. The poems were published anonymously and without her consent. Whether out of shyness or self-reliance, she did not seek publication. Whatever curiosity she felt about the literary marketplace was annulled by contempt:

> Publication – is the Auction
> Of the Mind of Man –
> Poverty – be justifying
> For so foul a thing

She seldom sought literary advice. She did write to the critic Thomas Wentworth Higginson in 1862, abruptly asking, "Are you too deeply occupied to say if my Verse is alive?" Higginson, an abolitionist and admirer of John Brown, was radical in politics but conservative in aesthetics. His taste can be discerned from his remark that "it is no discredit to Walt Whitman that he wrote 'Leaves of Grass,' only that he did not burn it afterwards." In spite of his instinct for poetic propriety, Higginson felt the life in the odd-looking verses Dickinson sent him, and he did his best to encourage her, but he was fuddled by the "slant" rhymes and peculiar punctuation. Though Dickinson had nothing to learn from Higginson, she may have been pleased to have been taken seriously by a relatively prominent writer and editor.

In one of her letters to Higginson, Dickinson described her reading: Keats and the Brownings in poetry; Ruskin, Sir Thomas Browne, and Revelation in prose. The list was typically partial. She was familiar with Emerson and Thoreau, and she studied Shakespeare with devotion. (After visiting her, Higginson reported to his wife that Dickinson "read Shakespeare & thought why is any other book needed.") Her deepest imaginative affiliations included a number of nineteenth-century women writers on both sides of the Atlantic: the Brontes, Helen Hunt Jackson, Elizabeth Barrett Browning, and George Eliot, whom she primly referred to as "Mrs. Lewes," as if the novelist had married the man she lived with. Dickinson wrote three poems on Barrett Browning, addressing her as a mentor who made "the Dark . . . beautiful." She likened *Middlemarch* simply to "glory," and she wrote a moving tribute to George Eliot after the novelist's death.

Whatever her affinities, the hallmark of Dickinson's poems is in fact their striking originality. They seem barely touched by precedent, constituting instead a series of assaults against midcentury poetic canons. Indeed, the poems as Dickinson wrote them, punctuated by dashes of varying lengths and often including alternative words in the margins, almost defy transcription. Only in 1955 did Thomas Johnson's three-volume edition of Dickinson's poetry offer something approximating her manuscript texts. Johnson arranged the poems in as much chronological order as he could reconstruct, numbered them, and carefully noted the variants. Some of the alternatives that Dickinson considered merely shade meaning, while others reorient entire poems. For example, Johnson calls particular attention to no. 1333, a splendidly complex invocation of spring:

> A little Madness in the Spring
> Is wholesome even for the King,
> But God be with the Clown –
> Who ponders this tremendous scene –
> This whole Experiment of Green –
> As if it were his own!

The work sheet for this poem survives, and it records the extraordinary spectrum of choices that Dickinson considered in writing the fifth line:

> fair Apocalypse of Green
>   whole

```
        gay
        bright
        fleet
        sweet
        quick
        whole
This whole Apocalypse of Green –
        experience –
        Astonishment –
        Periphery –
        Experiment
    wild experiment
```

This remarkable list illustrates what Adrienne Rich had in mind when she described Dickinson as "equivocal to the end." Spring is "experience" or "astonishment" or "periphery." The two favored choices – spring as an "apocalypse" or an "experiment" of green – are metrically interchangeable but in every other respect antithetical. "Apocalypse" looks back to religious assurance and is redolent of last things, while "experiment" is synonomous with the future and the uncertainties of science. Yet neither alternative has to be preferred exclusively. They coexist, enlarging the poem's possibilities and displaying the plentitude of a powerful mind (Figure 82).

For Dickinson, words had a mysterious power. She wrote to a friend, Joseph Lyman: "We used to think, Joseph, when I was an unsifted girl and you so scholarly that words were cheap & weak. Now I don't know of anything so mighty. There are [some] to which I lift my hat when I see them sitting princelike among their peers on the page. Sometimes I write one, and look at his outlines till he glows as no sapphire." Dickinson uses words as if she were inventing them. In her poetry, language remains itself and becomes at the same time brand new. Everything has to be rediscovered or created. Her poem on the story of Jason and the quest for the golden fleece hints at the elemental intentions of all her work:

> Finding is the first Act
> The second, loss,
> Third, Expedition for
> The 'Golden Fleece'

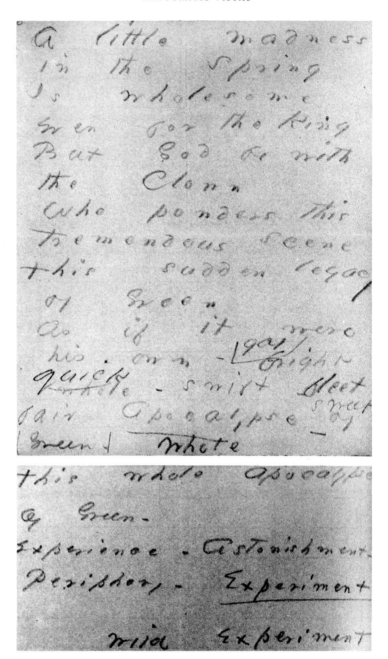

FIGURE 82 ❧ The work sheets for "A little madness in the spring," in Emily Dickinson's handwriting.

Fourth, no Discovery –
Fifth, no Crew –
Finally, no Golden Fleece –
Jason – sham – too.

This is witty sabotage, but its serious implications reach to Dickinson's task as an American, a woman, and a poet, the effort to build myth and meaning out of the native materials and homely experience of a New England household.

The tones of Dickinson's poems range from mild whimsy to impassioned delight to paralyzed despair. Pressing beyond the plausible limits of her metrical forms, her poems include unforgettable examples of satire, celebration, and elegy. She made extensive use of allegory, and she enjoyed riddles and puns. She handled abstractions as if they were familiar physical objects:

Presentiment – is that long Shadow – on the Lawn –
Indicative that Suns go down –
The Notice to the startled Grass
That Darkness – is about to pass –

Dickinson commemorated the fear that crouched in the corners of familiar rooms and the elation that attends the uncommon beauties of ordinary scenes. She could be cruelly funny. When she scrutinized the chilly decorum that masqueraded as piety in her community, she exposed it with evident relish:

What Soft – Cherubic Creatures –
These Gentlewomen are –
One would as soon assault a Plush –
Or violate a Star –

The greatest of Dickinson's poems contemplate the aching transience of joy, the brutality of pain, the inevitability of death. She rendered pain as if she were both patient and physician, reproducing its torment with a precision that stretches the capacity of language. She made anguish a sacrament and came closer to conveying the actual experience of death than any American writer. In several poems, the mouth of a dying woman is frighteningly described as "soldered." A poem that begins with a joke about a buzzing fly ends with the terrible moment when dying eyes "could not see to see." The funerals that occurred so often in Dickinson's Amherst enter her poetry repeatedly, sometimes as dramatic tableaux, sometimes as metaphors for unappeasable grief. Dickinson's darkest poems record the moment when the unaided, unsolaced soul confronts the threat of final vacancy, the dread that a fundamental emptiness gapes beneath the beams and girders of existence.

> I felt a Funeral, in my Brain,
> And Mourners to and fro
> Kept treading – treading – till it seemed
> That Sense was breaking through –
>
> And when they all were seated,
> A Service, like a Drum –
> Kept beating – beating – till I thought
> My Mind was going numb –
>
> And then I heard them lift a Box
> And creak across my Soul
> With those same Boots of Lead, again,
> Then Space – began to toll,
>
> As all the Heavens were a Bell,
> And Being, but an Ear,
> And I, and Silence, some strange Race
> Wrecked, solitary, here –
>
> And then a Plank in Reason, broke,
> And I dropped down, and down –
> And hit a World, at every plunge,
> And Finished knowing – then –

In poetry like this, Dickinson proved her citizenship in domains of tragedy and terror unexplored and even unsuspected by her New England contemporaries.

CHAPTER FOUR

❧ *An age of literary enterprise* ❧

THE DECADES following the Civil War seemed, to those who lived through them, a time of unprecedented acceleration and excess. The nation was transformed. In *The Gilded Age* (1873), coauthors Samuel Clemens and Charles Dudley Warner declared that "the eight years in America from 1860 to 1868 up-rooted institutions that were centuries old, changed the politics of a people, transformed the social life of half the country, and wrought so profoundly upon the entire national character that the influence cannot be measured short of two or three generations.'" The shocks that Clemens and Warner recorded were not so much measured as multiplied in the generations that followed.

From the Mississippi to the Pacific, new states were admitted, and territories were annexed and subdued in a frenzy of expansion and white settlement. Indians were penned in reservations, and Spanish towns of the South and West were absorbed into the continental empire. Enriched in numbers and diversity by a ceaseless arrival of immigrants, who numbered over ten million from Europe alone in the years from 1860 to 1900, America's population surged relentlessly westward. Early in the nineteenth century, Jefferson had predicted that it would take hundreds of years for Americans to people the western half of the country. Just three generations later, in 1893, Frederick Jackson Turner announced that the frontier was closed and in 1898 the United States commenced its career of overseas imperialism by provoking war with Spain and taking dominion over the Philippines.

Cities were swollen by immigrants and by those who left the farms and villages for the more alluring opportunities of urban life.

A GLIMPSE OF NEW YORK'S DRY GOODS DISTRICT
The Largest in the World.   Covering a Space of 135 Acres.   Containing 4,500 Firms.   Employing $800,000,000 Capital.

FIGURE 83 ❧ New York City dry goods district, 1880s. This photolithographic view of lower Broadway was produced by J. J. Fogerty.

In the four decades from 1860 to 1900, New York City grew fivefold, from three-quarters of a million people to three and one-half million (Figure 83). Chicago, a windswept cluster of wooden houses at the start of the Civil War, claimed a population of nearly two million by the turn of the century. Each census report documented the shift from countryside to metropolis. Cities, the focus of America's industry and commerce, became as well one of the chief facts of the country's imaginative life. With cities came the emergence of America's mass culture, which would become an increasingly inescapable fact of the nation's imaginative life. One index of the new relationship between cultural producers and consumers was the multiplication of magazines and newspapers, which grew from seven hundred periodicals in 1865 to thirty-three hundred twenty years later.

Though punctuated by periodic depressions in agriculture and the financial markets, the postwar years produced immense new wealth. The war's most destructive battles had been fought almost entirely on southern soil, and the South lay prostrate and impoverished for long years afterward. The North, on the other hand, was virtually untouched by the war, and its manufacturing was in some cases vitalized by the needs of a gigantic military enterprise. The war also taught lessons in organization and management which found lucrative application in the remainder of the nineteenth century. Led by northern industry, the nation rose out of the turmoil of the war to become by 1900 the world's leading industrial power. The country's economy and its daily life were simultaneously reshaped. Technology altered the relationship between people and nature and redefined the meaning of work.

Emerson confided to his journal in 1871 that "the splendors of this age outshine all other recorded ages. In my lifetime have been wrought five miracles, – namely, 1, the Steamboat; 2, the Railroad; 3, the Electric Telegraph; 4, the application of the Spectroscope to astronomy; 5, the Photograph; – five miracles which have altered the relations of nations to each other." Lists might differ, but Emerson's postbellum contemporaries all agreed that mechanical "miracles" were reshaping America's farms and factories and revolutionizing communication and transportation. In May 1869, amid much ceremony, the tracks of the Union Pacific and Central Pacific railroads were joined with a golden spike near Promontory Point, Utah, completing the first transcontinental rail system. What had been a harrowing four-week journey, involving travel by boat up and down the coasts and by mule train across Central America, was reduced to an uneventful ten days. In the 1870s and 1880s, the telephone, the electric light, and new machines for harvesting crops, making steel, and moving freight swiftly evolved from laboratory novelties into facts of commercial life.

America's leadership in manufactures and invention was taken as a material sign that the expectations of the founders were being fulfilled. The one hundredth anniversary of the Declaration of Independence, coming shortly after the future of the Union had been permanently assured, offered an irresistible opportunity to celebrate the country's new high place in the councils of world nations. In 1876, ten million people, nearly one-fifth of the entire population of the United States, visited the Centennial Exposition in Philadelphia, an entrepreneurial orgy of unctuous patriotism and moral uplift. Richard Wagner wrote the music for the exposition's opening events; President Grant led a procession of kings and commoners through each of the principal buildings. The vast exhibits that covered Fairmount Park, and the awestruck crowds that moved patiently through them, gave point to the New York *Times*'s editorial boast that America now stood "at the head of the phalanx of progress." The main building of the exposition, which measured 1,880 by 464 feet, was the largest structure in the world. In the thirteen acres of Machinery Hall, automated looms, sewing machines, and high-speed printing presses were on working display, all powered by the exposition's most conspicuous exhibit, the giant Corliss Engine (Figure 84). Forty feet high, and standing on a platform fifty-six feet across, the steam engine towered over its spectators. Its power was made impressively mysterious by its unlikely silence; the boilers were hidden in a separate building, and the great machine seemed to move with some hidden, inner life of its own. Walt Whitman, William Dean Howells, and the western poet Joaquin Miller were among those who stood before the Corliss Engine in abashed reverence, contemplating what they rightly took to be the future. To Howells, the exposition's painting and sculpture seemed paltry displays when measured against its machines. "It is in these things of iron and steel," Howells wrote, "that the national genius most freely speaks." Henceforward, the machine would compete with the pastoral garden as the emblem of America's most energetic imaginative longings.

In a revealing decision, the officers of the exposition ruled that *The Gross Clinic* (Plate 3), Thomas Eakins's first masterpiece and one of the strongest paintings ever produced in America, would hang in the medical exhibition, not in the fine arts section. Pain was, in effect, sequestered, and this one act of duplicity could stand for the point of view that presided over the entire event. The Centennial Exposition was a grand therapeutic spectacle, but its buoyant optimism contrasted with the dark places of the Republic and the hardships that assailed many of its citizens. In the 1870s, the country was subjected to a continuing series of tremors and alarms. The fair opened during the lingering depression brought on by the bank failures and financial panic of 1873. The national trauma was part of the weary cycle of boom and bust, but the public laid much of the blame at the door of Jay Gould, whose crooked speculations washed over Grant's cabinet and stained the presidency itself. The exposition was intended to distract the nation's attention from the venal opportunism of its leaders and the weaknesses of its political system. Sometimes, however, the fair's design itself unwittingly held a mirror up to the moral bankruptcy that crippled the country more profoundly than its collapsed banking houses. The separate Woman's Building, for example, was "very pretty and attractive," according to the fair's official history. Some acknowledgment was made of women's achievements in mechanics and

FIGURE 84 Corliss Engine, Hall of Machinery, Philadelphia Centennial Exposition (1876). This chromolithograph of the Corliss Engine appeared in the official history of the centennial exposition.

FIGURE 85 &ass; John Dost, *American Progress* (1872). This chromolithograph was published in 1873 by the New York firm of George A. Crofutt. It was, according to the publisher, "12 × 16 in size, painted in 19 colors, in the best manner, and is as richly worth $10 each, as any chromo that has ever been offered for sale in this country." A lengthy explanation of the picture's patriotic symbolism was printed on the reverse:

American Progress!

Subject, *The United States of America*

This rich and wonderful country – the progress of which at the present time, is the wonder of the old world – was, until recently, inhabited exclusively by the lurking savage and wild beasts of prey. If the rapid progress of the "Great West" has surprised our people, what will those of other countries think of the "*Far* West," which is destined, at an early day, to be the vast granary, as it is now the great treasure chamber of our country? How this change has been wrought, and by whom, is illustrated by our Chromo,

"American Progress."

Purely National in design, this beautiful painting represents the United States' portion of the American continent in its beauty and variety, from the Atlantic to the Pacific Ocean, illustrating at a glance the grand drama of Progress in the civilization, settlement and history of our own happy land.

In the foreground the central and principal figure, a beautiful and charming Female, is floating Westward through the air bearing on her forehead the "Star of Empire." She has left the cities of the East far behind, crossed the Alleghanies and the "Father of Waters," and still her march is Westward. In her right hand she carries a book – Common schools – the emblem of Education and the testimonial of our National enlightenment, while with the left hand she unfolds and stretches the slender wires of the Telegraph, that are to flash intelligence throughout the land. On the right of the picture is a city, steamships, manufactories, schools and churches, over which beams of light are streaming and filling the air – indicative of civilization. The general tone of the picture on the left declares darkness, waste and confusion. From the city proceed the three great continental lines of railway, passing the frontier settlers' rude cabin, and extending toward the Western Ocean. Next to these are the transportation wagons, overland stage, hunters, gold seekers, pony express, the pioneer emigrant and the war-dance of the "noble red man." Fleeing from "Progress," and towards the blue waters of the Pacific, which shows itself on the left of the picture beyond the snow-capped summits of the Sierra Nevadas, are the Indians, buffaloes, wild horses, bears, and other game, moving Westward, ever Westward the Indians, with their squaws, papooses, and "pony lodges," turn their despairing faces towards, as they flee from the presence of, the wonderous vision. The "Star"is *too much for them.*

What American man, woman or child does not feel a heartthrob of exultation as they think of the glorious achievements of *Progress* since the landing of the Pilgrim Fathers, on staunch old Plymouth Rock! What home, from the miner's humble cabin to the stately marble mansion of the capitalist, should be without this *Great* National Picture, which illustrates in the most artistic manner all the gigantic results of American Brains and Hands! Who would not have such a beautiful token to remind them of our country's grandeur and enterprise which have caused the mighty wilderness to blossom like the rose!!! One of the best art critics has pronounced this picture "*one of the grandest conceptions of the age.*"

---

engineering, but for the most part the Woman's Building was filled with embroidery, needlework, and flower arrangements. Thus, one hundred years after the founders had declared that all men were created equal, the centennial observance ratified the dogma that women's tasks would continue to be domestic and ornamental in the brave new technological world envisioned by the fair's planners.

Midway through the exposition, on June 26, 1876, national self-confidence was shaken when Gen. George A. Custer and a force

of two hundred sixty-four men were annihilated by the Sioux at the Battle of Little Big Horn. It was one of the few victories the Indians would win as the military and economic might of white America harassed them into reservations and extinction through the rest of the nineteenth century (Figure 85). Blacks, too, saw the fragile gains they had made since Appomattox and the commitments made to them evaporate together, in a sinister atmosphere of accommodation between North and South. The final days of the fair coincided with the notorious election of Rutherford B. Hayes, whose presidency was bound to the promise that the federal government would retreat from any effort to secure the rights of blacks. Working people who demanded their rights were fired, beaten, and sometimes shot. On June 21, 1877, for example, less than a year after the exposition closed, ten Irish coal miners in Pennsylvania, alleged members of the Molly Maguires, were hanged, primarily for the crime of union organizing. Pennsylvania's "Day with the Rope" was one of the most savage episodes of the labor warfare that would embroil the country for decades.

Trumpeting success and ignoring failure, the fair concealed the ominous divisions that separated the nation's classes. The wealth so prodigiously created in the postwar years was unequally shared. The chief beneficiaries of America's economic maldistribution were the heads of business, men who coined fortunes out of the new opportunities offered up by the country's land and resources. All three branches of the government put themselves at the service of money and the men who made it. In *Democracy* (1880), Henry Adams held a satiric mirror up to official Washington and titillated his readers with barely disguised sketches of cabinet secretaries, politicians, generals, and hostesses. "Democracy," he wrote, "rightly understood, is the government of the people, by the people, for the benefit of Senators." The senators, in their turn, were in the pay of business. The most powerful men in America bore names like Rockefeller, Morgan, Gould, and Hill, and they seemed to represent the highest achievements of a culture intoxicated by success. As the title of Andrew Carnegie's *Gospel of Wealth* (1889) suggests, stories of wealth were sometimes treated with the reverence usually reserved for Holy Writ. Russell Conwell, a Philadelphia minister, preached on behalf of success to packed halls all across the country. He is alleged to have delivered his most famous sermon, "Acres of Diamonds," over six thousand times; as a book, it was among the most widely read of the century. One of the most popular magazines of the later nineteenth century was called, simply and proudly, *Success*. Its pages were filled with biographies of the rich and famous, and it featured interviews between aspiring young journalists like Theodore Dreiser and such capitalist potentates as Carnegie, Morgan, and Philip Armour. *McGuffey's Readers* inspired conformity, self-discipline, and dreams of material comfort in generations of schoolchildren; adolescents read the same moral in the stories of Horatio Alger. Alger published over one hundred books for boys, repeatedly telling the glamorous tale of a young man's rise from shabbiness to affluence. Alger's interchangeable heroes included Ragged Dick, Tattered Tom, Dan the Detective, Tony the Hero. Some of his titles identify the themes: *Luck and Pluck, Strive and Succeed, Do and Dare, Brave and Bold, Paddle Your Own Canoe* (Figure 86).

The postwar years became synonomous with acquisitive lust and earned an assortment of colorful labels – it was the time of the "Great Barbeque," the era of the "Robber Barons." Samuel Clemens and Charles Dudley Warner attached the most durable tag to the period when they called it "The Gilded Age." The collusion between money and politics met some of its funniest and most effective resistance in the cartoons that became a staple of both the popular and the elite press. Thomas Nast, for example, helped to break New York City's Tweed Ring with a drawing that appeared in *Harper's Weekly*, just two days before the city elections of November 1871

"THIS IS YOUR LEGACY, HERBERT."

FIGURE 86 🔊
Illustration from Horatio Alger, *Herbert Carter's Legacy; or, The Inventor's Son. Herbert Carter's Legacy*, published in 1875, was the eighth and concluding volume in the "Luck and Pluck" series. Alger wrote in the preface that a single idea pervades the eight books: all the heroes "have met life manfully, and overcome by pluck and patience the obstacles which they found in their way." In this illustration from the first edition, the lawyer Spencer shows young Herbert Carter the clothing left to him as a legacy by the uncle for whom he was named.

The Tammany Tiger Loose. —"What Are You Going To Do About It?"

FIGURE 87 ❧ Thomas Nast, *The Tammany Tiger Loose*. Nast's most famous cartoon broadside against William ("Boss") Tweed appeared in *Harper's Weekly* in November 1871, on the eve of the New York City municipal elections. Partly as a result of journalistic opposition, including Nast's, the Tweed Ring was turned out by the voters.

(Figure 87). Joseph Keppler, who in 1876 founded *Puck*, the nation's first successful humor magazine, did his best to shame the greed and glut of the times in hundreds of stunning color caricatures.

In 1899, Thorstein Veblen dissected the values that accompanied prosperity and reported the results in the angry tones of a disappointed prophet. In his mordant classic, *The Theory of The Leisure Class*, Veblen spoke with contempt of the "pecuniary canons of taste" that deformed American standards and of the "conspicuous consumption" in which the rich indulged. For Veblen, the dominant figures of the period were the engineers and the bankers, who formed a tidy symbolic contrast between those who built and those who made deals. Engineers embodied the productive strength of America, the application of trained intelligence to the solution of significant problems, while the profit-driven bankers represented the corruption of greed. The crowds and buildings of New York became for Veblen, and for many other commentators, symbolic of the nation's future. The mansions of the rich, competing shamelessly with each other in size, rose above Fifth Avenue. They aped the splendor of European chateaus and villas and cast their battlemented shadows across the shacks and shanties that proliferated in the alleys behind them. Even more than other objects in the new consumer culture, Veblen concluded, buildings were designed under "the surveillance of expensiveness" and were thus especially well adapted "to the end of conspicuous waste."

Veblen's pages rehearsed the old debate over America's artistic destiny, raising once again the suspicion that the New World was still unready for serious art. This declared itself a major theme in the critical writing that followed the Civil War. Walt Whitman, chastened by the war's trivial moral consequences, lamented the failure of so much sacrifice to confer nobility on the survivors. Though he still looked forward to a day of fulfillment when the poets of democracy would write the grand poems of the people, Whitman was shocked by the spiritual malaise that seemed inevitably to infect material success. In *Democratic Vistas* (1871), he worried about the dichotomy between prosperity and poetry, and he scolded his fellow citizens for being content with a society that was "canker'd, crude, superstitious and rotten." Impatient and sometimes melancholy, Whitman fretted that the splendor of America's promise was at risk of being swallowed by the serpent of moneymaking.

Henry James found even less than Whitman to hope for in America's aesthetic prospect. James's views are fairly represented in an early story, "The Madonna of the Future" (1873). One of the story's characters is an American who is convinced that his nationality excludes him from the precincts of art: "He confessed . . . to his American origin. 'We are the disinherited of art!' he cried. 'We are condemned to be superficial! We are excluded from the magic circle. The soil of American perception is a poor little, barren, artificial deposit.' " A few years later, in his critical biography of

Hawthorne, James gave the indictment against America's artistic culture its definitive formulation when he listed all the attributes of civilization that the New World lacked:

> The negative side of the spectacle on which Hawthorne looked out, in his contemplative saunterings and reveries, might, indeed, with a little ingenuity, be made almost ludicrous; one might enumerate the items of high civilization, as it exists in other countries, which are absent from the texture of American life, until it should become a wonder to know what was left.

James then introduces a mock-epic catalog of complaint, comically long and detailed, deliberately reaching beyond climax to anticlimax:

> No State, in the European sense of the word, and indeed barely a specific national name. No sovereign, no court, no personal loyalty, no aristocracy, no church, no clergy, no army, no diplomatic service, no country gentlemen, no palaces, no castles, nor manors, nor old country-houses, no parsonages, nor thatched cottages, nor ivied ruins; no cathedrals, nor abbeys, nor little Norman churches; no great Universities nor public schools – no Oxford, nor Eton, nor Harrow; no literature, no novels, no museums, no pictures, no political society, no sporting class – no Epsom nor Ascot! Some such list as that might be drawn up of the absent things in American life.

When he wrote these words, James had just sailed away from the Great Barbeque to live for the rest of his life in Europe. The famous catalog was his seigneurial reply to the ringing choruses of patriots and boosters who insisted that America's racing economic indicators implied an elevated cultural station. In James's contrary view, America's imagination, such as it was, served the future, the individual, the dream of acquisition, and a commitment to indiscriminate mixing and leveling. But art, in James's understanding of it, required the past, a sense of community, the gift of reciprocity, and a devotion to high standards and fine discriminations. He concluded that there was simply nothing in America's untiring fascination with the here and now to nourish a significant literature, or painting, or sculpture, or even a decent conversation.

James's older brother William said that Henry was "a member

of the James family, and has no other country." The influence of that remarkable, intellectually competitive family on all its members was immense. Henry James, Sr., and his wife Mary Walsh James provided love and formidable stimulation to their five children. The elder James – rich, eccentric, hobbling on a cork leg from a childhood accident – was a familiar of Emerson, Lowell, and the other New England sages, a brilliant storyteller, an enthusiast of the arts, and a student of mystical religious experience (it was Howells who wrote that "Mr. Henry James has written a book called *The Secret of Swedenborg* and has kept it"). Brother William, after several false starts, pursued an academic career of exceptional distinction, influencing the development of American psychology and occupying a central place in Harvard's philosophy faculty during its so-called golden age (Figure 88). Alice James, the youngest of the five children and the only daughter, spent most of her life as an invalid. In spite of her illness, or perhaps because of it, she displayed an indomitable

FIGURE 88 𑁋
Photograph of Henry James (*left*) and William James (*right*) (ca. 1900).

intellectual vivacity; her letters and journals are among the high achievements of the James family.

From childhood on, the younger Henry James cultivated the habit of observation. By the time he was seventeen he had lived for several years in Europe, "gaping," as he liked to say, at the variegated manners and ceremonies of three or four different countries. He felt unfitted by artistic vocation for life in the hurly-burly of the postwar United States, but he was permanently suspicious of the moral price that Europe had paid for its luminous aesthetic achievements. His detachment from routine nationalist feelings served him well as a critic of comparative transatlantic manners. The contrast between America and Europe led to the principal themes of the fictional career in which James's life took its most significant shape. Yet precisely because his patriotism was all domestic, homelessness was an abyss that threatened his cosmopolitan assurance.

James consented to his literary vocation while he was still in his teens. His father, with a mixture of pride and dismay, called him a "devourer of libraries," and his reading, though eclectic, centered on the major and minor works of English and Continental fiction. With a self-conscious confidence that withstood the changing tastes of the marketplace and his reputation there, he set about to elevate the American novel to a higher and more professional level, to give it standing alongside the work of Balzac, George Eliot, and Turgenev. His first story appeared in New York's *Continental Monthly* in 1864, when he was barely twenty-one and the Civil War was still under way. When he died, over half a century later, in the midst of World War I, he was still at work, on novels, stories, reviews, and his autobiography. In his decades of writing, he produced over twenty novels and more than one hundred stories – in all several million words of fiction, together with scores of essays on art and literature, a dozen plays, travel books, biographies, memoirs, and literally thousands of letters.

James's earliest stories were American in setting, precocious and often witty tales of affluent people, typically at leisure, in New York, Boston, and Newport. In 1869 and 1870, he made his first adult trip to Europe, returning to England and France and traveling for the first time to Italy. His letters home glowed with his delighted reports of Europe's galleries, museums, and ancient buildings: "Venice is magnificently fair and quite, to my perception, the Venice of romance and fancy." Writing to his parents, his brother William, and such friends as Grace Norton and Thomas Sargent Perry, James reserved some of his most reflective passages for comments on the people he met and observed, especially the American tourists who so often taunted European reserve and sophistication with their raw transatlantic vulgarity. James had found his great subject, the encounter between the New World and the Old, and he announced his discovery in the tale "A Passionate Pilgrim," which appeared in the *Atlantic Monthly* in 1871. The story's title declares James's own ardor for Europe, and its young hero enacts his creator's cultural commitment to European history and values. In its theme and in its quality, the story was a rite of passage to James's mature undertakings; in dozens of subsequent novels and tales, he sifted the implications of what he called his "Americano-European legend."

In an era of multiplied middle-class traveling and of sensational marriages between American wealth and European titles, James's stories at first earned a measure of popular success. *Daisy Miller* (1878) made his fame. Indeed, the book became the narrow standard by which his more ambitious work would henceforward be measured, and it was rather ruefully that he later called it the "ultimately most prosperous child of my invention." James's tragicomic study of the young, free-spirited American woman in Europe, unbarnacled by convention and fatally ignorant of social codes, provoked amusement in England and resentment among his countrymen. "Daisy Miller" became a byword for a certain class of American innocent abroad, and James chafed with embarrassment when he was introduced as her inventor. To him, she was little more than a satiric sport, a "light, thin, natural, unsuspecting creature," sacrificed to a social rumpus beyond her understanding.

In 1880, James gave the international theme a far more complex statement in *The Portrait of a Lady*, the masterpiece of his middle years. Isabel Archer, the "lady" of the title, intelligent, curious, kind, and impressionable, arrives in Europe carrying only the baggage of her American naïveté. She has come, as James later wrote, for the purpose of "affronting her destiny," and she loses herself in the labyrinthine structure of a society at once cultivated and corrupt. Orphaned heiress of what seems at first to be a fairy tale, Isabel is ultimately stifled by a conspiracy that strips away her property, her illusions, and her freedom. Madame Merle, whom Isabel takes to be an ally and tutor, is in fact the architect of her undoing; an early conversation between the two women summarizes the debate between Old World and New as James dramatizes it here and in many of his other tales. Isabel asserts the irrelevance of material possessions, to which Madame Merle replies:

> "That's very crude of you. When you've lived as long as I you'll see that every human being has his shell and that you must take the shell into account. By the shell I mean the whole envelope of circumstances. There's no such thing as an isolated man or woman; we're each of us made up of some cluster of appurtenances. What shall we call our 'self'? Where does it begin? where does it end? It overflows into everything that belongs to us – and then it flows back again. I know a large part of myself is in the clothes I choose to wear. I've a great respect for *things*!

In response to this weary materialism, Isabel insists on the autonomy of the undisguised, unbending individual:

> "I don't agree with you. I think just the other way. I don't know whether I succeed in expressing myself, but I know that nothing else expresses me. Nothing that belongs to me is any measure of me; everything's on the contrary a limit, a barrier, and a perfectly arbitrary one. . . . My clothes may express the dressmaker, but they don't express me. To begin with it's not my own choice that I wear them; they're imposed upon me by society."

Madame Merle's description of the self as socially entangled stands face to face with Isabel's affirmation of the self-reliant Emersonian ego; the antithesis between civilization and innocence is drawn with almost allegorical single-mindedness. For his part, James's human sympathies were all with Isabel, but his conception of self and society accorded with Madame Merle's. As he said repeatedly (for example, in an 1884 essay on Balzac), his fictional method depended on a close reading of the textures and surfaces of human intercourse – the "cluster of appurtenances" that envelops each individual and knits men and women together in meaningful patterns of relation. That is why he chose Europe, where the protocols and ceremonies that accompanied old societies were more abundantly available to his inspection.

He worked inward, deducing what was morally and psychologically significant from what he sweepingly called the "manners" of a society. He was a realist ultimately of the inner rather than the outer life, as Joseph Conrad suggested when he called James "the historian of fine consciences." Thus, he accepted the obligation of the novelist to transcribe "experience," but he defined that elusive term by reference to perception, consciousness, and sensibility. "Experience," he wrote in "The Art of Fiction" (1888), "is never limited, and it is never complete; it is an immense sensibility, a kind of huge spider-web of the finest silken threads suspended in the chamber of consciousness, and catching every air-borne particle in its tissue. It is the very atmosphere of the mind." His interest was not in incident but in analysis: he cared passionately for what he called "the handling" of his materials. A letter that he wrote to H. G. Wells shortly before his death accurately declares the commitments of a long career: "It is art that *makes* life, makes interest, makes importance . . . and I know of no substitute whatever for the force and beauty of its process." Like his contemporary Henry Adams, James was bewildered by the clamorous and potent forces set loose by the Civil War, and he felt excluded from the nation's culture and its political arrangements. He turned in recoil to Europe and the transactions of the inner life.

In his pursuit of psychological truth, James perfected an imagistic style of densely ruminative subtlety, painstakingly sensitive to nuances of thought and feeling hitherto undetected in American fiction. His first great achievement in what would become his characteristic way of proceeding occurs in Chapter 42 of *The Portrait of a Lady*, where Isabel meditates, through a long evening, beside a dying fire, on the plot that has betrayed her. James himself called this episode "obviously the best thing in the book," and it demonstrates his capacity for fusing adventure and lucidity in the drama of consciousness.

Along with explorations of the international theme, James's characteristic subjects included ghosts, undervalued artists, ravaged innocence, and corrupted childhood. In the 1880s, he attempted to broaden the scope of his inquiry to include politics and reform in a series of ambitious novels, among them *The Princess Casamas-*

sima (1886), an unfriendly, unconvincing essay on European an-archism. When he did choose American materials, for example in *The Bostonians* (1886), an antagonistic account of New England feminism, his vantage point remained alienated. Above all, he never attempted to portray the "downtown" strongholds of business, the subject that he felt loomed largest in the buzzing, heedless democracy of late nineteenth-century America. He predicted that reputations would be made by those who could capture the turbulent worlds of commerce and industry for fiction; his own tastes and talents lay elsewhere.

James's quarrel with America was oddly and interestingly close to the position of those who put their faith in the nation's artistic promise. After all, his catalog in *Hawthorne* itemized nothing more or less than the cultural debris that a good many fervent democrats wanted to do without. Palaces and country houses and cathedrals and abbeys: was James not exposing the component parts of a caste-ridden, priest-ridden, senescent Old World? Was it not exactly the measure of the New World's more ennobling politics that it would dare to erect a society on less backward-looking terms? And if art were to be a casualty of the great instauration – "art," that is to say, as traditionally defined by European "high civilization" – more than a few Americans would welcome the loss.

Where James looked at America and found only blankness, writers like William Dean Howells and Samuel Clemens (Mark Twain) saw material enough to keep an army of novelists busy. James wondered "what was left" for a novelist in America; Howells answered, in effect, "everything." In a review of *Hawthorne*, Howells avowed that American novelists had "the whole of human life re-maining, and a social structure presenting the only fresh and novel opportunities left to fiction, opportunities manifold and inexhaus-tible." Clemens emphatically agreed. The job of "the native nov-elists," as Clemens called them, was not to generalize the nation but to depict each of the country's regions and peoples accurately. So marked are the differences, Clemens insisted, and so elusive the shadings of speech and manners, that it would take a thousand novels to capture them all. In a catalog of his own, written to refute the sneers of the French critic Paul Bourget, Clemens gives the answer as well to James's complaints about America's missing in-stitutions and traditions. The native novelist "lays plainly before you the ways and speech and life of a few people grouped in a certain place – his own place – and that is one book." Other novelists do the same. Gradually, the accumulation of these separate reports will begin to reveal "the life and the people of the whole nation":

> the life of a group in a New England village; in a New York village; in a Texan village; in an Oregon village; in villages in fifty states and territories; then the farm-life in fifty states and territories; a hundred patches of life and groups of people in a dozen widely separated cities.

Clemens is here speaking for one of the paramount features of America's postwar literary development. Though the vocabulary of reconciliation and unity pervaded the cultural prescriptions of journalists, preachers, and politicians after the war, the nation's literature in the latter part of the nineteenth century remained an incorrigibly regional affair. The plurality of American experience, the polyglot tongues of its people, the vastness of the continent, combined to affirm Clemens's democratic assessment of the nation's literary future:

> And the Indians will be attended to; and the cowboys; and the gold and silver miners; and the negroes; and the Idiots and Congressmen; and the Irish, the Germans, the Italians, the Swedes, the French, the Chinamen, the Greasers; and the Catholics, the Methodists, the Presbyterians, the Congregationalists, the Baptists, the Spiritualists, the Mormons, the Shakers, the Quakers, the Jews, the Campbellites, the infidels, the Christian Scientists, the Mind-Curists, the Faith-Curists, the train-robbers, the White Caps, the Moonshiners.

There is pride and defiance in this, along with its humor. "My choice," Henry James would write late in his life, "was the Old World." Samuel Clemens's choice was the New, in all of its ill-assorted, barely classifiable diversity. Often impatient with democracy and with humanity in the mass, Clemens grumbled against jury trials and widened voting rights, but he was instinctively loyal to America's common men and women. They filled his lecture halls, bought his books, provided the stuff out of which he fabricated his characters and stories. He had grown up poor himself, a child of the ragged frontier of antebellum Missouri. Self-educated skeptic and profane storyteller, he spent years drifting from job to job, among them journeyman printer and licensed riverboat pilot. Though he eventually made and lost more than one fortune, and ended up a legend, he always squirmed inside the starched shirts of decorum. Through Samuel Clemens, a new America pressed its claims to literary attention.

Clemens believed that the true road to what he called "the soul of the people, the life of the people" lay through their speech. In an age of nonstop talk, of oratory and sermons and lyceum lectures and traveling salesmen and carnival barkers, Clemens was the finest talker – and listener – in the land. More than any other writer of the nineteenth century, more even than Whitman, he recognized and exploited the literary possibilities of America's colloquial language. "There is no such thing as 'the Queen's English,' " he pugnaciously insisted, on behalf of his fellow Americans. "The property has gone into the hands of a joint stock company and we own the bulk of the shares." Clemens's prose is not merely an imitation or transcript of vernacular utterance but a selective, perfected new version of it. He had an uncanny ability to capture the swing and bite of ordinary speech, to reproduce its images, its vocabulary, and especially its rhythms. In an explanatory note prefaced to *Huckleberry Finn*, Clemens assumes a mock-pedagogical tone to make the serious point that seven different dialects have been used in the book, none of them "haphazard" or by guesswork but all with painstaking care. When Hemingway traced "all modern American literature" to "one book... called *Huckleberry Finn*," he was paying homage above all to the genius of Samuel Clemens's voice.

Clemens's antecedents lay in the tall tales and frontier humor of what came to be called the Old Southwest, an arc stretching from Georgia to Missouri. From the early years of expansion and settlement, the isolation, shapelessness, and routine violence of border life had been the forcing bed for a lively and luxuriantly vulgar oral culture. Humor provided a comic shield against the terrors that frontier dangers brought, and the tall tale offered an antidote to the absence of law and order. Ignoring the rules of grammar and of good behavior alike, frontier stories poked fun at the irrelevant pieties and the sedentary life of civilization. The typical heroes of these tales were larger than life but deliberately absurd, specimens of American individualism raised to an anarchic apotheosis. When the frontier's stories and characters made their way into printed texts, the results sounded like babble to some of the guardians of propriety; the New York critic E. C. Stedman, for example, complained about "the muddy tide of slang" that was deluging the country. Other readers, however, recognized the significance of the new voices.

Bret Harte, a dapper, fastidious man who had grown up in New York City, quarried an enormous if fleeting success out of the mountains and plains of the West. He edited San Francisco's *Overland Monthly* for two years, from 1868 to 1870, publishing his own work and that of other regional writers. Harte's sagebrush heroes and heroines broke new fictional ground, but his tales shrewdly appealed to the condescending curiosity of eastern readers by mingling realism and sentimentality. *The Luck of Roaring Camp and Other Sketches* (1870) included a gallery of exotic characters, caught up in melodramatic plots, who invariably disclose the natural virtue that their disreputable clothing and speech have disguised. Harte's stories brought him fame, but his most sensational success followed the publication of the poem *Plain Language from Truthful James*, universally known as *The Heathen Chinee*, which Harte himself described as "possibly the worst poem that anybody ever wrote." Regardless of its merit, Samuel Clemens said that the poem's publication in September 1870 made Harte "the most celebrated man in America today – the man whose name is on every single tongue from one end of the continent to the other." In sixty lines of rhyming narrative, in which two white men are cheated at cards by a Chinese man they set out to cheat, the poem exploits and subverts the stereotype that oriental ways are uncommonly tricky and dark (Figure 89).

As Harte's case suggests, most of the writers who made literary capital out of frontier humor kept a rather prim distance from the slang and bad spelling they recorded. Their tales typically included an introductory frame in which a well-spoken narrator carefully introduces himself as a visitor to the exotic hinterland and then tells a story in which assorted lowlifes are put on somewhat condescending display. One of the early frontier humorists, Augustus Baldwin Longstreet, opens many of the sketches in his *Georgia Scenes* (1835) with some little comment or other testifying to his detachment from the rustic comedy he is about to share. Nonetheless, whatever poses they insisted on, writers such as Longstreet, Johnson Jones Hooper, Thomas Thorpe, and (later in the century) Joel Chandler Harris in his tales of Uncle Remus performed the invaluable service of preserving what Samuel Clemens called "the hundred patches of life" that made up the heterogeneity of the United States. Longstreet himself wrote that the "leading object of the Georgia Scenes" was not humor but social and linguistic realism. In a letter to the editor of the *Southern Literary Messenger*, in which his book had been praised in an anonymous review (the notice was actually written by Poe), Longstreet said that he wanted "to enable those who came after us, to see us precisely as we are. . . . I have often desired to see the Greeks and Romans, as they saw each other. . . . The time will come perhaps, when the same desire will be felt to know all about us; and to gratify that desire, I am now writing."

Perhaps this was sincere – or perhaps Longstreet entered his polite, slightly defensive plea to justify his backcountry bumpkins to respectable readers. The distinction between high culture and low was still vigilantly enforced in many households, and the sketches and stories of the humorists were deemed inappropriate for family consumption. Much of the best work appeared in such news-

FIGURE 89 ❧ Cover of Bret Harte, *The Heathen Chinee* (1870).

BLOWN UP WITH SODA.

"Hole hit down, Mister Lovingood! hole hit down! hit s a cure for puppy luv; hole it *down!*"

Page 82.

papers as William T. Porter's New York City sporting journal, *Spirit of the Times*. It was in Porter's journal, in the 1840s, that George Washington Harris published his tales of Sut Lovingood, one of the most explosively vulgar characters in American literature. Sut is a scabrous vagabond, a creature of insatiable appetites for whom laws are made to be ignored, whisky is made to be drunk, and women are made to be abused. There is no endearing rustic charm concealed under Sut's spite and lust. Lazy except in pursuit of liquor or sex, he rails against any authority that gets between him and his carnal gratification (Figure 90). A cruelly brittle tone is one of the hallmarks of Sut's talk, as in this exchange about a burial:

FIGURE 90 ᐧᐁ *Blown up with Soda*, illustration from George Washington Harris, *Sut Lovingood's Yarns* (1867). Despite Dr. Goodman's advice, Sut is unable to "hole hit down."

> "Thar's one durn'd nasty mudy job, an' I is jis' glad enuf
> tu take a ho'n [drink] ur two, on the straingth ove hit."
> "What have you been doing, Sut?"
> "Helpin tu salt ole Missis Yardley down."
> "What do you mean by that?"

"Fixin her fur rotten cumfurtably, kiverin her up wif sile [soil], tu keep the buzzards frum cheatin the wurms."

"Oh, you have been helping to bury a woman."

"That's hit, by golly! Now why the devil can't I 'splain myself like yu?"

This passage gives a sample of Sut's nearly unreadable dialect, and it also implies, quite accurately, that Harris directs much of his character's bilious humor at women. Like many of his predecessors and followers, from Cooper to Samuel Clemens to Faulkner, Harris equates women with the constraints of adult society. Thus, his pranks are intermixed with misogyny, which takes the form, by turns, of injurious rage and contemptuous travesty. In this speech, Sut tells his interlocutor why he prefers the sexual company of widows:

"But then, George, gals an' ole maids haint the things tu fool time away on. Hits widders, by golly, what am the rale sensibil, steady-goin, never-skeerin, never-kickin, willin, sperrited smoof pacers. They cum clost up to the hoss-block [hitching post], standin still wif thar purty silky years playin, an' the naik-veins a-throbbin, an' waits fur the word, which ove course yu gives, arter yu finds yer feet well in the stirrup, an' away they moves like a cradil on cushioned rockers, ur a spring buggy runnin in damp san'. A tetch ove the bridil, an' they knows yu wants em tu turn, an' they dus hit es willin es ef the idear wer thar own. . . . Gin me a willin widder, the yeath [earth] over: what they dont know, haint worth larnin. They hes all been tu Jamakey an' larnt how sugar's made, an' knows how tu sweeten wif hit."

Prose such as this began as talk, talk that returned from the page to oral performance in the stand-up monologues of the itinerant comic lecturers whose postwar popularity signaled a seismic shift in taste. Antebellum lyceum lecturers had instructed their audiences in such weighty subjects as moral philosophy, English poetry, and classical architecture. After the war, these edifying topics were increasingly supplanted by political harangues and the lowbrow entertainment of men like Artemus Ward, Josh Billings, and Petroleum V. Nasby. Young Samuel Clemens learned the trade of humorous lecturing from Ward, and he toured with Ward, Nasby, and Billings

(Figure 91). Beginning as junior partner in the comic firm, Clemens rapidly eclipsed the competition and became the most successful platform performer in America. He mesmerized audiences with his shuffling walk, his superlative sense of timing, and his precarious but irresistible combination of worldliness and innocence. He delivered his "snappers," as he called them, deadpan and always seemed surprised at the commotion they caused. He quickly tired of the grinding travel that lecturing involved, but he was repeatedly seduced by the applause and money he could so lavishly earn. He enjoyed his fame. When he toured India, he reported that the only two Americans the Indians had heard of were George Washington and Mark Twain; when he walked down Fifth Avenue or stepped into a restaurant, he often received ovations. Clemens's experiences on the stages of a thousand concert halls and auditoriums had an inestimable value for his writing. Significantly, his first successful

FIGURE 91 ✌ *The American Humorists:* (*left to right*) Petroleum V. Nasby, Mark Twain, Josh Billings (1869). Taken by George M. Baker of Boston, this photograph of America's three leading humorists had a wide circulation.

story, "The Celebrated Jumping Frog of Calaveras County" (1869), reworked a well-known tall tale, and for half a century all his best prose, fiction and nonfiction, was filled with the sound of an authentic speaking voice. William Dean Howells, when he reviewed Clemens's second book, *The Innocents Abroad* (1869), said that he found an "amount of pure human nature . . . that rarely gets into literature." He also commented on the book's voice: "As Mr. Clemens writes of his experiences," Howells remarked, misspelling the author's name, "we imagine he would talk of them; and very amusing talk it would be: often not at all fine in matter or manner, but full of touches of humor, – which if not delicate are nearly always easy, – and having a base of excellent sense and good feeling."

The emergence of Clemens and other writers from the West and South marked the decline of New England's hegemony over America's literary standards. Bookmaking's commerce moved to New York City, and its imaginative energy diffused itself throughout the country. Howells himself voyaged east from Ohio, more like a pilgrim than a crusader, hoping to be admitted to the citadel of Boston rather than to topple it. Nonetheless, he was a Westerner, and his ascent to the editorship of the *Atlantic Monthly* in 1871 was widely understood as a portent of change. Howells's Brahmin mentors, Holmes and Lowell, spoke only half in jest of an "apostolic succession." For his part, Howells yearned for the approval of established literary authority, but he saluted the spontaneity and vigor that the West would bring to American letters, and he made the *Atlantic* a more ecumenical journal. Later, looking back on the eventful postwar years, Howells wrote: "The West, when it began to put itself into literature, could do so without the sense of any older or politer world outside of it; whereas the East was always looking fearfully over its shoulder at Europe, and anxious to account for itself as well as represent itself." A number of events might be invoked to summarize the watershed changes that were under way. One would be the January 1875 issue of the *Atlantic*, which included, along with poems by Longfellow and an essay by Holmes, chapters from Henry James's *Roderick Hudson* and the first pages of Samuel Clemens's "Old Times on the Mississippi." It was a table of contents that bridged much of the literary century.

"Old Times" was expanded eventually into one of Samuel Clemens's finest books, *Life on the Mississippi* (1883). It shimmers in the

glow of a recovered past, celebrating the unreflective joys of adolescence, glorying in the strong men who piloted the riverboats,
and above all paying tribute to the river that was so potently the
source of Clemens's inspiration: "the great Mississippi, the majestic,
the magnificent Mississippi, rolling its mile-wide tide along, shining
in the sun." Clemens often claimed, with a fond sadness, that the
steamboat pilot was the only truly free person on earth. His book
was an act of homage to a way of life that had, by the 1880s, become
obsolete. It was also a memorial to his own childhood before the
Civil War, the years in Hannibal when he stored up the experiences
and impressions out of which he created his most characteristic
fiction. From early manhood to old age, his reveries continually cast
him back to the days before the war and his own maturity had cut
him off from the past that he knew and loved. "School-boy days
are no happier than the days of after-life," he wrote in *The Innocents
Abroad*, "but we look back upon them regretfully because we have
forgotten our punishments at school, and how we grieved when our
marbles were lost and our kites destroyed – because we have forgotten
all the sorrows and privations of that canonized epoch and remember
only its orchard robberies, its wooden sword pageants and its fishing
holidays."

The willful mystification of his past explains the charms and the
limits of much of Clemens's work, including *The Adventures of Tom
Sawyer* (1876). This is "a boy's book," as Clemens correctly called
it, whose uncertain plot merely serves to carry Tom and his friends
from one comic or hair-raising escapade to another. *Adventures of
Huckleberry Finn* (1884), ostensibly the sequel to *Tom Sawyer*, begins
from similar premises but transcends them. It is Clemens's masterpiece, the novel in which his nostalgia coexists with a mature tragic
awareness. Huck's voice, one of the principal literary achievements
of the American nineteenth century, summons a world at once
earthy and mythic, in which America's promises stand in judgment
of what it has become. The journey that Huck and Jim take down
the Mississippi is a voyage into American history, a dissent from
the politics of opportunism that countenanced slavery. In *Huckleberry Finn*, Clemens wrote, "a sound heart and a deformed conscience come into collision and conscience suffers defeat." Huck's
sound heart and common sense pierce the shams under which America's greed and inhumanity lurked. When the members of the Con-

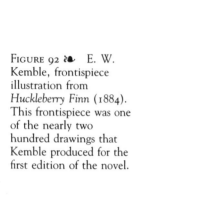

FIGURE 92 ❧ E. W.
Kemble, frontispiece
illustration from
Huckleberry Finn (1884).
This frontispiece was one
of the nearly two
hundred drawings that
Kemble produced for the
first edition of the novel.

HUCKLEBERRY FINN.

cord Library Committee banned the book, they called it "rough,
coarse and inelegant." To Clemens's credit, the indictment was
largely accurate (Figure 92).

Samuel Clemens's fiction is filled with orphans and strangers,
suggesting something of his own childhood and his divided relation
to American society. He was a drifter and a social critic who was
at the same time deeply rooted in the culture he satirized. He
complained that money had become the nation's God: "Gold and
Greenbacks and Stock – father, son, and the ghost of same – three
persons in one; these are the true and only God, mighty and supreme:
and William Tweed is his prophet." But Clemens worshiped the
golden calf he despised. While he lashed out at "the drive and push
and rush and struggle of the raging, tearing, booming nineteenth
century," he sized up his talent like a wary businessman and maintained a bookkeeper's vigil over his sales receipts. He wanted prop-

erty and freedom and comfort, and he also wanted the esteem that he bitterly conceded attended wealth in America. When his books and lecturing first made him rich, he built a grand house in Hartford, a Victorian extravaganza of gables and chimneys and porches. It was a seventy-thousand dollar advertisement for himself, dominating a five-acre hillside and declaring his unabashed contentment in success (Figure 93).

Spurred by dreams of profits, Clemens distributed his books by subscription, an indecorous but potentially lucrative system that involved squadrons of door-to-door salesmen fanning out across the country to peddle books, like other household commodities, in living rooms and kitchens in hundred of small towns. Boston disapproved of such hucksterism (which was also competition with Boston's publishing houses), but Clemens knew where his market was. "Anything but subscription publishing," he said to Howells, "is printing

FIGURE 93 ❧ Samuel Clemens's house: 351 Farmington Avenue, Hartford, Connecticut.

for private circulation." Clemens stalked the American dream into a hundred byways of investment and invention. He patented several gadgets, including a perpetual calendar and a history game, only one of which turned a (small) profit. He speculated continually in the stock market and in other people's ideas, until he lost nearly everything in the stillborn schemes of James W. Paige, whose type-setting machine was supposed to corner the printing market but only succeeded in ruining its principal investor in 1894.

Clemens always suspected that prosperity must inevitably lead to disaster, and the events of his own life seemed to confirm his fears. In a crushing year-long tour, he earned the money to pay off his creditors, but the shock of bankruptcy was succeeded by the tragedy of his daughter Susan's death, when she was just twenty-four, and his wife's decline into the permanent invalidism that led to her death a few years later. Another daughter, Jean, suffered from epilepsy. "The cloud is permanent now," he wrote in 1896, after Susan's death, and he came to think of his life more and more explicitly as a nightmare, a frightful dream from which there was no escape this side of the grave. In each day's papers he found new evidence of human barbarism, and he took an unhappy delight in constructing macabre allegories in which humanity is merely a col-lection of microbes in the intestines of some larger creature. He wrote feverishly, as if to exorcise his demons with his pen, com-pleting little and publishing less, page upon page of manuscript, continually revisiting the themes of disaster and guilt and death. Such fables as "The Man That Corrupted Hadleyburg" (1898) and "The Mysterious Stranger" (published posthumously) are tortured by a despair that verges toward nihilism and batters against ration-ality itself. Despite his private sorrows, Clemens remained an ad-ulated public figure in his last years. He made honorable use of his celebrity in the campaign against American imperialism, among other things contributing "To the Person Sitting in Darkness" (1901) to the antiimperialist cause. The frustration, guilt, and anger that seem to have been his daily companions occasionally gave way to the remembered joy and vigor he recorded in the autobiography he undertook near the end of his life.

For over half his life, Clemens enjoyed the friendship, the en-couragement, and the support of William Dean Howells. The con-nection began with Howells's kindly review of *Innocents Abroad*, which helped to gain notice for a book that might otherwise have been overlooked by established literary opinion. Howells and Clemens differed profoundly in temperament, but their western origins, limited formal schooling, and shared literary ambitions formed the common ground on which they stood together for forty years. When Clemens misbehaved, as he did in 1877 in a dreadfully miscalculated after-dinner speech lampooning Holmes, Emerson, and Longfellow as a trio of seedy drifters, Howells defended him. In his turn, Clemens almost always deferred to his friend's judgment and talent. "You are really my only author," he wrote to Howells; "I am restricted to you; I wouldn't give a damn for the rest." Clemens's estimate was more affectionate than discerning, but it overstates only a little the high regard in which Howells was held by his contemporaries. As author, editor, and patron, he more or less took charge of American letters after the Civil War and held his position through nearly two generations. In a career of daunting productivity, he filled over one hundred volumes with fiction, plays, verse, criticism, travel writing, biography, and memoirs. He became, in a widely repeated small joke, the "dean" of the nation's literature. When Howells was seventy, Henry Blake Fuller, one of the young writers he had promoted, wrote with plausible flattery that the last third of the nineteenth century was "the Age of Howells." A magazine poll in 1899 placed Howells first among living writers. He was, as Clemens gleefully wrote, "the head of the gang." When the American Academy of Arts and Letters met for the first time in 1908, he was elected president by acclamation and served in that honorific capacity until his death in 1920.

In his later years, Howells knew that in spite of his success critical opinion was passing him by. Two years before his eightieth birthday, he wrote to Henry James: "I am comparatively a dead cult with my statues cut down and the grass growing over me in the pale moonlight." Perhaps too readily, history accepted the dismissive verdicts of self-styled iconoclasts who fastened on Howells as a handy symbol of American Victorian gentility. Ambrose Bierce and H. L. Mencken began dismantling Howells's reputation while he was still alive, and Sinclair Lewis finished the job in his Nobel Prize address in 1930, when he sneered that Howells was "one of the gentlest, sweetest, and most honest of men, but he had the code of a pious old maid whose greatest delight was to have tea at the vicarage."

FIGURE 94 🙠
Photograph of William
Dean Howells (ca.
1910).

This sort of pique was graceless, and it was only partially deserved. Howells prospered rather too publicly for the taste of a later generation; he drove hard contractual bargains and even looked like a plump, bourgeois everyman. His enemies pilloried him as the busy shopkeeper of American letters, a man with a sharp eye on the till and a compliant sense of what his middle-class customers wanted. In addition, Howells was a man of undeniable sexual timidity, given to jittery recoils in the face of literary "uncleanness." He worried about being "smeared" with the physical in a poet like Chaucer, whom he otherwise tried hard to admire, and he found himself ridiculed, with some justice, as the fussy guardian of American morals (Figure 94).

Howells's condemnation by the heralds of literary toughmindedness is charged with a special irony, since he devoted the fiction, criticism, and influence of a long lifetime to the cause of realism. Along the way, he made indispensable contributions to the formulation of the post-Romantic aesthetic that America's new industrial and commercial preoccupations seemed to demand. "Howells is now monarch absolute of the *Atlantic*," Henry James wrote playfully to Charles Eliot Norton in 1871. Such as his journalistic kingdom was, Howells used the editorial power he inherited to expand its borders and enrich its expressive treasury. What is sometimes called his campaign for realism began with a long-meditated review of *The Hoosier Schoolmaster* (1871), in which Edward Eggleston blazed a rude literary trail to what Howells called "the intermediate West." Eggleston's Indiana, Howells wrote, was poised between pioneering and civilization – it was "the West of horse-thief gangs and of mobs, of protracted meetings and of extended sprees, of ignorance drawn slowly towards the desire of knowledge and decency in this world." Eggleston was only the first of a long list of postwar writers to whom Howells offered hospitality, either by publishing their work or reviewing it. Howells was a large-hearted patron, and he was often bravely independent, giving attention to those whom others had not yet discovered. In 1866, when Henry James had just a handful of stories to his credit, Howells wrote to E. C. Stedman that "young Henry James" was "extremely gifted – gifted enough to do better than any one has yet done toward making a real American novel." Over twenty-five years later, Howells was instrumental in legitimizing the work of Stephen Crane, and he offered patronage at one time or another to E. W. Howe, Hamlin Garland, Sarah Orne Jewett, Frank Norris, and Harold Frederic.

The realism for which Howells evangelized seemed to him a reasonably straightforward matter. It had various sources, among them local-color writing, which often became mired in dialect and sentiment but was based on the assumption that the daily life of common people was worth transcribing accurately. In contrast with romance, realism insisted on daylit explanations of cause and effect, and in this point of view showed its kinship with the ascendant empiricism of nineteenth-century science. The power of facts was asserting itself. Finally, the realist writers whom Howells promoted were typically fugitives from small towns who wrote of their rural beginnings out of a tensely ambivalent mixture of disenchantment and nostalgia. In short, realism for Howells involved both the choice of fictional subjects and authorial attitudes toward those subjects.

Though Howells was spacious in his judgments, his omissions

reveal his boundaries. In the twentieth century, to give the most famous example, he ignored Dreiser completely. Decades earlier, at the start of his own career, he had overlooked Rebecca Harding Davis. Unlike Dreiser, who found a host of supporters, Davis declined into relative obscurity for over a century after an auspicious literary debut. James T. Fields, Howells predecessor as editor of the *Atlantic*, had published Davis's first story, "Life in the Iron Mills," in the April 1861 issue of the magazine.

"Life in the Iron Mills" is an explosive study of the working poor, prophetic of the class struggle that would fill the main chapters of nineteenth-century labor history. Davis's story is remarkable for its solidarity with the cause of workers. Writers who took up the subject of the labor wars more typically enlisted on the side of corporate authority. In John Hay's *Bread-Winners* (1884), for example, the labor organizer is criminal, and property rights are endorsed as a stay against anarchy. Davis's allegiance, on the other hand, is altogether drawn to the human victims of the profit motive. In the flames and poisonous stench of the ironworks, bodies crack and lives drain away in the service of the new industrial order. The story's working men and women inhabit a closed, noisome world, moving as on a treadmill from the factory to the soot-covered company town where they snatch such comfort as they can from drink and sex and troubled sleep. Davis dramatizes the brutish conditions of labor from above, not within, but she addresses her subjects with passionate sympathy. Her proletarian characters are trapped in circumstances that later theorists would call naturalist. Reduced to an animal existence (her protagonist is even named Wolfe), the men and women of her story are pawns at once of fate and of a legal system that values their lives in pennies.

"You want something... to lift you out of this crowded, tobacco-stained commonplace," Davis lectured her readers in another of her tales. "I want you to dig into this commonplace, this vulgar American life, and see what is in it." This is instructive about Davis's democratic loyalties, but it suggests a more matter-of-fact attitude than she actually displayed in "Life in the Iron Mills." Her descriptions in that story, influenced by Dickens and the sensation novels of midcentury, are heightened toward melodrama by her urgent sense of moral responsibility:

> A cloudy day: do you know what that is in a town of iron-works? The sky sank down before dawn, muddy, flat, immovable. The air is thick, clammy with the breath of crowded human beings. . . .
>
> The idiosyncrasy of this town is smoke. It rolls sullenly in slow folds from the great chimneys of the iron-foundries, and settles down in black, slimy pools on the muddy streets. Smoke on the wharves, smoke on the dingy boats, on the yellow river, – clinging in a coating of greasy soot to the house-front, the two faded poplars, the faces of the passers-by. The long train of mules, dragging masses of pig-iron through the narrow street, have a foul vapor hanging to their reeking sides.

Like the later muckrakers, Davis is finally less interested in the artistic potential of "the commonplace" than she is in reforming an evil system. She has no political program to offer, just the example of her compassion and a fervent plea to Christian charity, but her anatomy of industrialism's human debris remains a moving testament of conscience. By the time she died, in 1910, Davis had been reduced to a literary footnote. Ironically, she had been supplanted in reputation by her own son. The pioneering searcher into social injustice was known principally as the mother of Richard Harding Davis, the glamorous journalist and hugely successful author of a long list of lightweight romances.

Howells had surely read "Life in the Iron Mills"; his apparent indifference to Davis's extraordinary work defines a circumspection in his critical judgments that is reflected as well in his own novels. He did not explore the worst of the nation's poverty, nor did he make the swollen cities and their slums his subjects. He did, on the other hand, patiently render the manners and customs of the unheroic, unexceptional men and women who had not previously been conspicuous in fiction. He said that "common, crude material" was "the right American stuff" and that his effort had always been "to fashion a piece of literature out of the life next at hand." James wrote confidentially to a friend that Howells lacked the "really *grasping* imagination" that could wrestle successfully with American subjects. Howells, who often met criticism with disarming modesty, might have agreed. His imagination was more scrupulous than grasping, carefully recording and preserving many of the surfaces of nineteenth-century American society. In a passage near the beginning of his first novel, *Their Wedding Journey* (1871), he writes: "I shall have nothing to do but to talk of some ordinary traits of American life . . . to speak a little of well-known and easily accessible places."

To those ordinary traits and accessible places, Howells remained loyal all his life, but his attitude toward his American materials darkened over the years. The most unfortunate opinion he ever delivered, that American novelists should concern themselves with "the smiling aspects of life," was in context merely a sensible contrast between the social circumstances of writers in America and Russia, and was in any case not typical of Howells's views. During the 1880s and 1890s, his unwavering democratic sympathies led him toward progressively more radical beliefs. He was disgusted by plutocratic greed and by the official complacency that ignored the suffering of the poor. Far from being a mouthpiece for comfortable pieties, he became one of the most eloquent opponents of the status quo. He began reading Tolstoy in 1885 and said that the "supreme art" of the Russian novelist had the effect of convincing him to "set art forever below humanity." Tolstoy's example helped turn Howells's steps toward socialism, and the trial and executions that followed the Haymarket bombing of 1886 pushed him farther along. The convicted anarchists, he wrote in 1888 to Hamlin Garland, had been "civically murdered . . . for their opinions." He adopted a vague, humanitarian socialism and used his novels increasingly as "bully pulpits" for the indictment of marketplace rapacity. In *A Hazard of New Fortunes* (1890), Basil March cries out against "this economic chance-world in which we live, and which we men seem to have created. . . . We go on, pushing and pulling, climbing and crawling, thrusting aside and trampling underfoot; lying, cheating, stealing; and when we get to the end, covered with blood and dirt and sin and shame." The century wore on, with no adequate reform in sight, and Howells wrote despairing letters to friends, expressing his abhorrence of "civilization" and predicting that a smash was inevitable unless society were rebuilt on the foundation of "a real equality."

The repeated political shocks of the late nineteenth century cut Howells loose from the hopeful democratic assumptions to which he had been tethered when he came east as a young man from Ohio. Like so many of his contemporaries, populist as well as patrician,

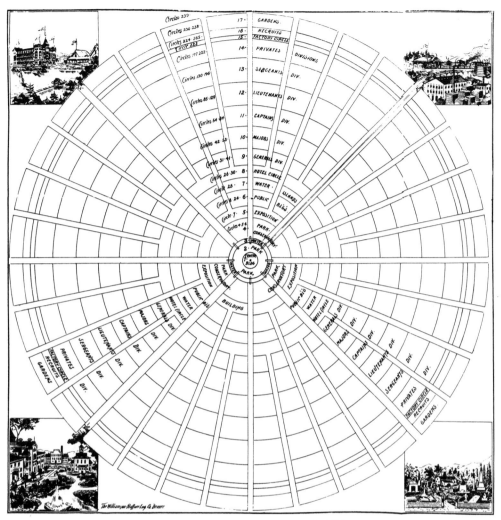

OUTLINE OF PLAN FOR NEW ERA MODEL CITY.

who had grown up in antebellum America and lived through the great changes of the postwar years, he drifted, turning for a while toward utopianism. Dozens of utopian tracts and novels were written in the 1880s and 1890s; they had little in common beyond a shared discontent with contemporary economic arrangements, and a tendency to earnest sermonizing. Charles W. Caryl's *New Era* (1897) proposed to solve urban problems by redesigning cities in a rational manner (Figure 95). The radically inclined Ignatius Donnelly, to give another example, used fiction as well as the Populist party to

FIGURE 95 ❧
Illustration from Charles W. Caryl's utopian tract *New Era* (1897). This map of a New Era model city was printed as an appendix to the book. The geometrical plan of the city, and its military hierarchy, were both typical of turn-of-the-century utopian designs.

battle plutocracy. In *Caesar's Column: A Story of the Twentieth Century* (1891), Donnelly extrapolated the technology and the deepening class divisions he saw around him into a shameful new world in which machines enable the rich to perfect their oppression of the masses.

By far the most successful of the utopian novels was Edward Bellamy's *Looking Backward, 2000–1887* (1888), which came to more optimistic conclusions than Donnelly's book and which Howells reviewed favorably in the June 1888 issue of *Harper's*. Bellamy's hero, Julian West, falls asleep in nineteenth-century Boston and awakens a century later to discover an America made ideal by human cooperation and the sane use of technology. The book had an enormous vogue, leading to the founding of Bellamy Clubs around the country and the brief flourishing of a Nationalist party. In Howells's own utopian romance, *A Traveler from Altruria* (1894), Mr. Homos, a visitor from the benevolent republic of Altruria, visits America and describes his homeland as a polity built on shared manual labor, full equality, and the collective ownership of property. Howells's utopianism, like his socialism, was more intuitive and hopeful than ideological, an expression of his honorably unprogrammatic kindness. In his last years, he settled reluctantly into pessimism, but he continued to speak out against injustice. He joined with William James and Samuel Clemens in opposition to American imperialism in the Philippines; he marched in support of women's rights; in 1909, when he was past seventy, he took part in the founding of the National Association for the Advancement of Colored People.

Twenty years earlier, convinced that Boston had become moribund, Howells had left New England for New York. His widely noted removal certified the end of Boston's literary dominance. The New England that succeeded the era of Brahmin hegemony was one among the many regions that made up the nation's loose cultural federation. Rose Terry Cooke, Mary E. Wilkins Freeman, and Sarah Orne Jewett were among those who best exemplified the work of late nineteenth-century New England. Each in her distinctive way wrote out of a consciousness of decline, an acknowledgment that Puritan rigor has stiffened into mere narrow-mindedness, and each exhibited a nervous fascination with the stunted lives of men and women left in the backwater of the great postwar changes. In the years after the Civil War, New England had lost prosperity, population, and political power, and the region's survivors were drawn by turns into resignation, satire, and nostalgia.

Cooke's stories, collected in such volumes as *Somebody's Children* (1881), *Root-bound* (1885), and *The Sphinx's Children* (1886), contain moments of fine comedy, but they deal more often in pathos. Convinced that something of value had disappeared from New England's life, Cooke simultaneously rejected and embraced the hard-dying myths of Puritan virtue. Her stories of brutal men and devastated women trapped in an unforgiving environment were a strong antidote to reverie and complacency, but they typically include concessions to the glory of a vanished past whose memory rebukes the present.

Mary Eleanor Wilkins Freeman was born in the small town of Randolph, Massachusetts, in 1851 and moved with her family to Brattleboro, Vermont, when she was fifteen. Freeman's memories, which she later shaped into fiction and poetry, were filled with images of long winters, stern religious preaching, families headed by tight-lipped fathers, and emotions kept always under watchful restraint. She began publishing her stories in the 1880s and continued writing through a long, productive life. In the tales and sketches she collected in *A Humble Romance* (1887) and *A New England Nun* (1891), she scrutinized the repressions that afflict village inhabitants, especially the women. Her stories, she said in the preface to one of her books, were "studies of the descendants of the Massachusetts Bay colonists, in whom can still be seen traces of the feature of will and conscience, so strong as to be almost exaggerations and deformities, which characterized their ancestors." In Freeman's barren settings, commitments have typically slipped free of principle; her characters are often trapped in the physical and emotional anguish of cropped and twisted identities (Figure 96).

Like most of the regional writers, Freeman was more successful as a story writer than a novelist. The men and women she wrote about are encumbered by the past and lamed by custom. Their days pass in an outwardly uneventful sequence; their dramas are intense but inward. Such unhurried, even motionless, lives are better suited to anecdotes, vignettes, and images than to the amplitude of novels. More than the men in her tales, it is Freeman's women who embody whatever remains of warmth and aspiration,

FIGURE 96 ❧ Pencil portrait of Mary E. Wilkins Freeman. The fantasticated dragon carries the calling card of Conscience, on which is inscribed: "At home/ Always – New England."

women like Louisa Ellis in the story "A New England Nun" and Sarah Penn, the title character in "The Revolt of 'Mother,' " whose outward shows of deference mask wills of iron and an unyielding sense of humane proportion. Their victories are often won by their quiet but emphatic resistance to the power of custom and tradition. The narrator of "The Revolt of 'Mother' " suggests that although Sarah Penn is a meek woman, her meekness is the "result of her own will, never of the will of another." She accepts her domestic role but never permits her independent spirit to be stifled. Sarah tells her daughter, Nanny, that women must accept their fate and must "reckon men-folks in with Providence" as implacable, inexplicable forces. However, instead of taking her own advice, Sarah bravely challenges her husband's misshapen values and secures a decisive triumph, an affirmation at once of her own dignity and her daughter's future.

In part because so many of the regional writers were women,

the strengths of their work long tended to be undervalued. "Local color" was inevitably used as a condescending epithet. Women such as Cooke, Freeman, and Jewett were banished to a rarely visited back parlor of allegedly quaint and merely antiquarian interest. Their work elicited grudging praise, in which certain recurring adjectives were combined to insinuate limits rather than accomplishment: "delicate," "sentimental," "exquisite," "charming." Such terms were not only diminishing; they were often wrong. Although Cooke and Freeman and Jewett certainly traded in melodrama and sentimentality, they also contributed their share to the realism that Harriet Beecher Stowe had pioneered, creating memorable portraits of small towns and their people. In particular, they sought out and commemorated the lives of women, and many of their stories are statements, sometimes of protest, sometimes of celebration, on behalf of obscure female lives. Another of Freeman's tales, "A Humble Romance," opens with an image of a woman defeated by the never-ending tasks of rural New England life:

> She was stooping over the great kitchen sink, washing the breakfast dishes. . . . The harmony between strength and task had been repeatedly broken, and the result was ugliness. Her finger joints and wrist bones were knotty and out of proportion, her elbows, which her rolled-up sleeves displayed, were pointed and knobby, her shoulders bent, her feet spread beyond their natural bounds – from head to foot she was a little discordant note.

The harassment and spiritual impoverishment implied in this woman's body was a common subject in regional fiction. Some stories, however, especially those of Jewett, declared the joy and power that resided in relationships among women. This was a theme repeated in the lives of the writers themselves. The lines of connection among New England's postwar storytellers were woven into a network of mutual inspiration and support. Sarah Orne Jewett chose her rural Maine subjects after reading Stowe's *Pearl of Orr's Island* (1862). Jewett praised Freeman's stories, and Freeman responded that she "never wrote any story equal" to Jewett's "A White Heron." Throughout much of her life, Jewett was friend and companion to Annie Adams Fields, the wife (and, after 1881, the widow) of publisher James T. Fields. The two women traveled together across America and Europe. On a trip to England in 1898, it was Annie Fields who brought Jewett to Rye and introduced her to James; ten years later, in Boston, it was also Fields who introduced Jewett to Willa Cather.

Jewett's imaginary New England places, among them Deephaven and Dunnet Landing, are the settings in which women reach out to each other across generations and form communities that stand in humane contrast to empty harbors and infertile soil. In Jewett's masterpiece, *The Country of the Pointed Firs* (1896), men are mostly absent; those who remain, like ancient Captain Littlepage, are back-looking wraiths. The matriarchal Mrs. Blackett observes that the men in the seacoast town went off to die at sea or in the West, and so "most of the home graves were those of women." Most of the stories in the town are those of women, too, tales of knitting, gardening, quilting, visiting, talking, and praying, which replace the gaudier adventures of Dunnet Landing's missing men. A family reunion becomes a ritual of integration, linking its members together in what Jewett's narrator calls "a golden chain of love and dependence." The idea of community, scanted in romances of frontier and flight, is here affirmed. It finds summary expression in Mrs. Blackett's small bedroom, lovingly described by the story's narrator. An old tufted rocking chair offers a view across Green Island to the sea:

> There was a worn red Bible on the lightstand, and Mrs. Blackett's heavy silver-bowed glasses; her thimble was on the narrow window-ledge, and folded carefully on the table was a thick striped-cotton shirt that she was making for her son. Those dear old fingers and their loving stitches, that heart which had made the most of everything that needed love! Here was the real home, the heart of the old house on Green Island! I sat in the rocking chair, and felt that it was a place of peace, the little brown bedroom, and the quiet outlook upon field and sea and sky.

There is a palpable sense of historical obligation in a passage like this, a duty to preserve scenes and lives that might otherwise disappear. While she was still a teenager, Jewett became indignant at the way in which visitors to rural Maine misconstrued the inhabitants. "I determined to teach the world," she later wrote, "that country people were not the awkward, ignorant set these people seemed to think. I wanted the world to know their grand, simple lives; and, as far as I had a mission, when I first began to write, I think that was it."

Jewett's work sometimes risked saccharine stock response, and some of her stories, for instance the overrated "White Heron," have the flat complacency of a smug fable. More typically, however, she avoided clichés, successfully endowing her rustic folk with dignified self-sufficiency and even heroism. Her characters, ordinary people absorbed in their daily tasks and satisfactions, correspond with the honest simplicity of their settings. Henry James had complained that America had no settings adequate for significant fiction: "no palaces, no castles, nor manors, nor old country-houses, no parsonages, nor thatched cottages," and so on. Jewett, who was rooted in the geography and architecture of New England places, proved that clapboard houses and country lanes could bear the full weight of tragedy.

Loyalty to America's plain and obscure people affirmed the democratic dignity of humble folks, but it could also slacken into teary sentimentality and pathos. Some of the most popular fiction of the later nineteenth century fed the national appetite for nostalgia, often equating the country's moral health with a vanishing rural simplicity. A fear of intellectual tumult, the consequence of Darwinism and other scientific threats to traditional verities, encouraged an imaginative retreat into the protective haven of the small town. So too did the enflamed nativism that greeted the millions of "new immigrants," as they were called, from southern and eastern Europe, who settled in seaboard and midwestern cities. The happy village life of such novels as Louisa May Alcott's *Little Women* (1868) and *Little Men* (1871) was also depicted in paintings that exploited patriotic and domestic themes and which included some of the century's best-loved images. Eastman Johnson's *Nantucket School of Philosophy* (1887), for example, paid pleasant deference to homely Yankee wisdom. Beginning in 1857, and continuing for years thereafter, Nathaniel Currier and J. Merritt Ives beguiled their middlebrow customers with lithographs on virtually every respectable subject, from country churchgoing and skating parties, to fashionable carriages in Central Park and steamboats on the Hudson and Mississippi. Thomas Hovenden's *Breaking Home Ties* (1890), which

FIGURE 97 🙐
Thomas Hovenden,
Breaking Home Ties
(1890).

circulated in numberless copies, was among the most widely familiar American paintings of its time. Hovenden's familial tableau, awash in the pain of farewell, was voted the most popular work of art at Chicago's Columbian Exposition of 1893 (Figure 97).

Cloying appeals of this sort to small-town sweetness and light also provoked strong counterstatements, a "revolt against the village," as it was called, that commenced in the years after the Civil War and continued into the mid-twentieth century. The cramped lives and values of Mary Wilkins Freeman's New England found counterparts in some of the writing that emerged from the Midwest and South as well. Hamlin Garland grew up in the Midwest, came east to try out his literary vocation, and returned to his family in South Dakota in 1887. That return, he later said, opened his eyes to the hard and bitter realities of life for the farmers and villagers of the country's heartland. The revelation of squalor propelled him into the stories of *Main-travelled Roads* (1891), in which he did what he could to demolish the Jeffersonian myth of agrarian virtue. In the preface to the book, he wrote that he had come to see rural life "from an entirely new angle. The ugliness, the endless drudgery, and the loneliness of the farmer's lot smote me with stern insistence." He intended his title to stand for his theme: the wearisome country roads are those that have "a dull little town at one end and a home of toil at the other." For Garland, as for Sinclair Lewis some thirty years later, small-town America offers neither escape nor a refuge from the welter of the changing world. Rather, rural people are crushed alike by their labor and their squinting prejudices; they scratch a meager subsistence from an unforgiving earth and huddle through bitter winters behind the faded curtains of their houses. Garland's method, as he described it somewhat ponderously in *Crumbling Idols* (1894), was "veritism," a version of realism dedicated in the spirit of Whitman to bettering the lot of ordinary men and women.

Southern literature in the later nineteenth century was surfeited with nostalgic romances that defended the Lost Cause and gazed wistfully back to the alleged sunny harmonies of plantation life before the Civil War. There were significant exceptions, including the work of George Washington Cable, Lafcadio Hearn, and Kate Chopin. As a teenager, Cable had served dutifully in the Confederate army. Shortly thereafter, in such northern magazines as *Scribner's* and *Appleton's*, he began to publish his sketches of Creole life. Seven of these were collected in *Old Creole Days* (1879), a volume that reveals Cable's humanitarian skepticism about provincial traditions as well as his considerable skill in reproducing vernacular. He soon came to reject the injustice of the South's racial caste system, and he became a spokesman for black civil rights. *The Silent South* (1885) and *The Negro Question* (1890) included lectures and essays that confronted the hypocrisy of southern culture as well as its politics. Southern literature, he said, had become a dishonest project, intended to sustain the morale of a beaten people by shielding them from reality and appealing to a mystified past. This sort of self-deluding literary commitment Cable could not honor. In his fiction and essays, and especially in his finest novel, *The Grandissimes* (1880), he stripped away the masks and pretenses under which the deformations of the South's moral life lay concealed. Though the novel was set in the prewar South, Cable wrote that it was also "a protest against the times in which it was written." He attacked the racism of his region with such gusto that he was more or less literally driven out; he moved from New Orleans to New England, where he wrote that he felt at home for the first time in his life.

Cable's odyssey was not unusual. The stultifying pressures of the southern myth and the bankrupt southern economy encouraged writers to seek air and opportunity elsewhere. Lafcadio Hearn, nomadic by circumstance and temperament, spent only a few years in the South. He was born in Greece of Irish-Greek parents, educated in Europe, and lived for a while in Cincinnati and New Orleans before settling finally in Japan. Hearn was a talented intellectual whose sheer delight in the alien, whether in Creole culture or in the Orient, alternated with more sober analytic responses. One of his earliest books, *Gombo Zhebes* (1885), was a collection of Creole proverbs. Among his last works was *Japan: An Attempt at Interpretation* (1904), written while Hearn was serving as professor of English literature at the Imperial University of Tokyo (Figure 98).

Kate Chopin, too, lived only for a while in New Orleans. She was born in 1851, raised in Saint Louis, and moved to Louisiana with her Creole husband. After his death in 1882, the thirty-year-old Chopin moved back to Saint Louis and began writing to support herself and her six children. Her most successful work, collected in *Bayou Folk* (1894) and *A Night in Acadia* (1897), was a series of sketches based on the Creole people and customs which she had

FIGURE 98 ❧ Lafcadio Hearn published "The Alligators," one of his "Creole sketches," in the September 13, 1880, issue of the New Orleans *Daily City Item*, the newspaper on which he had his first New Orleans job. According to Colonel John W. Fairfax, a Confederate veteran who was the owner-publisher of the *Item*, Hearn's woodcut illustrations were "the first newspaper cartoons in this part of the country."

observed during her marriage. Theirs was a society more European than American, in which canons of civility were more relaxed, and in which a langorous if cautious sensuality was regarded as the norm. Nonetheless, there were limits, imposed by racial prejudice and sexual double standards, and Chopin's tales often turn on the passions that break through surfaces of civilized restraint. Her stories find their analogy in the storms that sweep suddenly down on the bayous from the Gulf of Mexico, sometimes from deceptively clear skies. Her considerable early success was canceled by the scandal that greeted publication of her masterwork, *The Awakening* (1899). A frankly erotic and sympathetic exploration of female desire, Chopin's novella was denounced as obscene and then consigned to oblivion. There it remained for half a century.

Edna Pontellier, the main character in the book, is the young, Kentucky-born wife of an affluent Creole husband. She is a woman whose outwardly comfortable circumstances conceal a deepening though vague discontent. Confined by a society that will allow her anything except her autonomy, Edna experiments with art, with a separate residence, with adultery. After a friend gives birth to a child, Edna tells the woman's doctor as much as she can articulate of the sources of her unhappiness: "The years that are gone seem like dreams – if one might go on sleeping and dreaming – but to wake up and find – oh! well! perhaps it is better to wake up after all, even to suffer, rather than to remain a dupe to illusions all one's life." Edna's efforts to force an acknowledgment of her integrity are doomed; her subversive campaign of self-definition leads, with tragic inevitably, to her own death. The caged bird that cries out on the novel's first page, and the broken-winged bird that plunges toward the sea as Edna drowns, are conventional Romantic-naturalist images, but in context they are also poignant, efficient symbols of her catastrophe.

Chopin's stories, like those of Garland and Harte and Jewett, illuminated corners of nineteenth-century American experience that would otherwise have remained unseen. As Samuel Clemens had suggested, the sprawl of America could only be mastered by the combined diligence of a hundred native novelists. Only then would the nation's life be known in its particularity: "the life of a group in a New England village; in a New York village; in a Texan village; in an Oregon village; in villages in fifty states and territories; then the farm-life in fifty states and territories; a hundred patches of life and groups of people in a dozen widely separated cities." As Clemens had predicted, the city, too, became a fictional subject in the latter decades of the century. Resistance to the city had long been a cherished impulse in America's imaginative and political life. In the Republic's early days, Jefferson had exalted an agrarian ideal in which the country's care would be entrusted to its incorruptible small farmers. Suspicion of the urban masses was reflected in political arrangements that favored rural interests, even though each succeeding census declared that the expanding cities were to be the chief fact of America's demographic life. With their increasing numbers of immigrants, the polyglot cities seemed to genteel observers literally un-American. Whitman loved walking the streets of New York, and as early as midcentury he had incorporated the elbowing crowds, the organ-grinders, the street peddlers, the opera, and the ferry into his poetry, but his open-hearted precedent was largely ignored.

The burgeoning cities initially intruded themselves into the nation's consciousness more as problems than opportunities. Laissez-faire ideology made little provision for the welfare of the poor, but the investigations of academic and journalistic reformers added up the human costs of urban capitalism's unchecked greed. Some of the studies were statistical (it was the era of the new social sciences); others were anecdotal; almost all were shocking. In its own way, the point of view of these reports rather resembled that of regionalism and local-color writing. In particular, much of the work emphasized the distance between author and material. A book like Thomas de Witt Talmage's *Night Side of New York Life* (1885), for example, despite its author's uplifting intentions, threatened to substitute the urban poor for rural folk as picturesque subjects.

The most influential of the journalistic reformers was undoubtedly Jacob Riis, who published a series of landmark exposés, among them *The Children of the Poor* (1892) and *The Battle with the Slum* (1902). Though he was himself an immigrant, Riis felt only a blinkered sympathy for his largely immigrant subjects. He traded in ethnic stereotypes – Italians are inveterately greasy, Hester Street is the heart of "Jewtown" – and his zeal for justice was matched by a condescending and even scornful pity. Nonetheless, he forced his middle-class readers into closer contact than they had ever had with the festering slums of Bottle Alley, Five Points, and Mulberry Bend. His first book was a landmark: *How the Other Half Lives* (1890) stirred an outraged citizenry to action and led to corrective legislation and the eradication of some of New York's worst tenements. Riis spent years walking the streets of the Lower East Side and listening to its voices. As many as one million people were caged in a degradation that was always savage, and worst in summer:

> With the first hot night in June police despatches, that record the killing of men and women by rolling off roofs and window-sills while asleep, announce that the time of greatest suffering among the poor is at hand. It is in hot weather, when life indoors is well-nigh unbearable with cooking, sleeping, and working, all crowded into the small rooms together, that the tenement expands, reckless of all restraint. Then a strange and picturesque life moves upon the flat roofs. In the day and early evening mothers air their babies there, the boys fly their kites from the house-tops, undismayed by police regulations, and the young men and girls court and pass the growler [beer pitcher]. In the stifling July nights, when the big barracks are like fiery furnaces, their very walls giving out absorbed heat, men and women lie in restless, sweltering rows, panting for air and sleep. Then every truck in the street, every crowded fire-escape, becomes a bedroom, infinitely preferable to any the house affords.

Theodore Roosevelt called Riis the most useful citizen of New York; if the judgment was true, it derived in no small part from the illustrations included in Riis's books. Carrying his primitive and cumbersome equipment from one tenement or alley to another, he took his own pictures, dozens of images of blighted lives and ruinous buildings. Some were reproduced as facsimile drawings, but others were printed as Riis took them, and these photographs were among the pioneering works of American documentary journalism (Figure 99).

Urban America would have to be accounted for in any future national reckoning. In 1893, the skyscraper entered American literature in Henry B. Fuller's *Cliff-Dwellers*. Fuller turned the tall buildings of Chicago into symbols for the potent, prosperous future. The skyscraper gained recognition around the world as the quintessential American building, at once a technological marvel and a

coolheaded, economical response to rising real estate values. Over
the next generation, Fuller's emblematic use of tall buildings became
commonplace. Shortly after the turn of the century, for example,
in "The Genteel Tradition in American Philosophy," George Santayana declared that the skyscraper is "all aggressive enterprise," the
dwelling place of "the American Will."

A rather different comment on American cities and their buildings than those of either Riis or Fuller was embodied in the Columbian Exposition of 1893. The exposition, a slightly tardy tribute to
the four-hundredth anniversary of Columbus's voyage to the New
World, gave Chicago's city fathers the happy chance to say what
they would about their city and nation. Under the supervision of

FIGURE 99 ❧ Jacob
Riis, *Bandit's Roost*. Riis
photographed this alley
off Mulberry Street in
New York City in 1887
or 1888.

FIGURE 100 ❧ Court of Honor, World's
Columbian Exposition (1893). This panorama of
the White City includes several of the exposition's
principal structures. The Manufactures and Liberal
Arts Building, on the left, was connected to the
domed Agricultural Building by the Peristyle,
whose forty-eight pillars represented the states and
territories of the Union. On top of the Peristyle's
central water gate was the Quadriga group,
portraying the triumphal entry of Columbus into
the city. The colossal figure of the Republic stood
in front of the gate, at the east end of the Grand
Basin. In the right foreground, Frederick
MacMonnies's fountain and statuary group
presented Columbia enthroned on a barge of state,
with female figures representing the arts and
sciences at the oars and Father Time at the helm.

Daniel Burnham, one of the country's most prominent architects
and planners, the exposition simply annulled the modern city by
absorbing it into an idealized urban myth. The Court of Honor, the
colossal ensemble of buildings that dominated the Lake Michigan
site, was known as the White City (Figure 100). Here were acres
of neoclassical imitation, all confined to a uniform height, and all
made out of painted plaster. There were no skyscrapers here, though

the first Ferris Wheel loomed over the amusement parks of the fair's midway. While the antiseptic decor of the White City had no apparent connection with the actualities of America's urban life, nonetheless the grandiose utopianism of Burnham's three-dimensional dream was much welcomed. Frederick Douglass jibed that the exposition was "a whited sepulchre," but his dissent was an exception. Rather more typical was William Dean Howells, who thought the "Fair City" was like his fictional Altruria in its promise. Thirty years later, Theodore Dreiser still looked back in awe on the "vast and harmonious collection of perfectly constructed and snowy buildings" that he had seen as a young man. The beaux-arts columns and gilded statuary of the exposition offered reassurance that America had come of age and provided the stylistic vocabulary that the nation's imperial ambitions required. Louis Sullivan's dissonant Transportation Building was relegated to a back avenue.

Like all world's fairs, the Columbian Exposition was primarily festivity and spectacle. Among its many attractions were the exotic dancing of Little Egypt; an Alpine cyclorama lighted by electric bulbs and called, in the fair's official history, "the largest picture ever painted"; and an equestrian statue made completely out of dried prunes (California's contribution). The fair was a diversion from the intractable problems of American life in 1893, chief among them the financial panic of that year. At the same time, the planners felt an obligation to provide culture as well as titillation, and the exposition therefore offered a panoply of more sober and educational exhibits, including elaborate ethnographic displays instructing fair-goers in the superiority of the white race. Among the academic events was a meeting of the American Historical Association at which Henry Adams was elected president. During that same meeting, Frederick Jackson Turner delivered a paper of momentous consequence entitled "The Significance of the Frontier in American History." Turner argued that academic historians, who were almost all eastern in background and orientation, had revealed more of regional bias than of objectivity in their work. They had misconceived the country by studying only the East Coast and by interpreting American government and politics primarily as continuations of European institutions. "The true point of view in the history of this nation is not the Atlantic coast," he said, "it is the Great West." It was the frontier, that vast area of free land, constantly receding, that shaped America's development. Turner deduced the whole of America's character from the conditions that men and women faced on the frontier, and he enumerated them with evident relish: "That coarseness and strength combined with acuteness and inquisitiveness; that practical, inventive turn of mind, quick to find expedients; that masterful grasp of material things, lacking in the artistic but powerful to effect great ends; that restless, nervous energy; that dominant individualism, working for good and for evil, and withal that buoyancy and exuberance which comes with freedom – these are the traits of the frontier." Above all, by promoting individualism, by nourishing a habit of self-reliance in response to wilderness demands, the frontier had made democracy possible. In an irony of timing over which Turner himself lingered, he was announcing the seminal relationship of the frontier to democracy at precisely the moment when the frontier closed. Whatever the merits of his analysis, he was, willy-nilly, conferring privilege on the past. In short, though his paper was different in many obvious ways from the architecture of the building in which he delivered it, his views also served to nourish nostalgia and myth-making. Like Burnham's buildings, Turner's essay demanded a shift of attention away from the cities and their masses and toward the vanished edge of America's march westward.

Popular culture and the visual arts had swarmed westward on the heels of the pioneers and settlers. The Wild West tent shows of Buffalo Bill Cody and Annie Oakley offered a glamorized frontier as entertainment for eastern families (Figure 101). Owen Wister codified western formulas for fiction in *The Virginian: A Horseman of the Plains* (1902), a cowboy romance set in the cattle country of Wyoming in the 1870s and 1880s. Wister's novel is an elegy for "the cowpuncher, the last romantic figure upon our soil," part of a way of life gone from the land. "The mountains are there, far and shining, and the infinite earth, and the air that seems forever the true fountain of youth, – where is the buffalo, and the wild antelope, and the horseman with his pasturing thousands?" They are all part of "a vanished world." For Frederic Remington, too, the Old West became his subject when he realized that it was disappearing. In 1880, when the nineteen-year-old Remington was traveling through Montana to seek a nonartistic fortune, he suddenly realized that "the wild riders and the vacant lands" were about to be replaced by derby hats and machinery and thirty-day notes. "Without know-ing exactly how to do it," he later recalled, "I began to try to record some facts around me, and the more I looked, the more the pan-orama unfolded" (Figure 102).

Despite their apparent differences, western mythmaking and the back-looking consolations and evasions embodied in the Columbian Exposition reinforced each other by encouraging the substitution of wishful thinking for reality. The nation's best-selling books included a host of historical romances, pious religious allegories, and costume melodramas. Tales of Christ, of the Crusades, of General Wash-ington, rehearsed familiar stories and ratified familiar moral con-clusions. Many contemporary critics welcomed the triumph of romance, and its "spirit of idealism," over the realism of Howells and his even more graphic successors. Charles M. Sheldon's *In His Steps* (1896), Charles Major's *When Knighthood Was in Flower* (1898), F. Marion Crawford's *Via Crucis: A Romance of the Second Crusade* (1899): these were representative texts in the neoromantic revival, and critics applauded the public's return to the idealism and heroism of romance (Figure 103). In an essay in the *Independent* at the turn of the century, Maurice Thompson noted "a veering of

FIGURE 101 ❧ Advertisement, Buffalo Bill's Wild West Show. This poster, promising Colonel Cody's appearance at every show, dates from 1899.

FIGURE 102 🙋
Frederic Remington,
Mounting a Wild One.
This drawing appeared in
Harper's in March 1894.

popular interest from the fiction of character analysis and social problems to the historical novel and the romance of heroic adventure. We have had a period of intense, not to say morbid, introversion directed mainly upon diseases of the social, domestic, political and religious life of the world. . . . It has run its course." Thompson would have nominated his own work as a serviceable example of the healthy new trend; at the same time as this essay, he also published the best-selling *Alice of Old Vincennes*, a costume romance set on the Indiana frontier during the Revolutionary War. Heading the school of introversion and social disease, on the other hand, Thompson would surely have included the young, internationally celebrated Stephen Crane.

In 1893, while tourists were strolling through Daniel Burnham's White City, Crane published *Maggie: A Girl of the Streets*, which boldly led American literature into the dark city of Jacob Riis. The book was welcomed by Hamlin Garland and Howells as a blow in the battle for realism; in fact, as John Berryman recognized when he said that *Maggie* "initiated modern American writing," the book is less documentary than impressionist nightmare. The setting had its genesis in the Lower East Side, but all of its parts and contours are heightened toward extremity:

> Eventually they entered into a dark region where, from a careening building, a dozen gruesome doorways gave up loads of babies to the street and gutter. A wind of early autumn raised yellow dust from cobbles and swirled it against an hundred windows. Long streamers of garments fluttered from fire-escapes. In all unhandy places there were buckets, brooms, rags and bottles. In the street infants played or fought with other infants or sat stupidly in the way of vehicles. Formidable women, with uncombed hair and disordered dress, gossiped while leaning on railings, or screamed in frantic quarrels. Withered persons, in curious postures of submission to something, sat smoking pipes in obscure corners. A thousand odors of cooking food came forth to the street. The building quivered and creaked from the weight of humanity stamping about in its bowels.

Crane's slum is at last a state of mind, the vision of a universe governed solely by cruelty and violence. In an inscription on a copy

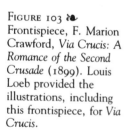

FIGURE 103 ❧ Frontispiece, F. Marion Crawford, *Via Crucis: A Romance of the Second Crusade* (1899). Louis Loeb provided the illustrations, including this frontispiece, for *Via Crucis*.

of *Maggie* that he gave to Garland, Crane wrote that he had tried "to show that environment is a tremendous thing in the world and frequently shapes lives regardless."

Crane was fascinated with randomness and determinism, and convinced that the anodynes of religion and morality are protective shams. He was a clinician probing human behavior in a world in which thought and motive have little connection to outcomes. He contemplated the ethical and psychological consequences of nature's impenetrable separateness: his urban and Civil War battlefields are the scenes of Darwinian struggles in which strength or cunning prevails and justice has no relevance. As the century wore toward its end, other writers and artists joined in the revelation of a nature that was more lethal than accommodating. Winslow Homer, for example, secluded in his later years at Prout's Neck, Maine, meditated on a natural world no longer available for human consolation. Homer's images of storms and shipwreck and barren coasts are formal compositions of great power, ruthless in their disclosure of the void that aches where certitude had once seemed to reside. In 1893, the year of *Maggie*'s publication, Homer painted one of his principal works, *The Fox Hunt* (Plate 4), in which a flock of black birds hover like a dark prophecy over the hunted animal in the center of the picture. Whether the fox escapes or not is of no interest or significance. Nature has become, as the correspondent in Crane's story "The Open Boat" says, "indifferent, flatly indifferent."

Crane began as a child of prosperity, the youngest of fourteen children in a ministerial family. Perhaps in reaction to the restrictions imposed by his parents, his search for experience was precocious and exhausting. Before he was eighteen, he had resigned from two colleges and begun writing notable journalism; before he was twenty, he was penniless and afflicted with the first symptoms of tuberculosis; before he was twenty-five, he was an author of international fame; he died before he was thirty. He projected a sense of studious and boyish fin-de-siècle decadence: cigarettte always dangling, a flamboyant getup (he wore a long white coat through the Spanish-American War), deliberately shocking his hearers with declarations of unbelief. Yet the disillusionment is real enough, and if Crane always seems very young, he also seems quite convincingly undone. The hallmark of his work is a universal irony, a repudiation of all the conventions and beliefs that formed the sinews of middle-class culture. Untaught, immature, hasty, Crane employed irony as a substitute for philosophical engagement. He glorified firsthand experience and scanted the value of reflection and instruction; he said that he had gotten his "artistic education on the Bowery." Needless to say, Crane's iconoclastic posture betrayed his commonplace intellectual descent and affinities. His impatience with book learning was in the Emersonian grain, while his celebration of physical experience resembled Theodore Roosevelt's preachments on "the strenuous life."

Crane was impatient with the demands of fictional structure, only occasionally successful in transcribing differentiated speech, and uncertain in his control of point of view. His imagination found its most eloquent expression in images, usually moments of devastation or terror that possess a riveting authenticity. Maggie's hallucinatory march to the river and death is made up of a cluster of such images. Another occurs in Chapter 7 of *The Red Badge of Courage* (1895), when Henry, "the youth" who is the book's hero, seized by fear, has deserted from a battle and fled to a forest for refuge. The landscape, a "fair field holding life," seems to promise safety and peace. He reaches a secluded place where the unbearable noise of the guns has receded and "the high, arching boughs made a chapel." Suddenly he falls back, horror-stricken, at the sight of "a thing": "He was being looked at by a dead man who was seated with his back against a columnlike tree. The corpse was dressed in a uniform that once had been blue, but was now faded to a melancholy shade of green. The eyes, staring at the youth, had changed to the dull hue to be seen on the side of a dead fish. The mouth was open. Its red had changed to an appalling yellow. Over the gray skin of the face ran little ants. One was trundling some sort of a bundle along the upper lip." Crane's weaknesses and strengths can both be detected in a passage like this. When his imagination of horror outstripped his skill, he relied on mere adjectives, such as "appalling," and on routine metaphors, like the skin of a dead fish. But the green color of the dead soldier's uniform, and the ant with its enigmatic bundle, are unforgettable physical correlatives for what Crane called "a psychological portrait of fear." The phrase accurately suggests the literary impressionism that was Crane's principal technique. The world exists not in itself but as it is apprehended by his characters, and his narratives consist of the sequence of impressions.

What he said of himself as a journalist applies to his characters as well: "I understand that a man is born into the world with his own pair of eyes, and he is not at all responsible for his vision – he is merely responsible for his personal honesty." Honesty to feeling and perception became Crane's leading motive and his chief criterion of judgment.

Though *The Red Badge of Courage* was actually written out of intuition rather than experience (Crane had not yet been near a battlefield when he wrote it), it spoke with masterful precision. Civil War veterans were among those who praised the novel as an authoritative rendering of war from the vantage point of the brutalized common soldier. The book was warmly reviewed on both sides of the Atlantic, went through nine editions in its first year, and its popularity led to the publication of Crane's poetry in a volume called *Black Riders* (1895). In their experimental form, his poems disclose the influence of Dickinson, especially, and of Whitman. They are gnomic, sometimes startling and sometimes ponderously oracular, bitter sketches and mocking epigrams that avow moral emptiness and the irrelevance of metaphysical questions. Crane's poems, which he called his "lines," obscurely summon a world of deserts, assassins, and blankness. At their most disillusioned, the poems in *Black Riders* and in a second volume, *War Is Kind* (1899), veer toward nihilism. What remains to balance humanity's insignificance is the integrity of the observing ego. His tone would be much admired by his disillusioned literary descendants, among them Ernest Hemingway.

The language of religion and epic intrudes on every page of Crane's work, but as nothing more than vestiges and memories of obsolete explanatory systems. His mock-heroic stance leads not to comedy or mere deflation but to terror. In a famous line from the story "The Blue Hotel," men and women are reduced to "lice," hanging onto a "whirling, fire-smitten, ice-locked, disease-stricken, space-lost bulb." Crane thought that science authorized this corrosive if slightly theatrical pessimism, in particular the hypotheses of popular Darwinism, which decreed the struggle for existence and replaced divine purposes with procreative spasms and adaptive mechanisms. Crane was a naturalist only by fits and starts, but he shared some of the premises that made naturalism a pervasive literary and philosophical attitude in the late nineteenth century.

Naturalism had both native and foreign sources. The Civil War had given undeniable testimony that life was a mortal struggle, and that the price of progress was spilled blood. Oliver Wendell Holmes, Jr., who was wounded three times in the war, went on to a long career that ended on the Supreme Court. He survived his wounds by seventy years, but he remained convinced that the battlefield was a parable for a society grounded on "the death of men." The rapacious laissez-faire capitalism that flourished after the war called forth defensive appeals to inevitability. Social theorists such as Yale's William Graham Sumner counseled that the linked phenomena of concentrated wealth and widespread poverty merely followed the operation of natural laws. John D. Rockefeller gave a legendary statement of this opinion when he told a Sunday school class at the turn of the century that the "growth of a large business is merely survival of the fittest. The American Beauty rose can be produced in the splendor and fragrance which bring cheer to its beholder only by sacrificing the early buds which grow up around it. This is not an evil tendency in business. It is merely a working out of a law of nature and a law of God."

Science transformed the intellectual as well as the physical life of the nation. Its palpable achievements, especially the technology that produced bridges and tunnels, railroads and electrification, sky-scrapers and photography, appealed to America's utilitarian temper and brought strong temptations to apply the models of science to the realms of society and politics. The effort to explain human behavior in putatively scientific terms led in many directions, from the vulgarity of social Darwinism to Henry Adams's search for math-ematical laws that could be applied to the sequence of historical events. When he was still a young man, Adams wrote of his firm belief that "the laws which govern animated beings will ultimately be found to be at bottom the same as those which rule inanimate nature." He concluded with a gesture that would become a fin-de-siècle commonplace: "I entertain a profound conviction of the lit-tleness of our kind."

Charlotte Perkins Gilman incorporated a Darwinist perspective to quite different ends in her book *Women and Economics* (1898). The most influential statement in turn-of-the-century feminism, Gilman's book comprises a wide-ranging inquiry into what she called

FIGURE 104 🙚
Photograph of Charlotte
Perkins Gilman.

the "sexuo-economic relation." She demanded the complete emancipation of women, not just particular reforms in voting laws, education, or wages. She demanded as well the redefinition of the
institutions of marriage and motherhood, which she believed served
as the chief instruments of a sentimentalizing but sinister oppression.
Gilman's story, "The Yellow Wallpaper" (1892), was the shattering
case study of a woman driven out of her mind by the isolation
imposed on her by a well-meaning physician-husband. The tale had
personal sources in Gilman's treatment by the prominent Philadelphia physician S. Weir Mitchell, who developed a "rest cure" for
women with psychological illnesses (Figure 104).

Gilman's work was part of a large-scale examination of the meaning of scientific hypotheses for human freedom. The inquiry was
cosmopolitan, and much of the impetus came from abroad. Emile
Zola, who was apparently more often invoked than read in America,
had influentially proposed that the methods of scientific analysis

could be imposed upon the novel and that fiction could be used to illustrate the explanatory power of inheritance and environment. Naturalism's adherents typically chose lower-class subjects, whose degradation exemplified determinist premises more persuasively than the comforts of the affluent would. These writers frequently employed a technique of saturation, knitting webs of inescapable circumstance through the multiplication of detail. The logic of naturalism, and its potential to shake the edifice of genteel assumptions, gave it a certain standing with the American avant-garde. At the same time, its emphasis on predestined outcomes and diminished individual responsibility threatened to cut the spine and vital organs out of fiction. Whether or not a strictly naturalist novel is a contradiction in terms, American writers tended toward eclectic and even anarchic combinations of naturalism's scientific vocabulary with older traditions of realism and romance. The case of Frank Norris is typical and instructive.

Norris was an almost exact contemporary of Stephen Crane, and the two men resembled each other in their middle-class backgrounds, their shared contempt for moderation, and their similar mixture of cosmic longings with an irrepressible itch for adventure. Norris studied painting in Paris, where he also went through a medieval interlude, and then enrolled in the University of California at Berkeley. In conventional terms, his education was inconclusive, but it was at Berkeley that he discovered the novels of Zola and came under the influence of a geology teacher, the self-styled "theistic evolutionist" Joseph Le Conte. He left San Francisco to take writing courses with Lewis Gates at Harvard, where his first novels began as class projects. From the beginning, Norris's work reveals his divided attraction to the scientific and the sensational. Indeed, in a character like the title figure of McTeague (1899), who degenerates into an inherited alcoholic bestiality, the rational and macabre merge.

Though Norris sometimes likened himself to Zola, there was a good deal of Richard Harding Davis in his globe-trotting style, and he labeled himself a romantic. By "romance," Norris had in mind more a point of view than a genre: "To Romance belongs the wide world for range, and the unplumbed depths of the human heart, and the mystery of sex, and the problems of life, and the black, unsearched penetralia of the soul of man." In the essay from which this comes, "A Plea for Romantic Fiction," he called for a literary frankness commensurate with the human truths being revealed by psychology, economics, and biology. He saw his own work as a kind of naturalist transcendentalism, a bold effort to search out the un-discovered countries that lay beneath familiar surfaces.

In the end, Norris was less interested in science, philosophy, or politics – indeed, less interested in literature – than he was in the interplay between force and individual lives. Power fascinated him, and he responded to it with a reverence that often bordered on a confused, panting mysticism. He thought in national and even global terms, and he was drawn to epic as the form needed to contain the bursting energy of a new imperial age. Only half jokingly, he suggested that a contemporary Richard the Lion-Heart would find work as a "leading representative of Amalgamated Steel" and that Andrew Carnegie, if he had lived in the Middle Ages, would have been a Crusader. Norris's major ambition was a projected "trilogy of wheat," a series that he intended as the modern epic. It was to be, collectively, the "great American novel" that would encompass the vastness of the nation and give shape to its past and future. Among them, the three novels were to present the growth of the wheat, the marketing of the wheat, and the distribution of the wheat to the hungry of the world. Norris completed only two volumes before his death, the first of which, *The Octopus* (1901), was his major achievement in fiction. The novel is loosely based on an episode in the long battle between California's wheat farmers and the encroaching railroad, but the economic and political issues are eventually submerged in Norris's besetting preoccupations. The several interlinked plots offer occasions for speculation on the function of literature, the efficacy of love, the order of reality, above all the mysteries of evolutionary forces. Nature is a machine and human beings "mere animalcules, mere ephemerides," but the universal force of nature moves always toward the good: "The good never dies; evil dies; cruelty, oppression, selfishness, greed – these die; but nobility, but love, but sacrifice, but generosity, but truth . . . these live forever, these are eternal." Despite his proclivity for this sort of rhetoric, the best scenes in *The Octopus* are pictorial and often panoramic: mass meetings, barn dances, gun duels. A speeding train slaughters a herd of peacefully grazing sheep that have wandered onto the tracks; hundreds of men and horses take part in a rabbit hunt that reaches from the foreground to the horizon. Norris's strength lay in his talent for big scenes and explosive action; it was a talent that far outweighed his uncertain stock of ideas.

Norris died in 1902, less than two years after Stephen Crane. Their deaths subtracted substantially from the literary aspirations of the postwar generation. They were survived by those who had preceded them, writers such as Howells and James and Samuel Clemens and Henry Adams.

CHAPTER FIVE

❧ Modernists and muckrakers ❧

I N 1900, at the Paris Exposition, Henry Adams stood before the great machines in the hall of dynamos and was seized with a secular insight approximating religious revelation. The forty-foot dynamo "became a symbol of infinity," a moral force demanding obedience and even reverence. Adams was sixty-two years old, the author of twenty volumes of history, biography, politics, and fiction, much honored by friends, colleagues, and former students for his scholarship, his intellectual audacity, his imaginative range, and his wit. His achievements enhanced an old and distinguished family name. His grandfather, John Quincy Adams, and his great-grandfather, John Adams, had risen to the American presidency; his great-grandmother, Abigail Adams, had been an eloquent voice for the rights of women in the early Republic; his father, Charles Francis Adams, had served as Lincoln's minister to England during the Civil War and had done much to affect the war's outcome through his shrewd diplomacy.

Looking back on his life from the vantage point of old age and the twentieth century, Adams concluded that his lineage had not been the auspicious gift it seemed. He judged himself a failure, unsuited by heredity, temperament, and training for any leading part in the rough-and-tumble world of American politics in the Gilded Age. Nor had his education provided him with the analytic and theoretical tools he needed to understand the new America. Adams acknowledged that his antecedents, along with his wealth and privilege, made his a special case, but he construed his life nonetheless as representative, and thus potentially instructive. He felt that his futility could serve to illustrate the abyss that separated human premises from their outcomes, an example made all the more convincing by his supposed advantages. Denied power, he became a student of power, tracking it through history and his own career, tracing its contours on the map of the past and projecting its consequences into the future.

To souls more optimistic than Adams, the dynamo whispered of a future bright with the hope of progress. Old dreams of human liberation seemed within reach of realization. Adams's generation had been born into an agrarian, preindustrial society. Those who lived long would see America transformed into full modernity: crowded cities, booming industries, inventions that seemed literally fabulous in their power. Journalist Mark Sullivan said that the metamorphosis was like "a fairy story" and that living through those years of change in the late nineteenth and early twentieth centuries was like being a character "in the Arabian Nights Tales." Little wonder that assorted wizards – of Tuskegee, of Menlo Park, of Oz – were among the most popular of Adams's real and fictional contemporaries. From automobiles to moving pictures, machines changed daily life, and they were welcomed by progressives of all sorts, who saw technology opening pathways toward a healthier democracy and even toward utopia.

For Adams, on the other hand, the dynamo foretold a future of uncontrolled technological power, a headlong rush toward chaos, and the triumph of directionless force over human will. Adams foresaw that the twentieth-century world would be a global village shadowed by the cloud of technological apocalypse. Having spent a lifetime searching for the laws that would explain the sequence of historical events, he was compelled to admit the supremacy of anarchy. Chaos is at last the rule of nature, logic only the trap of the mind. Such a vision left him lying flat on his metaphorical back in the Gallery of Machines, "his historical neck broken by the sudden irruption of forces totally new." He is the anguished figure of transition, the man who had lived in both the old and new worlds and who had felt the full shock of the radical discontinuity between them. Suddenly, in the late nineteenth century, history stopped moving steadily ahead and instead leaped crazily forward. This is the essence of Adams's situation and of his representative significance. His imagination is a seismograph registering, as if it were an earthquake, the rupture of history: "The year 1900 was not the first to upset schoolmasters. Copernicus and Galileo had broken many professorial necks about 1600; Columbus had stood the world on its head towards 1500; but the nearest approach to the revolution of 1900 was that of 310, when Constantine set up the Cross." Adams defended himself from the new century's welter behind a shield of irony. He declared himself obsolete, a primitive creature passed over by evolution, marooned in an antediluvian stage of development. Ostensibly to share the chastening lesson of his life, he wrote *The Education of Henry Adams*, one of the oddest and most valuable autobiographies in American letters, and one of the most pertinent introductions to the American twentieth century.

Privately published in 1907, the *Education* is a work of nearly perfected eccentricity, whose unorthodox form mirrors the intellectual experience of its principal character. The book's central figure is not presented in the first-person singular of most autobiography but is a carefully constructed "Henry Adams," the inept, fumbling, but ultimately valorous hero of a latter-day *Pilgrim's Progress*, searching for solutions, answers, meaning, and finding only confusion and doubt. The voice which describes the doings and disappointments of this Adams is arch, occasionally lacerating, always ironic. In the disillusioned world of the *Education*, everything, even love, is subsumed in this leveling tone.

The following passage is typical, in its arcane references, its piling on of paradoxes, its self-regarding and finally self-destructive irony. In this paragraph, from the chapter called "Teufelsdrökh" (after the main character in Carlyle's *Sartor Resartus*), Adams is allegedly defining what he calls the Conservative Christian Anarchist party":

> This wing of the anarchistic party consisted rigorously of but two members, [Henry] Adams and Bay Lodge. The conservative Christian anarchist, as a party, drew life from Hegel and Schopenhauer, rightly understood. By the necessity of their philosophical descent, each member of the fraternity denounced the other as unequal to his lofty task and inadequate to grasp it. Of course, no third member could be so much as considered, since the great principle of contradiction could be expressed only by opposites; and no agreement could be conceived, because anarchy, by definition, must be chaos and collision, as in the kinetic theory of a perfect gas. Doubtless this law of contradiction was itself agreement, a restriction of

personal liberty inconsistent with freedom; but the "larger synthesis" admitted a limited agreement provided it were strictly
confined to the end of larger contradiction. . . .

Adams proclaimed that in the last synthesis, order and
anarchy were one, but that the unity was chaos.

Stiffly comic, almost smug, the passage delights in its mock pedantry
and in the play of broad wit over serious issues. Despair becomes a
labored joke. At the same time, the issues remain serious, lying
indeed near the heart of the *Education*. Though his assessment was
dark, Adams continued to explore the uses of the mind in discovering pattern in the multiform contradictions of the world and its
history. Adams's rather precious humor is an effort to deflect anxiety,
revealing the distress of a man schooled to believe in the meaning
of history and instead finding only impenetrable obscurity. Repeatedly in the *Education* Adams calls himself the last of the Puritans,
and he is right. From those Puritan ancestors he had learned the
providential conception of America's story, and he had seen, furthermore, the way in which that Providence is enacted in the lives
of particular men and women. Though the old religious assumptions
no longer hold, the same heavy responsibility lies upon Adams as
upon earlier historians: to probe through biography and autobiography for the meaning of the nation. Whereas their inquiry ended
in victory, his ends always in defeat.

In his search for explanatory hypotheses that might make sense
of the cacophony of events, Adams turned to science. He would
have relished deriving laws governing historical sequence from the
very discoveries which had proved so completely deranging to older
systems. The outcome of his investigations into evolution, atomic
physics, chemistry, and mathematics, however, only confirmed
skepticism. A law of historical acceleration, a dynamic theory of
the past, a mathematics of political force – all these collapse into
the same confusion. The last chapter of the book opens with a visit
to an anarchic, exploding New York City, and it closes with the
death of Adams's friend John Hay. "There it ended," Adams writes.

The failure with which the book concludes tolls through all its
pages like a funeral bell, and it is the key to the book's significance.
At a time when the nation was absorbed in the reach and strength
of its grasp and intoxicated with its material well-being, Adams
uttered a monitory counterstatement. In some undeniable measure,

Adams's judgment of his failures is an encoded indictment of the society around him. His mind was well furnished with the prejudices of his embattled Brahmin caste, including an ugly anti-Semitism, and he was repelled by the polyglot democracy of the new America. Beyond that, however, Adams had the detachment to confess his own responsibility for his irrelevance. The Henry Adams whose story is told in the *Education* sounds like a premeditated parody of Horatio Alger's heroes. Where Alger's young men start life poor and barely educated, and win through to affluence and respected status, Adams was born to wealth and prestige, and spent a lifetime snatching defeat from the jaws of victory. Thus the recurring, almost stylized structure of the book, in which each chapter tells of some experience in journalism or teaching or travel and then concludes by pronouncing, epitaphlike, Adams's failure to learn anything of use from the episode.

In spite of its apparent candor, reticence coexists with revelation in the *Education*. Unspoken in the book, but lying like a weight across the last three decades of Adams's life, was the suicide of his wife, Marion Hooper Adams, in 1885. The Adams marriage had, by all accounts, been happy. Marion Adams was a woman of strong opinions and agile intelligence. Henry James, who had been a frequent houseguest of the Adamses during their marriage, sketched the most memorable impression of Marion's conversation and personality in his story "Pandora" (1884). Her death was an emotional calamity for her husband. The event is hidden in the *Education*, missing, along with everything else that had happened in the years between 1871 and 1892. The single reference to the tragedy of Marion Adams's death is characteristically oblique. When Adams returned to the United States in 1892, after extended travel in Europe, the South Seas, and Japan, he went first to Rock Creek Cemetery in Washington, D.C., "to see the bronze figure which St. Gaudens had made for him in his absence." This is the memorial to Marion Adams, by Augustus Saint-Gaudens, that became known as *Grief*, though Adams preferred *Peace of God* (Figure 105). (Since the "peace of God" traditionally surpasses human understanding, the title may be an especially embittered example of Adams's irony).

Though Adams hid the torment of his intimate life from the scrutiny of readers, those private sufferings enlarged his authority as a witness to modern malaise. The fault lines along which both

FIGURE 105 ❧
Augustus Saint-Gaudens,
Adams Memorial (1897).

the twentieth century and his own life had fractured seemed to him
to correspond. In his later years, he turned to the distant past for
consolation. According to its subtitle, the *Education* was a study in
"twentieth-century multiplicity." The book was intended as sequel
and complement to *Mont-Saint-Michel and Chartres*, which is a study
in "thirteenth-century unity." *Mont-Saint-Michel* (privately published in 1904) was Adams's main contribution to the ubiquitous
medievalizing that swept across turn-of-the-century culture on both
sides of the Atlantic. Architecture, city planning, educational theories, painting, and theology were all influenced by a revival of
interest in the gothic. The Middle Ages beckoned the new Goths,
as they called themselves, as the repository of coherence, simplicity,
and order, precisely the values driven out by the industrial and
commercial noise of the twentieth century. Henry Adams paid tribute to the human vitality and the spiritual integrity of Europe's
medieval civilization in *Mont-Saint-Michel*, evoking its sentimentalized past more colorfully and convincingly than any other American writer. At the center of his reverent attention, he placed the
Virgin: "Illusion for illusion – granting for the moment that Mary
was an illusion – the Virgin Mother . . . repaid to her worshippers

a larger return for their money than the capitalist has ever been able to get, at least in this world, from any other illusion of wealth which he has tried to make a source of pleasure and profit." It is the Virgin to whom Adams pays homage again in the *Education*, the woman whose humanity he opposes to the indifferent power of machinery. She stands on the far edge of the chasm that has opened across history (Figure 106).

Among those who shared the alarm Adams felt as he surveyed the new century was his friend and correspondent, Henry James. James called the period between the Civil War and World War I "the Age of the Mistake." His dismay at the imperiled state of culture and society was exacerbated by his "essential loneliness," as he called it in a letter of 1900 to his young friend, Morton Fullerton. Loneliness, James wrote, was the port from which he had set out and to which he found himself returning as he neared old age. When he offered that desolate self-appraisal, the success that had greeted his early work had long since yielded to increasing public neglect. His alienation from his audience had reached a humiliating climax in 1895, when he had literally been hooted from the stage on the opening night of his play, *Guy Domville*. James never slipped

FIGURE 106 ❧ The nave of Chartres Cathedral, from Henry Adams, *Mont-Saint-Michel and Chartres* (1904).

CHARTRES: THE NAVE

FIGURE 107 ❧ John Singer Sargent, portrait of Henry James (1913).

into obscurity, and he retained the loyalty of many fellow writers who acknowledged his primacy and flattered his vanity by referring to him as the Master. Nonetheless, he saw himself as an isolated figure, single-minded in his dedication to his craft, surrounded by incomprehension (Figure 107).

After 1900, James returned to his international subject in three final novels of great scope and ambition: *The Wings of the Dove* (1902), *The Ambassadors* (1903), and *The Golden Bowl* (1904). In these books, the drama of consciousness reaches a sustained and subtle apotheosis. Narrative attention is drawn irresistibly inward, as James minutely scrutinizes the minds of his characters in the act of reflection and choice. Consequently, the familiar elements of fiction yield to an absorbed psychological attention, and the centripetal density that results virtually cuts James's men and women off from the material world. They exist only in their self-scrutiny and in their contemplation of each other. Edith Wharton asked James, "What was your idea in suspending the four principal characters in *The Golden Bowl* in the void? What sort of life did they lead when they were not watching each other, and fending with each other?" James reacted with bewilderment to Wharton's question, but she had accurately assessed the abandonment of social surface in James's late work. Visual imagery is no longer deployed as traditional novelistic reportage but gives expression instead to an elusive system of symbolic communication. Buildings and objects speak with a complex clarity that discursive abstractions could only approximate. In *The Golden Bowl*, to give an example from the novel Wharton found so frustrating, James uses an oriental pagoda, a strange and exotic structure of the sort that might be seen at Kew Gardens, to suggest both the allure and the sinister mystery of Maggie Verver's situation as Prince Amerigo's wife:

> This situation had been occupying, for months and months, the very center of the garden of her life, but it had reared itself there like some strange, tall tower of ivory, or perhaps rather some wonderful, beautiful, but outlandish pagoda, a structure plated with hard, bright porcelain, colored and figured and adorned, at the overhanging eaves, with silver bells that tinkled, ever so charmingly, when stirred by chance airs. She had walked round and round it – that was what she felt; she had carried on her existence in the space left her for circulation, a space that sometimes seemed ample and sometimes narrow; looking up, all the while, at the fair structure that spread itself so amply and rose so high, but never quite making out, as yet, where she might have entered had she wished. She had not wished till now – such was the odd case; and what was doubtless equally odd, besides, was that, though her raised eyes seemed to distinguish places that must serve, from within, and especially far aloft, as apertures and outlooks, no door appeared to give access from her convenient garden level. The great decorated surface had remained consistently impenetrable and inscrutable.

Much of James's late fiction is concerned, as this example suggests, with the vexed question of knowing and judging in a social world of deceptive appearances. His characters estimate nuance with laborious care, and the result is a verbal style that is spaciously ruminative, endlessly ramifying and qualifying. The labyrinthine indirections of James's late style perplexed even his most sympathetic readers, including Edith Wharton. William James complained of his brother's "curlicues," urging Henry to "say it *out*, for God's sake, and have done with it." For his part, James persevered in the belief that his manner was no mere mannerism. He sought a style that could dramatize a sophisticated consciousness in the arduous and gradual process of illumination. As a gesture of confidence in the tendency of his mature prose, James spent several years meticulously revising much of his earlier work, bringing it into closer conformity with his later preferences. The results were collected and published in two dozen volumes by Scribner's (1907–9). The New York Edition, as it was called, attested in part to James's admiration for and emulation of Balzac, whose *Human Comedy* had so greatly influenced James's first conception of himself as a writer. The prefaces James wrote for his collected edition make up a manifesto for his art, an unprecedented attempt to establish the theoretical foundation upon which serious fiction might be based (Figure 108).

Shortly before his death in 1916, James adopted British citizenship as a statement of his loyalties in World War I, and a statement as well of his impatience with American neutrality. In the final thirty years of his life, he returned to his homeland just once, in 1904–5, when he made an extended tour and filled several notebooks with his observations. The book that resulted from his visit, *The American Scene* (1907), repeated and elaborated his lifelong quarrel with his native country. Everywhere James went, he concluded that his pessimism about the cultural possibilities of America had been sadly confirmed. It was a country ruled tyrannically by monetary values alone, whose ceaseless change forbade contemplation. New York is evoked as a frightening kaleidoscope of ceaseless movement and rapacious, buccaneering greed. Immigrants have made James a stranger in his own house: he contends that "brotherhood" with immigrants "in the first grossness of their alienism" is unthinkable. The crowded streets of American cities, especially of New York, left him shaken and grieving for the smaller past. James's case illuminates the limits of his own sympathies, and it illustrates as well the nativist resentment that met the massive influx of new immigrants who entered the United States in the early twentieth century (Figure 109).

One of the rare moments of respite James found on his American tour came during a visit with his friend Edith Wharton at "The Mount," the home she had designed for herself in Lenox, Massa-

chusetts. In a letter to Howard Sturgis, James wrote that the Mount was "an exquisite and marvellous place . . . a delicate French Chateau mirrored in a Massachusetts pond." Handsomely throned in its splendid gardens, the house paid a grand tribute to "the almost too impeccable taste of its so accomplished mistress." Thirty years later, in her memoirs *A Backward Glance* (1934), Wharton recalled James's visit with amused but genuine affection. Their friendship had been strong enough to survive Wharton's impatience with James's late books and James's mistrust of Wharton's popular success. She was never, as she rightly protested, merely "an echo of Mr. James," but the two writers were kindred spirits. They had in common a New York City background, a cosmopolitan outlook, a preference for Europe, and a distaste for the new worlds of mass culture and dem-

FIGURE 108   Alvin Langdon Coburn, *Portland Place* (1907). Coburn provided the two dozen photographs that serve as frontispiece illustrations for the New York Edition of Henry James's novels and tales. This view of Portland Place, in London, appears in the second volume of *The Golden Bowl*. James collaborated closely with Coburn on the selection of subjects, giving him written instructions and accompanying him in the search for appropriate London locations.

FIGURE 109 ❧ Hester Street, New York City (1899).

ocratic politics. Brought face-to-face with what she took to be the vulgarity that followed in the wake of an advancing industrial capitalism, Wharton took refuge in satire and expatriation. Like James, she was devoted to the craft of prose (one of her books is called *The Writing of Fiction*), and she believed that manners were an infallible instrument of social analysis (Figure 110, Figure 111).

The manners of a society, Wharton said, represent its history, "the long process of social adaptation," and they offer the novelist an inexhaustible field of inquiry. Wharton, whose early books in-

FIGURE 110 🦚 Photograph of Edith Wharton (1905).

FIGURE 111 🦚 "The Mount," Lenox, Massachusetts (1905).

cluded *The Decoration of Houses* (coauthored with Ogden Codman in 1897) and *Italian Villas and Their Gardens* (illustrated by Maxfield Parrish and published in 1904), was a penetrating student of society's physical signs and visible gestures. Under her interrogation, clothing, flowers, paintings, furnishings, and houses themselves all disclose their moral secrets. In her fictions, surfaces are endowed with resonance, and buildings are gifted with eloquence.

Her strength led her to her subject, after an initial false start. Her first novel, *The Valley of Decision* (1902), was a historical romance set in eighteenth-century Italy, competently tailored to fit the well-known formulas of costume melodrama. Henry James wrote with praise but admonished her to direct her fictional attention to the society around her, the world she had known from childhood. He argued in favor of "the *American Subject*": "Don't pass it by — the immediate, the real, the one that's yours, the novelist that it waits for. Take hold of it, and keep hold, and let it pull you where it will. . . . Profit, be warned by my awful example of exile and ignorance. . . . *Do New York!* The 1st hand account is precious." Wharton was born into the prestige and affluence of Old New York. She enjoyed the material comfort her circumstances bestowed, but she was stifled by the cultural aridity of America's higher castes. The puzzled contempt with which her family and friends treated her literary apprentice work was appalling proof to her that philistinism was an article of faith among her class. No one was more clear-eyed in detecting and deflating the pretensions of New York's genteel aristocracy. At the same time, she was repelled by the new people and new money who were demanding social recognition in the years of her growing up. Expatriated, estranged for years from her dim husband Teddy and ultimately divorced, Wharton was in several senses uprooted and homeless. Such a life held particular poignance for a woman who regarded stability and tradition as the necessary basis of a coherent existence.

Wharton held firmly to "that 'sense of the past,' " as she called it in *French Ways and Their Meaning* (1919), which enriches the present by binding generations together in the continuity of art and knowledge. In *The Custom of the Country* (1913), one of her European characters, the French aristocrat Raymond de Chelles, complains that Americans "come from hotels as big as towns, and from towns as flimsy as paper, where the streets haven't had time to be named, and the buildings are demolished before they're dry, and the people are as proud of changing as we are of holding to what we have." Yet Wharton was also sensitive and, as a woman, far more sensitive than James to the constricting pressure of traditional codes and arrangements. Much of her life, and a good deal of her most representative fiction, took its stimulus and its theme from her frustrated sense of dislocation. Dissent and compliance are often counterposed in her best works. Though her novels and tales are seldom autobiographical in any literal way, they often dramatize the contest between obedience and independence that defined her own life's choices. Professional writing was itself a subversive activity for a woman of her class. From her youth through the first years of her marriage, she had made conformity her habit and tried dutifully to comply with the expectations of others. Her first volume of stories, *The Greater Inclination* (1899), was not published until she was thirty-seven years old. Looking back on that event decades later, she wrote that publication "broke the chain which had held me so long in a kind of torpor. For nearly twelve years I had tried to adjust myself to the life I had led since my marriage; but now I was over-mastered by the longing to meet people who shared my interests." The vocabulary of chain and torpor, the antithesis between adjustment and desire, the assertion of self and the yearning for community: these were the elements at once of Wharton's own life and of her fictional world.

Privation was her absorbing study. One of the symptoms of Wharton's recurring nervous disorder was an inability to breathe; her characters are continuously threatened with moral and spiritual suffocation. As a woman, she was particularly convinced of the compelling power of environment, and the apparent naturalism of her fiction is often in fact a parable of gender. The images that describe Lily Bart in *The House of Mirth*, (1905), for example, bespeak her fate specifically as a woman in the money-driven society of turn-of-the-century New York. Lily "was like some rare flower grown for exhibition, a flower from which every bud had been nipped except the crowning blossom of her beauty." She has been trapped by gender and material circumstances into cooperating with her own spiritual impoverishment: "Inherited tendencies had combined with early training to make her the highly specialized product she was; an organism as helpless out of its narrow range as the sea-anemone torn from the rock. She had been fashioned to adorn and delight; to what other end does nature round the rose leaf and paint the humming-bird's breast?" In these passages, the language of evolution and romance is entangled. Beauty, a criterion imposed by society rather than nature, is the selective mechanism in Lily's struggle for survival; as a woman, she is reduced to the marginality of ornament (Figure 112).

True to the biblical echoes of its title ("The heart of the fool is in the house of mirth," Ecclesiastes), Wharton's novel presents a devastating satire on the cruelly vacuous world of New York society. Overweight men and overdressed women wallow placidly in an allegory of waste, finding such satisfaction as they can in gambling, sexual intrigue, pointless travel, and conspicuous display. Moral standards have been replaced by expediency and a frantic respectability. Wharton's abundant and brilliantly epigrammatic contempt reaches even to the minor residents of her house of fools, to Lily Bart's aunt Mrs. Peniston, for instance, who keeps "her imagination shrouded" like furniture in the summer and who finds

FIGURE 112 ❧ A. B. Wenzell, illustration from *The House of Mirth* (1905). Wenzell's illustrations accompanied the novel's serial publication in *Scribner's Magazine*. This impression of the meeting between Lily Bart and Lawrence Selden in the grounds of Bellomont appeared in the March 1905 installment of the novel.

the idea of immorality as offensive "as a smell of cooking in the drawing-room." Lily, who despises this world even as she aspires to rise in it, can conceive of no significant alternative. Her occasional confidant Lawrence Selden appeals to her with heady talk of a "republic of the spirit," an ideal realm of self-sufficiency, but this is an idle and irrelevant fancy. Selden, like so many of the male characters in Wharton's stories, is a moral trifler. She knew that fine sentiments come more readily to the well fed. Defending her choice of subject matter, Wharton later wrote that "a frivolous society can acquire dramatic significance only through what its frivolity destroys." Lily is destroyed long before she half-willingly takes an overdose of her sleeping draught in the novel's closing pages.

The struggle announced in *The House of Mirth* between freedom and disabling circumstance is enacted in much of Wharton's subsequent fiction, including *Ethan Frome* (1911), *Summer* (1917), and *The Age of Innocence* (1920). Though their settings vary from New York to Paris to the bleak loneliness of a poor New England farm, each of these novels traces a collision between spontaneity and convention, in which generosity is crushed by calculation. Her principal characters, usually women, are trapped within systems that deprive them of light and air, sometimes of life itself. Her fiction gained much of its texture from her anxious and even baffled concern with the connections between sexual identity and integrity, and her acute but tentative insight into the social construction of personality. Most of her best work was finished by 1920. In the last two decades of her life, the years following the First World War, she settled her accounts by simplifying them. Her distaste for the modern world stiffened into a crotchety nostalgia for the old, vanished world of her New York youth.

A long with its meditations on class and gender, Wharton's work made substantial contributions to America's imaginative discovery of the city. In the twentieth century, the nation's political and imaginative path would inevitably lie on city streets; the American scene would be urban. Some artists, and a good many politicians, resisted the metamorphosis; others welcomed their new opportunities. The city was embraced by reformers who interpreted the congestion and deprivations of urban life as curable anomalies. More fundamentally, many progressives and socialists – men and women who might be called the new urban ideologists – believed that the city represented the future and democracy. In 1905, the year of Henry James's outraged return to America, the social scientist Frederick C. Howe published his influential book, *The City: The Hope of Democracy*, which became a textbook for hopeful urban reformers. "To the city, we are to look for a re-birth of democracy," wrote Howe, and many of his fellow progressives agreed. Jane Addams, founder of Hull House, also celebrated the urban and democratic future in her lectures and articles. Artists such as John Sloan, George Luks, and the somewhat younger George Bellows made the city their subject, and they argued for the democratic logic of their choice. They insisted that the city was where reality could be found, and they insisted, like other American writers and painters, that they preferred reality to art. When George Luks fulminated against art and declared that he wanted "Guts! Guts! Life! Life!", he sounded like Frank Norris, who had written a few years earlier: "We don't want literature, we want life." The techniques of the so-called Ash Can painters were largely untouched by the revolutions of European modernism, but their images redirected American culture by demanding artistic recognition for the tenements, back alleys, and disheveled people of the nation's cities (Figure 113).

Theodore Dreiser's first novel, *Sister Carrie* (1900), offered a primitive and yet decisive account of the city's seductions and dangers. Through his young title character, Dreiser expressed his own dazzled reaction when he came to Chicago for the first time, in 1889, and saw the new city that had been built on the ashes of the 1871 fire. "Hail, Chicago! First of the daughters of the new world!", he wrote later of that first visit. The city was itself a "strange illusion of hope and happiness." With its cascade of immigrants, its daily changing skyline, its gargantuan appetites, its mingling of slaughterhouses and countinghouses, Chicago was perhaps the quintessential American city. When he was twenty-three, Dreiser returned to Chicago to cover the Columbian Exposition for the Saint Louis *Republic*, and his sense of intoxicated delight was renewed and multiplied.

More completely than any writer before him, Dreiser discovered the fictional possibilities of the new urban America. The clogged streets and gaudy show that provoked other American writers to contempt, despair, and exile provided Dreiser with rich resources, correlatives for his lifetime of confused, passionate preoccupation with desire, fulfillment, and fate. American cities, he wrote in *A Hoosier Holiday* (1916), were charged with a "young, hopeful seeking atmosphere." In them, he found "something which I have . . . missed abroad . . ., a crude, sweet illusion about the importance of all things material." Dreiser spent a career both recording and reflecting the spectacle of that crude sweetness. When he distilled his goggle-eyed wonder into fiction, he spoke for a previously undocumented sensibility. His fiction was ungainly, but it seemed to possess an unrehearsed candor that vibrated with authenticity. These were the qualities that would give him special standing with the iconoclasts of a later generation. Sinclair Lewis, who won America's first Nobel Prize for literature in 1930, used the occasion of his acceptance address to discuss some of the other Americans who might have won. He named Dreiser first, an act of homage reaching back three decades to the publication of *Sister Carrie*.

FIGURE 113 ❧ George Bellows, *The Lone Tenement* (1909).

Dreiser was the ill-educated son of impoverished parents, the ninth child of a tyrannically Catholic immigrant father and a more indulgent, illiterate mother to whom he gave such love as he would ever feel. The family was mired in poverty and bad luck. The only notable success was that of Dreiser's older brother Paul, who, under the name "Paul Dresser," did well in show business. One of his songs, "My Gal Sal," memorialized a brothel-keeping mistress; another, "On the Banks of the Wabash," was coauthored with his younger brother Theodore. Dreiser was never more than badly educated. Abetted and supported by a local schoolteacher, he managed to complete a year at Indiana University. There and later, his desultory reading in Nietzsche, Darwin, and Herbert Spencer filled his impressionable, receptive mind with half-formed, contradictory notions of supermen and determinism; the language of power and passivity spoke to his own condition and would be written into much of his fiction (Figure 114).

Dreiser had nothing more in mind than a title when he jotted

FIGURE 114 ❧ Dreiser in his studio, 16 St. Luke's Place, New York City, in 1923. The large desk in the rear was made from a piano that had been owned by Dreiser's older brother, Paul Dresser.

the words "Sister Carrie" at the top of a blank sheet of paper. He made up her story as he went, appropriating pieces of it from the lives of friends and family, among them his sister Emma, who had eloped with a bartender. Carrie's spirit Dreiser deduced from his own. She is the seeker, the dreamer who yearns with an inarticulate hunger for the glamour that might lift her out of the commonplace: "She realized in a dim way how much the city held – wealth, fashion, ease – every adornment for women, and she longed for dress and beauty with a whole heart." At the same time, Carrie is a creature in an allegory of destiny; the first chapter of her story is prophetically titled "The Magnet Attracting: A Waif amid Forces." She acts out Dreiser's puzzled fascination with freedom and fate. Factory work, she quickly finds, will yield only shabbiness and physical pain. She becomes the mistress of two men in turn, the first a flashy salesman, the second a saloon manager named Hurstwood. Like all of Dreiser's characters, those in *Sister Carrie* obey the dictates of reality rather than literary decorum. The consequence of Carrie's immorality is not punishment or death but a well-paid job on the New York stage. It is Hurstwood, not Carrie, who slides into failure and despair and finally takes his own life by turning on the gas in a flophouse room. Dreiser's indifference to the rules of fictional propriety prompted his publisher, Frank Doubleday, to the virtual suppression of a novel that he had initially accepted with enthusiasm. (Doubleday's second thoughts made him a reluctant sponsor; the book received only desultory distribution and promotion.) In the much rearranged version of the novel that Doubleday published, Hurstwood's suicide is followed by Carrie's concluding meditation, a vague sigh of discontent that is untouched by remorse:

> On, Carrie, Carrie! Oh, blind strivings of the human heart! Onward, onward, it saith, and where beauty leads, there it follows. Whether it be the little tinkle of a long sheep bell o'er some quiet landscape, or the glimmer of beauty of sylvan places, or the show of soul in some passing eye, the heart knows and makes answer, following. It is when the feet weary and hope seems vain that the heartaches and the longings arise. Know then, that for you is neither surfeit nor content. In your rocking-chair, by your window, dreaming, shall you long, alone. In your rocking-chair, by your window, shall you dream such happiness as you may never feel.

A passage like this illustrates Dreiser's strange amalgam of a fumbling diction, timidly tied to literary precedent, and a completely emancipated moral vision. *Sister Carrie* was an affront to genteel cultural values, all the more inflammatory because Dreiser seemed so guileless in his candor. He could be charged with obscenity, but never with dishonesty. The novel received a few respectful reviews, but its initial commercial failure pushed Dreiser toward desperation and the edge of suicide.

Rejected as a writer, he found work as an editor. He took a job at Butterick's, whose magazines served mainly to promote dress patterns. The work brought him a substantial salary, a measure of prestige, and a chance to sample the rewards of American success. He illuminated his seeking self on a grandiose scale when he created the character Frank Cowperwood, the central figure in *The Financier* (1912) and *The Titan* (1914), the first two novels in a projected "trilogy of desire." (The final volume, *The Stoic*, was published only posthumously in 1947.) Nearly a century earlier, de Tocqueville had written that in America all personal relations are pecuniary relations and that the love of money is either the beginning or the end of every democratic passion. Cowperwood is towering evidence that the allegation might be true; his triumph in the jungles of commerce is a victory for the talented, ambitious common man of the democratic myth, and his every gesture obeys the stage directions of the American dream. Cowperwood is the heir to men like Philip D. Armour and Andrew Carnegie, whose lives Dreiser had breathlessly celebrated in the 1890s in profiles for the magazine *Success*. Cowperwood's nerveless courage and his instinct for leadership, modeled on the character of the swindling and charismatic tycoon Charles T. Yerkes, endeared him to his creator. Furthermore, he appealed to Dreiser's fantasies of intermingled financial and erotic domination. In Dreiser's fiction, as in his life, women were censors, termagants, irritants, or conveniences. He groped after completion and the reassurance that he could not find by following a career of sad, indefatigable promiscuity. His dazzled response to men like Cowperwood signaled the strength of his affiliation with the ruling assumptions of American society.

It has often been said that it took America's taste about a generation to catch up with Dreiser. In any case, when he published his masterpiece, *An American Tragedy* (1925), critical opinion and the marketplace were both ready to offer him the approval they had previously withheld. The book has most of the faults of his earlier novels: the stylistic ineptitude, the undiscriminating accumulation of detail, the half-digested, paltry philosophy. But *An American Tragedy* abundantly reveals Dreiser's strengths as well. More precisely, the novel demonstrates how closely allied his defects and achievements were. The heaped up, miscellaneous detail, for example, ultimately produces an atmosphere of elemental factuality. All this clutter, Dreiser's prose seems to say, is the unavoidable burden of urban life in twentieth-century America. Rather than selecting and summarizing, as most novelists do, Dreiser seems to transcribe events in numbing, repetitive detail. Yet if his prose is often lumpish, it can also be unexpectedly compelling, investing the commonplace and even the sordid with a kind of lyric intensity. His legendary gaucherie is vindicated as a testament of his total identification with the culturally lamed and often ill-favored men and women that people his novels.

Clyde Griffiths, the main character of *An American Tragedy*, is a peculiarly modern hero, selfish without a sense of self, predatory and yet weakly passive. His brief life altogether lacks the nobility that defines traditional heroes, and his death is hardly "tragic" in any conventional sense. From his early years reluctantly following his mountebank parents, the shabby purveyors of a noisy fundamentalism, to his final months on the death row of a New York prison, Clyde is trapped by the collusion between circumstance and desire. He is vivid only in the sheer energy of his primitive and tawdry lusts. His doom is inescapable; even the murder he commits is finally more instinctual than willed. *An American Tragedy* is a "naturalist" book, and Dreiser's naturalism is a nineteenth-century survival, yet Clyde's destruction is a strikingly twentieth-century phenomenon. He is an unwelcome everyman, at once alien and familiar. His unsavory story brings nearer to the surface murderous questions about the economic and sexual appetite of modern America that might otherwise have remained subterranean.

Though Dreiser spent his life fleeing from his past, he never broke faith with the impoverished victims of America's economic injustices. The earlier realists had been middle class in origin, attracted to the temperate climes of experience. Dreiser had first viewed the American scene from the bottom, and he had felt the crushing weight of the status quo. His response to suffering, however, was typically emotional rather than programmatic, a mixture of fatalism and unschooled sympathy. He had grown up assuming the world to be a violent, cruel place, a conspiracy of forces that could be opposed only with a strength unsullied by sentiment. "We live in an age," he wrote in *Jennie Gerhardt* (1911), "in which the impact of materialized forces is well-nigh irresistible; the spiritual nature is overwhelmed by the shock." Though Dreiser's politics were typically belated (it was not until the end of the 1920s, at about the time of a visit to the Soviet Union, that he began to think of himself as a political radical), his insights into the deformities of the American system corresponded with the findings of his reform-minded contemporaries, among them the progressive politicians and muckraking journalists of the early twentieth century.

The muckrakers appeared at the juncture of impatient democratic aspirations and the technology of a new journalism. Their antecedents lay in the work of such writers and artists as Henry Demarest Lloyd, Samuel Clemens, and Thomas Nast, but where their predecessors had come singly, they were a battalion. Making an index of American institutions, they poked into every corporate and government cranny they could find, in search of corruption and conspiracy. They were given their derisive label by an exasperated Theodore Roosevelt, who tired of their zeal and their taste for sensation; alluding to *Pilgrim's Progress*, he denounced "the man with the muckrake" who slanders "men engaged in public work." In fact, the motives of the muckrakers were mixed, and their relationship to the established structures was ambivalent. Nonetheless, they successfully orchestrated a clamor of protest that directly influenced the course of legislative and political events. Merely to list a few of the essays and books the muckrakers published is to suggest something of the scale of their ambition: Ida M. Tarbell's *History of the Standard Oil Company* (1902); Edward Bok's " 'Patent-medicine' Curse" (1904); Lincoln Steffens's *Shame of the Cities* (1904); G. W. Galvin's "Our Legal Machinery and its Victims" (1904); Thomas Lawson's *Frenzied Finance* (1905); Robert Hunter's "Children Who Toil" (1905); David Graham Phillips's *Treason of the Senate* (1906); Louis D. Brandeis's "Greatest Life Insurance

FIGURE 115 ❧ John Sloan, *The Ludlow Massacre* (1914). In the four years that Sloan was associated with *The Masses*, from 1912 to 1916, he produced sixty or so political cartoons. *The Ludlow Massacre* was his response to the murder of Colorado miners and their wives and children by John D. Rockefeller's hired police.

Wrong" (1906); and Charles Edward Russell's *Lawless Wealth* (1908). The magazines that demanded reform or (in some cases) revolution included *Cosmopolitan, Appeal to Reason, McClure's,* and *The Masses* (Figure 115).

Muckraking's propagandistic masterpiece was Upton Sinclair's *The Jungle,* a fictionalized exposé of Chicago's meat-packing industry, originally serialized in the radical journal *Appeal to Reason* in 1906. The novel is told from the point of view of Jurgis Rudkus, a Lithuanian immigrant, and his family, whose hopes and lives are mutilated by the knives of the slaughterhouses and the greed of the owners. In Packingtown, as Sinclair called it, the struggle for survival is waged with the stark and simplifying clarity of a morality play. Human beings confront the same resistless fate as the animals they butcher in the meat factories. *The Jungle* is an encyclopedia of horrors, whose most lurid scenes gained instant notoriety: a baby drowning in a puddle of filthy water; a little boy eaten by rats; workers slipping into the rending vats. Sinclair dedicated his book to "the Workingmen of America," and his design was socialist. At the end of the novel, Jurgis is revivified by a revolutionary call to arms and marches with his comrades into the proletarian dawn, chanting: "Chicago will be ours!" America's middle-class readers drew a rather different moral from Sinclair's tale. They demanded government inspection of their meat. Sinclair later ruefully recalled that he had aimed for the public's head and hit its stomach instead.

Sinclair's socialist frustrations exemplify the balked career of radical ideologies in the early twentieth century. Socialism had moments of electoral success and gained a number of important converts among intellectuals and labor leaders, but revolutionary aspirations invariably stumbled over combinations of patriotism and pragmatism. One of the most famous (if least coherent) of the literary socialists was Jack London, who lectured across the country as president of the Intercollegiate Socialist Society, signed his correspondence "Yours for the Revolution," and published a shelf of stories and essays predicting the apocalyptic final battle between labor and capital. London's socialism, however, was more instinctive than premeditated, an opportunity for excitement rather than a program. He was interested in novelty and self-expression, not consistency, and he tried on by turns virtually every intellectual fashion of his time, from Darwinism to primitivism to vegetarianism to Nietzchean ideas of supremacy. His adventure stories, including *The Call of the Wild* (1902), *The Sea-Wolf* (1904), and *White Fang* (1906), made him one of the world's most widely read writers. By the time he died at forty, he had written nearly fifty books. His best novel, the patently autobiographical *Martin Eden* (1909), is bitter and wishful at once, a portrait of a mental and physical superman whose suicide condemns a society too stupid to appreciate him (Figure 116).

Legend associates the conscious beginnings of muckraking with *McClure's Magazine*. The January 1903 issue contained Lincoln Steffens's exposé of municipal graft in Minneapolis, a chapter of Ida Tarbell's history of the Standard Oil Company, and Ray Stannard Baker's article "The Right to Work." In a famous editorial on the front page of that issue, McClure and his colleagues called attention to this "coincidence" and thereby introduced the public to the investigative role of the press. Dozens of other periodicals, among them *Everybody's*, *Collier's*, and *Cosmopolitan*, earned honorable places in the new journalism of opposition and reform, but *McClure's* remained a leader. Jack London, O. Henry, David Graham Phillips, and Theodore Dreiser were all published in the magazine; its editors included Tarbell and, from 1906 to 1912, Willa Cather.

Cather came to *McClure's* from Pittsburgh, where she had spent several years editing a smaller magazine and teaching high school English. She was born in Virginia but had moved as a child to the frontier town of Red Cloud, Nebraska, a raw settlement barely a decade old when she and her family had emigrated there. Both her grandmothers were still alive when she was growing up, literate and educated women, and from them she received an early training in English and Latin. Throughout her life, women would continue to provide Cather's most consequential personal and professional re-lationships. She admired Flaubert and Henry James, but she felt a closer affiliation for the work of Sarah Orne Jewett, whom she met in Boston in 1908. Significantly, the most important advice she received as a writer came from Jewett, who recalled their meeting in a letter. "You must find a quiet place," Jewett wrote. "You must find your own quiet center of life and write from that. . . . The thing that teases the mind over and over for years, and at last gets itself

Figure 116 &ra; Jack London, dressed as a tramp for his research on *The People of the Abyss.*

FIGURE 117 ❧ Willa Cather (n.d.).

put down on paper – whether little or great, it belongs to Literature" (Figure 117).

In 1912 she gave up her career as editor and journalist to write the fiction whose subjects had long teased her mind. She wrote best about the frontier she had come from and about what Sinclair Lewis called the "obvious heroisms" of its past. Her novels are loose in structure, sometimes episodic, chronicles of the combat between courage and human waste. She celebrated the efforts of the prairie people, especially the women, to live decently and even to find fulfillment, despite the relentless toil and the harsh conditions that ground them down. The winters of the Midwest, she often wrote, are cold and lonely. In *O Pioneers!* (1913), Alexandra Bergson, a strong-willed immigrant daughter, takes command of a prairie farm when her father dies and masters it through the force of her commitment. She embodies the grandeur and integrity that are the hallmarks of the past. So, too, does the title character of My Antonia (1918), whose competence, faith, and quiet perseverance prove that she "was a rich mine of life, like the founders of early races." Much of Cather's fiction was productively shaped by the tension between the valued past and the fallen present. Especially after the First World War, however, her rejection of the urban and technological sometimes drifted into caricature. In 1926, in comments prefatory to a collection of her essays, she declared that "the world broke in two in 1922 or thereabouts, and the persons and prejudices recalled in these sketches slide back into yesterday's seven thousand years."

Cather sought solace against the contemptible present in the rituals, beliefs, and coherence of the past. Many of her contemporaries, including the reform-minded women and men she worked with at McClure's, sought rather to remake society along more humane lines. Large numbers of women enlisted in the cause of sexual equality in marriage and the workplace or worked to secure the right to vote in federal elections. Margaret Sanger risked abuse and arrest by promoting birth control, especially among poor women, in lectures and in a magazine called Woman Rebel. Immigrant Emma Goldman traveled the country, tirelessly campaigning for her anarchist vision of human liberation, until her deportation to Russia at the end of the First World War. Jane Addams founded Hull House as a refuge for Chicago's malnourished poor and eventually expanded its interests to encompass the whole range of social and political reform that stirred America in the early twentieth century. The Women's Trade Union League was founded in 1903 to secure for women the organizing mechanisms that the men of the American Federation of Labor (AFL) refused to share. Leaders like Rose Schneidermann, who led New York's hat and cap makers in a dangerous strike, emerged from the ranks of the women workers.

For blacks, the early years of the century were a time of triumphant white intransigence and hardening racial divisions. In Plessy v. Ferguson (1896), the Supreme Court had affirmed the constitutionality of segregation, and a legalized system of separation was imposed in the decades that followed. In the North as well as the South, blacks were trapped in a maze of proliferating discrimination. The spectrum of black response reached from cooperation to counsels of revolution. "In all things purely social we can be as separate as the fingers," Booker T. Washington told a largely white audience

FIGURE 118 ✒︎
Frontispiece photographs,
Booker T. Washington,
My Life and Work
(1900). The caption
underneath these photos
of Booker T.
Washington, President
William McKinley, and
Governor J. F. Johnston
of Alabama refers to
"Mr. Washington and
two of his distinguished
friends and supporters."

at the Atlanta Exposition of 1895, just a year before *Plessy*. Until
his death in 1915, Washington continued to press for friendship
between the races grounded mainly upon black conciliation and
compromise. His accommodating tone, along with his undeniable
accomplishments, gave him exceptional influence on white opinion
(Figure 118).

Washington's autobiography, *Up from Slavery* (1901), surveys a
career of uncommon achievement. Against daunting odds, he lifted
himself out of poverty and illiteracy, enacting America's dream of
success more dramatically than the white precedents on whom his
career was patterned. As a child, he had lived in a one-room log
shack with a dirt floor and no windows, eating his meals with his
fingers out of the common pot. His clothes were hand-made, and
he was forbidden by his stepfather to learn to read or write. Such
beginnings could have led to a lifetime of peonage; instead they

inspired Washington with a passion for learning and improvement. He moved forward with a quiet tenacity as unadorned and single-minded as the prose in which he tells of it. President of Tuskegee Institute for many years, he proved to be an unparalleled fundraiser and a shrewd administrator. Tuskegee also served as his political base, the headquarters of the "Tuskegee machine," through which he promoted his own prestige and the careers of his allies. The prominence he gained made him an international figure, but it also provoked the opposition, and in many cases the contempt, of other black leaders, who felt that he was willing to pay too high a price in political accommodation for modest economic gains.

Washington's chief critics included W. E. B. Du Bois, who responded sharply and unequivocally to the Atlanta Exposition speech, to *Up from Slavery*, and to the common use of Tuskegee's vocational training as a model for black education. Du Bois excoriated Washington for consenting to black inferiority and collaborating with the system that denied blacks their fundamental rights, including the right to vote. Du Bois laid out the terms of his argument in a review of Washington's autobiography and then in the essay entitled "Of Mr. Booker T. Washington and Others," which was included in the volume *The Souls of Black Folk* (1903). Where Washington offered himself as a representative figure, typifying the spacious opportunities open to American blacks, Du Bois attacked what he took to be Washington's timidity and his preemptive concern with his own prestige (Figure 119).

In his life as well as his ideas, Du Bois stood as Washington's antithesis. He was born just after the close of the Civil War and grew up in a middle-class Massachusetts family. He graduated from Fisk University and became the first black to earn a Ph.D. from Harvard, submitting a dissertation on the slave trade. In seven decades of research, teaching, and activism (he died in Ghana in 1963, at the age of ninety-five), Du Bois established himself as one of the principal radical figures of the twentieth century. He was an organizer of the militant Niagara Movement in 1905 and of the National Association for the Advancement of Colored People (NAACP); he served as the influential first editor of the NAACP journal, the *Crisis*.

Du Bois spoke truth to power, and he used what he called "the plainest English" in protesting the manifold evils of racism. At the

FIGURE 119 ❧ (*Seated*) W. E. B. Du Bois; (*behind him, left to right*) Freeman H. M. Murray; Lafayette M. Hershaw; William Monroe Trotter. The photograph was taken in about 1906, at an early meeting of the Niagara Movement.

same time, his analysis of black life in white America was informed as deeply by compassion as by anger, encompassing the psychological as well as the economic and political consequences of living behind "the veil." "Of Our Spiritual Strivings," the first essay in *The Souls of Black Folk*, provides the book's central themes and elaborates Du Bois's seminal insight into the singularity of a racial system which permits blacks "no true self-consciousness." Rather, they can see themselves only "through the revelation of the other world":

> It is a peculiar sensation, this double-consciousness, this sense of always looking at one's self through the eyes of others, of

measuring one's soul by the tape of a world that looks on in amused contempt and pity. One ever feels his twoness, – an American, a Negro; two souls, two thoughts, two unreconciled strivings; two warring ideals in one dark body, whose dogged strength alone keeps it from being torn asunder.

The Souls of Black Folk displays a remarkable range of genres and tones. The book's fourteen sections include fable, elegy, cultural history, bitter protest, and moving evocations of the black family and community. Music, education, religion, and economics are among his diverse subjects, but his unvarying demand is for liberation and untrammeled black participation in American politics and commerce. Du Bois detected no racial progress in the decades of the so-called Progressive Era, and his alienation grew in proportion. In later essays, including those collected in *Darkwater: Voices from within the Veil* (1921), he would show himself less patient, and less forgiving of white bigotry.

Du Bois struggled long against the stereotypes that throttled black aspirations, and he came to believe that his exertions were largely unavailing. Science conspired with prejudice to cement venomous conceptions of black inferiority. In the years before the First World War, such books as William P. Calhoun's *The Caucasian and the Negro* (1902), Carlyle McKinley's *Appeal to Pharaoh* (1907), and William Pickett's *Negro Problem* (1909) all justified the vulgar dogma of white supremacy by reference to one or another purportedly scientific system. With a few exceptions, the blacks who appeared in white literature were denied their humanity and cast as fools or beasts, contentedly shiftless or carnally insatiable. The nineteenth-century plantation tradition flowered again, for instance in the genially benighted work of Thomas Nelson Page, whose essays and novels in praise of the old order and the Lost Cause were more enthusiastically read in the North than in the South. The fictional diminishment of blacks reached a savage apotheosis in the novels of Thomas Dixon, Jr., who began his career as a Baptist minister and itinerant lecturer preaching the gospel of racial hierarchy. In rapid sequence, Dixon produced three volumes mourning the South's defeat in the Civil War, denouncing Reconstruction, and celebrating the vigilante justice of the Ku Klux Klan. Stimulated by the commercial success of *The Leopard's Spots* (1902), Dixon followed with *The Clansman* (1905), and *The Traitor* (1907). When

The Clansman was used by D. W. Griffith as the basis for the film *The Birth of a Nation* in 1915, Dixon's ideology found a forum of unprecedented scope.

For their part, black writers recognized that plain speaking about racial injustice would alienate the predominantly white book-buying public. Belittled by the pressure of white expectations, including an axiomatic association of black life with primitivism, a poet like Paul Laurence Dunbar met rebuke when he stepped outside dialect verse. It was only in dialect, William Dean Howells wrote, that Dunbar could wield a "direct and fresh authority . . . expressive of a race-life within the race." Dunbar, who died in 1906 while still in his midthirties, only occasionally pierced the barriers of polite restraint with poems of anger and protest. In "The Haunted Oak" (1903), a conventional poetic diction heightens by its formality the shock of a lynching, and "We Wear the Mask" (1896) is an anguished psychological sketch that condemns bigotry and capitulation at once:

> We smile, but, O great Christ, our cries
> To thee from tortured souls arise.
> We sing, but oh, the clay is vile
> Beneath our feet, and long the mile;
> But let the world dream otherwise,
>   We wear the mask.

Charles Waddell Chesnutt made opposition to the color line his subject in many of the stories and novels he wrote; for overstepping the genteel boundaries of accommodation, he found his promising career cut short. One of his earliest stories, "The Goophered Grapevine," was published in the *Atlantic* in 1887, marking the first appearance by a black writer in that most prestigious magazine (though his race was not disclosed to readers for several years). Chesnutt conceived of literature as a didactic instrument in the battle against caste and racism: the "province of literature," he wrote, is to open the way to social recognition and political equality for blacks and to help redress the "ever-lengthening record of Southern wrongs and insults." Chesnutt assailed racism with satire, pathos, and anger. Uncle Julius McAdoo, the old exslave who is the main character in "The Goophered Grapevine" and the other stories collected in *The Conjure Woman* (1899), subverts the several submissive traditions he seems to exemplify and establishes himself as a wily self-promoter. In *The House behind the Cedars* (1901), the light-skinned Rowena Walden's death is assignable to the murderous prejudice that makes her freedom in the South unimaginable. *The Marrow of Tradition* (1901), mingling documentary and romance, records Chesnutt's despairing recognition that segregation was intensifying and mob violence increasing in the early twentieth century. In short, conditions for black people were deteriorating rather than improving: racial history seemed to be going backward rather than forward. The hostile climate of racial opinion ensured the failure of Chesnutt's major novels and of his cause. For the last thirty years of his life, he remained active in civil rights work, but he wrote almost no fiction. His blighted career and enforced silence remain an eloquent indictment of America's racial beliefs.

A surging desire to renovate the nation linked demands for black civil rights and woman suffrage, and the struggle to improve the conditions of labor and the quality of city life. Reforms were typically grudging and tentative, sometimes collapsing into opportunism, but the premises of American politics were gradually revised. Progressives, to label them all summarily, required little formal theory; they stood in the line of utilitarian tinkerers and social problem solvers who constituted America's nearest approach to a native intellectual tradition. That legacy was codified and named by William James in a series of lectures that were subsequently collected in the book *Pragmatism* (1907). James, whose long career at Harvard included pathbreaking work in psychology, defined pragmatism as a cast of mind that appealed to results as the proper test of speculation. "The pragmatic method," James wrote, "is to try to interpret each notion by tracing its respective practical consequences. What difference would it practically make to anyone if this notion rather than that notion were true?" In James's view, beliefs are really rules for action, and consequences, rather than alleged first principles, ought to be placed at the center of philosophical inquiry.

The spirit of renewal that breathed through American politics and philosophy in the early twentieth century touched literature and the other arts as well. On both sides of the Atlantic, manifestos and movements flourished: cubism, fauvism, vorticism, constructivism, and futurism competed with each other for primacy and (no less important) for attention. In the main, these versions of modernism, which constituted a tumultuous and full-scale assault on received artistic traditions, were European developments; the battle was principally joined in Rome, Berlin, London, and, above all, Paris. Nonetheless, Americans played decisive roles. America no longer clung to "the circumference of civilization" to which Henry James had consigned it not so many years before. A country in which improvisation had always mediated between intention and act provided fertile soil for an emerging culture of slipping moments and fragments, an aesthetic in which the interrogatory replaced the declarative. In Paris, the expatriated Gertrude Stein settled at 27, rue de Fleurus, and gathered about her the men and women who "were to create the twentieth century art and literature," as she put it without undue modesty. In England, the young Americans Ezra Pound and Thomas Stearns Eliot launched a campaign to rescue poetry from what they took to be the encrustations of Victorian restraint and convention. In Chicago, a small, self-conscious renaissance took place under the leadership of Margaret Anderson, who put out the *Little Review*, and Harriet Monroe, editor of *Poetry: A Magazine of Verse*.

Gertrude Stein, the daughter of assimilated and affluent German-Jewish parents, was initially attracted to the intellectual rigor of philosophy and science. Surmounting the bias that restricted her to segregated classes and assorted "female annexes," she consistently distinguished herself in her studies with William James at Harvard, and she completed two years of medical school at Johns Hopkins. Shortly after the turn of the century, she moved to France and commenced the career of writing, patronage, art collecting, and theorizing that would make her one of modernism's pivotal figures. The home she shared with her lover Alice B. Toklas became a crowded gallery of postimpressionist painting, an indispensable place of pilgrimage for those in search of the avant-garde. Stein's prose, constructed according to all sorts of abstract notions and hermetic codes, was idiosyncratic and often indecipherable, but her editorial judgments, her imperious personal style, her advice, and her example enriched a generation of disciples. Her attempt to locate what she called the "bottom nature" of human identity led to linguistic experiments in which close observation was linked to image clusters and patterns of repetition that are sometimes stunning and sometimes merely bizarre. Stein was celebrated as an eccentric per-

sonality but her work was little read. Only one of her books achieved a measure of popularity, the self-portrait she wrote from the assumed point of view of her companion, *The Autobiography of Alice B. Toklas* (1933). Though it is sly and often funny, the *Autobiography* is little more than opinionated chat, a sustained self-advertisement proclaiming Stein's rightful place in the front ranks of twentieth-century genius. Her most durable work had come much earlier, especially in the short novels gathered in *Three Lives* (1905), where the prose is tempered by a steady simplicity and the stories of immigrant and black women are told directly, without condescension (Figure 120).

Shortly after Stein decamped from Baltimore for Paris, Ezra Pound and T. S. Eliot arrived in London, where they took upon themselves the task of sweeping away prevailing poetic values and rebuilding on new foundations in the space they had cleared. The English writer Richard Aldington said that Pound wanted to be London's "literary dictator," a phrase that could be applied to Eliot as well and suggests the authoritarian ground note of their critical

FIGURE 120 ❧ Man Ray, photograph of Alice B. Toklas and Gertrude Stein (1923). This picture was taken in the studio of 27, rue de Fleurus, Paris.

pronouncements. The flamboyant Pound and fastidious Eliot were altogether different in temperament, but they were kindred in their contempt for what they judged to be the spongy sentimentality, "emotional slither," and "painted adjectives" of contemporary verse and the general decadence of mass and middlebrow culture. Over the course of long and increasingly divergent careers, they sought refuge in a procession of solutions, Eliot eventually settling into the consolations of Anglo-Catholicism, Pound becoming the rabid propagandist of anti-Semitism and fascism. Like all evangelical theorists, they believed that elevated aesthetic opinions could somehow repair the world's political and economic injuries, a delusion that tempted them both into versions of autocracy in the years between the two world wars. Their significance for literature lay elsewhere and earlier, when they brought a searching light to poetic practice and engineered what Eliot grandly but accurately called a "revolution in taste." Pound proved to be the supreme literary patron and politician of the century, campaigning tirelessly for those who met his demands for authenticity and a rejection of the prevailing fashions: he championed Yeats, Joyce, Frost, Marianne Moore, Hemingway, the sculptor Gaudier-Brzeska, the composer George Antheil (Figure 121).

Pound had arrived in Europe at the end of a long journey that had begun in Hailey, Idaho, and led through the University of Pennsylvania and teaching jobs in New York and Indiana. Though he held no academic positions after 1914, Pound remained a teacher all his life, lecturing and hectoring the fit few on subjects ranging from oriental linguistics to constitutional law to economics. He was foreign editor for Harriet Monroe's *Poetry* magazine. Early in 1913, upon his recommendation, three poems were published in *Poetry* over the signature "H. D., Imagiste." These were the work of another expatriate, the Pennsylvanian Hilda Doolittle, who had come to Europe in 1911 after two unhappy years of study at Bryn Mawr College. Anticipating and exemplifying the short-lived but influential movement that would be called "imagism," Doolittle's first poems demonstrated her gifts for concentration, clarity, and novel rhythms suited to her subjects. Her early poetry – and the fiction she began to write in the twenties – also revealed her abiding interest in classical myth. *Sea Garden* (1916), her first collection, included paraphrases and translations from Sappho, Euripides, and Meleager.

Just before the First World War, Pound edited the anthology
Des Imagistes (1914), in which he included, along with his own
work, the poems of H. D., William Carlos Williams, F. S. Flint,
and Amy Lowell. In that volume, and in a manifesto published in
Poetry the preceding year, Pound codified imagist ideas in a series
of influential formulas and dicta. Poetry, he announced, must be
liberated from soft sentimentality, "superfluous" words, and pallid
abstraction; it must become a matter of "hard light, clear edges."
The flexible rhythm of speech is henceforth to be valued above the
regular beat of the metronome, and the core of poetry's identity is
now deemed to consist in its economy, concrete precision, and truth
of statement. In *A Few Don'ts by an Imagiste*, he defined an image
as "that which presents an intellectual and emotional complex in
an instant of time." His explanations of the image were punctuated
with talk of vigor and energy and illumination; his examples included some of Hilda Doolittle's work, and his own poem "In a
Station of the Metro," modeled in part on Japanese haiku:

FIGURE 121 &. Henri
Gaudier-Brzeska, pencil
sketch of Ezra Pound.
Gaudier-Brzeska drew
this profile before carving
his "Hieratic Head" of
Pound.

The apparition of these faces in the crowd;
Petals on a wet, black bough.

"Make it new," Pound famously decreed, but he and Eliot conceived of significant innovation as rooted in a reconstructed past. They ransacked several historical traditions, searching for precedents, for ideas of order, for legitimacy. They were conscious of themselves as radically modern yet radically alienated from the modern scene, and their poetry tensely groped after structures in which that complex awareness could be adequately expressed. The explosive originality of their poetic forms was thus a means of defending the elite cultures of the past against the headlong and heedless rush of the present. The first incontestable masterpiece of American modernism was Eliot's "Love Song of J. Alfred Prufrock" (1915). Opening with an epigraph from Dante's *Inferno*, "Prufrock" tries to capture the sensibility of the twentieth century in an extended, ironic confession that proceeds by way of allusive contrasts between the heroic past and the shrunken present. Eliot was still in his early twenties when he created the superbly realized voice of a timorous, middle-aged man whose fidgety introspection parodies and condemns the idle hours and fatuous cocktail party chatter of a generation (Figure 122). Prufrock is enveloped in a claustrophic atmosphere of sexual panic, and his purposeless life is redeemed only by his flickering awareness of his own moral and emotional vacancy:

> Let us go then, you and I,
> When the evening is spread out against the sky
> Like a patient etherised upon a table.

Beginning as a vanguard raid on gentility, modernism soon hardened into a triumphant orthodoxy; idiosyncratic preferences were elevated into indisputable assertions, and hierarchies were established that would dominate critical estimates for decades. Nonetheless, good work was being produced on other assumptions, including those of a more recognizably native tradition. In the years around the turn of the century, for example, Edwin

FIGURE 122 🍂 T. S. Eliot, outside the publishing firm of Faber & Gwyer (1927). Faber & Gwyer became Faber & Faber in 1929; Eliot worked for the firm for forty years.

Arlington Robinson labored obscurely at a series of volumes in which the defeated men and women of a joyless New England contemplate the dry bones of transcendentalism's vanished glory. The fictional "Tilbury Town" of Robinson's early poems is a place of cold north-eastern winds and clouds that block the sun. Emersonian "light" has become a mere figure of speech, a mocking reminder of hope withdrawn. Rather like Henry James, whose fiction he especially admired, Robinson was attracted to the drama that resided in rec-ollected missed chances and in loneliness. His irony could sometimes be merely clever, as in "Richard Cory" (1896), or mean-spirited, as in "Miniver Cheevy" (1910), a sketch of a boozy malcontent who longs for the glamour of the Middle Ages. A poem like "Isaac and Archibald" (1902), on the other hand, balances affection and detachment with uncanny sensitivity. The title characters are two old men, long since dead, whom the poem's adult narrator recalls from his childhood. His patient, retrospective meditation is a poign-ant masterpiece of blank verse, an utterly persuasive evocation of characters and setting. In this and in much of his work, Robinson made use of rather conventional forms, and long sentences, often suspended, which tend to create the effect of a carefully controlled prose. His writing could sometimes simply be slack, but his techniques were impeccably suited to his psychological preoccupations. A poem like "Eros Turannos" (1916), which renders a woman's desperate and self-destructive love for the man she knows will betray her, comes near the pity and terror of genuine tragedy.

Aside from the support of a few friends, and the admiration of Theodore Roosevelt (which led to a job as customs inspector in New York for four years), Robinson's work was met by a nearly unanimous indifference. He eventually won ample recognition, including three Pulitzer Prizes, but the rewards came years and even decades after his best work was finished, as if an embarrassed literary establishment wanted to repay him for such long neglect. An Arthurian trilogy made up the bulk of his work in the postwar years. The thematic links that bind the medieval and modern worlds in *Merlin* (1917), *Lancelot* (1920), and *Tristan* (1927) were forged out of Robinson's far-reaching disillusion, a conviction of human frailty that was only deepened by the bloodshed of the First World War. Robinson was immune to the nostalgia that transmuted the Middle Ages into a consoling anodyne for so many of his contemporaries; he was struck more by the likeness than the difference between his legendary heroes and the scene around him. He was, in a word, not so much a medieval revivalist as a medieval realist. For him, the human story has always been crowded with episodes of failure and betrayal, and the past teaches the same demoralizing lessons as the present.

Robinson's early poetry proved that the resources of traditional forms and homely talk were unexhausted. Among those who learned from his example, none exploited native materials more shrewdly or successfully than Robert Frost. "We must write with the ear on the speaking voice," he once said, a dictum which his poetry obeyed and vindicated. Born in California, Frost lived most of his long life in New England, and his poetry is anchored in that region. He became the best-known American poet of the twentieth century, but his popularity was based on a simplifying equation. W. H. Auden said, admiringly, that Frost had the temperament of a "smallholder," the farmer who owns and personally works his modest piece of ground. Frost's poetry was taken by his public to personify a cluster of stereotypical Yankee qualities. It seemed to invoke a familiar regional mythology, in which upright New Englanders are moral outcroppings of their rocky soil, a landscape whose flinty poverty demonstrates its value. Frost's characters are taciturn but thoughtful, reluctant speakers whose rare comments are larded with a rustic wisdom that underscores their authenticy. The silence of his close-mouthed men and women reproves the rising tide of garrulity associated with twentieth-century city life, the mass media, and the manipulative culture of advertising (Figure 123).

Such images embody the resilient pastoral longings of the American imagination, embraced all the more fervently as the center of the nation's life shifted from country to city. Frost's poetry is often superb on its own terms, but his outsized success had explanations beyond his achievement. For nearly half a century, he ministered to the needs that an urban civilization felt for an alternative, anterior vision, a conception of the nation rooted in the birches, frozen lakes, and plain people of its first and oldest wilderness. In fact, Frost's nostalgia, though palpable, is typically blunted by clarity, realism, and an awareness of tragedy, dimen-

FIGURE 123 ❧
Photograph of Robert Frost (ca. 1915). This picture, taken in Franconia, New Hampshire, shows Frost working at a writing desk he built for himself.

sions that many of his enthusiasts ignored. Nonetheless, he learned to enjoy the role assigned to him, consenting to perform in countless lectures and readings as an American sage, a latter-day "Good Gray Poet" whose character and private life were notoriously at variance with the artfully groomed benevolence of his public persona.

Frost was nearly forty when he first came to public notice. His long apprenticeship had included work as a bobbin boy in a Massachusetts mill; a semester at Dartmouth; two years at Harvard; teaching; marriage to Elinor White; several children; and a failed effort to live self-sufficiently on a New Hampshire farm. For two decades he wrote steadily, but only a few of his poems found their way into print. The turning point came in 1912, when he sold the farm and took his family to England. His expatriation was brief, but it was in England that he found a publisher for his first volume, *A Boy's Will* (1913), which received several approving notices. In an influential review in *Poetry*, Ezra Pound wrote that Frost was a man with "the good sense to speak naturally and to paint the thing, the thing as he sees it." *North of Boston* (1914), which Frost described as "a book of people," enlarged his reputation among the critics and brought him the public attention he would command for nearly fifty years.

Frost was consciously indebted to his New England predecessors, including Robinson, Thoreau, and especially Emerson. Like them, he believed that the language and rhythm of poetry consisted of "natural words in the natural order." Like them, too, he assumed that the visible world was suggestive; he said that the goal of his poetry was "metaphor," and he defined metaphor as "saying one thing in terms of another." Thus, his unequaled powers of observation result in a profusion of natural details caught and preserved, images which also carry the burden of moral and psychological insight. Most of his finest poems appeared in his early volumes, among them the narratives, dialogues, and dramatic monologues that perfected colloquial speech and sought out the joys and griefs of hidden country lives: "Mending Wall," "Home Burial," "A Servant to Servants," and "The Black Cottage" (all published in 1914). In "The Wood-Pile" (1914), a speaker walking in a frozen swamp turns the trees around him into a landscape of loneliness:

> The view was all in lines
> Straight up and down of tall slim trees
> Too much alike to mark or name a place by
> So as to say for certain I was here
> Or somewhere else: I was just far from home.

The tension of the coiled lines builds toward its climactic statement of homelessness and separation. The voice here is typical in its self-denial and carefully controlled emotion. When Frost wrote that "I prefer the synecdoche in poetry – that figure of speech in which we use a part for the whole," he suggested the sense of restraint that gives an instantly recognizable texture to his writing. The oven bird, a woodland surrogate for the poet, is a creature that "knows in singing not to sing":

> The question that he frames in all but words
> Is what to make of a diminished thing.

Frost's poetry, and especially the matchlessly authentic voice in which his speakers address their isolation, was his answer to the oven bird's question.

Frost and Robinson, whatever their affinities, stood apart from each other and from other formal groups and movements. First by circumstance and then by choice, they adopted a style of studious New England self-reliance. The new writers of the Midwest, on the other hand, gathered in force, making Chicago the most concentrated scene of American poetic experiment in the years before the First World War. Chicago in the prewar years was also the site of America's most consequential new architecture. A succession of architects, among them Louis Sullivan and Frank Lloyd Wright, made their headquarters in Chicago and redefined the vocabulary and grammar of American design (Figure 124).

The most useful index to literary developments was the magazine *Poetry*, whose tables of contents represented Harriet Monroe's eclectic but canny editorial judgments. *Poetry* rather resembled the Armory Show of 1913 in its catalytic effect and in symbolizing the emergence of avant-garde aesthetic possibilities in America. Modernism was "going to occur" (as Meyer Shapiro put it years ago) with or without *Poetry* or the Armory Show, but the magazine and the exhibition had much to do with the particular texture and

FIGURE 124   Frank Lloyd Wright, *The Larkin Building* (1905). This drawing, of one of Wright's most important buildings, was included in *The Wasmuth Portfolio*, published in Germany by the Wasmuth Press in 1910. The one hundred plates in the book influenced European architecture for a generation.

nuance of modernist performance in America, and they had much to do, as well, with creating an audience sympathetic to the new work.

Alongside the early poems of Eliot, Pound, and Frost, Monroe published the quite different work of Vachel Lindsay, Carl Sandburg, and Edgar Lee Masters. Lindsay was driven by the rather odd desire "to be the great singer of the Y.M.C.A. Army," and he more or less satisfied his ambition in 1913, when "General Booth Enters into Heaven" appeared in *Poetry*. A preacher by inclination, and an enthusiastic populist, Lindsay produced poetry more suited for public performance than for reading and contemplation. Indeed, his most famous poems make absolutely no intellectual demands, contenting themselves with urgent oratorical appeals measured in the booming, insistent rhythms of a bass drum. Appropriating and vulgarizing Afro-American antiphonal strategies, Lindsay constructed an aesthetic of deliberated primitivism, and he referred to his work, without irony, as episodes in "the Higher Vaudeville."

Carl Sandburg was a better poet than Lindsay, though his verse also suffers from bardic pretensions and he was subject to a mechanical populism that too often confused art with democratic noises. He came by his politics early and altered his views only slightly during a long life. The son of Swedish immigrants, he grew up poor and ill educated, spent a little time in the army, then worked as an organizer for Wisconsin's Social Democratic party, as secretary to the socialist mayor of Milwaukee, and as a writer for the radical Milwaukee *Leader*. The title of one of his later volumes, *The People, Yes* (1936) summarized his commitment to ordinary folk. In the service of those people, he devised a sort of roughneck aesthetic, an affair of prosy rhythms; street-smart, slangy diction; and direct, emphatic statement. Nuance was not in Sandburg's line. "Chicago," which was published in *Poetry* in 1914, remains one of his best-known works, and its opening lines typify his practice:

> Hog Butcher for the World,
> Tool Maker, Stacker of Wheat,
> Player with Railroads and the Nation's Freight Handler;
> Stormy, husky, brawling,
> City of the Big Shoulders:
> They tell me you are wicked and I believe them, for I have
>   seen your painted women under the gas lamps luring
>   the farm boys.

Whitman's influence is clear enough in Sandburg's poems, but so are the differences that separate the two writers. Whitman's broad and deep identification with human diversity has been reduced to a narrow polemical point, his intoxicated engagement with language has shrunk to earnest verbal gesture. Furthermore, the declamatory tone of "Chicago," which is typical of Sandburg's work, usually accompanies Whitman's weakest lines (Figure 125).

Recognition came late but abruptly. Sandburg was thirty-eight when *Chicago Poems* appeared in 1916 and made him famous. In that volume and in the many that followed, his bounce and brag made an undeniable if modest contribution to the reclamation of American poetry. Beyond that, his celebrations of city lowlifes and prairie immigrants proved irresistible to an audience that mistrusted refinement and craved an opportunity to admire its own crudity. His devotion to America attracted him to the study of folklore,

FIGURE 125   Edward
Steichen, photomontage
of Carl Sandburg (1936).

history, and biography. Like Lindsay and other midwestern writers,
he revered Lincoln as the preeminent American hero. His devotion
led to a sprawling, adulatory biography, *Abraham Lincoln*, published
in two parts: *The Prairie Years*, whose two volumes appeared in 1916,
and the four volumes of *The War Years*, published in 1939. The
biography is probably his best work.

Along with Lindsay and Sandburg, the third of the poets whose
work served notice that Chicago intended to take its literary place
was Edgar Lee Masters. In a literary career that began in conventional lyrics and ended in drab naturalism, Masters produced one
exceptional book. *The Spoon River Anthology* (1915) immortalizes
his hatred of the small Illinois towns in which he grew up. Inspired
by the epigraphs and gnomic verses of the *Greek Anthology*, Masters's
volume is a sequence of over two hundred poems, confessions spoken
by the men and women buried in the cemetery of a small midwestern
town. Candid and sometimes shocking, these verse epitaphs are
designed to tear away the masks of village life and disclose closely
guarded secrets of sin and regret and grief. Petit the Poet missed his
artistic chance by contenting himself with "little iambics, / While

Homer and Whitman roared in the pines." Knowlt Hoheimer died in the Civil War, "the first fruits of the battle of Missionary Ridge"; he lies under a patriotic Latin inscription that he cannot understand. Like Petit and Hoheimer, many of Spoon River's dead citizens are trapped in the eternal contemplation of lives cut short or wasted, grain by grain, in futility. Masters sometimes makes his satiric argument by contrasting sketches, the dismal moral of which is the routine success of corruption over the outnumbered forces of virtue. Newsman Carl Hamblin, who protested the hanging of the Haymarket anarchists, was tarred and feathered for his courage, his press wrecked by the mob. Editor Whedon, on the other hand, had the ethics of a sneak thief and prospered thereby, using privileged information for revenge and personal profit. There is occasional release from bitterness in Spoon River, and even moments of exaltation, but such interludes only emphasize the prevailing despair. A rueful disappointment fills these pages, linking one vignette to another in a shared sigh of disappointment and stunted dreams.

Sherwood Anderson complained that Spoon River was too squarely "founded on hatred" and that Masters had lamed himself with his sneering attitude toward his subjects. Nonetheless, Spoon River helped Anderson solve the structural problems confronting his own writing by suggesting how a sequence of separate tales could be coherently knit together. The result, after several more years of experimentation, was Winesburg, Ohio (1919), Anderson's third book and his one masterpiece, a work that served for a generation as the definitive report on the vanishing American small town. More accurately, Winesburg is Anderson's testament of youth, his ambivalent memorial to the midwestern village from which he had only partially escaped (Figure 126).

When he reconstructed his own life in his conversations and memoirs, Anderson placed a dramatic story at the center, a kind of secular conversion experience in which he found the nerve to abandon his middle-class responsibilities and commit himself to art. He was thirty-five years old, and up to that point had followed a modestly successful career that led from a boyhood in Clyde, Ohio, to the presidency of a paint company. On November 27, 1912, as Anderson told it, he literally walked out of his office, leaving his job, his wife, and his children behind. "For the rest of my life," he recalled whispering to himself, "I will be a servant to words alone."

FIGURE 126 ⫸ Alfred Stieglitz, photograph of Sherwood Anderson (1923).

The anecdote is only partly true, but its appeal to Anderson and his contemporaries is probably more relevant than its accuracy. Rather like the alleged suppression of *Sister Carrie*, Anderson's revolt against convention took its cherished place in the avant-garde allegory that pitted the sensitive and alienated artist against the marketplace and its conformities.

Anderson had a gambler's passion for literature; that, along with the candor of his fiction, made him a model for younger writers. Some, like Hemingway, eventually repaid him in condescension and parody, but his influence was far-reaching. He expanded the range of what could be said in fiction, and his technical innovations encouraged others to go beyond his example in redefining literary practice. Life itself, he once wrote, "is a loose, flowing thing. There are no plot stories in life." This recognition of the flux of experience was a central motif of modernism, an aesthetic axiom that Anderson shared with writers and artists on both sides of the Atlantic. Gertrude Stein's *Three Lives* and *Tender Buttons* (1914) demonstrated that language had to be broken down and reconstructed to capture life's formless flow with precision. The paintings of the Postimpressionists, which Anderson saw in Chicago in 1914, taught a complementary lesson. The violent disregard that Cézanne, Gauguin, and Van Gogh showed for academic canons of imitative accuracy persuaded him that the truth of existence had to be sought beyond or beneath the surface of received convention.

Such assumptions were too volatile to be contained within the confines of the traditional novel or the well-made short story. What Anderson sought was a fiction that would renounce the contrivances of plot but would still have its own internal logic, a structure of impression and metaphor and deep motivation. *Winesburg* represented his nearest approach to the kind of book his conception of literature demanded. Though many of the two dozen tales that make up the volume had been published separately in such magazines as the *Little Review* and *The Masses*, they nonetheless became, when gathered together, convincing elements in a mosaic of loneliness and repressed desire. The book is unified by its setting: by its central character, the apprentice writer, George Willard; and by Anderson's notion of "the grotesque." The term, which is somewhat obscurely described in a prefatory essay, is made clearer in the sketches themselves. The grotesques are men and women locked into a claustrophobic isolation by some wound that will not heal or an obsession that topples normal reason. Communication shrinks to the vanishing point; even talk becomes impossible, and touch is dangerous. Ironically, the impenetrable barriers between the people of Winesburg are doubled by the proximity of neighbor to neighbor. In Anderson's rendering, the peaceable kingdom of small-town myth gives way to a grimmer drama; the town is revealed as the locale in which parallel but unshared individual tragedies are enacted. Only George Willard escapes from the emotional blight, making contact with each of Winesburg's citizens in turn and offering the redemption of understanding. Joyfully confused in his adolescent sexual awakening and his devotion to writing, Willard challenges the town's death-in-life with his naive vitality. His moments of illumination are the portals of epiphany through which the future is glimpsed like lamps on a darkened street. His departure for the city, for adulthood and a career as a writer, brings the book to its inevitable close (Figure 127).

Anderson had been working on the sketches of *Winesburg* for years, but the book was not published until after the First World

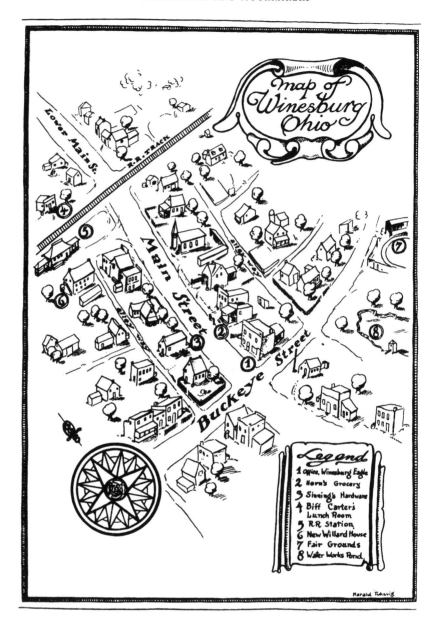

FIGURE 127 ❧ Harald Toksvig drew this map of Winesburg, Ohio, for the first edition of Sherwood Anderson's book.

War, an accident of chronology that enriched its significance. The town stands on the edge of a new America, its eighteen hundred citizens a collective memorial to the bygone world that preceded the transformations of technology, industry, and urban growth. Contesting with Anderson's flinch of distaste for his small-town youth is a pervasive nostalgia that looks back to a time and place in which the measures of existence were smaller and slower. Though the streets of Winesburg make up a landscape of emotional aridity and twisted souls, they have also been for George Willard the scene of dawning insight, companionship, and even love. The town's absorption into the mechanical, urban civilization of the twentieth century was aptly announced in the wake of history's most mechanized and destructive war.

CHAPTER SIX

❧ Between the wars ❧

THE WAR, concluded in 1918 after four years of unimaginable slaughter, loomed over the decade of the twenties, doing much to shape the attitudes of writers on both sides of the Atlantic. "After the war," said Gertrude Stein, "we had the twentieth century." On the third anniversary of the armistice, November 11, 1921, President Harding led a delegation of dignitaries to Arlington National Cemetery to bury the Unknown Soldier. Perhaps no event of the twenties so compactly symbolizes the rupture that the war created between the windy bromides of politicians and the disillusion of private citizens. Cabinet officers and Supreme Court justices and congressmen, along with generals and diplomats from all the Allied nations, attended the solemn service. They heaped the coffin with medals and wreaths, and they listened attentively as the president assured the nameless dead soldier that "his sacrifice, and that of the millions dead, shall not be in vain."

A good many Americans thought otherwise. Thorstein Veblen wrote what many others thought when he jeered at "the rant and bounce of Red Cross patriotism." Revulsion from the war, and from the Versailles peace, became a major fact of the moral life of the twenties, a leading motive behind some of the decade's most characteristic and most powerful work. Even before Harding crooned that "we return this poor clay to its native soil garlanded by love and covered with the decorations that only nations can bestow," Ezra Pound had given the angry answer in "Hugh Selwyn Mauberley" (1919):

> Died some, pro patria,
>   non "dulce" non "et decor"...

believing in old men's lies, then unbelieving...
There died a myriad,
And of the best, among them,
For an old bitch gone in the teeth,
For a botched civilization.

For the writers who took part in it – among them Edith Wharton, Ernest Hemingway, E. E. Cummings, John Dos Passos, Edmund Wilson – and for many who did not, the calamity of the war resided not merely in its appalling brutality but, even more tragically, in the distance between that reality and the pieties in which it had been disguised. As writers, they felt that their language had been stolen from them and abused.

John Dos Passos had served as a medical corpsman in the war and returned to the United States with a suffocating anger against the established order that had ordained so much death. His *Three Soldiers* (1921) was among the first of the war's novels, and it was among the most savage in its repudiation of war and the military. In the stories of three young men who go to France to fight, and especially in the fate of John Andrews, a sensitive and talented musician condemned to death for desertion, Dos Passos dramatized the war's irredeemable barbarism. "The lies! The lies," Andrews weeps, summing up the complaint of a generation against its leaders. The sense of betrayal was indelible. Years later, Dos Passos re-created the scene at Arlington in the final pages of *Nineteen Nineteen* (1932), the second volume of his *U.S.A.* trilogy. He unmasked the hypocrisy of the event by locating his point of view inside the coffin, with the dead, nameless soldier, and he replaced patriotic platitudes with pain. A staccato sequence of sometimes gruesome images overwhelms Harding's unctuous rhetoric:

The shell had his number on it.
The blood ran into the ground. . . .
The blood ran into the ground, the brains oozed out of the cracked skull and were licked up by the trenchrats, the belly swelled and raised a generation of bluebottle flies, and the incorruptible skeleton, and the scraps of dried viscera and skin bundled in khaki...
Where his chest ought to have been they pinned the Congressional Medal.

The novel closes with a glimpse of the crippled and dying Woodrow Wilson, a bouquet of poppies in his hand, flowers that signify both the death of America's heroes and the obliteration of the naive trust they carried with them to the western front.

E. E. Cummings also served as an ambulance driver in the war and spent six months in the French concentration camp of La Ferté Macé, under suspicion for "treasonable correspondence." The charge was a mistake, a symptom of the bureaucratic bungling that seemed as central to the war as wounds and death. Cummings shaped the squalor and fear of his experience into *The Enormous Room* (1922), a nightmare in prose, in which the prison becomes the frightening symbol of the mindless, ubiquitous state and its power to intrude into private lives. As the prisoners wait in the camp's enormous central room to be called before the dreaded commission, they are guarded by a jailer with "the Wooden Hand." Conversation is forbidden but goes on sporadically, interrupted by threats from the "amiable Wooden Hand":

> Twice the door SLAMMED open, and *Monsieur le Directeur* bounced out frothing at the mouth and threatening everyone with infinite *cabinot*, on the grounds that everyone's deportment or lack of it was menacing the aplomb of the commissioners. Each time the Black Holster appeared in the background and carried on his master's bullying until everyone was completely terrified – after which we were left to ourselves and The Wooden Hand once again.

Life in the enormous room is a surreal mingling of slapstick and terror. The bureaucracy in charge of this madness embodies Cummings's protest against the so-called civilization in whose service so many millions died (Figure 128).

No one felt more acutely than Ernest Hemingway that the war had drawn a line across history. He was a respectable child of the middle-class suburbs of Chicago who had spent some of the most memorable hours of his boyhood camping and fishing in the northern Michigan woods with his physician father. After high school, he took his first job as a reporter for the Kansas City *Star*, where he learned the rudiments of his craft: "Avoid the use of adjectives," he read in the *Star*'s style sheet, "especially such extravagant ones as splendid, gorgeous, grand, magnificent, etc." He covered Kansas

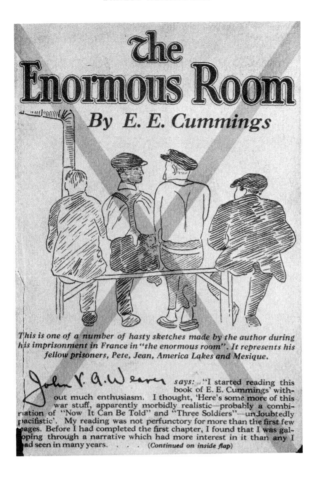

FIGURE 128 ❧ Dust jacket, E. E. Cummings, *The Enormous Room* (1922). Cummings drew this cartoon, which appeared on the dust jacket of the first edition.

City's fires and gangsters for two years, but he knew that the war was where the big stories and the action were.

In 1918, Hemingway traveled to the Italian front in search of copy and adventure and was wounded while driving an ambulance. Personal injury shocked him into a reappraisal of the meaning of power and the fate of the individual trapped within the mass bureaucracies of the twentieth century. What he now saw was the skull beneath the skin of modern politics. In a famous passage in *A Farewell to Arms* (1929), Lt. Frederic Henry laments that the subjection of language to militarist ambition has murdered truth. According to Lieutenant Henry, words like "sacrifice" and "glorious" have become embarrassing: the battlefields are like "the stockyards at Chicago." Only proper names and unanalyzed physical experiences retain their dignity:

Certain numbers were the same way and certain dates and these with the names of the places were all you could say and have them mean anything. Abstract words such as glory, honor, courage, or hallow were obscene words beside the concrete names of villages, and the numbers of roads, the names of rivers, the numbers of regiments and the dates.

As Hemingway picked through the war's debris, he decided that nothing remained intact save the self and the objects of the self's regard. Recording the unembellished names of rivers and streets and taverns became the burden of Hemingway's prose. It was therefore a prose of rigorous selectivity and strenuous compression, stripped of the usual ornaments of literary convention. Narrow in its range, Hemingway's style always teetered on the edge of self-parody, but it could be compelling in its single-minded concentration:

In the late summer of that year we lived in a house in a village that looked across the river and the plain to the mountains. In the bed of the river there were pebbles and boulders, dry and white in the sun, and the water was clear and swiftly moving and blue in the channels.

In sentences like these, Hemingway was creating the most influential style of the twentieth century; he was the only writer after Samuel Clemens to alter the literary language of the nation. Young writers, women as well as men, envied his career and emulated his prose (Figure 129).

"You are all a lost generation," Gertrude Stein had said in a legendary remark, and Hemingway hoisted the comment like a banner over his fiction. In one of his few extended comments on American literature, in *Green Hills of Africa* (1935), he wrote that "a new classic does not bear any resemblance to the classics that have preceded it." As a critical statement the remark is silly, but it sums up Hemingway's desire to produce a fiction that would cut its ties to the past, deny its literary debts, and be fundamentally new. Abandoned by history, Hemingway communicated both his despair and his sense of existential obligation to his most sensitive and watchful characters. These are men and women who refuse the consolations of traditional values, including those of religion, and seek comfort instead in the pleasures of alcohol, sport, and sex. Jake

the author *wood-cut from portrait by* henry strater

in our time
by

ernest hemingway

FIGURE 129 ❧
Frontispiece and title
page, Ernest Hemingway,
In Our Time (1924).

paris:
printed at the three mountains press *and for sale
at* shakespeare & company, *in the rue de l'odéon;*
london: william jackson, *took's court, cursitor street, chancery lane.*

1924

Barnes, in *The Sun Also Rises* (1926), has been emasculated in the war. His injury serves as an emblem for the decade's worldly but world-weary survivors, men and women who drift back and forth from one European city to another in an aimless but representative odyssey, knowledgeable, cynical, spiritually exhausted. They place the small faith they can muster in the rigorous demands of a stoic code, and snatch what remains of honor from the fallen world by behaving with decorum and a sense of elementary decency. Action and language alike must be disciplined to maintain their grace under the inescapable pressure of reality's violence. Complaint and emotional expression are the marks of inadequacy. Characters like Jake Barnes, Brett Ashley, and Bill Gorton, who recognize the code's demands, are bound together by their disillusioned acceptance of limits and by their shared reticence. A character such as Robert Cohn, on the other hand, who makes a clamor on behalf of personal feelings, is condemned to the exile of obsolete gestures and conventions.

A primitive concept of masculinity, surely hardened by his own uncertain sense of sexual identity and his inclinations toward androgyny, impels much of Hemingway's fiction. Shaken by the pointless cruelty of the war and by his father's suicide shortly afterward, Hemingway adopted a glamorized, stylized violence as his own first principle. He presents situations of extremity as if they were the most reliable crucibles of human testing, yet his struggle to master undignified sentiment often leads to its own sentimentality. Warfare, African exploration, fishing, boxing, and big-game hunting offer the kinds of romantic terrain in which men can affirm their manliness. In one of Hemingway's best-known short stories, "The Short Happy Life of Francis Macomber" (1936), the title character justifies his existence in a momentary but fully achieved manhood that permits him to dominate his fears of both death and women. Similarly, in "The Killers" (1927), Ole Anderson accepts his own murder with a fatalism that confers a measure of secular sanctity on him. In *Death in the Afternoon* (1932), a nonfictional account of bullfighting, Hemingway elaborates his belief that courage and restraint can transform what would otherwise be bloody slaughter into the meaningful patterns of ritual.

At the same time, it was not victory so much as stalemate and defeat that attracted Hemingway. The struggle against fear that fills his stories and novels with anxious tension is perhaps his characteristic subject, and his rendering of moments of challenge and loss remains his most authentic and durable achievement. His best work came early. *The Sun Also Rises* was his first and probably his finest novel. In the second half of his life, he played the lead in a kind of cultural morality play, acting out his own sour prophecies about the ways in which good writers lose their talent. Indulging in the satisfactions of wealth and international celebrity, he produced stories that grew progressively weaker, little more than weary imitations of himself. *The Old Man and the Sea* (1952) demonstrated something of the patient concentration that had distinguished Hemingway's fiction in the twenties and early thirties, and it provided the occasion for the award of the Nobel Prize that he received in 1954. However, the personal and artistic losses were irreversible, and within a few years he was dead by his own hand.

Edmund Wilson suggested that the landscapes of Hemingway's fiction, like his characters, are wounded. Though often brightly lit and agreeable, they are shadowed by suffering, by "the undruggable consciousness of something wrong." The wound that Hemingway's work so often contemplates recurs as a thematic motif in much of postwar poetry and fiction. T. S. Eliot's Fisher King, the mythical ruler of *The Waste Land* (1922), has suffered the same emasculating injury as Jake Barnes, a maiming that inflicts sterility upon the soil and signifies a universal moral exhaustion. At the time of the poem's publication, Eliot was thirty-four years old, on leave from his work at Lloyd's Bank in London, recovering in a sanatorium in Lausanne, Switzerland, from a breakdown. His own suffering had much to do with the desperate tone of the poem, but many readers seized on it as the brilliantly unnerving testament of a shattered culture. Years later, in 1934, Eliot briskly rejected such a reading: "When I wrote a poem called *The Waste Land* some of the more approving critics said I had expressed 'the disillusionment of a generation,' which is nonsense." Nonetheless, *The Waste Land* caused a sensation when it was first published in the *Dial*, and it was read for decades as a fiercely compressed encyclopedia of the collapse of postwar values.

Many of the characteristics and devices of *The Waste Land* had appeared in Eliot's earlier poetry: the fluent use of literary and mythic pasts, the fascination with final causes, the nervous energy, the uncanny control of rhythm. From his beginnings as a writer, Eliot was driven by an urge to recapture for poetry the centrality he believed had seeped away from it into the stony ground of Victorian materialism. In the poems leading up to and away from *The Waste Land*, a satiric gallery of modern urban characters passes in review, hollow men and women caught in loveless, pointless monotony:

Birth, and copulation, and death.
That's all the facts when you come to brass tacks:
Birth, and copulation, and death.
I've been born, and once is enough.

Sweeney draws that mordant conclusion from his life, in "Sweeney Agonistes" (1927). This is the same man who, in an earlier poem ("Sweeney among the Nightingales," 1920), "spreads his knees, / Letting his arms hang down to laugh," while the "zebra stripes along his jaw" swell grotesquely to resemble those of a giraffe. "Gerontion" (1920) is spoken in a dry month by an old man, the tenant of a rented, draughty house, barely able to force his muttered curses against the decaying modern world (and its Jews) through grimly clenched teeth.

Eliot had planned to reprint "Gerontion" as a sort of prelude to *The Waste Land*. It was Pound who talked him out of it, and Pound who made some of the most extensive and celebrated editorial suggestions ever offered by one poet to another. Eliot accepted much of Pound's advice, in particular making substantial cuts in the typescript, which had a good deal to do with the poem's final shape and texture. Densely allusive, startling in its contrasts and transitions, uncommonly learned in its appearance, *The Waste Land* made unprecedented academic and emotional demands on its readers. The opening lines became famous as the signature of a generation's mood:

> April is the cruellest month, breeding
> Lilacs out of the dead land, mixing
> Memory and desire, stirring
> Dull roots with spring rain.

The poem's tone modulates from the timorous sigh of these opening phrases, through fear and anguish and confusion, finally resolving into an ambiguous, provisional affirmation: "These fragments I have shored against my ruins."

The fragments which the Fisher King shores up against the ruin of the wasted land are cause for fragile hope. They are also the key to Eliot's method in the poem, his kaleidoscopic résumé of a culture in crisis. His effort was to master the discontinuities of postwar society by incorporating them into an idiosyncratic but deliberated structure. In this *The Waste Land* typifies the long poems of the twenties and later. Many of the landmarks of American literary modernism – from Pound's *Cantos* to Hart Crane's *Bridge* and William Carlos Williams's *Paterson* – would be similarly cobbled together out of history's broken pieces.

These and other writers in the years between two world wars recorded heightened anxieties, a conviction of some fundamental split in the culture. One response to the pervasive sense of dislocation was a multiplied migration from America to Europe. To be sure, the new expatriates were part of a long history. Over the years, many American artists had found their native land inhospitable and sought in Europe the aesthetic nourishment they could not find in the United States. Pound and Eliot, Gertrude Stein, Edith Wharton, and Henry James, Mary Cassatt and John Singer Sargent, to name only the most prominent in the years before the war, had found shelter in England or France or Italy. However, the torpid years of "normalcy" intensified the alienation that divided some of America's best artists and writers from their home. In 1913, Pound had written that "there are just two things in the world, two great and interesting phenomena: the intellectual life of Paris and the curious teething promise of my own vast occidental nation." After the war, as if on Pound's cue, Paris became the special place of American pilgrimage, and the figure of the expatriate joined the other sights on the Left Bank. Not all of these self-elected artists would do important work; not all would even try. In 1922, in a commentary published in the Toronto *Star Weekly*, Hemingway ridiculed what he called the "American Bohemians" in Paris:

> You can find anything you are looking for at the Rotonde [café] – except serious artists. The trouble is that people who go on a tour of the Latin Quarter look in at the Rotonde and think they are seeing an assembly of real artists of Paris. I want to correct this in a very public manner, for the artists of Paris who are turning out creditable work resent and loathe the Rotonde crowd.

But along with the poseurs and the crackpots and the tourists came serious artists in numbers. They came because the postwar franc stood at fifteen to the dollar and because so many others from other countries came, too. Painters, poets, and musicians from all the countries of Europe and from North and South America made Paris the cosmopolitan and artistic capital of the Western world. Gertrude Stein found an aphorism to fit the circumstances when she said that "America is my country but Paris is my home town."

Harold Stearns sailed for France in 1921. Just before his departure, he finished editing and sent to his publisher the anthology *Civilization in the United States* (1922). The essays that Stearns collected, by thirty-three writers, anatomized the state of American society under headings ranging from "The City" to "Poetry" to "The Alien" to "Nerves." The contributors to this minor classic of cultural history included Van Wyck Brooks, Lewis Mumford, Ring Lardner, and H. L. Mencken. While there are differences in emphasis and disagreements over detail, the articles in Stearns's volume are striking chiefly for their broad and gloomy consensus. With few exceptions, the essays are angry, even embittered, estimates of the American scene. "The most moving and pathetic fact in the social life of America today," Stearns wrote in the preface, "is emotional and aesthetic starvation." Editor and contributors alike deemed America's air provincial, utilitarian, thin. In short, in a critique that brings forward the earlier opinions of de Tocqueville, Hawthorne, Henry James, and others, "civilization" was assumed to be a misnomer for the social structures and values the United States had produced.

These are the testimonies of internal exiles. Van Wyck Brooks, in "The Literary Life," remarked on "the singular impotence" of America's "creative spirit." H. L. Mencken, the caustic critic of middle-class values and propagandist for tough-minded skepticism, fulminated against American politicians:

> What they know of sound literature is what one may get out of McGuffey's Fifth Reader. What they know of political science is the nonsense preached in the chautauquas and on the stump. What they know of history is the childish stuff taught in grammar-schools. What they know of the arts and sciences – of all the great body of knowledge which is the chief intellectual baggage of modern man – is absolutely nothing.

Along with most other social critics in the twenties and thirties, the participants in Stearns's symposium identified three forces as primarily responsible for America's cultural impoverishment: puritanism, the pioneer spirit, and business. In countless articles and books between the two world wars, these three abstractions were personified in assorted allegorical tableaux. The Puritan's hypocrisy and joyless bigotry, the pioneer's rootless wandering and casual lawlessness, the businessman's philistinism and insatiable greed: these were the recurring targets of satire. Stearns himself, to give one example, vigorously pummeled the pioneer (along with women) in his essay "The Intellectual Life." The American, in Sterns's puckish phrase, is "the pioneer *toujours*," unencumbered by idealism, suspicious of mind, indifferent to spirit.

The Puritan elicited even more of the scorn of postwar intellectuals than the pioneer. The bumptious Mencken again led the charge, impaling puritanism on the rather blunt edge of his contempt in essay after essay. In the *American Mercury*, the influential journal of literature and opinion that he coedited with George Jean Nathan, Mencken famously defined "puritanism" as "the haunting fear that somewhere, someone may be happy" (Figure 130). The Puritan, who had previously been held in rather high esteem, was transformed in the opening decades of the new century into an emblem of

FIGURE 130 ℘
Photograph of George Jean Nathan and H. L. Mencken (1924).

intolerance, repression, and sterility. Apparently, the age demanded a more sinister Puritan. Writers who were self-consciously separating themselves from traditional pieties insisted, somewhat predictably perhaps, that the pieties were polluted at their source. Brooks Adams, John Jay Chapman, and Randolph Bourne in "The Puritan's Will to Power" (1917) were among the prewar writers who contributed to the revision. After the war, the leveling gathered momentum. Vernon L. Parrington's *Main Currents of American Thought* (1927) diagnosed many of America's cultural ailments as Puritan in origin. And Waldo Frank, in *The Re-discovery of America* (1929), included puritanism among the "cults" that had sapped whatever vitality America might have had. Frank claimed that American puritanism, shorn of its original religious dimensions, had shrunk to a mere ideology, a habit of regulation, a need "to say No."

For William Carlos Williams, the witchcraft trials of 1692 marked out a dark avenue leading directly to the underside of the American character. *In The American Grain* (1925), Williams's eccentric prose masterpiece, condemns the Puritans in large measure by simply transcribing several of the trial reports verbatim. The Puritans' own accounts, in Williams's view, prove them "spiritless, thus without grounds on which to rest their judgments of this world." Heir to the long tradition of Romanticism, Williams counseled a prodigal generosity and defined "morality" away from the rigid puritanic moralism. "It is *this* to be *moral*," Williams declared: "to be *positive*, to be peculiar, to be sure, generous, brave – TO MARRY, *to touch* – to give because one HAS." To touch. Antipathy toward the Puritan tells much about the postwar years. The burden of the complaint was more than sexual, of course, but it encompassed sexuality. Young men and women wrote about sex as if it were being discovered for the first time. Sexual candor, impatience with euphemism, dissent from the double standard were all reiterated themes in the writing of the twenties. The long American romance with Freud had begun, and the steeple-hatted, sable-mantled, sexually squeamish puritan – caricature or not – had to go.

Neither the Puritan nor the pioneer roused the postwar writers to as much vehemence as did the businessman. Indeed, a simplifying imaginative calculus derived the businessman out of the unhappy coupling of the Puritan's crabbed devotion to false duty and the pioneer's feckless individualism: from Cotton Mather and Daniel

Boone to George F. Babbitt. The business of America might be business, in Calvin Coolidge's deathless phrase, but the business of America's writers and intellectuals was clerkly skepticism.

One of the most prolific of the skeptics was Sinclair Lewis. Lewis's reputation has grown steadily smaller in the second half of the twentieth century, but he was for a time regarded as the voice of literary iconoclasm. Red-haired and awkward in appearance, Harry Sinclair Lewis was a country doctor's son who found no more companionship at Yale, from which he graduated in 1908, than he had at home, back in the new prairie town of Sauk Centre, Minnesota. Like so many other Americans, Lewis spent enormous energy to win the success and popularity his books scorned. *Main Street* (1920), his fifth novel, brought him that success; with its publication, he was famous. The book's much-quoted and once much-admired prefatory note set the tone for a decade's writing:

> Main Street is the climax of civilization. That this Ford car might stand in front of the Bon Ton Store, Hannibal invaded Rome and Erasmus wrote in Oxford cloisters. What Ole Jenson the grocer says to Ezra Stowbody the banker is the new law for London, Prague, and the unprofitable isles of the sea; whatsoever Ezra does not know and sanction, that thing is heresy, worthless for knowing and worthless to consider.

Gopher Prairie memorializes Sauk Centre. It is a cluster of undignified though sometimes pretentious buildings huddled together incongruously in the immensity of the fields. The prevailing rule in Gopher Prairie is conformity, the prevailing ethos dull. Carol Kennicott, the alert young woman through whose eyes the town is seen, is a less coherent figure than Lewis seems to have realized, but she speaks clearly enough his distaste for "the village virus" (Figure 131, Figure 132).

Lewis's most important book may have been *Babbitt* (1922), whose title character almost instantly entered America's folklore. Babbitt exemplifies to the thickness of parody just about every vice stereotypically associated with the middle-class culture of commerce. In Babbitt's city, the rising, raw, midwestern Zenith, heroism has shrunk to hustle, and the smooth-talking salesman is the new preacher, filled with zeal for the gospel of success. To Babbitt and his friends, "the Romantic Hero was no longer the knight, the wandering poet, the cowpuncher, the aviator, nor the brave young

FIGURE 131 &ent; Carl Van Vechten, photograph of Sinclair Lewis (1930).

district attorney, but the great sales manager, who had an Analysis of Merchandising Problems on his glass-topped desk, whose title of nobility was 'Go-Getter'!" Babbitt proudly wears a lapel button decorated with the words "Boosters – Pep!", and he reverently regards the Second National Tower as "a temple spire of the religion of business."

As these excerpts from his prose indicate, Lewis's satire was rarely subtle or tentative. His major work, almost all of it accomplished in the twenties, methodically took up and exposed one after another of the beliefs, prejudices, and rituals of the contemporary bourgeoisie. If his characters are often types rather than complex realities, that is in part because of the limits of his talent and in part because he wanted to present types. He was more interested in surveying the varieties of provincial folly than in the men and women who happened to exemplify each kind. Furthermore, he wanted to portray a broad cross section of American professionals; thus there is a doctor-novel, a preacher-novel, a salesman-novel. (A long-projected labor novel was never written.) Lewis hoped to become a satiric Balzac. As one consequence of that far-reaching ambition, his method was documentary. Each novel was preceded by travel, research, interviews. In common with other American realists, Lewis displayed a large enthusiasm for recording the surfaces of modern life. He enjoyed making catalogs and lists; he delighted in the names of people and towns and products; he liked getting his facts straight. His stories are told in an undemanding style, hardy if not versatile, attuned perhaps too well to the accents of America's provincial speech.

Lewis's disapproving treatment of his subjects was typically rough, but then much of the vulgarity of American life in the 1920s deserved rough handling. The images that have lingered, created in large part by Mencken, Lewis, Fitzgerald, Cummings, and their contemporaries, are shopworn now, but they still disclose part of the truth. A procession of high-collared Republican chief executives celebrated "Normalcy" and presided over an apparently endless prosperity. Gangsters battled in city streets to control the profits of vice, while a resurgent fundamentalism collaborated with a bigoted nativism to punish difference and impose conformity and pious ignorance. In 1925, John Scopes was fined one hundred dollars for teaching evolution in a Tennessee high school, and in 1927 the anarchists Sacco and Vanzetti were executed in Massachusetts in the midst of international protests on their behalf. A revitalized Ku Klux Klan enrolled thousands of members and went about its job of terrorizing blacks, Jews, and Catholics. Lewis's *Elmer Gantry* (1927), a portrait of the preacher as hypocritical huckster, was inspired by the orgiastic revival festivals that have produced gen-

FIGURE 132 ❧ This photograph of Sauk Centre, Minnesota, shows Main Street as it looked in the early twentieth century, about the time that Lewis left for Yale.

erations of ministerial millionaires. To Lewis, America's religious life, like its politics and business, seemed an arid landscape of sham that reached to the horizon. In 1925, the advertising executive Bruce Barton unintentionally demonstrated the truth of Lewis's charge when he published his remarkable book, *The Man Nobody Knows*. According to this enormously popular best-seller, Jesus Christ was "the founder of modern business," a go-getter who turned twelve ordinary and unpromising men into the most formidable sales organization in world history. Announcing triumphantly that Christianity is good for business, Barton's chapters spell out Christ's "recipe for success" and the main elements of his "business philosophy." Christ as Rotarian: it was this sort of travesty that Lewis tried to expose.

And yet, though *Elmer Gantry* was dedicated "with profound admiration" to Mencken, Lewis was less alienated from America's people and values than the tribute to Mencken implies. His iconoclasm was more affectionate than his contemporaries understood. His prose rubs tirelessly, like a rasp, against all the institutions and customs of what Mencken called "the booboisie," but at bottom his response was as much amused as outraged. In his most characteristic work, he lampooned American excess with the buoyancy and optimism of a reformer. When George Babbitt empties his pockets, the contents are to be taken as the flotsam and jetsam of a spiritless materialism, but the tone of the revelation is more or less good-hearted:

> He was earnest about these objects. They were of eternal importance, like baseball or the Republican Party. They included a fountain pen and a silver pencil. . . . On his watch-chain were a gold pen-knife, silver cigar-cutter, seven keys (the use of two of which he had forgotten), and incidentally a good watch. Depending from the chain was a large, yellowish elk's-tooth — proclamation of his membership in the Benevolent and Protective Order of Elks.

And so on. Like so many of America's homegrown critics, Lewis measured the nation's failures against the standard of its own aspirations; his impatience was tempered by nostalgia, the hope of a reformation that would return the country's government and citizenry to the ideals of an earlier day.

In 1930, Lewis became the first American to win the Nobel Prize in Literature, an honor that had been denied to Henry James, Samuel Clemens, and William Dean Howells, among others. The naming of Lewis to the award was controversial, but it signaled a new international attitude toward American letters, a recognition that American writers had earned the European esteem so long denied them. Lewis understood the symbolic significance of the prize, and he used the occasion of his Nobel address to salute some of the other Americans who might have won, among them Theodore Dreiser and Eugene O'Neill.

The literary realignment that took place in the 1920s and was signified by Lewis's Nobel Prize encouraged revisions in received historical opinion as well. The most fundamental of these re-appraisals led to the recovery of Melville from the obscurity that had enveloped him for several generations. Novels and poems that had been forgotten were reclaimed, and work that had been previously uncollected or unpublished was printed. *The Apple-Tree Table*, a collection of sketches and stories, appeared in 1922, followed by *Billy Budd* in 1924, the same year as Raymond Weaver's path-breaking biography, *Mariner and Mystic*. Melville's mordant rejection of national complacency, his stylistic innovations, his inclination toward metaphysical ambiguity, and his mingling of pathos with a grim, tight-lipped humor all suited the taste of a postwar sensibility steeped in disillusionment and dissent. Writers as diverse as Hart Crane, W. H. Auden, Charles Olson, and Lewis Mumford responded to Melville's example and conceded his influence on their thought and work. Crane's poem "At Melville's Tomb" (1926), which records that influence, has endured as one of the handful of splendid elegies in American letters.

The reassessment of Melville also suggested, accurately, that the pervasive irony and nihilism of the postwar years had not erased a longing for the more spacious experience of literary tragedy. No writer of the period came closer to realizing the tragic potential of modern materials than Eugene O'Neill. O'Neill was engrossed by the contest between dream and disabling circumstance, fascinated by the combination of banality and terror that lies at the heart of ordinary experience. He was haunted by the strict Catholicism in which he had been brought up and which he had imperfectly abandoned, and he traced the malaise of his time to the aching absence left by the disappearance of God. "The sickness of today as I feel it," he wrote to George Jean Nathan, is "the death of the old God and the failure of science and materialism to give any satisfying new one for the surviving primitive religious instinct to find a meaning for life in, and to comfort his fears of death with."

From the day of his birth in a Broadway hotel room, O'Neill's life was woven of the threads of theater, family, Catholicism, and disappointment. His father James had been one of America's leading serious actors, praised by Edwin Booth, but he was ultimately trapped by his huge, endlessly repeatable success as Edmund Dantes in *The Count of Monte Cristo*. (James played the role six thousand times over forty years, earning nearly one million dollars from it.) O'Neill's tragic temperament was forged by his father's anger and self-loathing, his mother's dreamy faith and morphine addiction, his older brother's corrosive and alcoholic despair – this accumulation of pain and the failure of "the old God" to console him. He mapped the wintry landscape of the human spirit in dozens of plays over a quarter-century of writing, beginning with the one-act plays he wrote for the Provincetown Players during and just after the First World War. His first full-length play, *Beyond the Horizon*, appeared in 1920 and earned him the first of his four Pulitzer Prizes (Figure 133).

The nineteenth-century American stage had been a setting primarily for melodrama, farce, musical revues, and countless productions of Shakespeare. It was only after 1900, and especially in the years following World War I, that American writers began to produce significant theatrical work in abundance. O'Neill created the best plays of the 1920s and 1930s, but many other writers also contributed to the virtual creation of the modern American theater in those years. The new plays included the comedies of George S. Kaufman and his several collaborators and the expressionist satire of Elmer Rice's *Adding Machine* (1923), John Howard Lawson's *Roger Bloomer* (1923), and E. E. Cummings's *him* (1927), which Cummings called a "phantasmagoria" in twenty-one scenes. Maxwell Anderson's *What Price Glory?* (1924), written with Laurence Stallings, was a sardonic comment on war, and the dramas of Sidney Howard, including *The Silver Cord* (1926), attempted to domesticate Freudian ideas. These were some of the productions that invigorated the American theater by replacing the costume romances, melo-

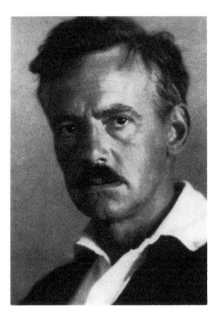

FIGURE 133 ❧
Photograph of Eugene
O'Neill (1927).

dramas, narrowly topical "problem" plays, and genteel versatility of writers like Clyde Fitch that had crowded America's stages in the years before the First World War. A substantial accomplishment, by any measure, they also provided the context for O'Neill's larger achievement.

Out of his need to lay bare the hidden places of the psyche, O'Neill experimented constantly, risking masks, choruses, symbolic figures, tom-toms, asides, monologues of fifteen minutes and more. Out of his equivalent need to put the unadorned truth on stage, he created characters of memorable verisimilitude who spoke with a realism seldom heard before in American plays. Writing of Strindberg, he referred to "that self-defeating self-obsession which is the discount we moderns pay for the loan of life." That grim insight also lay behind his own work. The search for commensurate forms led him, throughout his career, to test differing combinations of the symbolic and the real. Categories are treacherous, but it might be said that the generally realistic texture of the early plays gave way to extended innovation throughout the twenties, a series of experiments that yielded, in turn, to the realism and naturalism of the final plays. The expressionism of *The Emperor Jones* (1920) and *The Hairy Ape* (1922) was pushed to a schematic but successful conclusion in *The Great God Brown* (1926), in which masks were used to disclose what O'Neill called "those profound hidden conflicts of the mind which the probings of psychology continue to disclose to us."

Because of the variety of his experiments, no single play of O'Neill's is typical of his work in the twenties. *Desire under the Elms* (1924) was among the most important. Desire in its multiple forms – as lust, as will to power, as a yearning for beauty – propels the play's three characters on their tragic courses. A story of repression, passion, adultery, and murder unfolds within the walls of a cheerless nineteenth-century New England farmhouse. The setting is at once starkly realistic and a symbolic stage for the dramatization of the subconscious. Along with his characteristic interest in the psychology of motivation, the play also exemplifies O'Neill's merging of carefully constructed actualities with symbolism and his absorption in family tragedy. In frankly reworking an ancient legend (the tale of Theseus, Hippolytus, and Phaedra), O'Neill demonstrates his willingness to have his own work and the plight of modern men and women measured against both the art and the myths of antiquity. For O'Neill, the sordid contemporary scene could have a dignity equal to the heroic tales of the past; the job of the playwright was to find or invent it.

"The theater," O'Neill wrote, "should give us what the church no longer gives us – a meaning. In brief, it should return to the spirit of Greek grandeur. And if we have no Gods or heroes to portray, we have the subconscious, the mother of all gods and heroes." This was the high task O'Neill repeatedly chose for himself. He often failed, in part because his Freudian apparatus tempted him into murky and fashionable attitudinizing, in part because he was prone to tedious, intrusive explanations that claimed more insight than his dramas had actually earned. Nonetheless, his perception of his place in the traditions of tragedy and epic encouraged him to work on a scale worthy of that responsibility, often with unprecedented results. The trilogy *Strange Interlude* (1928), which chronicles three decades of national and family history, is nine acts in length and ran from 5:30 P.M. to nearly midnight (with an eighty-minute dinner break). Though O'Neill used the dramatic aside in the play on a scale never before attempted on the modern stage, he returned to a version of realism and perfected the distinctive dialogue, theatrical but persuasively realistic, that imprinted itself on so much subsequent American drama.

In his Nobel Prize address in 1930, Sinclair Lewis told the Swedish Academy that O'Neill had "done nothing much in American drama save to transform it utterly in ten or twelve years from a false world of neat and competent trickery to a world of splendor and fear and greatness." In 1936, O'Neill received the prize himself, but he had by then already withdrawn into the seclusion that would conceal the last two decades of his life from the public. Though he continued writing, no new play of his was produced between 1934 and 1946, when *The Iceman Cometh* opened on Broadway. That play, and *Long Day's Journey into Night*, which was produced and published posthumously, were the principal works of O'Neill's last years, the bitter results of a mature and deliberated commitment to despair and failure. Both plays belong to the naturalist tradition that O'Neill had earlier broken away from; both make use of the classical unities of time, place, and action to intensify a remorseless investigation of the destruction that follows in the wake of intimacy. The "pipe dreams" that *Iceman*'s characters cling to, and the fog that surrounds the Tyrone family in *Long Day's Journey*, signify the narcotic dreams in which men and women try to find shelter from a pitiless reality (Figure 134). Within such materials, O'Neill sought and found tragedy. Mary Tyrone's final speech, uttered as she slips back into drug addiction, is the confession of a lost soul, but her suffering transcends pathos and confers nobility on the closing moments of *Long Day's Journey*:

> I went to the shrine and prayed to the Blessed Virgin and found peace again because I knew she heard my prayer and would always love me and see no harm ever came to me as I never lost my faith in her. That was in the winter of senior year. Then in the spring something happened to me. Yes, I remember. I fell in love with James Tyrone and was so happy for a time.

O'Neill's final works possess the strength of confidently rediscovered conventions, but it was his more evidently experimental plays of the 1920s that seemed liberating to his contemporaries. His technical innovations typified the testing of artistic boundaries that went on in all the literary genres in that decade. "New thresholds! New anatomies!" Hart Crane exuberantly wrote: new subjects and insights demanded new forms. Significant experiments in the arts included the work of several painters associated with the photographer Alfred Stieglitz. In the years before the First World War, Stieglitz's "291" Gallery had housed the first American exhibitions of such European artists as Matisse, Toulouse-Lautrec, Cézanne, and Picasso. The American painters Stieglitz sponsored included Marsden Hartley, Arthur Dove, Alfred H. Maurer, and Georgia O'Keeffe (Plate 5).

The twenties, whose politics exhibited many of the surface features of conservatism and reaction, also served as seedbed for the luxuriant growth of literary innovation. It was innovation often linked with varieties of tradition, and the connection is no more than superficially puzzling. Impatient with the status quo in both art and politics, writers frequently looked backward. Like other avant garde episodes, the literary experimentation of the twenties was bound up with the effort to find a usable past and to identify

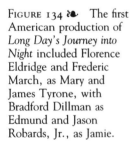

FIGURE 134 ❧ The first American production of *Long Day's Journey into Night* included Florence Eldridge and Frederic March, as Mary and James Tyrone, with Bradford Dillman as Edmund and Jason Robards, Jr., as Jamie.

FIGURE 135 ❧
Brooklyn Bridge appears
in the background of this
photograph of Hart
Crane.

the elements that might constitute an invigorated national, regional, or ethnic identity.

Crane's own poetry made an important contribution to the
search. The son of ferociously unhappy parents who fought their
battles in his presence, Crane dropped out of high school and left
his Cleveland home for New York when he was just seventeen.
Within a year he had published a poem in the *Little Review*, but he
took a miscellany of odd jobs, including the occasional manufacture
of advertising copy for tires and furnaces to support himself in the
early 1920s. The two years from 1924 to 1926 were his anni mi-
rabiles, a period of matchless creativity during which he completed
most of the poems in his first volume, *White Buildings* (1926), a
masterful collection of meditations on subjects ranging from the
myth of Faust to Melville to Charlie Chaplin. In those years, too,
he drafted many of the sections of his long work in progress, *The
Bridge*, which was completed and published in 1930 (Figure 135).
Alcoholic, unsure of his talent, and alternately inspired and

tormented by his homosexuality, Crane lived at a frantic, self-destructive pace. In 1932, when he was just thirty-three years old, he committed suicide by jumping into the Caribbean during the passage back to the United States from a Guggenheim Fellowship sabbatical in Mexico.

Crane believed that his intensity could dye words with meanings beyond their conventional definitions. His poetry is built out of knotty images connected by the sensational leaps of what he called a "logic of metaphor": patterns deeper than those of rational discourse and relying on the emotional associations of words rather than their literal signification. Consequently, while his poems are always bravura performances, displaying sensuous surfaces and voluptuous rhythms, the sense of them is sometimes hidden inside an obscurity that resists decoding. At their best, nonetheless, in "Chaplinesque," "For the Marriage of Faustus and Helen," "At Melville's Tomb," and half a dozen sections of *The Bridge*, Crane approached the "ecstasy" that he claimed as his poetic goal. The six poems of the "Voyages" sequence, which explore the pain and passion of Crane's love for the seaman Emil Opffer, Jr., are among the handful of indispensable love poems in American letters. The last stanza of the sixth poem rests in the assurance of the permanence which love, and the poetry of love, confer:

> The imaged Word, it is, that holds
> Hushed willows anchored in its glow.
> It is the unbetrayable reply
> Whose accent no farewell can know.

In one of his letters, Crane referred to himself as "the Pindar for the dawn of the machine age." It was his choice to absorb the technology of the new American civilization, to go beyond what he called the "negations" of Eliot and stand with Whitman in affirming the nation and its works. The Brooklyn Bridge, completed in 1883 and visible from Crane's apartment window, was his central symbol for the quintessentially American marriage of art and technology. *The Bridge* was to present a myth of America, rooted in its legends and history, but a vision that would also have its own autonomy. In Crane's epic, the arching span of the bridge represents the search through time and space — into the past and across the nation — for values that will suffice. Thus, the poem's principal characters include predecessor explorers, among them Columbus and Rip Van Winkle, along with predecessor poets, especially Whitman. There is much of exhilaration in the poem, but there is also fear, a haunting counter-theme which reaches a climax in the subway ride of "The Tunnel," with its glimpses of the "retching flesh" and "trembling hands" of Edgar Allan Poe. Out of the darkness of disintegration the poem rises to the transcendence of its eighth and final section, "Atlantis," a hymn to the dream of unity that beckons the singer on his quest.

Crane acknowledged Eliot's initial influence on his poetry, but his mature poetry was shaped by resistance to Eliot. William Carlos Williams, too, who shared Eliot's commitment to the renovation of poetry, snappishly rejected Eliot's erudite and edgy meditations on the decline of the West, and he rejected Eliot's expatriation as well. The son of immigrant parents, an English father and a Puerto Rican mother, Williams made just two trips to Europe and lived almost all of his long life in New Jersey. He insisted that "the local is the universal," and he was therefore personally affronted by the decisive impact of Eliot's verse, which he regarded as stagy cosmopolitanism. "The *Dial* brought out *The Waste Land* and all our hilarity ended. It wiped out our world as if an atom bomb had been dropped upon it and our brave sallies into the unknown were turned to dust." He condemned Eliot's "exquisite" work as a conformist rehash of European predecessors, and he scorned Pound's "paraphrases," his "cribbing" from the Renaissance, Provence, and the modern French. It was, in short, the old argument between Anglo-European bookishness and American populism. Williams acknowledged that America was "primitive," but it was essential to his life and art (Figure 136).

Williams was a hard-working physician whose profession allowed him access to the "secret gardens of the self." As he wrote in his *Autobiography* (1951), his "medical badge" permitted him "to follow the poor, defeated body into those gulfs and grottos." In moments of torment, "foul as they may be with the stinking ischio-rectal abscesses of our comings and goings," he had glimpses of a fundamental beauty. No American poet saw more of the joy and the misery of his fellow humans than Dr. Williams, and none was more clear-eyed in recording what he saw. For him, the fittest classroom was experience. Like so many other Americans, he was uncomfortable with the very idea of a capitalized and segregated Art. "I don't want to be thought an artist," he said. "I much prefer to be an ordinary fellow. I never wanted to be separated from my fellow mortals by acting like an artist." Hilda Doolittle complained about the frivolous "hey-ding-ding touch" running through his verse, and Wallace Stevens tried to convince him that "a book of poems is a damned serious affair," but Williams went his own democratic way. His patients and his own animal instincts taught him that "there is nothing sacred about literature." Affirming poetry and ordinariness simultaneously, Williams was discovering what a complex fate it is to be an artist in America.

"Say it, no ideas but in things," he several times wrote, summarizing his poetic credo. Placing himself in the line of Whitman, who, he said, "broke through the deadness of copied forms," Williams argued for the integrity of the commonplace and the primacy of the object. A friend of the Precisionist painters Charles Demuth and Charles Sheeler, he sought to achieve in his poetry the clarity

FIGURE 136 ❧ Charles Sheeler, photograph of William Carlos Williams (1938). This study of Williams appeared in a retrospective exhibit of Sheeler's paintings, drawings, and photographs at the Museum of Modern Art in 1938. Williams wrote the introduction to the exhibit catalog. "I think Sheeler is particularly valuable," Williams wrote, "because of the bewildering directness of his vision, without blur, through the fantastic overlay with which our lives so vastly are concerned, 'the real,' as we say, contrasted with the artist's 'fabrications.'"

of edge and outline that he appreciated in much modern painting. Demuth's painting "I Saw the Figure 5 in Gold" takes its title from one of Williams's poems (Plate 6). Williams's ideas about poetry inspired the Objectivist group, the only formal poetic movement that he ever participated in. He met with Louis Zukofsky, George Oppen, and a few others in Zukofsky's Brooklyn Heights apartment to debate theory and read poems. The job of the poet, Williams repeatedly insisted, was to illuminate the here and now, to lift up to the imagination "those things which lie under the direct scrutiny of the senses, close to the nose." Illustrating, he wrote these much-debated lines, which appeared in section xxi of *Spring and All* (1923):

> so much depends
> upon
>
> a red wheel
> barrow
>
> glazed with rain
> water
>
> beside the white
> chickens.

Rigorous in its modesty and reserve, the poem is at the same time defiant, proclaiming that the commonplace can be the stuff of art. The job of the poet is to pierce the haze of stock response and received opinion that clouds perception; to consent to the finality that clings to each of the world's objects. Williams's poems are filled with moments like this, sharply etched images and vignettes that invest daily life with high privilege.

Beginning in 1946, when he was past sixty, Williams began publishing the successive volumes of his most ambitious poem, the epic *Paterson*. He wrote that he wanted to "find an image large enough to embody the whole knowable world about me." Counterpointing verse with historical documents, newspaper stories, personal letters, and scientific reports, and exhibiting an improvisatory form that mirrors the unpredictable meandering of the river that provides its chief image, *Paterson* records the inconclusive but invigorating attempt to wrest human community and artistic utterance from the chaos of the twentieth-century city. It was in *Paterson II* that Williams first used what he called the "variable foot" and the "triadic line," a poetic measure more regular than free verse but more responsive to idiomatic speech than the metrical systems of traditional English poetry:

> The descent beckons
>   as the ascent beckoned
>   Memory is a kind
> Of accomplishment
>   a sort of renewal
>   even
> an initiation, since the spaces it opens are new
> places
>   inhabited by hordes
>   heretofore unrealized,
> of new kinds —

The variable foot became the unit of some of Williams's richest late work, including the long love poems in *The Desert Music and Other Poems* (1954) and *Journey to Love* (1955).

In a fine phrase, Marianne Moore said that Williams used "a language dogs and cats could understand." Moore herself typically preferred a more demanding vocabulary, encompassing archaisms and the recondite terms of natural science, but she resembled Williams in her fidelity to the concrete things of the world. She took prose as one of her models, seeking to reproduce in her verse the "unbearable accuracy" of such writers as Francis Bacon, Thomas Browne, and Henry James. Consequently she subordinated rhyme, relied on syllabic rather than accentual verse, and considered the stanza (by analogy to the prose paragraph), rather than the line or word, to be the basic unit of poetic construction. Much of her poetry exhibits an essayistic quality, along with an interest in definition and discursive argument.

Elizabeth Bishop called Moore "the World's Greatest Living Observer," and what Moore observed found expression in subtle, sometimes elusive formal arrangements. Beginning with what she called "a felicitous phrase," she invented structures in which complex patterns provide order for insight without annulling the spontaneity of her starting point. Along with the dignity of artistic premeditation, she said that she wanted "to secure an effect of flowing continuity." Especially in passages of description, like this evocation of the bird-filled sky over a seaside town in "The Steeple-Jack" (1932), she often succeeded:

> One by one in two's and three's, the seagulls keep
>   flying back and forth over the town clock,
> or sailing around the lighthouse without moving their
>   wings –
> rising steadily with a slight
>   quiver of the body – or flock
> mewing where
>
> a sea the purple of the peacock's neck is
>   paled to greenish azure. . . .

Rarely have seagulls been rendered with such elaborate, even ceremonial care.

To apprehend means both to see and to grasp. In Moore's poems the world is vigorously apprehended, wit complementing sight. She was "a literalist of the imagination," and she wrote with a painstaking devotion to craft. Her second volume of poems, *Observations*, won the *Dial* prize in 1924, shortly after which she accepted the editorship of the *Dial* and served until the magazine ceased publication in 1929. Her decisions were sometimes controversial – she altered a poem of Hart Crane's and rejected excerpts from Joyce's *Finnegans Wake* because of its ribald obscurity – but she more often exhibited the tolerant patience and the undeceivable good taste that made her one of the most influential poets and critics of her generation (Figure 137).

From her childhood on, Moore was interested in almost everything. A 1909 graduate of Bryn Mawr College, she received better grades in biology than in literature and briefly considered a medical career. She chose writing instead, but she claimed that a successful poem should have the "impact and exactitude" of surgery. She never lost her indefatigable curiosity, which brought into her poems everything from botany, to newspaper gossip, to Gieseking's interpretations of Scarlatti, to the Brooklyn Dodgers. (Her regular attendance at Dodger home games, invariably wearing a hat of splendid audacity, brought her more attention than her poems.) Moore's al-

FIGURE 137 &. George Maillard Kesselère, photograph of Marianne Moore (1938).

lusions and quotations are sometimes obscurely arcane, as her technique is sometimes merely fastidious. At its more typical, however, her poems mingle a sense of play and of vital poetic purpose. Her definition of poems as "imaginary gardens with real toads in them" is so well known that its sly subversiveness is often overlooked. The "reality" she embraced in her poetry was no mere abstraction but included much that was common and even unsightly – the numberless toads of the world (Figure 138).

Like other modern poets, Marianne Moore was fascinated by the reciprocal relations between imagination and reality. Wallace Stevens too, made those transactions his lifelong study, but he more typically placed his emphasis on the shaping power of the imagination and on the resulting autonomy of art. His poems are elegant, ingenious, dazzling in their imagery and filled with virtuoso aural effects. The palpable quality of hedonism in some of his poetry has led to the charge that Stevens was often merely fanciful or even precious. These are the opening lines of "Bantams in Pine-Woods":

FIGURE 138 🍋
Marianne Moore, sketch
of a diamondback turtle
(1936). Moore made this
sketch of a turtle, whose
zoological name she
recorded as *Macalemys
terrapin*, in Norfolk,
Virginia.

Chieftain Iffucan of Azcan in caftan
Of tan with henna hackles, halt!

Damned universal cock, as if the sun
Was blackamoor to bear your blazing tail.

Fat! Fat! Fat! Fat! I am the personal.
Your world is you. I am my world.

Stevens has been called the preeminent dandy in American letters, and with some justice. While Williams and Frost created a new poetry out of America's street-corner speech, Stevens chose to "whisper / Heavenly labials in a world of gutturals." He reveled in outré expressions and foreign phrases, filling his verses with what he called "the gaiety of language": concupiscent curds, brune figures, enfantillages, envious cachinnations, and apostrophizing wreaths. In his *Adagio*, he said that "reality is a cliché from which we escape by metaphor," and his fantastic style is sometimes taken to prove that he meant what he said. After all, from 1916 until his death in 1955, Stevens was employed by the Hartford Accident and Indemnity Company. Poetry – especially elaborate, exotic, voluptuous poetry – might provide a therapeutic retreat.

This construction of Stevens's life and work is tidy, but it fails to meet the facts of the case, and for at least two reasons. To begin with, it rests on a view of business that Stevens did not share. He did not glamorize insurance selling in the manner, for instance, of Charles Ives, but he wanted to be a success, and he was. Second, and more important, whatever the highly polished surfaces of his verse might suggest, the body of Stevens's poetry is in no way frivolous. He used his prodigious technique to probe serious issues. In many of his poems, including the bitterly ironic "Emperor of Ice Cream" (1923), he looked at death unblinkingly. And much of his poetry confronts the fundamental questions – of belief and value, of war and the prospects for survival – raised by the pervasive violence of modern life. Though his voice was unmistakably his own, he shared with his contemporaries the need to discover what would suffice in the midst of so much twentieth-century loss. He found his answers in poetry and in the affirmation of life itself (Figure 139).

Where Eliot lamented the decay of religious tradition and eventually adopted Anglo-Catholicism as his creed, Stevens celebrated the liberation of the modern spirit from the oppression of ancient

FIGURE 139 &▲ Alfred A. Knopf, photograph of Wallace Stevens (1938).

tombs and myths. Christianity, he wrote, in "A High-toned Old Christian Woman" (1923), is a thing of "tink and tank and tunk-a-tunk-tunk." He urged human self-sufficiency against dependence on the pallid ghost of dead gods. He drew the contrast repeatedly, most memorably in the meditative "Sunday Morning" (1915). The poem asks what divinity is, "if it can come / Only in silent shadows and in dreams." Upending the claims of religion to rule the realm of permanence – claims Stevens considered usurpations – the poem argues that life in its transience is more durable than any supernatural abstraction:

> There is not any haunt of prophecy,
> Nor any old chimera of the grave,
> Neither the golden underground, nor isle
> Melodious, where spirits gat them home,
> Nor visionary south, nor cloudy palm
> Remote on heaven's hill, that has endured
> As April's green endures.

In one of his *Adagia* Stevens bluntly observed: "After one has abandoned a belief in God, poetry is that essence which takes its place as life's redemption." He opposed what he called the tyranny of all codified systems, whether in religion, morality, or politics. These are all imprisoning illusions, outworn and second-rate to boot, the lifeless debris that litters history's junkyard. Poetry, on the other hand, is "the supreme fiction," the imagination's only competent defense against the violent welter of the world. It is imagination that deposits the famous jar on a Tennessee hilltop and tames the slovenly surrounding wilderness ("Anecdote of the Jar," 1923). And it is imagination, like the singer's voice, that makes the sky "acutest at its vanishing" ("The Idea of Order at Key West," 1935).

Like Stevens, E. E. Cummings, Harvard graduate and son of a Cambridge, Massachusetts, preacher, took his stand with love and the vanishing individual: "Buffalo Bill's defunct." An admirer of machinery, burlesque, and the comic strip "Krazy Kat," he delighted in puns and coinages, enjoyed shocking middlebrow readers with smut, and devised eccentric typographic patterns that made his poems distinctive visual as well as verbal artifacts:

in Just-
spring   when the world is mud-
luscious the little
lame balloonman

whistles   far   and wee

and eddieandbill come
running from marbles

A celebrant of spontaneity and physical pleasure, Cummings thought of his poems as vital parts of the natural and human world, honorably competing with "roses and locomotives (not to mention acrobats Spring electricity Coney Island the 4th of July the eyes of mice and Niagara Falls)." He proselytized for life and growth in all their unpredictable variety and, as a correlative, he fancied himself a reckless crusader in the war against conformity. His particular targets were advertising agents and other purveyors of the homogenized, assembly-line culture that exhorted men and women to rest in an ignoble material comfort. In "Poem, or Beauty Hurts Mr. Vinal" (1922), America has become the land of Gillette razor blades and Arrow shirts, the land of Lydia E. Pinkham:

land above all of Just Add Hot Water And Serve –

from every B.V.D.

let freedom ring

amen.

By 1925, when Cummings won the *Dial* Award, he was already beginning to enjoy the considerable popularity that would make his tone and mannerisms widely imitated. Over time, however, his innovations began to seem rather gaudy, more like self-indulgent puzzles than substantial formal experiments, and his conception of political institutions failed to advance beyond a set of rudimentary slogans. His perception of twentieth-century threats against liberty was acute, but his smirking superiority trivialized his sense of crisis. His love poems, earthy and high-spirited, have retained more of their freshness than his social criticism. His satire often has the look of graffiti daubed proudly but harmlessly across the walls of received opinion.

Cummings brought out his first volume, *Tulips and Chimneys*, in 1923. That was two years after Marianne Moore's first collection, *Poems*; a year after *The Waste Land*; and the same year in which William Carlos Williams published *Spring and All*. In 1923, too, Wallace Stevens's first book, *Harmonium*, appeared. The following year Robinson Jeffers published *Tamar and Other Poems*, his third volume of poetry, and the one that announced his distinctive voice. The collective creativity represented by this body of work was broadened and deepened by the new work of black artists and writers. "The 1920s," Langston Hughes wrote in his autobiography, *The Big Sea* (1940), "were the years of Manhattan's black Renaissance. It began with *Shuffle Along*, *Running Wild*, and the Charleston. Perhaps some people would say even with *The Emperor Jones*, Charles Gilpin [the black actor who played the lead in *Emperor*], and the tom-toms of Provincetown."

Other beginnings have been suggested as well, such as the publication of Jean Toomer's *Cane* (1923) or of Alain Locke's trailblazing anthology *The New Negro* (1925). Whatever the exact date (and of course no single date or event can be singled out as the starting point), the movement usually called the Harlem Renaissance witnessed an unprecedented outpouring of black prose and poetry. Postwar black writing had a long prologue and foreground, to be sure, generations of artistic accomplishment reaching back to America's colonial period and ahead to the early twentieth century. The writers of the renaissance, however, produced work on a new scale, and they were fully aware that they were doing so.

At the same time, although the movement was, self-consciously, a communal gathering of forces, it was not monolithic in its point of view or ideology. Indeed, much of the vigor of the renaissance resided precisely in the energy with which key questions were debated. Was there, in fact or theory, an "Afro-American art"? Were black literary norms the same as white? If not, what was different and what was held in common? What was the political function of black literature? In short, while Alain Locke was right to proclaim that "the New Negro [is] vibrant with a new psychology; the new spirit is awake in the masses," it was not a spirit that spoke in one voice only. Bitterness coexisted with aspiration, as Wallace Thurman's *Infants of the Spring* (1932) documents more reliably than any other novel. James Weldon Johnson's tentative prophetic optimism in *Black Manhattan* (1930) is expressive of the renaissance, but so too is the resolute anger of Claude McKay's call to judgment, "If We Must Die" (1922):

> If we must die, O let us nobly die,
> So that our precious blood may not be shed
> In vain; then even the monsters we defy
> Shall be constrained to honor us though dead.

Conventional formality – for example, the use of the sonnet form here by McKay and also by Countee Cullen in such poems as "From the Dark Tower" (1927) – is typical of the movement. Yet no less typical are the dreamlike interior monologues of Richard Bruce, such as "Smoke, Lilies and Jade" (1926), and the efforts of Langston Hughes to create rhythms in verse that would approximate the feel of jazz. Toomer's *Cane* sought analogs for psychological experience in a form that alternated and mixed verse, narrative, and character sketches (Figure 140).

The range of subjects was as wide as the spectrum of tones and styles. The literature of protest multiplied. Poems and broadsides and essays, angry and ironic by turns, assailed Jim Crow, segregation, and antiblack violence. Some of this publishing, for instance the grim statistical surveys of lynching in the magazine *Crisis*, continued into the twenties from before the First World War. Other work struck a new, characteristically postwar note. In "The Pathology of Race Prejudice," for example, E. Franklin Frazier applied contemporary psychological theory to race relations and diagnosed white racism as a form of collective insanity.

Protest and assertions of racial pride were often closely joined, as were politics and history. "The American Negro must remake his past in order to make his future." With this sentence, Arthur A. Schomburg began his essay, "The Negro Digs up His Past," printed in Locke's *New Negro*. Schomburg was the leading collector of African and Afro-American printed materials. His scholarship was part of a spreading and searching inquiry into black history and folklore. For the first time on a large scale, also, Africa drew the attention of America's black writers. Countee Cullen's long poem,

"Heritage" (1925), was one of many works that derived both sorrow and strength from contemplation of the African homeland of American blacks. The flamboyant Marcus Garvey, founder of the Universal Negro Improvement Association, campaigned for a return to Africa. "I have a vision of the future," Garvey wrote in "Africa for the Africans" in the early 1920s, "and I see before me a picture of a redeemed Africa, with her dotted cities, with her beautiful civilization, with her millions of happy children, going to and fro." Garvey was often ridiculed by other black leaders. For A. Philip Randolph, to give one example, "Garveyism" was a term of reproach, summarizing the accusation that the movement had distracted blacks from the hard, practical job of improving conditions in America. Randolph wrote that "Garveyism is spiritual; the need now, however, is a Negro renaissance in scientific thought." In fact, the Harlem Renaissance encompassed something of both science and spirit.

FIGURE 140 ❧ Writers of the Harlem Renaissance (1925). The photograph includes (*left to right*) Langston Hughes, Charles S. Johnson, E. Franklin Frazier, Rudolph Fisher, and Hubert Delany.

The city made the renaissance possible. In 1927, in an essay called "Blades of Steel," Rudolph Fisher described Harlem in terms that abstract literary significance from geography: "Negro Harlem's three broad streets form the letter H, Lenox and Seventh Avenues running parallel northward, united a little above their midpoints by east-and-west 135th Street." Joining the streets of Harlem as a sign, Fisher was acknowledging that much of the writing of the renaissance bears the unmistakable stamp of the city.

Insofar as it was an urban phenomenon, the Harlem Renaissance was part of the general development of postwar American society. America had grown increasingly urban throughout the nineteenth and early twentieth centuries, but it was the census of 1920 that first counted more than half of the country's population as city dwellers. Since any settlement of twenty-five hundred people or more was considered a city, the meaning of this demographic revelation was not quite as self-evident as it has sometimes been taken to be. Millions of citizens continued to live in small towns and on farms, and the constellation of values conventionally associated with rural America survived tenaciously in the nation's political and literary discourse. Nonetheless, American society had reached a turning point of undeniable cultural significance, and the perennial debate between the small town and the city was renewed with considerable clamor. The argument encapsulated a contest between the past and the future, between history and hope. In one version or another, it would form a principal motif of American literature throughout the following decades.

No one was more sensitive than F. Scott Fitzgerald to the tensions between America's past and future. "My point of vantage," he later wrote, "was the line between the two generations, and there I sat – somewhat self-consciously." He was always self-conscious, self-absorbed, anxiously self-evaluating. It was the key at once to his strength and weakness. In 1920, he decided that America was about to go on "the greatest, gaudiest spree in history," and he realized that he had found his subject. He gave the name "the Jazz Age" to the twenties, and he more or less invented the flapper and the sheik in his early stories. Both in his rise and fall, he was the consummate representative figure of the twenties: handsome and spendthrift; hard-drinking but (for a while, at least) resilient; boyish in spite of a precocious gift for irony; passionately, publicly in love with his wife, Zelda Sayre; devoted to the enchantment of the American dream, even as he felt it shift like sand under his feet. He said that all the stories that came into his head "had a touch of disaster in them," and the phrase described his own life as well. His titles declare something of his preoccupations: *This Side of Paradise* (1920); *The Beautiful and the Damned* (1922); "The Diamond as Big as the Ritz" (1922); *All the Sad Young Men* (1926); *Taps at Reveille* (1935). He was irresistibly drawn to the spectacle of illusion shadowed by tragedy (Figure 141).

In "The Rich Boy," he wrote that "the very rich . . . are different from you and me," a remark which, though it provoked a famous jeer from Hemingway, is simply true. More to the point, Fitzgerald's wealthy characters served him well as emblems of America's frantic culture of consumption. For them, life was a matter of proprietary privilege and of casual indifference to consequence. "They were

FIGURE 141 ❧ The Fitzgeralds – F. Scott, Zelda, and Scottie – in Paris (1925).

careless people," Nick Carraway says of Daisy and Tom Buchanan near the end of *The Great Gatsby* (1925). "They smashed up things and creatures and then retreated back into their money and their vast carelessness . . . and let other people clean up the mess." Fitzgerald himself was at once seduced and repelled by the glitter he chronicled. The "chance of having anything you wanted," as Edmund Wilson put it, fascinated him. After an undistinguished undergraduate career at Princeton, he joined the army in the late stages of the First World War, but he got no closer to the front than Camp Sheridan, Alabama. He regarded the war as a missed literary opportunity, a typical (if meretricious) response among young people who did not participate in "the late unpleasantness," as Fitzgerald called it. The loss was gain, since the manners of the advantaged classes better suited his talent and temperament than the brutalities of trench warfare.

He had chosen his literary vocation early. He was still an undergraduate when he announced to his bemused friend Edmund Wilson: "I want to be one of the greatest writers who ever lived, don't you?" That mixture of charm and gaucherie was one of Fitzgerald's hallmarks. His behavior could be maddeningly childish, as when he tried to shock Edith Wharton with leering allusions to brothels, but his dedication to his craft was altogether mature from the start. He set out to become a writer, and to become rich and famous into the bargain. He accomplished all that before he was twenty-five, and he also married Zelda, the aristocratic and beautiful young woman he had met and fallen in love with in Alabama. "I was in love with a whirlwind," he said later, in a metaphor that exaggerated only a little. He and Zelda were evenly matched in their extravagance, their emotional neediness and arrested adulthood, and in the premonitory desperation that darkened their earliest joy. Zelda Fitzgerald's own novel, *Save Me the Waltz* (1932), was to be written in a period of respite from the schizophrenic nightmare that imprisoned her through much of the last two decades of her life.

Fitzgerald was, in his own phrase, a mediocre caretaker of his talent. He wanted to live well, and he spent his abilities accordingly, producing in quantity the stories that the *Saturday Evening Post* and *Liberty* magazine would pay high prices for. Nonetheless, his fictions remain the most enduring snapshots left behind from the twenties, smaller perhaps than they once seemed, and faded, but still conveying a sense of immediacy, a feeling that the tawdry, twitching lives of his characters are being seen from the inside. And in *The Great Gatsby* Fitzgerald produced a masterpiece, a book that T. S. Eliot called "the first step the American novel has taken since Henry James."

Taken literally, Gatsby is merely a gangster and a sinister charlatan, a hustler of limitless appetite who engorges everything in his path. In Nick Carraway's rendering of him, however, Gatsby's story widens into epic. Notwithstanding Fitzgerald's shaky command of history, he managed to invest Gatsby with the resonance of America's mythic past. Gatsby "sprang from his own Platonic conception of himself," but it was a conception sewn together, almost touchingly, out of the scraps of national legend. His antecedents reach back to Benjamin Franklin, Hopalong Cassidy, the heroes of Horatio Alger, characters from history and fiction whose competence and heady confidence routinely drive circumstance to the wall and seize victories against long odds. It is America's past, and not just his own, which Gatsby madly assures Nick Carraway he can relive. Nick, filled with Fitzgerald's own awe in the face of absolute intensity, ultimately senses how much was at stake when Gatsby's trashy but gorgeous dream shattered against the hard rock of reality. At the end of the novel, watching Gatsby's empty house dissolve under the moonlight of a summer night, Nick "became aware of the old island here that flowered once for Dutch sailor's eyes," a piece of infinite promise that "had once pandered in whispers to the last and greatest of human dreams." Briefly, perhaps only for the space of a heartbeat, America's promise seemed to lie open and accessible: "For a transitory enchanted moment man must have held his breath in the presence of this continent, compelled into an aesthetic contemplation he neither understood nor desired, face to face for the last time in history with something commensurate to his capacity for wonder."

The Great Gatsby was the last novel Fitzgerald would write until after the Crash of 1929 had ended the long spree that he had done so much to define. He felt that uncanny links bound him to his era, links that held as strong in the bitter thirties as they had in the momentary gaiety of the twenties. His early triumph, he later wrote, had been "unnatural – unnatural as the Boom." He continued, "my recent experience" (by which bland phrase he meant alcoholism; a shattered marriage and a wife reduced to mental invalidism; a blocked and perhaps even vanished talent; and attempted suicide) "parallels the wave of despair that swept the nation when the Boom was over."

In those dreadful last years, which ended with what he considered Hollywood hackwork, Fitzgerald produced his second fine novel, *Tender Is the Night* (1934). Eloquently elegiac, the story follows the decline of an American psychiatrist, Dick Diver, from promise into failure. Diver's doomed relationship with his schizophrenic wife, Nicole Warren, had its obvious biographical sources, but that pain has been transmuted with an unusually complex sensitivity. Along with his last fiction, Fitzgerald also wrote a series of autobiographical sketches, most of them for *Esquire*, which were collected and published posthumously as *The Crack-Up* (1945). These are the sad, confessional chapters of a penitent's life, often startling in their candor, and taking a kind of pornographic delight in clinically observed details of suffering and disintegration. One of them, "Auction – Model 1934," written with Zelda, seems to be little more than a list of the contents of fifteen packing cases, which contain all the objects, the treasures and junk, that the Fitzgeralds had collected in their life together. Each case is unpacked, item by item; each item is offered for sale at an imaginary auction and finds no buyers. Despite its bouncy tone, "Auction" is a devastating glimpse into lives coming apart. The catalog is a funeral of exhausted objects, standing in turn for the human exhaustion of Scott and Zelda Fitzgerald. As their success had been expressed in accumulation, so their collapse is told in a stripping away.

The Crash precipitated the most divisive and wrenching domestic crisis since the Civil War. An economic structure that had seemed unshakable simply collapsed, and neither experts nor ordinary citizens were ever sure why. Responding only marginally to the therapies of the New Deal, the Depression ravaged the country for a decade. Unadorned statistics can capture something of the scope of failure in the thirties, though only abstractly. In late 1932, three years after the Depression had begun, American industries were performing at less than half of their peak rates of production in 1929. In 1932 wages paid to American workers amounted to barely half those of 1929. Unemployment rose from four million, in 1930, to over twelve million in 1934, the latter figure representing fully 20 percent and more of the work force. Stock prices fell by as much as 90 percent: General Motors slid from seventy-two dollars a share, in 1929, to eight dollars a share in 1932; United States Steel declined from two hundred sixty-one to twenty-one dollars. Concealed within the aggregated numbers lay millions of individual tragedies. Families were torn apart; lives were blighted and shortened; the premises upon which American society was based were discredited.

For three years, President Hoover assured the citizenry that the economy was "fundamentally sound" and that nothing need be done to bring recovery. Kenneth Fearing, perhaps the most durable of the radical bards of the thirties, satirized Hoover's blithe confidence in a poem called "Devil's Dream." Along the way, Fearing also caught the continuing sense of bewilderment that so many Americans felt in the thirties, their inability to understand where the Depression had come from and why it lingered:

> But it could never be
> > how could it ever happen if it never did before and it's
> > > not so now . . .

> But what if it is, what if it is, what if the
> > thing that cannot happen really happens just the same
> > suppose the fever goes to a hundred, then a hundred
> > > and one
> what if the Holy Savings Trust goes from 98 to 88 to 78 to
> > 68, then drops
> > > down to 28 and 8 and out of sight . . .

> But now there's only the wind and the sky and sunlight and
> > clouds,
> > with everyday people walking and talking as they
> > > always have before
> > > along the everyday street

doing ordinary things with ordinary faces and ordinary
   voices in the
   ordinary way
just as they always will . . .

Because it is not, will not, never could be true
   that the whole wide, bright, green, warm, calm world
   goes
   CRASH.

When that bright green world did crash, it shook America's collective sense of purpose. Multiplied joblessness, increased poverty, and tremors of political unrest collaborated with acts of nature, especially the most severe drought of the century, to produce an atmosphere of unparalleled anxiety. The dust that triumphed over the middle states symbolized betrayal: the inexorable laws of nature had conspired with the inscrutable laws of economics to defeat America's myth of omnipotence. The Depression created the central political and literary challenge faced by the writers of the 1930s. It is probably the case that American writers had never before taken their social responsibility so seriously. Or, to put it more accurately, never before had so many writers tried to define their jobs as writers in social and political terms.

To be sure, much of the literature and art of the decade, including much of the most popular work, declined any direct engagement with the crisis. The historical romance, for example, long a staple of bestseller lists, found a growing audience amid economic deprivation. Hervey Allen's *Anthony Adverse* (1933) traced the life of its glamorous hero from Napoleonic Europe through the far corners of the world, taking more than twelve hundred pages to do so. Within three years of its publication, the novel sold nearly one million copies, but those extraordinary figures were soon eclipsed by the sales of *Gone with the Wind* (1936), one of the most popular novels ever published in America. At one point the publisher, Macmillan, was shipping fifty thousand copies a day of Margaret Mitchell's thousand-page tale of love and courage in the Civil War. The movie that followed has remained a fixture of whatever imaginative culture Americans have in common.

The reasons for the enormous success of these historical romances, and of others such as Kenneth Roberts's *Northwest Passage*

FIGURE 142 ⫷ Grant Wood, *Overmantel Decoration* (1930).

(1937), are not far to seek. In a period of turmoil and uncertainty, there was an avid market for the solace of nostalgia and the anodyne of action. The allure of lost causes and lost worlds expanded in the vacuum left by a bankrupt economy and a politics of futility. Film, in its perfection of melodramatic formulas and its numberless love stories, musicals, and comedies, also offered oases of entertainment and escape. Walt Disney's *Snow White* (1937), the first feature-length cartoon, used one million separate drawings to animate a fairy tale and inculcate the happy ending of connubial bliss. The paintings of the American Scene group, midwestern realists like Grant Wood, John Steuart Curry, and Thomas Hart Benton, celebrated the values of religion and family and the fertile soil of the plains at a time when drought had turned the fields to dust and revolution was in the air. The regional painters were neither simpleminded nor humorless patriots, but their work strode assertively on the broad track of consensus and affirmation. In the influential opinion of their chief propagandist, Thomas Craven, the pictures of the American Scene were a rebuke to dissent, a demonstration of American genius, and a healthy native antidote to the corrupt foreign example of the School of Paris (Figure 142).

Escapism and jaunty romance represented an oblique way of dealing with the convulsions of the Depression, but the crisis also elicited more explicit and politically committed responses. While some writers rallied in support of the homegrown fascism that aroused the followers of demagogues like Huey Long and Father Charles Coughlin, far more of them moved left. There is some justice in the tag that has labeled the thirties as the "Red Decade." In 1932, the bottommost year of the Depression, over fifty writers jointly issued a pamphlet endorsing the Communist candidate for president, William Z. Foster. The signatories of *Culture and Crisis* included some of the most important names in American letters: Edmund Wilson, Langston Hughes, Sherwood Anderson, John Dos Passos, Malcolm Cowley, and Lincoln Steffens were among them. The pamphlet declared that capitalist America had become "a house rotting away; the roof leaks, the sills and rafters are crumbling." The writers claimed alliance with the nation's workers and encouraged others to join them in rejecting "the lunacy spawned by grabbers, advertisers, traders, speculators, salesmen, the much-adulated, immensely stupid and irresponsible 'business men.' " The pamphlet concluded with a call to vote "for the frankly revolutionary communist party, the party of the workers." Not since Jack London, at the turn of the century, had signed his correspondence "Yours for the revolution" had writers shown such enthusiasm for proletarian insurrection.

Many writers determined to put their talent as well as their vote at the service of the class struggle. "Proletarian literature" achieved a centrality it had not known before in America. Some was actually written by workers themselves; more of it, however, was produced by bourgeois writers self-consciously attempting to declass themselves. In 1935 Granville Hicks, Michael Gold, and several others published the anthology *Proletarian Literature in the United States*, a collection that achieved quasi-doctrinal status on the Left. Joseph Freeman wrote a pugnacious introduction to the volume, which opens with the announcement that "whatever role art may have played in epochs preceding ours, whatever may be its function in the classless society of the future, social war today has made it the subject of partisan polemic." Ridiculing the "Man in White" – a ham-fisted caricature of the middle-class liberal – Freeman demands the subordination of art to experience, specifically to the political and economic demands of the working class.

The debate over the proper role of literature was sharpened in the thirties by crisis, but the argument had a long history. American culture has from its beginnings harbored generous quantities of an-tiintellectualism and of suspicion against art. Long before the Depression, many American writers had felt alienated and even stigmatized by their calling, marginal to a society that valued the utilitarian and the factual and regarded the aesthetic as frivolous. The political and moral welter of the thirties gave this dilemma an unprecedented urgency. For some writers, the pressure to subordi-nate craft to dogma became irresistible. The literary results of their efforts to unite the social and artistic revolutions were not always fortunate. A considerable amount of forgettable prose and poetry was produced, politically correct and otherwise undistinguished. The work was at least earnest; some of it was good; and all of it remains as a lively testament to the conflicts of that receding but decisive decade. The titles alone offer a thumbnail index to the preoccupations of the time: Jack Conroy's *Disinherited* (1933); Mi-chael Gold's *Jews without Money* (1930); Clara Weatherwax's *March-ing! Marching!* (1935); Albert Halper's *Union Square* (1933); Edward Dahlberg's *Bottom Dogs* (1930).

The radical books often adopted conservative techniques. This could follow logically from a proletarian stance, since an unde-manding style would make a book accessible – at least in theory – to a less-educated audience. The most reductive instance of this strategy was probably Giacomo Patri's *White Collar* (1940), a "novel in linocuts." Patri tells the story of one family's decline from pros-perity into poverty and ruin, and he uses no prose at all, just one hundred twenty cartoonlike pictures (Figure 143). A more typical example of proletarian writing is Tom Kromer's *Waiting for Nothing* (1935). Kromer employs a style of almost primitive simplicity to tell of life in the lower depths of the hobo jungle. One horrific anecdote follows another:

This is good wood. It makes a good blaze. We do not have to huddle so close now. It is warm, too, except when the wind whistles hard against our backs. Then we shiver and turn our backs to the fire and watch these rats that scamper back and forth in the shadows. These are no ordinary rats. They are big rats. But I am too smart for these rats. I have me a big piece of canvas. This is not to keep me warm. It is to keep these rats from biting a chunk out of my nose when I sleep.

For writers like Kromer and Patri, the cultural enemy was bourgeois modernism, derided by doctrinaire leftists for its finicky absorption in mere technique.

Other radicals, however, tried to make use of the literary innovations of the twenties, while putting them to more progressive purposes. After all, the commitment to fact which so dominated literary discussion in the thirties had already received superlative expression before the Crash, in the work of such writers as Hemingway and William Carlos Williams. To put it summarily, some of the writers of the revolutionary thirties hoped to appropriate what they had learned from the twenties and apply it to the task of rescuing America simultaneously from its economic misery and its spiritual torpor.

Robert Cantwell's *Land of Plenty* (1934) and Edward Dahlberg's *From Flushing to Calvary* (1932) exemplify this combination of proletarian politics and experimental technique. Part I of Cantwell's novel, called "Power and Light," takes place during a power failure and blackout in a West Coast factory. In the total darkness, Cant-

FIGURE 143 ❧ Linocut from Giacomo Patri, *White Collar* (1940).

well uses only voices to portray his characters and to dramatize their situation. The voices – disembodied, discordant, initially cacophonous – eventually blend in a kind of proletarian chorus that catches with at least some success the anger, humor, and humanity of the workers. Dahlberg's *From Flushing to Calvary* is an autobiographical novel that ends in private and public disaster: the cruel death of the central character's mother is followed by a police riot. The vocabulary of the book is colloquial, even slangy, but the mother's death is rendered in an elaborate, almost Joycean stream of consciousness. The style is calculated to make the chaos and fear of the dying woman's last moments palpable and to involve the reader in the personal and social significance of her fate.

Playwrights, too, counted revolutionaries among their numbers in the 1930s. Lillian Hellman's early work, though not confined within proletarian definitions, vigorously engaged some of the decade's central social and political questions (Figure 144). Elmer Rice's *We the People* (1933) and *Judgment Day* (1934), Sidney Kingsley's *Dead End* (1935), and Marc Blitzstein's radical "opera" *The Cradle Will Rock* (1937), whose first production was directed by John Hous-

FIGURE 144 ❧ Lillian Hellman, *The Children's Hour* (1934). In this climactic scene, a schoolgirl charges two of her teachers with lesbianism; the play's considerable success was connected in part with its controversial theme. *The Children's Hour* was Hellman's first play, and the first of her many Broadway productions. Several of her other works appeared in the late 1930s and early 1940s, including *Days to Come* (1936), which dramatizes a strike; *The Little Foxes* (1939), which traces the disintegration of a reactionary white southern family; and the anti-Fascist *Watch on the Rhine* (1941).

man, were just a few of the plays that brought the hardships of the Depression to varying degrees of theatrical life. The theater, with its opportunities for collective effort, amateur production, and audience participation, bristled with dissent and propaganda. Ben Blake, in a pamphlet to which he gave the naively optimistic title *The Awakening of the American Theatre* (1935), explained that the popularity of agitprop plays among workers' theater groups in New York City in the early Depression years signified both the liberation of the stage and of proletarian consciousness. The Sacco and Vanzetti case, the Scottsboro trial, episodes from the labor wars, satires of plutocrats and politicians, utopian scenes from communized Russia, and hymns to working-class solidarity were the typical stuff of agitprop productions.

The most consistently successful of the left-wing playwrights was undoubtedly Clifford Odets. Though he was only in his early twenties when the Depression began, he was already an experienced if struggling actor and writer. The turn his work took after 1930 was precipitated by circumstance and personal conviction, but it also had much to do with his membership in the Group Theatre. The Group, founded in 1930 by Harold Clurman, Lee Strasberg, and Cheryl Crawford, was based on a conception of theater as a truly collective enterprise (Figure 145). Its members included a good many actors, actresses, and directors who would later earn prominent places in American drama, often leaving their fervently left-wing positions behind as they did so. The alumni of the Group included Lee J. Cobb, Jules (later John) Garfield, Elia Kazan, Stella Adler, Howard Da Silva, Frances Farmer, and Karl Malden. In the ten disputatious years of the Group's existence, none of its productions achieved more notoriety than Odets's *Waiting for Lefty*, which opened on January 5, 1935.

The Communist *Daily Worker* called *Lefty*, which Odets wrote in three nights in a Boston hotel room, the "most effective agitprop play written in this country." (One of its earliest reprintings was in Granville Hicks's *Proletarian Literature* anthology.) Loosely based on a New York City taxi strike, *Lefty* pits the corrupt leader of the drivers' union, a cigar-chomping thug named Harry Fatt, against his more militant rank and file. As in much other radical literature before and after the thirties, the play's battle with capitalism is a battle as well with comfortable and discredited union

FIGURE 145 ❧ The directors of the Group Theatre (1931). Taken at Brookfield Center, this photograph includes (*left to right*) Cheryl Crawford, Lee Strasberg, and Harold Clurman. Photograph by Ralph Steiner.

leadership. Harry Fatt counsels patience, and cooperation with the New Deal. But the play, through a series of brief vignettes which dramatize the just grievances of the workers, insists on the irrelevance of small, orthodox solutions. The famous final scene is a call for revolutionary action:

> AGATE. It's war! Working class, unite and fight! Tear down the slaughter house of our old lives! Let freedom really ring!
> These slick slobs stand there telling us about the bogeymen. That's a new one for the kids – the reds is bogeymen! But the man who gave me food in 1932, he called me Comrade! The one who picked me up where I bled – he called me Comrade too! What are we waiting for. . . . Don't wait for Lefty! He might never come.

Though it relied almost completely on stereotype and slogan, the play was a triumph. The exalted response of its first-night audience became part of legend. Harold Clurman described the concluding, shouted lines – "STRIKE! STRIKE! STRIKE!" – as "the birth cry of the thirties" (Figure 146).

Given the diligence with which the proletarian voice was sought, it is something of an irony that the most authentic novel to come out of the slums in the Depression decade was more or less overlooked. Henry Roth's *Call It Sleep* (1934) received warm initial reviews, went through a respectable first and second printing, and

FIGURE 146 ❧ Scene from *Waiting for Lefty* (1935). Elia Kazan is third from the left in this photograph of the play's final scene.

then dropped from sight along with its author. In fact, despite its immersion in the lives of ghetto immigrants, the book is not "proletarian," at least not in the narrow and usual sense. *Call It Sleep* is indifferent to party ideology, and that was surely part of the reason for its obscurity. It stood in a different tradition, not yet visible to criticism, of books and essays that dramatized immigrant experience. Starting before the turn of the century, Abraham Cahan, founder and long-term editor of the *Jewish Daily Forward*, had evoked the Lower East Side in such novels as *Yekl: A Tale of the New York Ghetto* (1896), which attracted favorable comment from William Dean Howells, and *The Rise of David Levinsky* (1917). Following the First World War, the Russian immigrant Anzia Yezierska published a series of stories and novels whose main characters are often the women of the ghetto. Her first collection of stories, *Hungry Hearts* (1920), which was made into a film by Samuel Goldwyn, long remained her best-known volume. Her later work included *Bread Givers* (1925), a novel whose central conflict is compactly indicated in its subtitle, "A struggle between a father of the Old World and a daughter of the New." These are the fictions with which *Call It Sleep* might most usefully be compared (Figure 147).

FIGURE 147 ❧ Cover, Anzia Yezierska, *Bread Givers* (1925).

Roth reproduced in meticulous detail the hunger and fear that attend poverty. Above all, no writer more faithfully transcribed the cruelty with which the hapless denizens of the urban jungle prey on each other. However, Roth's interest is less in social institutions than in psychology. His point of view throughout the book is that of a child. And to David Schearl, who grows from six years old to eight in the course of the story, the realities of poverty are not problems in political economics but mysterious wonders in an untrustworthy world. Fleeing from a gang of older boys, for example, David stumbles blindly into an urban wasteland:

> David climbed up the junk heap and threaded his way cautiously over the savage iron morraine. . . . Before him the soft, impartial April sunlight split over a hill of shattered stoves, splintered wheels, cracked drain pipes, potsherds, marine engines split along cruel and jagged edges. Eagerly, he looked beyond – only the suddenly alien, empty street and the glittering cartracks, branching off at the end.

This litter may be the excrement of capitalism, but protest is irrelevant to Roth's use of it. Rather, the vacant lots and their garbage, along with the cellars and streets of Brownsville and the Lower East Side, are the arena in which young David grows up, and grows into knowledge. David learns much of fear and pity, but he has glimpses of beauty, too. The possibility of enchantment, which separated *Call It Sleep* from the politics of its time, stamps the novel's tone as well. Improbably but effectively, Roth's prose alternates between gritty realism and something like song, a lyricism true to David's wide-eyed ebullience and unquenchable hope. Where the more formulaic proletarian novel concludes with an obligatory call to arms and a strike, *Call It Sleep* ends with David, half-killed by the electric jolt of a trolley's live rail, rapt by a strange and funny vision of God.

For writers more politically engaged than Henry Roth, the Depression years seemed to prove beyond argument some version or other of the old naturalist hypothesis: human destiny was being brutally shaped by forces that could neither be contained nor controlled. Where Roth stood outside this consensus, James T. Farrell practically personified it. Like the earlier naturalists, Farrell understood that life, including its dreams, is the product of social forces. Unlike the earlier naturalists, however, Farrell's subject was not poverty but imaginative, moral, and spiritual oppression. His characters are creatures of the system, groping without joy or even interest after pleasure, respectability, power. He wrote about what he had seen and lived through as a child: the gangs and crooks, policemen, politicians, and priests of South Chicago. Above all, he wrote about the lower middle-class, Irish Catholic family in which he had grown up. He often said that he had paid with his youth for what he had learned about life, and he became the hard-boiled laureate of the city streets.

Though his prose often seems as uncalculated as automatic writing, Farrell thought a good deal about matters both of substance and style. He was much influenced by Joyce and especially by Sherwood Anderson. Anderson's sympathy "for the grotesque, the queer, the socially abnormal," as Farrell put it, encouraged the younger writer to have confidence in his own back-alley subjects. "Perhaps my own feelings and emotions," he later wrote, "and the feelings and emotions of those with whom I had grown up were important.

... I thought of writing a novel about my own boyhood, about the neighborhood in which I had grown up. Here was one of the seeds that led to *Studs Lonigan*."

Farrell dropped in and out of the University of Chicago several times, staying long enough to absorb something of Chicago's social sciences and to write a first draft of *Studs* in Professor James Weber Linn's composition course. He kept writing for half a century. Unlike many of the other left-wing novelists and poets of the thirties, Farrell survived the decade and kept working. By the time he died, in 1979, he had published some forty volumes of fiction, essays, and poetry. His later novels included two additional multivolume fictional lives, that of Danny O'Neill in five volumes and the Bernard Carr trilogy; over time, he moved away from radicalism toward accommodation and a version of stoicism. Nonetheless, Farrell is indivisibly linked to the thirties, and the Studs Lonigan trilogy remains the work which his name immediately evokes.

The novels of the trilogy appeared in just three years, from 1932 to 1935. In *Young Lonigan: A Boyhood in Chicago Streets*, Studs is an attractive boy of fifteen, experimenting with sex, smoking, and petty theft, rebellious and already surrounded by unmistakable signs that he is doomed. *The Young Manhood of Studs Lonigan* follows Studs across the 1920s, as he waits for his big break, dissipated but making occasional weak promises to reform. The book concludes with one of Farrell's famous set pieces, an orgiastic New Year's Eve party that ends with Studs drunk and unconscious in a gutter. The lurid scene is Farrell's emblem of individual and national excess, encapsulating the violence and hopelessness that Studs represents. *Judgment Day* finishes the story as it must, bringing Studs through bitterness and illness to his death at twenty-nine.

Studs is a memorably sleazy hero, a self-absorbed bully, a prurient adolescent who grows into a dissolute adult. He is redeemed only by the energy Farrell expends on him and by his irrepressible longings for what he vaguely calls "something else." If Studs has a soul, it is a scarred receptacle of violence and discontent. He inhabits a world that Farrell builds sentence by tedious sentence, piling nondescript images one on top of another. Farrell's style is a deliberated assault against genteel decorum. He transcribes, in all of their banality, the clichés and endlessly reiterated catchphrases that his characters use in place of language. Thick to the point of near suffocation with the stale, repetitive texture of the city's monotonous streets, Farrell's flattened prose virtually becomes what it tells. To take just one example, Farrell can devote over fifteen pages of *Judgment Day* to the utterly pointless chatter of a dance marathon. Contestant Squirmy Stevens has this to say to the audience when he steps up to the ballroom microphone:

> Hello, everybody, I want to say that I thank you one and all for your interest in me and in our World's Championship Super Dance Marathon out here at the Silver Eagle Ballroom and I'd like to say that I'd like to invite you, one and all, to come out here any time and see us do our stuff. And, folks, I wanna say this. A dance marathon is a fight, and the winner in a high-class field like this one we got here in our World's Championship battle has got to be a fighter, and stick to it, and that's what we're all out here trying to do. So long, Squirmy Stevens signing off.

And so on, for nearly ten thousand words. In no other book are such pages even conceivable; here they are merely typical. The event, and the numbing prose in which it is created, add their portion to the tedium of Studs's life and come to symbolize it – a competition for a cheap prize, significant only for sheer endurance.

Farrell thought of Studs as an American everyman, "the story of an American destiny in our time." That concern with national destiny was a leading theme in the 1930s. The postwar twenties had already witnessed a flowering of history and biography, a body of distinguished works of reconstruction, including Van Wyck Brooks's *Ordeal of Mark Twain* (1920); James Truslow Adams's New England trilogy, whose first volume, *The Founding of New England* (1921), won a Pulitzer Prize; Carl Sandburg's *Abraham Lincoln: The Prairie Years* (1926); the first volumes of Mark Sullivan's *In Our Times* (1926); Mary and Charles Beard's *Rise of American Civilization* (1927); and the first volumes of the *Dictionary of American Biography* (1928). This busy inquiry into the national character was accelerated by the shock of the Depression. Scores of writers traveled the country, by car or train, even on foot, interviewing, watching, listening, recording. Some of them, including Dreiser, Dos Passos, and Cowley, took part in veterans' marches or union-organizing rallies. More typically they searched out the hidden lives of individual men and women as a way of discovering the meaning of the Depression for America's national life. They filled a shelf with their books and articles, angry, disillusioned, and sentimental by turns. Among them, they offered a sustained exploration into the national mood. Sherwood Anderson's *Puzzled America* (1935), Edmund Wilson's *American Jitters* (1932) and *American Earthquake*, Theodore Dreiser's *Tragic America* (1932) – the titles alone suggest the difference between these books and those of the preceding decade.

Some of the books that documented the Depression made extensive use of photographs. Enabled by improved technology, photojournalism was a product of the thirties, and Depression America was its first great subject. The new *Life* magazine, which began publication in 1936, hired the country's best photographers, reduced its text to brief, exclamatory captions, and used its "picture essays" to become one of the best-selling periodicals in the nation's history. The camera offered access to a potent immediacy that seemed responsive to both the aesthetic and political demands of the thirties, and photography attracted some of the most talented visual artists of the decade. Margaret Bourke-White and her husband Erskine Caldwell published *You Have Seen Their Faces* (1937), and Dorothea Lange and Paul Taylor collaborated on *An American Exodus* (1939).

In 1936, James Agee and Walker Evans accepted a commission from *Fortune* magazine to write a series of articles on the condition of poor whites in the rural South. The two men spent about six weeks in Alabama, mostly with three families, Agee taking notes, Evans taking pictures. The articles and photographs they produced were rejected by *Fortune*; revised and expanded, the material was eventually published in 1941 in book form, under the title *Let Us Now Praise Famous Men*. The book was just about forgotten for twenty years after its first printing. Its rediscovery in the 1960s, along with *Call It Sleep* and other neglected books of the Depression decade, signaled a general reappraisal of the cultural achievement of the 1930s.

The three families in *Famous Men* are called the Ricketts, the Gudgers, and the Woods. Every detail in their bleak lives is rendered with laboriously close attention. The meager furniture, the tattered clothing, the flyblown coops in which scrawny chickens are kept – each small, undistinguished item is reproduced with unexpected affection and even reverence, with a patience out of all proportion to the values usually assigned to such scenes and people. The nearly identical palings in a split-pine fence are described one by one, each tiny difference a matter of mystery and significance. The cheap calendars and magazine advertisements that decorate a fireplace wall are reproduced with the painstaking care of illustrations in a museum catalog. However unlikely, Agee's intentions are celebratory and epic. Forty-six pages, and nearly twenty thousand words, are devoted to the word-picture Agee draws of the dilapidated Gudger home.

Agee was deeply ambivalent about his work. He wanted to communicate the pathos of what he had seen, but he recoiled from violating the privacy and dignity of the three families whose hospitality he had shared. His solution was to reproduce what he had seen with elaborate care, to show strength coexisting with shabby suffering, and thus to invest these ordinary, anonymous people with tragic scope. Ultimately, the title of the book is not ironic: the men and women of the Ricketts, Gudger, and Woods families deserve praise. Agee's credo in *Famous Men*, which he shared with many other documentary writers, was to tell the truth. "It seems to me," he writes in a typical aside to the reader, "there is . . . considerable value (to say nothing of joy) in the attempt to see or to convey even some single thing as nearly as possible as that thing is." And again: "All I want to do is tell this as exactly and clearly as I can and get the damned thing done with." His contempt for what he called "mere art" was altogether in the American grain, as was his assertion that facts are not only more important than poetry or fiction; they are more beautiful as well: "The forms of these plainest and most casual actions are the hardest I can conceive of to set down straight as they happen; and each is somewhat more beautiful and valuable, I feel, than, say, the sonnet form." In fact, in spite of Agee's continuous polemic against literary artifice, *Famous Men* is a carefully contrived, thoroughly artful book. His rumblings against ornament constitute a political statement, a pledge of solidarity with the luckless people for whose existence he felt somehow responsible (Figure 148).

Agee's response to suffering was instinctive, unprogrammatic, and sometimes explosive. Like many of his forebears in the American radical tradition, he was not patient with theory. In the summer of 1939, *Partisan Review*, founded a few years earlier to encourage Marxist politics and avant-garde art, sent a survey to a number of

writers, asking their opinions on seven questions "which face American writers today." Along with inquiries about class and audience and "the next world war," the writers were asked to summarize "the political tendency of American writing as a whole since 1930." The brief essays that Agee wrote in response to the survey were so angry that the magazine refused to print them. Agee denounced *Partisan Review* for turning literature and life into abstractions, and he invoked the figure of the autonomous self as his political and literary ideal, praising "men who do not breathe one another's breath nor require anything of one another . . . but are the only free human beings."

Among the other writers who responded to the *Partisan Review* survey, Sherwood Anderson described himself as an isolationist; James T. Farrell pointed out that the Irish had little interest in

FIGURE 148 ☙ Walker Evans, photograph from *Let Us Now Praise Famous Men* (1941). Agee wrote that "any body of experience is sufficiently complex and ramified to require (or at least to be able to use) more than one mode of reproduction." For that reason, he wrote, "the photographs are not illustrative. They, and the text, are coequal, mutually independent, and fully collaborative."

keeping the world safe for the British Empire if war should come; and Gertrude Stein doubted that a general war was imminent. John Dos Passos answered the questions with something of Agee's contempt for political dogma. Dos Passos struck a populist note: "My sympathies, for some reason, lie with the private in the front line against the brass hat; with the hodcarrier against the strawboss, or with the walking delegate for that matter; with the laboratory worker against the stuffed shirt in a mortar board; with the criminal against the cop." This was the democratic faith to which, in his own eyes at least, Dos Passos remained loyal throughout his five decades of writing. His ideological career was a complicated odyssey. After graduating from Harvard in 1916 he went to Europe, intending to study architecture in Spain but shortly thereafter volunteering to serve as a medic and driver in the legendary Norton-Harjes Volunteer Ambulance Service on the western front. The war catalyzed his contempt for the institutional straitjackets of modern life. Later, in the twenties, the trial of Sacco and Vanzetti completed his alienation from the established structures of American politics and justice. He went to jail to protest the Sacco and Vanzetti executions, shared a cell with the Communist Michael Gold, and emerged as a briefly committed left-wing activist. The militance of his work in the thirties followed from the radicalism of his earlier antiwar novels but gave way to an increasing conservatism in the years after the Second World War. By the time he completed his *District of Columbia* trilogy (1952) and *Mr. Wilson's War* (1963), Dos Passos had practically reversed his earlier judgments. Through it all, he claimed that he consistently honored the individual, and he claimed as well to speak in the accents of earlier American thinkers and writers, including Lincoln and Emerson, and, above all, Whitman. Whatever the continuity or swerving in his politics, his most important fiction was accomplished in the thirties with the *U.S.A.* trilogy.

Inquiring into the present by way of the past, Dos Passos was the preeminent historian among the novelists of the Depression decade. *U.S.A.*, which swarms and sprawls across three volumes and nearly fifteen hundred pages, is a panoramic chronicle of the country from the turn of the century to the mid-1930s. *The Forty-Second Parallel* (1930), *Nineteen Nineteen* (1932), and *The Big Money* (1937), collectively enact the nation's decline and fall. Occasionally exuberant, *U.S.A.* is finally a dispiriting morality play in which national greed earns the retribution of the Crash. The protagonist of the trilogy is none of its individual characters; it is American social and political history. That in turn determined the technique Dos Passos used in the books. Weaving fact and fiction together, U.S.A.'s hundreds of separate sections employ an alternation of strikingly various narrative devices. A cluster of fairly conventional fictional stories is surrounded by fragmented, impressionistic biographies, "Newsreels," and first-person, stream-of-consciousness meditations that appear under the title "The Camera Eye."

The newsreels, nearly seventy of them, compress the current events of the passing scene into a montage of headlines and paragraphs torn from newspapers, along with snatches from popular songs. This one, near the end of *Nineteen Nineteen*, offers glimpses of prohibition and the red-baiting that followed World War I:

NEWSREEL XLIII

the placards borne by the radicals were taken away from them, their clothing torn and eyes blackened before the service and exservicemen had finished with them

Thirty-four die after drinking wood alcohol   trains in France may soon stop

GERARD THROWS HIS HAT INTO THE RING

SUPREME COURT DASHES LAST HOPE OF MOIST MOUTH

LIFEBOAT CALLED BY ROCKET SIGNALS SEARCHES IN VAIN FOR
SIXTEEN HOURS

America I love you
You're like a sweetheart of mine

The two dozen or so brief biographies included in U.S.A. make up a cross section of the politicians, entrepreneurs, intellectuals, and bunco artists who personify America's heterogeneity. William Jennings Bryan is here, and so are Isadora Duncan, Frank Lloyd Wright, and J. P. Morgan. The opinionated portraits in which these men and women are sketched work with the newsreels to enhance the novel's documentary feel, but they also serve Dos Passos's thematic purposes. His distaste for Woodrow Wilson ("Meester Veelson") and for William Randolph Hearst ("Poor Little Rich Boy") is no more veiled than his admiration for Thorstein Veblen and for Joe Hill, the songwriter and organizer for the Industrial Workers of the World (IWW):

> At Bingham, Utah, Joe Hill organized the workers of the Utah Construction Company in the One Big Union, won a new wage scale, shorter hours, better grub. (The angel Moroni didn't like organizers any better than the Southern Pacific did.)
>
> The angel Moroni moved the hearts of the Mormons to decide it was Joe Hill shot a grocer named Morrison.... [Joe] was in jail a year, went on making up songs. In November 1915 he was stood up against the wall in the jailyard in Salt Lake City.
>
> "Don't mourn for me organize," was the last word he sent out to the working stiffs of I.W.W. Joe Hill stood up against the wall of the jailyard, looked into the muzzles of the guns, and gave the word to fire.

In between the newsreels and biographies, Dos Passos inserted sections that he called "The Camera Eye," somewhat murky autobiographical reflections, as well as long chapters of generally conventional narration describing the lives of the novel's many characters (Figure 149). Throughout *U.S.A.*, the rhythmic movement between the several forms of storytelling provides an impressive

FIGURE 149 ❧ Reginald Marsh, drawing for *U.S.A.* (1946). Marsh produced several hundred drawings for Houghton Mifflin's illustrated edition of the trilogy. This sketch of patrons at the Café de la Paix in Paris appears in *Nineteen Nineteen*.

mechanism for examining both the inner and outer identities of the nation. The constant shifts among the novel's voices splendidly mimic the drive and staccato pace of twentieth-century American life, its restless, agitated, nonstop motion. Don Passos admired the gleaming engines that powered America's cars and trains and airplanes, and his fictional forms offer his homage to native ingenuity and workmanship. At its frequent best, *U.S.A.* came nearer than any other novel of the thirties to containing the interplay between imagination and social institutions.

At the end of the trilogy, a young man called only "Vag" stands at the edge of a road trying to thumb a ride. Hungry, dirty, betrayed by America's failed promises, the vagabond watches a plane soar overhead, a symbol of opportunity and progress now turned into an ironic taunt by the country's general collapse in the Depression. The scene summarizes Dos Passos's bitterness and aptly closes his unhappy epic. Much of the American twentieth century is contained in *U.S.A.*, but it is a chronicle of defeat: from the wreck of idealism in the First World War, through the judicial murder of anarchists in the twenties, to the unexampled misery of the thirties. Earlier American heroes journeyed by choice, in proof of their self-sufficiency. The vagabond, their beaten descendant, is a creature of circumstance; he stands as lonely sentry beside a road that goes nowhere.

In the first half of the thirties, Dos Passos was a literary lion on the Left, including the Communist Left. As early as 1934, however, when he signed a letter condemning Communist disruption of a socialist meeting in New York City, his partisan reliability came into question. His final break with the doctrinaire Left occurred, as it did for so many others, in the later thirties in response to the Moscow purge trials, the Soviet sellout of the republican forces in the Spanish civil war, and the Nazi–Soviet nonaggression pact. By 1937, he had decided (as he told Dreiser) that he did not want to "Russianize" America, that America was "probably the country where the average guy has got the better break."

Charges and countercharges about Russianizing America would fill a thick volume in the political history of the thirties. The programs of the New Deal, which seem both modest and pragmatic in retrospect, were regularly denounced as elements in some Soviet master strategy or other. One of the principal targets of right-wing

FIGURE 150 ❧ Raphael Soyer, *The Mission* (1935). This lithograph was part of the portfolio *The American Scene.*

critics was the Federal Writers Project, which was set up in 1935. Under the auspices of the project, writers for the first time received federal subsidies, pathetically small in most cases, but enough to keep pens in their hands. Not all the men and women who received this unprecedented support would go on to major careers, but the roster includes Richard Wright, Saul Bellow, Margaret Walker, John Cheever, Arna Bontemps, and Ralph Ellison. The small checks bought food and shelter and also, perhaps more important, a measure of dignity. "Actually to be *paid* for writing," Ellison recalled, "why that was a wonderful thing!" The government's financial involvement in art, reluctant and temporary though it was, attracted the vigilant hostility of the political Right. The whole undertaking, together with the corresponding Federal Theatre Project and the Federal Arts Project, seemed suspect, even un-American. To be sure, conservatives distrusted government payments to artists on principle, but it was also true that many of the artists in question had accumulated longer or shorter records of left-wing activity (Figure 150).

On the Left as well as the Right, the debate over politics and literature became more shrill as the thirties progressed. Attacks by right-wing politicians on the patriotism of dissident writers were matched on the Left by the gibes of communist apparatchiks, who scolded novelists and poets for each hint of deviance. For their part, most of the writers drifted away, sooner or later disenchanted by the sterility of politicized aesthetics or the excesses of Stalinism. As in all sectarian struggles, those who kept the faith reserved their special scorn for those who deserted. The Writers' Congresses, patterned on gatherings of workers in America and the Soviet Union and intended as staging grounds for organized left-wing creativity, became instead dreary arenas for accusations of bad faith. At the fourth and last of the congresses, in 1941, Mike Gold discoursed irrelevantly but fervently on the need for ideological purity, and he used Thornton Wilder and John Steinbeck to illustrate what he considered the polar oppositions of contemporary writing. Gold had been pummeling Wilder since the late twenties as a decadent escapist. In a review called "Wilder: Prophet of the Genteel Christ" (1927), Gold had charged Wilder with presiding over a romantic junk shop, had accused him of retreating into political indifference, and – worst of all – had charged him with writing like Henry James. In his Writers' Congress speech fourteen years later, Gold pressed the same indictment. Gold cheered Steinbeck, on the other hand, as the bearer of a true "people's culture." In particular, according to Gold, *The Grapes of Wrath* proved that the "proletarian spirit had battered down the barricades set up by the bourgeois monopolists of literature."

Aside from the tired melodrama of its metaphors, this estimate of Steinbeck was both right and wrong. Certainly Steinbeck infused his novels with an almost evangelical populist enthusiasm and created characters whose deprivations seemed real rather than formulaic. However, like most of the other major writers of the 1930s, he chafed under the halter of any rigorous discipline. Steinbeck was given to moral simplification, but it was a homegrown variety, the sentimentality that has long attached itself to the plain people and the good land. *In Dubious Battle* (1935), his strike novel, was mistakenly called Marxist by several critics. In fact, the book's sympathies are reserved for the untutored workers, whose courage and suffering alike transcend the explanation of abstract systems. A longtime observer of California seapools, Steinbeck fancied himself an amateur scientist, but his unscientific passion for rectitude and his attachment to the primitive almost always dictated his fictional choices (Figure 151).

California, both as setting and symbol, provided the axis around which Steinbeck's life and imagination revolved. In his work, the venerable westering myth was given a colorful and sometimes moving restatement. He was born in the Salinas Valley and studied at Stanford for several years. After a couple of false fictional starts, including a pirate romance, he found his subject and his first success with *Tortilla Flat* (1935), a good-humored if rather one-dimensional portrayal of the allegedly carefree and picturesque paisanos of Monterey. Steinbeck remained a partisan of the disadvantaged throughout the rest of his career, of people like the hulking but gentle half-wit Lenny in *Of Mice and Men* (1937), of the Joads and the Okies they represent in *The Grapes of Wrath* (1939), of the poor Mexican fisherman in *The Pearl* (1948). He was capable of vivid realism, but his reverence for nature tempted him continuously toward a romantic lyricism that often verged on mysticism. In the end, his strength probably lay neither in rhapsody nor in protest but in the broadly conceived and often funny characters that live in the fly-blown cabins of his rural settlements and loiter on the streets of his backwater villages.

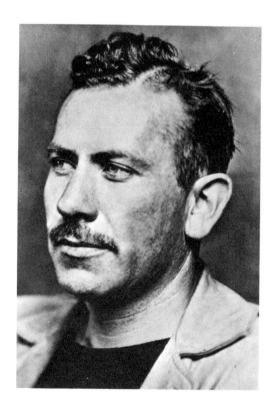

FIGURE 151 🌶
Photograph of John
Steinbeck (n.d.)

In the late thirties, the influx of midwestern migrants into California reached flood tide, and Steinbeck saw the harsh treatment of suffering families by police and business as the saddest consequence of the Depression. Moved to anger by the brutality that scarred the relations among fellow human beings, he determined to make a suitable, politically useful record. Journalism was his first choice, as it was frequently the choice of writers in the thirties. It has often been suggested that the most characteristic literary genre of the Depression decade was the documentary. The success of the photojournalists was matched and exceeded by the popularity of the filmed weekly newsreels that played to millions in movie theaters. The sheer weight of American reality sometimes seemed too heavy a burden for fiction or poetry to carry. Needless to say, fidelity to what appears to be fact does not ensure good writing, but much of the decade's strongest prose took the form of reportage. A comment of Steinbeck's, in a letter of 1938, can be taken as representative: "I want to put a tag of shame on the greedy bastards who are responsible for this but I can best do it through newspapers." He did use newspapers, but he also reworked his reporting in *The Grapes of Wrath*, and he produced the most controversial and influential novel of the 1930s. Among earlier fictional works, only Upton Sinclair's *Jungle* and Harriet Beecher Stowe's *Uncle Tom's Cabin* were so inextricably linked to the social history of their times as Steinbeck's chronicle of the Joad family and their endurance (Figure 152).

The Joads belong at once to history and myth. Exiled from their failed Oklahoma farm by the collusion between the drought and the bankers, and straggling westward in search of a new life, they are the representative figures of a dispossessed decade. At the same time, they are the last, unlikely pioneers, and their story rings with the intermittent echoes of Jefferson, Emerson, and Whitman. They travel across half a continent to find whatever still remains of the American dream. Like Dos Passos in *U.S.A.* and Agee in *Let Us Now Praise Famous Men*, Steinbeck attempted to enhance the authority of *The Grapes of Wrath* by employing a multiplicity of voices. To reinforce the novel's larger significance, he regularly interrupts the Joad family's adventures to insert a series of "interchapters." Hoovervilles, used-car lots, tractors, and banks are some of Steinbeck's subjects in these sections. Some of these pages are abstract,

FIGURE 152 ☙ Dorothy Lange, *Ditched, Stalled, and Stranded, San Joaquin Valley, California* (1935).

most are anecdotal, but all are intended to broaden the novel's scope, generalize its themes, and confirm its documentary claims. The Joads, conceived with monumental simplicity to illustrate the plight and the underlying integrity of America's victims, are memorable characters, but they never escape the sentimental premises on which they are based. Their indomitable decency is intended to prove the justice of their cause. Rev. Casy gives up preaching to learn from these unlettered people, and his choice implies Steinbeck's comradely preference for instinct over the so-called civilization that has made the Depression possible: "I ain't gonna baptize.

I'm gonna work in the fiel's, in the green fiel's, and I'm gonna be near to folks. I ain't gonna try to teach 'em nothin'. I'm gonna try to learn. Gonna learn why the folks walks in the grass, gonna hear 'em talk, gonna hear 'em sing. Gonna listen to kids eatin' mush. Gonna hear husban' an' wife a-pounding the mattress in the night. Gonna eat with 'em an' learn."

The Grapes of Wrath was denounced on the floor of the Senate and in the pulpits of the Midwest, reviled as a travesty by affronted Oklahomans, and banned in dozens of libraries. It also won the Pulitzer Prize. Both sorts of response are instructive. Not far beneath its surface of melodrama and dissent lies a network of comfortable American verities. The reputed proletarianism of the novel subsides at last into a celebration of the endurance of ordinary folk. It is the traditional democratic faith, almost religious in Steinbeck's formulation of it. The book's message is inscribed in its images rather than its discourse: a geranium plant that improbably survives by the side of a road; sunshine on wet leaves after a shower; Rose of Sharon wordlessly nourishing a starving old man with the breast milk meant for her stillborn child.

The economic troubles that engulfed the country in the 1930s had bedeviled the South long before 1929. For three generations following the Civil War, America's gigantic industrial and urban growth had bypassed the South almost completely. The states of the old Confederacy continued to be rural, poor, agrarian, precariously tied to a single crop, and morally impoverished by a systematized racism. Literary culture was virtually nonexistent. A flippantly mournful couplet was passed from hand to hand for decades: "Alas, poor South, her poets get fewer and fewer; / She never was much given to literature." Ellen Glasgow, looking back on her childhood in late nineteenth-century Virginia, later wrote that "southerners did not publish, did not write, did not read." Northern observers agreed with that assessment, and they lacked altogether any counterbalancing sympathy. In 1920, Mencken published an essay on southern civilization festooned with the audaciously insulting title, "The Sahara of the Bozart." He likened the South to the Gobi Desert, Asia Minor, Lapland, and other places he considered cultural wastelands. He discerned within this "gargantuan paradise of the fourth-rate" only one writer of merit, James Branch Cabell. Mencken had Cabell's *Jurgen* in mind, which had been published the preceding year and had created a flutter of scandal on the grounds of obscenity. Under the pressure of Mencken's influential opinion, Cabell's arch and mincing aestheticism was sometimes credited with ushering in the new literature of the South. A more persuasive case can be made for the novels of Ellen Glasgow.

Glasgow's novels appeared in tireless succession for over forty years, the first in 1897, the last in 1941. Her particular subject was the history of her region; her particular contribution was to liberate southern history from the defensive and disabling cult of the Lost Cause, that pious anthology of shibboleths and slogans which falsified the Civil War as a doomed but knightly Confederate quest. In her best novels, Glasgow replaced nostalgia with a realism that was often ironic and was always critical. In *The Deliverance* (1904), for example, set in the years following the Civil War, she debunked southern mythmaking by means of a superb satiric invention. In that novel, Mrs. Blake is a blind and paralyzed old woman who believes that the South won the war. Her family shields her for decades from the actual outcome, giving her detailed reports drawn from a consoling and utterly fictitious postbellum history, in which a sequence of southern presidents follows the victory of the Confederacy. Mrs. Blake is a representative thematic figure. In many of Glasgow's stories and novels, she diagnosed the besetting southern disease as blindness, and she exposed the South's incorrigible inability to look at the facts of life. Dinwiddie, the southern city in which several of her novels are set, is suffused in a false and foglike calm so pervasive that "an axe could hardly have dispelled it" (Figure 153).

In several books, including *Virginia* (1913), *The Life of Gabriella* (1916), and *Barren Ground* (1925), Glasgow attended to the status of women in the changing South. In *Barren Ground*, one of her best novels, the career of the central character could be said to recapitulate the South's literary development in the early twentieth century. Dorinda Oakley is the daughter of defeated parents who scratch

FIGURE 153 ❧
Photograph of Ellen
Glasgow (n.d.).

a hard living out of the meager soil of their small Virginia farm, and she longs for marriage as escape and fulfillment. Instead, the man she loves seduces and jilts her. These initial premises seem conventionally romantic. As the novel progresses, however, it moves steadily away from such melodrama toward a more mature realism. Dorinda neither pays for her sexual transgression with death, nor does she collapse into matrimonial contentment with some forgiving man at the end of her story, nor does she magically transform the lesser characters around her. She is not interested in anyone's forgiveness or sympathy. Rather, she chooses work over passion and spends thirty years quietly mastering the "barren ground" of the book's title. She becomes successful and independent. The novel's structure is straightforward, in many ways undramatic, but the book is potent in its celebration of female integrity and endurance. Out of a prose that moves with the methodical pace of repetitive but productive working days, Glasgow created in Dorinda Oakley one of the sturdier characters of twentieth-century fiction.

Glasgow's novels made a turning point. What is sometimes called the southern literary renaissance may be dated to her early work. However, the renaissance became a self-conscious movement after the First World War, with the gathering of the Nashville Fugitives in and around Vanderbilt University. The magazine they put out, *The Fugitive*, first appeared in 1922 and was published for just three years. The group's members carried on, and they played seminal roles in the reassessment of the south's past and prospects that so conspicuously took place between the two world wars. They included the poets Donald Davidson, Allen Tate, and John Crowe Ransom, whose verses sought out the strength that might still reside in traditional values. In some cases, the tradition was southern only by appropriation. Davidson's "On a Replica of the Parthenon in Nashville," for example, harshly condemns the busy materialism of modern city life by contrasting it with the tranquil simplicity of classical Greece. Davidson implies that the South is the only contemporary region in which that nurturing tranquility is likely to be rediscovered (Figure 154).

In the familiar manner of literary pastoral, the Fugitives wedded the personal virtues of their region's rural citizens to the nobility of their history. Davidson's "Tall Men" contrasts the virile backwoodsmen of Tennessee with the thin-blooded inhabitants of modern southern cities. John Crowe Ransom's "Antique Harvesters" abstracts the quality of ceremony from southern talk and from the soul-rewarding labors of planting and hunting:

> We pick the spindling ears and gather the corn.
> One spot has special yield? "On this spot stood
> Heroes and drenched it with their only blood."
> And talk meets talk, as echoes from the horn
> Of the hunter – echoes are the old men's arts,
> Ample are the chambers of their hearts.
>
> Here come the hunters, keepers of a rite;
> The horn, the hounds, the lank mares coursing by
> Straddled with archetypes of chivalry.

As in this poem, much of Agrarian verse is filled with the retreating echoes of Civil War heroism. Plain soldiers and leaders are called

FIGURE 154 ❧ The Fugitives (1923). The front page of the May 27, 1923, *Nashville Tennessean* included the photographs of several leading Fugitives.

up from the shadows, their images deckle-edged with authority and pathos. Davidson's best-known poem, "Lee in the Mountains," pictures the defeated general in retirement and idealizes him and the cause he fought for. Ransom's "Captain Carpenter" is treated with gentle irony as he goes down to defeat before the forces of modernity, but his outmoded gallantry is shown to be clearly preferable to the savage efficiency of his opponents. The most affecting of these historical meditations is Allen Tate's "Ode to the Confederate Dead," first published in 1926. In the poem, a speaker standing by a cemetery gate ponders the rows of headstones lined up, soldierlike, which mark the graves of those who fell in the service of the Old South:

> Autumn is desolation in the plot
> Of a thousand acres where these memories grow
> From the inexhaustible bodies that are not
> Dead, but feed the grass row after row.
> Think of the autumns that have come and gone!

Hart Crane thought he detected the influence of T. S. Eliot on Tate, before Tate had yet read any of Eliot's poetry. The error was understandable. Rather like Eliot, Tate and the other new southern poets typically employed dense and challenging formal inventions to record their rediscovery of the values of the past and their dissent from the industrial and urban trends of the twentieth century. Their themes were given expository statement in 1930 in a book called *I'll Take My Stand*. The dozen essays in this controversial volume range across economy and art, religion and race. Detailed, often sentimental sketches of happy rural life alternate with root-and-branch assaults on the technology and mass culture of the North. The book was subtitled "The South and the Agrarian Tradition." As Donald Davidson said in the introductory "Statement of Principles," all the essays in the book "tend to support a Southern way of life against what may be called the American or prevailing way; and all as much agree that the best terms in which to represent the distinction are contained in the phrase, Agrarian *versus* Industrial." The polemical tone of the book is economically suggested by the title of some of the individual essays: "Reconstructed but Unregenerate," "A Critique of the Philosophy of Progress," and "Not in Memoriam, but in Defense."

In terms of twentieth-century politics, the Agrarians were fighting a rear-guard and losing action, and much of what they said seemed even at the time more quaint than pertinent. But their emphases and priorities identify some of the qualities of the resurgent literary activity they helped to inaugurate. Directly or by implication, all the contributors insisted on the primacy of the concrete and particular over the abstract and general. Agrarian preferences, masked as aesthetic principles transcending ideology, shaped much of critical practice over the next several decades. In the name of a rigor that was designed to rescue literary texts from the tyranny of mere opinion, the tenets of the New Criticism urged a scrupulously careful analysis. The textbook *Understanding Poetry* (1938), in which Cleanth Brooks and Robert Penn Warren explained and exemplified the new approach, instructed generations of students in its formal methods. Despite its detached and self-sufficient demeanor, the New Criticism was embedded in assumptions that included an admiration for irony, deference to the authority of received literary hierarchies, and a straitened view of literary texts that narrowed the range of permissible questioning. Inquiry into literature's sources and ends tended to be disparaged as irrelevant, if not propagandistic.

In their poetry and fiction, as well as their criticism, southern writers created the most significant body of regional writing in the first half of the twentieth century. Literature repaid the debts of military defeat and sustained economic privation. Walker Percy, putting to himself the question, "Why has the south produced so many good writers?" answered with a kind of gallows humor: "Because we got beat." Failure nourished pride in a vanquished territory that held itself aloof, as if it were a separate country, until the Second World War. Allen Tate ventured the opinion that "the very backwardness of Mississippi, and of the South as a whole, might partially explain the rise of a new literature which has won the attention not only of Americans but of the Western world." Tate was a partisan, to be sure, but the list of writers he referred to is indeed formidable. To name just a few, beginning with Tate himself and Ransom and Warren: Eudora Welty, Katherine Anne Porter, Flannery O'Connor, Tennessee Williams, James Agee, Truman Capote, Carson McCullers.

Though the estimate has long since been abandoned, many readers in the 1930s judged the major southern writer to be Thomas Wolfe. The seventh of seven children, Wolfe grew up unhappily in the hills of North Carolina, in the town of Asheville, the son of a tombstone carver and a boardinghouse manager. He attended college at the state university and went on from there to graduate study at Harvard, European travel, and two decades of almost uninterrupted writing. Born at the turn of the century, he published only two novels before he died in 1938, leaving millions of unpublished words behind. Sinclair Lewis was among those who admired Wolfe's first novel, *Look Homeward, Angel* (1929), and the book had a considerable success. Wolfe's second novel, *Of Time and the*

River (1935), secured his fame. In the last few years of his life he enjoyed the status of an outsized prose bard, a man of unquenchable appetites and epic ambitions. In fact, Wolfe's lunging eagerness too often overwhelmed whatever talent he had. He disparaged literary discipline and mistook excited effusions for acts of imagination. He wrote too much and revised too little. His big books were quarried out of bigger drafts, sometimes by him, more often by editors. His novels are swarming chronicles of sensibility, knit together only by the cravings and emotions of their autobiographical heroes, among them Eugene Gant and George Webber.

Faulkner, making Wolfe sound a little like one of his own brooding, baffled characters, said that "Tom Wolfe was trying to say everything, the world plus 'I', or filtered through 'I' or the effort of 'I' to embrace the world in which he was born and walked a little while and then lay down again." Robert Penn Warren complained about the overwrought rhetorical explosions that "steamed and bubbled" from the surface of Wolfe's prose. Wolfe's grandiose yearning to embrace the world led him, probably willy-nilly, to adopt a style of inclusion, multiplication, saturation. Everything is named and listed and annotated, then named and listed again. This is just a small fraction of what young Eugene Gant remembers as he thinks back to the smells of his childhood in *Look Homeward, Angel*:

> the exciting smell of chalk and varnished desks; the smell of heavy bread-sandwiches of cold fried meat; the smell of new leather in a saddler's shop, or of a warm leather chair; of honey and of unground coffee; of barrelled sweet pickles and cheese and all the fragrant compost of the grocer's; the smell of stored apples in the cellar, and of orchard-apple smells, or pressed-cider pulp; of pears ripening on a sunny shelf, and of ripe cherries stewing with sugar on hot stoves before preserving; the smell of whittled wood, of all young lumber, of sawdust and shavings; of peaches stuck with cloves and pickled in brandy; of pine-sap, and green pine-needles; of a horse's pared hoof; of chestnuts roasting, of bowls of nuts and raisins; of hot cracklin, and of young roast pork; of butter and cinnamon melting on hot candied yams.

Wolfe told Fitzgerald that "a great writer is not only a leaver-outer but also a putter-inner," and he seemed to work on the hypothesis

that he could possess all of America if he accumulated it in his prose.

In 1927, two years before Wolfe published his first novel, Katherine Anne Porter set to work on a biography that was to be called *The Devil and Cotton Mather*. The book was never finished, but its title gives a sense of the anger that animates the dozen or so chapters Porter wrote. To Porter, Mather represented evil, in a peculiarly conscious and therefore dangerous form, and his career dramatized for her the calamitous results that follow when power links arms with a fanatical ideology. It was also in 1927 that Porter joined in the protests against the execution of Sacco and Vanzetti. Her comments on the case, published fifty years later in *The Never-ending Wrong* (1977), suggest that she read the same sinister lesson in the political and judicial events of America's past and present. She was drawn to scenes of starkly contrasted good and evil, and her work has affinities with the allegorical dramas of Hawthorne (Figure 155).

Born in west Texas in 1890, amid still-potent memories of the Civil War, Porter made homes across the country and around the world in the course of her long life: Denver, New York, California,

FIGURE 155 ❧ Katherine Anne Porter (1927). Arrested in a protest against the execution of Sacco and Vanzetti, Porter is shown (*fourth from left*) being escorted to the Joy Street police station in Boston. The woman in front of her carries a placard on which is printed: "Equal and exact justice to all men of whatever state of persuasion, religious or political. Not in Massachusetts!"

Bermuda, Mexico, Paris, Germany. Though she worked for over twenty-five years on her novel, *Ship of Fools* (1962), her most enduring achievement was probably the remarkable stories she published in the 1920s and 1930s. Gathered in such volumes as *Flowering Judas and Other Stories* (1935) and *Pale Horse, Pale Rider* (1939), Porter's stories came to be regarded as a standard of craftsmanship and influenced the prose of such writers as Kay Boyle, Flannery O'Connor, and Eudora Welty.

Porter believed in her talent, but she feared, rightly, that the label of "stylist" threatened to trivialize her themes and subjects. She was a fearless student of human extremity, and her stories record her firsthand observations of brutality, cruelty, and betrayal. "Flowering Judas" traces the tragic, comic decline of revolutionary commitment into economic and erotic opportunism. "Noon Wine" powerfully evokes the marginal lives of subsistence farmers and reproduces the mysterious terror that accompanies a sudden, inexplicable eruption of violence. "The Leaning Tower" offers a grimly engaging sketch of Berlin in the thirties, demoralized, wobbling on the brink of the abyss.

Porter's own eventful life provided the materials for "Old Mortality" and the sequence "The Old Order." Her main character, Miranda, grows into sad knowledge amid multiplied images of decay, death, and racial and sexual conflict. In the opening episode of "The Grave," the last story in "The Old Order," nine-year-old Miranda leaps "into the pit that had held her grandfather's bones." When, shortly afterwards, her older brother kills and opens a pregnant rabbit, the tiny bodies of the unborn animals elicit Miranda's astonished pity and serve as summary images of a universal death-in-life.

Unlike Porter, William Faulkner rarely left the South. He went to Canada in the latter days of the First World War, in an unsuccessful effort to fly with the Royal Canadian Air Force, and he made an obligatory but unproductive sojourn in Europe in the early twenties. In 1929, after bringing out a volume of poetry and two competent novels, Faulkner published *Sartoris* and *The Sound and the Fury*, and with those books began the exploration of his invented Mississippi county, Yoknapatawpha, which would occupy him across thirty years and nearly twenty volumes. The astonishing reach of his fictional experiments, arising in part from his early fascination with Symbolist poetry, marks Faulkner as a writer of the twenties (Figure 156). But his most distinctive work, beginning with the first Yoknapatawpha novels, appeared throughout the 1930s and early 1940s. Those were the years in which Faulkner produced *As I Lay Dying* (1930), *Light in August* (1932), *Absalom, Absalom!* (1936), *The Unvanquished* (1938), and *Go Down, Moses* (1942). With the single exception of Henry James, no American novelist has sustained such a level of writing in so many books. With the exception of Melville, none has pushed against the limits of fictional convention with such restless and prodigal fertility.

"It has been argued that the Southerner lives in the past," Robert Penn Warren once wrote. "That is not true; the past lives in him." By that standard, as by almost any other, Faulkner's fiction was as

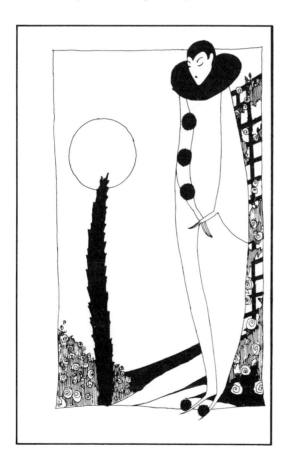

FIGURE 156 &· William Faulkner, *Pierrot Standing*, from *The Marionettes* (1920). Faulkner himself drew the illustrations for his early one-act play *The Marionettes*.

typical as it was preeminent. At the beginning of *Absalom, Absalom!*, the young Quentin Compson sits listening through "a long hot weary dead September afternoon" in 1909 to the anguished tale Miss Rosa Coldfield tells him. Like so many of Faulkner's characters, Quentin spends much of his time listening, and listening, to the same stories told over and over again. Faulkner writes that Quentin's "very body was an empty hall echoing with sonorous, defeated names; he was not a being, an entity, he was a commonwealth. He was a barracks filled with stubborn back-looking ghosts." Something like that could be said of Faulkner himself, who grew up, like Quentin, hearing the exciting, hair-raising, sometimes lurid stories that told the rise and fall of his family and place.

He was descended from colonels and heroes who were descended in their turn from Scottish immigrants, refugees from English persecution. His family had borne its share of the glory and the shame that make up the burden of southern history, a chronicle of wastage and decline that had led from prosperity to war and devastation. The Old South had been a dream colored in the garish but seductive hues of chivalry and rooted in the crimes of expropriation and chattel slavery. Its legacy was a bankrupt economy, barbaric racial codes, inertia that alternated with spasms of cruelty, nostalgia for blightd honor, reverence for the unspoiled land, contempt for the intellect, and a passion for talk. In the 1920s, as Faulkner took up his fictional vocation, he demurred from the metropolitan gospel of the "New South" which was being promoted by the businessmen of Oxford, Mississippi, and other southern towns. Like the Fugitives, Faulkner had no interest in joining the American mainstream. While his Rotarian neighbors looked to the future and planned for what was to happen next, Faulkner accepted the task of explaining what had happened before, how so much promise had led to such unappeasable futility and disappointment.

Faulkner's early years in and around Oxford were a time of desultory effort and no discernible accomplishment. He took up drinking, dropped out of high school, enlisted in the Royal Canadian Air Force during the First World War but never got overseas, worked without interest at a sequence of small jobs, and took a few courses at the University of Mississippi, where he was also fired from his position as university postmaster. In the midtwenties he lived for a time in New Orleans, taking part in the marathon discussions of poetry and culture that animated the city's literary colony and accepting Sherwood Anderson's hospitality. It was Anderson, Faulkner later acknowledged, who helped him published his first novel, a war story called *Soldier's Pay* (1926), and guided him to his subject, the "little postage-stamp of soil" that he knew best and out of which he produced, in his fiction, a commonwealth. Yoknapatawpha is a fictional world at once self-contained and filled with outward reference. What Faulkner says of the McCaslin ledger in "The Bear" is true as well of Yoknapatawpha: it is "a whole land in miniature, which, multiplied and compounded, was the entire South" (Figure 157).

Faulkner's compulsion to preserve and explain had precise historical sources. For white southerners, the future had ended at Gettysburg. On the day of that battle, Faulkner suggested in *Intruder in the Dust* (1948), freedom became a memory:

> For every Southern boy fourteen years old, not only once but whenever he wants it, there is the instant when it's still not two o'clock on that July afternoon in 1863, the brigades are in position behind the rail fence, the guns are laid and ready in the woods, and the furled flags are already loosened to break out and Pickett himself with his long oiled ringlets and his hat in one hand probably and his sword in the other looking up the hill waiting for Longstreet to give the word and it's all in the balance, it hasn't happened yet.

But of course it has all happened, and nothing of that day is in the balance. This hopeful conjuring of the instant before catastrophe, the moment before disaster struck white southern history, is only possible for children – for fourteen-year-old boys. The mature imagination returns to such scenes with pathos rather than hope, bewildered and fascinated by what has irrevocably taken place. Thus Yoknapatawpha, to use a phrase from *As I Lay Dying*, becomes a land of "weary gestures wearily recapitulant." Faulkner's stories are tales of memory and doom. Joe Christmas, in his mad flight to embrace death in *Light in August*, "enters again the street which ran for thirty years." For Joe, as for the rest of Faulkner's characters, the streets of Jefferson lead into a labyrinth of inescapable cause and effect. Faulkner's continual evocation of fatality, like the theatrical images of dark dicemen and puppeteers that fill his pages as

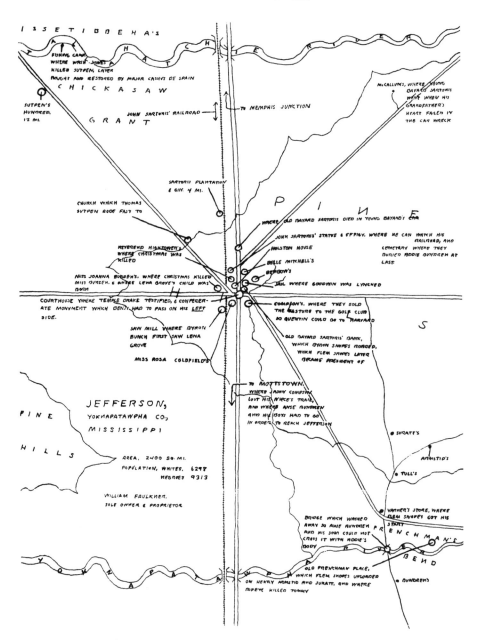

FIGURE 157 William Faulkner, map of Yoknapatawpha County. Faulkner produced this map, in which he identifies himself as the "sole owner and proprietor" of the county, for the first edition of *Absalom, Absalom!* (1936).

emblems of relentless destiny, derives from his resignation to the inscrutable forces that mock human will. He was fond of saying that "the past isn't dead; it isn't even past." At its most potent, as in the Benjy section of *The Sound and the Fury*, the past simply replaces the present. More precisely, the present is reduced to the vanishing point, serving as little more than a transparent theater scrim through which the past can always be perceived. Thirty-three-year-old Benjy, arrested at the mental age of three, trudges through a repetitive daily round that provides only a series of provocations to reenter the past.

The Sound and the Fury was perhaps Faulkner's finest novel, the book in which he created some of his most affecting images for the collaboration of choice and fate that has ruined the South and its people. The Compsons have sold their pasture in order that the favored son, Quentin, may attend Harvard. On the day of the novel's opening, nearly twenty years later, Quentin and his suicide are a mocking memory, like the fence that separates the Compsons from their land, now turned into a golf course. Quentin's idiot brother Benjy spends much of each day mooning beside the fence, a hulking symbol of his family's decayed fortunes. Usually inert, Benjy is shocked into rhapsody whenever he hears a golfer shout the word "caddie," which he hears as "Caddie," the nickname of his beloved but long-vanished sister Candace, who was the only person ever to treat him with tenderness. The cruel comedy of Benjy's plight serves as prologue and synopsis for the Yoknapatawpha saga, in the distance between his delusions and the shabby reality around him, in the sense of loss that he embodies. Trapped in the changeless vault of his own mind, Benjy can only revisit the treasured scenes of childhood, which are as real to him as the jimson weed that grows by the fence and the fire in which he burns his hand.

Faulkner's characteristic fictional methods rose directly out of his central themes. He needed to subject the past to continuous scrutiny, to hold it in his hand like a familiar but still puzzling object and turn it around repeatedly in the light. Each of his novels records a newly conceived strategy to capture reality, and each therefore expands, absorbs, and perhaps annuls what has gone before. He said that the four chapters of *The Sound and the Fury* were really a single story that he had tried (unsuccessfully) to tell four times, in four different ways. Like all of Faulkner's comments about his own work, this one was at least a little perverse, intended to thwart pursuit instead of explaining. Nonetheless, it hints at an important perception. Faulkner's technique in *The Sound and the Fury* allowed him to enter into the mysteries of consciousness, to reproduce the rush and twisting of thought – in Benjy's case, the chaotic stratum beneath thought – and at the same time to raise the inner experience of the Compson brothers to the level of modern dynastic myth. Much of his most abundant fiction sought to document this interweaving of private defeat and general catastrophe.

Though it represented a turning in his own work and in American letters, *The Sound and the Fury* did not erupt inexplicably out of Faulkner's earlier fiction. In his youthful poems and first novels, he had already demonstrated a capacity for experiment. He had, as well, discovered his subject matter in the country people of Mississippi: the beggared but still defiant white aristocracy; the closefisted traders and scalawags; the drunks and half-wits and conscience-stricken preachers; the hunters, farmers, blacks, and Indians of Jefferson County, and their ancestors as well. He had also begun to perfect the language and cadence of the distinctive rhetoric in which his major stories would be told. It was a voice that he himself described as a self-taught "oratory out of solitude," built of long, fluid, mesmerizing sentences, sometimes running a page or longer, that mix colloquialism and coinage with arcane and archaic vocabulary. This passage is from the narrator's introduction of Dilsey in the fourth section of *The Sound and the Fury*:

> She had been a big woman once but now her skeleton rose, draped loosely in unpadded skin that tightened again upon a paunch almost dropsical, as though muscle and tissue had been courage or fortitude which the days or the years had consumed until only the indomitable skeleton was left rising like a ruin or a landmark above the somnolent and impervious guts, and above that the collapsed face that gave the impression of the bones themselves being outside the flesh, lifted into the driving day with an expression at once fatalistic and of a child's astonished disappointment, until she turned and entered the house again and closed the door.

In spite of her frailty and the pain she has seen and suffered, Dilsey holds the novel's black and white families together. The unhurried but crowded sentences in which she is portrayed illuminate her commanding but precarious stature and prepare for the events that await her and the Compsons.

At its best, Faulkner's prose invests his interior monologues and anecdotes with the grandeur of tragedy, uniting experience and annotation in implacable rivers of talk. At its worst, on the other hand – and Faulkner himself could not always tell the difference – his eloquence is bloated into a gassy grandiloquence that has been ridiculed as "Dixie Gongorism." Nor can his sentences always redeem his grotesque characters, melodramatic plots, and bizarre incidents from gothic excess. His stories are rank with sadism, with episodes of bloodshed, rape, murder, suicide, decapitation, incest, castration, and lynching. A ligature of violence binds Faulkner's characters to each other in a parody of brotherhood, and his efforts to turn brutality directly into thematic statement sometimes tempted him into mere extremity. His affection, real though almost furtive, was reserved for the marginal and cast-off, the very young and very old, people excluded from the exercise of authority and even from respectability by age, race, or class.

In the political and ideological struggle over race, Faulkner's position was complex. He equivocated. He announced his support for states' rights, including the prerogatives of state governments to enforce segregation. In his fiction, however, some of his strongest characters are black. In *Go Down, Moses*, Lucas Beauchamp is the legatee of whatever courage and integrity has survived in the McCaslin family. And of Dilsey, Faulkner wrote with elliptical admiration, in the genealogy that he constructed as a putative commentary on *The Sound and the Fury*: "They endured." Sharing the paternalism that often poisoned white southern attitudes, Faulkner nevertheless paid his tribute to the stamina that had outlasted centuries of abuse and oppression.

For many black Americans, the Crash merely intensified hardships they had already known. Competition for jobs intensified, and racial scapegoating became fiercer. Black intellectual response to the Depression took shape as an ongoing debate between those who kept racial questions at the center of their analysis and those who adopted a Marxist viewpoint and shifted their emphasis from race to economics and class structure. The arguments were often bitter, and the poets and novelists who engaged in them reflected the same divisions as the historians and political scientists.

The Harlem Renaissance, with its aesthetic and exotic overtones, was finished. Looking back on it, radical critics sometimes accused the renaissance writers of an accommodating gentility and of a politically irrelevant absorption in technical issues. Wallace Thurman's *Infants of the Spring* (1932), for example, lampoons Countee Cullen under the thin disguise of DeWitt Clinton. Thurman's spokesman in the novel, a character named Raymond Taylor, demolishes Clinton / Cullen by picturing him at work: "eyes on a page of Keats, fingers on the typewriter, mind frantically conjuring African scenes, and . . . a Bible nearby." Richard Wright was especially offended by the subservience of many renaissance writers to white standards. In an important essay called "Blueprint for Negro Writing" (1937), Wright described the renaissance writers as

> prim and decorous ambassadors who went a-begging to white America. . . . They entered the Court of American Public Opinion dressed in the kneepants of servility, curtsying to show that the Negro was not inferior, that he was human, and that he led a life comparable to that of other people. For the most part these artistic ambassadors were received as though they were French poodles who do clever tricks.

According to Wright, in the 1930s the job of the black writer was to identify himself with the masses and then use literature to "create the values by which his race is to struggle, live and die." Wright adhered to a more or less dogmatic Marxism for only a few years, but during the late thirties he regularly measured black literature by the yardstick of revolutionary utility. He elaborately praised Arna Bontemps's *Black Thunder* (1936), for example, a good political novel which Wright valued as the first work of black proletarian fiction. Similarly, Wright attacked Zora Neale Hurston's work because he found it insufficiently concerned either with race or the class struggle.

Wright underestimated Hurston. Racial conflict is not typically at the center of her work because she chose to create narratives of self-contained black experience, stories that tell of life within black communities, and her testimony has proved valuable, enduring, and fertile. Trained as an anthropologist, she made distinguished con-

FIGURE 158 ❧ Carl
Van Vechten,
photograph of Zora Neale
Hurston (1934).

tributions to black folklore studies, recording and analyzing folk
customs and tales across the South and in the Caribbean. The essays
in *Mules and Men* (1935) and the recollections in her autobiography,
Dust Tracks on a Road (1942), are rich with the evidence she gathered of African-American culture. She brought her considerable
social-scientific skills to her fiction. She had a remarkable ear for
the varieties of speech, and one of the particular strengths of her
novels and her nonfiction is her use of dialect with convincingly
human, rather than eccentric, effect. Her second novel, *Their Eyes
Were Watching God* (1937), was one of the more significant books
of the Depression decade (Figure 158).

The novel follows the life of its central character, a black woman
named Janie, from childhood into middle age. Despite Wright's
strictures, the novel is not racially indifferent. It includes, among
other episodes, a chilling scene of the segregated burial of blacks
and whites after a disastrous flood, an episode that eloquently
condemns the lunacy of racism. But Hurston's main interest is in
Janie's relations with the black men and women around her. Un-
aware that her poverty and illiteracy are burdens, Janie conducts
her life with assurance, dignity, and humor. She wants companionship and fulfillment, and she insists on equality in love and on
her right to think and choose for herself. Words that her grandmother once spoke to her, telling her that the black women is "de

mule uh de world," become the unforgotten warning that guides her life.

Though he was impatient with Hurston's work, Richard Wright acknowledged the central importance of folklore to black culture. In his "Blueprint," he wrote that it was "in a folklore molded out of rigorous and inhuman conditions of life that the Negro achieved his most indigenous and complete expression." But Wright's understanding of folklore was different from Hurston's, as were the politically specific purposes to which he put it. His *12 Million Black Voices* (1941), for example, an angry documentary account of black life in Depression America, is subtitled "A Folk History of the Negro in the U.S." In fact, the book is a history of the exploitation of blacks by whites, a chronicle in which all whites are reduced to one of two allegorical figures: the southern "Lords of the Land" and the northern "Bosses of Buildings." (At about the same date as *12 Million Black Voices*, in pictures such as *They Live in Fire Traps*, (Plate 7), the artist Jacob Lawrence used his work to protest racial injustice.) As he enumerates the crimes of whites against blacks, Wright's prose ascends to a kind of lyric scream. The one-room kitchenette apartment of northern ghettos is "our prison, our death sentence," imposed without a trial.

> The kitchenette, with its filth and foul air, with its one toilet for thirty or more tenants kills our black babies so fast that in many cities twice as many of them die as white babies. . . .
>
> The kitchenette, with its crowded rooms and incessant bedlam, provides an enticing place for crimes of all sorts — crimes against women and children or any stranger who happens to stray into its dark hallways. The noise of our living, boxed in stone and steel, is so loud that even a pistol shot is smothered. . . .
>
> The kitchenette is the funnel through which our pulverized lives flow to ruin and death on the city pavements, at a profit.

Wright had grown up with poverty. He was born on a plantation near Natchez, Mississippi, and spent part of his childhood in an orphanage. Few American writers have risked or endured as much simply to learn to read and write. His stories, essays, and novels distill his firsthand experience of the varieties of legally sanctioned American oppression. He joined the Communist party in 1934 and remained a member until 1942. He first came to notice on the Left as a poet, publishing, among some two dozen poems, "I Have Seen Black Hands," a call for the interracial revolution of exploited workers, and "Between the World and Me," an appallingly successful re-creation of a lynching.

The violence Wright had seen and felt in his boyhood and later in Chicago became the hallmark of his fiction. In his memoir, *Black Boy* (1945), he observed that "all my life had shaped me for the realism, the naturalism of the modern novel." His own climactic addition to the accomplishment of naturalism was *Native Son* (1940), a book that permanently enlarged the possibilities for black literature in America. Bigger Thomas, the novel's protagonist, is descended neither from the racial idealizations nor the passive victims who populate most earlier fiction. He is not class conscious nor indeed conscious of much of anything except the universal white injustice that suffocates his vague dreams of happiness. Virtually trapped into murdering his first victim, a white woman, he later murders again, a black woman this time, and in cold blood. Bigger inevitably acts out the violence that has stifled his humanity. He goes further, accepting his own actions and defining his freedom in terms of the murders he commits:

> There remained to him a queer sense of power. He had done this. He had brought all this about. In all of his life these two murders were the two most meaningful things that had ever happened to him. He was living, truly and deeply, no matter what others might think, looking at him with their blind eyes. Never had he had the chance to live out the consequences of his actions; never had his will been so free as in this night and day of fear and murder and flight.

It was this moral stance, and not the excess of its individual scenes, that gave *Native Son* the power of a physical blow. Bigger Thomas belies comforting assertions that might be offered about America's racial future. In a lecture at Fisk University, in 1942, Wright said: "I had accidentally blundered into the secret, black, hidden core of race relations in the United States. That core is this: nobody is ever supposed to speak honestly about this problem." Bigger is not the whole of America's racial truth, but he was a part of it that had not been spoken before. He was also, at least in Wright's intentions,

FIGURE 159 ❧ Richard Wright wrote the screenplay and played the role of Bigger Thomas in the 1950 film version of *Native Son*.

a figure symbolic of America's future, a prophecy of "what we would encounter on a vast scale in the days to come" (Figure 159).

As the thirties progressed, the violence that lies at the center and circumference of Wright's vision seemed increasingly a true finding. The atmosphere of economic and racial crisis was further darkened by predictions of war. One European country after another was ingested by totalitarian governments, and the defeat of republicanism by the Fascists in Spain – along with the betrayal of republicanism by the Communists – signaled the end of democratic hope. The political and moral consequences of Versailles, which so many writers on both sides of the Atlantic had foretold, were being irresistibly realized.

Nathanael West (Figure 160), perhaps the least documentary of the major writers of the 1930s, may nonetheless be the surest guide to the dislocations of Depression America and the calamity that loomed ahead. The maimed dreamers who people West's peculiar half-worlds are the creatures of their own nightmares. Their deformities and the surreal plots they act out seem more proportionate than patient realism to the anxieties and alarms of their times. Riots, crucifixion, dismemberment: in West's fictions, the open road so cherished by generations of American writers ended in a dark cul-de-sac. West's preoccupation with violence, unlike Richard

Wright's, did not have obvious sources in his own life. The son of relatively prosperous immigrant parents, he attended Tufts and Brown, conniving toward a degree by receiving credit for courses he did not take. It was after college that West changed his name from Nathan Weinstein, spent six months in Paris, and found a job as assistant manager of a New York City hotel. His four novels appeared between 1931 and his death in an automobile accident in 1940.

His first book, a novella called *The Dream Life of Balso Snell* (1931), satirized the leading modernist figures and was for West a sort of literary rite of passage. *Miss Lonelyhearts* (1934) gives first expression to West's main themes: "Men have always fought their misery with dreams. Although dreams were once powerful, they have been made puerile by the movies, radio and newspapers. Among many betrayals, this one is the worst." This is the insight of Miss Lonelyhearts, the newspaperman hero of the story, who writes the advice column of his paper. He originally took on the column as a joke, but the letters he gets have pierced his ironic armor with their anguished revelations. Like a distorting mirror, these letters reflect lives twisted by irremediable emptiness and gratuitous cruelty. In such a world, even the spring landscape shimmers with death: "It was very sad under the trees. Although spring was

FIGURE 160 ❧
Photograph of Nathanael West (1938).

well advanced, in the deep shade there was nothing but death –
rotten leaves, gray and white fungi, and over everything a funereal
hush."

In each of West's books, he subverts the clichés of America's
verbal and emotional junkyard by copying them down and then
frantically inflating them. His tone is a compound of comedy and
terror, as his ribald delight in the absurdity of childish dreams dissolves into panic in the face of the murderous energies those dreams
release. He alternates between pity for the victims of modern society
and contempt for the trivial values they so desperately embrace.

In the mid-1930s, West moved to Hollywood to work as a screen-
writer for Columbia Pictures and R.K.O. Other writers, among them
Hemingway, Faulkner, and Fitzgerald, accepted Hollywood salaries
in exchange for the use of their names and even occasionally for
their writing. But it was West who found his subject in the dream
factories on the edge of the continent. In *The Day of the Locust*
(1939), his last book, Hollywood is revealed as the macabre cemetery of American illusions, the final resting place of the American
myth. Everything is faked, and everything is monstrous; reality itself
has turned into masquerade. What remains is death, repeatedly
engraved in the lethal stares of the people who have come to California to die. An atmosphere of hallucination breathes through the
novel, as one ghastly image follows another: a life-size rubber replica
of a bloated dead horse floating in a swimming pool; a drunken
gang-rape; a cockfight's bloody details.

Tod Hackett, a graduate of the Yale School of Fine Arts, has
come to Hollywood to design sets, but his more serious ambition is
to paint. He fills his sketchbook with the faces he has seen in
California: "the cultists of all sorts, economic as well as religious,
the wave, airplane, funeral and preview watchers – all those poor
devils who can only be stirred by the promise of miracles and then
only to violence." The key to the ubiquitous violence is boredom,
the emotional vacancy of people who never had anything but hopes
and realize that their hopes are doomed to disappointment. A dim
but universal awareness that the exotic promises of the movies will
not be fulfilled engenders resentment and then hate. Tod's big
project is a painting called *The Burning of Los Angeles*, a huge canvas
that will show the city in flames, its frenzied lunatics and imitation
architecture consumed in one final holocaust.

In *The Day of the Locust*, West wrote his apocalyptic epitaph to the thirties. A continent away, the 1939–40 New York World's Fair unintentionally reached the same conclusion. What had been a swamp in Flushing, Long Island – the "valley of ashes" of *The Great Gatsby* – had been briefly transformed into the World of Tomorrow. The fair's inspirational symbolism was calculated and timely. Fully ten years after the Crash, the nation's crippled economy continued to resist the palliatives of the New Deal. The fair counseled hope: like its sleek, modern buildings, America would rise out of stagnation and discover a prosperous carefree future. For a few hours at least, visitors could leave behind the dreariness of unemployment and class struggle and enter an ideal world of rational planning in which social problems found elegant solutions (Figure 161).

History, as usual, had other plans. A few months after the fair opened, Hitler invaded Poland, and the dream of tomorrow became the nightmare of blitzkrieg and Holocaust. In the fall of 1940, as America inched closer to entering the war, the fair quietly closed, and demolition of its buildings commenced more or less immedi-

FIGURE 161 ❧ The Trylon and Perisphere, which stood on the site of "Democracity," became the symbols of the 1939 New York World's Fair.

ately. The Trylon and Perisphere, those famous linked symbols of the future, had been made of pressed paper and gypsum board; their gleaming surfaces had offered only the illusion of solidity. The ersatz World of Tomorrow was returned to its swamp. Like the crash of the German airship Hindenburg at Lakehurst, New Jersey, in 1936, the destruction of the fair's technological showplaces taught the dispiriting lesson that the effort to soar above the jumble of the world usually leads to catastrophe.

CHAPTER SEVEN

❧ Midcentury and beyond ❧

FROM MAY THROUGH OCTOBER of 1952, in three consecutive issues, the editors of *Partisan Review* published a series of commissioned essays under the heading, "Our Country and Our Culture." The contributors included over twenty members of the New York intellectual scene, and the general tone of their essays was conciliatory. The symposium rested on the assumption that American writers, who had until quite recently thought of their country as hostile to art and culture, now regarded the nation and its institutions with a measure of esteem. According to *PR*'s editors, American intellectuals no longer felt disinherited from their native soil, no longer felt themselves adrift, as had their predecessors, from Henry James to Pound to Mencken. In their assembled brief statements, such men and women as Lionel Trilling, Jacques Barzun, Louise Bogan, and Richard Chase affirmed – though usually with misgivings and reservations, and sometimes with a confession of surprise – that literary artists conceived of America in a new way, with a heightened sympathy and sense of identification.

One measure of the shift in attitude, as C. Wright Mills pointed out in his own essay, was "available to those who try to imagine 'the old *PR*' running the title 'Our Country . . . ,' etc. in 1939. You would have cringed." Mills was reminding the editors and readers of the magazine's earlier affiliations with a cosmopolitan Marxism. In the 1930s and early 1940s, *Partisan Review* had bristled with dissent and had subjected the pieties as well as the premises of American culture to strenuous criticism. Now, in the midst of the Cold War and on the eve of the election of Dwight D. Eisenhower to the presidency, upwards of two dozen influential voices were raised

in tribute to a set of arrangements that earlier generations had judged
to be discredited by the weight of a grasping materialism.

To be sure, a few of *PR*'s contributors refused to join the celebration. Irving Howe found more of bewilderment, skepticism, and
lassitude than of hope or affirmation in the mood of his contemporaries, and he numbered himself among the opponents of the
status quo. Norman Mailer began his combative remarks by announcing: "I think I ought to declare straightway that I am in almost
total disagreement with the assumptions of this symposium." Not
yet thirty-five years old as he wrote, Mailer surveyed the commitments of those he called "the older American intellectuals." Among
these, he singled out Dos Passos, Farrell, Faulkner, Steinbeck, and
Hemingway as writers who had journeyed from alienation to "varying degrees of acceptance, if not outright proselytizing, for the American Century."

Mailer's choice of targets indirectly but valuably offered an index
to the hesitant, even stalled character of literary culture in the
postwar years. The most prominent writers of the fifties were actually
representative of America's prewar literature. Hemingway, Faulkner, Dos Passos, and Steinbeck had long since accomplished their
best and most characteristic work, but they kept publishing and kept
accumulating the honorary degrees and Nobel Prizes that ratified
their public stature. The endurance of canonical opinion was in
part a laggard tribute, in part a token of continuity, a way of arguing
the proposition that the war had not after all turned the world
upside down.

Similarly, popular writers such as John O'Hara and John P.
Marquand remained content, in their postwar novels, to scrutinize
the same suburban scenes that had occupied their first books in the
1930s, and they employed the same conservative fictional techniques. It would be hard to infer, from comparing *Appointment in
Samarra* (1934) with *Ten North Frederick* (1955), for example, even
a hint of the two decades that separated them. O'Hara's fascination
with the pointlessly ferocious excesses of country club and pent-
house, his genius for recording boozy chat, and his hard-boiled
sentimentality repeated themselves from book to book, virtually
indifferent except in superficial ways to the world's upheavals.

What Mailer called the American Century had begun in earnest in August 1945 with the atomic bombs that annihilated Hiroshima and Nagasaki, ended the Second World War, and inaugurated a generation of American dominion in the economic, political, and military affairs of the world. An estimated fifty million persons, most of them civilians, had died in six years of battle, starvation, and genocide. The United States counted its dead along with the rest but emerged from the global conflagration intact and even flourishing. Where the various schemes of the New Deal had failed to lift the country out of depression, the war had energized the national will and had sharply expanded employment, productivity, and capital investment. Keyed to military priorities that prevailed into the postwar years, America's rejuvenated economy brought with it an era of prosperity without precedent in the history of any industrial society. Consumer goods multiplied, and sectors of the populace that previously had been excluded gained increased access to education and medical care. Interstate highways and intercontinental airliners transformed travel into a middle-class prerogative. The mass-produced tract houses of builder William Levitt brought homeownership within reach of the majority of workers (Figure 162).

The war itself had elicited some of the strongest fiction of the forties and early fifties. *Dangling Man* (1944), Saul Bellow's first novel, explored the misgivings and meditations of a young man named Joseph as he nervously awaits his draft notice. Bellow was still in his twenties when he wrote *Dangling Man*, and the book's gestures and tone have their sources in a young man's extended engagement with Dostoyevsky and Kafka. Despite its indebtedness, the book is a precocious demonstration of imaginative authority, and a forecast as well of Bellow's characteristic preoccupations. Warily, the book asks whether anything can be affirmed for humanity, for dignity, in a century that has abandoned itself to regimented violence.

Norman Mailer and James Jones both made use of their wartime experiences in the South Pacific in their first novels. Mailer's *The Naked and the Dead* (1946) offers a naturalist inquiry into the contest between will and force. Men on patrol are presented as players in an existential allegory, and their loyalties and betrayals are lavishly defined as a microcosm of human behavior under pressure. Uncertain

FIGURE 162 ❧
Levittown, Long Island,
in the 1950s.

in his handling of most of the novel's characters, Mailer deploys a
prose better suited to reproducing action than talk or thought. The
book discloses Mailer's early affiliations with Hemingway and Stephen Crane and his fascination with extremity. The novel's large
size is a consequence of Mailer's epic designs and also of the fictional
technique he would continue to favor, his effort to tell it all by
telling it all. In Mailer's work over the succeeding four decades,
there would not be much of indirection or economical selectivity.

James Jones's *From Here to Eternity* (1951) was set on the eve
of the war, rather than on its battlefields. Jones pushed one tradition
of naturalism to its limits, turning the barracks of Pearl Harbor in
the days and hours before the Japanese attack into a complete,
closed, and doomed world. Lacking Mailer's talent, Jones nonetheless achieved an ungainly fidelity to experience that gave memorable

life and a provocative range of significance to his account of a community on the brink of disaster.

Finally, John Horne Burns's *The Gallery* (1947), set in wartime Italy, surrounds a bombed glass temple in Naples with a series of elusively but powerfully juxtaposed "portraits" and "promenades." Using an experimental technique of daring leaps and contrasts, Burns suggests something of the war's kaleidoscopic lacklogic and its ultimately deadening significance for its participants.

It had been "the good war," fought to erase the unmitigated evils of Hitler and fascism, but its outcome was clouded with doubt, and its legacy included the relentless international tension of the Cold War and the permanent threat of nuclear extinction. The victory over fascism seemed too quickly spoiled, yielding to a malaise that Faulkner tried to capture in *A Fable* (1954), his brave if cumbersome allegorical meditation on the war. The nervous peace that followed the war tempted men and women who had endured nearly two decades of ceaseless turmoil to turn toward the satisfaction of cultivating their backyard gardens, and many of them did so.

Wright Morris, to give one example, combined fiction and fact in nostalgic efforts of return and recovery. *The Home Place* (1948), a novel describing Clyde Muncy's one-day visit to his rural childhood home in Lone Tree, Nebraska, is told through the combination of Morris's lean prose and eighty or so of his photographs. Virtually every two-page opening in the book includes one of these pictures, some a direct illustration of the text, others related by association. Significantly, few of the scenes include people. The men and women of the novel are to be found in Morris's prose; the photographs create the settings and in doing so lend *The Home Place* an evocative sense of reality (Figure 163).

In a 1947 poem, W. H. Auden spoke of the retreat of battered sensibilities into the whimpers of an "Age of Anxiety." There was much evidence to support Auden's disquiet. Senator Joseph McCarthy built an odious career out of red-baiting and the search for treason in high places. Hollywood produced a numbing proliferation of pious biblical epics that merchandised an ethic of thinly veiled authoritarianism. Norman Vincent Peale's *Power of Positive Thinking* (1953) linked boosterism with self-esteem for its millions of readers. Women, displaced from the jobs that the war had made temporarily

FIGURE 163 ❧ Wright
Morris, photograph from
The Home Place (1948).

available, were summoned back to the hearth and the nursery,
harassed by the demands of what Betty Friedan was about to call
The Feminine Mystique (1963). Television evolved almost overnight
from a technological novelty into an instrument for the propagation
of packaged humor and retrograde cultural assumptions. Novels and
volumes of popularized sociology, among them Sloan Wilson's *Man
in the Gray Flannel Suit* (1955) and William Whyte's *Organization
Man* (1956), took as their subject the culture of an affluent but
timid middle class.

On June 15, 1953, in the face of worldwide protest, Ethel and
Julius Rosenberg were electrocuted in Sing Sing prison. Like Sacco
and Vanzetti a generation before them, and the Haymarket anarchists forty years earlier still, the Rosenbergs were executed less
to punish their individual guilt than to signal the triumph of a
dominant ideology. The death of the Rosenbergs, to which E. L.
Doctorow would turn in *The Book of Daniel* (1971) and Robert
Coover a few years later in *The Public Burning* (1977), became for
many writers an emblem for the shrunken domain of spirit that lay
at the icy core of the fifties: the transformation of politics into
pandering Cold War spectacle; the flight from moral responsibility

FIGURE 164 ❧ "I Have a Dream." Martin Luther King, Jr., speaks at the Lincoln Memorial in Washington, on August 28, 1963.

into therapeutic evasions; and the flimsiness of a civilization which consults above all the demands of mere appetite.

At some point, impossible to date with precision, the 1950s gave way to the assorted phenomena that would become known as "the sixties." A series of shocks strained the country's ideological fault lines. Consensus was replaced by protest along a broad front, and energy multiplied as separated dissenters gathered in a fragile but potent coalition of resistance. The challenges were cultural as well as political. Blacks who campaigned for civil rights, women who demanded equality, and the men and women of all races who organized to stop the war in Vietnam joined to insist on the reconstitution of the nation's underlying assumptions. In August 1963, the Reverend Martin Luther King, Jr., led a march of over two hundred and fifty thousand people to Washington, D.C., the first of many mass gatherings and rallies that dramatized dissent and the demand for change in the sixties (Figure 164). Virtually every received value was subjected to interrogation in an unprecedented search for alternatives.

The final significance of the convulsions of the sixties remains imponderable. The war ended, but not until 1975, and perhaps more out of national exhaustion than in response to a decade of protest. The gains made by blacks and women, at least those of the middle class, were undeniable but partial, and in the seventies and eighties the nation's leadership seemed indifferent to the unfinished business of civil rights and equality. In 1980 and again in 1984, to give a single example, Ronald Reagan ran as the first presidential candidate of either party since 1940 to oppose the Equal Rights Amendment.

If subsequent events have left the meaning of the sixties uncertain, lengthening retrospect has disclosed the sources of the decade's dissent more precisely. It is now rather clearer than it was to contemporaries that the texture of America's cultural and political life in the 1950s was neither as homogeneous nor as insipid as the residual imagery sometimes suggests. Much of what occurred in the sixties had its origins in the preceding years. Indeed, the tightened grip of orthodoxy itself bred resistance. In 1955, a year after the Supreme Court had belatedly acknowledged that segregation in schooling was unconstitutional, Rosa Parks refused to move to the back of a bus in Montgomery, Alabama, and in that act precipitated the modern civil rights revolution. The National Committee for a Sane Nuclear Policy (SANE) and other organizations opposed to war and nuclear weapons grew slowly but steadily. Teenagers discovered the defiant and erotic pleasures of rock-and-roll: Bill Haley's "Rock around the Clock" was a major hit in 1952, and Elvis Presley released "Heartbreak Hotel," the first of his more than sixty "gold" records (awarded for sales of one million or more), in 1956.

Varieties of upheaval also shook the visual arts before the sixties commenced. Beginning in the 1940s, for example, the painters of the New York School earned international recognition for a body of work that turned away from representation and transformed the surface into an arena for action and self-expression. The drip paintings of Jackson Pollock and the contemplative canvases of Mark Rothko and Barnett Newman, different in many ways from each other, shared in the project of withdrawing the visual arts from their traditional allegiance to representation, an allegiance to which American painting had clung more tenaciously than that of Europe. (Pollock's *#1, 1950* is reproduced as Plate 8.) Andrew Wyeth's exhibitions attracted the largest crowds of the fifties and sixties, but his nostalgic subjects and traditional techniques were increasingly isolated in the battle over taste.

❧ Poetry ❧

The brio and calculated self-reference of action painting found counterparts and affinities in a group of New York poets, among them Frank O'Hara, Kenneth Koch, and John Ashbery. They shared an absorption in the urban scene and its contingencies, as well as a fascination with the making of poetry as a subject. Ashbery said that his poems were "snapshots" of whatever was going on in his head as he thought about writing. "Not thoughts, exactly," he wrote, "but ideas, maybe: / Ideas about thoughts. Thoughts is too grand a word." Ashbery is the consummate diarist of the mind in motion. His poems, densely allusive juxtapositions of city clatter with the sublime, attempt, in his description of them, to reproduce "the actions of a mind at work or at rest."

The title poem in Ashbery's *Self-portrait in a Convex Mirror* (1975) is ostensibly a response to a mannerist Renaissance painting:

> As Parmigianino did it, the right hand
> Bigger than the head, thrust at the viewer
> And swerving easily away, as though to protect
> What it advertises.

These are the opening lines, brilliantly initiating the interplay between revelation and concealment that lies at the heart of the poem and demanding a strong and agile interaction (with promises of rich meaning) between the painting, the painter, the poet-viewer, and the reader. Thus the poem is no mere act of homage or imitation. Rather, it charts the commitments and reversals that accompany the act of artistic creation, linking painting and poetry, past and present, in a complex network of signification. The resultant shifts and slidings, in this and in many of Ashbery's poems, can lead, as he himself admits, to opacity. It is the cost of breaking down the generalizations and conventions that falsify experience by making it tidy. Ashbery's poems are grounded in the daring acknowledgment that days have no margins and that consciousness is undisciplined, quirky, and peculiar.

A different set of postwar poetic experiments took place at Black

Mountain College, a radical refuge perched incongruously on a North Carolina hillside. The survival and brief flourishing of a community like Black Mountain demonstrates the persistence of nonconformity, even amid the intensification of the Cold War. Founded in 1933, Black Mountain College in the 1950s was workplace, and sometimes home, to such artists and writers as John Cage, Mary Caroline Richards, Merce Cunningham, Josef Albers and Anni Albers, Robert Rauschenberg, Buckminster Fuller, Robert Creeley, Francine Du Plessis, and Willem de Kooning. Joining idiosyncracy with real talent, and embracing a generally progressive politics, Black Mountain presaged the communitarian dreams of the sixties. In 1952, just four years before it closed, the college was the scene of the first "happening," a legendary collaboration among Cage, Olson, Richards, Cunningham, and Rauschenberg, each of them reading or dancing or playing music in a sequence of uncoordinated events instigated by Cage.

Charles Olson stood at the center of Black Mountain in its last years, and at the center of the loosely affiliated clutch of writers who made up the Black Mountain "school" of poetry. Before he came to the college, Olson had already achieved a certain notoriety with his first book, *Call Me Ishmael* (1947), an idiosyncratic but important inquiry into the "MYTH...SPACE...TRAGEDY" (Olson had a weakness for the upper case) of *Moby-Dick*. Olson was an amateur archaeologist, and his excavations can serve as metaphor for his search into the instrumental sources of art. In the influential essay "Projective Verse" (1950), he declared that poetry involved the "transfer of energy" from artist to reader. Consequently, the poem would find its measure in the breath of the poet, whose verses would take shape by "field," rather than in the lines and stanzas of convention. *The Maximus Poems*, published in a complete edition only in 1983, twelve years after Olson's death, represent his own lifetime of effort to produce the poetry that his theory demanded (Figure 165).

Olson insisted that a poet was not free to be part of any sect, but ten or so poets were eventually gathered, along with Olson, under the Black Mountain label, among them Robert Duncan, Robert Creeley, Denise Levertov, and Joel Oppenheimer. They shared more of outlook than technique. Opposed to the formalism of the New Criticism, and to what they considered the stuffy academic

FIGURE 165 ᘐ
Jonathan Williams,
photograph of Charles
Olson (1951). Olson is
shown in his apartment
at Black Mountain
College, working on the
Maximus poems.

provinciality of prevailing taste, they looked to Whitman and the
more recent examples of Pound and William Carlos Williams for
alternative conceptions of voice and line. Just seven issues of the
Black Mountain Review were published between 1954 and 1957, but
the magazine achieved a remarkable influence on literary opinion.

An occasional visitor to Black Mountain was Paul Goodman,
who attacked the complacency of the fifties in a series of impassioned
articles and books. *Growing up Absurd* (1960) was to serve in the
sixties as a kind of testament, but in the fifties it expressed a frustration shared by many of the nonconforming dissidents. Similarly,
in the overwrought novel *One Flew Over the Cuckoo's Nest* (1962),
Ken Kesey surveyed the spiritual world of the fifties and saw a lunatic
asylum. Nurse Ratched, the asylum's manager and presiding evil
genius, is Kesey's paranoid tribute to the crushing demands of
normality:

> I see her sit in the center of this web of wires like a watchful
> robot, tend her network with mechanical insect skill, know
> every second which wire runs where and just what current to
> send up to get just the result she wants. What she dreams of
> there in the center of those wires is a world of precision effi-
> ciency and readiness like a pocket watch.

A more significant cultural saboteur than Kesey, the poet Allen Ginsberg cataloged the sins of the established political and sexual order in a rhetoric of studious excess, denouncing the bourgeois idols of marketplace and decorum with the apocalyptic zest of a minor prophet. *Howl* (1956) was intended at once as a shout of protest and an anthem of liberation:

> I saw the best minds of my generation destroyed by
> madness, starving hysterical naked,
> dragging themselves through the negro streets at dawn
> looking for an angry fix,
> angelheaded hipsters burning for the ancient heavenly
> connection to the starry dynamo in the
> machinery of night.

Whitman, Blake, and the Bible lie behind *Howl*'s long lines and chantlike rhythms, and Ginsberg said that Charlie Chaplin, too, had something to do with the coexistence of comedy and tragedy in his poetry. Above all, he traced the origins of his method to what he called "the inspired prose line" of Jack Kerouac. William Carlos Williams introduced *Howl* by warning a startled audience that "we are going through hell."

The government's decision to prosecute *Howl* as an obscene book ensured its sales and also conferred an outsize stature on Ginsberg and the group of poets, poseurs, pamphleteers, novelists, and bardic hangers-on known as the Beats. The Beats, among them Ginsberg (Figure 166), Kerouac, Gregory Corso, and Lawrence Ferlinghetti, appealed to the haphazard antinomianism that has always fretted under the demands of group solidarity in American ideology. Taking their name from their search for "beatitude," perhaps, or from the rhythms of jazz, or from their posture of fatigued dissent, the Beats anticipated the shifted political and cultural moods of the sixties. They tunneled under the lackluster surface of the Eisenhower years and gave voice to a simplified but energizing primitivism. They championed the integrity of unbuttoned instinct against the inhibitions and spiritual anemia that allegedly turned middle-class lives into treadmills of routine. At the same time, the Beats demonstrated a sense of audience and a mastery of publicity that was altogether in the American grain. Not for nothing was one of Ginsberg's first paying jobs in market research.

FIGURE 166 ❧ Robert Frank, photograph of Allen Ginsberg (1980).

Couched in a vocabulary of mystical populism, the Beat aesthetic had trouble discriminating literary work except on the ground of truth to personal experience. John Clellon Holmes's *Go* (1952) and Jack Kerouac's immensely successful *On the Road* (published in 1957 but essentially complete by 1951) both demonstrate the artistic misfortunes that attended the effort to use Ginsberg's yawp as a principle of structure. The cross-country roving of Sal Paradise, Kerouac's autobiographical alter ego in *On the Road*, collapses, under the weight of narrative demands, into foggy meandering. Despite its limits, however – its childish self-absorption, its utter shape-lessness, its misogyny and meager intellectual and moral furnishings – Kerouac's novel compelled attention through its energy. Its sheer overwrought urgency gave *On the Road* status as the signature piece of the decade's discontent. Smaller than his predecessors, Sal Paradise nonetheless stands in a line of opposition that reaches back through Jack London's Martin Eden to Huck Finn and Thoreau.

The lurching romanticism of the Beats bore witness to the feeling that postwar individualism was imperiled in a world of multiplied and hostile force. The centralized authority, military power, and increasingly efficient technology that defined postwar society collaborated to infuse the old tropes of naturalism with a rejuvenated relevance. The federal government, by designating thousands of school basements as bomb shelters, inadvertently propagated a tragi-comic symbol of despair: children were taught that prospects for mere survival were, even officially, slim. Under the weight of such circumstances, histories of victims, and of marginal men and women, assumed a resonant cultural significance. The literary vogue of outsiders, losers, and lost souls may be understood not only as a reflection of social and political fact but also as an effort to cope imaginatively with the vertigo of postwar cultural fracturing.

The noisy testimony of the Beats notwithstanding, there was much talk of a postwar retreat from the rigors of intellectual and political commitment. In a book published at the start of the sixties, Daniel Bell influentially announced *The End of Ideology* (1962). The postwar years were labeled "the tranquillized Fifties," in Robert Lowell's "Memories of West Street and Lepke" (1956). It was an era, Lowell's enduring phrase suggested, in which principled public concern was anesthetized by abundance, patriotism, and a pervasive conformity.

Lowell was the resisting heir of ten generations of New England achievement; his ancestors and relations reached back to the *Mayflower* and included scholars, poets, ambassadors, and Harvard presidents. In response to these strong predecessors, Lowell's first adult choices were stamped in a pattern of repudiation: after two years at Harvard, he transferred to Kenyon College in 1937 to study poetry with John Crowe Ransom (Figure 167); he converted to Roman Catholicism in 1941; he refused induction in World War II and was sentenced to a year in jail. Lowell's melancholy dissent from the Pax Americana of the postwar years was intensified by the nation's continuing indifference to civil rights and its habit of imperialism. In the 1960s, he stepped forward as an early and significant opponent of the Vietnam War, a man whose gravity helped to turn middle-class opinion. After the 1967 March on the Pentagon, Norman Mailer recorded his awed irritation at the deference that Lowell's great earnestness automatically elicited. Mailer wrote that Lowell possessed "the unwilling haunted saintliness" of a man who was repaying centuries of moral debts.

Lowell was shaken by inner turmoil as well as public controversy. Married three times, he was repeatedly institutionalized for "recur-

FIGURE 167 ❧ Kenyon School of English (1950). (*Front row, left to right*) Philip B. Rice, William Empson, John Crowe Ransom, L. C. Knights, and Charles M. Coffin; (*back row*) Arthur Mizener, Robert Lowell, Kenneth Burke, and Delmore Schwartz.

ring manic-depressive psychosis." His stature as the leading poet of his generation coexisted with a universe of scars. Indeed, the poetry was grounded in the private pain. Lowell called his dozen volumes an "autobiography in verse." His presentation of self was direct in the later poems, those of *Notebook 1967–68* (1969); the three 1973 volumes, *History, For Lizzie and Harriet,* and *The Dolphin;* and his last book, *Day by Day* (1977). In the early poems, autobiography presses more obliquely on the verse. *Lord Weary's Castle* (1946), his second volume, is steeped in the precepts and practice of Ransom, Tate, and Eliot. Urgent, sometimes apocalyptic emotion is held in check by an elegant, mannered, self-indicating technique. Prodigious in craftsmanship, these dense, often furious early poems piece together shards of history, theology, myth, nautical lore, and biography in formal structures of considerable complexity. "Mr. Edwards and the Spider," built out of quotations from the writings of Jonathan Edwards, concludes by recalling the suicide of Joseph Hawley, Edwards's uncle, who killed himself by cutting his own throat at the height of the Great Awakening. Hawley's gruesome fate is invoked as a warning to believer and nonbeliever alike:

> But who can plumb the sinking of that soul?
> Josiah Hawley, picture yourself cast

Into a brick-kiln where the blast
Fans your quick vitals to a coal.

In the postwar sortings devised by critics and anthologists, a great divide seemed to stand between the "open" verses of the Beats and Projectivists and the "closed," more traditional forms of Lowell, John Berryman, Delmore Schwartz, Elizabeth Bishop, and Randall Jarrell. In fact, similarities and differences were more idiosyncratic and less categorical, and the points of contacts between the groups sometimes produced profound and formative encounters. Such a moment occurred for Lowell when he toured the West Coast in the late fifties and heard readings of Ginsberg's *Howl* and sections of Gary Snyder's unpublished *Myths and Texts* (1960). Shortly thereafter, Lowell complained about the stilted precision and heavy-handed symbolism of his own poetry, and he began writing in what he called "a new style." That style, looser in structure, more intimate in focus, received its full expression in *Life Studies* (1959), a volume of dazzling effects and shocking revelations, one of the key texts of the postwar years. Sylvia Plath, who was briefly Lowell's student, spoke of the "intense breakthrough into very serious, very personal emotional experience." These were poems that took Lowell's family, his illnesses, and his sexuality as their subjects, and Allen Tate urged Lowell not to publish them. "My mind's not right," the speaker declares flatly in "Skunk Hour," the final poem and, in Lowell's view, the anchor of *Life Studies*.

The title poem of his next volume, *For the Union Dead* (1964), synthesized and summarized Lowell's main preoccupations, drawing the map of history along the perpendicular axes of self and the power of the state. Written in 1963, on the one hundredth anniversary of the Emancipation Proclamation, the poem is an elegy at once for the soldiers killed in the Civil War and the ideals betrayed by the nation's subsequent generations of racial bad faith. It memorializes the common fate of a white colonel, Robert Gould Shaw, and the black infantrymen of his Fifty-fourth Massachusetts Regiment, who died in a brave but futile attack on Fort Wagner in South Carolina, the most massive earthworks fortification ever built. In 1897, after decades of debate and false starts, the sculptor Augustus Saint-Gaudens completed a memorial bronze relief, which was installed, amid much ceremony, on Boston Common (Figure 168).

Figure 168 ❧
Augustus Saint-Gaudens,
Shaw Memorial (1897).

William James and Booker T. Washington were among the speakers
at the unveiling, and fragments of their pious speeches echo ironically through the poem. The emptiness of public rhetoric is contrasted to the idealism of the soldiers' silent valor. In *History*, Lowell
wrote that "a nihilist has to live in the world as it is," but Shaw's
doomed heroism is a glimpse of grandeur:

> He is out of bounds now. He rejoices in man's lovely
> peculiar power to choose life and die –
> when he leads his black soldiers to death,
> he cannot bend his back.

Saint-Gaudens's Shaw memorial also figures as the center of
response in John Berryman's "Boston Common," a lesser poem than
"For the Union Dead," even darker in its intimations of personal
and national failure. Berryman was born in 1913, just four years
before Lowell, and like Lowell, Jarrell and Schwartz (all contemporaries) his life was troubled by childhood turmoil, periods of in-
stitutionalization, sexual misadventure, incapacitating depression,
and episodes of despair that led, in Berryman's case, to suicide.

As a young poet, Berryman said that he wanted to be Yeats.
After a long literary apprenticeship, which included a brilliant pi-

oneering biography of *Stephen Crane* (1950), he found his own style in *Homage to Mistress Bradstreet* (1956). A poem at once of tribute and improbable seduction, *Mistress Bradstreet* enacts Berryman's allegiance to poetry and to its marginalized makers. The poem's fractured syntax and irregular rhythms create an unexpectedly resilient instrument for describing affection and historical inquiry alike. In an early stanza, the poet summons Bradstreet from the past, telling her, "We are on each other's hands / who care"; the single voice gives way to a dialogue, which yields in turn to Bradstreet's confessional monologue (Figure 169).

The major work of Berryman's final decade was the *Dream Songs*, a sequence extending eventually to hundreds of poems, a kind of diary made up of slapstick comedy, self-revelation, divided and coalescing voices, wisdom in strange places, and a taste for the bizarre. Originally published in two volumes, entitled *77 Dream Songs* (1964) and *His Toy, His Dream, His Rest* (1968), the poems throw the spotlight of a minstrel show over a straight man named Henry – Henry Pussycat, Huffy Henry, Crucified Henry, Stammering Henry, Henry Gravedigger – and his alter ego, Mr. Bones.

The poet's coy disclaimers notwithstanding, the several Berry-

FIGURE 169 ❧ Ben Shahn, drawing for John Berryman, *Homage to Mistress Bradstreet* (1956).

mans are one, in all measurable respects. Saul Bellow wrote that Berryman drew his art "out of his vital organs, out of his very skin," until there was nothing left. He went to pieces, as one of the songs concedes, but "the pieces sat up & wrote. They did not heed their piecedom" but went on turning private torment into shareable significance. Though the tone is often jaunty, the *Dream Songs* are, in the main, the chronicle of a long and downward curve. It is a dismal record, years "of mostly labor & scrounge," clouded by a father's suicide, the deaths of friends and fellow poets, alcoholism, and a tenacious commitment to failure: "He stared at ruin. Ruin stared straight back."

Berryman's personal ruin also attached itself, in one degree or another, to several of the poets in what is often called "the middle generation," among them Theodore Roethke, Anne Sexton, Randall Jarrell, and Sylvia Plath. Facile generalizations will distort the separate facts of each case, but one of Berryman's own *Dream Songs* puts into the form of a peevish elegy the mysterious tug toward self-hurt that these men and women shared:

> I'm cross with god who has wrecked this generation.
> First he seized Ted, then Richard, Randall, and now Delmore.
> In between he gorged on Sylvia Plath.
> That was a first rate haul. He left alive
> fools I could number like a kitchen knife.

Anne Sexton, a suicide at forty-six in 1974, would also become part of the human wreckage that Berryman's sad litany commemorates. Sexton was raised a Roman Catholic, and, though she gave up that faith, the yearning for supernatural assurance remained an urgent motive in her life and poetry. She studied briefly with Lowell (Plath was a classmate), but she acknowledged the greater influence of W. D. Snodgrass's early and self-revealing *Heart's Needle* (1959). The style she often chose, a prosy verse of deliberate simplifications, reflected her feeling of vulnerability and her dissent from the massed forces of convention and control, but it left little room for analytic maneuver. Poetry, she said, should be "a shock to the senses"; and it should give pain.

Sexton's books comprise a dark autobiography, the testament of a suffering soul entangled in a labyrinth of dread and depression. *To Bedlam and Part Way Back* (1960), her first volume, uses her own experiences in a mental hospital as its materials. In the chilling self-portrait "Ringing the Bells," she describes herself within "the circle of the crazy ladies," women who compliantly grope through pointless lives "like bees caught in the wrong hive." Later books, including *All My Pretty Ones* (1962), share the intimate pains and losses of daily life as daughter, wife, and mother. Death is increasingly the subject. Driven repeatedly to a fatal precipice, Sexton's speakers frequently assume the voices of the dying and even the dead – sometimes with relish. "The Starry Night," which quotes from a letter of Van Gogh as epigraph, transforms the famous painting into a visualized death wish:

> The old unseen serpent swallows up the stars.
> Oh starry starry night! This is how
> I want to die.

"Sylvia's Death" is Sexton's tribute to Sylvia Plath, who took her own life in 1963, when she was just thirty years old. Plath's poetry, like Sexton's, hovers over an abyss of extinction, and the best of her poems, collected and published posthumously in *Ariel* (1965), were written in a fury of production, at the rate of one or more a day, in the weeks preceding her death. A quarter-century after their publication, these remorseless poems have lost little of their power to shock. Personal in subject but often cruelly impersonal in their point of view, Plath's poems bind together her punished status as a woman with the apocalyptic derangements of twentieth-century politics.

This is a world of excess, filled with images of operating theaters, trepanned soldiers, glass eyes, rubber crotches, madhouse shrieks, miscarried fetuses bottled in formaldehyde, vampires, and Nazi crematoriums. A poem like "Daddy," barely in control of its own rhetoric, protests against the interlocking patriarchies of an autocratic father, a treacherous husband, and a god who has abetted (or at least condoned) the atrocities of genocide. The lover who hands a woman the heart of a corpse, in "Two Views of a Cadaver Room," typifies Plath's capacity to charge cliché with gruesome energy. Death is everywhere in Plath, and death is at once repellent and alluring, often invested with a macabre erotic intensity. Though Plath's poems traffic in sensational effects, her shudders of terror and anger seldom merely erupt. Her emotional equations were calculated. She deployed her lurid materials quite bravely, as a way of trying to break through surfaces to the deeper, sinister strata that threaten and beckon under each day's deceptive ordinariness. Minor kitchen accidents provide the unlikely occasions for hallucinatory visions into the hidden fabric of reality.

Versions of transcendentalism, most of them not as grotesque as Plath's manic sorceries, have formed a persistent base of much postwar poetry. Early and late, for example, Robert Bly has culled the scenes of rural Minnesota for the spare but passionate poems that make up *Silence in the Snowy Fields* (1962) and *This Tree Will Be Here for a Thousand Years* (1979). Gary Snyder said that the poems of woods and seas in his first volume, *Riprap* (1959), were written "under the influence of the geology of the Sierra Nevada." In a later poem, "What You Should Know to Be a Poet," he advises poets to learn "all you can about animals as persons / the names of trees and flowers and weeds / names of stars."

The strongest of Theodore Roethke's poems draw upon the remembered landscapes of northern Michigan and the greenhouses full of plants that both his father and grandfather tended. Proceeding with the premeditation of a latter-day Wordsworth, Roethke sought to discern the significance in a child's fascinated encounters with the tiny mysteries of botany. *The Lost Son and Other Poems* (1948), his second volume, is piled high with vines, bulbs, cuttings, roots, weeds, and flowers of every sort, blossoms that sing of preconscious joys and of "waking" into initiatory insight. Roethke longed to lose himself in the sensuous forms of nature and there find a stay against the inner turmoil that bedeviled him. He wanted "to hum in pure vibration" with nature's rhythms.

In a quite different way, Elizabeth Bishop used the whole globe, and her travels on it, as the stimulus to a poetry of exacting precision. She was orphaned as a young child: her father died when she was an infant, and her mother was institutionalized a few years later. She was raised by relatives in New England and Nova Scotia and became patiently, precociously watchful. Later she chose to live in Florida, Brazil, New York, and again New England. The significance of place to her work is rather obviously signaled in the titles of her books, which she called *North and South* (1946), *Questions of Travel* (1965), and *Geography III* (1976). The contrast of north and south, of arctic and tropics, suggests the dialectical play between familiarity and strangeness that enlivens Bishop's perceptions. A "tremendous fish," caught and brought to the side of a boat in one of her early poems, earns its freedom without fighting when the poem's speaker notices the five hooks embedded in its jaw, relics of old battles, the five broken lines trailing out like "medals with their ribbons / frayed and wavering." The fish, with its large shallow yellowed eye, is memorably seen but is also a spectral presence, an emblem of nature's independence. As in the work of Marianne Moore, which she had come to early, Bishop's menagerie is a place of instruction.

Bishop's voice, which approaches that of colloquial speech, has been called companionable, but it is in fact typically detached and self-possessed. Even her jokes are aloof and armed with knowledge: "We'd rather have the iceberg than the ship, / although it meant the end of travel." Bishop's world, hemispheres of carefully realized, finely graded chiaroscuro, contains its regions of doubt as well as light. Nonetheless, her poems insist, with confidence, that sight can yield vision and that life can provide satisfactions. In "The Moose," that great animal, "high as a church," gently bumps against a bus, sending a small thrill of rapture like an electric current through the passengers:

> Taking her time,
> she looks the bus over,
> grand, other-worldly.
> Why, why do we feel
> (we all feel) this sweet
> sensation of joy?

Bishop's balance, like that of such otherwise dissimilar poets as Howard Moss, James Merrill, and Richard Wilbur, represents an alternative to the bardic line of Black Mountain and San Francisco. Merrill, for example, claims that feelings reveal themselves accurately only when distanced by the "translations" of time and space. The poems of his first three decades, including those of *The Black Swan* (1946) and *Water Street* (1962), are distinguished by a careful shaping of autobiography into meditation, and sometimes narrative. In recent years he has chosen a more vatic utterance, writing a verse trilogy, collected in *The Changing Light at Sandover* (1983), with the aid of a ouija board, but he continues to distill the mysteries of spirit and flesh in poems of consummate poise.

Merrill's masters included Wystan Hugh Auden, who emigrated to the United States from England in 1939 and exerted a detectable influence on the American poetic scene in the decades following the war. Auden's conception of poetry as "heightened speech" and of poems as the clear expressions of mixed feelings, his characteristic irony, and his superb technical skills made his works widely imitated models. Something of his tone and idiom can be found in the work of Richard Wilbur, a discriminating spokesman for the traditions belittled by a throwaway culture. In a long career that began with the heralded publication of *The Beautiful Changes* (1947), when he was twenty-six, Wilbur has held steadily to the norms of decorum, restraint, and contemplation. In rebuttal to the "raw events" of the war and its following tremors, Wilbur abides by the values of intelligence, believing in the power of civilized discourse to be civilizing. The mind at play, he has written in an early poem, is like a bat swooping through a darkened cave, which somehow contrives "not to conclude against a wall of stone."

As this example suggests, Wilbur's nature poems and his emblem poems assume that old systems of correspondence remain, at least partially, intact. So, too, in these poems, the heritage of Europe is still accessible, from its baroque fountains to the plays of Molière, such as *The Misanthrope* (1955) and *Tartuffe* (1963), which Wilbur has translated so successfully. Identifying his poetics as a "public quarrel" with Edgar Allan Poe – the Poe, presumably, of abstracted, "pure" poetry – Wilbur has sought a spirituality closely tied to the concrete facts of existence. According to the title of one poem, a close paraphrase from the seventeenth-century religious poet Thomas Traherne, "A world without objects is a sensible emptiness."

Along with Wilbur's measured lucidity and the intensity of confessional introspection, the commodious achievement of postwar poetry also included direct response to the contemporary politics of protest and reformation. Opposition to the Vietnam War, and the liberation movements of minority people and women, catalyzed some of the most distinctive poetry of recent years. Lyric, fused with social awareness, was enlisted in the struggles to reconceive the nation's governing assumptions about race, gender, and class.

The work was produced equally by new writers and writers in mid-career who shifted their stance. Robert Bly, for example, joined Lowell, Ginsberg, Adrienne Rich, and others in writing against America's calamitous adventuring in Vietnam.

Gwendolyn Brooks, whose second volume of poetry, *Annie Allen* (1949), won the first Pulitzer Prize awarded to a black writer, took an increasingly militant stance in the years after 1967. She became a participant and a presiding spirit in the Black Arts Movement and a voice for fundamental change. To the ample technical facility of her early verse, Brooks added an increasingly impatient demand for justice. The irony of a poem such as "The Lovers of the Poor," from the early sixties, in which "the Ladies from the Ladies' Betterment League" descend on a noisy tenement to inflict their benevolence, yielded to the anger of "Boy Breaking Glass" from the late sixties, in which a broken window can be "a cry of art . . . / If not an overture, a desecration."

Robert Hayden, who said that poetry offered him the means of "coming to grips with both inner and external realities," probed history for the precedents and sources of twentieth-century racial conflict. "Runagate, Runagate" pays tribute to Harriet Tubman's escape from slavery, the prelude to her career in leading other blacks to freedom. "Frederick Douglass" and "The Ballad of Nat Turner" commemorate nonviolent and violent black resistance.

Michael Harper, who has also searched out racism through the historical record in his poetry, has described Hayden in a graceful and much-cited phrase as "the poet of perfect pitch." The long poem "Middle Passage" exemplifies Hayden's virtuosity. The poem's title refers to the transporting of slaves from Africa to the New World on ships with such names as *Jesus, Esperanza,* and *Mercy.* On these ships, the human cattle were stowed "spoon-fashion": "Some went mad of thirst and tore their flesh and sucked the blood." The poem is based on the mutiny of the captives aboard the slave ship *Amistad* and their subsequent trial for murder. Hayden summons a disparate chorus of voices, historical and imagined, in the slaves' defense. The texts he arrays include fragments of ships' logs, Christian hymns, trial transcripts, and a dying slaver's confession:

> Twenty years a trader, twenty years,
> for there was wealth aplenty to be harvested

from those black fields, and I'd be trading still
but for the fevers melting down my bones.

Only the slaves are silent, but the absence of their voices ultimately represents the poem's highest eloquence.

The poetry of ideological engagement risks becoming, as Robert Lowell warned in "Epilogue," his last poem, "paralyzed by fact." But poetry can also be nourished and energized by fact, when knowledge about the order of things releases writing into a less confined expressive or imaginative space. In any case, many writers have shared the belief that political implication is literature's inescapable burden, regardless of intention or design. In an essay of 1981, "Notes for a Magazine," Adrienne Rich wrote that "no art exists that is not ultimately political." Language has the capacity either "to bolster privilege and oppression or to tear away at their foundations." Especially in the past two decades, Rich has dedicated her own poems, her activism, and her influential essays to the double task of renouncing the given and creating a language, a history, and a mythology answerable to the re-visions of women about themselves and the world. She has aspired to discover the "common language" of female solidarity, or at least to dream of it.

Even in her early poems, those collected in *A Change of World* (1951) and *The Diamond Cutters* (1955), with their euphonies and dutiful reminders of Yeats and Auden, Rich was sounding prophetic tones of discord and resistance. Auden remarked with approval on how "neatly and modestly dressed" the early verse was, but one of the best poems in the first volume bore the premonitory title "Storm Warnings." Looking back in the seventies on the formalism of her early work, Rich wrote that it was a strategy: "Like asbestos gloves, it allowed me to handle materials I couldn't pick up barehanded." Those explosive materials and the new, irregular forms needed to contain them became paramount concerns in *Snapshots of a Daughter-in-Law* (1963) and *Necessities of Life* (1966). *Snapshots* announced her bitter judgment on a marriage that had become a union of "two strangers, thrust for life upon a rock." In both *Snapshots* and *Necessities*, the pain of impasse and doubt was lightened by an expanding awareness. The poems include Rich's candid, exhilarating reports on a new coming to be: "Piece by piece I seem / to re-enter the world" (Figure 170).

Each of Rich's books has pushed beyond its predecessors, risking critical censure for an increasingly severe refusal to respect the demarcations that defined poetry's function and woman's place. An empathic "dream of tenderness" wrestles with all the sad knowledge Rich has gleaned from her lifetime of experience in the patriarchy. She has concluded that "men – in so far as they are embodiments of the patriarchal idea – have become dangerous to children and other living things." The first poem in *Diving into the Wreck* (1973) is called "Trying to Talk with a Man," and the foolhardiness of that effort is likened to standing too near atomic-bomb tests in the desert. In "Diving into the Wreck," the volume's title poem, the poet descends into the dark waters of history to search for the treasures that have endured amid the debris of a wrecked ship. Relying on words themselves as both map and purpose, she seeks "the wreck and not the story of the wreck / the thing itself and not the myth."

Filled with anger, compassion, and promises of revolution, *Diving* summarizes twenty years of awakening. It also anticipates the themes to which Rich would subsequently turn, her commitment to tracing and celebrating the connections among women, across barriers of class and race. The sources of those connections, she said in an important talk that she gave at the Modern Language Association convention in 1976, was "The Lesbian in Us." Many of her later poems record real and imagined conversations between women or letters sent by women to each other; the women include Rich's relatives – her mother, grandmother, and sister – as well as historical figures: Marie Curie, Willa Cather, the artists Paula Modersohn-Becker and Clara Westhoff, Ethel Rosenberg, and Simone Weil.

ε**ℯ**

Each month, nearly five thousand poems are sent to the editors of *The New Yorker*; incalculable thousands of others arrive in the offices of the hundreds of magazines and journals that share the unassigned responsibility of estimating, selecting, and publishing America's contemporary poetry. Final judgments within that outpouring are impossible, but a few tendencies can perhaps be discerned, and a few examples offered.

Continuity with the recent and even distant poetic past coexists with new directions or emphases. Modernism's fascination with the transactions between imagination and a fractured reality persists in some writers but has yielded in the work of others to a postmodern suspicion that language itself is reality's untrustworthy creator. The confessional self survives, but has more typically given place to rather guarded autobiographical performances and to an increased sense of solidarity with ethnic or sexual or regional groups. History remains a recurrent subject – the history of families, the ancestral past, rather than the official history of public events. Speech, often in its most local and colloquial particularity, is the preferred medium: acts of historical recovery encompass a commitment to rescue and use the many voices in which immigrants, or minorities, or workers, or rural people express themselves.

Amy Clampitt's poems were not published in book form until she was past fifty. *The Kingfisher* (1983) and *What the Light Was Like* (1985) contain her fully mature recollections of adolescence in Iowa, her meditations on the life and poetry of John Keats, her vividly realized renderings of landscape and seacoasts. Mark Strand, in a verse of deliberate compression, dramatizes the loneliness and dreamlike, sometimes hallucinatory quality imposed on life by the crowded isolation of the modern urban scene. "I am what is missing," Strand wrote in "Keeping Things Whole" (1969), and that problematic subject has remained one of his chief concerns.

The title of Michael Harper's first volume, *Dear John, Dear Coltrane* (1970), identified the musical sources of his verse in jazz. Harper's subjects include personal loss and the betrayals committed repeatedly in America's racial history against the dream of equality. Narrative survives in Harper's work and in the work of other poets, among them Dave Smith, who has insisted on the importance of "event" to his poems. Robert Pinsky has written verse that provides discursive, urbane, and accessible accounts of an eclectic range of American topics, while Rita Dove has chosen to explore "the history-within-the-history of Blacks in America." Among them, writers as diverse as these illustrate the range and versatility that warn against unduly confident generalizations about recent American poetry.

ë Drama ë

In the years following the war, perhaps no work of literature better reproduced the feel, the texture, of disaffection and malaise than Arthur Miller's *Death of a Salesman*. After its Broadway opening on February 10, 1949, the play ran for 742 performances and won a Pulitzer Prize and several other awards. Today it survives as one of the dominant plays produced on the American stage in the past four decades. Willy Loman, embodied for the original Broadway audience in the virtuoso performance of Lee J. Cobb, almost instantly became one of the emblematic figures of the period.

According to Miller's stage directions, the Loman home is "small, fragile-seeming" and surrounded by "a solid vault of apartment houses." Wandering through the brilliantly sinister maze of Jo Mielziner's set, Willy is lost and bewildered, defeated by a conspiracy of circumstance and personal weakness. Combining realism and expressionist techniques – the play was originally called *The Inside of His Head*, and it moves fluidly through the walls that separate past and present – *Salesman* relentlessly dismantles Willy's illusions about himself and his family and traces his inexorable collapse from Rotarian heartiness to despair and suicide. His fate is

personal and domestic, but his cry of pain is a reverberating rebuke to the values and assumptions of American society (Figure 171).

Within two weeks of the play's opening, Miller published an essay, "Tragedy and the Common Man," in the *New York Times*. Neither Willy Loman nor *Salesman* is mentioned in the essay (a coy affectation), but Miller's intention was obviously to recapture for his play, and for the theater and culture of America's polyglot urban democracy, the high value that surrounds the word "tragedy" like an archaic halo. Earlier in the century, Joseph Wood Krutch and others had pronounced the death of tragedy as a corollary of Western culture's shift from religious and aristocratic bases to those of secular science. Responding to such pontifications, Miller rejected the idea that midcentury men and women were necessarily "below tragedy – or tragedy above us." On the contrary, in a defense and gloss on his own work, Miller shifts the terms of tragic experience from status

FIGURE 171 ✍ Jo Mielziner's set for the first production of Arthur Miller's *Death of a Salesman* (1949).

to personal authenticity. The genuine tragic character is one who chooses dignity, even at the cost of life itself.

Miller's fascination with the doom that pursues choice links *Salesman* to several of his other plays, as does his weaving together of private lives and public questions. Though Miller has been attuned to the political upheavals of his time – he was convicted of contempt of Congress in the late fifties and stoutly defended student radicals in the late sixties – he does not write out of a strict ideological program. His absorption in the family as a subject has coexisted with his political inquisitiveness, and this conjunction between the domestic and the public has offered opportunities for complex patterns of interaction. In a dismissive comment on the serenity of Thornton Wilder's *Our Town*, Miller said that the family can be a vehicle for exploring "the disturbance of social wracks"; so it is in his own work.

His first major play, *All My Sons* (1947), set in the midst of the Second World War, unmasks the evil that lies festering under the dim, amiable opportunism of its central character. Joe Keller is husband; father of a son; and manufacturer of defective parts for military aircraft. Joe's barely conscious criminality causes distant deaths whose eventual revelation shatters the bonds of illusion and affection between father and son. The wounds that betrayal inflicts on love are laid open again in *Salesman*. The disclosure of Willy's infidelity completes an agony of disintegration, cutting off for good the havens of pretense and self-deception. Late in the play, shuffling about the stage planting seeds that cannot survive in his failed, tiny garden, Willy's hunched body testifies to the mocking victory of personal insufficiency and hard reality over dreams.

A different sort of mockery, crueler and more lethal, inhabits *The Crucible* (1953). Miller has always deferred to the dramatic power of facts. Both *All My Sons* and the earlier play *The Man Who Had All the Luck* (1944) were derived from anecdotes; later plays would put versions of Miller's life on stage. In the introduction that he wrote in 1957 for his *Collected Plays*, he argued that the most colorful and breathtaking pages of "that great book of wonder, *The Brothers Karamazov*" are those filled with the thickest concentration of facts. *The Crucible* took shape at the intersection of two bodies of fact: the Salem witchcraft trials of the 1690s, and the government investigations of alleged Communist subversion in the early 1950s.

Miller insisted on the historical accuracy of his play – "the reader will discover here the essential nature of one of the strangest and most awful chapters in human history" – and he insisted as well on the contemporary political reference.

There is melodrama, to be sure, in *The Crucible*'s high-pitched tone, in its rather artificial seventeenth-century language, and in the confrontation between John Proctor's unyielding heroism and the massed hysteria that destroys him. Miller conceived of the witchcraft judges as pure evil, and Proctor, in spite of the adultery Miller invented to humanize him, is quite without defect. Nonetheless, for all its simplifying satisfactions, the play has outlasted its topical context and has proved to be, after *Salesman*, Miller's most popular and most frequently produced work. One reason is the courtroom setting, that scene of familiar but dread ceremonial which licenses the play's clenched intensity. The trial, as an image for the testing of life and conscience, is a recurring device in Miller's plays. Among other examples, Miller described *After the Fall* (1964) as "a trial; the trial of a man by his own conscience, his own values, his own deeds."

Some of the voices on the postwar stage belonged to an older dramatic generation. Many of O'Neill's late plays, for example, written before and during World War II, had their first performances in the later 1940s and 1950s, including *The Iceman Cometh* (1946), *A Moon for the Misbegotten* (1947), *A Long Day's Journey into Night* (1956), and *A Touch of the Poet* (1957). Other older writers, among them Clifford Odets, Elmer Rice, Lillian Hellman, and Robert E. Sherwood, had new plays produced, not as strong in most cases as their earlier work but a collective effort that provided context and continuity for the American theater.

Musical comedy, which in the twenties and thirties had established itself as the distinctively American descendant of European light opera, commanded a substantial share of the postwar Broadway audience. Much of the work seemed saccharine, a falling-off from the glamorous best of Cole Porter, George Gershwin, or Richard Rodgers and Lorenz Hart. Generally more interesting for its tunes than its characters or ideas, the postwar musical stage was dominated by Rodgers's long second collaboration with Oscar Hammerstein II. Between them, Rodgers and Hammerstein produced a generation of mammoth hits, including *Oklahoma!* (1943), *South Pacific* (1949), and *The Sound of Music* (1959). Leonard Bernstein, following the example of Gershwin's *Porgy and Bess* (1935), successfully blended art music and popular appeal in *Candide* (1956) and *West Side Story* (1957).

The diversity of America's postwar theater was also enlarged by the traffic between Broadway and Hollywood and by writers such as Paddy Chayevsky and Tad Mosel who had done pioneering scripts for the new medium of television. Among the most prominent of the newer playwrights, William Inge enjoyed a brief success with such plays as *Picnic* (1953) and *Bus Stop* (1955). Inge had a reliable ear for strong scenes and realistic dialogue, but he found himself trapped in minor formulas. He was too eager to console his audience with sharply outlined, simplified emotional crises that are resolved by characters who learn to accept love and responsibility.

Along with Arthur Miller, the principal new playwright in the years following the war was Tennessee Williams. More prolific than Miller, Williams wrote over two dozen full-length plays, along with a number of one-act plays, poetry, fiction, occasional essays, and memoirs. From *The Glass Menagerie* (1944) through *The Night of the Iguana* (1961), Williams had a remarkable run of success, critical as well as commercial. Not all his work was enthusiastically received, but such plays as *A Streetcar Named Desire* (1947), *The Rose Tattoo* (1951), and *Cat on a Hot Tin Roof* (1955) kept him near the high place he had first earned with *Menagerie*. The last twenty years of his life (Williams died in 1983) saw hardly less productivity, but the later work too routinely repeated what had gone before.

When he confessed his fascination with the barbarous cruelty of Shakespeare's *Titus Andronicus*, Williams was also identifying one of his own preoccupations. His is a world of dark suspicions and lurid appetite, in which longing leads to frustration and intimacy is a savage rite. "There is a horror in things," Williams said in an interview in 1962; "we are in this jungle with whatever we can work out for ourselves. It seems to be that the cards are stacked against us." The best that can be hoped for are interludes of solace, usually sexual or alcoholic, or moments of forgetfulness. Vulnerability and difference, the recurring hallmarks of his characters, bring the penalties of hatred and hurt.

Williams is master of a rhetoric that shifts between sonorous declamation and barking vulgarity; his language sometimes overreaches, but it is always premeditated, and its range is an index to Williams's theatrical ambitions. In part because evasion is the stuff of his characters' reality, Williams repeatedly attempted to merge the realistic and its several alternatives onstage. This involved continual experiments in stagecraft and in the handling of character. Williams's men and women are vividly realized, but their gestures and speeches, like the images that turn into symbols of their predicaments, give access to levels of psychological truth that realism alone would have left hidden.

The Glass Menagerie is a memory piece. It is bittersweet, poignant, often dreamlike, a relatively gentle unveiling of the different illusions that have trapped a mother, Amanda Wingfield, and her daughter Laura. Lying in wait to smash their hopes like the fragile glass animals that Laura collects is a reality described by Tom Wingfield, Amanda's son: "the slow and implacable fires of human desperation." That desperation engulfs many of Williams's characters, from Blanche Du Bois, in A *Streetcar Named Desire*, to Brick Pollitt in *Cat on a Hot Tin Roof.*

Streetcar is perhaps Williams's strongest play. Elia Kazan, who directed the first production, thought of the play as "poetic tragedy" and of Blanche Du Bois as a butterfly in a jungle. The most predatory animal that she confronts is Stanley Kowalski, brought to menacing life in the original production by the young actor Marlon Brando. Stanley's braying, potent sexuality represents the passion that will ultimately tear away the consolations of pretense (Figure 172).

Williams, Inge, Miller, and their contemporaries in the earlier postwar years all estimated their success by Broadway standards. Subsequent decades saw a shift of theatrical energy away from Broadway. The causes were in part economic. The cost of producing a Broadway play grew prohibitively; by 1960 there were just over thirty Broadway theaters, down by nearly two-thirds from prewar figures. The financial risks created a cautious theatrical climate, which rewarded well-tested formulas and broad appeal. Experimental work moved to Off-Broadway, and afterward to Off-Off-Broadway, and then to the provinces and the streets, as alternatives to the escalating costs and generally predictable limits of the commercial theater. The numbers of Off- and Off-Off-Broadway productions in New York City grew in the 1960s and 1970s from fewer than two dozen to more than one hundred twenty-five each week.

Several events in the late fifties anticipated, and indeed helped to stimulate, the theatrical history of the subsequent decades. In 1956, the San Francisco Actors' Workshop mounted a legendary production of Samuel Beckett's *Waiting for Godot* at San Quentin prison. Younger writers responded enthusiastically to Beckett and other representatives of the European avant-garde, including Antonin Artaud, whose influential book *The Theater and Its Double* was published in an English translation in 1958. In the following year, Jack Gelber's *Connection* was the first Off-Broadway production to earn nomination as one of the season's officially designated "best plays." *The Connection* makes up a Chinese box of layered fictions and plays-within-plays, all illustrating the theme of human addiction. In fact, the narcotic that Gelber's characters need is not heroin but hope, a theme that locates the play in the fifties, in spite of its tough talk and rather daring structure.

FIGURE 172 ❧ Scene from Tennessee Williams, *A Streetcar Named Desire* (1947). Among the principal actors in this scene from the play's opening production are Kim Hunter (*second from left*), as Stella; Karl Malden (*head on table*) as Mitch; Jessica Tandy (*behind table*) as Blanche; and Marlon Brando (*second from right*) as Stanley.

Drama shared with other postwar genres an interest in the varieties of alienation and the internal divisions that seemed a sad concomitant of life in the oversized bureaucracies of the late twentieth century. Erich Fromm, in a much-cited book *The Sane Society* (1955), defined alienated persons as those who are out of touch with themselves and who are regarded by others as merely objects. Like all pop-psychological constructions, Fromm's diagnosis threatened to turn reality into jargon. But his insight was widely shared, and it was enacted on many stages. Arthur Kopit's remarkable *Indians* (1969), to give just one example, presents Buffalo Bill as a man who happily merchandises his own myth and who accepts the genocide inflicted on the Indians as the inevitable consequences of abstract historical forces.

More significant than Kopit, Edward Albee appeared at the end of the fifties with a series of short plays in which irredeemably separated people grope toward each other in alternate spasms of desire and hatred. Albee's settings, beginning with the Off-Broadway productions of *The American Dream* and *The Zoo Story* in 1959, are bleak, unfurnished, vaguely specified boxes. Whether indoors or not, the atmosphere is closed and airless. In each play a handful of characters, sometimes just two, engage in verbal and even physical assault, usually for no conventional reason. There is an echo of the theater of the absurd in these plays, and of slapstick as well. Events and their resonances, according to Albee, are more important than explanations.

In Albee's own reading of his work, his plays are chapters in a volume of social criticism, an anatomy of a disordered culture from which love and heroism have, understandably, fled. The analysis is never quite clear, but capitalist greed seems to bear much responsibility for the emotional and spiritual torpor of Albee's characters. In a prefatory comment on *The American Dream*, he argued that the play is "an attack on the substitution of artificial for real values in our society." In fact, the early plays were less memorable as social comment than as dirges for a gallery of grotesque lost souls, fumbling to break out of their isolation but ultimately subsiding into it.

Who's Afraid of Virginia Woolf?, the most naturalistic of Albee's plays, was also the first to premiere on Broadway. It opened in October 1962 and quickly established itself as one of the indispensable works of the postwar years. Set on the campus of a small New

England college, *Virginia Woolf* is the brutal record of the relationship between a middle-aged couple, George and Martha, who have invented an imaginary son to replace the child they could not have and whose decades of savage recrimination have brought them to the edge of physical violence. The play's theatrical achievement lies in its dialogue, a witty, articulate, ultimately dangerous and scarifying language that pierces all the facades that protect each naked soul from the assault of others. For whatever sentimental reasons, the play lapses into an unearned optimism at the end; hatred is redefined by compassion. In the final crisis, the characters apparently face reality and outgrow self-deception. The titles of the play's three acts summarize something of its weakly affirmative intentions: "Fun and Games"; "Walpurgisnacht"; and "The Exorcism." Albee intends no irony in this sequence. Violence leads to a ritual cleansing and "a hint" of communion between George and Martha.

Tiny Alice (1964) shared with *Virginia Woolf* a fascination with the blurred but essential line that separates illusion from reality. The play's main character, a lay brother named Julian, asks at one point if he was actually most sane during his six years in a mental institution: "WAS THAT WHEN I WAS RATIONAL? THEN?" A less accessible play than its predecessor, *Tiny Alice* initiated a long series of increasingly opaque work that has had difficulty finding an audience. Committed to testing the limits of conventional theatrical experience, Albee has refused to turn his early success into formula. His absorption in the tension between reality and pretense remains profound, but his inquiry into his themes has relied on experiments that have proved sealed in obscurity.

Sam Shepard's work has followed a somewhat different path, moving from the startling and often inexplicable juxtaposition of images that defined his early work in the sixties, toward the naturalism of the later plays, beginning with *Curse of the Starving Classes* (1976). Shepard is a Westerner, a musician, and a talented actor, and each of these facts is significant for his work. He is often drawn to the contrast between the Old West of frontier and open spaces and the New West of freeway and shopping mall. Throughout all his writing, he has exploited rock music and the movies as reference points, situating his characters in the electric atmosphere of the only mythologies most of them will ever know. Bob Dylan, Mick Jagger, James Dean, Marlene Dietrich, and Jesse James are the icons who preside over Shepard's drama. Glamor and danger are closely allied. In *Operation Sidewinder* (1970), one of the characters warns of "headline oppression": the domination of the people by pundits and politicians. *The Tooth of Crime* (1970), Shepard's most frequently produced play, pits two characters, Hoss and Crow, in a lethal duel that builds inexorably outward in its significance. What begins as personal encounter ultimately becomes a history of violence, embracing nineteenth-century gun battles, contemporary urban gang wars, and superpowers teetering on the edge of a macho apocalypse.

Apocalypse, whether as explosion or as a grinding, degrading entropy, is a thread that ties the work of Shepard to that of several contemporaries, including David Mamet. Mamet is another of the theater's poets of loss, a writer who finds a kind of blank lyric in the inarticulateness and silences of his characters. His drifters and chiselers and losers are never redeemed from their nastiness, but they are made poignant by the very intensity of their failure. Mamet's first success, *Sexual Perversity in Chicago* (1974), contained many marks of his later work, including its paranoid texture of menace and its sense of incurable loneliness, but including as well its irrepressible, ribald humor. The play is constructed of brief, staccato episodes and uses language as a solvent to eradicate deception.

Mamet's abiding curiosity about the nature of reality and the relation of perception to truth takes shape as a continuing conversation about the metaphorical nature of the theater itself. He claims for his plays an affinity with fairy tales, and he is drawn to the destructive consequences of American make-believe. In a comment on his play *American Buffalo* (1975), he described his disgust at the "great and small betrayals and ethical compromises called business." Many of his plays are angry attacks on the engine of greed that drives the machinery of American public life. Betrayals are enacted in all of Mamet's settings, from the junk shop of *American Buffalo*, to the real estate office of *Glengarry Glen Ross* (1983), to the Hollywood of *Speed-the-Plow* (1988). In each of these plays, Mamet unmasks an amoral jungle of struggle and self-interest.

The movement away from Broadway has enabled an unprecedented plurality of dramatic voices to be heard. Black theater quickly moved from the sentimental social realism of Lorraine Hansberry's *Raisin in the Sun* (1959) to the comic satire of Ossie Davis's *Purlie*

Victorious (1961) and Douglas Turner Ward's *Day of Absence* (1965), to the unquenchable outrage of Le Roi Jones (later Imamu Amiri Baraka). In Baraka's *Dutchman* (1964), the murder of a black man by a white woman in a New York subway car is offered as the emblem of the fatal distance that separates the races.

The recovery of black history has been the task of much recent black drama. Charles Fuller's *Brownsville Raid* (1976) and *A Soldier's Story* (1980) oppose hard racial truths to the patriotic myths that have long dominated schoolbook versions of America's military past. August Wilson, in *Ma Rainey's Black Bottom* (1979), *Fences* (winner of the Pulitzer Prize for Drama in 1987), and *Joe Turner's Come and Gone* (1988), has combined mysticism and naturalism, blues and lyric ritual, to trace the odysseys of blacks and women toward self-definition and freedom. *Joe Turner*, set in a black boardinghouse in Pittsburgh in 1911, brings together a group of disconnected characters whose intersecting stories become the material of revelation and of a fragile but luminous communion.

Along with the flowering of black theater, one of the signal phenomena of recent American theater has been the ascendance of women playwrights. Encouraged by the success of Ntozake Shange's *For Colored Girls Who Have Considered Suicide / When the Rainbow is Enuf* (1976) and inspirited by the earlier work of Lillian Hellman and Lorraine Hansberry, women in abundance began in the seventies and eighties to find acceptance on the commercial stage. Many had begun as actresses and felt the need to create better roles than they found. Mary Gallagher's *Dog Eat Dog* (1982) is a painfully funny chronicle of the decline and fall of suburban contentment when bad times suddenly overtake prosperity. Tina Howe's *Painting Churches* (1981) divides its sympathies between a young artist and the aging parents who stand as obstacles to her commitment to herself and her talent.

These playwrights offered stories of daughters instead of sons, and of women on their own, liberated but often bewildered by feminism. They offer valuable witness to a culture that has been dedicated to the continuing subordination of women. Some, like Wendy Wasserstein, work in comic tones, while others, like La-vonne Mueller, whose *Little Victories* presents a debate between Joan of Arc and Susan B. Anthony, approach allegory. The Pulitzer Prize for Drama went to Beth Henley in 1981, for *Crimes of the Heart*, and then to Marsha Norman, in 1983, for her remarkable 'Night Mother. Just two characters appear in Norman's long single-act play, a mother and a daughter who live together in rather ordinary circumstances. Near the beginning of the play, the daughter announces that she is going to kill herself, and the rest of the drama leads relentlessly toward its fated outcome. Probing pitilessly and yet compassionately beneath the surfaces of commonplace lives, Norman has produced one of the important images of recent American theater.

The emergence of women playwrights had its source partly in individual talent, partly in the productive coupling of art and ideology that has attended movements of self-definition across the whole spectrum of American minority groups. Blacks, Hispanics, Asians, Indians, and gay men and women have reinforced their demands for equality by appropriating theater's uniquely intimate engagement with its audience. El Teatro Campesino, to give an important example, began in the mid–1960s explicitly as a means of aiding the political struggle of Spanish-speaking migrant workers in California. In such productions as *The Conscience of a Scab* (1965), played in the fields and using workers as actors, the group crossed the line dividing theatrical illusion from daily reality.

❧ Fiction ❧

The early postwar mood of alienation and disengagement found its fictional analog in J. D. Salinger's *The Catcher in the Rye* (1951). Holden Caulfield is Salinger's pouting Peter Pan, burdened with a superior sensitivity to cant and eager to take on all the world's phonies single-handedly. Holden's voice snaps with a contempt for propriety that has beguiled millions of young readers for decades:

> If you really want to hear about it, the first thing you'll probably want to know is where I was born, and what my lousy childhood was like, and how my parents were occupied and all before they had me, and all that David Copperfield kind of crap, but I don't feel like going into it, if you want to know the truth. In the first place, that stuff bores me, and in the second place, my parents would have about two hemorrhages apiece if I told anything pretty personal about them.

In fact, Holden's clamorous innocence is the wispy stuff of day-dream, a simplified Rousseauean fantasy linking childhood with wisdom. His ambition to shield children from danger or from the contamination of obscene graffiti is at bottom a species of self-defense, a withdrawal from the messy world of grownup sexual and ideological entanglements. Seventeen years old, Holden furiously resists his own adulthood; his rebellion is finally more a poignant gesture than a profound act.

Salinger followed *The Catcher in the Rye* with a handful of small books: *Nine Stories* (1953); *Franny and Zooey* (1961); and *Raise High the Roof Beam, Carpenters and Seymour: An Introduction* (1963). At the center of each story lies some version of the same lament over the alleged emptiness of contemporary culture. Salinger's frightened longing for purification led to a series of religious gesticulations, including appeals to universal love, Jesus, Taoism, and Zen. He prefers a moral terrain of shadowless clarity; his evaluations are blinkered by an adolescent impatience with ambiguity. As an antidote to America's spiritual distemper, he offered a couple of saintly characters warmed by his own sticky affection, images of innocence imperiled by the world's assorted snares.

Following *Seymour*, Salinger virtually disappeared. Only Thomas Pynchon has carried the argument against publicity to greater lengths. Salinger stopped publishing and went into seclusion in New England, where he has remained for over a quarter of a century, silent except in defense of his privacy. In 1987, he won a court suit against publication of a biography that he believed intruded on him unfairly.

Most of Salinger's work appeared first in *The New Yorker*, a magazine whose distinctive style he found congenial. *The New Yorker*, antimodernist but sophisticated in its literary preferences, nurtured a prose of high finish: arch, unflappable, laconic, tremendously knowing. *The New Yorker* has only a tourist's interest in politics, but, ironically, the magazine's lineage can be traced back to the journalism of more populist and even more radical turn-of-the-century periodicals. In particular, *The Masses*, a monthly concatenation of drawings by John Sloan and George Bellows, essays by Randolph Bourne and Max Eastman, and advertisements for Karl Marx Cigars, was a pioneering venture in graphics and design that imprinted its innovations upon less engagé successors. From its founding in 1911 until it expired in 1917, a casualty of the First World War, *The Masses* was devoted to dreams of socialist revolution. The radical politics have long since vanished, and the legacy of *The Masses* was dispersed in the country's middlebrow visual culture.

Begun in 1925, *The New Yorker* has in sixty-five years published an anthology of well-wrought prose and poetry, much of it in response to the unease of modern urban life. Along with Salinger, the magazine's authors in the postwar years included John Hersey, whose *Hiroshima* took up the entire issue of August 31, 1946, Peter Taylor, John Cheever, John Updike, Vladimir Nabokov, and Donald Barthelme, writers who established and repeatedly met high standards of technical mastery.

All the stories in Cheever's first two books, *The Way Some People Live* (1943) and *The Enormous Radio* (1953), had been published in the *New Yorker*. There and in his later Wapshot novels, Cheever touched one after another of the bruised places that trouble the successful businessmen and golf widows who inhabit contemporary suburbia. He often seemed surprised at how much sadness can coexist with material comfort and stability. He was interested in the disappointment, sometimes the actual terror, that lies hidden behind the tailored curtains of affluent St. Botolph's. To push those curtains back, Cheever never hesitated to introduce gothic, myth, and fable into the ordinary bedrooms and backyards of Hitching Post Lane and Coventry Circle.

Everything in Cheever is disoriented; in *Bullet Park* (1969), even the birds are rattled out of their migratory instincts by the overflowing birdfeeders that permit them to fill their small bellies and misplace their destinies through the fall and winter.

In his later years, Cheever deliquesced into hopefulness. The violence and bad dreams of *Falconer* (1977) culminate in a call for rejoicing, and *Oh What a Paradise It Seems* (1982), Cheever's last novel, is swaddled in a nimbus of affirmation. Beginning by the edge of a polluted lake, an emblem of Walden's insulted fate in technologyland, the tale moves toward the consolations of a transcendental vision: "The sense of the hour was of an exquisite privilege, the great benefice of living here and renewing ourselves with love."

Like Cheever, John Updike has taken for his subject the discontented men and women whose lives occupy the puzzling, un-defined space between older inhibitions and contemporary permissiveness. These are people whose sexual and spiritual gropings are signs of a frustration bequeathed by new freedoms. They drift, they couple and uncouple and couple again, they run. In the fore-word to *Hugging the Shore* (1983), a collection of his essays and reviews, Updike writes that his critical touchstone is a "fervent relation to the world." In the essays, he repeatedly circles back to religious questions and to the difficulty of investing fiction with seriousness in a culture of multiplying counterfeit.

As those essays also demonstrate, Updike has read widely, and he tends to use quotation and allusion to document his large pur-poses. His novels are larded with mythology, saints' lives, citations from the Bible, Dante, Pascal, nineteenth-century novels, and the philosophy of Karl Barth, Paul Tillich, Alexander Blok, and Sartre. The fiction comprises an anthology of solemn reference that often misfires by merely confirming his suburban sufferers in their small-ness. *The Centaur* (1963), for example, is split in two by Updike's ambitions. A poignant rendering of a buoyantly pessimistic, doomed high school teacher named George Caldwell, the book finally dis-appears behind the scaffolds and ladders of its elaborate crosscutting to the legend of Chiron (Figure 173).

With increasing explicitness, from *Couples* (1968) forward, Up-dike has made sex one of the central nodes of his work: often acrobatic, typically joyless, invariably misogynist. His intentions, at least professedly, are not to titillate but to explore, in the manner of a latter-day, pornographic Emerson. In search of the spirit, Up-dike conducts repeated forays into the flesh. Fittingly, though he was raised in rural Pennsylvania, he has lived most of his adult life in New England. He is the temperamental heir of the Puritans and transcendentalists: the women of *The Witches of Eastwick* (1984) descend from seventeenth-century Salem, and *Roger's Version* (1987) reenacts *The Scarlet Letter* from Reverend Dimmesdale's point of view.

Updike's first books, the poems of *The Carpentered Hen* (1958) and the short novel *The Poorhouse Fair* (1959), appeared when he was in his midtwenties. Since then he has published a prodigious list of fiction, essays, and poetry. *Rabbit, Run* (1960), Updike's second novel, is the tale of Harry ("Rabbit") Angstrom, a car salesman who has fallen from the pleasures of high school basketball excellence into the mediocrity of remorse and fleshly panting. The first Rabbit novel was eventually joined by two others, *Rabbit Redux* (1971) and *Rabbit Is Rich* (1981), to comprise a trilogy of postwar discontent, a sexual-political odyssey reaching from the waning days of Eisenhower's presidency to the outset of Reaganism.

Updike's restless talent has encouraged him to push into unfamiliar territories in search of subjects, structures, and voices. *Bech: A Book* (1970), for example, presents the middle age of a written-out but durable Jewish author, and *The Coup* (1978) tells the tragicomic history of the poverty-stricken African country of Kush. In all his diverse work, and in spite of his efforts to objectify myth, to encompass national and global politics, and to discern the motions of grace in his characters' nonstop gulpings and lickings and plungings, Updike's principal achievement has been bound up in his management of the visible and local. He is gifted with apparently inexhaustible verbal resources, and he displays them most prodigally in summoning up the here and now. Self-regarding, calculated, his sentences move with a confident

FIGURE 173 ❧ Steve Liss, photograph of John Updike (1982).

swagger, one brilliant image following another like polished objects. The sheer numbers of them, over hundreds of pages, can produce a glut of "fine writing." In the end, Harry Angstrom and Bech and the Maples of *Too Far to Go* (1979) are excuses for Updike's expenditures of talent, poor souls not redeemed from banality by the prose that engenders and eventually overpowers them. The final point of Updike's writing is itself.

The literature of the postwar South was a various achievement, but was still – much of it, in any case – regionally self-conscious. A sense of common origin and place united writers otherwise as unlike as Robert Penn Warren, Eudora Welty, Flannery O'Connor, Carson McCullers, and Walker Percy. The South was no longer the nation's "number one economic problem," as Franklin D. Roosevelt had put it in one of his fireside chats during the Depression. Nonetheless, while the South moved some distance toward the metropolitan mainstream, it retained a sense of sectional difference, a distinct attitude toward the ideas of community, history, and race. Southern writers tended toward a more guarded view than Northerners of the power of individual will to assert itself against circumstance. Consequently, these writers valued the authority of specified place, what Eudora Welty, in her essay *Place in Fiction* (1957), has called "the named, identified, concrete, exact and exacting, and therefore credible, gathering-spot of all that has been felt."

Most of Tennessee Williams's settings and principal characters are southern: A *Streetcar Named Desire* is set in a New Orleans slum, as is *The Rose Tattoo*; the events of *Summer and Smoke* (1948) transpire in Glorious Hill, Mississippi, while *Cat on a Hot Tin Roof* is also placed in Mississippi, on an enormous plantation. Even *The Glass Menagerie*, set in Saint Louis, derives some of its texture of bewildered despair from the turmoil of a recent move from the South. Williams spent the first twelve years of his life in Mississippi, and the odor of decay that clings to so many of his plays can be traced to the ashes of a peculiarly southern gentility. He shared his sympathy for the dispossessed with many of his southern literary contemporaries, and he shared as well the suspicion that history is a nightmare.

The twin legacies of place and fate have shaped the writing of Robert Penn Warren, whose career has spanned most of this century. Born in Guthrie, Kentucky, in 1905, Warren published his first book, an ungenerous, acidly debunking biography called *John Brown: The Making of a Martyr*, in 1929; his fifth volume of *Selected Poems* appeared in 1985. In the half-century and more that separates his first and his most recent books, Warren has published upwards of thirty volumes of poetry, fiction, criticism, history, and drama. His collaboration with Cleanth Brooks influenced a generation of critical ideas and practice through the textbooks they coauthored, and through the *Southern Review*, which they founded and edited at Louisiana State University in the midthirties.

Warren's strongest novels were probably his earlier ones. *Night Rider* (1939), *At Heaven's Gate* (1943), and especially *All the King's Men* (1947), stories driven by a propulsive narrative energy and peopled by consummately vicious characters. Although Warren was a founder of New Critical formalism, his own concerns have been unvarying historical; much of his major work records his meditations on the ironic lessons that history teaches. Warren values responsibility and continuity above innovation, and he regards notions of human perfectibility with professorial skepticism. Emerson and Jefferson stand, arm in arm, at the antipodes of Warren's moral universe. In a poem mischievously called "Homage to Emerson," set aboard a night flight to New York, Warren's speaker decides that "at 38,000 feet Emerson / is dead right"; a sturdier philosophy is needed for walking on the ground.

Brother to Dragons, a "tale in verse and voices," which was first published in 1953 (a substantially revised and shortened version appeared in 1979), retells the story of Jefferson's nephews, who butchered a black slave for breaking a water pitcher. With an almost unseemly relish, Warren measures the grotesque distance between the murder and Jefferson's dreams of democratic beatitude. To Jefferson's protests that he "tried to be innocent" of cruelty to his own slaves, the poem's interlocutor, "RPW," returns:

> You lived
> In the lean, late years by the skill of some colored mechanics,
> Nailmakers I think, that luckily you'd trained up.
> Well, this is impertinent, but to build Monticello,
> That domed dream of our liberties floating
> High on its mountain, like a cloud, demanded
> A certain amount of black sweat.

Debate over ideas is common in Warren's fiction and poetry. He has described the "philosophical novelist" as a writer "for whom the documentation of the world is constantly striving to rise to the level of generalization about values, for whom the image strives to rise to symbol, for whom images always fall into a dialectical configuration." This discloses Warren's rather schoolmasterly approach to his material, and it suggests as well the appeal that both melodrama and contemplation have for him. His effort, sometimes all too visible, has been to align the concrete facts of fictional or personal experience within the organizing grids of moral or political categories. The surveyor's transit, an image that occurs several times in his novels and poems, might serve as an emblem for his stance and technique: his effort to see the raw material of geography and human behavior with precision and, at the same time, to fix the meaning of their relationships.

RPW of *Brother to Dragons* and Jack Burden of *All the King's Men* typify at once Warren's searching intelligence and the somber delight he takes in paradox and unanswered questions. He has always been impatient with social and political engineering. His attack on his fellow southerner, T. S. Stribling, is instructive. Stribling earned considerable acclaim, including clamorous support from Mencken, for his iconoclastic and socially committed fictional accounts of the impoverished poor whites of Arkansas and Tennessee. *The Store*, the second volume of Stribling's trilogy on the Vaiden family, won a Pulitzer Prize in 1933, one of the worst years of the Depression.

Warren prefers a sense of tragedy to technocratic solutions, an insular point of view in the 1930s, to be sure, but a spring of his fiction and poetry. Willie Stark's corrupt efficiency proves ultimately as irrelevant to the deepest needs of men and women as Adam Stanton's romantic rites of purification. At the end of *All the King's Men*, Jack Burden, who has been educated beyond cynicism by the shock of experience and death, is left to engage the world anew:

FIGURE 174 🍋 In 1986, Robert Penn Warren was named the nation's first poet laureate.

"We shall go out of the house and go into the convulsion of the world, out of history into history and the awful responsibility of Time." The prose is deliberately grandiloquent. Jack's willingness to take on the obligations of historical consciousness enacts Warren's own commitments.

The weight of the past has freighted Warren's verse, as well as his fiction, from the beginning. He first heard poetry recited, "by the yard," when he visited the farm of his maternal grandfather, a Confederate veteran. Warren's first publications were poems, and he has rededicated himself to poetry in his later years. He began as a modern metaphysical, influenced by Eliot and Ransom. The verse of *Thirty-six Poems* (1935) and *Eleven Poems on the Same Theme* (1942) is careful, artful, even mannered, much given to the elaboration of dense and complex metaphors (Figure 174).

In the poems since *Promises* (1957), and especially since *Incarnations* (1968), Warren has forged a different style and idiom, meditative, more colloquial, more firmly anchored in the natural world and in his own past:

> When I was a boy I saw the world I was in.
> I saw it for what it was. Canebrakes with
> Track beaten down by bear paw. Tobacco,
> In endless rows, the pink inner flesh of black fingers
> Crushing to green juice tobacco worms plucked
> From a leaf. The great trout,
> Motionless, poised in the shadow of his
> Enormous creek-boulder.

Warren's later poems are filled with intimations of a mortality only imperfectly redeemed in knowledge. Transactions between the human and animal worlds are by turns consolatory and shocking, the record of a long inner debate between logic and fear.

During Warren's years at the *Southern Review* in the late 1930s, the magazine published the early work of many writers who later took leading parts in postwar literature in both the North and the South. Stories by Caroline Gordon appeared alongside Delmore Schwartz's long review of Dos Passos; the poetry of Randall Jarrell and John Berryman shared space with the political speculations of Sidney Hook and I. F. Stone. Seven of the seventeen stories collected in Eudora Welty's first book, *A Curtain of Green and Other Stories* (1941), first appeared in *Southern Review*. Welty was born in Jackson, Mississippi, in 1909 and has lived there all her life. No one has reproduced the landscape and people of the South more memorably. She has a perfect ear for speech, and she is a superb maker of images, economically rendered, not upholstered with adjectives and adverbs. "The Whistle" tells of Jason and Sara Morton, a desperately poor elderly sharecropper couple whose meager existence is threatened by a hard frost. As the cold night descends on their darkened farmhouse, they are lying together:

> between the quilts of a pallet which had been made up close
> to the fireplace. A fire still fluttered in the grate, making a
> drowsy sound now and then, and its exhausted light beat up
> and down the wall, across the rafters, and over the dark pallet
> where the old people lay, like a bird trying to find its way out
> of the room.

In a story such as "A Worn Path," the quiet passion of Welty's attention to each detail turns a trivial anecdote into an action at once lyric and epic. Phoenix Jackson, an old, nearly blind black woman, walks for hours across cold December fields to bring home medicine for her permanently disabled grandson. A life in which nothing of outward consequence happens is seen from the inside to radiate with courage and even joy. This story, like most of Welty's best, is rooted in its southern soil. She has repeatedly insisted, for example in the essay *Place in Fiction*, that fidelity to the known scene provides the source and motive for her work. "I am," she has written, "touched off by place. The place where I am and the place I know, and other places that familiarity with and love for my own make strange and lovely and enlightening to look into, are what set me to writing my stories."

Welty's fiction emerges out of her long-held convictions about the relationship of setting to feeling and about the writer's need for a fixed and stable point of view. These values are numbered among her principal themes. Bowman's death in her first published story "Death of a Traveling Salesman" – alone, next to his car, his sample cases his only companions – encapsulates his life of frustrated, sterile journeying. His loneliness and placelessness are counterpointed by the poor, taciturn country couple who give him shelter, a man and woman whose anonymous rural lives are whole and fruitful.

While Welty's terrain is familiar, her explorations of it encompass a kaleidoscope of forms and techniques. Katherine Anne Porter, in her introduction to *A Curtain of Green*, rightly remarked on the "extraordinary range of mood, pace, tone." Welty's breadth has several sources. She is drawn to the subtle connections between apprehension and discovery. In consequence, some of her stories and novels, including "Livvie," "Moon Lake," and *Delta Wedding* (1946), her first full-length novel, adopt children's observations as their focus; others, among them "Lily Daw and the Three Ladies," "The Key," and *Losing Battles* (1970), confer a sometimes comic but always moving amplitude on the lives of handicapped, elderly, half-witted persons, men and women conventionally dismissed as grotesque. A sharp, irrepressible humor, unsentimental but forgiving, is the lens through which Welty typically views her characters and their fates.

In describing the photography she did for the Works Progress Administration during the Depression, Welty has remarked on the camera's ability to stop a moment from running away and thus to capture transience. She has approached fiction with the same purpose and has therefore created complex fictional patterns that weave the local together with history and myth (Figure 175). The novella *The Robber Bridegroom* (1942), set in the Mississippi wilderness of the early nineteenth century, combines frontier humor, history, tall tales, and fairy story. *The Golden Apples* (1949), a sequence of related stories set in and around the invented town of Morgana, Mississippi, locates the tragedy and farce of the twentieth-century South within the framework of classical and Celtic myth. Perseus, Leda, and Odysseus inhabit the same small-town houses and backyards as the MacLains, Starks, and Morrisons of Morgana. The links are elusive, often ironic, but they suggest the depth and significance of Welty's seemingly slight subjects.

In *One Writer's Beginnings* (1984), Welty elaborated on her conviction that seeing is unavoidably attached to memory. In line with that assumption, her fiction often traces the process through which recollection leads to clarifying or shattering insight. One of her narrators says that memory lives "in the patterns restored by dreams," and her stories and novels dramatize the implications of this insight. In *Optimist's Daughter* (1972), Laurel McKelva Hand

FIGURE 175 ❧ Eudora Welty, *The Fortune-teller's House/Jackson*, from *One Time, One Place* (1971).

persistently, loyally pursues the ancient causes of present loss behind the veil of time. The gathered descendents of Granny Vaughn, who have come together to celebrate her ninetieth birthday in *Losing Battles*, join voice to voice in evocation of past incidents, choruslike, building a monument of collective memory.

The gothic overtones that sound in Welty's fiction recur with more persistence and centrality in the work of Flannery O'Connor. O'Connor's stories are filled with images of the grotesque, and her characters include a gallery of men and women who are mentally or physically twisted, misshapen. In a well-known essay entitled "The Grotesque in Southern Fiction," she acknowledged that she had chosen "the way of distortion" in her narratives rather than the way of realism. A devout if ironic Catholic, she believed in both evil and grace, and she chose extremity as her subject in order to probe the mystery that she felt lay beneath all of life's plausible explanations. O'Connor died in 1964, at thirty-nine, a victim of the lupus that had crippled her and kept her tied to her Milledgeville, Georgia, home for fifteen years. Her illness and increasing immobility contributed to her attitudes, as did her devotion to the town and countryside where she spent virtually all her life.

She found in the South a metaphor for her theology, and her tales set out the consequences of Original Sin and the Fall. She gave her paramount intellectual allegiance to the church, but her affiliations reached widely. She was deeply moved by the mystical evolutionary meliorism of the Jesuit theologian-scientist, Pierre Teilhard de Chardin. She wrote admiringly of Hawthorne and Melville as masters of romance. She accepted the literary advice of Caroline Gordon, and if her stories display little of Gordon's nostalgia for vanished southern virtue, they do share a concern for structure and the crafts of fiction. Finally, she recommended *Miss Lonelyhearts* and *As I Lay Dying* to friends, and toward the end of her life she corresponded with John Hawkes. (Hawkes named her, along with Nathanael West and Djuna Barnes, as the important experimental voices in modern American fiction.)

O'Connor's South is a place of primitive emotion, ugliness, and bad luck, relieved only at long intervals by beauty or hope. The brace shop in "The Lame Shall Enter First" is a storeroom of affliction, culminating in nameless misery: "Wheel chairs and walkers covered most of the floor. The walls were hung with every kind of

FIGURE 176 ❧ Ralph Morrisey, photograph of Flannery O'Connor (1955).

crutch and brace. Artificial limbs were stacked on the shelves, legs and arms and hands, claws and hooks, straps and human harnesses and unidentifiable instruments for unnamed deformities." O'Connor published two novels, *Wise Blood* (1952) and *The Violent Bear It Away* (1960), but her power increased as her focus narrowed (Figure 176). Like Mrs. Turpin, in her story "Revelation," O'Connor sees everything fiercely and at a distance: "as if she were looking . . . through the wrong end of a telescope." In the story "Parker's Back," the tale of a man who has a portrait of Christ tattooed on his back, Parker's wife is described as "plain, plain." The skin of her face was "thin and drawn as tight as the skin on an onion and her eyes were grey and sharp like the points of two icepicks." Such imagery separates O'Connor's characters from their humanity, reducing them to shrunken, parched automatons gazing blankly over vistas of disappointment. These are men and women whose calamities sear their souls and bodies like brands; they betray little of any inner complexity.

In one story after another, O'Connor explored the frustration – sometimes the sheer boredom – that leads to violence, to murder, suicide, or cold despair. Good intentions are few and are almost always divorced from outcomes. The peacocks that she kept as pets on her Milledgeville farm appeared to her to be gaudy emblems of transfiguration, images of her unshakable belief in the Holy Ghost. But in her stories, even moments of visionary access dissolve into dark, ironic comedy. In "Greenleaf," Mrs. May is killed by a bull that her ne'er-do-well hired hand has forgotten to pen securely. As

she is impaled on the bull's horns, "she had the look of a person whose sight has been suddenly restored but who finds the light unbearable."

Like Flannery O'Connor, Carson McCullers was born and raised in Georgia; like O'Connor's, her last years were afflicted by the illness from which she died (in 1967), just after her fiftieth birthday. McCuller's fiction, even more than O'Connor's and Welty's, teems with a distinctively grotesque vitality. Her strange characters and scenes are calculated affronts to normality, skillfully drawn caricatures whose pain and deformities continually push against the borders of plausibility. Above all, McCullers intended to render the radical isolation of modern life. Loneliness is the crushing weight that defeats love and drains the savor from experience.

McCullers published her first novel, *The Heart Is a Lonely Hunter* (1941), when she was just twenty-three. Set in a small southern town in the Depression, the novel is a combination of closely observed social detail and an allegorically symmetrical action. That mixture of the real with versions of fable would recur throughout her work. The novel's opening lines introduced the flat, journalistic voice in which she chose to narrate difference, or eccentricity, or obsession: "In the town there were two mutes, and they were always together. Early every morning they would come out from the house where they lived and walk arm in arm down the street to work."

In the center of the moribund town is the ironically named New York Café, bravely offering some hope of companionship, "the only store on all the street with an open door and lights inside." In fact, the café is hope's tomb, and McCullers returned to a similar setting in her most accomplished work, *The Ballad of the Sad Café* (1951). Influenced in part by Isak Dinesen's *Seven Gothic Tales*, this novella enacts McCullers's symbolic equation between disfigurement, whether physical or spiritual, and the failure of love. Muscular, cross-eyed Miss Amelia Evans, whose competence and independence lead inevitably to defeat, is the main actor in a frightening parable about the dangers of female power.

Parable, with its precedents in southern folktales and the Bible, has attracted many postwar southern writers, among them William Styron, John William Corrington, and Cormac McCarthy. Styron's novels, he said in a comment following the publication of *Sophie's Choice* (1979), have all been reflections on "human institutions:

humanly contrived situations which cause people to live in wretched unhappiness." Within the constraints of that persistent theme, his subjects have been diverse, ranging from surburban family conflict, to a nineteenth-century slave revolt, to the Nazi death camps. His first book, *Lie Down in Darkness* (1951), ponders the suicide in New York City of a young southern woman. Excavating under the deed to its sources, working backward from the moment of irrecoverable loss, Styron employs a style of elaborate exertions, replete with pauses, modifiers, dependent clauses, long suspensions, baroque oratory, and a regular alternation of outer and inner, present and past. Everything is named, and everything named is laden with significance. There was some justice in the charge that Styron made his debut with a kind of copybook Faulkner, straining to encompass universality by heaping immense explanations on top of exhausting descriptions.

Styron's later work has addressed history and its outrages more directly. *The Confessions of Nat Turner* (1967), which Styron called a "meditation on history" rather than a historical novel "in the conventional sense," retells the story of Nat Turner, leader of a slave rebellion in 1831, from Turner's point of view. Styron's Turner is memorably misconceived, his courage reduced to paranoia and fanaticism, his outrage twisted into the lunging paroxysms of his lust for white women. Rather than offering access to the great tragedy of race, Nat Turner becomes a clinical case study, his motives cankered by stereotype. Styron's prose in the novel is consistently powerful, but his rhetoric is as alien as his vision from whatever of reality or mystery might actually be signified in the historical Nat Turner's life and death.

In *Sophie's Choice*, Styron attempted his most sweeping recapitulation of history and personal experience. The writer Stingo is the instrument through which Styron reveals Sophie's story, her survival in Auschwitz, and the terrible moment that annulled her soul. The choice she was forced to make, in deciding which of her children was to be spared and which murdered, encapsulates Styron's flawed but frightening inquiry into absolute evil. The fact of Auschwitz mocks the pretensions of civilization, and *Sophie's Choice* asks what is possible after such knowledge.

Employing nonsouthern materials, *Sophie's Choice* pushes to its limits the apocalyptic urgency that marks much of the postwar southern fiction. Styron shares with David Madden, William Goyen, and Walker Percy a consciousness of history as fractured and unhealable. Percy's third novel, *Love in the Ruins* (1971), is in fact set, according to its subtitle, "at a Time Near the End of the World" – which is to say, the 1980s. The book's narrator and hero is Dr. Thomas More, like Percy a physician and a Catholic, and like Percy a man given to diagnosing the political and spiritual diseases that have brought modern America to the verge of anarchy. All of Percy's major figures, from Binx Bolling in *The Moviegoer* (1961) to the title character of *Lancelot* (1977), are seekers, trying to find an answer to a question Percy himself has raised: "Why does man feel so sad in the twentieth century?"

Percy's pilgrims are misfitted by sensibility or religion for any place in their society, and Percy uses their wayfaring as the fictional excuse for one satiric itinerary after another. Percy is appalled by the culture of shopping mall, country club, and split-level house. This is the New South, the South that swallowed up Faulkner's in its frenzy to join the prosperous North. Binx Bolling describes his opposition to the modern wasteland in overwrought images that have found restatement in nearly all of Percy's subsequent novels. Binx says that, at thirty-one, he knows less than he knew before but that he has learned "to recognize merde when I see it." And that is what he sees, and smells, all around him:

> merde from every quarter, living in fact in the very century of merde, the great shithouse of scientific humanism where needs are satisfied, everyone becomes an anyone, a warm and creative person, and prospers like a dung beetle, and one hundred percent of people are humanists and ninety-eight percent believe in God, and men are dead, dead, dead; and the malaise has settled like a fall-out and what people really fear is not that the bomb will fall but that the bomb will not fall.

Percy's novels are filled with characters at or beyond the borders of lunacy, creatures of his scowling suspicion that "the shithouse of scientific humanism" is also a madhouse and that only the crazy are sane. Percy's fondness for oddballs and antinomians conveniently relieves him of too nice a concern for motives and plausible structures; it also licenses the frequent plotlessness of his novels and justifies his sermonizing.

The text of Percy's preaching is quite simple: old virtues have become obsolete, and new virtues are unthinkable. Will Barrett, the gentleman of *The Last Gentleman* (1966), is subject to what are called "fugue states," fits of amnesia that cut him off, literally and symbolically, from his surroundings. He often wakes from these states to find himself wandering alone on Civil War battlefields. A combination of Bunyan's Christian, southern everyman and twentieth-century Huck Finn, Will travels across a good portion of the United States, engaged on a quest he does not choose, in search of values he does not understand. A novel of large invention and flamboyant, funny episodes, *The Last Gentleman* is finally less than the sum of its parts, held together mainly by Percy's unappeasable anger at modernity.

The persistence of southern literature exemplifies the striking resilience of geographic and ethnic identification across the postwar years. Despite the oft-rumored homogenization of American culture, the alleged result of national magazines, middle-class mobility, television, and the statistical reduction of diversity to the averaging of random sampling, the nation's politics and literature remained largely the property of clan, group, and increasingly, of gender. So, although the flourishing of Jewish and black writing had much to do with individual energy, it also expressed the power of the local, the familial, the familiar. At stake, too, was a retreat from the totalizing ideologies that had helped to breed total chaos. When the atrocities of the Holocaust became known, history and culture stood unmasked as problematic and perhaps treacherous, flimsier bulwarks against anarchy than they had seemed, and bearing the livid, unblinkable bruises of humanity's capacity for evil.

Circumstances called for skepticism and new styles. One cluster of responses came from a loosely assembled group of intellectuals in New York, including Lionel Trilling, Philip Rahv, Harold Rosenberg, Alfred Kazin, Irving Howe – mostly Jewish and the children of immigrants. They shared a fondness for ideological speculation, and they had a common political temperament which led most of them to early radicalism and later disillusionment. They believed in the future, but they also believed in the links that bind individuals to their pasts. They had a taste, says Nathan Zuckerman in Philip Roth's *Anatomy Lesson* (1983), for scrutinizing a social event as though it were a dream or a work of art. They took literature's social importance for granted and searched for an aesthetic spacious enough to encompass both passion and discrimination.

The New York intellectuals had begun to coalesce amid the turmoil of the 1930s. If one figure could represent the group it would be Delmore Schwartz, brilliant, ambitious, combative, intellectually omnivorous. He published his first novel, *In Dreams Begin Responsibilities* (1938), when he was twenty-four and achieved a considerable éclat among makers of advanced opinion. An editor of *Partisan Review* from 1943 to 1955, Schwartz fell into fearful disasters. His pugnacity disintegrated into brawling, alcoholic paranoia; his talent deserted him; he drove away his friends. He died at fifty-three, alone, in a bad New York hotel. His career, from its precocious beginning to its shabby end, was sadly cherished as a kind of morality play by the survivors he left behind. In *Humboldt's Gift* (1975), Saul Bellow used Schwartz's fictionalized biography to investigate the fate of the artist in America. The country is so immense, so indifferent: "Maybe America didn't need art or inner miracles. It had so many outer ones. The USA was a big operation, very big. The more *it*, the less *we*."

The contest between "it" and "we" has occupied all of Bellow's attention throughout more than forty years of fiction; the contest, that is to say, between state and self, force and spirit, between all the assorted bureaucratic filing systems, noises, redundant junk, and quick fixes of twentieth-century existence and the vulnerable, shrinking domain of individual freedom. "I thought of the variation on Gresham's famous Law," muses the title character of *Herzog* (1964): "Public life drives out private life." And, in a passage later in the novel, Herzog finds a synoptic and sinister symbol in a routine act of urban destruction. Turning a corner in midtown New York (New York is always more dangerous than Chicago for Bellow), Moses Herzog sees a wrecking crew at work:

> The great metal ball swung at the walls, passed easily through brick, and entered the rooms, the lazy weight browsing on

kitchens and parlors. Everything it touched wavered and burst, spilled down. There rose a white tranquil cloud of plaster dust. The afternoon was ending, and in the widening area of demolition was a fire, fed by the wreckage. Moses heard the air, softly pulled toward the flames, felt the heat. The workmen, heaping the bonfire with wood, threw strips of molding like javelins. Paint and varnish smoked like incense. The old flooring burned gratefully – the funeral of exhausted objects.

According to the quietly bitter irony of Bellow's prose, modern destruction is above all routine, almost genial, and the objects of traditional regard have become too fatigued to resist (Figure 177).

From Asa Leventhal in *The Victim* (1947), to Herzog, to Albert Corde in *The Dean's December* (1982), all of Bellow's main characters are men of great feeling also burdened with mind. The discord between heart and head makes them comic (Bellow is one of the funniest writers America has produced), but they prove their value through a tenacious, often naive fidelity to human dignity. They

FIGURE 177 &. Michael Maurey, photograph of Saul Bellow (1970). Bellow is shown among the shops and markets of Chicago's Maxwell Street.

understand that history is different from sophisticated talk about history and that the living owe tribute to the dead. They open themselves to the answers that humanity might give to the massed forces of positivism, irrationality, and coercion.

Bellow's embrace is not ecumenical. His novels are seldom civilized in their treatment of women, and his war against the sixties has led him into cranky arrogance. (His endorsement of Allen Bloom's mean-spirited manifesto *The Closing of the American Mind* (1987) signaled a further narrowing of Bellow's sympathies.) Nor has he been willing to experiment much with fictional form. His receipt of the Nobel Prize in 1976 confirmed his special status, and it also paid tribute to his cautious but ultimately affirmative alliance with a traditional literary humanism. Viewing the twentieth century as "an unending cycle of crises . . . disappointing ideologies . . . and madness," Bellow has put his faith in what he calls "certain durable human goods," a set of values derived from the past. Suspicious of utopian scheming, his books are a series of meditations on the relevance of past to present.

Bellow enjoys wearing the regalia of moralist and metaphysician. Ideas are important to him and to his characters, many of whom are intellectuals or professional academics, much given to rumination and dispute. Indeed, Bellow's large task has been to rehabilitate thinking for a culture suspicious of mind. His books have simultaneously earned popularity and critical esteem by making contemplation interesting and accessible to a wide audience. Still, his contribution to American fiction lies less in his opinions than in his extraordinary novelistic gifts. No one better than Bellow has caught the sights and sounds of urban life in America: the ethnic variety, the ordinary citizens and the gangsters, mountebanks, saints, and crazies, the feel of the seasons in city streets, the co-existence of nightmare and farce.

Henry James demanded of novelists that they provide "solidity of specification." That is only one way to define fiction, to be sure, but within its terms no writer has reproduced America in this century more solidly or more convincingly than Bellow. Whether he is focusing on the parched claustrophobia of Tommy Wilhelm's despair, in *Seize the Day* (1956), or expanding to accommodate the shouts of his hero's appetite in *Henderson the Rain King* (1959) – "I want, I want!" – Bellow's voice is his supple and nearly faultless instrument. He mingles slang and learned discourse, jokey dialogue, reporting, and rapturous vision in a tone-perfect image of the frantic, dislocated quality of contemporary American life.

In 1944, in the midst of the war, Isaac Rosenfeld first speculated on the Jew's paradoxical role as both outsider and insider in American culture. The hypothesis would receive increasing assent in the postwar years, as the country absorbed the contributions of the Jews who had fled the genocide of Hitler's Europe. By most counts, two-thirds of the European exiles were Jewish, and the list of refugees is a roll call of excellence in virtually every field of science, letters, and the arts. Albert Einstein, Erwin Panofsky, Arnold Schoenberg, Bruno Bettelheim, Hannah Arendt, Erich Fromm, Maurice Abravanel, Paul Lazarsfeld, Ernst Cassirer, Max Horkheimer: these were among the men and women who came in their thousands. It was an unprecedented phenomenon, which changed the direction of America's intellectual and political history.

Isaac Bashevis Singer arrived from Poland in 1935, a journalist and storyteller whose tales and novels circulated for years only among the Yiddish-speaking. Most of Singer's work is set in the vanished world of European Jewry, a world of shtetl and ghetto, yeshiva and synagogue, but of dybbuk and black magic too, darkly luminous with mysticism, illusion, and metamorphosis. Krochmalna Street, the Warsaw block that was home to Singer as a child, is a place in which anything can happen, and often does. Rather than enshrining a culture in the pastel shades of nostalgia, Singer's stories exult in bawdy vitality and cavort in the routines of low comedy and gothic melodrama.

Though he has lived in the United States for fifty years and sometimes sets his stories in New York City, Singer has continued to write in Yiddish, a language that has been stumbling toward extinction in the years since the Holocaust. He is the only Yiddish writer whose work, in translation, has attracted a large American audience; he began to find that larger readership in 1953, when Saul Bellow published his own translation of "Gimpel the Fool" in *Partisan Review*. Bellow's fiction has little in common with Singer's; his translation was an act at once of homage and exploration, and a reminder of the diversity that is to be found under the rubric of Jewish writing.

In many ways, the postwar writer closest to Singer in subject and sensibility was Bernard Malamud. Son of Russian immigrants, Malamud was a teller of moral folktales, many of them rich with reference to the Jewish culture of Eastern Europe. His novels and stories are blendings of naturalism and fable, parables in which the larger meaning of an absurd existence is glimpsed not in precept but in images. In "The Mourners," two old men, unassimilated and impoverished, use bed sheets for prayer shawls as they recite the kaddish on the bare floor of a barren New York City apartment. Like that apartment, all of Malamud's settings – his baseball diamonds, rural college campuses, and Edenic islands, as well as the shops and crowded apartments of the Lower East Side – are symbolic places. They are densely real, but they are also locales which can accommodate such a figure as Angel Levine, a zoot-suited, jive-talking, black Jewish messenger from God.

The people who inhabit Malamud's tales are defeated seekers, trapped in uneven contests between conscience and desire, rationality and violence. They ask the old questions, about suffering and redemption, but they expect no answers from a God whose puzzling purposes humble the good and the wicked equally. Malamud's subject is bad luck, treated sometimes with pathos, sometimes with a shrug. His short stories, especially those collected in *The Magic Barrel* (1958), infuse the mischances of their gullible schlemiel-heroes with a surprising, inspiriting comedy. His novels tend to be more sober, more philosophically assertive. He examined the politics and theology of anti-Semitism in *The Fixer* (1966), in which Yakov Bok's fate encapsulates the savagery of Christian intolerance in prerevolutionary Russia. A few years later, *The Tenants* (1971) offered Malamud's response – nervous but more generous than Bellow's in *Mr. Sammler's Planet* (1970) – to the confrontations between blacks and whites in the 1960s.

The Assistant (1957) was Malamud's second novel, and probably his best. Morris Bober, a small-time grocer, struggles, only to fail. The fourteen hours he works each day behind the counter of his tiny, tunnellike store yield only pennies of profit, and everything he gains is lost to competition, bad debts, and petty theft. The sour odor of frustration touches all of Morris's few possessions, and a barely suppressed hysteria threatens to rip through the patched fabric of his self-denial and self-restraint. "He sat in a chair at the round wooden table in the rear of the store and scanned, with raised brows, yesterday's Jewish paper that he had already thoroughly read. From time to time he looked absently through the square windowless window cut through the wall, to see if anybody had by chance come into the store."

Morris is preyed upon by landlord, neighbors, and the Italian hooligan Frank Alpine, whom he takes on as an assistant. He loses his business and, in the book's final pages, dies of the heart attack that has pursued him from the opening scene, yet in the end he achieves a kind of victory. Frank Alpine, who has for months ridiculed Jewish conscience and Jewish suffering, is transformed by Morris's inexplicable but unyielding integrity. Frank takes over the store and also takes responsibility for the family. When he has himself circumcised and becomes a Jew, Frank replaces Morris's long-dead son as well. The outcome is perhaps more wishful than plausible, but it expresses the ache of a post-Holocaust yearning that dignity be possible even in defeat and that moral distinctions matter.

The Holocaust outstripped the imagination's power to bargain with reality. Genocide was not quite impossible as a subject: the Polish writer Tadeusz Borowski's shattering stories, including "This Way for the Gas, Ladies and Gentlemen" and "Auschwitz, Our Home," published just after the war, and Polish-born Jerzy Kosinski's *Painted Bird* (1965), written in English, prove the point. But the Holocaust was a calamity that American fiction usually chose to approach from an oblique angle, allegorically in John Barth's *Giles Goat-Boy* (1966) or through the memories and tribulations of survivors like Styron's Sophie Zawistowska, Bellow's Artur Sammler, or Sol Nazerman, the title character of Edward Lewis Wallant's *Pawnbroker* (1961). In a portentous act of recovery, the novels and tales of Franz Kafka were propelled into the postwar canon. Kafka had died, of tuberculosis, a decade before Hitler came to power. However, after nazism had turned the unthinkable into an accomplished fact, Kafka's bizarre fables of imprisonment, torture, and mysterious guilt were endowed with the stature of prophecy.

In an important essay written in 1973, "Looking at Kafka," Philip Roth describes the pain of his reaction to a photograph taken of Kafka in 1924, the year of his death. The pain is engendered by Roth's knowledge that the noose of history was tightening around the dying man. Even if he had survived his illness, he would soon

FIGURE 178 ❧ Thomas Victor, photograph of Philip Roth (1983). Franz Kafka appears in the photograph on the wall of Roth's studio.

have been dead: "Skulls chiseled like this one were shoveled by the thousands from the ovens; had he lived, his would have been among them, along with the skulls of his three younger sisters." It is, Roth adds, no more horrifying to think of Kafka in Auschwitz than to think of anyone else in Auschwitz: "It is just horrifying in its own way" (Figure 178).

Roth's affiliation with Kafka, and with the Eastern European novelists he has sponsored in an influential series entitled "Writers from the Other Europe," bespeaks the ethical and political concerns that he has engaged in his writing for over thirty years. Roth the public figure is a paradox: a decorous, nearly reclusive figure who has produced some of the most exhibitionist fiction of the postwar years. Even Roth was surprised by the success and the scandal that attended *Portnoy's Complaint* (1969), but the outcry, as usual, blurred the serious point. Underneath their sexual gymnastics, Roth's novels represent probes into a postwar Jewish culture cut adrift in currents of prosperity and assimilation. His assaults on decency – often hilarious, consistently misogynist – are in the end frantic expressions of nostalgia, bawdy laments for an unrecoverable moral order that might have some legitimacy.

In an essay on *The Great American Novel* (1973), Roth declared his abiding interest in the "problematic nature" of moral authority, social restraint, and regulation. These are questions that take on a special urgency in a society whose tendency toward messianic self-indulgence coexists with a grinding pressure toward conformity, and

Roth has studied them with unusual candor and wit. His main characters are locked in endless internal debate, a habit of intro-spection that sometimes leads to narrative paralysis. Furthermore, Roth's preoccupation with self reduces all of his secondary characters to ciphers and sounding boards. The female characters, especially, are one-dimensional, divided too easily between complaisant nym-phomaniacs and scolds. But the continuous self-watchfulness also confers an unusual quality of awareness.

Roth's first book, a collection of short stories and the title novella *Goodbye, Columbus* (1959), sketched conflicts among Jews, exam-ining in a variety of tones the tension between cultural intransigence and forgetfulness. Written in the first of the many virtuoso styles Roth would perfect over the years, the book's satire was carefully calculated and targeted. The reach of Roth's discontent was not yet evident, nor would it be in the formally disciplined novels he pub-lished in the 1960s, *Letting Go* (1962) and *When She Was Good* (1967). Yet, as early as 1960, Roth had begun to complain about the oversized awfulness of contemporary America, which beggars the skills of mere novelists: "The actuality is continually outdoing our talents, and the culture tosses up figures almost daily that are the envy of any novelist." Alexander Portnoy's cacophonous libido was one response to excess, and what Roth called the "farcical, blatant, and coarse-grained" anti-Nixon satire of *Our Gang* (1971) was another. *The Great American Novel*, an answer to Malamud's *Natural* and a long stand-up comedy routine on baseball, is a re-minder that Roth has claimed kinship with Henny Youngman as well as Kafka.

In the two decades since *Portnoy*, Roth's absorption in the mul-tiple anomalies of his vocation have led to an unfolding portrait of the artist, a sequence of books whose main character lives out a life rather like Roth's own. *The Ghost Writer* (1979), *Zuckerman Un-bound* (1981), and *The Anatomy Lesson* (1983) follow the career of Nathan Zuckerman from his twenty-three-year-old fictional aspi-rations, through the fame and wealth that accompany publication of *Carnovsky* (a dirty but hilarious novel), to the physical and psychic debilities that lure him toward the comically desperate decision to leave the miseries of writing behind.

When Roth gathered the Zuckerman books together and re-published them under the punning title *Zuckerman Bound* (1985), he added as epilogue a novella called "The Prague Orgy." This fierce, funny parody of Henry James's "Aspern Papers" finds Zuckerman in Prague, Kafka's city, searching for the unpublished stories of one Sinovsky, the Yiddish Flaubert, whose papers are zealously guarded by his alcoholic, deserted daughter-in-law. Prague's tragic past and dispirited present illuminate a sad contrast between the permissively indifferent cultures of the West, which license everything and listen to nothing, and the police states of Eastern Europe, which tax moral agency at the high rate of imprisonment, or exile, or death.

The cross-references, internal allusions, backward glances, and the teasing autobiographical games of hide-and-seek that fill the Zuckerman books reached a masterful climax in *The Counterlife* (1987), a kind of summa of Roth's preoccupations with the transactions between reality and art. The novel is structured around a series of postmodern turns in which the dead return to life, the living turn out to be dead, and, as Roth said in describing it, the contract between author and reader "gets torn up at the end of each chapter." According to *The Counterlife*, the Zuckerman who wrote *Carnovsky* was "in fact [sic]" the fictional creation of Peter Tarnapol, the professor-writer of *My Life as a Man* (1974). Inventing, explaining, revising, revising again, the novel resembles Roth's description of the geography of Kafka's story "The Burrow"; "an elaborate and ingeniously intricate system of underground chambers."

The trope of the "underground" life, with its echoes of Dostoyevsky as well as Kafka, has been a staple of modern literature, a metaphor of existence as well as a figure for the formal experiments of fiction and poetry. "The Man Who Lived Underground" (1944) is Richard Wright's version of the image, the tale of an innocent black man wrongly accused of murder. Wright's victim-hero Fred Daniels escapes from the police, plunges into Chicago's sewers, crawls into a basement, and Crusoe-like, harvests the necessities of a self-sufficient life beneath the city streets. He finds food, shelter, clothing, and a temporary haven affording the rudimentary autonomy denied to a black person in a racist society. In a parody of capitalist accumulation, he even papers the walls of his cellar with money stolen from a safe.

Although wrapped too tightly around the armature of its ideas, the story vividly exploits the suggestions of flight, exile, and marginality that its underground setting offers. Anticipating the more philosophical dread of Wright's *Outsider* (1953), "The Man Who Lived Underground" presents a central character whose innocence is tainted by a nameless, forgotten crime: "a gigantic shock that had left a haunting impression upon one's body which one could not forget or shake off, but which had been forgotten by the conscious mind, creating in one's life a state of eternal anxiety."

Fred Daniels embodies the existential anxiety of race; his "crime" is his color, and his predicament is at once exotic and merely typical. Wright's example in "The Man Who Lived Underground" was fruitfully bequeathed to other black writers, to Le Roi Jones (Imamu Amiri Baraka), for example, who translated the cosmology of medieval Christianity into contemporary racial terms in the subterranean phantasmagoria of *The System of Dante's Hell* (1963), and, more significantly, to Ralph Ellison.

Ellison started writing *Invisible Man* in 1945 and published the book in 1952. The novel's narrator is unnamed, a fact that emphasizes his anonymity as well as his invisibility in white America. All blacks, as Ellison later pointed out in his essay "Hidden Name and Complex Fate" (1964), bear "names originally possessed by those who owned our enslaved grandparents," and *Invisible Man* is an extended inquiry into the linkages among name and identity, possession and dispossession. "When I discover who I am, I'll be free," the novel's narrator declares at one point. He lives in a basement cave that he has saturated with light – 1,369 electric light bulbs, to be precise – and he plans to install more. The flood of light within which he lives and the associated images of veils, curtains, masks, blankness, and blindness, offer Ellison's annotations on white America's willful, destructive sightlessness. Ralph Waldo Emerson, for whom Ellison was named, had diagnosed America's besetting disease as opthalmia, a failure of vision; *Invisible Man* reformulates Emerson's transcendental complaint in the anguished and historically grounded terms of race. "I am an invisible man," the narrator announces in the book's opening lines, "invisible, understand, simply because people refuse to see me."

The novel's sprawl of episodes records the narrator's several initiations and his moments of expanding insight, and they also comprise an encyclopedia of American racial oppression. Ellison called the episodic, reiterative structure "boomeranging," a line of motion simultaneously forward and recursive. He also described the technique as a deliberate progression from naturalism through expressionism to surrealism. The individual scenes have their sources in oral literature and folklore, jazz, current events, literary precedent, nightmare, and autobiography. The "battle royal"; Jim Trueblood's tale of incest; the racially accommodating and blind Reverend Barbee; the Liberty Paint Company's "Optic White" (ten drops of black paint disappear into each vat of white); the lobotomizing box; the black nationalism of Ras the Exhorter and Destroyer; Brother Jack's glass eye – these are some of the characters and incidents that transform the narrator's youthful gullibility into sardonic racial wisdom.

When he published *Invisible Man*, Ellison had known Richard Wright for nearly twenty years. They had worked together in the thirties to raise funds for the Loyalists in the Spanish civil war, and it was Wright who introduced Ellison to both Malraux and Leadbelly, each of whom represented elements of Ellison's intellectual and artistic commitments. In a review of *Black Boy* (1945), Ellison praised Wright's autobiography for converting "the American Negro impulse toward self-annihilation and 'going-underground' into a will to confront the world, to evaluate his experience honestly and throw his findings unashamedly into the guilty conscience of America." Over time, however, Ellison's response to Wright modulated toward disaffection. In an exchange with Irving Howe nearly two decades after his admiring remarks on *Black Boy*'s toughmindedness, Ellison insisted on distancing himself from Wright's naturalism and his bleak conception of black life.

James Baldwin had preceded Ellison in acknowledging and disavowing Wright. In essays that he wrote in the forties and early fifties, Baldwin argued that *Native Son*, though it marked a significant turning point, opening fictional possibilities heretofore closed, nonetheless fails in the end because it chooses to rest in categories rather than in life. Bigger Thomas, Baldwin wrote, is "Uncle Tom's descendant, flesh of his flesh." The title Baldwin chose for his first collection of essays, *Notes of a Native Son* (1955), is an act at once of homage and resistance. Wright, like Baldwin's own father, was a powerful but smothering figure who must be opposed and overcome.

Baldwin was the oldest of nine children of a storefront preacher, a violent man who died in 1943, on the day his youngest child was born. A few hours after his death, Harlem exploded in a race riot; his funeral took place on his son James's nineteenth birthday. Long after his death, Baldwin's father remained the central force in his son's imaginative life: "He could be chilling in the pulpit and indescribably cruel in his personal life and he was certainly the most bitter man I have ever met." Relations between fathers and sons are the frequent subject of Baldwin's fiction, beginning with his first and perhaps best novel, *Go Tell It on the Mountain* (1953). Gabriel Grimes, the tyrannical stepfather who looms over that book's youthful hero, is a man consumed by bitterness and self-hatred. He is split almost in two by the conflict between his appetites and his fanatical religious vocation.

John Grimes, Gabriel's stepson and the novel's teenage main character, is growing up in a milieu thick with danger. He is threatened at home by his stepfather's punishing rage and outside by the injustices engendered by a racist society. Crowded with incident, the novel is organized in terms of a shrewdly paced alternation between past and present, and between John and the adults around him. John's awakening into sexuality and racial awareness leads him toward self-discovery, but the novel's final scenes show him seized by the convulsions of religious conversion. The forging of identity, this conclusion suggests, cannot be disentangled from the vexed issues of loyalty to family and heritage and race.

John Grimes's odyssey is eloquently told, in a rhetoric blended out of lyric, meditation, pulpit oratory, and street talk. In the subsequent thirty-five years of his career, until his death in 1988, Baldwin's language remained his chief gift. His later novels, among them *Giovanni's Room* (1956), *Another Country* (1962), and *Just Above My Head* (1979), were moderately audacious but emotionally unconvincing juxtapositions of race and art and homosexuality. His essays, on the other hand, constituted an accumulating body of brilliant polemic almost without parallel in American letters.

Baldwin, like Wright before him, lived for many years in France, and his essays bear witness to exile and increasing estrangement. Collected in such volumes as *Nobody Knows My Name* (1961) and *The Devil Finds Work* (1976), Baldwin's essays make up a passionate, unanswerable indictment of racial injustice. His pitiless insight into

FIGURE 179 ❧ Carl Mydans, photograph of James Baldwin (1962).

the profoundly institutional nature of American racism permanently changed the discourse between black and white, eliminating any further appeal to the naive half-truths of individual good deeds and good will. He wrote and spoke out of an unappeasable anger that deepened with age and expatriation (Figure 179).

In November 1962, on the eve of the one-hundredth anniversary of the Emancipation Proclamation, Baldwin published his "Letter from a Region of My Mind" in *The New Yorker*; the essay was a watershed, for Baldwin and for the nation's recognition of the real meaning of its racial dilemma. Baldwin's "Letter" excavates under oppressed black lives and spirits to the layers of hypocrisy that have concealed the consequences of racism from white understanding. Black children are taught "from the moment their eyes open on the world" to despise themselves because of their color, a lesson that all of society's institutions inculcate with relentless efficiency thereafter. The daily humiliations inflicted by white power on black powerlessness will never be defeated by trust in mere kindness. Neither the brutality of police nor the complacent, casual bigotry of "everyone else – housewives, taxi drivers, elevator boys, dishwashers, bartenders, lawyers, judges, doctors, and grocers" – will ever yield to civilized reason or "Christian love."

In America, it is a crime and a sin to be black, and the wages of that sin "were visible everywhere, in every wine-stained and urine-splashed hallway, in every clanging ambulance bell, in every scar on the faces of the pimps and their whores, . . . in every knife and pistol fight on the Avenue." America's past, "the Negro's past, of rope, fire, torture, castration, infanticide, rape," of fear by day and night, fear "as deep as the marrow of the bone," all of this, Baldwin warned, was leading the nation to an apocalyptic reckoning. When the "Letter" was published in book form, along with the "Letter to My Nephew," Baldwin chose as his title *The Fire Next Time* (1963).

Baldwin's prophetic rhetoric helped to crystallize an emerging black consciousness. The March on Washington in 1963, the civil rights and voting rights acts of 1964 and 1965, the riots of the late sixties, and the assassination of the Reverend Martin Luther King, Jr., were public signposts of a journey that was also inward, a long struggle accompanied and nourished by increasing evidence of cultural self-assertion. For example, the three dozen essays gathered together by Addison Gayle in *The Black Aesthetic* (1971) sought to define the distinctive racial identity of black literature and music. In Gayle's view, the hegemony of what he called "the white aesthetic" ensured the "strangulation" of black culture. A few of the essays he collected (those by Richard Wright and W. E. B. Du Bois, for example) had been written earlier in the century, but most were contemporary efforts to forge an authentic artistic position out of anger, black nationalism, and a unanimously shared refusal to sunder art from politics. "The Black Arts Movement," Larry Neal wrote, "is radically opposed to any concept of the artist that alienates him from his community." Unity with black people would require separate myths and icons, and separation as well from the white critical mainstream. As a corollary, these acts of dissociation brought accusations of accommodation against black writers, principally Ellison, who had found substantial white approval.

Pitched in a lower key, the debate over the black aesthetic has continued through the seventies and eighties, often in conjunction with other arguments among contending literary theories. Mutually inspiriting acts of recovery and innovation have sustained a postwar black literary renaissance.

The abundant accomplishment of black women, including Margaret Walker, Paule Marshall, Mari Evans, Nikki Giovanni, and Gayl Jones, has formed a principal chapter in the collective literary enterprise. Alice Walker's journey to Florida in search of Zora Neale Hurston's grave might serve as a symbolic summary for the commitment these writers shared, to reclaim a legacy from the silences of official histories.

Walker is the daughter of Georgia sharecroppers. She grew up in the knowledge of the differences that caste, color, and gender make. As a child, she lived near the home of Flannery O'Connor, whose work she has always admired, but a visit to O'Connor's house merely confirmed the distance between aesthetic accomplishment and political reality. "Standing there knocking on Flannery O'Connor's door," Walker writes, "I do not think of her illness, her magnificent work in spite of it; I think: it all comes back to houses. To how people live. There are rich people who own houses to live in and poor people who do not. And this is wrong."

The "Womanist" essays that Walker collected in the volume *In Search of Our Mothers' Gardens* (1983) celebrate the generations of female creativity and endurance, the cooking, gardening, and quilting, whose beauty is tied to human use. The obligation to preserve the stories she has heard, and with them the oral tradition they come from, has formed one of the axioms of her fiction and essays. She has traced the origins of *The Color Purple* (1982) to Celie's voice and described the writing of the novel as an act of obedience to the demands of that voice (Figure 180).

The novel, written as a series of letters, pays tribute in its form to the literary mode in which, historically, women most often expressed themselves. The letters record the untranslated experiences of Celie's oppression and liberation. Sexually abused by a man who may be her father, the fourteen-year-old Celie writes to God. Eventually she will find the comradeship she needs in women, in the letters she writes to her sister Nettie, and in her love for Shug Avery, her husband's mistress. Her letters, which begin in bewilderment and rise toward affirmation, serve as an emblem and an instrument of identity.

"Black people's grace," Toni Morrison has said, "has been what they do with language." Much black writing declares its fidelity to speech; it aspires, in Morrison's phrase, "to be both print and oral literature." At the core of Morrison's own achievement lies a conception of shared language as the seal of community. Stories that are handed down are also the avenue to the past, the realm of ancestors. Her first novel, *The Bluest Eye* (1970), identified her communal concerns with almost allegorical clarity. In the book's opening pages, the squalor that contaminates Pecola Breedlove's adolescent life is methodically contrasted to the white prosperity that teases her from the pages of Dick and Jane schoolbooks. Mother, Father, Dick, and Jane live in a green and white house with a happy cat; Mother smiles, Father laughs. Pecola, raped by her father, lives in a festering slum that beats the lesson of self-hatred into all its victims. Her hopeless desire for blue eyes enacts her choice of criteria and categories that efface her humanity. Her final madness is a moving image of fundamental despair: "Elbows bent, hands on shoulders, she flailed her arms like a bird in an eternal, grotesquely futile effort to fly. Beating the air, a winged but grounded bird, intent on the blue void it could not reach – could not even see – but which filled the valleys of the wind."

FIGURE 180 ❧ Alice Walker (1984).

FIGURE 181 ⪩ Toni Morrison (1985).

Pecola's yearning toward flight reverberates in Morrison's later novels, in particular *Song of Solomon* (1977), which is centered on the ancient fable of a flying African. The links between flight and identity are proposed in the book's epigraph, "The fathers may soar / And the children may know their names," but the full significance of the correlation is only gradually disclosed, at the end of a many-layered, multigenerational tale. Macon Dead, Jr., ("Milkman") journeys from north to south in pursuit of his origins, his maturity, his place in the community. His discoveries are hard won, and the novel's intricate structure of narrative and symbol reflects the difficulties of unearthing truth. Neither linear logic nor conventional causality is adequate to the task of explanation. The abundantly realized episodes have roots, by turns, in the real and the supernatural. Both realms, as they are rendered in the amplitude of Morrison's prose, are equally plausible, and equally astonishing (Figure 181).

By breaching the solid-seeming walls that separate the factual and the fantastic, Morrison's novels gain a vantage point from which the extremity bequeathed by history can be viewed whole and mastered. *Beloved* (1987) originated in such extremity, in the true story of a black woman who escaped from slavery with her four children in 1855. Faced with recapture, Margaret Garner (Sethe, in the novel) tried to murder her children and succeeded in killing her baby daughter with a handsaw. Death is a lesser horror than slavery.

The novel takes place in 1873, after Sethe's release from jail. She shares her small house with her daughter's ghost, who appears as a pool of red and undulating light, "not evil, just sad."

Beloved is, among other things, a remorseless recreation of the casual and daily barbarism of slavery. One episode after another gives substance to the systematized brutality that was intended to deny slaves any portion of rights and dignity. A slavetracker explains that a recaptured runaway was liable to do "disbelievable things" and had to be guarded with care: "Leave the tying to another. Otherwise you ended up killing what you were paid to bring back alive. Unlike a snake or a bear, a dead nigger could not be skinned for profit and was not worth his own dead weight in coin." The numbing tonelessness of this speech is perhaps more effective than scenes of cruelty themselves in documenting the moral abyss from which Sethe saved her child. Paul D., a former slave from Sweet Home, the same Kentucky plantation where Sethe had lived, hears Sethe's story and decides, correctly, that "to love anything that much was dangerous."

The dangers of such love, and the challenges of the reality it confronts, are subjects that demand an extraordinary array of narrative devices and modes. *Beloved* is a book made up of dreams, myth, folktale, lyric, and a fully actualized American reality. History remains Morrison's inescapable starting point, but history is revealed as nightmare, demanding a narrative technique that can accommodate the hard surfaces of naturalistic actuality and a universe of experience that transcends nature. In effect, *Beloved* creates its own genre and in doing so encapsulates many of the multiform tendencies of postwar fiction.

History," Mailer wrote in *St. George and the Godfather* (1972), "has moved from a narrative line to a topological warp." The pressures of history and of contemporary politics have led, on the one hand, toward a range of technical innovations that pushed the novel's form far from conventional definitions and, on the other hand, toward a flourishing nonfiction, the result of a compact that placed prose at the service of fact. The diversity of the work drove critics to the expedient of multiplied categories, a frank confession that analysis was not keeping pace with fictional creativity. Popular pigeonholes included "metafiction," "transfiction," "minimalism," "the literature of exhaustion," "neorealism," "new journalism," "factions," and the ubiquitous "postmodernism."

Much of the experimenting of the postwar years had been anticipated – and some was directly influenced – by the earlier work of Henry Miller. *Tropic of Cancer*, published in Paris in 1934, was banned in the United States until 1961, and its notoriety added to its stature as a major text in the aesthetic and sexual revolutions of the twentieth century. Miller claimed that he used obscenity to struggle against inertia, and he wrote, near the beginning of *Tropic of Cancer*, that the only thing that interested him was the "recording of all that which is omitted in books." Miller conceived of his book as an antibook, a conception that impelled his lyrically clinical accounts of sexual action and his hostility to the disciplines of conventional fiction. Body, bed, room, street, and city are all rendered with accomplished journalistic vigor, but all are absorbed in the surrealist monodrama of Miller's fictionalized confession. Starting as a radical from Brooklyn, Miller moved through an endless succession of odd jobs and disappointments that merely confirmed his rejection of America and its values. In his case, expatriation was a vocation, a considered act of permanent disaffiliation from the land he called, in the title of another book, *The Air-conditioned Nightmare* (1945).

Miller's postwar heirs included Kerouac and the prophets of the urban and sexual underground, among them John Rechy, in *City of Night* (1963); Hubert Selby, in *Last Exit to Brooklyn* (1964); Norman Mailer, in his more scabrous and self-parading moods: and William S. Burroughs. Burroughs's *Naked Lunch* (1959) retailed an exclamatory, paranoid fantasy, a bad dream in which heroin addiction is at once the graphic subject and the metaphor for a system of total control. Burroughs's dadaist "cut-up" or "fold-in" method of storytelling works against story by turning narrative into an aleatory collaboration with the reader. *Naked Lunch* and its sequels *The Soft Machine* (1961), *The Ticket That Exploded* (1962), and especially *Nova Express* (1964), carried the Beat indictment of American mores to the avant-garde frontier. At the same time, the hatred and self-hatred of these books repeatedly spill over into mechanical efforts to overtop shock with shock. Perhaps by design, pornography becomes detached from nerve endings and becomes, at last, boring. In retrospect, Burroughs's noisy vulgarity and willed wildness seem quite touchingly out of date, less radical than histrionic.

More significant explorations into literary form were undertaken by Vladimir Nabokov, an exile from the Russian Revolution who emigrated to the United States in 1940 and whose first novels were written in Russian and German. Using parody, multilingual puns, fictitious scholarly citations, and elaborate cross-reference as his instruments, Nabokov was at once fiction's closest student and its subversive antagonist. A recognized entomologist and butterfly collector, he focused the lens of a prodigious attention on the nature of fictionality itself and scrutinized the problematic relationship of words to reality.

Everything in Nabokov's fiction is doubled and repeated and then denied and negated, suggesting at once the power of fictional representation and its patent artifice. Artifice, indeed, is Nabokov's subject. His complexly allusive novels have the demanding structures of well-made acrostics or puzzles. *Lolita* (1955), the seriocomic saga of middle-aged Humbert Humbert's infatuation with a young girl, provoked a scandal when it was published, but the erotic center of the book is actually to be found in its textuality rather than in sex. In *Lolita*, as in the more densely ambitious *Pale Fire* (1962) and *Ada* (1969), Nabokov lavishes his invention on the idea of invention, not only questioning the power of language to deliver a reliable report of the world but raising doubts about the alleged stability of the world outside of novels as well. A good deal of nostalgia coexists with Nabokov's ironic fabulations. He was, as the narrator of *Pnin* (1957) says, "battered and stunned by thirty-five years of homelessness." His metaphysical disquiet had its biographical sources in the house and property and homeland he had lost as a child and to which he knew he would never return. At the same time, Nabokov's views rhymed with the surrounding turmoil of the sixties and seventies. His opinions, and his fiction, were part of a widening assault on received aesthetic certitudes.

The French theoretician Roland Barthes wrote an essay entitled "The Death of the Author" (1968), and the American writer Ronald

Sukenick carried the metaphor several steps farther in his novella "The Death of the Novel" (1969). In Sukenick's catalog of absences "reality doesn't exist, time doesn't exist, personality doesn't exist." God, the omniscient author, has died and taken all the plots with him. These "antiassumptions," as they might be called, have engendered a generation of experiments. Robert Coover's *Origin of the Brunists* (1965), William Gass's *In the Heart of the Heart of the Country* (1968), John Barth's *Giles Goat-Boy* (1966), and Donald Barthelme's *Dead Father* (1975) challenged each of the traditional elements of fiction, replacing authority with skepticism, embracing self-parody, and putting signification at the service of its own denial. Where modernism had appealed to the artist to impose coherence on a fractured or wasted landscape, postmodernism demurred from that high task and retreated into a hundred feints and dodges. In place of modernism's aspiration to create the conscience of a people, postmodernism embraced its own marginality. Fiction, like the world that it refused to reflect, represent, subsume, redeem, or even deny, was lost in the funhouse. What is outside the funhouse often seems worse.

Joseph Heller's *Catch–22* (1961) enshrined the inexplicable power and the logic-defying logic that forbid genuine communication in technologyland's total institutions. Which is to say that Heller's novel, ostensibly a black-comedy routine about the lunacy of World War II, is in fact a complaint against the war's legacies of universal control and coercion. Catch–22: any bomber pilot certified as insane is excused from further bombing missions, but anyone who seeks to be excused must be sane and must therefore keep flying. "That's some catch, that Catch–22," says Yossarian, the book's hero, with real respect in his voice. Not especially daring in its techniques, *Catch–22* reached millions of readers with its paranoid unmasking of history as a manipulable commodity. American participation in the Vietnam War began in earnest just two years after Heller's novel was published, and the book seemed a foretelling of what citizens would slowly conclude about their government's capacity for deception and cynicism.

Heller's humor had a nihilist point. Kurt Vonnegut, Jr., on the other hand, has toyed with apocalypse but has always tried to finesse Armageddon with a punch line. Vonnegut, a young prisoner of war who survived the Allied fire bombing of Dresden, fully earned his opinion that history is a pulverizing conspiracy, but he has consistently trivialized his convictions by retreating into the comfort of moral bromides and well-rehearsed fictional formulas. To attribute the design of earthly history to creatures on the planet Tralfamadore, for example, as Vonnegut has in several novels, is to offer a pulp-fiction answer to a serious question. As Vonnegut himself said, at about the time he published *Breakfast of Champions* (1973): "I've gotten into the joke business." His arch cleverness flits on the surface of ideas. His laconic, telegraphic style creates books that are clusterings of "tiny little chips; and each chip is a joke." So it goes.

The bad dreams that Vonnegut dissembles have been for four decades the home ground of John Hawkes's much more disturbing fictions. Hawkes has said that he began writing on the assumption that the true enemies of fiction were "plot, character, setting, and theme." Out of these denials he has furnished a violent, grotesque fictional world whose only constant seems to be fear. His first novel, *The Cannibal* (1949), broods over a devastated postwar Germany. It is a land whose future is encoded in the illegible scrawls of American military-intelligence communiques. Illegibility becomes a metaphor for the novel's formal process, its deliberate distortion of daylit reality, and its transformation of history into hallucination. The kaiser (Hitler) and new dictator (Zizendorf) merge in a vision of eternally recurring fascism.

Hawkes's later work has extended the territory of nightmare – to the American West, Italy, England, and an island in the Atlantic – but the wounded psychic landscape remains essentially unchanged. The horrific images that Hawkes invents externalize the gothic derangements of lives in which desire and disgust are permanently entangled. *The Lime Twig* (1961) is a multivoiced parable of love's inevitable defeat by violence and death. Three later books – *The Blood Oranges* (1971), *Death, Sleep & the Traveler* (1974), and *Travesties* (1976) – were conceived as a "triad" addressed to sex and the imagination. They sharpen the terms of Hawkes's investigation of modern darkness, presenting a triptych in which orgasm, death, and art are linked in ceaseless variations.

Hawkes's extremity is personal, but the implications of his work can be generalized. The myriad strategies that he and other writers devised to dismantle fiction's traditional mimetic function sprang from a suspicion that the old conventions were used up. John Barth, in an essay that gained wide and influential circulation, spoke of "The Literature of Exhaustion" (1967). He meant, by this much-quoted phrase, that the received genres and forms, after centuries of honorable service, could no longer be expected to yield significance. The writer's job, under such circumstances, was to reinvent the fundamental terms of perception and literary discourse. Appropriately, the opening novella of Barth's *Chimera* (1972) journeys back to "the springs of narrative," the tales of Scheherazade. *The 1001 Nights*, as Barth's narrator observes, is not only the story of Scheherazade; it is also "the story of the story of her stories." Barth's own novels and tales are an anthology of experiments, each of them also telling its own story. *The Sot-Weed Factor* (1960) is a brilliant invented history of seventeenth-century Maryland, in which each character takes on a dizzying number of disguises; *Giles Goat-Boy, or the Revised New Syllabus* (1966) is a fictive book of revelation, in which a goat-man, child of a computer, enacts an elaborate satire on the machinery and politics of contemporary America.

In *Letters* (1979), Barth offered an encapsulation of his central preoccupation, not with story but with storytelling. The book is an encyclopedia of devices, including multiple narrators, parody and pastiche, coded messages, layered meanings, suspense that is often unresolved, texts within texts, intricate doublings, patterns of allusion, elaborate self-quotation, and intertextual reference. The labyrinthine mazes of Barth's fictions lead inexorably toward their own inwardness, toward resolutions that vanish as they are grasped and meanings that prove chimerical. Facts themselves evade apprehension or prove fantastic. Refracted through the lens of a consuming self-consciousness, Barth's novels incorporate libraries of history and myth, the trove of unreliable documents and fables that document, in the end, only the unreliability of knowledge.

Barth's prolifically unfolding fictions send one set of signals across the chasm that separates language from its referential conventions. Quite different inferences from similar premises are contained in the radical eliminations of Donald Barthelme's minimalism. The narrator of Barthelme's "Dolt" says that "endings are elusive, middles are nowhere to be found, but worst of all is to begin, to begin, to begin." So much for plot. And the questions and answers of "The Explanation" include the following exchange, which does away with description and setting:

Q: Are you bored with the question-and-answer form?
A: I am bored with it but I realize that it permits many valuable
   omissions: what kind of day it is, what I'm wearing, what
   I'm thinking.

The self evaporates in this world, leaving behind traces of language like the shards and hieroglyphs of an alien and unknowable
civilization.

The staccato rhythms, banished transitions, and bizarre juxtapositions are sometimes merely coy; the tired formulas and cant
phrases Barthelme likes to use sometimes remain tired formulas.
More often, however, they succeed in creating funny and frightening
images, bits and pieces of broken mirror in which contemporary
anxiety is reflected. "Fragments," Barthelme has written, "are the
only forms I trust." Along with its thoroughly ironizing language,
Barthelme's fragments sometimes include visual images such as black
boxes, large-type slogans, copies of old woodcuts: the postmodern
legacy of modernist collage. Instead of narrative, Barthelme arranges
his sentences and nonsentences in mosaics, analogs for the mysteries
that lurk underneath the clichés of modern life: "This Paraguay is
not the Paraguay that exists on our maps" (Figure 182).

Nor are Joan Didion's California (or Miami, or El Salvador) the
places on ordinary maps. "All I knew," Didion wrote in *The White
Album* (1979), "was what I saw: flash pictures in variable sequence,
images with no 'meaning' beyond their temporary arrangement."
Didion began as the chronicler of California's freaks, freeways, rock
concerts, and mass murderers, a self-nominated descendant of Nathanael West who discovered that narrative line had become a
casualty of contemporary pace and violence. The images simply
follow one another: "not a movie, but a cutting-room experience."
Whether she travels to war-ravaged Central America or to the re-
made Miami of the 1980s, Didion's subject has been the simultaneous, and probably interdependent, deterioration of self and society. Her anecdotes and stories are often apocalyptic parables,
declaring her fear of personal and national breakdown. In some
mysterious but literal sense, the stress that will someday tear open
California at its fault lines and the stress of surviving in the eddies
of late twentieth-century America are the same.

Raymond Carver, Bobbie Ann Mason, and Ann Beattie have

affinities with Didion, but their focus has generally been closer and their restraint more pronounced. Carver referred to his desire "to write about commonplace things and objects using commonplace but precise language, and to endow these things – a chair, a window curtain, a fork, a stone, a woman's earring – with immense, even startling power." The echo of transcendentalism in this manifesto is ironic, since Carver's revelations are more usually of pain and loss than hope. Carver's fictional world is narrow and airless, defined by absences that mirror the dislocated lives and inarticulacies of his characters. His subject is often marriage, and his marriages are usually troubled or finished. The men and women in his stories huddle together in an intimacy that leaves them essentially untouched, waiting for the good luck that does not come. Surprises are few, and disruptive.

The disruption in Bobbie Ann Mason's stories are traceable to the relentless pressures that change brings to the working-class people of rural Kentucky. Stable but straitened lives are tempted and threatened by the novelties pumped into country homes by the

Tolstoy's coat

FIGURE 182 ❧
Illustration from Donald Barthelme's "At the Tolstoy Museum."

media each day. Describing herself as an exile from her rural setting, Mason is also its advocate. She gives voice to the men and women whose dialect measures the distance between their backwater anonymity and the glitter that television and the movies promise. In "Detroit Skyline, 1949," which was included in Mason's first collection, *Shiloh and Other Stories* (1982), a woman from western Kentucky takes her young daughter to Detroit so that she can see the tall buildings. The daughter's anticipation can stand for the yearning that many of Mason's characters feel: "I couldn't sleep for thinking about Detroit. Mama had tried in vain to show me how high the buildings were, pointing at the straight horizon beyond the cornfields. I had the impression they towered halfway to the moon."

Mason's nonfiction includes a book called *The Girl Sleuth: A Feminist Guide to the Bobbsey Twins, Nancy Drew, and Their Sisters* (1975). One of Raymond Carver's most famous stories, "Cathedral," tells of a man's effort to describe a cathedral for his wife's blind friend, who uses his fingers to sense a building he has never seen. Both works are reminders that many postwar writers, whether minimalist or expansive in technique, have inhabited the common ground of a fascination with detection, codes, deciphering, and conspiracy. *The Recognitions* (1955), for example, is William Gaddis's massive meditation on forgery in life and in art, and on the undeniable centrality of deceit and disguise to all aesthetic and social relations, indeed to perception itself. Two decades later, in *JR* (1975), Gaddis created hundreds of pages of dialogue, often opaque and usually interrupted, to expose the links between wealth and conspiracy in America.

There is abundant good reason for fiction's suspicious interest in conspiracy, a motif which reached a kind of apotheosis in the three novels of Thomas Pynchon. Filled with warehouses of a rampant consumer culture's junk, Pynchon's fiction obsessively tests the hypothesis that every plastic spoon, canned-soup label, television commercial, postage stamp, windshield decal, or spray-painted wall may be an element in a message, a glimpse of the fathomless teleologies of the unidentified Others who control humanity's destiny. But Pynchon admits the counterhypothesis, too, as equally plausible: that his seekers may be the hallucinating victims of their own fears. Each of them may be – as Oedipa Maas puts it, almost lyrically, in

The Crying of Lot 49 (1966) – a "true paranoid for whom all is organized in spheres joyful or threatening about the central pulse of himself."

The paths that lead through contemporary clutter in Pynchon's books trace plots of breathtaking complexity. Plot, after all, in the most reductive, sinister, and totalizing sense, may be what the world is all about. The novelistic structures are deliberately kaleidoscopic and chaotic, defying final clarity, but they continually intersect, overlap, even merge. Events, though they are tied to historical data (Fashoda, World War II, the alligators infesting the sewers of New York City), also float in a surreal miasma beyond the grasp of academic explanation. In *V.* (1963), everything depends on a quest that may be mad. V. may or may not be alive, may or may not have ever lived, may or may not have played a role in a great conspiracy. Clues outnumber, overwhelm meaning. V. is linked to Victoria Wren, Veronica Manganese, Valletta, the capital of Malta, the Edenic Vheissu, and more.

Gravity's Rainbow (1973) opens with the scream of a V-2 rocket approaching London in the last days of World War II, which precipitates a bewildering search. The object of the quest is called, in the novel's linguistic metaphor for its own doubts, "the Real Text," which is never found or proved to exist. With its seven hundred sixty pages, its four hundred or so characters, its uncountable allusions and quotations, its technical scientific references, and its vast historical reach, *Gravity's Rainbow* deepens the fictional debate between meaning and indeterminacy and brings to a climax Pynchon's fascination with the encroachments of technology upon the spirit. The phallic V-2 rocket, arcing across the rainbow commanded by gravity, remains the inescapable, prophetic, fatal fact.

As always in Pynchon's work, evidence of a master plan is visible everywhere, hints of a plan to reduce all of organic life to zero, but certitude remains tantalizingly out of reach. The search for the proof of conspiracy becomes a harrowing but exhilarating forced march into a fictional landscape of disintegration and counterfeit. The possibility of a counterforce is raised but ultimately abandoned as the V-2 finishes its deadly business on the novel's last page.

John Barth once said that "reality is a nice place to visit but you wouldn't want to live there, and literature never did, very long." This is amusing, and even useful, as a comment on some versions of experimental fiction, including Barth's. On the other hand, a good many novelists, among them John Irving, E. L. Doctorow, Joyce Carol Oates, John Wideman, Robert Stone, Tim O'Brien, and Cynthia Ozick, whose work in other respects has little in common, express a different point of view. These writers make calculated use of postmodernism's self-referential and epistemologically subversive maneuvers but do so on behalf of a more direct engagement with reality and its facts. Indeed, a major literary phenomenon of the postwar period has been the emergence and flourishing of several nonfictional genres.

While it comprises a response to contemporary circumstances, recent nonfiction is also heir to a long line of descent, a lineage that reaches from the artist-explorers of the eighteenth and nineteenth centuries to the muckraking of turn-of-the-century reformers, the photojournalism of the thirties, and the battlefield dispatches of generations of war correspondents. What has differentiated the new nonfiction has been its generic self-consciousness, the conviction, among at least some of its practitioners, that adherence to fact would produce a literature that could replace a wornout fiction. Tom Wolfe, mandarin of the movement, insisted that the new journalism would supply what novels could not. Borrowing and adapting whatever fictional technique he found congenial, Wolfe created reportage out of his own observations and put himself and his self-regarding, ironic, extravagant rhetoric in the privileged center of attention. In two decades of writing, from his Day-Glo chronicles of Ken Kesey's Merry Pranksters in *The Electric Kool-Aid Acid Test* (1968), through dissenting essays on modern painting and architecture, to the urban paranoia of his first novel, *The Bonfire of the Vanities* (1988), Wolfe has been a mordant, supremely smug critic of novelty in culture and of the allegedly Left-leaning politics of establishment intellectuals.

The postwar flourishing of nonfiction has included several versions of personal history that have virtually redefined the autobiographical genre. Some of the most significant instances have been the testaments of women and persons of color, committed to making their different voices heard. In these books, identity and discourse have been simultaneously reenvisioned. *The Autobiography of Malcolm X* (1964), for example, edited by Alex Haley, transforms several familiar literary modes, including the edifying tales of self-improvement that have filled so many American volumes. Malcolm's journey was ideological rather than entrepreneurial, from the trammels of crime and self-hatred to the liberation bequeathed by self-knowledge. Born Malcolm Little, his life until he discovered Islam was a picaresque and incoherent sequence of episodes leading to theft and prison. His birth into the new identity of Malcolm X did not secure him either from uncertainty or from violence – he predicted his own assassination – but it conferred an almost messianic sense of purpose, firing the eloquence that made him one of the principal spokesmen for an aroused resistance. Malcolm's story remains a key text in any listing of postwar black autobiography, a major collective achievement that includes Maya Angelou's *I Know Why the Caged Bird Sings* (1969), George Jackson's *Soledad Brother* (1970), Angela Davis's *Autobiography* (1974), and even Eldridge Cleaver's inflamed, misogynist *Soul on Ice* (1968).

Malcolm's evolution was evidence of a large-scale postwar sifting and appraisal of America's traditional claims. In the autobiographical novel *Bless Me, Ultima* (1972), the Chicano writer Rudolfo A. Anaya also dramatizes the conflict over cultures out of which personal identity is formed. Myths are central to Anaya, since they provide vessels within which the past can be contained. From Ultima, a healer and teacher, Anaya's hero Antonio learns to build strength on the bedrock of tradition and continuity.

The lore and wisdom of "old ones" is also celebrated in the work of Leslie Marmon Silko, whose ancestry is a mixture of Pueblo Indian, Mexican, and white. Silko has traced the source of her fiction to the stories her grandmother told her. Her memories of that telling and listening have inspired her commitment to honor the oral tradition in her writing. Her novel *Ceremony* (1978) combines realistic narrative with the songs and legends of Indian tradition to tell the story of an Indian veteran of World War II, spiritually devastated by the death of his half-brother and by the war, who must come to terms with his heritage and its rites before he can become whole and reenter the world.

A quite different but equally illuminating record of the struggle between past and present can be found in Maxine Hong Kingston's *Woman Warrior: Memoirs of a Girlhood among Ghosts* (1976). The ghosts are the Americans and their machines, among whom Kingston has grown up: Taxi Ghosts, Bus Ghosts, Police Ghosts, Fire

Ghosts, Meter Reader Ghosts, Tree Trimming Ghosts, Five-and-Dime Ghosts. "Once upon a time," Kingston writes, "the world was so thick with ghosts, I could hardly breathe; I could hardly walk, limping my way around the White Ghosts and their cars." But the ghosts are also the customs and stories of China, a legacy of pain and beauty that Kingston receives from her mother's years of "talk-story." America, with its opportunities but its indifference to spirit, is her future, while China, which makes room for magic but values girl-children at nothing, is her past.

The Woman Warrior weaves together the old tales with contemporary experience, finding in each the metaphor that clarifies the other. Kingston defies her mother's prohibitions and rejects her self-denying superstitions, but she also engages in an act of piety by preserving and writing down her mother's stories and life. The book effectively dissolves the line between fiction and nonfiction.

The term "nonfiction novel" might have been invented in connection with any number of postwar books. In fact, the phrase originated with Truman Capote, who used it as a subtitle for *In Cold Blood* (1965). Capote, who had specialized in the melancholy southern gothic of *Other Voices, Other Rooms* (1948) and the social comedy of *Breakfast at Tiffany's* (1958), joined the sixties by reporting on a specific act of violence, the savage murder of a Kansas farm family by a pair of rootless psychopaths. Though it is soiled by Capote's misplaced sympathies, *In Cold Blood* is an intermittently impressive assemblage of masses of information, which are used to build a naturalist case study in the hidden sources of gratuitous brutality. The murders which Perry Smith and Richard Hickock commit encapsulate lives twisted by insult, failure, and self-loathing.

Fifteen years after it was published, *In Cold Blood* was inevitably compared to a bigger and more significant book, Norman Mailer's *The Executioner's Song* (1979). Mailer described his recreation of Gary Gilmore's crimes and death as "A True Life Novel." The book is a slab of prose, one thousand pages of toneless, featureless writing, patched together from interview transcripts, trial records, and newspaper stories. Banality and grotesque revelation merge into each other in literally thousands of separate paragraph-units. Mailer's long fascination with existential outlaws compelled him to hope that Gilmore was more than a motiveless hoodlum, that he might in fact be a protagonist entitled to all the attention he receives in this book. Gilmore ought to be the dark descendant of the hipster, the defier of "square" morality whose heroic nonconformity Mailer once praised in a dozen stories and articles, beginning with the notorious essay "The White Negro" in the late fifties. Such overreaching propositions collapse under the inert weight of Gilmore's meager awfulness. What remains is Mailer's immense journalistic effort and his apparent complicity in packaging and selling Gilmore to the several media.

Despite his rigorous refusal of almost every ordinary novelistic opportunity in the book, the central figure in *The Executioner's Song*, as always in Mailer's work, is Mailer: choosing, selecting, editing, brooding, writing. Decades earlier, in *Advertisements for Myself* (1959), he had committed himself to making "a revolution in the consciousness of our time." That romantic ambition proved untenable for Mailer's fiction, tempting him into one novelistic cul-de-sac after another, from *The Deer Park* (1955) to *Ancient Evenings* (1983). But Mailer's self-appointed role as the scribe and perhaps the agent of apocalypse has given significance to his nonfiction, urging him to chronicle the major political stories of the postwar era.

Mailer's novels are redolent with a fear that masquerades as strut. His tiresomely thrusting, dominating, macho heroes disclose a contempt for women almost luminous in its single-mindedness. Sergius O'Shaughnessy and the murderous Rojack of *An American Dream* (1965) are figures of fantasy, to be sure, but a villainous fantasy nonetheless. Ironically, the revolution intimated in Mailer's novels has been mainly a rearguard action, a stand against the fundamental upheavals in ideology and especially in sexual attitudes, that have marked the postwar years.

His books of reporting, on the other hand, occupy a space less confined by the solipsistic geometry that constrains his fiction. If he has trouble inventing figures commensurate with contemporary absurdity, he has no trouble finding them in each day's headlines.

His finest prose takes shape at the intersection of public event and inner response. He has been too eager a participant, too oracular an explainer, and he has been too infatuated with theories of conspiracy. With all that granted, his indefatigable paranoia has given his observation an uncommon tenacity.

Mailer's books on the political conventions of 1968 and 1972 remain the necessary guide to the two most interesting presidential seasons of the past forty years. In *Miami and the Siege of Chicago* (1969) and *St. George and the Godfather* (1972), a thousand engrossing details cohere in the scripts of modern morality plays. *Of a Fire on the Moon* (1970) ponders the fusion of potency and passivity that traps the astronauts within their life-supporting capsules. The brute power of unshielded flesh is the subject of *The Fight* (1975), a long essay on the title bout between Muhammad Ali and George Forman in Zaire.

Aside from *The Executioner's Song*, Mailer's major work of reporting remains *The Armies of the Night* (1968). Subtitled "History as a Novel / The Novel as History," the book recreates the March on the Pentagon that took place in late October 1967, one of the major public protests against the Vietnam War. Like most of Mailer's work, indeed like most significant postwar literature, the book is a meditation on power: the concentration of power in bad hands, and the powerlessness of the opposition. The ragtag coalition marching against the war has nothing to throw into the battle but truth and its own rage. Mailer – heckler, cheerleader, spokesman, observer – knows how little the truth avails against the Pentagon's fortress walls: "the symbol, the embodiment, no, call it the true and high church of the military-industrial complex, the Pentagon, blind five-sided eye of a subtle oppression which had come to America out of the very air of the century... greedy stingy dumb valve of the worst of the Wasp heart" (Figure 183).

Mailer has sought new forms because he believes that late twentieth-century life is qualitatively different, and he believes as well that experience and expression are umbilically linked. Because he sees himself as the indispensable diagnostician of the contemporary, he desperately wants his work to matter. His frantic, splintered life has that single motive. Consequently, his actions as a public figure are not diversions. His clowning, his loopy preachments about contraception, cancer, and reincarnation, his ill-conceived

films, his comically strenuous campaign for mayor of New York City (and, in fairness, one should add, his useful presidency of the writers' organization PEN and his tireless prosecution of censorship around the world) have the same sources as his novels and journalism. His career is an instance of what he once called the perpetual transit of the modern ego "from the tower to the dungeon and back again." For over four decades, he has been searching for a style that might suit the gargantuan scale of contemporary confusion. His missteps are themselves instructive (Figure 184).

The interplay between imagined and historical events has served as the wellspring for much recent fiction, including such commercially successful entertainments as E. L. Doctorow's *Ragtime* (1975) and *World's Fair* (1986) and Gore Vidal's multivolume revisionist history of the United States, his smirking revenge on two hundred years of America. Paul Theroux, in *The Great Railway Bazaar*

FIGURE 183 ❧ Fred McDarrah, *The March on the Pentagon* (1967). (*Left to right*) Marcus Raskin, Noam Chomsky, Norman Mailer, Robert Lowell, Sidney Lens, Dwight McDonald.

(1975), helped to rediscover the travelogue and directed that once-harmless genre into the more lurid corners of a troubled, postimperial American psyche.

Several of Joyce Carol Oates's novels represent a formidable effort to negotiate between fictional form and the requirements of an impinging reality. In an essay on modern fiction, Oates has rebuked the "stubbornly monastic" vision of Henry James and Virginia Woolf and has defined her allegiances in terms of social engagement. After James and Woolf, she wrote, "after the experiments of the mind's dissection of itself and its dissociation from the body, perhaps we are ready to rediscover the world."

One of Oates's first acts of rediscovery, and still one of her most powerful, was the novel *them* (1969). An author's note printed as preface to the book announces that "this is a work of history in fictional form." The novel, Oates claimed, is based directly upon the life, and often upon the verbatim remarks, of the woman who appears in the book as "Maureen Wendall," a student in one of the

FIGURE 184 🗫 Norman Mailer (1969). Mailer speaks to the press during his 1969 campaign for mayor of New York City.

classes Oates taught at the University of Detroit in the 1960s. The lives recounted in *them* are deadened by violence and violation, naturalist case studies retrieved like sad mementos from the larger chaos of a disintegrating Detroit. Oates's acute description of Flannery O'Connor's world can serve as a summation of her own as well: it is a "primitive landscape" in which there is "nothing to be recognized – there is only an experience to be suffered." The novel includes two letters from "Maureen Wendall," an exceptional act of candor and courage, since the letters are a cry of anguish that tie Maureen's devastated life to her experience in Oates's class: "You failed me. You flunked me out of school" (Figure 185).

Oates has said that she writes "in flurries." Aside from documenting her versatility and scope, her fifty or so books put exceptions in the way of most generalizations. She has occasionally provided her own version of her work in comments that reaffirm her sense of temporal and societal connection. "I have tried to give a shape," she has written, "to certain obsessions of mid-century Americans – a confusion of love and money, of the categories of public and private experience, of the demonic urge I sense all around me, an

FIGURE 185 ❧ Jerry Bauer, photograph of Joyce Carol Oates (n.d.).

urge to violence as the answer to all problems, an urge to self-annihilation, suicide, the ultimate experience and the ultimate surrender."

Among other valuable suggestions, this comment documents the source of the ubiquitous violence in Oates's work. She has complained that the repeated questions about the violence she narrates are "always insulting, always ignorant, always sexist." In her own view of it, her violence is quite simply a faithful transcript of the time's temper. Her grotesque episodes are born in the numberless forms of compulsion, danger, threat, and destruction that form the boundaries of contemporary existence. Melodrama has become the genre of daily life. In the epigraph she chose for *Angel of Light* (1981), Oates conveyed her sense that the late twentieth century is merely driving an old truth to its farthest reach. She quotes from Bernard de Mandeville, an eighteenth-century moral philosopher, who claimed that evil is the grand principle that makes us social creatures. We must look to Evil "for the true Original of all Arts and Sciences. ... The Moment Evil ceases, the Society must be spoiled." This is less a paradox than a fall into realism; it offers one way of defining the social and familial traps within which so many of Oates's characters find themselves.

Discovering what remains of the self's identity under such circumstances, what she has called "the phantasmagoria of personality," provides one of Oates's abiding concerns. That pursuit, in turn, has stimulated her to explore the forms of fiction. In the 1980s, she investigated the genres of gothic and romance in *Bellefleur* (1980), *A Bloodsmoor Romance* (1982), and *Mysteries of Winterthurn* (1984). This remarkable trilogy, together with her poetry, her essays in criticism, and her virtuoso nonfiction, including *Boxing* (1987), suggests Oates's ambition to command virtually all the styles and genres of contemporary literature.

In one of her recent novels, *You Must Remember This* (1987), Oates has returned to the 1950s, the site of some of her strongest fiction. Her account of those early postwar years summons chiefly an atmosphere of dread and foreboding. The failure that is stamped on the faces and the souls of her characters mirrors the failure of history itself, which brings a universe of purposeless and random violence. The novel is a backward glance not only at the fifties but at the naive promises of an earlier generation that were extinguished by the war. The book's title is taken from the popular song of the late 1930s, "As Time Goes By," which in the early 1940s became the theme of the buoyantly patriotic and optimistic movie *Casablanca*. In Oates's vision of the 1950s, love and pride have sunk into the sadness of knowledge.

The awareness that troubles this and Oates's other novels has been widely shared, and her prolific disquietude may serve to conclude – and, at least in part, to represent – a survey of America's postwar literature. In its rich inventiveness, its contemplation of dislocation and pain, its immersion in popular culture, its sensitivity to divisions of class and gender, above all in its anxious assessments of history, Oates's fiction identifies the questions to which much of America's recent writing has been addressed.

✿ Literary chronology ✿

1640   *Bay Psalm Book*

1644   *The Bloudy Tenent of Persecution* by Roger Williams (1603–83)

1650   *The Tenth Muse Lately Sprung up in America* by Anne Bradstreet (1612–72)

1662   *The Day of Doom* by Michael Wigglesworth (1631–1705)

1702   *Magnalia Christi Americana* by Cotton Mather (1663–1728)

1729   Edward Taylor (ca. 1642–1729) dies (work remains unpublished until 1939)

1732   *Poor Richard's Almanack* by Benjamin Franklin (1706–90)

1741   *Sinners in the Hands of an Angry God* by Jonathan Edwards (1703–58)

1754   *Freedom of the Will* by Jonathan Edwards

1773   *Poems* by Phillis Wheatley (1753–84)

1776   *Common Sense* by Thomas Paine (1737–1809)

1782   *M'Fingal* by John Trumbull (1750–1831)
         Letters from an American Farmer by St. Jean de Crèvecoeur (1735–1813)

1783   *American Spelling Book* by Noah Webster (1758–1843)

1786–7   *The Ararchiad* by the Connecticut Wits

1787   *The Contrast* by Royall Tyler (1757–1826)

1787–8   *The Federalist* by Alexander Hamilton, John Jay, and James Madison

1790   First U.S. copyright law

1792	*Modern Chivalry* by Hugh Henry Brackenridge (1748–1816)
1798	*Wieland* by Charles Brockden Brown (1771–1810)
1807	*The Columbiad* by Joel Barlow (1754–1812)
1819–20	*The Sketch Book* by Washington Irving (1783–1859)
1823	*The Pioneers* by James Fenimore Cooper (1789–1851)
1826	*The Last of the Mohicans* by James Fenimore Cooper
1828	*An American Dictionary of the English Language* by Noah Webster
1831	*Poems* by Edgar Allan Poe (1809–49)
1835	*The Yemassee* by William Gilmore Simms (1806–70)
1836	*Democracy in America* by Alexis de Toqueville
1837	*Twice-Told Tales* by Nathaniel Hawthorne (1804–64)
1838	"Divinity School Address" by Ralph Waldo Emerson (1803–82)
1840	*Tales of the Grotesque and Arabesque* by Edgar Allan Poe
1841	Horace Greeley founds *New York Tribune*
1843	*History of the Conquest of Mexico* by W. H. Prescott (1796–1859)
1845	*Narrative of the Life of Frederick Douglass* by Frederick Douglass (1817–95)
1846	*Typee* by Herman Melville (1819–91)
1847	*Evangeline* by Henry Wadsworth Longfellow (1807–82)
1849	*The Oregon Trail* by Francis Parkman (1823–93) *Civil Disobedience* by Henry David Thoreau (1817–62)
1850	*The Scarlet Letter* by Nathaniel Hawthorne
1851	*The House of the Seven Gables* by Nathaniel Hawthorne *Moby-Dick* by Herman Melville *New York Times* founded
1852	*Uncle Tom's Cabin* by Harriet Beecher Stowe (1811–96)
1854	*Walden* by Henry David Thoreau
1855	*Leaves of Grass* by Walt Whitman (1819–92)

1867   *Ragged Dick* by Horatio Alger (1832–99)

1869   *Innocents Abroad* by Samuel L. Clemens (Mark Twain)
        (1835–1910)

1870   *The Luck of Roaring Camp* by Bret Harte (1836–1902)

1875   *Science and Health* by Mary Baker Eddy (1821–1910)

1880   *The Grandissimes* by George Washington Cable (1844–1925)

1881   *The Portrait of a Lady* by Henry James (1843–1916)

1884   *Adventures of Huckleberry Finn* by Samuel Clemens

1885   *The Rise of Silas Lapham* by William Dean Howells (1837–
        1920)

1888   *Looking Backward* by Edward Bellamy (1850–98)

1890   *Poems* by Emily Dickinson (1830–86)

1891   *Main-travelled Roads* by Hamlin Garland (1860–1940)

1895   *The Red Badge of Courage* by Stephen Crane (1871–1900)

1896   *The Damnation of Theron Ware* by Harold Frederic (1856–
        98)

1899   *The Awakening* by Kate Chopin (1851–1904)
        McTeague by Frank Norris (1870–1902)
        The Theory of the Leisure Class by Thorstein Veblen (1857–
        1929)

1900   *Sister Carrie* by Theodore Dreiser (1871–1945)

1903   *The Ambassadors* by Henry James
        The Call of the Wild by Jack London (1876–1916)
        The Souls of Black Folk by W. E. B. Du Bois (1868–1963)

1905   *The House of Mirth* by Edith Wharton (1862–1937)

1906   *The Jungle* by Upton Sinclair (1878–1968)

1907   *The Education of Henry Adams* by Henry Adams (1838–
        1918)

1907   *Pragmatism* by William James (1842–1910)

1909   *Martin Eden* by Jack London
        Three Lives by Gertrude Stein (1874–1946)

1912	*Poetry: A Magazine of Verse* founded by Harriet Monroe (1860–1936)
1913	*A Boy's Will* by Robert Frost (1875–1963) *O Pioneers!* by Willa Cather (1873–1947)
1915	*Spoon River Anthology* by Edgar Lee Masters (1869–1950)
1917	"The Love Song of J. Alfred Prufrock" by T. S. Eliot (1888–1965)
1918	*My Antonia* by Willa Cather
1919	*Winesburg, Ohio* by Sherwood Anderson (1876–1941)
1920	*The Age of Innocence* by Edith Wharton *Main Street* by Sinclair Lewis (1885–1951) *Hugh Selwyn Mauberley* by Ezra Pound (1885–1972)
1921	*Collected Poems* by Edwin Arlington Robinson (1869–1935)
1922	*Babbitt* by Sinclair Lewis *The Waste Land* by T. S. Eliot *Anna Christie* by Eugene O'Neill (1888–1953)
1923	*Cane* by Jean Toomer (1894–1967) *Harmonium* by Wallace Stevens (1879–1955) Henry R. Luce founds *Time*
1924	First publication of *Billy Budd* by Herman Melville *Desire under the Elms* by Eugene O'Neill
1925	*Manhattan Transfer* by John Dos Passos (1896–1970) *An American Tragedy* by Theodore Dreiser *In Our Time* by Ernest Hemingway (1898–1961) *The Great Gatsby* by F. Scott Fitzgerald (1896–1940) *The Cantos* by Ezra Pound Harold Ross founds *The New Yorker*
1926	*The Sun Also Rises* by Ernest Hemingway
1929	*The Sound and the Fury* by William Faulkner (1897–1962) *Look Homeward, Angel* by Thomas Wolfe (1900–38)
1930	*The Bridge* by Hart Crane (1899–1932) *A Draft of XXX Cantos* by Ezra Pound Sinclair Lewis receives the Nobel Prize

1931   *The Good Earth* by Pearl S. Buck (1892–1973)

1934   *The Ways of White Folks* by Langston Hughes (1902–67)
        Tender Is the Night by F. Scott Fitzgerald
        Collected Poems, 1921–31 by William Carlos Williams
        (1883–1963)

1935   *Waiting for Lefty* by Clifford Odets (1906–63)
        Tortilla Flat by John Steinbeck (1902–68)

1936   *Absalom, Absalom!* by William Faulkner
        The People, Yes by Carl Sandburg (1878–1967)
        Eugene O'Neill receives the Nobel Prize

1938   *Our Town* by Thornton Wilder (1897–1975)
        Pearl Buck receives the Nobel Prize
        U.S.A. (trilogy) by John Dos Passos

1939   *The Grapes of Wrath* by John Steinbeck
        The Day of the Locust by Nathanael West (1903–40)

1940   *Native Son* by Richard Wright (1908–60)

1943   *Four Quartets* by T. S. Eliot

1945   *The Glass Menagerie* by Tennessee Williams (1911–1983)

1946   *Paterson* by William Carlos Williams
        All the King's Men by Robert Penn Warren (1905–)

1947   *A Streetcar Named Desire* by Tennessee Williams

1948   *The Naked and the Dead* by Norman Mailer (1923–)
        T. S. Eliot receives the Nobel Prize

1949   *Death of a Salesman* by Arthur Miller (1915–)

1950   William Faulkner receives the Nobel Prize

1951   *The Catcher in the Rye* by J. D. Salinger (1919–)

1952   *Invisible Man* by Ralph Ellison (1914–)
        Wise Blood by Flannery O'Conner (1925–64)

1953   *The Adventures of Augie March* by Saul Bellow (1915–)
        Go Tell It on the Mountain by James Baldwin (1924–88)

1954   Ernest Hemingway receives the Nobel Prize

1955   *Notes of a Native Son* by James Baldwin
        The Recognitions by William Gaddis (1922–)

1956   *Homage to Mistress Bradstreet* by John Berryman (1914–72)
        Howl by Allen Ginsberg (1926–)
        First production of *Long Day's Journey into Night* by Eugene
        O'Neill

1957   *On the Road* by Jack Kerouac (1922–69)
        The Assistant by Bernard Malamud (1914–1986)

1958   *Lolita* by Vladimir Nabokov (1899–1977)

1959   *Life Studies* by Robert Lowell (1917–77)

1960   *The Sot-Weed Factor* by John Barth (1930–)

1961   *Catch–22* by Joseph Heller (1923–)

1962   *Who's Afraid of Virginia Woolf?* by Edward Albee (1928–)
        John Steinbeck receives the Nobel Prize

1964   *Herzog* by Saul Bellow

1966   *The Crying of Lot 49* by Thomas Pynchon (1937–)

1968   *The Armies of the Night* by Norman Mailer
        Couples by John Updike (1932–)

1969   *Portnoy's Complaint* by Philip Roth (1933–)

1973   *Gravity's Rainbow* by Thomas Pynchon
        Burr by Gore Vidal (1925–)
        Breakfast of Champions by Kurt Vonnegut, Jr.

1975   *Ragtime* by E. L. Doctorow (1931–)

1976   Saul Bellow receives the Nobel Prize

1977   *Song of Solomon* by Toni Morrison (1931–)

1978   *The Dream of a Common Language* by Adrienne Rich
        (1929–)

1980   *The Collected Stories* of Eudora Welty (1909–)

1983   First complete edition of *The Maximus Poems* by Charles
        Olson (1910–70)
        The Color Purple by Alice Walker (1944–)

1984   *A Wave* by John Ashbery (1927–)

1986   *What the Light Was Like* by Amy Clampitt (1920–)

1987   *The Counterlife* by Philip Roth
        Beloved by Toni Morrison

Chronology of American events

1112	First Bishop of America appointed
1492	Columbus's first voyage to the New World
1564	Fort Caroline founded by French (Saint Johns River)
1565	Spanish build Saint Augustine (Florida)
1583	Humphrey Gilbert voyages to Newfoundland
1584	Sir Walter Raleigh founds the unsuccessful colony of Roanoke (North Carolina)
1603–35	Champlain's voyages
1607	Virginia Company of London lands colonists at Jamestown
1609	Henry Hudson explores the Hudson River
1619	African blacks brought as slaves to Jamestown Virginia House of Burgesses founded
1620	Pilgrims sign Mayflower compact and disembark at Plymouth (Massachusetts)
1626	Dutch establish New Amsterdam
1628	Massachusetts Bay Colony chartered; officers elected (1629)
1630	John Winthrop and Puritans arrive aboard the *Arbella* and found the Massachusetts Bay Colony at Salem
1634	Lord Baltimore establishes a settlement in Maryland
1636	Harvard College founded (first college in English-speaking colonies)
1637	Anne Hutchinson tried and convicted of heresy in Massachusetts
1638	Swedish settle in Wilmington (Delaware)

1639	Margaret Brent begins movement for woman suffrage
1644	Roger Williams secures royal charter for Providence, Rhode Island
1648	First woman executed for witchcraft in America (Margaret Jones)
1649	Toleration Acts
1662	Puritans devise Halfway Covenant to facilitate new church membership
1664	British capture New Amsterdam and rename it New York
1669–80	Charleston founded
1675–6	King Philip's War against Indians in New England
1676	Bacon's Rebellion in Virginia
1681	William Penn granted charter for Pennsylvania
1689–97	King William's War against French
1690	First newspaper printed in English North America (Boston)
1692	Salem witchcraft trials
1693	College of William and Mary founded
1698–1702	French settle Louisiana
1701	Yale College founded
1702–13	Queen Anne's War against French
1731	Library Company of Philadelphia founded
1732	General James Oglethorpe granted charter for the colony of Georgia
1734	Jonathan Edwards preaches and Great Awakening begins
1735	John Peter Zenger tried and acquitted for seditious libel of New York's governor
1741	First symphony orchestra organized (Pennsylvania)
1744–8	King George's War against French
1746	College of New Jersey founded (Princeton)
1754–63	French and Indian wars

1754	Albany Congress outlines plans for union of colonies King's College founded in New York City; becomes Columbia College in 1784
1755	The College and Academy of Philadelphia founded; medical school established in 1675
1763	Peace of Paris
1764	Sugar Act, first act to raise revenue from colonies
1765	Stamp Act
1767	Townshend Revenue Act
1770	Boston Massacre; British troops fire on mob in Boston and kill five civilians Thomas Jefferson builds Monticello
1773	Tea Act levies taxes against tea imported into colonies; Boston Tea Party in December
1774	First Continental Congress meets in Philadelphia
1775	Colonial militia and British troops battle at Lexington and Concord (April 19) and Bunker Hill (June 17)
1775–83	American Revolutionary War (independence of the colonies formally recognized by the Treaty of Paris, 1783)
1775	First abolitionist society organized (Philadelphia)
1776	Declaration of Independence (signed July 2)
1781	Articles of Confederation ratified Defeat of British under General Cornwallis at Yorktown
1782	First seal of the United States adopted
1783	First daily newspaper published (Philadelphia)
1784	*Empress of China* sails from New York in February and begins direct trade with China
1785	Ordinance passed for sale of western lands U.S. adopts decimal system
1787	Constitutional Convention meets in Philadelphia Shay's Rebellion Northwest Ordinance passed to provide for government of national domain

1788	Constitution ratified
	First settlement in Northwest Territory (Marietta, Ohio)
1789–97	Presidency of George Washington (Federalist; inaugurated April 30)
1789	First session of Congress meets
	Virginia Capitol built at Richmond
1790	First U.S. census shows population of 3.9 million
	Samuel Slater introduces power-driven cotton spinning
1791–6	Hamilton–Jefferson conflict fosters beginnings of American party system (Federalists and Democratic-Republicans)
1791	Bill of Rights passed
	Bank of the United States opens (Philadelphia)
ca. 1792	L'Enfant designs plans for Washington, D.C.
1793	Eli Whitney invents the cotton gin
	First national coinage issued (Philadelphia Mint)
1797–1801	Presidency of John Adams (Federalist)
1799	George Washington dies
1800	Washington, D.C., becomes site of national government
1801–9	Presidency of Thomas Jefferson (Democratic-Republican)
1802	U.S. Military Academy established at West Point, N.Y.
1803	*Marbury* v. *Madison* establishes right of Supreme Court to judicial review
	Jefferson acquires Louisiana Territory and doubles size of United States (Louisiana Purchase, from which thirteen new states were eventually formed)
1804	Lewis and Clark expedition (reaches Pacific on November 7, 1805)
1805	Zebulon M. Pike expedition to the Rockies
	Pennsylvania Academy of Fine Arts founded
1807	Robert Fulton builds *Clermont* steamboat
1808	United States prohibits further importation of slaves
1809–17	Presidency of James Madison (Democratic-Republican)

1812–14   War of 1812

1814   Washington, D.C., burned by the British (August 24)
Robert Fulton launches steam frigate in New York

1817–25   Presidency of James Monroe (Democratic-Republican)

1818   Northern boundary (from the Great Lakes to the Rocky
Mountains) fixed at the forty-ninth parallel of latitude
U.S. flag adopted

1819   Florida purchased from Spain

1820   Missouri Compromise outlaws slavery north of latitude 36°
30′ (Missouri admitted as a slave state, Maine admitted as a
free state)
University of Virginia founded by Jefferson

1821   Davy Crockett elected to the Tennessee legislature (elected
to Congress in 1827)

1823   Monroe Doctrine affirms America's hegemony in the Western Hemisphere

1825–9   Presidency of John Quincy Adams (Republican)

1825   Erie Canal links Hudson River and Great Lakes

1826   Robert Owen founds community at New Harmony, Indiana

1829–37   Presidency of Andrew Jackson (Democrat)

1831   Nat Turner's slave insurrection
McCormick Reaper invented

1832–3   Nullification Crisis leads to decreased tariffs on imported
goods

1833   American Antislavery Society founded
Oberlin College founded as first coeducational institution of
higher learning

1836   Texas declares independence from Mexico and establishes
the "Lone Star Republic"
Battle of the Alamo
Building of Washington Monument begins
Colt pistol patented

1837–41   Presidency of Martin Van Buren (Democrat)

1837   Samuel F. B. Morse files telegraph experiments at Patent Office
        Financial panic
        John Deere develops plow for prairie lands

1838   Regular steam travel across the Atlantic begins with arrival of the British *Sirius and Great Western* (crossing time a little more than sixteen days)

1839   Invention of the daguerreotype
        Abolitionists found the Liberty Party

1841   Presidency of William Henry Harrison (Whig; dies after one month in office)

1841–5 Presidency of John Tyler (Whig)

1841   Brooke Farm community established

1844   Telegraph line from Washington to Baltimore opens

1845–9 Presidency of James Knox Polk (Democrat)

1845   Texas annexed to the United States

1846–8 Mexican War (United States acquires territory between Rocky Mountains and Pacific)

1846   Oregon Territory acquired by agreement with Britain
        Smithsonian Institution established

1847   Mormons settle at Great Salt Lake (Utah)
        Elias Howe invents first practical sewing machine
        Pennsylvania Railroad chartered

1848   Seneca Falls Convention
        Free Soil party formed
        Gold discovered at Sutter's Mill, California

1849–50 Presidency of Zachary Taylor (dies in 1850)

1850–3 Presidency of Millard Fillmore (Whig)

1850   Compromise of 1850

1851   Maine becomes first state to enact prohibition
        Telegraph lines extended across the Mississippi

1853–7 Presidency of Franklin Pierce (Democrat)

1853	Commodore Perry sails to Japan; Treaty of 1854 opens Japan to world trade The Exhibition of the Industry of All Nations opens in New York (New York Crystal Palace)
1854	Kansas-Nebraska Act repeals the Missouri Compromise
1856	Republican party nationally organized (replaces Whig party in northern sections)
1857	Illinois Central Railroad system extends from Chicago to Cairo, Illinois First kindergarten in United States established Founding of *Atlantic Monthly*
1857–61	Presidency of James Buchanan (Democrat)
1857	Dred Scott Decision (Supreme Court denies blacks standing in court)
1858	Lincoln–Douglas debates
1859	John Brown's raid on Harper's Ferry (Virginia) Petroleum discovered in Pennsylvania Colorado gold rush, "Pikes Peak or Bust" (mass migration to the West throughout the 1860s)
1860	Confederation of Southern States formed
1861–5	Presidency of Abraham Lincoln (Republican; assassinated April 14, 1865)
1861	Secession of southern states April 12, Fort Sumter attacked (beginning of war between Confederacy and Union)
1862	Homestead Act
1863	Emancipation Act frees slaves in areas of Confederate control
1865	Slavery abolished by Thirteenth Amendment Founding of Freedmen's Bureau
1865–9	Presidency of Andrew Johnson (Democrat)
1865–77	Reconstruction
1867	Alaska purchased from Russia

1869–77   Presidency of Ulysses S. Grant (Republican)

1869   First transcontinental railroad completed

1870   Metropolitan Museum of Art and Boston Museum of Fine Arts founded

1871   Chicago fire

1872   Yellowstone National Park established

1875–6   Second Sioux War (Custer's calvary defeated at the Battle of Little Big Horn, 1876)

1876   Telephone invented by Alexander Graham Bell
Centennial Exposition, Philadelphia

1877–81   Presidency of Rutherford B. Hayes (Republican)

1879   Incandescent light bulb perfected by Thomas Alva Edison
John D. Rockefeller's Standard Oil Trust founded

1881   Presidency of James A. Garfield (Republican; assassinated four months after taking office)
American National Red Cross founded

1881–5   Presidency of Chester A. Arthur (Republican)

1883   Brooklyn Bridge opened
First National College Football Championship

1884   National Equal Rights Party nominates Belva Lockwood as first woman candidate for president

1885–9   Presidency (first term) of Grover Cleveland (Democrat)

1886   Formation of the American Federation of Labor (AFL)
Haymarket bombing in Chicago

1888   George Eastman introduces Kodak camera

1889   Jane Addams establishes Hull House in Chicago

1889–93   Presidency of Benjamin Harrison (Republican)

1890   Ellis Island, New York, designated as immigration depot
Sherman Anti-Trust Act
Eleventh U.S. census declares frontier closed

1891   Formation of Populist party

1893   World's Columbian Exposition in Chicago
Financial panic

1893–7   Presidency (second term) of Grover Cleveland

1895   J. P. Morgan and Company founded

1896   Supreme Court, in decision *Plessy* v. *Ferguson*, declares
"separate but equal" the law of the land
First moving pictures shown on a public screen

1897–1901 Presidency of William McKinley (Republican; assassinated
in first year of his second term)

1898   February 15, USS Maine blown up in Havana Harbor,
Spanish-American War (Puerto Rico ceded to United
States; Hawaii annexed; Philippines occupied)

1901   United States Steel Company founded

1901–9   Presidency of Theodore Roosevelt (Republican)

1903   Wright brothers make world's first successful heavier-than-
air flight
Panama Canal treaty signed (canal opened to commerical
traffic in 1914)
First baseball World Series

1904   American Academy of Arts and Letters founded

1905   First nickelodeon opens in Pittsburgh

1906   Pure Food and Drug Act passed
Theodore Roosevelt becomes first American to win Nobel
Prize (for peace)

1907   Peak year of immigration (1,285,000 immigrants enter
United States)

1908   Henry Ford introduces Model T

1909   National Association for the Advancement of Colored People (NAACP) established

1909–13 Presidency of William Howard Taft (Republican)

1911   Triangle Shirtwaist Fire in New York City

1912   New Mexico and Arizona, forty-seventh and forty-eighth
states, admitted to Union

1913   Federal income tax introduced
Armory Show in New York City

1913–21   Presidency of Woodrow Wilson (Democrat)

1914   World War I begins
Eight-hour day and $5.00 daily wage introduced in Ford plants

1915   Opening of D. W. Griffith's *The Birth of a Nation*
Sinking of *Lusitania*

1917   April 6, United States declares war on Germany

1918   November 11, armistice ends war in Europe

1919   Prohibition instituted by Eighteenth Amendment (repealed by Twenty-first Amendment in 1933)
Senate rejects U.S. membership in League of Nations

1920   Federal voting rights for women secured by Nineteenth Amendment
Fourteenth U.S. Census indicates that urban population exceeds rural
First commercial radio station begins operation (KDKA in Pittsburgh)

1921–3   Presidency of Warren G. Harding (Republican)

1923–9   Presidency of Calvin Coolidge (Republican)

1923   Oklahoma placed under martial law because of terrorist activities of Ku Klux Klan

1925   Trial of John T. Scopes for teaching evolution in Tennessee

1926   Admiral Richard Byrd flies over North Pole
National Broadcasting System creates first permanent radio network

1927   Charles Lindbergh flies across Atlantic
First scheduled passenger air service established, between New York and Boston
The Jazz Singer, starring Al Jolson, popularizes moving-picture sound
Sacco and Vanzetti executed

1929–33   Presidency of Herbert Hoover (Republican)

1929	Stock market crashes, October 29; Great Depression begins
1931	Nobel Peace Prize won by Jane Addams and Murray Butler
1933–45	Presidency of Franklin D. Roosevelt (Democrat)
1933	National Industry Recovery Act passed (replaced in 1935 by National Labor Relations Act)
1934	Invention of nylon
1935	Social Security Act passed
1935–7	Neutrality legislation passed to prevent U.S. involvement in foreign wars
1937	The airship *Hindenburg* destroyed by fire in a crash at Lakehurst, N.J.
1938	Congress of Industrial Organizations (CIO) formed
1939	World War II begins
1940	Regular television broadcasting begins
1941	December 7, Japan bombs Pearl Harbor; United States enters war
1942	UN Declaration signed in Washington
1943	Italy surrenders to Allies
1944	Allied invasion of Normandy
1945–53	Presidency of Harry S. Truman (Democrat)
1945	Germany surrenders to Allies United States drops atomic bombs on Hiroshima and Nagasaki; Japan surrenders, September 2 United Nations Conference in San Francisco and signing of UN Charter
1946	Fulbright Act permits scholarships for study abroad
1947	Taft-Hartley Act restricts trade union power Edward Land introduces Polaroid camera
1948–9	Berlin blockade and airlift
1948	Long-playing phonograph records introduced Transistor invented

1949   NATO established

1950–60   Advent of mass television

1950   United States begins police action in Korea (ends in 1953)
            Alger Hiss convicted of perjury
            Senator Joseph McCarthy launches anticommunist crusade
            McCarran Internal Security Act passed

1951   CBS originates television broadcasts in color

1953–61   Presidency of Dwight D. Eisenhower (Republican)

1953   Julius and Ethel Rosenberg executed for espionage

1954   Supreme Court rules doctrine of "separate but equal" un-
            constitutional (*Brown* v. *Board of Education*), directs end of
            racial segregation in public schools
            J. Robert Oppenheimer denied security clearance

1955–6   Rosa Parks refuses to give her seat to white riders in Mont-
            gomery, Alabama; bus boycott begins

1956   Suez Crisis

1957   Federal troops enforce school desegregation in Little Rock,
            Arkansas

1958   Stereophonic phonograph records marketed

1959   Admission to statehood of Alaska and Hawaii (forty-ninth
            and fiftieth states of the Union)

1960   U.S. population reaches 180 million

1961–3   Presidency of John F. Kennedy (Democrat; assassinated No-
            vember 22, 1963)

1961–8   Birth-control pill comes into general use

1961   Black students sit in to desegregate lunch counters in
            Greensboro, North Carolina
            Bay of Pigs invasion

1962   Cuban missile crisis
            International live telecasts by satellite
            James Meredith attends University of Mississippi, escorted
            by U.S. marshals

1963–9   Presidency of Lyndon B. Johnson (Democrat)

1963   United States, Soviet Union, and Great Britain approve nuclear test ban treaty
Medgar Evers assassinated

1964   Gulf of Tonkin Resolution begins buildup of U.S. ground forces in South Vietnam

1965–7   Race riots in Los Angeles, Chicago, Newark, Detroit, and other major cities

1965   March on Washington in support of equal rights for blacks
Bombing of North Vietnam begins, combat troops sent in
National Foundation for the Arts and Humanities established by Congress

1966   National Organization for Women founded

1968   Rev. Martin Luther King, Jr. assassinated
Robert Kennedy assassinated

1968–72 Students protest on U.S. campuses

1969   U.S. astronauts land on moon

1969–74 Presidency of Richard M. Nixon (Republican; resigned)

1970   Four students killed by National Guard in protest at Kent State University

1971   Twenty-sixth Amendment gives voting rights to eighteen-year-olds

1972   Watergate break-in

1973   Price of oil quadruples

1974–7   Presidency of Gerald Ford (Republican)

1977–81 Presidency of Jimmy Carter (Democrat)

1978   Egypt and Israel sign peace agreement at Camp David

1979   Islamic revolution in Iran

1981–9   Presidency of Ronald Reagan (Republican)

1984   Geraldine Ferraro becomes first woman nominated for the vice-presidency by major political party

1986   Space shuttle *Challenger* explodes seventy-four seconds after takeoff
      Harvard celebrates three hundred fiftieth anniversary

1987   Dow Jones Industrial average loses 508 points (October 19), worst one-day decline in market history
      United States and Soviet Union reach agreement to ban medium-range nuclear missiles

1988   Worst heat wave and drought since Depression

1989–   Presidency of George Bush (Republican)

Books for further reading

Some of the books listed are general in scope; others are most relevant to particular chapters in this book, as indicated in parentheses.

Aaron, Daniel. *Writers on the Left: Episodes in American Literary Communism.* New York: Harcourt Brace & World, 1961. (Chapters 5 and 6)

Aldridge, Alfred Owen. *Early American Literature: A Comparatist Approach.* Princeton: Princeton University Press, 1982. (Chapter 1)

Allen, Gay W. *The Solitary Singer: A Critical Biography of Walt Whitman,* rev. ed. New York: New York University Press, 1967. Originally published 1955. (Chapter 3)

Allen, Margaret V. *The Achievement of Margaret Fuller.* University Park, Pa.: Pennsylvania State University Press, 1979. (Chapter 3)

Anderson, Quentin. *The Imperial Self: An Essay in American Literary and Cultural History.* New York: Knopf, 1971.

Asselineau, Roger. *The Evolution of Walt Whitman* (2 vol.). Cambridge, Mass.: Harvard University Press, 1960. (Chapter 3)

Baker, Carlos H. *Ernest Hemingway: A Life Story.* New York: Scribner's, 1969. (Chapter 6)

Baker, Houston A., Jr. *The Journey Back: Issues in Black Literature and Criticism.* Chicago: University of Chicago Press, 1980.

Banta, Martha. *Failure and Success in America: A Literary Debate.* Princeton: Princeton University Press, 1978.

Baym, Nina. *Woman's Fiction: A Guide to Novels by and about Women in America, 1820–1870.* Ithaca: Cornell University Press, 1978. (Chapter 3)

Bell, Millicent. *Edith Wharton and Henry James: The Story of Their Friendship.* New York: Braziller, 1965. (Chapter 5)

Bercovitch, Sacvan. *The American Jeremiad*. Madison: University of Wisconsin Press, 1978. (Chapters 1 and 2)

The Puritan Origins of the American Self. New Haven: Yale University Press, 1975. (Chapters 1 through 3)

Berryman, John. *Stephen Crane*. New York: Sloane, 1950. (Chapter 4)

Berthoff, Warner. *The Ferment of Realism: American Literature, 1884–1919*. New York: Free Press, 1965. (Chapters 4 and 5)

A Literature without Qualities: American Writing since 1945. Berkeley and Los Angeles: University of California Press, 1979. (Chapter 7)

Bigsby, C. W. E. *A Critical Introduction to Twentieth-century American Drama* (3 vols.). Vol. 1: *1900–1940*, 1982; vol. 2, *Tennessee Williams, Arthur Miller, Edward Albee*, 1985; vol. 3, *Beyond Broadway*, 1985. Cambridge University Press. (Chapters 6 and 7)

Bradbury, Malcolm. *The Modern American Novel*. New York: Oxford University Press, 1983. (Chapters 6 and 7)

Bridgeman, Richard. *The Colloquial Style in America*. New York: Oxford University Press, 1966.

Brodhead, Richard H. *Hawthorne, Melville, and the Novel*. Chicago: University of Chicago Press, 1976. (Chapter 3)

Brooks, Cleanth. *William Faulkner: The Yoknapatawpha Country*. New Haven: Yale University Press, 1963. (Chapter 6)

Charvat, William. *The Profession of Authorship in America, 1800–1870: The Papers of William Charvat*, ed. Matthew J. Broccoli. Columbus: Ohio State University Press, 1968.

Chase, Richard Volney. *The American Novel and Its Traditions*. Garden City, N.Y.: Doubleday, 1957.

Clurman, Harold. *The Fervent Years: The Story of the Group Theatre and the Thirties*. New York: Knopf, 1945. (Chapter 6)

Conarroe, Joel. *William Carlos Williams' Paterson: Language and Landscape*. Philadelphia: U. of Pennsylvania Press, 1970. (Chapters 6 and 7)

Conn, Peter. *The Divided Mind: Ideology and Imagination in America, 1898–1917*. Cambridge University Press, 1983. (Chapter 5)

Cook, Bruce. *The Beat Generation*. New York: Scribner's, 1971. (Chapter 7)

Cowley, Malcolm. *Exile's Return: A Literary Odyssey of the 1920's*. New York: Norton, 1934. (Chapter 6)

Think Back on Us: A Contemporary Chronicle of the 1930's, ed. Henry Dan Piper. Carbondale, Ill.: Southern Illinois University Press, 1967. (Chapter 6)

Davis, Richard B. *Intellectual Life in the Colonial South* (3 vols.). Knoxville: University of Tennessee Press, 1978. (Chapter 2)

Dickstein, Morris. *Gates of Eden: American Culture in the Sixties.* New York: Basic Books, 1977. (Chapter 7)

Donoghue, Denis. *Connoisseurs of Chaos: Ideas of Order in Modern American Poetry.* London: Faber & Faber, 1966. (Chapters 5 through 7)

Reading America. New York: Knopf, 1987.

Douglas, Ann. *The Feminization of American Culture.* New York: Knopf, 1977. (Chapters 3 and 4)

Duberman, Martin. *James Russell Lowell.* Boston: Houghton Mifflin, 1966. (Chapter 3)

Duffey, Bernard. *The Chicago Renaissance in American Letters.* East Lansing: Michigan State University Press, 1954. (Chapter 5)

Edel, Leon. *Henry James* (5 vols.). Philadelphia: Lippincott, 1953–72. (Chapter 4)

Elliott, Emory. *Revolutionary Writers: Literature and Authority in the New Republic, 1725–1810.* New York: Oxford University Press, 1982. (Chapters 2 and 3)

Elliott, Emory, ed. *Columbia Literary History of the United States.* New York: Columbia University Press, 1988.

Feidelson, Charles S., Jr. *Symbolism and American Literature.* Chicago: University of Chicago Press, 1953. (Chapter 3)

Ferguson, Robert A. *Law and Letters in American Culture.* Cambridge, Mass.: Harvard University Press, 1984. (Chapter 3)

Fiedler, Leslie A. *Love and Death in the American Novel*, rev. ed. New York: Stein & Day. Previously published 1960.

What Was Literature? Class, Culture and Mass Society. New York: Simon & Schuster, 1982.

Fliegelman, Jay. *Prodigals and Pilgrims: The American Revolution against Patriarchal Authority, 1750–1800.* Cambridge University Press, 1982. (Chapter 2)

Gibson, William M. *The Art of Mark Twain.* New York: Oxford University Press, 1976. (Chapter 4)

Givner, Joan. *Katherine Anne Porter: A Life.* New York: Simon & Schuster, 1982. (Chapter 7)

Hamilton, Ian. *Robert Lowell: A Biography.* New York: Random House, 1982. (Chapter 7)

Hart, James D. *The Popular Book: A History of America's Literary Taste.* New York: Oxford University Press, 1950.

Hassan, Ihab. *Radical Innocence: Studies in the Contemporary American Novel.* Princeton: Princeton University Press, 1961. (Chapter 7)

Hendin, Josephine. *Vulnerable People: A View of American Fiction since 1945.* New York: Oxford University Press, 1978. (Chapter 7)

Hoffman, Daniel G. *Form and Fable in American Fiction.* New York: Oxford University Press, 1961.

Hoffman, Daniel G., ed. *Harvard Guide to Contemporary American Writing.* Cambridge, Mass.: Harvard University Press, 1979. (Chapter 7)

Howard, Leon. *Literature and the American Tradition.* New York: Doubleday, 1960.

Howe, Irving. *William Faulkner: A Critical Study,* 3rd, rev. ed., Chicago: University of Chicago Press, 1975. (Chapter 6)

   World of Our Fathers: The Journey of the East European Jews to America and the Life They Found and Made. New York: Simon & Schuster, 1976. (Chapter 5)

Howells, William D. *My Mark Twain: Reminiscences and Criticisms.* New York: Harper, 1910. (Chapter 4)

Huggins, Nathan. *Harlem Renaissance.* New York: Oxford University Press, 1971. (Chapter 6)

Irwin, John T. *American Hieroglyphics: The Symbol of the Egyptian Hieroglyphics in the American Renaissance.* Baltimore: Johns Hopkins University Press, 1983. (Chapter 3)

   Doubling and Incest / Repetition and Revenge: A Speculative Reading of Faulkner. Baltimore: Johns Hopkins University Press, 1975. (Chapter 6)

Jones, Howard Mumford. *The Literature of Virginia in the Seventeenth Century.* Charlottesville: University Press of Virginia, 1968. (Chapter 1)

   O Strange New World: American Culture: The Formative Years. New York: Viking Press, 1964. (Chapter 1)

Kammen, Michael. *A Season of Youth: The American Revolution and the Historical Imagination.* New York: Knopf, 1978. (Chapter 2)

Kaplan, Justin. *Mr. Clemens and Mark Twain.* New York: Simon & Schuster, 1966. (Chapter 4)

Walt Whitman: A Life. New York: Simon & Schuster, 1980, (Chapter 3)

Karl, Frederick. *American Fictions, 1940–1980: A Comprehensive History and Critical Evaluation.* New York: Harper & Row, 1983. (Chapter 7)

Kazin, Alfred. *Bright Book of Life: American Novelists and Storytellers from Hemingway to Mailer.* Boston: Little, Brown, 1973. (Chapters 6 and 7)

On Native Grounds: An Interpretation of Modern American Prose Literature. New York: Reynal & Hitchcock, 1942. (Chapters 5 and 6)

Kelley, Mary. *Private Woman, Public Stage: Literary Domesticity in Nineteenth-century America.* New York: Oxford University Press, 1984. (Chapter 3)

Kenner, Hugh. *A Homemade World: The American Modernist Writers.* New York: Knopf, 1975. (Chapters 5 and 6)

Kerber, Linda K. *Federalists in Dissent: Imagery and Ideology in Jeffersonian America.* Ithaca: Cornell University Press, 1970. (Chapter 2)

King, Richard H. *A Southern Renaissance: The Cultural Awakening of the American South, 1930–1955.* New York: Oxford University Press, 1980. (Chapters 6 and 7)

Kirkpatrick, D. L., ed. *Reference Guide to American Literature.* London: St. James Press, 1987.

Klein, Marcus. *After Alienation: American Novels in Mid-century.* Cleveland: World Publishing, 1962. (Chapter 7)

Foreigners: The Making of American Literature, 1900–1940. Chicago: University of Chicago Press, 1981. (Chapter 5)

Kolodny, Annette. *The Land before Her: Fantasy and Experience of the American Frontier, 1630–1860.* Chapel Hill: University of North Carolina Press, 1984. (Chapters 1 through 3)

Lawrence, D. H. *Studies in Classic American Literature.* New York: Seltzer, 1923. (Chapters 3 and 4)

Lawson-Peebles, Robert. *Landscape and Written Expression in Revolutionary America: The World Turned Upside Down.* Cambridge University Press, 1988. (Chapter 3)

Lee, Robert A. *Black Fiction: New Studies in the Afro-American Novel since 1945.* New York: Barnes & Noble, 1980. (Chapter 7)

Lehmann-Haupt, Helmut, Lawrence Wroth, Rollo Silver et al. *The Book in America: A History of the Making and Selling of Books in the United States*, rev. ed. New York: Bowker, 1952. Originally published 1939.

Levin, David. *History as Romantic Art: Bancroft, Prescott, Motley, and Parkman.* Stanford: Stanford University Press, 1959. (Chapter 3)

Levin, Harry. *The Power of Blackness: Hawthorne, Poe, Melville.* New York: Knopf, 1958. (Chapters 2 and 3)

Lewis, David L. *When Harlem Was in Vogue.* New York: Knopf, 1981. (Chapter 6)

Lewis, R. W. B. *The American Adam: Innocence, Tragedy and Tradition in the Nineteenth Century.* Chicago: University of Chicago Press, 1959. (Chapters 3 and 4)

   Edith Wharton: A Biography. New York: Harper & Row, 1975. (Chapter 5)

Leyda, Jay. *The Melville Log: A Documentary Life of Herman Melville* (2 vols.). New York: Harcourt Brace, 1951; supplement, 1969. (Chapter 3)

Lowance, Mason I. *The Language of Canaan: Metaphor and Symbol in New England from the Puritans to the Transcendentalists.* Cambridge, Mass.: Harvard University Press, 1983. (Chapters 1 through 3)

Ludington, Townsend. *John Dos Passos: A Twentieth-century Odyssey.* New York: Dutton, 1980. (Chapter 6)

Lynen, John F. *The Design of the Present: Essays on Time and Form in American Literature.* New Haven: Yale University Press, 1969.

Lynn, Kenneth S. *William Dean Howells: An American Life.* New York: Harcourt Brace Jovanovitch, 1971. (Chapter 4)

McConnell, Frank D. *Four Postwar American Novelists: Bellow, Mailer, Barth, and Pynchon.* Chicago: University of Chicago Press, 1977. (Chapter 7)

McKinsey, Elizabeth R. *Niagara Falls: Icon of the American Sublime.* Cambridge University Press, 1985. (Chapters 3 and 4)

McNally, Dennis. *Desolate Angel: Jack Kerouac, the Beat Generation and America.* New York: Random House, 1979. (Chapter 7)

McWilliams, John P., Jr. *Hawthorne, Melville, and the American Character: A Looking Glass Business.* Cambridge University Press, 1984. (Chapter 3)

Martin, Jay. *Harvests of Change: American Literature, 1865–1914.* Englewood Cliffs, N.J.: Prentice-Hall, 1967. (Chapters 4 and 5)

Martin, Ronald E. *American Literature and the Universe of Force*. Durham, N.C.: Duke University Press, 1981. (Chapter 4)

Marx, Leo. *The Machine in the Garden: Technology and the Pastoral Ideal in America*. New York: Oxford University Press, 1964. (Chapters 3 and 4)

Matthiessen, Francis Otto. *American Renaissance: Art and Expression in the Age of Emerson and Whitman*. New York: Oxford University Press, 1941. (Chapter 3)

Mazzaro, Jerome. *Postmodern American Poetry*. Urbana: University of Illinois Press, 1980. (Chapter 7)

Mellow, James R. *Nathaniel Hawthorne in His Times*. Boston: Houghton Mifflin, 1980. (Chapter 3)

Mencken, H. L. *The American Language*, 4th ed. New York: Knopf, 1937.

Miller, Perry. *The New England Mind: The Seventeenth Century*. Cambridge, Mass.: Harvard University Press, 1953. (Chapter 2)

   The New England Mind: From Colony to Province. New York: Macmillan, 1939. (Chapter 1)

Millgate, Michael. *American Social Fiction: James to Cozzens*. New York: Barnes & Noble, 1965. (Chapters 4 through 6)

Moers, Ellen. *Two Dreisers: The Man and the Novelist*. London: Thames & Hudson, 1970. (Chapter 5)

Morison, Samuel Eliot. *The Intellectual Life of Colonial New England*. Ithaca: Cornell University Press, 1960. (Chapter 1)

Mott, Frank Luther. *A History of American Magazines* (5 vols.). Vol. 1: *1741–1850*; New York: Appleton, 1930. Vol. 2: *1850–1865*; vol. 3, *1865–1885*; vol. 4, *1885–1905*; vol. 5, *Sketches of 21 Magazines, 1905–1930*; Cambridge, Mass.: Harvard University Press, 1938–68.

Murdoch, Kenneth. *Literature and Theology in Colonial New England*. Cambridge, Mass.: Harvard University Press, 1949. (Chapter 1)

Nevius, Blake. *Cooper's Landscapes: An Essay on the Picturesque Vision*. Berkeley and Los Angeles: University of California Press, 1976. (Chapter 3)

Norton, Mary B. *Liberty's Daughters: The Revolutionary Experience of American Women, 1750–1800*. Boston: Little, Brown, 1980. (Chapter 2)

O'Brien, Michael. *The Idea of the American South, 1920–1941*. Baltimore: Johns Hopkins University Press, 1979. (Chapter 6)

Ostriker, Alicia Suskin. *Stealing the Language: The Emergence of Women's Poetry in America.* Boston: Beacon Press, 1986.

Parrington, Vernon Louis. *Main Currents in American Thought: An Interpretation of American Literature from the Beginnings to 1920* (3 vols.). New York: Harcourt Brace & World, 1927–30.

Pearce, Roy Harvey. *The Continuity of American Poetry.* Princeton: Princeton University Press, 1961.

Pease, Donald E. *Visionary Compacts: American Renaissance Writings in Cultural Contexts.* Madison: University of Wisconsin Press, 1987. (Chapter 3)

Perkins, David. *A History of Modern Poetry: From the 1890s to the High Modernist Mode.* Cambridge, Mass.: Harvard University Press, 1976. (Chapter 5)

    A History of Modern Poetry: Modernism and After. Cambridge, Mass.: Harvard University Press, 1987. (Chapters 6 and 7)

Pizer, Donald. *Realism and Naturalism in Nineteenth-century American Literature.* Carbondale, Ill.: University of Southern Illinois Press, 1966; rev. ed., 1984. (Chapter 4)

Poirier, Richard. *The Performing Self: Compositions and Decompositions in the Languages of Contemporary Life.* New York: Oxford University Press, 1971.

    A World Elsewhere: The Place of Style in American Literature. New York: Oxford University Press, 1966.

Porte, Joel. *Emerson and Thoreau: Transcendentalists in Conflict.* Middletown, Conn.: Wesleyan University Press, 1966. (Chapter 4)

Pritchard, William H. *Frost: A Literary Life Reconsidered.* New York: Oxford University Press, 1984. (Chapter 6)

Railton, Stephen. *Fenimore Cooper: A Study of His Life and Imagination.* Princeton: Princeton University Press, 1978. (Chapter 3)

Reynolds, David S. *Beneath the American Renaissance: The Subversive Imagination in the Age of Emerson and Melville.* New York: Knopf, 1988. (Chapter 3)

Rideout, Walter B. *The Radical Novel in the United States, 1900–1954: Some Interrelations of Literature and Society.* Cambridge, Mass.: Harvard University Press, 1956. (Chapters 5 through 7)

Rose, Anne C. *Transcendentalism as a Social Movement, 1830–1850.* New Haven: Yale University Press, 1982. (Chapter 3)

Rosenblatt, Roger. *Black Fiction*. Cambridge, Mass.: Harvard University Press, 1974.

Rosenthal, M. L. *The New Poets: American and British Poetry since World War II*. New York: Oxford University Press, 1967. (Chapter 7)

St. Armand, Barton L. *Emily Dickinson and Her Culture: The Soul's Society*. Cambridge University Press, 1984. (Chapter 3)

Samuels, Ernest. *The Young Henry Adams; Henry Adams: The Middle Years; The Major Phase*. Cambridge, Mass.: Harvard University Press, 1948, 1958, 1964. (Chapter 5)

Schorer, Mark. *Sinclair Lewis: An American Life*. New York: McGraw-Hill, 1961. (Chapter 6)

Seelye, John. *Prophetic Waters: The River in Early American Life and Literature*. New York: Oxford University Press, 1977. (Chapter 3)

Segal, Howard P. *Technological Utopianism in American Culture*. Chicago: University of Chicago Press, 1985. (Chapters 4 and 5)

Sewall, Richard B. *The Life of Emily Dickinson* (2 vols.). New York: Farrar, Straus & Giroux, 1974. (Chapter 3)

Seyersted, Per. *Kate Chopin: A Critical Biography*. Baton Rouge: Louisiana State University Press, 1969. (Chapter 4)

Shaw, Peter. *American Patriots and the Rituals of Revolution*. Cambridge, Mass.: Harvard University Press, 1981. (Chapter 2)

Shea, Daniel B. *Spiritual Autobiography in Early America*. Princeton: Princeton University Press, 1968. (Chapter 1)

Silverman, Kenneth. *A Cultural History of the American Revolution: Painting, Music, Literature, and the Theatre in the Colonies and the United States from the Treaty of Paris to the Inauguration of George Washington, 1763–1789*. New York: Crowell, 1976. (Chapter 2)

Sinclair, Andrew. *Jack: A Biography of Jack London*. New York: Harper & Row, 1977. (Chapter 4)

Slotkin, Richard. *Regeneration through Violence: The Mythology of the American Frontier, 1600–1860*. Middletown, Conn.: Wesleyan University Press, 1973.

Smith, Henry Nash. *Virgin Land: The American West as Symbol and Myth*. Cambridge, Mass.: Harvard University Press, 1950. (Chapters 3 and 4)

Spencer, Benjamin T. *The Quest for Nationality: An American Literary Campaign*. Syracuse: Syracuse University Press, 1957. (Chapter 3)

Spiller, Robert E., ed. *The American Literary Revolution, 1783–1837.* Garden City, N.Y.: Doubleday (Anchor Books), 1967. (Chapter 3)

Spiller, Robert E., Willard Thorp, Thomas Johnson et al., eds. *Literary History of the United States,* 4th ed. (2 vols.). New York: Macmillan, 1974.

Spindler, Michael. *American Literature and Social Change: William Dean Howells to Arthur Miller.* Bloomington: University of Indiana Press, 1983. (Chapters 4 through 7)

Stepanchev, Stephen. *American Poetry since 1945: A Critical Survey.* New York: Harper & Row, 1971. (Chapter 7)

Stepto, Robert. *From behind the Veil: A Study of Afro-American Narrative.* Urbana: University of Illinois Press, 1979.

Story, Ronald. *The Forging of an Aristocracy: Harvard and the Boston Upper Class, 1800–1870.* Middletown, Conn.: Wesleyan University Press, 1980. (Chapter 3)

Strouse, Jean. *Alice James: A Biography.* Boston: Houghton Mifflin, 1980. (Chapter 4)

Strout, Cushing. *The Veracious Imagination: Essays on American History, Literature, and Biography.* Middletown, Conn.: Wesleyan University Press, 1981.

Sundquist, Eric J., ed. *American Realism: New Essays.* Baltimore: Johns Hopkins University Press, 1969. (Chapters 4 and 5)

Susman, Warren I. *Culture as History: The Transformation of American Society in the Twentieth Century.* New York: Pantheon Books, 1984. (Chapters 5 and 6)

Tanner, Tony. *City of Words: American Fiction, 1950–1970.* New York: Harper & Row, 1971. (Chapter 7)

The Reign of Wonder: Naivety and Reality in American Literature. Cambridge University Press, 1965.

Taylor, Gordon O. *The Passages of Thought: Psychological Representation in the American Novel, 1870–1900.* New York: Oxford University Press, 1962. (Chapter 4)

Taylor, William Robert. *Cavalier and Yankee: The Old South and American National Character.* Cambridge, Mass.: Harvard University Press, 1979.

Tichi, Cecelia. *New World, New Earth: Environmental Reform in American Literature from the Puritans through Whitman.* New Haven: Yale University Press, 1979. (Chapters 1 through 3)

Trilling, Lionel. *The Liberal Imagination: Essays on Literature and Society.* New York: Viking Press, 1950.

Turnbull, Andrew. *Scott Fitzgerald.* New York: Scribner's, 1962. (Chapter 6)

Unterecker, John. *Voyager: A Life of Hart Crane.* New York: Farrar, Straus & Giroux, 1969. (Chapter 6)

Vendler, Helen. *On Extended Wings: Wallace Stevens' Longer Poems.* Cambridge, Mass.: Harvard University Press, 1969. (Chapter 6)

Part of Nature, Part of Us: Modern American Poets. Cambridge, Mass.: Harvard University Press, 1980. (Chapters 6 and 7)

Waggoner, Hyatt H. *American Poets from the Puritans to the Present.* Baton Rouge: Louisiana State University Press, 1958; rev. ed., 1984.

Weales, Gerald. *American Drama since World War II.* New York: Harcourt Brace & World, 1962. (Chapter 7)

The Jumping-off Place: American Drama in the 1960s. New York: Macmillan, 1969. (Chapter 7)

Weaver, Michael. *William Carlos Williams: The American Background.* Cambridge University Press, 1971. (Chapter 6)

Webster, Grant. *The Republic of Letters: A History of Postwar American Literary Opinion.* Baltimore: Johns Hopkins University Press, 1979. (Chapter 7)

Weintraub, Stanley. *London Yankees: Portraits of American Writers and Artists in England, 1894–1914.* New York: Harcourt Brace Jovanovitch, 1979. (Chapter 5)

Wilson, Edmund. *The American Earthquake: A Documentary of the Twenties and Thirties.* New York: Doubleday, 1958. (Chapter 6)

Patriotic Gore: Studies in the Literature of the American Civil War. New York: Oxford University Press, 1962. (Chapter 4)

Wolff, Cynthia G. *A Feast of Words: The Triumph of Edith Wharton.* New York: Oxford University Press, 1977. (Chapter 5)

Woodress, James L. *A Yankee's Odyssey: The Life of Joel Barlow.* Philadelphia: Lippincott, 1958. (Chapter 2)

Ziff, Larzer. *The American 1890s: Life and Times of a Lost Generation.* New York: Viking Press, 1966. (Chapter 4)

Puritanism in America: New Culture in a New World. New York: Viking Press, 1973. (Chapter 1)

❧ Index ❧

Abraham Lincoln: The Prairie Years (Carl Sandburg), 342
Abraham Lincoln: The War Years (Carl Sandburg), 342
Abravanel, Maurice, 502
Absalom, Absalom! (William Faulkner), 427–8
"Acres of Diamonds" (Russell Conwell), 238
Acushnet, The, 205
Ada (Vladimir Nabokov), 518
Adagia (Wallace Stevens), 381
Adams, Abigail, 86, 295
Adams, Brooks, 360
Adams, Charles Francis, 295
Adams, Henry, 146, 157, 166, 192, 238, 247, 282, 290, 294–301
Adams, James Truslow, 404
Adams, John, 86, 87, 112, 295
Adams, John Quincy, 169, 295
Adams, Marion Hooper, 299
Addams, Jane, 312, 323
The Adding Machine (Elmer Rice), 366
Addison, Joseph, 97, 115, 147, 158
"An Address to the Slaves of the United States of America" (Henry Highland Garnet), 186
Adler, Stella, 398
Adventures of Huckleberry Finn (Samuel Clemens), 250, 257
The Adventures of Tom Sawyer (Samuel Clemens), 257
Advertisements for Myself (Norman Mailer), 529
Advice to the Privileged Orders (Joel Barlow), 97
After the Fall (Arthur Miller), 473
"Age of Anxiety" (W. H. Auden), 447
The Age of Innocence (Edith Wharton), 311
Agee, James, 405–7, 415, 423
The Air-conditioned Nightmare (Henry Miller), 517
Al Aaraaf (Edgar Allan Poe), 134
Albee, Edward, 477–8
Albers, Anni, 452
Albers, Josef, 452
Alcott, Bronson, 165, 195
Alcott, Louisa May, 165, 195, 273
Aldington, Richard, 331
Alger, Horatio, 239, 299, 389
The Alhambra (Washington Irving), 117
Alice of Old Vincennes (Maurice Thompson), 285
All the King's Men (Robert Penn Warren), 487, 488–9
All My Pretty Ones (Anne Sexton), 462

All My Sons (Arthur Miller), 472
All the Sad Young Men (F. Scott Fitzgerald), 387
Allan, John, 134
Allen, Hervey, 392
Allen, Richard, 185
"The Alligators" (Lafcadio Hearn), 276
Almanac (Benjamin Banneker), 80
The Ambassadors (Henry James), 302
America (Theodor de Bry), 4
American Academy of Arts and Letters, The, 261
American Buffalo (David Mamet), 479
An American Dream (Norman Mailer), 529
The American Dream (Edward Albee), 477
The American Earthquake (Edmund Wilson), 405
An American Exodus (Dorothea Lange and Paul Taylor), 405
American Federation of Labor, 323
The American Jitters (Edmund Wilson), 405
American Mercury magazine, 359
American Progress (John Dost), 236–7
The American Scene (Henry James), 304
"The American Scholar" (Ralph Waldo Emerson), 168
The American School (Matthew Pratt), 66
An American Tragedy (Theodore Dreiser), 317
Ames, Fisher, 96
Ames, William, 10, 13–14
Amistad, The, 466
The Anatomy Lesson (Philip Roth), 499, 506
Anaya, Rudolfo A., 527
Ancient Evenings (Norman Mailer), 529
Anderson, Margaret, 330
Anderson, Maxwell, 366
Anderson, Sherwood, 342–7, 394, 402, 405, 407, 429
"Anecdote of the Jar" (Wallace Stevens), 381
Angel of Light (Joyce Carol Oates), 534
Angelou, Maya, 527
"Annabel Lee" (Edgar Allan Poe), 137
Annie Allen (Gwendolyn Brooks), 466
Another Country (James Baldwin), 510
Anthiel, George, 332
Anthony Adverse (Hervey Allen), 392
Anthony, Susan B., 480
"Antique Harvesters" (John Crowe Ransom), 420
Anti-Slavery Almanac, 183
Appeal to the Colored Citizens of the World (David Walker), 185–6

An Appeal to Pharoah (Carlyle McKinley), 327
Appeal to Reason magazine, 319
Appleton's magazine, 275
The Apple-Tree Table (Herman Melville), 365
Appointment in Samarra (John O'Hara), 444
Arbella, The, 8, 197
Arendt, Hannah, 502
The Armies of the Night (Norman Mailer), 530
Armory Show, The, 339
Armour, Philip, 238, 316
The Art of Fiction (Henry James), 247
Artaud, Antonin, 476
Arthur Mervyn (Charles Brockden Brown), 105
"As I Ebb'd With the Ocean of Life" (Walt Whitman), 214
As I Lay Dying (William Faulkner), 427, 429, 493
Ashbery, John, 451
"The Aspern Papers" (Henry James), 507
The Assistant (Bernard Malamud), 503–4
At Heaven's Gate (Robert Penn Warren), 487
"At Melville's Tomb" (Hart Crane), 365, 372
"At the Tolstoy Museum" (Donald Barthelme), 523
Atlantic Monthly, 147, 149, 245, 256, 263, 264, 328
"Auction – Model 1934" (F. Scott and Zelda Sayre Fitzgerald), 390
Auden, W. H., 336, 365, 447, 465, 467
"Auschwitz, Our Home" (Tadeusz Borowski), 504
An Autobiography (Angela Davis), 527
Autobiography (Benjamin Franklin), 83–4
Autobiography (William Carlos Williams), 373
The Autobiography of Alice B. Toklas (Gertrude Stein), 331
The Autobiography of Malcolm X (Alex Haley), 526–7
The Autocrat of the Breakfast Table (Oliver Wendell Holmes), 147–8
The Awakening (Kate Chopin), 277
The Awakening of the American Theatre (Ben Blake), 398

Babbitt (Sinclair Lewis), 361–4
A Backward Glance (Edith Wharton), 305
Bacon, Francis, 138, 170, 376
Baker, Ray Stannard, 320
Baldwin, James, 509–12
"The Ballad of Nat Turner" (Robert Hayden), 466
The Ballad of the Sad Café (Carson McCullers), 495
Balzac, Honore de, 244, 246, 304, 362
Bancroft, George, 114
Banneker, Benjamin, 80
Baraka, Imamu Amiri (Le Roi Jones), 480
"The Barefoot Boy" (John Greenleaf Whittier), 160
Barlow, Joel, 97–8, 101–2, 113, 125
Barnes, Djuna, 493
Barren Ground (Ellen Glasgow), 418–20
Barrett Browning, Elizabeth, 225–6
Barth, John, 504, 519, 520–1, 525–6
Barth, Karl, 484
Barthelme, Donald, 483, 519
Barthes, Roland, 518
"Bartleby the Scrivener" (Herman Melville), 209

Barton, Bruce, 364
Bartram, William, 74–5
Barzun, Jacques, 443
The Battle with the Slum (Jacob Riis), 278
Battle-Pieces (Herman Melville), 217
Baudelaire, Charles, 133
Baxter, Richard, 13
Bay Psalm Book, 40–2, 99
Bayou Folk (Kate Chopin), 276
Beard, Charles, 404
Beard, Mary, 404
Beattie, Ann, 522
The Beautiful Changes (Richard Wilbur), 465
The Beautiful and the Damned (F. Scott Fitzgerald), 387
Bech: A Book (John Updike), 485
Beckett, Samuel, 476
Bell, Daniel, 456
Bellamy, Edward, 268
Bellefleur (Joyce Carol Oates), 534
Bellow, Saul, 412, 445, 461, 499–502
Bellows, George, 312, 313, 482
Bellows, J.N., 113
"The Bell-Tower" (Herman Melville), 209
Beloved (Toni Morrison), 515–6
"Benito Cereno" (Herman Melville), 209
Benton, Thomas Hart, 393
Bernstein, Leonard, 474
Berryman, John, 285, 458, 459–61, 490
Bettelheim, Bruno, 502
"Between the World and Me" (Richard Wright), 437
Bierce, Ambrose, 261
The Big Money (John Dos Passos), 408
The Big Sea (Langston Hughes), 383
The Biglow Papers (James Russell Lowell), 153–4
Billings, Josh, 254
"Billy Budd" (Herman Melville), 209, 365
Bingham, George Caleb, 110, 128–9
The Birth of a Nation, 328
"The Birthmark" (Nathaniel Hawthorne), 199
Bishop, Elizabeth, 376, 458, 463–4
The Black Aesthetic (Addison Gayle), 512
"The Black Arts Movement" (Larry Neal), 512
Black Boy (Richard Wright), 437, 509
"The Black Cottage" (Robert Frost), 338
Black Manhattan (James Weldon Johnson), 384
Black Mountain Review, 453
The Black Riders (Stephen Crane), 289
The Black Swan (James Merrill), 464
Black Thunder (Arna Bontemps), 434
"Blades of Steel" (Rudolph Fisher), 386
Blair, Robert, 124
Blake, Ben, 398
Blake, William, 454
Bless Me, Ultima (Rudolfo A. Anaya), 527
The Blithedale Romance (Nathaniel Hawthorne), 197
Blitzstein, Marc, 397
Blodget, Samuel, 112
Blok, Alexander, 484
The Blood Oranges (John Hawkes), 520
A Bloodsmoor Romance (Joyce Carol Oates), 534

Bloom, Allen, 501
"The Blue Hotel" (Stephen Crane), 289
"Blueprint for Negro Writers" (Richard Wright), 434, 436
The Bluest Eye (Toni Morrison), 514
Bly, Robert, 463, 466
"Body of Liberties" (Massachusetts), 10
Bogan, Louise, 443
Bok, Edward, 318
The Bonfire of the Vanities (Tom Wolfe), 526
Bonifacius (Cotton Mather), 37–8
Bontemps, Arna, 412, 434
The Book of Daniel (E. L. Doctorow), 448
Boone, Daniel, 110, 360
Booth, Edwin, 366
Borowski, Tadeusz, 504
"Boston Common" (John Berryman), 459
Boston *Courier*, 153
The Bostonians (Henry James), 248
Bottom Dogs (Edward Dahlberg), 395
Bourget, Paul, 248
Bourke-White, Margaret, 405
Bourne, Randolph, 360, 482
Bowles's Moral Pictures, 82
Boxing (Joyce Carol Oates), 534
"Boy Breaking Glass" (Gwendolyn Brooks), 466
Boyle, Kay, 426
A Boy's Will (Robert Frost), 338
Bracebridge Hall (Washington Irving), 117
Brackenridge, Hugh Henry, 85, 105–7
Bradford, William, 25–7, 29, 30, 35, 84, 190
Bradstreet, Anne, 39, 50–8, 73, 83
Bradstreet, Simon, 51
Brady, Matthew, 152, 222
Brandeis, Louis D., 318
Brando, Marlon, 475
Brave and Bold (Horatio Alger), 239
Bread and Cheese Club, 120, 145
Bread Givers (Anzia Yezierska), 400
Breadwinners (John Hay), 264
Breakfast at Tiffany's (Truman Capote), 528
Breakfast of Champions (Kurt Vonnegut, Jr.), 520
Breaking Home Ties (Thomas Hovenden), 273–4
The Bridge (Hart Crane), 357, 371–3
"The Bridge" (Henry Wadsworth Longfellow), 143
Brook Farm, 195–6
Brook Farm in 1844 (painting), 196
Brookes, The, 94
Brooklyn Dodgers, 377
Brooks, Cleanth, 423, 487
Brooks, Gwendolyn, 466
Brooks, Van Wyck, 358, 404
Brother to Dragons (Robert Penn Warren), 487–8
The Brothers Karamazov (Fyodor Dostoyevsky), 472
Brown, Charles Brockden, 104
Brown, John, 160, 180–2, 217, 225, 487
Browne, Sir Thomas, 225, 376
Browning, Robert, 225
Brownson, Orestes, 165
Brownsville Raid (Charles Fuller), 480

Bruce, Richard, 384
Bry, Theodor de, 4
Bryan, William Jennings, 409
Bryant, William Cullen, 120, 124–8, 145
The Buffalo's Back Fat (George Catlin), 130
Bullet Park (John Cheever), 483
Bunyan, John, 198
Burke, Kenneth, 457
Burnham, Daniel, 281–3
Burns, Anthony, 180
Burns, John Horne, 447
Burns, Robert, 159
Burroughs, George, 22
Burroughs, William, 517–8
"The Burrow" (Franz Kafka), 507
Bus Stop (William Inge), 474
Byrd, William II, 71–3
Byron, George Gordon, 115

Cabell, James Branch, 418
Cable, George Washington, 275–6
Caesar's Column (Ignatius Donnelly), 268
Cage, John, 452
Cahan, Abraham, 400
Caldwell, Erskine, 405
Calhoun, William P., 327
Call It Sleep (Henry Roth), 399–402, 405
Call Me Ishmael (Charles Olson), 452
The Call of the Wild (Jack London), 320
Candide (Leonard Bernstein), 474
Cane (Jean Toomer), 383
The Cannibal (John Hawkes), 520
Cannibals All! (George Fitzhugh), 108
Cantos (Ezra Pound), 357
Cantwell, Robert, 396–7
Capote, Truman, 423, 528
"Captain Carpenter" (John Crowe Ransom), 421
Carlyle, Thomas, 164, 167, 190, 195, 297
Carnegie, Andrew, 238, 293, 316
The Carpentered Hen (John Updike), 484
Carrier, Martha, 22
Carter, Robert, 36
Carver, John, 25
Carver, Raymond, 522–4
Caryl, Charles W., 267
Casablanca, 535
Cassatt, Mary, 357
Cassirer, Ernst, 502
Cat on a Hot Tin Roof (Tennessee Williams), 474, 486
The Catcher in the Rye (J. D. Salinger), 481–2
Catch–22 (Joseph Heller), 519
"Cathedral" (Raymond Carver), 524
Cather, Willa, 272, 321–3, 469
Catlin, George, 129
The Caucasian and the Negro (William P. Calhoun), 327
"The Celebrated Jumping Frog of Calaveras County" (Samuel Clemens), 255–6
"The Celestial Railroad" (Nathaniel Hawthorne), 197
The Centaur (John Updike), 484

Centennial Exposition of 1876 (Philadelphia), 234
Ceremony (Leslie Marmon Silko), 527
Cézanne, Paul, 345, 370
A Change of World (Adrienne Rich), 467
The Changing Light at Sandover (James Merrill), 464
Channing, William Ellery, 162
Chaplin, Charles, 371, 454
"Chaplinesque" (Hart Crane), 372
Chapman, John Jay, 171, 360
Charlotte Temple, a Tale of Truth (Susanna Haswell
    Rowson), 103–4
Chase, Richard, 443
Chaucer, Geoffrey, 262
Chayevsky, Paddy, 474
Cheever, Ezekiel, 35
Cheever, John, 412, 483
Chesnut, Mary Boykin, 219–20
Chesnutt, Charles Waddell, 328–9
"Chicago" (Carl Sandburg), 341
Chicago Poems (Carl Sandburg), 341
Child, Lydia Maria, 187
The Children of the Poor (Jacob Riis), 278
"Children Who Toil" (Robert Hunter), 318
The Children's Hour (Lillian Hellman), 397
Chimera (John Barth), 521
Chomsky, Noam, 531
Chopin, Kate, 275–7
"The Christmas Dinner" (Washington Irving), 116
Cilley, Jonathan, 198
Cinque, Joseph, 186
The City: The Hope of Democracy (Frederick C. Howe),
    312
City of Night (John Rechy), 517
"Civil Disobedience" (Henry David Thoreau), 182
Civilization in the United States (Harold Stearns), 358
Clampitt, Amy, 469
The Clansman (Thomas Dixon, Jr.), 327–8
Clare, Ada, 145
Cleaver, Eldridge, 527
Clemens, Jean, 260
Clemens, Samuel, 122, 131, 157, 221, 231, 248–60,
    268, 277, 294, 318, 352, 365
Clemens, Susan, 260
Cliff-Dwellers (Henry B. Fuller), 279
The Closing of the American Mind (Allen Bloom), 501
Clurman, Harold, 398–9
Cobb, Lee J., 398, 470
Coburn, Alvin Langdon, 305
Codman, Ogden, 308
Cody, Buffalo Bill, 283–4
Coffin, Charles M., 457
Cole, Thomas, 126–8
Coleman, Anne, 197
Coleridge, Samuel Taylor, 115, 135, 164
Collected Plays (Arthur Miller), 472
Collier's magazine, 320
The Color Purple (Alice Walker), 513
The Columbiad (Joel Barlow), 101–2
Columbian Exposition of 1893 (Chicago), 274, 280–2,
    312

Columbus, Christopher, 101–2, 280, 373
Commentaries (Julius Caesar), 221
Common Sense (Thomas Paine), 85
The Confessions of Nat Turner (William Styron), 496
The Confidence Man (Herman Melville), 209
Confucius, 165
The Conjure Woman (Charles Waddell Chesnutt),
    328–9
The Connection (Jack Gelber), 476
The Conquest of Granada (Washington Irving), 117–8
Conrad, Joseph, 247
Conroy, Jack, 395
The Conscience of a Scab (El Teatro Campesino), 481
Continental Monthly (New York), 244
The Contrast (Royall Tyler), 99–100
Conwell, Russell, 238
Cooke, Ebenezer, 73
Cooke, John Esten, 108
Cooke, Rose Terry, 268–71
Coolidge, Calvin, 361
Cooper, James Fenimore, 71, 118–24, 125, 129, 145,
    158, 254
Coover, Robert, 448, 519
Copley, John Singleton, 64–5
The Coquette (Hannah Foster), 103
Corey, Giles, 31
Corrington, John William, 495
Corso, Gregory, 454
Cosmopolitan magazine, 319, 320
Cottage Residences (Andrew Jackson Downing), 156
Cotton, John, 10, 12, 13, 14, 15, 30, 35, 40–1, 46–7,
    52–3
Coughlin, Charles, 394
The Counterlife (Philip Roth), 507
The Country of the Pointed Firs (Sarah Orne Jewett),
    272–3
The Coup (John Updike), 485
Couples (John Updike), 484
Cowley, Malcolm, 394, 404
The Crack-Up (F. Scott Fitzgerald), 390
The Cradle Will Rock (Marc Blitzstein), 397
Crane, Hart, 357, 365, 370–3, 377, 422
Crane, Stephen, 263, 285–9, 292, 446
Craven, Thomas, 393
Crawford, Cheryl, 398–9
Crawford, F. Marion, 284, 286
Creeley, Robert, 452
Crimes of the Heart (Beth Henley), 480
Crisis magazine, 325, 384
"Crossing Brooklyn Ferry" (Walt Whitman), 214
The Crucible (Arthur Miller), 472–3
Crumbling Idols (Hamlin Garland), 275
Crummell, Alexander, 185
The Crying of Lot 49 (Thomas Pynchon), 525
Cullen, Countee, 384, 434
Culture and Crisis, 394
Cummings, E. E., 349–51, 363, 366, 381–3
Cunningham, Merce, 452
Curie, Marie, 469
Currier, Nathaniel, 273

Curry, John Steuart, 393
Curse of the Starving Classes (Sam Shepard), 478
A Curtain of Green and Other Stories (Eudora Welty), 490–1
Custer, George A., 236
The Custom of the Country (Edith Wharton), 308–9

Da Silva, Howard, 398
"Daddy" (Sylvia Plath), 462
Dahlberg, Edward, 395, 396–7
The Daily Worker, 398
Daisy Miller (Henry James), 245
Dana, Richard Henry, Jr., 146, 206
Dangling Man (Saul Bellow), 445
Darkwater: Voices from within the Veil (W. E. B. Du Bois), 327
Darley, F.O.C., 113, 118
Darwin, Charles, 314
Davidson, Donald, 420–1
Davis, Alexander Jackson, 157
Davis, Angela, 527
Davis, Ossie, 479
Davis, Rebecca Harding, 264–5
Davis, Richard Harding, 265, 292
Davis, Theodore R., 188
Day by Day (Robert Lowell), 457
Day of Absence (Douglas Turner Ward), 480
The Day of Doom (Michael Wigglesworth), 19, 40, 49–50
The Day of the Locust (Nathanael West), 440–1
Days to Come (Lillian Hellman), 397
De Forest, John William, 218
De Hooch, Peter, 161
De Kooning, Willem, 452
Dead End (Sidney Kingsley), 397
The Dead Father (Donald Barthelme), 519
Dean, James, 478
The Dean's December (Saul Bellow), 500
Dear John, Dear Coltrane (Michael Harper), 470
Death in the Afternoon (Ernest Hemingway), 354
"The Death of the Author" (Roland Barthes), 518
"The Death of the Novel" (Ronald Sukenick), 519
Death of a Salesman (Arthur Miller), 470–2
"Death of a Traveling Salesman" (Eudora Welty), 491
Death, Sleep & the Traveler (John Hawkes), 520
The Decoration of Houses (Edith Wharton), 308
The Deer Park (Norman Mailer), 529
The Deerslayer (James Fenimore Cooper), 121
Delany, Hubert, 385
The Deliverance (Ellen Glasgow), 418
Delta Wedding (Eudora Welty), 491
Democracy (Henry Adams), 238
Democratic Vistas (Walt Whitman), 241
Demuth, Charles, 374–5
Des Imagistes (Ezra Pound), 333
Description of New England (John Smith), 3
The Desert Music and Other Poems (William Carlos Williams), 376
Desire Under the Elms (Eugene O'Neill), 368

The Devil and Cotton Mather (Katherine Anne Porter), 424
The Devil Finds Work (James Baldwin), 510
"Devil's Dream" (Kenneth Fearing), 391–2
Dial magazine (1840–1844), 166, 171
Dial magazine (1880–1929), 355, 373, 377, 382
"The Diamond as Big as the Ritz" (F. Scott Fitzgerald), 387
The Diamond Cutters (Adrienne Rich), 467
Dickens, Charles, 103, 264
Dickinson, Austin, 225
Dickinson, Emily, 222–30
Dickinson, Lavinia, 225
Dictionary of American Biography, 404
Didion, Joan, 522–3
Dietrich, Marlene, 478
Dinesen, Isak, 495
The Disinherited (Jack Conroy), 395
Disney, Walt, 393
District of Columbia trilogy (John Dos Passos), 408
Ditched, Stalled, and Stranded (Dorothea Lange), 416
The Divine Comedy (Dante), 157, 334
Diving Into the Wreck (Adrienne Rich), 468
"The Divinity School Address" (Ralph Waldo Emerson), 168–9
Dixon, Thomas, Jr., 327–8
Do and Dare (Horatio Alger), 239
Doctorow, E. L., 448, 526, 531
Dog Eat Dog (Mary Gallagher), 480
"Dogood Papers" (Benjamin Franklin), 84–5
The Dolphin (Robert Lowell), 457
"Dolt" (Donald Barthelme), 521
Don Quixote (Miguel de Cervantes), 107
Donne, John, 62
Donnelly, Ignatius, 267
Doolittle, Hilda [H.D.], 332–3, 374
Dos Passos, John, 349, 394, 404, 408–11, 415, 444, 490
Dost, John, 236–7
Dostoyevsky, Fyodor, 445, 472, 507
Doubleday, Frank, 315
Douglass, Frederick, 145, 187–90, 282, 466
Dove, Arthur, 370
Dove, Rita, 470
Downing, Andrew Jackson, 156, 178
The Dream Life of Balso Snell (Nathanael West), 439
Dream Songs (John Berryman), 460–1
Dreiser, Emma, 315
Dreiser, Theodore, 238, 264, 282, 312–8, 321, 365, 404–5, 411
Dresser, Paul, 314
Drum Taps (Walt Whitman), 217
Dryden, John, 63
Du Bois, W. E. B., 325–7, 512
Du Plessis, Francine, 452
Dudley, Thomas, 45
Dunbar, Paul Laurence, 328
Duncan, Isadora, 409
Duncan, Robert, 452
Dunlap, William, 120

Dunster, Henry, 42
Durand, Asher B., 126–7
Dust Tracks on a Road (Zora Neale Hurston), 435
Dutchman (Imamu Amiri Baraka), 480, 508
Duyckinck, Everett, 144, 152
Dwight, Timothy, 97, 99, 103, 113
Dylan, Bob, 478

Eakins, Thomas, 215, 234
Eastman, Max, 482
Edgar Huntley (Charles Brockden Brown), 105
Edinburgh Review, The, 113
The Education of Henry Adams, 297–300
Edwards, Jonathan, 65–8, 457
Eggleston, Edward, 154, 263
Einstein, Albert, 502
Eisenhower, Dwight D., 443, 454, 485
El Teatro Campesino, 481
The Electric Kool-Aid Acid Test (Tom Wolfe), 526
Eleven Poems on the Same Theme (Robert Penn Warren), 489
Eliot, George, 226, 244
Eliot, John, 35, 43
Eliot, T. S., 133, 330–4, 340, 355–7, 373, 380, 389, 422, 457
Ellison, Ralph, 412, 508–9, 512
Elmer Gantry (Sinclair Lewis), 363–4
Elsie Venner (Oliver Wendell Holmes), 146, 148
"The Embargo" (William Cullen Bryant), 125
Emerson, Ralph Waldo, 104, 133, 143, 145–6, 157–8, 163–71, 174, 175, 176, 190, 195, 210, 226, 233, 243, 261, 408, 415, 487, 508
The Emperor Jones (Eugene O'Neill), 367, 383
"The Emperor of Ice Cream" (Wallace Stevens), 380
Empson, William, 457
The End of Ideology (Daniel Bell), 456
The Enormous Radio (John Cheever), 483
The Enormous Room (E. E. Cummings), 350–1
"Epilogue" (Robert Lowell), 467
Equiano, Olaudah [Gustavus Vassa], 92–3
"Eros Turannos" (Edwin Arlington Robinson), 336
Esperanza, The, 466
Esquire magazine, 390
"Ethan Brand" (Nathaniel Hawthorne), 199
Ethan Frome (Edith Wharton), 311
Euripides, 333
Evans, Hanna, 104
Evans, Mari, 513
Evans, Walker, 405–7
Everybody's magazine, 320
The Executioner's Song (Norman Mailer), 528–9
"The Exile's Departure" (John Greenleaf Whittier), 159
"The Explanation" (Donald Barthelme), 521–2

A Fable (William Faulkner), 447
A Fable for Critics (James Russell Lowell), 126, 154, 157–8
Falconer (John Cheever), 483

"The Fall of the House of Usher" (Edgar Allan Poe), 138
A Farewell to Arms (Ernest Hemingway), 351
Farmer, Frances, 398
Farrell, James T., 402–4, 444
Faulkner, William, 254, 424, 426–33, 440, 444, 447, 496
Fearing, Kenneth, 391–2
Federal Arts Project, 412
Federal Theatre Project, 412
Federal Writers Project, 412
The Feminine Mystique (Betty Friedan), 448
"Fenimore Cooper's Literary Offenses" (Samuel Clemens), 122
Ferlinghetti, Lawrence, 454
A Few Don'ts by an Imagiste (Ezra Pound), 333
Fichte, Johann Gottlieb, 165
Fielding, Henry, 103, 107, 198
Fields, Annie Adams, 271–2
Fields, James T., 145, 264, 271
Fields, John, 178
The Fight (Norman Mailer), 530
The Financier (Theodore Dreiser), 316
"Finding is the first Act" (Emily Dickinson), 227
Finnegans Wake (James Joyce), 377
The Fire Next Time (James Baldwin), 512
"The Fire of Drift-Wood" (Henry Wadsworth Longfellow), 144
Fisher, Rudolph, 385–6
Fiske, John, 42
Fitch, Elizabeth, 58
Fitzgerald, F. Scott, 363, 386–90, 424, 440
Fitzgerald, Zelda Sayre, 387–9
The Fixers (Bernard Malamud), 503
Flaubert, Gustave, 321, 507
Flint, F. S., 333
Flowering Judas and Other Stories (Katherine Anne Porter), 426
Fogerty, J. J., 232
For Colored Girls Who Have Considered Suicide (Ntozake Shange), 480
For Lizzie and Harriet (Robert Lowell), 457
"For the Marriage of Faustus and Helen" (Hart Crane), 372
For the Union Dead (Robert Lowell), 458–9
"A Forest Hymn" (William Cullen Bryant), 126
Fortune magazine, 405
The Fortune-teller's House/Jackson (Eudora Welty), 492
The Forty-Second Parallel (John Dos Passos), 408
Foster, Hannah, 103
Foster, William Z., 394
The Founding of New England (James Truslow Adams), 404
"Fourth of July" (Margaret Fuller), 175
The Fox Hunt (Winslow Homer), 287
Frank, Robert, 455
Frank, Waldo, 360
Franklin, Benjamin, 38, 47, 65–6, 76–84, 113, 178, 389

Franklin, James, 77
Franny and Zooey (J. D. Salinger), 482
Frazier, E. Franklin, 384–5
Frederic, Harold, 263
"Frederick Douglass" (Robert Hayden), 466
Freeman, Mary E. Wilkins, 268–71, 274
French Ways and Their Meaning (Edith Wharton), 308
Freneau, Philip, 85, 89, 125
Frenzied Finance (Thomas Lawson), 318
Friedan, Betty, 448
"Friendship" (Henry David Thoreau), 166
"From the Dark Tower" (Countee Cullen), 384
From Flushing to Calvary (Edward Dahlberg), 396–7
From Here to Eternity (James Jones), 446–7
Fromm, Erich, 477, 502
Frost, Robert, 332, 336–9, 340, 379
The Fugitive magazine, 420
The Fugitives, 420–2
Fuller, Buckminster, 452
Fuller, Charles, 480
Fuller, Henry Blake, 261, 279
Fuller, Margaret, 165, 166, 171–3, 175
Fullerton, Morton, 301

Gaddis, William, 524
Gallagher, Mary, 480
The Gallery (John Horne Burns), 447
Galvin, G. W., 318
Gandhi, Mohandas, 182
Gardner, Alexander, 220–2
Garfield, John, 398
Garland, Hamlin, 263, 266, 274–5, 285
Garner, Margaret, 515
Garnet, Henry Highland, 186
Garrison, William Lloyd, 152, 154–5, 159, 160, 180
Garvey, Marcus, 385
Gass, William, 519
Gates, Lewis, 292
Gaudier-Brzeska, Henri, 332, 333
Gauguin, Paul, 345
Gay, John, 142
Gayle, Addison, 512
Gelber, Jack, 476
"General Booth Enters into Heaven" (Vachel Lindsay), 340
General Historie of Virginia (John Smith), 4
"The Genteel Tradition in American Philosophy" (George Santayana), 280
"The Gentle Boy" (Nathaniel Hawthorne), 202
Geography III (Elizabeth Bishop), 463
Georgia Scenes (Augustus Baldwin Longstreet), 251
"German Literature" (Theodore Parker), 166
"Gerontion" (T. S. Eliot), 356
Gershwin, George, 473
The Ghost Writer (Philip Roth), 506
Gibbon, Edward, 171
Gieseking, Walter, 377
The Gilded Age (Samuel Clemens and Charles Dudley Warner), 231
Giles Goat-Boy (John Barth), 504, 519, 521

Gilman, Charlotte Perkins, 290–1
Gilmore, Gary, 528–9
Gilpin, Charles, 383
"Gimpel the Fool" (Isaac Bashevis Singer), 502
Ginsberg, Allen, 454–5, 458
Giovanni, Nikki, 513
Giovanni's Room (James Baldwin), 510
The Girl Sleuth (Bobbie Ann Mason), 524
Glasgow, Ellen, 417–20
The Glass Menagerie (Tennessee Williams), 474–5, 486
Glen Ellen, 156
Glengarry Glen Ross (David Mamet), 479
Go (John Clellon Holmes), 455
Go Down, Moses (William Faulkner), 427, 433
Go Tell It on the Mountain (James Baldwin), 510
"God's Controversy with New England" (Michael Wigglesworth), 48
God's Determinations (Edward Taylor), 59–60
Godwin, William, 105
"Goethe" (Margaret Fuller), 166
Goethe, Johann Wolfgang von, 165, 172
Gold, Michael, 394, 395, 408
The Golden Apples (Eudora Welty), 492
The Golden Bowl (Henry James), 302–3
Goldman, Emma, 182, 323
Goldsmith, Oliver, 97, 115, 147
Goldwyn, Samuel, 400
Gombo Zhebes (Lafcadio Hearn), 276
Gone with the Wind (Margaret Mitchell), 108, 392
"Good News from New England" (Edward Johnson), 44
Good, Sarah, 33
Goodbye, Columbus (Philip Roth), 506
Goodman, Paul, 453
"The Goophered Grapevine" (Charles Waddell Chesnutt), 328
Gordon, Caroline, 490, 493
Gospel of Wealth (Andrew Carnegie), 238
Gottschalk, Louis, 145
Gould, Jay, 235
Goyen, William, 497
Graham's Magazine, 135
The Grandissimes (George Washington Cable), 275
Grant, Ulysses S., 219–22, 234
The Grapes of Wrath (John Steinbeck), 413–7
"The Grave" (Katherine Anne Porter), 426
Gravity's Rainbow (Thomas Pynchon), 525
Gray, Thomas, 124
Grayson, William, 108
The Great American Novel (Philip Roth), 505, 506
The Great Gatsby (F. Scott Fitzgerald), 388–90, 441
The Great God Brown (Eugene O'Neill), 368
The Great Railway Bazaar (Paul Theroux), 531–2
The Greater Inclination (Edith Wharton), 309
"The Greatest Life Insurance Wrong" (Louis D. Brandeis), 318–9
The Greek Anthology, 342
Green Hills of Africa (Ernest Hemingway), 352
"Greenleaf" (Flannery O'Connor), 494
Greenough, Horatio, 201

Griffith, D. W., 328
Grimké, Angelina, 183
Grimké, Sara, 183
Griswold, Rufus W., 133
The Gross Clinic (Thomas Eakins), 234
"The Grotesque in Southern Fiction" (Flannery O'Connor), 493
Group Theatre, The, 398–9
Growing Up Absurd (Paul Goodman), 453
The Guardian Angel (Oliver Wendell Holmes), 148
Guy Domville (Henry James), 301

The Hairy Ape (Eugene O'Neill), 367
Haley, Alex, 526–7
Haley, Bill, 450
Halleck, Fitz-Greene, 113, 120, 125
Halper, Albert, 395
Hammerstein, Oscar, II, 473–4
Hammon, Jupiter, 92
Hansberry, Lorraine, 479, 480
Harding, Warren G., 348
Harmonium (Wallace Stevens), 383
Harper, Michael, 466, 470
Harper's magazine, 219, 239, 268
Harris, George Washington, 253
Harris, Joel Chandler, 252
Hart, Lorenz, 473
Harte, Bret, 251, 277
Hartley, Marsden, 370
The Hasty Pudding (Joel Barlow), 97–8
Hathorne, John, 197
Hathorne, William, 33, 197
"The Haunted Oak" (Paul Laurence Dunbar), 328
Hawkes, John, 493, 520–1
Hawley, Joseph, 67, 457
Hawthorne (Henry James), 203, 241–2, 248
"Hawthorne" (Henry Wadsworth Longfellow), 144
Hawthorne, Nathaniel, 104, 135, 158, 196–203, 358, 425, 493
Hawthorne, Sophia Peabody, 198, 202
Hay, John, 264, 298
Hayden, Robert, 466–7
Hayes, Rutherford B., 131, 238
A Hazard of New Fortunes (William Dean Howells), 266
Heade, Martin Johnson, 173
Hearn, Lafcadio, 275–6
Hearst, William Randolph, 409
The Heart is a Lonely Hunter (Carson McCullers), 495
"Heartbreak Hotel" (Elvis Presley), 450
Heart's Needle (W. D. Snodgrass), 461
"The Heathen Chinee" (Bret Harte), 251
Hedge, F. H., 165
Hegel, Georg Wilhelm, 296
Heller, Joseph, 519
Hellman, Lillian, 397, 473, 480
Hemingway, Ernest, 289, 332, 344, 349, 350–5, 387, 440, 444, 446
Henderson the Rain King (Saul Bellow), 502
Henley, Beth, 480

Henry James (John Singer Sargent), 302
Henry, Patrick, 108
Herbert Carter's Legacy (Horatio Alger), 239
Herbert, George, 62
"Heritage" (Countee Cullen), 385
Herman Melville: Mariner and Mystic (Raymond Weaver), 365
Hernshaw, Lafayette M., 326
Hersey, John, 483
Herzog (Saul Bellow), 499–500
Hiawatha (Henry Wadsworth Longfellow), 143
Hickock, Richard, 528
Hicks, Granville, 394, 398
"Hidden Name and Complex Fate" (Ralph Ellison), 508
Higginson, Francis, 3
Higginson, Thomas Wentworth, 225
"A High-toned Old Christian Woman" (Wallace Stevens), 381
Hill, Joe, 410
him (E. E. Cummings), 366
Hindenburg, The, 442
"The Hireling and the Slave" (William Grayson), 108
Hiroshima (John Hersey), 483
His Toy, His Dream, His Rest (John Berryman), 460–1
History (Robert Lowell), 457, 459
The History of the Conquest of Mexico (William Hickling Prescott), 193
Histories of the Dividing Line (William Byrd II), 74
The History of New York (Washington Irving), 115–6
The History of the Standard Oil Company (Ida M. Tarbell), 318
Hitler, Adolf, 441, 447, 504
Holme, John, 4–5
Holmes, John Clellon, 455
Holmes, Oliver Wendell, 114, 146–8, 214, 256, 261, 290
"Homage to Emerson" (Robert Penn Warren), 487
Homage to Mistress Bradstreet (John Berryman), 460
"Home Burial" (Robert Frost), 338
Home of a Rebel Sharpshooter (Alexander Gardner), 220–1
The Home Place (Wright Morris), 447–8
Homer, Winslow, 287
Hook, Sidney, 490
Hooker, Thomas, 12, 14, 16
Hooper, Johnson Jones, 252
A Hoosier Holiday (Theodore Dreiser), 313
The Hoosier Schoolmaster (Edward Eggleston), 154, 263
Hoover, Herbert, 391
Hopkins, Edward, 51–3
Hopkins, Lemuel, 97
Horkheimer, Max, 502
The House behind the Cedars (Charles Waddell Chesnutt), 329
The House of Mirth (Edith Wharton), 309–11
The House of the Seven Gables (Nathaniel Hawthorne), 199–200
Housman, John, 397–8
Hovenden, Thomas, 273

How the Other Half Lives (Jacob Riis), 279–80
Howard, Sidney, 366
Howe, E. W., 263
Howe, Frederick C., 312
Howe, Irving, 444, 498, 509
Howe, Tina, 480
Howells, William Dean, 145, 222, 234, 243, 248, 256, 259–68, 282, 285, 294, 328, 365
Howl (Allen Ginsberg), 454, 458
Hugging the Shore (John Updike), 484
"Hugh Selwyn Mauberley" (Ezra Pound), 348–9
Hughes, Langston, 383–5, 394
Hull House, 312, 323
The Human Comedy (Honore de Balzac), 304
A Humble Romance (Mary E. Wilkins Freeman), 269, 271
Humboldt's Gift (Saul Bellow), 499
Hume, David, 84
Hungry Hearts (Anzia Yezierska), 400
Hunter, Robert, 318
Hurston, Zora Neale, 434–6, 513
Hutchinson, Anne, 52–3
Hutchinson, Thomas, 91

"I felt a Funeral, in my Brain" (Emily Dickinson), 230
"I Have Seen Black Hands" (Richard Wright), 437
I Know Why the Caged Bird Sings (Maya Angelou), 527
I Saw the Figure 5 in Gold (Charles Demuth), 375
The Iceman Cometh (Eugene O'Neill), 369, 473
"Ichabod" (John Greenleaf Whittier), 160
"The Idea of Order at Key West" (Wallace Stevens), 381
"If We Must Die" (Claude McKay), 384
I'll Take My Stand, 422
In the American Grain (William Carlos Williams), 360
In Cold Blood (Truman Capote), 528
In Dreams Begin Responsibilities (Delmore Schwartz), 499
In Dubious Battle (John Steinbeck), 413
"In the Heart of the Heart of the Country" (William Gass), 519
In His Steps (Charles Sheldon), 284
In Our Time (Ernest Hemingway), 353
In Search of Our Mothers' Gardens (Alice Walker), 513
"In a Station of the Metro" (Ezra Pound), 333–4
Incidents in the Life of a Slave Girl (Harriet Jacobs), 187
The Independent, 284
Indians (Arthur Kopit), 477
Industrial Workers of the World (IWW), 410
Infants of the Spring (Wallace Thurman), 384, 434
Inge, William, 474, 475
The Innocents Abroad (Samuel Clemens), 256, 257
Intercollegiate Socialist Society, 320
The Interesting Narrative of the Life (Olaudah Equiano), 92–3
Intruder in the Dust (William Faulkner), 429
Invisible Man (Ralph Ellison), 508–9
Irving, John, 526
Irving, Washington, 113–8, 125, 145, 158
Irving, William, 115

"Isaac and Archibald" (Edwin Arlington Robinson), 335
Italian Villas and Their Gardens (Edith Wharton), 308
Ives, J. Merritt, 273

Jackson, Andrew, 119, 156, 201
Jackson, George, 527
Jackson, Helen Hunt, 226
Jackson, Lydia, 164
Jacobs, George, 22
Jacobs, Harriet, 187
Jagger, Mick, 478
James, Alice, 243
James, Henry, 71, 133, 199, 202–3, 241–9, 256, 261, 263, 271, 273, 294, 299, 301–5, 312, 321, 330, 335, 357, 365, 376, 389, 427, 443, 501, 507, 532
James, Henry, Sr., 243
James, Jesse, 478
James, Mary Walsh, 243
James, William, 242–3, 245, 268, 303, 329, 330, 459
Japan: An Attempt at Interpretation (Lafcadio Hearn), 276
Jarrell, Randall, 458, 459, 461, 490
Jay, John, 119
Jeffers, Robinson, 383
Jefferson, Thomas, 84–9, 99, 105, 110, 112, 151–2, 155, 186, 231, 278, 415, 487–8
Jennie Gerhardt (Theodore Dreiser), 318
Jesus, The, 90, 466
Jewett, Sarah Orne, 263, 268–71, 277, 321
"The Jewish Cemetery at Newport" (Henry Wadsworth Longfellow), 144
Jewish Daily Forward, 400
Jews Without Money (Michael Gold), 395
Joan of Arc, 480
Joe Turner's Come and Gone (August Wilson), 480
John Brown Going to His Hanging (Horace Pippin), 181
John Brown: The Making of a Martyr (Robert Penn Warren), 487
Johnson, Charles S., 385
Johnson, Eastman, 109, 273
Johnson, Edward, 15, 28–9, 43, 44
Johnson, James Weldon, 384
Johnson, Robert, 2
Johnson, Thomas, 226
Johnston, J. F., 324
Jones, James, 445–6
Jones, John Paul, 120
Jones, Le Roi, *see* Baraka, Imamu Amiri
Journal (John Woolman), 159
Journey to Love (William Carlos Williams), 376
Joyce, James, 332, 402
JR (William Gaddis), 524
Judgment Day (James T. Farrell), 403–4, 407
Judgment Day (Elmer Rice), 397
The Jungle (Upton Sinclair), 319–20, 415
Jurgen (James Branch Cabell), 418
Just Above My Head (James Baldwin), 510
Justice and Expediency (John Greenleaf Whittier), 158

Kafka, Franz, 445, 504–5, 507
Kant, Immanuel, 165
Kaufman, George S., 366
Kazan, Elia, 398, 400, 475
Kazin, Alfred, 498
Keats, John, 105, 225, 434, 469
"Keeping Things Whole" (Mark Strand), 469
Kennedy, John Pendleton, 107–8
Keppler, Joseph, 240
Kerouac, Jack, 454–5, 517
Kesey, Ken, 453
Kesselere, George, 378
"The Key" (Eudora Welty), 491
"The Killers" (Ernest Hemingway), 354
"The Kind Master and the Dutiful Servant" (Jupiter Hammon), 92
Kindred Spirits (Asher B. Durand), 126–7
King, Martin Luther, Jr., 182, 449, 512
The Kingfisher (Amy Clampitt), 469
Kingsley, Sidney, 397
Kingston, Maxine Hong, 527–8
Knight, Sarah Kemble, 74
Knights, L. C., 457
Koch, Kenneth, 451
Kopit, Arthur, 477
Kosinski, Jerzy, 504
Kromer, Tom, 395–6
Krutch, Joseph Wood, 471

"The Lame Shall Enter First" (Flannery O'Connor), 493
Lancelot (Walker Percy), 497
Lancelot (Edwin Arlington Robinson), 336
Land of Plenty (Robert Cantwell), 396
Lane, Fitz Hugh, 173
Lange, Dorothea, 405, 416
Lardner, Ring, 358
Last Exit to Brooklyn (Hubert Selby), 517
The Last Gentleman (Walker Percy), 498
The Last of the Mohicans (James Fenimore Cooper), 121
"The Latest Form of Infidelity" (Andrews Norton), 169
Latrobe, Benjamin Henry, 155
Lawless Wealth (Charles Edward Russell), 319
Lawrence, D. H., 122
Lawrence, Jacob, 436
Lawson, John Howard, 366
Lawson, Thomas, 318
Lazarsfeld, Paul, 502
Leadbelly, 509
Leaves of Grass (Walt Whitman), 210–5
Le Conte, Joseph, 292
"Lee in the Mountains" (Donald Davidson), 421
"The Legend of Sleepy Hollow" (Washington Irving), 116–7
Lens, Sidney, 531
The Leopard's Spots (Thomas Dixon, Jr.), 327
"The Lesbian in Us" (Adrienne Rich), 468
Let Us Now Praise Famous Men (James Agee and Walker Evans), 405–7, 415

"Letter from a Region of My Mind" (James Baldwin), 511
"Letter to My Nephew" (James Baldwin), 512
Letters (John Barth), 521
Letters from an American Farmer (St. Jean de Crèvecoeur), 95–6
"Letters of Jonathan Oldstyle, Gent." (Washington Irving), 115
Letting Go (Philip Roth), 506
Levertov, Denise, 452
Levitt, William, 445
Lewis, Richard, 70–1
Lewis, Sinclair, 261, 275, 313, 322, 361–5, 369, 423
Liberator, 152, 154–5, 180
Liberty magazine, 388
Lie Down in Darkness (William Styron), 496
Life magazine, 405
Life in the Iron Mills (Rebecca Harding Davis), 264–5
The Life and Memorable Actions of George Washington (Mason Locke Weems), 190–1
The Life of Gabriella (Ellen Glasgow), 418
Life on the Mississippi (Samuel Clemens), 256
Life Studies (Robert Lowell), 458
Light in August (William Faulkner), 427, 429
"Lily Daw and the Three Ladies" (Eudora Welty), 491
The Lime Twig (John Hawkes), 520
Lincoln, Abraham, 97, 125, 185, 194, 217–8, 342, 408
Lindsay, Vachel, 340–1
Linn, James Weber, 403
Literary World, 144–5
"The Literature of Exhaustion" (John Barth), 521
The Little Foxes (Lillian Hellman), 397
"A little Madness in the Spring" (Emily Dickinson), 226–8
Little Men (Louisa May Alcott), 273
Little Review magazine, 345, 371
Little Victories (Lavonne Mueller), 480
Little Women (Louisa May Alcott), 273
"Livvie" (Eudora Welty), 491
Lloyd, Henry Demarest, 318
Locke, Alain, 383–4
Locke, John, 1, 63
Lodge, Henry Cabot, 192
Loeb, Louis, 286
Lolita (Vladimir Nabokov), 518
London Company, The, 6
London, Jack, 320–1, 394, 455
The Lone Tenement (George Bellows), 313
Long Day's Journey into Night (Eugene O'Neill), 369–70, 473
Long, Huey, 394
Longfellow, Henry Wadsworth, 141–4, 146, 157, 256, 261
Longstreet, Augustus Baldwin, 251–2
Look Homeward, Angel (Thomas Wolfe), 423–4
"Looking at Kafka" (Philip Roth), 504–5
Looking Backward (Edward Bellamy), 268
Lord Baltimore, 6
Lord Calvert, 70

Lord Say and Seal, 10
Lord Weary's Castle (Robert Lowell), 457–8
Losing Battles (Eudora Welty), 491–2
The Lost Son and Other Poems (Theodore Roethke), 463
Love in the Ruins (Walker Percy), 497
"The Love Song of J. Alfred Prufrock" (T. S. Eliot), 334
"The Lovers of the Poor" (Gwendolyn Brooks), 466
Lowell, Amy, 333
Lowell, James Russell, 126, 142, 145–6, 147, 148–55, 169, 243, 256
Lowell, Robert, 456–9, 466, 467, 531
Luck and Pluck (Horatio Alger), 239
The Luck of Roaring Camp (Bret Harte), 251
Luks, George, 312
Lyman, Joseph, 227
Lyon, Richard, 42
Lyrical Ballads (Wordsworth and Coleridge), 124

Ma Rainey's Black Bottom (August Wilson), 480
Madden, David, 497
Madison, James, 86, 97
"The Madonna of the Future" (Henry James), 241
Maggie: A Girl of the Streets (Stephen Crane), 285–6
Magnalia Christi Americana (Cotton Mather), 30–35
Mailer, Norman, 444–6, 456, 516, 517, 528–32
Main Currents of American Thought (Vernon L. Parrington), 360
Main Street (Sinclair Lewis), 361
Main-travelled Roads (Hamlin Garland), 274–5
Major, Charles, 284
Malamud, Bernard, 503–4
Malcolm X (Malcolm Little), 526–7
Malden, Karl, 398
Mallarmé, Stéphane, 133
Malraux, Andre, 509
Mamet, David, 479
The Man in the Gray Flannel Suit (Sloan Wilson), 448
The Man Nobody Knows (Bruce Barton), 364
"The Man That Corrupted Hadleyburg" (Samuel Clemens), 260
"Man the Reformer" (Ralph Waldo Emerson), 166
The Man Who Had All the Luck (Arthur Miller), 472
"The Man Who Lived Underground" (Richard Wright), 507–8
The Marble Faun (Nathaniel Hawthorne), 200–1
Marching! Marching! (Clara Weatherwax), 395
Mardi (Herman Melville), 207
The Marionettes (William Faulkner), 427
Marquand, John P., 444
The Marrow of Tradition (Charles Waddell Chesnutt), 329
Marsh, Reginald, 410
Marshall, Paule, 513
Martin Eden (Jack London), 320
Martineau, Harriet, 172
Mason, Bobbie Ann, 522–4
The Mason Children (the Freake-Gibbs painter), 65

"Massachusetts to Virginia" (John Greenleaf Whittier), 159–60
The Masses magazine, 319, 345, 482–3
Masters, Edgar Lee, 342–3
Mather, Cotton, 13, 30–36, 48, 54, 63, 71, 80, 163, 360
Mather, Increase, 30. 163
Mather, Richard, 30, 35
Matisse, Henri, 370
"Maud Muller" (John Greenleaf Whittier), 160
Maurer, Alfred H., 370
The Maximus Poems (Charles Olson), 452
Mayflower, The, 456
McCarthy, Cormac, 495
McCarthy, Joseph, 447
McClure's magazine, 319, 320–1
McCullers, Carson, 423, 490, 495
McDonald, Dwight, 531
McGuffey's Reader, 238
McKay, Claude, 384
McKinley, Carlyle, 327
McKinley, William, 324
McTeague (Frank Norris), 292
Meleager, 333
Melville, Herman, 145, 203–10, 217, 365, 371, 493
Memorable Providences (Cotton Mather), 31
"Memories of West Street and Lepke" (Robert Lowell), 456
Mencken, H. L., 261, 358–9, 363, 364, 417–8, 443, 488
"Mending Wall" (Robert Frost), 338
Mercy, The, 466
Merlin (Edwin Arlington Robinson), 336
Merrill, James, 464–5
Miami and the Siege of Chicago (Norman Mailer), 530
"Michael" (William Wordsworth), 124
"Middle Passage" (Robert Hayden), 466–7
Middlemarch (George Eliot), 226
Mielziner, Jo, 470–1
Milk for Babes (John Cotton), 13
Miller, Arthur, 470–3, 475
Miller, Henry, 517
Miller, Joaquin, 234
Mills, C. Wright, 443
Milwaukee Leader, 341
"The Minister's Black Veil" (Nathaniel Hawthorne), 199
"Miniver Cheevy" (Edwin Arlington Robinson), 335
The Misanthrope (Moliere), 465
Miss Lonelyhearts (Nathanael West), 439, 493
Miss Ravenel's Conversion (John William de Forest), 219
The Mission (Raphael Soyer), 412
Mitchell, Jonathan, 40
Mitchell, S. Weir, 291
Mizener, Arthur, 457
Moby-Dick (Herman Melville), 207–9, 452
"A Model of Christian Charity" (John Winthrop), 8
Modern Chivalry (Hugh Henry Brackenridge), 105–7
Modersohn-Becker, Paula, 469

Moliere, 465
Monroe, Harriet, 330, 332, 339, 340
Montaigne, Michel de, 170
Montcalm and Wolfe (Francis Parkman), 193
Monticello, 155
Mont-Saint-Michel and Chartres (Henry Adams), 300–1
A Moon for the Misbegotten (Eugene O'Neill), 473
"Moon Lake" (Eudora Welty), 491
Moore, Marianne, 223, 332, 376–9, 383, 464
"The Moose" (Elizabeth Bishop), 464
The Moral Argument Against Calvinism (William Ellery Channing), 162
Morgan, J. P., 238, 409
Morris, Wright, 447–8
Morrison, Toni, 514–6
Morse, Samuel F. B., 120
A Mortal Antipathy (Oliver Wendell Holmes), 148
Morton, Thomas, 27
Mosel, Tad, 474
Moss, Howard, 464
Mosses from an Old Manse (Nathaniel Hawthorne), 203
Motley, John Lothrop, 146, 191–2
The Mount, 304–7
Mount, William Sidney, 128–9
"The Mourners" (Bernard Malamud), 503
The Moviegoer (Walker Percy), 497
"Mr. Edwards and the Spider" (Robert Lowell), 457–8
Mr. Sammler's Planet (Saul Bellow), 503, 504
Mr. Wilson's War (John Dos Passos), 408
Mueller, Lavonne, 480
Mules and Men (Zora Neale Hurston), 435
Mumford, Lewis, 358, 365
"Murders in the Rue Morgue" (Edgar Allan Poe), 139
Murray, Freeman H. M., 326
Murray, Judith Sargent, 172
My Antonia (Willa Cather), 323
My Life As a Man (Philip Roth), 507
My Life and Work (Booker T. Washington), 324
The Mysteries of Winterthurn (Joyce Carol Oates), 534
The Mysterious Stranger (Samuel Clemens), 260
Myths and Texts (Gary Snyder), 458

Nabokov, Vladimir, 483, 518
The Naked and the Dead (Norman Mailer), 445–6
Naked Lunch (William Burroughs), 517–8
The Nantucket School of Philosophy (Eastman Johnson), 273
Narrative of the Adventures and Escape of Moses Roper, 186–7
The Narrative of Arthur Gordon Pym (Edgar Allan Poe), 206
Narrative of the Life of Frederick Douglass, 187–90
Nasby, Petroleum V., 254
Nashville Tennessean, 421
Nast, Thomas, 239–40, 318
Nathan, George Jean, 359, 366
National Anti-Slavery Standard, 149, 153
National Association for the Advancement of Colored People (NAACP), 268, 325

National Committee for a Sane Nuclear Policy (SANE), 450
National Era, 159, 184
Native Son (Richard Wright), 437, 509
Nature (Ralph Waldo Emerson), 166–8
Neal, Larry, 512
Necessities of Life (Adrienne Rich), 467
The Negro Christianized (Cotton Mather), 92
"The Negro Digs up His Past" (Arthur A. Schomburg), 384
The Negro Problem (William Pickett), 327
The Negro Question (George Washington Cable), 275
The Never-ending Wrong (Katherine Anne Porter), 424
New England Canaan (Thomas Morton), 27
New England Monthly, 147
A New England Nun (Mary E. Wilkins Freeman), 269–70
New England Primer, 69
New Englands Plantation (Francis Higginson), 3
New Era (Charles W. Caryl), 267
New Harmony, 195
The New Negro (Alain Locke), 383–4
New York *Daily Tribune*, 175
New York Edition, The (Henry James), 304–5
New York *Evening Post*, 125
New York *Times*, 209, 234
New York World's Fair (1939–40), 441–2
The New Yorker magazine, 469, 482–3, 511
Newburyport *Free Press*, 159
"Newes from Virginie" (Richard Ruth), 3
Newman, Barnett, 450
Newton, Sir Isaac, 63
Niagara Movement, The, 325–6
Nietzsche, Friedrich, 314
A Night in Acadia (Kate Chopin), 276
'*Night Mother* (Marsha Norman), 481
The Night of the Iguana (Tennessee Williams), 474
Night Rider (Robert Penn Warren), 487
The Night Side of New York Life (Thomas de Witt Talmage), 278
Nine Stories (J. D. Salinger), 482
Nineteen Nineteen (John Dos Passos), 349, 408
Nixon, Richard, 506
Nobody Knows My Name (James Baldwin), 510
"Noon Wine" (Katherine Anne Porter, 426
Norman, Marsha, 481
Norris, Frank, 263, 292–4, 312
North American Review, 149
North of Boston (Robert Frost), 338
North and South (Elizabeth Bishop), 463
Northwest Passage (Kenneth Roberts), 392
Norton, Andrews, 169
Norton, Charles Eliot, 142, 263
Norton, Grace, 245
Notebook 1967–68 (Robert Lowell), 457
"Notes for a Magazine" (Adrienne Rich), 467
"Notes of a Native Son" (James Baldwin), 509
Notions of the Americans (James Fenimore Cooper), 121
Nova Britannia (Robert Johnson), 2
Nova Express (William Burroughs), 517

Noyes, John Humphrey, 195
Number 1, 1950 (Jackson Pollock), 450

O Pioneers! (Willa Cather), 322
Oakes, Urian, 25, 47
Oakley, Annie, 283
Oates, Joyce Carol, 526, 532–5
O'Brien, Tim, 526
Observations (Marianne Moore), 377
O'Connor, Flannery, 423, 426, 490, 493–5, 513
The Octopus (Frank Norris), 293
"Ode to the Confederate Dead" (Allen Tate), 421–2
Odets, Clifford, 398–9, 473
Of a Fire on the Moon (Norman Mailer), 530
Of Mice and Men (John Steinbeck), 414
"Of Mr. Booker T. Washington and Others" (W. E. B. Du Bois), 325
"Of Our Spiritual Strivings" (W. E. B. Du Bois), 326–7
Of Plymouth Plantation (William Bradford), 25–6
Of Time and the River (Thomas Wolfe), 423–4
Oh What a Paradise It Seems (John Cheever), 483
O'Hara, Frank, 451
O'Hara, John, 444
O'Keeffe, Georgia, 370
Oklahoma! (Richard Rodgers and Oscar Hammerstein, II), 473
Old Creole Days (George Washington Cable), 275
"Old Ironsides" (Oliver Wendell Holmes), 146
Old Kentucky Home (Eastman Johnson), 109
The Old Man and the Sea (Ernest Hemingway), 355
"Old Mortality" (Katherine Anne Porter), 426
"The Old Order" (Katherine Anne Porter), 426
"Old Times on the Mississippi" (Samuel Clemens), 256
Olson, Charles, 365, 452–3
"On Being Brought from Africa to America" (Phillis Wheatley), 91–2
"On a Replica of the Parthenon in Nashville" (Donald Davidson), 420
On the Road (Jack Kerouac), 455
One Flew Over the Cuckoo's Nest (Ken Kesey), 453
One Writer's Beginnings (Eudora Welty), 492
O'Neill, Eugene, 365–70, 473
O'Neill, James, 366
"The Open Boat" (Stephen Crane), 287
Operation Sidewinder (Sam Shepard), 479
Opffer, Emil, Jr., 372
Oppen, George, 375
Oppenheimer, Joel, 452
The Optimist's Daughter (Eudora Welty), 492–3
The Ordeal of Mark Twain (Van Wyck Brooks), 404
The Organization Man (William Whyte), 448
The Origin of the Brunists (Robert Coover), 519
O'Sullivan, John L., 153
O'Sullivan, Timothy, 222
Other Voices, Other Rooms (Truman Capote), 528
Otis, James, Jr., 90
Our Gang (Philip Roth), 506
"Our Legal Machinery and Its Victims" (G. W. Galvin), 318

Our Old Home (Nathaniel Hawthorne), 198
Our Times (Mark Sullivan), 404
Our Town (Thornton Wilder), 472
"Out of the Cradle Endlessly Rocking" (Walt Whitman), 216
The Outsider (Richard Wright), 508
"The Oven Bird" (Robert Frost), 339
Overland Monthly, 251
Overmantel Decoration (Grant Wood), 393
Owen, Robert, 195
Owl's Head, Penobscot Bay (Fitz Hugh Lane), 173
Ozick, Cynthia, 526

Paddle Your Own Canoe (Horatio Alger), 239
Page, Thomas Nelson, 108, 327
Paige, James W., 260
Pain, Philip, 42
Paine, Thomas, 85–6, 97
The Painted Bird (Jerzy Kosinski), 504
The Painter's Triumph (William Sidney Mount), 128–9
Painting Churches (Tina Howe), 480
Pale Fire (Vladimir Nabokov), 518
Pale Horse, Pale Rider (Katherine Anne Porter), 426
Palladio, Andrea, 88
"Pandora" (Henry James), 299
Panofsky, Erwin, 502
The Panorama and Other Poems (John Greenleaf Whittier), 160
Paradise Lost (John Milton), 59
Paris Exposition (1900), 295
Parker, Theodore, 145, 166
"Parker's Back" (Flannery O'Connor), 494
Parkman, Francis, 191–4
Parks, Rosa, 450
Parrington, Vernon L., 146, 360
Parris, Samuel, 33
Parrish, Maxfield, 308
Partisan Review, 406–8, 443–4, 499, 502
Pascal, Blaise, 165, 484
"A Passionate Pilgrim" (Henry James), 245
"The 'Patent-Medicine' Curse" (Edward Bok), 318
Paterson (William Carlos Williams), 357, 375–6
The Pathfinder (James Fenimore Cooper), 121
"The Pathology of Race Prejudice" (E. Franklin Frazier), 384
Patri, Giacomo, 395–6
"Paul Revere's Ride" (Henry Wadsworth Longfellow), 144
Paulding, James K., 114, 115
The Pawnbroker (Edward Lewis Wallant), 504
Peabody, Elizabeth, 172
Peale, Norman Vincent, 447
The Pearl (John Steinbeck), 414
The Pearl of Orr's Island (Harriet Beecher Stowe), 271
The People of the Abyss (Jack London), 321
The People, Yes (Carl Sandburg), 341
Percival, James Gates, 149
Percy, Walker, 423, 490, 497–8
Perkins, William, 10
Perry, Thomas Sargent, 245

The Personal Memoirs of U. S. Grant, 219–20
Personal Narrative (Jonathan Edwards), 68
Phillips, David Graham, 318, 321
Picasso, Pablo, 370
Pickett, William, 327
Picnic (William Inge), 474
Pierce, Franklin, 198, 201
Pierre (Herman Melville), 207
Pierrot Standing (William Faulkner), 427
Pilgrim's Progress (John Bunyan), 59, 297, 318
The Pilot (James Fenimore Cooper), 120
Pindar, 372
Pinkham, Lydia E., 382
Pinsky, Robert, 470
The Pioneer magazine, 148–50
The Pioneers (James Fenimore Cooper), 120, 121–2
Pippin, Horace, 181
Place in Fiction (Eudora Welty), 486, 491
Plath, Sylvia, 458, 461, 462–3
"A Plea for Captain John Brown" (Henry David Thoreau), 181
"A Plea for Romantic Fiction" (Frank Norris), 292–3
Plessy v. Ferguson, 323
Pnin (Vladimir Nabokov), 518
Pocahontas, 3, 4
Poe, Edgar Allan, 105, 115, 133–40, 145, 155, 158, 171, 252, 373, 465
"Poem, or Beauty Hurts Mr. Vinal" (E. E. Cummings), 382
Poems (William Cullen Bryant), 125
Poems (James Russell Lowell), 152
Poems (Marianne Moore), 383
Poems on Various Occasions (Phillis Wheatley), 91–2
Poems, Second Series (James Russell Lowell), 154
"The Poet" (Ralph Waldo Emerson), 170–1
"The Poetic Principle" (Edgar Allan Poe), 135
Poetry magazine, 332, 333, 338–41
Pollock, Jackson, 450
Poor Richard's Almanack (Benjamin Franklin), 79
The Poorhouse Fair (John Updike), 484
Pope, Alexander, 63, 97, 142, 147
Porgy and Bess (George Gershwin), 474
Porter, Cole, 473
Porter, Katherine Anne, 423, 425–6, 491
Porter, William Sidney [O. Henry], 321
Porter, William T., 253
Portland Place (Alvin Langdon Coburn), 305
Portnoy's Complaint (Philip Roth), 505, 506
The Portrait of a Lady (Henry James), 245–7
Pound, Ezra, 330–4, 340, 348, 357, 373, 443, 453
The Power of Positive Thinking (Norman Vincent Peale), 447
Powers, Hiram, 201
Powhatan, 3
Pragmatism (William James), 329
"The Prague Orgy" (Philip Roth), 506
The Prairie (James Fenimore Cooper), 121
Pratt, Matthew, 66
Precaution (James Fenimore Cooper), 118–9
Preparatory Meditations (Edward Taylor), 60–64

Prescott, William Hickling, 114, 191–3
"Presentiment—is that long Shadow" (Emily Dickinson), 229
Presley, Elvis, 450
The Princess Casamassima (Henry James), 247–8
Proctor, John, 22
"Projective Verse" (Charles Olson), 452
Proletarian Literature in the United States, 394, 398
Promises (Robert Penn Warren), 489
"A Psalm of Life" (Henry Wadsworth Longfellow), 144
The Public Burning (Robert Coover), 448
"Publication—is the Auction" (Emily Dickinson), 225
Puck magazine, 240
Pugin, A. W. N., 155
"The Puritan's Will to Power" (Randolph Bourne), 360
Purlie Victorious (Ossie Davis), 479–80
"The Purloined Letter" (Edgar Allan Poe), 139
Puzzled America (Sherwood Anderson), 405
Pynchon, Thomas, 482, 524–5

Queen Victoria, 141
Questions of Travel (Elizabeth Bishop), 463
Quidor, John, 117

Rabbit is Rich (John Updike), 485
Rabbit Redux (John Updike), 485
Rabbit, Run (John Updike), 485
Ragtime (E. L. Doctorow), 531
Rahv, Philip, 498
Raise High the Roof Beam, Carpenters (J. D. Salinger), 482
A Raisin in the Sun (Lorraine Hansberry), 479
Raleigh, Sir Walter, 56
Randolph, A. Philip, 385
Ransom, John Crowe, 420, 423, 456, 457
"Rappaccini's Daughter" (Nathaniel Hawthorne), 197
Raskin, Marcus, 531
Rauschenberg, Robert, 452
"The Raven" (Edgar Allan Poe), 134, 137
Ray, Man, 331
Reagan, Ronald, 450
"Receipt to Make a New England Elegy" (Benjamin Franklin), 78
Rechy, John, 517
The Recognitions (William Gaddis), 524
The Red Badge of Courage (Stephen Crane), 288–9
The Rediscovery of America (Waldo Frank), 360
Remington, Frederic, 283–5
"Resistance to Civil Government" (Henry David Thoreau), 182
"Revelation" (Flannery O'Connor), 494
"The Revolt of 'Mother' " (Mary E. Wilkins Freeman), 270
Rice, Elmer, 366, 397, 473
Rice, Philip B., 457
Rich, Adrienne, 227, 466, 467–9
"The Rich Boy" (F. Scott Fitzgerald), 387
"Richard Cory" (Edwin Arlington Robinson), 335
Richards, Mary Caroline, 452
Richardson, Samuel, 103, 198

Richter, Jean Paul, 165
"The Right to Work" (Ray Stannard Baker), 320
The Rights of the British Colonies (James Otis, Jr.), 90
The Rights of Man (Thomas Paine), 85
Riis, Jacob, 278–80
"Ringing the Bells" (Anne Sexton), 462
"Rip Van Winkle" (Washington Irving), 116–7
Ripley, George, 195
Riprap (Gary Snyder), 463
The Rise of American Civilization (Charles and Mary Beard), 404
The Rise of David Levinsky (Abraham Cahan), 400
The Rise of the Dutch Republic (John Lothrop Motley), 193
"The Rising Glory of America" (Brackenridge and Freneau), 85
The Robber Bridegroom (Eudora Welty), 492
Roberts, Kenneth, 392
Robinson, Edwin Arlington, 157, 334–6, 339
"Rock Around the Clock" (Bill Haley), 450
Rockefeller, John D., 238, 290
Roderick Hudson (Henry James), 256
Rodgers, Richard, 473–4
Roethke, Theodore, 461, 463
Roger Bloomer (John Howard Lawson), 366
Roosevelt, Franklin D., 486
Roosevelt, Theodore, 279, 288, 318, 336
Root-bound (Rose Terry Cooke), 269
Roper, Moses, 186–7
The Rose Tattoo (Tennessee Williams), 474, 486
Rosenberg, Ethel, 448, 469
Rosenberg, Harold, 498
Rosenberg, Julius, 448
Rosenfeld, Isaac, 502
Roth, Henry, 399–402
Roth, Philip, 499, 504–7
Rothko, Mark, 450
Rousseau, Jean-Jacques, 206
Rowlandson, Mary, 30
Rowson, Susanna Haswell, 103–4
Royal Council for Virginia, The, 6
Royal Society of England, The, 80
"Runagate, Runagate" (Robert Hayden), 466
Rush, Benjamin, 90
Ruskin, John, 225
Russell, Charles Edward, 319
Russell, Daniel, 39
Ruth, Richard, 3, 5

Sacco, Nicola, 363, 398, 408, 425, 448
Saffin, John, 42
"The Sahara of the Bozart" (H. L. Mencken), 418
Saint Louis *Republic*, 312
Saint-Gaudens, Augustus, 299–300, 458–9
Salinger, J. D., 481–2
Salmagundi, 115
Salt Marshes: Newport, Rhode Island (Martin Johnson Heade), 173
San Francisco Actors' Workshop, 476
Sandburg, Carl, 340–2, 404

The Sane Society (Erich Fromm), 477
Sanger, Margaret, 323
Santayana, George, 148, 280
Sappho, 333
Sargent, John Singer, 302, 357
Sartor Resartus (Thomas Carlyle), 297
Sartoris (William Faulkner), 426
Sartre, Jean-Paul, 484
Saturday Club, 145
Saturday Evening Post magazine, 388
Saul and the Witch of Endor (Benjamin West), 133
Save Me the Waltz (Zelda Sayre Fitzgerald), 388
Scarlatti, Alessandro, 377
The Scarlet Letter (Nathaniel Hawthorne), 197, 199, 203, 484
"Scented Herbage of My Breast" (Walt Whitman), 216
Scheherazade, 521
Schelling, Friedrich Wilhelm von, 165
Schleiermacher, Friedrich Ernst, 165
Schneidermann, Rose, 323
Schoenberg, Arnold, 502
Schomburg, Arthur A., 384
The School for Scandal (Richard Brinsley Sheridan), 99
Schopenhauer, Arthur, 296
Schussele, Christian, 113
Schwartz, Delmore, 457, 458, 459, 461, 490, 499
Scopes, John, 363
Scott, Sir Walter, 107, 115, 119, 157, 193, 198
Scribner's magazine, 275, 310
"Sea Garden" (Hilda Doolittle), 332
The Sea-Wolf (Jack London), 320
The Secret of Swedenborg (Henry James, Sr.), 243
Sedgeley, 155
Sedgwick, Catherine, 104
Seize the Day (Saul Bellow), 501
Selby, Hubert, 517
Selected Poems (Robert Penn Warren), 487
Self-Portrait in a Convex Mirror (John Ashbery), 451
Seneca Falls Convention, 172
"A Servant to Servants" (Robert Frost), 338
Seven Gothic Tales (Isak Dinesen), 495
77 Dream Songs (John Berryman), 460–1
Sewall, Mrs. Hannah, 13
Sewall, Samuel, 20–4, 74
Sexton, Anne, 461–2
Sexual Perversity in Chicago (David Mamet), 479
Seymour: An Introduction (J. D. Salinger), 482
Shahn, Ben, 460
Shakespeare, William, 149, 151, 226, 474
The Shame of the Cities (Lincoln Steffens), 318
Shange, Ntozake, 480
Shapiro, Meyer, 339
Shaw, Robert Gould, 458–9
Sheeler, Charles, 374
Sheldon, Charles, 284
Shepard, Sam, 478–9
Shepard, Thomas, 14–15, 17–19, 20, 47, 83
Sherman, William T., 219
Sherwood, Robert, 473
Shiloh and Other Stories (Bobbie Ann Mason), 524

Ship of Fools (Katherine Anne Porter), 426
"The Short Happy Life of Francis Macomber" (Ernest Hemingway), 354
"The Significance of the Frontier in American History" (Frederick Jackson Turner), 282–3
Silence in the Snowy Fields (Robert Bly), 463
The Silent South (George Washington Cable), 275
Silko, Leslie Marmon, 527
The Silver Cord (Sidney Howard), 366
Simms, William Gilmore, 107, 114
Sims, Thomas, 180
Sinclair, Upton, 319–20, 415
Singer, Isaac Bashevis, 502
Sister Carrie (Theodore Dreiser), 312–6, 344
The Sketch Book (Washington Irving), 114–6, 125
"Skunk Hour" (Robert Lowell), 458
A Slave Auction at the South (Theodore R. Davis), 188
"Slavery in Massachusetts" (Henry David Thoreau), 180
"The Sleeper" (Edgar Allan Poe), 137
"The Sleepers" (Walt Whitman), 214
Sloan, John, 312, 319, 482
Smibert, John, 21
Smith, Dave, 470
Smith, John, 2–3, 7
Smith, Perry, 528
Smith, Sydney, 113–4
Smith, Thomas, 36–7
"Smoke, Lilies and Jade" (Richard Bruce), 384
Snapshots of a Daughter-in-Law (Adrienne Rich), 467
Snodgrass, W. D., 461
Snow White (Walt Disney), 393
"Snowbound" (John Greenleaf Whittier), 160–1
Snyder, Gary, 458, 463
The Soft Machine (William Burroughs), 517
Soldier's Pay (William Faulkner), 429
A Soldier's Story (Charles Fuller), 480
Soledad Brother (George Jackson), 527
Somebody's Children (Rose Terry Cooke), 269
"Song of Myself" (Walt Whitman), 212–4
"Song of Slaves in the Desert" (John Greenleaf Whittier), 159
Song of Solomon (Toni Morrison), 515
Sophie's Choice (William Styron), 495–6, 504
"The Sot-weed Factor" (Ebenezer Cooke), 73
The Sot-Weed Factor (John Barth), 521
Soul on Ice (Eldridge Cleaver), 527
The Souls of Black Folk (W. E. B. Du Bois), 325–7
The Sound and the Fury (William Faulkner), 426, 431–2
The Sound of Music (Richard Rodgers and Oscar Hammerstein, II), 474
South Pacific (Richard Rodgers and Oscar Hammerstein, II), 473
Southern Literary Messenger, 252
Southern Review, 487, 490
Southworth, E. D. E. N., 104
The Sovereignty and Goodness of God (Mary Rowlandson), 30
Soyer, Raphael, 412
Sparks, Jared, 162, 191

Specimen Days (Walt Whitman), 214–5
The Spectator, 115
Speed-the-Plow (David Mamet), 479
Spencer, Herbert, 314
Spenser, Edmund, 198
The Sphinx's Children (Rose Terry Cooke), 269
Spirit of the Times, 253
Spoon River Anthology (Edgar Lee Masters), 342–3
Spring and All (William Carlos Williams), 375, 383
The Spy (James Fenimore Cooper), 119–20
St. George and the Godfather (Norman Mailer), 516, 530
St. Jean de Crèvecoeur, Hector, 95–6
Stallings, Laurence, 366
Standish, Myles, 27
"The Starry Night" (Anne Sexton), 462
Stearns, Harold, 358–9
Stedman, E. C., 251, 263
Steele, Sir Richard, 158
Steen, Jan, 161
"The Steeple-Jack" (Marianne Moore), 377
Steere, Richard, 42
Steffens, Lincoln, 318, 320, 394
Steichen, Edward, 342
Stein, Gertrude, 222, 330–1, 344, 348, 352, 357–8, 408
Steinbeck, John, 413–7, 444
Stephen Crane (John Berryman), 460
Sterne, Laurence, 107, 115, 142
Stevens, Wallace, 374, 379–81
Stieglitz, Alfred, 344, 370
Stiles, Ezra, 58, 95
The Stoic (Theodore Dreiser), 316
Stone, I. F., 490
Stone, Robert, 526
The Store (T. S. Stribling), 488
"Storm Warnings" (Adrienne Rich), 467
Stowe, Harriet Beecher, 183–5, 190, 271, 415
Strand, Mark, 469–70
Strange Interlude (Eugene O'Neill), 368
Strasberg, Lee, 398–9
A Streetcar Named Desire (Tennessee Williams), 474–6, 486
Stribling, T. S., 488
Strindberg, August, 367
Strive and Succeed (Horatio Alger), 239
Stuart, Gilbert, 89
Studies in Classic American Literature (D. H. Lawrence), 122
Studs Lonigan trilogy (James T. Farrell), 403–4
Sturgis, Howard, 305
Styron, William, 495–7
Success magazine, 238, 316
Sukenick, Ronald, 518–9
Sullivan, Louis, 282, 339
Sullivan, Mark, 296, 404
Summer (Edith Wharton), 311
Summer and Smoke (Tennessee Williams), 486
Sumner, William Graham, 290
The Sun Also Rises (Ernest Hemingway), 353, 354

"Sunday Morning" (Wallace Stevens), 381
Survey of the Sum of Church Discipline (Thomas Hooker), 12
Sut Lovingoods Yarns (George Washington Harris), 253–4
Swallow Barn (John Pendleton Kennedy), 108
"Sweeney Agonistes" (T. S. Eliot), 356
"Sweeney Among the Nightingales" (T. S. Eliot), 356
Swift, Jonathan, 63, 142
"Sylvia's Death" (Anne Sexton), 462
The System of Dante's Hell (Imamu Amiri Baraka), 508

Tales of the Grotesque and Arabesque (Edgar Allan Poe), 134
Tales of a Traveller (Washington Irving), 117
"Tall Men" (Donald Davidson), 420
Talmage, Thomas de Witt, 278
Tamar and Other Poems (Robinson Jeffers), 383
Tamerlane (Edgar Allan Poe), 134
The Tammany Tiger Loose (Thomas Nast), 240
Tapping, Joseph, 46
Taps at Reveille (F. Scott Fitzgerald), 387
Tarbell, Ida M., 318, 320
Tartuffe (Moliere), 465
Tate, Allen, 420–2, 457, 458
Taylor, Bayard, 145
Taylor, Edward, 20, 39, 50, 54, 58–64
Taylor, Paul, 405
Taylor, Peter, 483
Teilhard de Chardin, Pierre, 493
Ten North Frederick (John O'Hara), 444
The Tenants (Bernard Malamud), 503
Tender Buttons (Gertrude Stein), 344
Tender is the Night (F. Scott Fitzgerald), 390
Tennyson, Alfred, 151
The Tenth Muse (Anne Bradstreet), 54–8
Thackeray, William Makepeace, 115
"Thanatopsis" (William Cullen Bryant), 124–5
The Theater and Its Double (Antonin Artaud), 476
Their Eyes Were Watching God (Zora Neale Hurston), 435
Their Wedding Journey (William Dean Howells), 266
Them (Joyce Carol Oates), 532
The Theory of the Leisure Class (Thorstein Veblen), 240–1
"There Was a Child Went Forth" (Walt Whitman), 214
Theroux, Paul, 531–2
They Live in Fire Traps (Jacob Lawrence), 436
Thirty-six Poems (Robert Penn Warren), 489
This Side of Paradise (F. Scott Fitzgerald), 387
This Tree Will Be Here for a Thousand Years (Robert Bly), 463
"This Way for the Gas, Ladies and Gentlemen" (Tadeusz Borowski), 504
Thomas à Kempis, 165
Thompson, Maurice, 284–5
Thoreau, Henry David, 165, 173–82, 190, 226, 455
Thorpe, Thomas, 252
Three Lives (Gertrude Stein), 331, 344

Three Soldiers (John Dos Passos), 349
Thurman, Wallace, 383–4, 434
The Ticket That Exploded (William Burroughs), 517
Tillich, Paul, 484
"Tintern Abbey" (William Wordsworth), 124
Tiny Alice (Edward Albee), 478
The Titan (Theodore Dreiser), 316
Titcomb, Mary Sarah, 106
Titus Andronicus (William Shakespeare), 474
To Bedlam and Part Way Back (Anne Sexton), 461–2
"To the Memory of the Brave Americans" (Philip Freneau), 85
"To the Person Sitting in Darkness" (Samuel Clemens), 260
Tocqueville, Alexis de, 111, 113, 178–9, 205, 316, 358
Toklas, Alice B., 330–1
Toksvig, Harald, 346
Tolstoy, Count Leo, 266
Tompson, Benjamin, 42
Too Far to Go (John Updike), 486
Toomer, Jean, 383
The Tooth of Crime (Sam Shepard), 479
Toronto *Star Weekly*, 357
Tortilla Flat (John Steinbeck), 414
A Touch of the Poet (Eugene O'Neill), 473
Toulouse-Lautrec, Henri de, 370
Town and Country Club, 145
"Tragedy and the Common Man" (Arthur Miller), 471
Tragic America (Theodore Dreiser), 405
Traherne, Thomas, 465
The Traitor (Thomas Dixon, Jr.), 327
Transcendental Club, 145, 172
Transcendental Wild Oats (Louisa May Alcott), 195
A Traveler from Altruria (William Dean Howells), 268
Travels through North and South Carolina . . . (William Bartram), 74
Travesties (John Hawkes), 520
The Treason of the Senate (David Graham Phillips), 318
Trilling, Lionel, 443, 498
Tristan (Edwin Arlington Robinson), 336
Tropic of Cancer (Henry Miller), 517
Trotter, William Monroe, 326
"A True Relation of the Flourishing State of Pennsylvania, " (John Holme), 4–5
Trumbull, John, 97, 99, 101–2
Truth, Sojourner, 185
"Trying to Talk with a Man" (Adrienne Rich), 468
Tubman, Harriet, 185, 466
Tucker, Ellen, 164
Tuckerman, Henry, 114
Tulips and Chimneys (E. E. Cummings), 383
Turgenev, Ivan, 244
Turner, Frederick Jackson, 231, 282–3
Turner, Nat, 186, 466, 496
Twain, Mark: see Clemens, Samuel
Tweed, William, 239, 258
12 Million Black Voices (Richard Wright), 436
Twice-Told Tales (Nathaniel Hawthorne), 135, 198
"Two Views of a Cadaver Room" (Sylvia Plath), 462

Two Years Before the Mast (Richard Henry Dana, Jr.), 206

Tyler, Royall, 99–100

Typee (Herman Melville), 206–7

U.S.A. trilogy (John Dos Passos), 349, 408–11, 415

U. S. S. *Constitution*, 146–7

"Ulalume" (Edgar Allan Poe), 137

Uncle Remus (Joel Chandler Harris), 252

Uncle Tom's Cabin (Harriet Beecher Stowe), 108, 183–5, 190, 271, 415

Understanding Poetry (Cleanth Brooks and Robert Penn Warren), 423

Union Square (Albert Halper), 395

"The United States Elevated to Glory and Honor" (Ezra Stiles), 95

United States Magazine, 85

Universal Negro Improvement Association, The, 385

The Unvanquished (William Faulkner), 427

Up From Slavery (Booker T. Washington), 324–5

Updike, John, 483–6

V. (Thomas Pynchon), 525

"The Valley of Baca" (Cotton Mather), 13

The Valley of Decision (Edith Wharton), 308

Van Buren, Martin, 201

Van Gogh, Vincent, 345, 462

Van Vechten, Carl, 362, 435

Vanzetti, Bartolomeo, 363, 398, 408, 425, 448

Veblen, Thorstein, 240–1, 348, 410

Very, Jones, 165

Vezey, Denmark, 186

Via Crucis: A Romance of the Second Crusade (F. Marion Crawford), 284, 286

The Victim (Saul Bellow), 500

Vidal, Gore, 531

"The Village Blacksmith" (Henry Wadsworth Longfellow), 144

The Violent Bear It Away (Flannery O'Connor), 494

Virginia (Ellen Glasgow), 418

Virginia Comedians (John Esten Cooke), 108

Virginia Company, The, 6

The Virginian (Owen Wister), 283

The Vision of Sir Launfal (James Russell Lowell), 154–5, 157

Voices of Freedom (John Greenleaf Whittier), 159

Vonnegut, Kurt, Jr., 519–20

"Voyages" (Hart Crane), 372

Wagner, Richard, 234

Waiting for Godot (Samuel Beckett), 476

Waiting for Lefty (Clifford Odets), 398–400

Waiting for Nothing (Tom Kromer), 395–6

Walden (Henry David Thoreau), 175–80

Walker, Alice, 513–4

Walker, David, 185–6

Walker, Margaret, 412, 513

Walker, Timothy, 194

Wallant, Edward Lewis, 504

Walpole, Horace, 105

Walt Whitman (Thomas Eakins), 215

War is Kind (Stephen Crane), 289

Ward, Artemus, 254

Ward, Douglas Turner, 480

Ward, Nathaniel, 54

Warner, Anna, 104

Warner, Charles Dudley, 231

Warner, Susan, 104

Warren, Robert Penn, 423, 427, 486–90

Washington, Booker T., 323–5, 459

Washington, George, 89, 91, 95, 97, 115, 117, 125, 190–1, 255

Wasmuth Portfolio, 340

Wasserstein, Wendy, 480

The Waste Land (T. S. Eliot), 355–7, 373, 383

Watch on the Rhine (Lillian Hellman), 397

Water Street (James Merrill), 464

The Way Some People Live (John Cheever), 483

"The Way to Wealth" (Benjamin Franklin), 79

"We Are Seven" (William Wordsworth), 124

We the People (Elmer Rice), 397

"We Wear the Mask" (Paul Laurence Dunbar), 328

Weatherwax, Clara, 395

Weaver, Raymond, 365

Webster, Daniel, 160, 180

Webster, Noah, 100–1

Weems, Mason Locke, 190–1

Weil, Simone, 469

Weir, Robert W., 201

Wells, H. G., 247

Welty, Eudora, 423, 426, 490–3

Wenzell, A. B., 310

West, Benjamin, 64, 78, 133

West, Nathanael (Nathan Weinstein), 438–41, 493

West Side Story (Leonard Bernstein), 474

Westhoff, Clara, 469

Wharton, Edith, 302–11, 349, 357, 388

Wharton, Edward, 308

What the Light Was Like (Amy Clampitt), 469

What Price Glory? (Maxwell Anderson and Laurence Stallings), 366

"What Soft – Cherubic Creatures" (Emily Dickinson), 229

"What You Should Know to Be a Poet" (Gary Snyder), 463

Wheatley, John, 91

Wheatley, Phillis, 90–2

When Knighthood Was in Flower (Charles Major), 284

"When Lilacs Last in the Dooryard Bloom'd" (Walt Whitman), 217

When She Was Good (Philip Roth), 506

"The Whistle" (Eudora Welty), 490

The White Album (Joan Didion), 522

White Buildings (Hart Crane), 371

White Collar (Giacomo Patri), 395–6

White, Elinor, 338

White Fang (Jack London), 320

"A White Heron" (Sarah Orne Jewett), 271, 273

White, Maria, 151

"The White Negro" (Norman Mailer), 529

Whitman, Walt, 140, 145, 171, 210–6, 225, 234, 241, 250, 278, 341, 374, 408, 415, 454
Whittier, John Greenleaf, 146, 158–61
Who's Afraid of Virginia Woolf (Edward Albee), 477–8
Whyte, William, 448
Wideman, John, 526
Wieland (Charles Brockden Brown), 105
Wigglesworth, Michael, 19, 40, 49–50, 72
Wilbur, Richard, 464–5
"Wilder: Prophet of the Genteel Christ" (Michael Gold), 413
Wilder, Thornton, 413, 472
Williams, John, 22
Williams, Roger, 42, 53
Williams, Tennessee, 423, 474–6
Williams, William Carlos, 333, 357, 360, 373–6, 383, 396, 453–4
Willis, Nathaniel Parker, 114
Wilson, August, 480
Wilson, Edmund, 349, 355, 388, 394, 405
Wilson, Sloan, 448
Wilson, Woodrow, 350, 409
Winesburg, Ohio (Sherwood Anderson), 342–7
The Wings of the Dove (Henry James), 302
Winthrop, John, 8–10, 30, 35, 51–2, 83, 190
Winthrop, Katherine, 23–4
Wise Blood (Flannery O'Connor), 494
Wister, Owen, 283
The Witches of Eastwick (John Updike), 484
Wolfe, Thomas, 423–5
Wolfe, Tom, 526
Woman in the Nineteenth Century (Margaret Fuller), 172
Woman Rebel magazine, 323
Woman Warrior (Maxine Hong Kingston), 527–8
Women and Economics (Charlotte Perkins Gilman), 290–1
Women's Trade Union League, 323
Wonders of the Invisible World (Cotton Mather), 31, 34
The Wonder-working Providence of Sion's Saviour in New England (Edward Johnson), 28–9

Wood, Grant, 393
Woodbridge, Benjamin, 46
Woodbridge, John, 54
"The Wood-Pile" (Robert Frost), 338
Woolf, Virginia, 532
Woolman, John, 159
Wordsworth, William, 124–6, 151, 164, 463
Works Progress Administration, 491
World's Fair (E. L. Doctorow), 531
"A Worn Path" (Eudora Welty), 490–1
Wright, Frank Lloyd, 339–40, 409
Wright, Richard, 412, 434–9, 507–8, 509, 512
The Writing of Fiction (Edith Wharton), 306
Wyeth, Andrew, 450–1
Wyllys, Ruth, 58

A Year's Life (James Russell Lowell), 150–1
Yeats, William Butler, 332, 459, 467
Yekl: A Tale of the New York Ghetto (Abraham Cahan), 400
"The Yellow Wallpaper" (Charlotte Perkins Gilman), 290–1
The Yemassee (William Gilmore Simms), 107
Yerkes, Charles T., 316
Yezierska, Anzia, 400–1
You Have Seen Their Faces (Margaret Bourke-White and Erskine Caldwell), 405
You Must Remember This (Joyce Carol Oates), 534
Young, Edward, 142
Young Lonigan: A Boyhood in Chicago Streets (James T. Farrell), 403
The Young Manhood of Studs Lonigan (James T. Farrell), 403

Zola, Emile, 291–2
The Zoo Story (Edward Albee), 477
Zuckerman Bound (Philip Roth), 506
Zuckerman Unbound (Philip Roth), 506
Zukofsky, Louis, 375

CHESTNUT HILL

NOC 6/90